Chinese Politics in the
Hu Jintao Era

Chinese Politics in the Hu Jintao Era

New Leaders, New Challenges

Willy Wo-Lap Lam

An East Gate Book

M.E.Sharpe
Armonk, New York
London, England

An East Gate Book

Copyright © 2006 by Willy Wo-Lap Lam

Library of Congress Cataloging-in-Publication Data

Lam, Willy Wo-Lap.
  Chinese politics in the Hu Jintao era : new leaders, new challenges / by Willy Wo-Lap Lam.
    p. cm.
  "An East Gate book."
  Includes bibliographical references.
  ISBN-13 978-0-7656-1773-6 (cloth : alk. paper); ISBN-13 978-0-7656-1774-3 (pbk. : alk. paper)
  ISBN-10 0-7656-1773-0 (cloth : alk. paper); ISBN-10 0-7656-1774-9 (pbk. : alk. paper)
  1. China—Politics and government—2002– 2. Hu, Jintao, 1942– I. Title.

DS779.46.L35 2006
951.06092—dc22   2006015454

For Grace, Ching-Wen, and Wen-Chung

Contents

Preface

While China's economic success is ringing alarm bells and arousing protectionist sentiments around the world, the Chinese Communist Party (CCP) leadership under President Hu Jintao is aware of the fact that the flipside of the coin called the "world factory" is the proverbial *xuelei gongchang*, a work mill filled with blood, sweat, and tears. Not only are laborers—many of them underaged and not protected by the law—underpaid and working extra-long hours, the nation's resources are being depleted. Industrial accidents are commonplace and China's environment is a mess. The country is consuming so much energy and raw materials that questions of sustainability are being raised with increasing intensity. For example, China's energy use per gross domestic product (GDP) unit is five times that of Germany and six times that of Japan. The Eleventh Five-Year Plan (2006–2010) has mandated that energy efficiency be boosted by 20 percent; yet in the 2000–2005 period, the country barely cut fuel wastage by 7 percent.[1] By late 2005, twenty-seven years after Deng Xiaoping first began the country's reform and open-door policy, officials and opinion leaders in the country admitted that the economy was still dominated by *cufangxing* (rough and quantitative-oriented) production.

A fast-rising and somewhat glamorous China has dominated the world media in the past two years or so in a way that may have hidden its multiple problems. It is true that the People's Republic of China (PRC) has been extremely successful with trade—which accounts for about 70 percent of GDP. The country is also piling up foreign exchange surpluses to the tune of $800 billion. Yet its leaders understand that even as protectionist pressures are mounting in both developed and developing countries, profit margins are getting razor thin due to mounting factor costs. As Minister of Commerce Bo Xilai put it, "China needs to sell 800 million shirts before it can earn enough to buy one Airbus A380."[2] While discussing the nation's Eleventh Five-Year Plan, Premier Wen Jiabao noted that China must dramatically boost its domestic consumption: "Expanding domestic demand is a long-term strategic policy that we must stick to," he said. President Hu repeatedly urged industrialists and researchers to do more in coming up with innovative, cutting-edge products whose intellectual property rights belong solely to the Chinese.[3] Calls have also been made to boost the share of services in the nation's economy. Yet experts are not optimistic that much progress can be made in the rest of the Hu-Wen team's tenure in areas including boosting innovation and increasing domestic spending (see Chapter 7).

Compared to predecessors ranging from Deng to ex-president Jiang Zemin, the Hu-Wen leadership has been paying substantially more attention to the welfare of disadvantaged classes, meaning peasants and sectors that have lost out in the course of reform. The first three years of the Hu administration were suffused with political slogans ranging from "putting people first" to "constructing a harmonious society." As pointed out in Chapters 2 and 3, concrete benefits for disadvantaged sectors of society, particularly farmers, have increased. Agrarian taxes have been abolished in the majority of provinces. The Maoist household registration regime has been liberalized to some extent, and plans have been unveiled to move up to 300 million peasants to urban areas. Yet the harmony that has been the ideal of sages and rulers since the time of Confucius hardly seems within reach.

Social injustice—one of whose most obvious manifestations is the yawning gap between rich and poor—has kept increasing. With the abolition of the cradle-to-grave social-welfare system, essential services in medicine and education have become so expensive that many in the hinterland areas cannot afford to go to either a hospital or a university. Even China's highly controlled media have admitted that, as the liberal (and often censored) *Beijing News* put it in late 2005, "the rich–poor gap is tearing asunder the consensus of society." Minister of Public Security Zhou Yongkang admitted that in 2005, there were 87,000 "mass incidents"—a euphemism for riots, disturbances, and civil unrest—nationwide, up 6.6 percent from the year before. The central authorities reckon that economic losses owing to so-called unexpected events—natural disasters, traffic and industrial accidents, as well as riots and disturbances—amounted to 650 billion yuan in 2004, or about 6 percent of GDP.[4]

The government's labyrinthine bureaucracy seems ill equipped to handle the growing—and deepening—contradictions plaguing the country. Premier Wen has been called a latter-day Zhou Enlai thanks to his administrative and trouble-shooting skills. Yet the State Council's response to various problems seems slow and haphazard. For example, it wasn't until several thousand coal miners had perished in the pits that Beijing started in late 2005 to strictly enforce regulations closing mines with inadequate safety measures.[5] Seen in this perspective, Hu and Wen seem more like rookie firefighters scurrying to put out blazes than the visionary architects of a more humane, more harmonious new world. Since becoming head of government in March 2004, Wen has called numerous meetings to improve the country's ability to counter risks and tackle emergencies. For example, in a mid-2005 national conference, Wen asked cadres to do a better job "perfecting early warning systems and strengthening management work regarding emergencies."[6] As of 2005, there were early-warning and crisis management systems to handle mishaps including—you name it—floods and epidemics, mine explosions, traffic accidents, and political disturbances caused by laid off workers, overtaxed peasants, and petitioners. Yet the "mass incidents" and disasters keep happening with mind-numbing frequency.

It seems clear that short of cutting the Gordian knot called political liberaliza-tion, the Hu-Wen team cannot hope to make much advancement in either restruc-turing the economy or alleviating sociopolitical woes. As the official *Outlook Weekly* put it, China "could only achieve progress through innovation in institu-tions."[7] Both ex-president Jiang and President Hu have called on cadres and ordi-nary citizens to "make progress with the times." It is hardly a secret that the institution that needs retooling most is the antediluvian system called one-party dictatorship. Unless and until the CCP is ready to cede more power to the people by, for example, allowing non-party-controlled labor unions, media, and political NGOs to appear, the entire modernization process can hardly take off.

Take for instance, innovation in technology and industry. Given that China produces more than 250,000 science and engineering graduates a year, the coun-try should be a powerhouse in high-tech wizardry. Yet the country lacks the free atmosphere deemed indispensable for first-class research. The universities are still subject to the tight control of CCP apparatchiks; the Internet is heavily po-liced; and intellectuals are not allowed to openly express views deemed politi-cally incorrect. No wonder the cream of China's college graduates have continued to seek their fortunes in the West. And as economics professor Qiao Xinsheng put it in the *People's Daily,* "we should really reflect deeply over the fact that while South Korea had started more than ten years later than China, it has now sur-passed us in science and technology." Qiao blamed excessive "bureaucratic inter-ference" for stunting Chinese innovation.[8] Or consider the reasons behind Chinese's extremely high savings rate, which militates against Beijing's bid to encourage consumer spending. It has been suggested that apart from the lack of social-welfare benefits, one reason Chinese are reluctant to spend is their lack of faith in the CCP administration, as well as fear of possible political upheavals.[9]

The authorities have resorted to two excuses—one openly stated, and the other couched in euphemisms—for dragging their feet on real change. The first pretext is that "radical" reform, in economic and especially political matters, will be de-stabilizing. In the words of *Outlook Weekly,* "harmony should be achieved in the course of institutional reform." No matter that reform is by nature an effort to upset the status quo, and by definition, disharmonious! The other, even more fundamental reason, could be that thoroughgoing reform will undermine the CCP's authority. And preserving the party's hold on near-absolute power is the bottom line for cadres from all factions and backgrounds.

Twenty-seven years after the start of Deng's reform, the party-and-state appa-ratus still maintains a tight grip on almost all aspects of life, including the economy. Despite genuflection to the rules of the global marketplace, CCP and government authorities still control about 170 so-called aircraft carrier–type enterprises that the CCP hopes to nurture into South Korean–style *chaebols* that are capable of penetrating the world market. Part of the reason for the anemic conditions of the Chinese stock market is that the state is still holding on to about 60 percent of the shares of most of the companies listed on the Shanghai and Shenzhen bourses.[10]

In terms of political reform, the Hu-Wen cabal of firefighters has a clear preference for stop-gap, half-hearted measures. They have licked the bureaucracy into better shape through a more efficient enforcement of the "cadre responsibility system" and through implementing anti-corruption regulations more vigorously. Measures have been taken to boost government transparency to some degree. Most significantly, Beijing has dramatically expanded the base from which the party and government leadership picks cadres and civil servants (see Chapter 4). However, "socialist democracy with Chinese characteristics" is basically a top-down model: the pro-democracy tendencies of the Hu-Wen team do not seem to go much beyond seeking a more efficient and "scientific" way to gauge popular opinion and to consult more experts in the interest of "scientific decision making." As a commentator for the official China News Service put it, the leadership would in the rest of the decade be more conscientious in "listening to public opinion, showing concern for people's livelihood, reflecting people's views, and synthesizing the people's wisdom."[11]

But how about the real thing, such as letting people take part in politics through means including standing for elections, as well as enlarging the scope of checks and balances within the system by allowing political parties to be formed and to compete with the CCP? As usual, the leadership hides behind clichés and platitudes to the effect that China is not ready for it. In a late-2005 interview with the French paper *Figaro,* Premier Wen rehashed this familiar message: "Like other countries, the development of democracy [in China] requires a process [of evolution]."[12] He then cited the not very relevant—and perhaps politically incorrect—example of black Americans having to wait for 100 years before acquiring full political rights in the United States. Did Wen mean, then, that ordinary Chinese are to the CCP mandarins what African Americans were to the Caucasian, Anglo-Saxon elite?

Equally damaging has been the CCP leadership's failure to foster—some would say eagerness to suppress—a Chinese civil society and related trappings such as a relatively free media and information superhighway (see Chapter 6). The police and state-security apparatus have employed chillingly brutal methods to tame the Internet and arrest "Net-dissidents." Particularly after the series of "velvet revolutions" in Central Asian states such as Ukraine and Kyrgyzstan, the Hu administration has redoubled efforts to crack down on NGOs and semi-independent research institutes, particularly those suspected of having received aid from the West. This is despite the fact that quite a few NGOs, such as legal and environmental groups, have been instrumental in helping defuse social conflicts. It is also disturbing that about the only political NGOs that the Hu administration tolerates are those pushing nationalism, seen by some party cadres as the only cohesive force that could hold the nation together. Excessive reliance on nationalism—and even xenophobia—however, is a dangerous way to prop up the regime; this would also compromise the Hu-Wen team's long-standing effort to project the image of the "peaceful rise" of China.

The absence of a healthy and pluralistic civil society has thrown into relief a phenomenon most inimical to the ideal of a harmonious society: the collusion of vested-interest groupings such as the cadre-mandarins, "princeling" businessmen, as well as a new generation of "red capitalists." These power blocs are eagerly joining hands to make a fast buck out of China's "primitive stage of capitalism." And particularly at the rural level, these privileged classes are helped by mushrooming gangs of triads, or Chinese-style mafia. Some of the most vicious cases of confrontation between peasants and the authorities in 2004 and 2005 involved land disputes: cadres, in collusion with property developers or the bosses of mines and hydroelectric companies, forced farmers to vacate their plots. And those peasants who resisted—in addition to lawyers who were helping the suppressed—were beaten up by police as well as village thugs.[13]

As honchos such as Hu and Wen grapple with the problem of when—and how much—to liberalize the system, however, time is not on their side. In a globalized world where China is assuming bigger significance by the day, the leadership needs to realize that whatever decisions they make will affect not only 1.3 billion Chinese but well-nigh everybody else. Officially, CCP theoreticians still subscribe to the 1950s-vintage Five Principles of Peaceful Coexistence, especially the fact that no country, however powerful, can interfere in the internal affairs of others.[14] However, the corollary of this argument, that the CCP leadership is free to do pretty much what it likes within China's boundaries, is becoming more hollow by the day.

Moreover, the extent to which China's economy, jobs, stability—and ultimately the CCP's mandate of heaven—has become dependent on international factors such as trading patterns means that China's Fourth-Generation chieftains can no longer disregard what major countries like the United States think about them. Take the phenomenon, much discussed in the CCP's internal councils, called "America's anti-China containment policy" (see Chapter 5). While opinions are divided as to whether this is a mere bogeyman conjured by the CCP leadership to stir up Chinese nationalism, the United States is indeed in a position, if it so chooses, to "make trouble" for China on fronts including trade and energy supplies. And if, as President George W. Bush has indicated, a key part of American diplomacy is to spread democracy in Asia, Washington could well argue that China has become such a major force that Americans and other concerned global citizens can no longer afford not to pay attention to what's happening inside the country.

Certainly, in a globalized world, the international community has an obligation to be concerned about whether the once and future Middle Kingdom would abide by globally accepted norms. Way back in the 1990s, the hot-button issue was "Who will feed China?" Well, Beijing seems to have solved the problem of food and basic necessities quite well. Now, legitimate questions include: How will China's vaunted 'world factory' be fueled and sustained? And perhaps even: What will happen if the 87,000 "mass incidents" that plagued China in 2005 were to increase to, say 150,000 a year? What will happen if the CCP were to collapse?

So far there are no clear-cut signs to indicate that the party-government-army apparatus cannot go on muddling through for a couple of decades more, as it has done since the 1989 June 4 crisis. However, it is true that in the more than three years that they have been in power, Hu, Wen, and their Politburo colleagues have not yet demonstrated the kind of foresight and courage needed to push forward bold, far-reaching changes to their archaic system. Some Chinese intellectuals have in disappointment started pinning their hopes on the so-called Fifth Generation of cadres—younger, better educated, and in many cases Western-trained officials ranging in age from the late thirties to the early fifties—who are set to succeed the likes of Hu and Wen in the early 2010s (see Chapter 7). However, the world is spinning at a speed exponentially faster than that of the days of Mao, Deng, or even Jiang. Whether the CCP leadership likes it or not, it must initiate real and substantive liberalization of both the economic and political systems in the rest of this decade. To procrastinate further is to invite the possibility of a lose-lose situation for China and the world. And the globe has become too small and too integrated, and China too important, for any worthy Citizen of the World to afford this outcome.

Acknowledgments

Watching, analyzing, and writing about China all require patience, forbearance, clairvoyance, and occasionally, a spark from the heavens. Having studied China intensely—and fairly patiently—since the mid-1970s, and written about figures including Deng Xiaoping, Hu Yaobang, Zhao Ziyang, Jiang Zemin, and Hu Jintao, I can perhaps be forgiven for feeling somewhat put off by the sense of *plus ça change* that the three-year-old Hu Jintao administration has evoked. When, just when, will real change come about? More patience, it seems, is mandatory. I can perhaps console myself with the fact that, at least, I have company aplenty while pursuing this sometimes frustrating, other times mind-blowing chore called China-watching.

In the course of researching and writing this tome, I have benefited from the expert advice and timely tips, tea and sympathy, and much more from the following friends and colleagues: Rick Baum, John Beeston, Jason Blatt, Claudia Bowring, Richard Bush, Jean-Pierre Cabestan, Alfred Chan, May Chan, Timothy T.Y. Chan, Chan Yuen-ying, Gordon Chang, Joseph Caron, Nicholas V. Chen, Windson Chen, Joseph Cheng, Helen Cheng, Cheung Kin-bor, Peter Cheung, Sharon Cheung, Oliver Chou, Linda Choy, Jeremy Connell, Maurice Copithorne, X.L. Ding, Earl Drake, Isaac Ehrlich, Janet Fan, David Faure, Harvey Feldman, Jonathan Fenby, Joseph Fewsmith, David Finkelstein, Terry Foster, Ed Friedman, Fung Wai-kong, Danny Gittings, Brad Glosserman, David Hale, Ryoichi Hamamoto, Robin Hart, Gordon Houlden, Hung Ching-tin, Linda Jakobson, Ken Jarrett, Jin Zhong, Jing Jun, Yoshi Kobayashi, Lut Lams, Carol P.Y. Lai, Jimmy Lai, Diana Lary, Johnny Lau, Dinah Lee, Martin Lee, Theresa Leung, Leung Tin-wai, Angela Li, Linda Li, Joseph Y.Z. Lian, Perry Link, Baopu Liu, Liu Dawen, Kin-ming Liu, Paul Loong, Bernard Luk, Andrew Lynch, Sheila McNamara, Grace Mak, Mak Yin-ting, Man Cheuk-fei, Pamela Mar, Mau Chi-wang, Andrew Mertha, Jonathan Mirsky, Jeanne Moore, Robert Morton, Robin Munro, Kit-Fai Naess, Andrew Nathan, Chris Nelson, Douglas Ng, Ng Ka-Po, Phil Pan, David Ransom, Gary Rawnsley, Ming-Yeh Rawnsley, Norio Saitoh, Orville Schell, Sin-ming Shaw, Masaru Soma, James Tang, Hideo Tarumi, Eric Teo, John Tkacik, K.K. Tse, T.L. Tsim, Toshiya Tsugami, Tu Wei-ming, Willem van der Geest, Steve Vines, Jim Walker, Arthur Waldron, Wang Yan, Wang Ying, Jennifer West, Louis Won, John Wong, Gracia Wong, Linda Wong, Wing Thye Woo, Wu Jiaxiang, Harry X.Y. Wu, Xia Taining, Dali Yang, Yang Fan, Yang Lujun, Yu Maochun, Ray Yep, Zhang Weiguo,

Zheng Yongnian, Arnold Zeitlin, and David Zweig. (For the sake of simplicity, their titles and honorifics have been omitted.) There are also many good friends in China whose names unfortunately have to remain anonymous.

Special thanks are due to President Mineo Nakajima of Akita International University, Japan, with which I have been associated since early 2005. Administrators, faculty, and staff of AIU, a refreshingly innovative liberal-arts, English-speaking university, have given me enormous support. I must also thank President Glen Howard, as well as the board and staff of Jamestown Foundation, the distinguished think tank in Washington, D.C., for years of help and encouragement.

Professors David Wall and Wu Guoguang, plus a number of Sinologists, kindly read parts of the manuscript and offered suggestions for improvement. Heartfelt thanks are due to long-time friends John Hoffman and Frankie Leung for advice on negotiating the cunning corridors of Chinese affairs. I would like to note my appreciation for the friendship of schoolmate and colleague Ching Cheong, who was detained by Chinese authorities in April 2005 while trying to obtain a manuscript about revered reformer Zhao Ziyang.

I am very much obliged to the management and staff of M.E. Sharpe, Inc., for their tremendous help. In particular, Asian Studies editor Patricia Loo has furnished me with much encouragement in addition to brilliant suggestions. I am indebted to Managing Editor Angela Piliouras, copyeditor Susanna Sharpe, Editorial Coordinator Maki Parsons, as well as other editing, production, and marketing specialists at the distinguished publishing house, for generous assistance on different fronts.

Above all, I must express my gratitude for the spiritual and other support given me over so many years by my dear, sweet wife Grace. We are very thankful to have two loving, smart, and kind-hearted kids, Michelle Ching-wen and Julian Wen-chung. I am reasonably confident that they will see a China that is more humane, more harmonious, and above all, more democratic.

Chinese Politics in the
Hu Jintao Era

1

Introduction

The Rise of Hu Jintao and the
Traits of the Fourth-Generation Leadership

Great Expectations for the Hu Jintao Administration

China—and the world—had great expectations of the Fourth-Generation leadership that was ushered into place at the Sixteenth Chinese Communist Party (CCP) Congress in November 2002. While the nation, or at least its "gold coast," had largely prospered during the thirteen-year stewardship of ex-president Jiang Zemin, the *Shanghaibang* (Shanghai Faction) honcho did not exactly impress domestic or foreign observers with his visionary statecraft or commitment to thoroughgoing reform. Moreover, there was evidence from 2000 onward that Jiang and his *Shanghaibang* protégés such as Zeng Qinghong were more concerned with holding onto power than pushing forward with reform. This was fully demonstrated by Jiang's refusing to yield perhaps his most important post—chairman of the policy-setting Central Military Commission (CMC) at the end of the congress.[1]

It is fair to say that Chinese, particularly the intelligentsia, have projected their hopes about an enlightened, pro-reform CCP on two relatively young leaders who acceded to the Politburo Standing Committee (PSC) at the congress: Hu Jintao, who was made CCP general secretary, and Wen Jiabao, premier-designate. Neither Hu nor Wen (both born in 1942) are members of the Shanghai Faction, which has pretty much overstayed its welcome at least in the eyes of cadres and residents outside of the Greater Shanghai Region. And despite subsequent—and largely unconfirmed—rumors about the business dealings of their children, both Hu and Wen have a well-deserved reputation as Mr. Clean.

This chapter will trace the rise of Hu from his humble origins as a political instructor at Tsinghua University and later a hydraulic engineer in remote Gansu Province. Circumstances that prompted Hu's meteoric rise—particularly his close ties with patrons Song Ping and late party chief Hu Yaobang, as well as his "resolute" suppression of the Lhasa riots of 1989—will be examined in detail. Focus will also be put on the difficult relationship between Hu and his immediate predecessor, ex-president Jiang, as well as the power struggle between Jiang's Shanghai Faction and Hu's own Communist Youth League Faction.

Particular attention will be paid to how the president's experience and exposure has shaped his worldview and political philosophy. While Hu's decades of training as a political functionary and commissar have inculcated in him a respect for socialist orthodoxy, he also seems to attach a lot of importance to the CCP making necessary adaptations to meet the challenges of the new century. The careers and political orientations of other Fourth-Generation cadres such as Wen, as well as members of the Shanghai Faction and "Gang of Princelings," will be analyzed. The chapter will end by asking the overwhelming question of whether China under a Hu administration will make bold departures, particularly in political, structural, and institutional reforms.

Hu's Meteoric Rise and His Power Base

Hu's Humble Beginnings

It was clear from the outset that Jiang and Hu had radically different personalities, styles, and philosophies. Ex-president Jiang had an expansive—his critics would even say buffoon-like—style. He liked to sing karaoke—and his repertoire ranges from Elvis Presley love songs to the classical aria "O Sole Mio." Jiang made international headlines while singing this aria together with Pavarotti during the maestro's visit to Beijing in 2001. Hu is polite and correct—but hardly effusive—in public. Yet Hu—the putative "core" of the *disidai* or Fourth-Generation leadership—is known to be an accomplished dancer, at least in his younger days. While a Communist Youth League (CYL) instructor at Tsinghua University, he was a star in song-and-dance troupes at that elite institute of higher learning. It was also his fancy footwork that reportedly helped him win the favor of classmate Liu Yongqing, who would later become Mrs. Hu. And until his emergence as party general secretary at the Sixteenth Congress, Hu mainly preserved his helmsman-in-waiting status by dancing to Jiang's music.[2]

Indeed, one of the characteristics of Hu—and to some extent, Wen Jiabao, who was named premier in March 2003—was his willingness to prance and gyrate to the tune of party elders or top honchos. Hu's numerous patrons included the governor of Gansu Province in the early 1970s, Li Dengying; "Godfather of Gansu Province" Song Ping; former party chief Hu Yaobang; late patriarch Deng Xiaoping; and to some extent, even Jiang. The ability to play the role of faithful understudy—and an unusual knack for avoiding mistakes—helped propel Hu to the very top. Yet these qualities might not help him spin out bold visions for running the party or country.

It is not for nothing that many Western observers have this standard joke about Hu Jintao: "Who's Hu?" or "Hu's on top?" Hu's enigmatic persona began with his birthplace. The Fourth-Generation stalwart's official biographies said he was born in Jixi County, Anhui Province, a rural township that had produced a number of senior officials and literary figures. They included modern China's great philosopher and writer, Dr. Hu Shih—"China's Bertrand Russell." The truth, however, is that while the ancestors of the Hu family had hailed from Jixi, his forebears left the place about 180 years ago. Hu was actually born in Taizhou, Jiangsu Province, where he attended primary and secondary schools. Hu has been reluctant to point to his connection with Taizhou for various reasons. Taizhou is only a stone's throw from Yangzhou, the hometown of Jiang Zemin; it is also close to the home village of another Politburo Standing Committee member of the 1990s, former vice-premier Li Lanqing. For Hu to list his hometown as Taizhou, Jiangsu, would give rise to criticism that too many present-day leaders hail from the same part of China.[3]

Hu's family was not well off: his father—who did not attend university—and mother were humble teachers. However, his grandfather and great-grandfather were tea merchants—and according to Communist Chinese "blood-line" theories, Hu should have been classified a capitalist or at least the descendant of a capitalist clan. Luckily, Hu's nonproletariat background did not stand in the way of his getting into Tsinghua University—usually referred to as China's MIT—in 1959, partly because he did so well at school. There can be little doubt about Hu's above-average IQ: he has a photographic memory that became evident in his high school days. After gaining national prominence in 1992, he has impressed foreign guests mostly by being able to deliver long speeches or cite complicated data without referring to "prompt notes."

Hu's four years at Tsinghua University coincided with the worst famine in Chinese history, in which more than 10 million people starved to death. Food available at the elite university was minimal and Hu lived in a spartan dormitory with four other students. At that time hydraulic engineering was all the rage because of the call for building better and stronger infrastructure for the new China; and so Hu enrolled in this subject. His first patrons were the top administrators in Tsinghua, including President Jiang Nanxiang. This enabled him to be inducted into the CYL and also to have a good citation—a "red and expert youth"—written in his dossiers when he became a party member in college. After graduation in 1964, just two years before the start of the Cultural Revolution (1966–76), Hu stayed behind in Tsinghua as a political instructor. There is no record of his becoming excessively involved in the internecine bickering—sometimes even physical combat—among factions in the famous university. However, as a political instructor he was identified with the discredited establishment of college bureaucrats. And the young Hu was bitterly unhappy, particularly during the first, violent phase of the Cultural Revolution.[4]

At the end of 1968, Hu was recruited by the Ministry of Hydraulic Engineering. The young engineer was sent to "learn from the masses" in poor northwestern Gansu Province, where he assumed positions as technician, secretary, and head of lower-level party cells in various hydraulic stations along the upper reaches of the Yellow River. Hu was to stay in Gansu for fourteen years. Of course, he had little choice at the time and was probably glad to be away from the centers of power struggles during the Cultural Revolution. Hu did not know at that time that he had made a superb career move. Given the poverty and remoteness of Gansu, it is surprising that a good number of top cadres first earned their spurs there. Among current Politburo members they include Premier Wen Jiabao and "strongwoman" Vice-Premier Wu Yi. For Hu, the only consolation during that period was that his girlfriend Liu was also in Gansu—and they were married in 1970. The Hus were given a tiny apartment and they had to share a kitchen and toilet with other families living along the same corridor. Mrs. Hu gave birth to a son in 1971 and a daughter in 1972.[5]

Hu's reputation as both red (meaning politically reliable) and expert stood him in good stead. In 1973, the young man left the hydraulic stations and became a bureaucrat at the provincial Construction Commission, which was in charge of infrastructure projects, construction materials, and energy. Hu's big break came in 1980, when he rose to become a vice-chief of the Gansu Construction Commission. This was a senior position for a thirty-eight-year-old cadre, equivalent to a deputy head of department in a central-level ministry. Hu's main patron was Governor Li Dengying, who was a wartime comrade of the uncle of Mrs. Hu's.

Hu also benefited from his substantial—though relatively indirect—connection with Song Ping, then party secretary of Gansu. Song was also a graduate of Tsinghua; and Song's wife was a senior party official at Tsinghua when Hu was studying there. Hu, then a student CYL leader and political instructor, impressed Song's wife with his good grades and political zeal. Song became a member of the Politburo Standing Committee in 1989 and his influence in high-level politics remained until the early 2000s. Song is a conservative who is opposed to market reforms, and he and his wife helped instill in Hu a firm belief in the imperative of party supremacy. Song's influence on Hu has also been demonstrated by the number of cadres who have become the latter's allies. For example, Premier Wen (see following section), who also spent the first part of his career in Gansu, benefited from Song's patronage. And Zhang Xuezhong, the current party boss of Sichuan Province, served as one of Hu's deputies during the latter's stewardship of Tibet. Zhang had earlier been a personal secretary of Song Ping's.[6]

Compared to his immediate forebears—including Jiang Zemin and Zhu Rongji, both of whom were relative late bloomers—Hu had a series of lucky breaks early in his career. Another big opportunity awaited Hu in 1981, when he was sent for one year's training at the Central Party School. By sheer luck, the young turk was put in the same class as Hu Deping, the ultra-liberal son of Hu Yaobang, who was to become party chief in 1982. Thanks to the introduction of Hu Deping, Hu Jintao got to know the party chief—perhaps his biggest patron—quite well. And owing to Hu Yaobang's recommendation, Hu returned to Gansu as head of the provincial CYL—and he became a rising star not only in Gansu but nationally.[7]

Briefly afterward, in 1982, Hu was appointed a secretary of the national CYL party committee, a vice-ministerial position. After fourteen years, the Tsinghua graduate finally moved back to the comforts—and opportunities—of the capital. Just four years previously, Deng had unseated the Gang of Four and kicked off the open-door policy. Thanks to Hu Yaobang's patronage, Hu became First Secretary of the CYL party committee in 1984. He had assumed a ministerial-level position at the tender age of forty-two—one of the youngest ministerial-level cadres in the post–Cultural Revolution era. For such a bright young man, the sky was the limit.

While at the league, Hu also got on good terms with Hu Qili, another former CYL chief who later became Politburo Standing Committee member in charge of ideology. The Three Hus—Hu Yaobang, Hu Qili, and Hu Jintao—were considered a liberalizing influence in Chinese politics. While Hu spent no more than three years at the CYL, it was a vital opportunity for him to gain access to the vast talent pool that the league represented. For the first time, Hu was able to build up a national network of fellow cadres and intellectuals: many of his friends and associates of that time became important members of the Hu Jintao or CYL Faction, which coalesced in the mid-1990s. Also at the CYL, Hu became universally known as a polite, courteous young cadre who did not put on airs and who was friendly to young men and women who were carving out their careers in the capital.[8]

To prepare Hu for a major promotion, Hu Yaobang sent his protégé in 1985 to another poor province, Guizhou, to gather more regional experience. At the Chinese New Year in early 1986, Hu Yaobang showed his concern for the younger Hu by spending Spring Festival in Guiyang, capital of the province. Again, fate—and circumstances—was kind to Hu Jintao, who stayed in the province until 1998. If he had remained in the capital, the hotshot cadre might have been badly hit by the disgrace of his mentor Hu Yaobang, who was ousted in January 1987 for failing to properly handle the student movement a month earlier.

While in Guizhou, Hu Jintao did his best to improve the economy of the land-locked province. He personally visited the eighty-six counties and cities in the province, thus earning the nickname the "walking map of Guizhou." The young party boss was also praised for his willingness to talk to—and empathize with—junior cadres as well as ordinary peasants. However, local officials were sometimes frustrated with Hu's unwillingness to give his own views on policy matters. They used the expression *dishui bulou*—a reference to a container that is so airtight not even a drop of water can leak—to describe the tight-lipped senior cadre. Guizhou folks said then that they still preferred Hu's predecessor Zhu Houze, another protégé of Hu Yaobang's. During Hu Yaobang's tenure as general secretary, Zhu was head of the Propaganda Department—and he played a big role in liberalizing party ideology as well as lifting the party's straitjacket on the media and the arts. While Hu was deemed an honest, noncorrupt cadre, he conscientiously toed the line from Beijing. Zhu, on the other hand, was noted for his originality of thinking and willingness to consider measures more liberal than those recommended by the central party authorities.[9]

Deng's "Hu Yaobang Complex": How Hu Became the Heir Apparent

Why was Hu designated a potential "core" of the Fourth-Generation leadership in 1992, when the unheralded cadre surprised practically all China watchers by being inducted into the Politburo Standing Committee? The roots of Hu's rise to real prominence lay in his transfer to Tibet in late 1988. In itself, the move to the poor western province was not a good omen for any cadre's rise to the top. If Hu's star had been ascending at that time, he would have been posted to a rich coastal province such as Jiangsu or Guangdong, given that he had already served long years in hard-scrabble Gansu and Guizhou. Immediately after Hu Yaobang's downfall in January 1987, Hu enraged a number of party elders, particularly Bo Yibo, by refusing to join in an all-out critique of his former boss. So his transfer to destitute Tibet was in a sense a punishment if not demotion.[10]

Moreover, the young party secretary was to have a hot potato on his hands. Lhasa and other Tibetan cities had by late 1986 already been simmering with unrest and even small-scale anti–Han Chinese demonstrations. A few months before Hu's transfer to Lhasa, Beijing decided to defuse the time bomb by sending the revered Panchen Lama—the second most important religious figure in Tibet after the Dalai Lama—back to his homeland. The Panchen Lama had long been faithful to Beijing, and the CCP authorities hoped his return to Tibet would help stabilize the situation. Unfortunately for Beijing—and for Hu—the Panchen Lama suffered a heart attack while preaching and died in January 1989. The situation began to get out of hand. Anti–Han Chinese sentiments culminated in a bloody insurrection on March 5.[11]

Hu was flabbergasted—but very soon decided he had no choice but to act tough. The party boss was concurrently political commissar of the Tibet People's Liberation Army (PLA) District and the Tibet People's Armed Police (PAP) District. Hu ordered the police and PAP officers to restore order—and persuaded Beijing to declare martial law on March 8, 1989. With streets full of uniformed security personnel, Lhasa experienced perhaps its tensest moment since the Dalai Lama fled the region in the late 1950s.[12]

While Hu is generally credited with brandishing the iron fist in Lhasa, what happened the night of March 5—which marked the climax of anti–Han Chinese and anti-Beijing demonstrations—reveals a level of cunning and political maturity rare for a forty-seven-year-old cadre. According to sources close to the Hu camp, the then Tibet party boss played a crafty game. Earlier on that fateful day, angry Tibetans had been surrounding the police headquarters of Lhasa. By early evening, there were signs that the police and PAP guards were no longer able to maintain control. The head of police had sought instructions from Hu by telephone since the late afternoon. The police chief wanted to know whether they could use force to disperse the mob. Hu's reply was: "Keep a close watch on the situation. Don't act yet—wait for my instructions." By early evening, however, the protestors had started throwing stones into the premises and some policemen were hurt. And still Hu's instruction on the phone was the same: "Remain on high alert and wait for my instructions." Then, shortly after nightfall, the police chief called again saying the rioters were trying to burn the place down. Hu's reply was the same. After this, the party boss ordered his aides to unplug the telephone so that the police chief could no longer get through.[13]

What happened later was expected. Even without an explicit authorization from the party secretary, the police chief had no choice but to order his men to use force—and shoot to kill if necessary—to chase away the rioters. He also called for help from the PAP officers. The "rebellion" was quickly suppressed because the protestors did not have heavy weapons and were badly outgunned. Late that night, Hu reported to Beijing that the situation had come under control after some "valiant action" by the police and the PAP. The credit for this successful restoration of order would of course go to Hu. However, should something terrible have happened—for example, if the draconian police action were to backfire and the rioting worsen the next day—Hu could always put the blame on the police chief on the grounds that he had never given his personal approval for use of force.

A rare picture of Hu in military helmet and anti-riot gear—taken by a senior New China News Agency (NCNA) journalist named Tian Congming, who would later become president of the state news agency—appeared in the March 8 edition of *Tibet Daily*. Friends and superiors of Hu who saw the photo were surprised: the scholarly, kind-hearted Confucianist cadre suddenly assumed the air of a tough, belligerent hatchet man. In the course of the "crush-the-rebellion" crusade that week, more than sixty pro-independence "splittists" were killed mainly by police and PAP officers.[14]

In the eyes of Western politicians and commentators, Hu's participation in—if not masterminding of—the bloody suppression of the pro-independence movement became an indelible blot on his record. Many diplomatic analysts are convinced that the crushing of the Lhasa "rebellion" in March 1989 became a model for the CCP leadership's even more ruthless crackdown of the democracy movement in Beijing and other cities a few months later. Hu, as well as Chinese authorities, was reluctant to release detailed information about the senior cadre's Tibet years. The NCNA picture of Hu in military gear, for example, is no longer available. However, there was little question that Hu's "bold and resolute" stance against the pro–Dalai Lama activists earned him the respect of central leaders, particularly Deng Xiaoping. Not long after the March incident, Hu developed high-altitude sickness—whose after-effects, in the form of acute headaches, still haunt him today. In late 1989 Hu was forced to move back to Beijing—and he ran Tibet by remote control. In total, Hu spent no more than a year and a half in Tibet.[15]

The surprise at Hu's ascent was perhaps shared by Hu himself when he was made a member of the ruling Politburo Standing Committee (PSC) during the Fourteenth Party Congress in late 1992. At that time, Jiang had already been party chief for three years. Since Hu was associated with the discredited CYL Faction—and he had had few prior dealings with Jiang—the latter's original idea was to name Hu minister of water resources or minister of education. These positions would suit Hu's background as a technocrat. But Jiang was overruled by Deng, who said Hu deserved a much higher post. Deng reportedly told Jiang that "it would be a mistake to waste such a big talent."[16]

Why did Deng pick Hu as a potential successor to Jiang—as well as head of the Fourth-Generation leadership? First of all, there was the "Hu Yaobang complex."

Deng had felt guilty all along for unceremoniously dumping Hu Yaobang in January 1987. It was well known to cadres as well as intellectuals that the removal of Hu was, strictly speaking, unconstitutional since it was done in an "enlarged Politburo meeting" and without formal approval of the full Central Committee. Moreover, Bo Yibo, Chen Yun, and other elders who bitterly criticized Hu Yaobang in that fateful meeting had already retired and occupied no important positions in the party.

Deng hoped the appointment of Hu Jintao—a man associated with the liberal traditions of Hu Yaobang, Hu Qili, and the CYL—would signify to the world that China would soon have a Fourth-Generation leader different from—and more reform-oriented than—Jiang, the "core" of the Third Generation. In January and February of 1992, Deng had made known his disapproval of Jiang's conservative ways by going to southern China and giving a series of speeches on the imperative of no-holds-barred reform. The patriarch had complained to his family members and aides that the atmosphere in Beijing was too stifling—hence the need for him to go south to speak his mind. In 1992, Deng also briefly entertained the idea of sacking Jiang and finding another general secretary.[17] Moreover, Deng, who was nearing the end of his career, had turned slightly mellow. He reportedly told associates that Hu Jintao "has a good heart" because after Hu Yaobang's disgrace, the younger Hu was only one of two associates of the disgraced party chief who did not engage in an open criticism of their former boss. (The other was Li Ruihuan, also a CYL alumnus. Deng also had a favorable impression of Li, a former Tianjin mayor who made it to the PSC in 1997.)[18]

Equally important, Hu Jintao lived up to Deng's criterion of "being tough with both fists": Hu had liberal and pro-market inclinations; yet at critical moments when the CCP was threatened, he was bold and resolute in crushing the party's enemies, which was demonstrated by his Tibet career. Thus, in Deng's mind, the young man was even more capable than either Hu Yaobang or Zhao Ziyang—the party general secretary disgraced soon after the June 4 massacre—in the difficult task of striking a balance between liberalization and repression. After all, Hu Jintao had cultivated his "red and expert" credentials even when he was a lowly student at Tsinghua. Other key criteria for the Fourth-Generation leadership "core" that Hu Jintao satisfied included age and "geographical distribution." In 1992, he was the only below-fifty cadre with substantial experience in both Beijing and the provinces. And while the former CYL boss hailed from eastern China, he was one of the few top-level cadres who had served for long years in Gansu, Guizhou, and Tibet.

Hu's Personality and Traits: A Man for All Seasons

Hu's Tricks for Survival: Self-Effacement and Accommodation of His Bosses

On his one-day visit to Malaysia in April 2002, then vice-president Hu was besieged by a number of international reporters. "You are really a mysterious man," said one journalist. "It's not fair to call me mysterious," Hu replied. Nonetheless, for the then Number 2—and now Number 1—leader of a nation of 1.3 billion people, Hu's personality, beliefs, and worldview were and are steeped in mystery.

According to an expert on Chinese politics, Zong Hairen (aka Zhang Liang, the author of the bestselling *Tiananmen Papers*), party authorities including the CCP Organization Department conducted an internal assessment of the former CYL chieftain before he was inducted into the PSC in late 2002. Four points were made about Hu's political traits: (1) Hu has a strong faith in Marxism; he is totally loyal to the party; (2) he is good at linking theory to practice; he goes deeply among the people and has good relations with the masses; (3) Hu has the big picture of the well-being of the nation at heart; he has a democratic work style and is willing to listen to views from different sectors—after which he can make tough decisions; (4) he is clean and noncorrupt; he has a plain lifestyle and a strong sense of responsibility.[19]

The contrast between Jiang and Hu is clear. Jiang had a "Shanghai-style" personality of expansiveness; he liked to talk and gesticulate wildly, to show off, to be the star of every occasion, and to throw big parties. Despite his frequent outings to poor areas in China to demonstrate his "concern for the masses," Jiang thrived in metropolises such as Beijing and Shanghai. He had little personal knowledge of— or feel for—the impoverished countryside. By contrast, Hu is quiet, introverted, and prone to serious thought. Yet thanks to more than fifteen years working in the poorest parts of China, he has a genuine understanding of the common man. According to a Western diplomat who accompanied Hu during parts of his trip to Europe in late 2001, Hu felt at home while visiting peasant families in Germany. "Hu asks the relevant questions about farming," the diplomat said. "This shows he is a man of the countryside, not the big cities."[20]

One thing is certain about Hu: he has a gentle disposition, does not like to put on airs, and he is very approachable. According to cadres who knew him when he was at the CYL, Hu acted as a big brother to young party members as well as professionals. He would never turn down requests from provincial CYL members who wanted to take pictures with their "young and smart leader." "Wang Zhaoguo, his immediate predecessor as CYL chief, behaved like a grand mandarin," said one former CYL official. "Yet Hu Jintao is close to the masses." At that time, Hu's personal secretary was Ling Jihua (now the Number 2 at the General Office of the CCP Central Committee). The official recalled that at one point, he tried to call up Ling. But Ling was not in and it was Hu who answered the phone. "Hu said on the phone, 'I am Jintao,' in a mild and friendly tone," the official recalled. "Because the connection was bad, I couldn't hear him properly and I kept on shouting, 'Who are you?' Yet every time, it was the same gentle reply, 'I am Jintao; what can I do for you'?" Most senior cadres in China would never pick up the phone and take messages for their underlings, let alone assume such a pleasant telephone manner.[21]

After his surprising induction into the PSC in 1992, Hu began a ten-year career of self-effacement—and did a splendid job of not outshining more senior members of the supreme council, especially Jiang. According to the division of labor of the five-man PSC, Hu should have been in charge of party affairs. However, Hu would always defer to not just first-among-equals Jiang, but other more experienced PSC members such as then premier Li Peng and then vice-premier Zhu Rongji. After the Fifteenth Party Congress in 1997—and despite the death of possibly his last mentor, Deng—Hu gained additional titles and influence: he became state vice-president in 1998 and CMC vice-chairman 1999.

Yet it was precisely in the late 1990s that Hu adopted a markedly more subservient attitude in the area of what Chinese pundits call "making propaganda" for his boss, Jiang. For example, from late 1998 through 1999, Hu was at the forefront of giving publicity to Jiang's "Theory of the Three Emphases" ("emphasis on politics, on studying [the Marxist canon] and on righteousness"). The same was true for efforts by Hu to popularize the "Theory of the Three Represents" (see Chapter 3). This is despite the fact that Jiang more often than not consulted his cronies and aides rather than Hu when it came to formulating new ideas and slogans. For example, both the "Three Emphases" and "Three Represents" could be ascribed to suggestions made by Zeng Qinghong and Wang Huning, the vice-chief (and later chief) of the Central Committee Policy Research Office.[22]

However, Hu is neither Lin Biao—at one time Mao's Number 2—nor Hua Guofeng, Mao's designated successor. Both General Lin, a career soldier, and Hua, a public security official, climbed the ladder through currying the favor of Mao and protesting their "undying loyalty" to the Great Helmsman. Hu, a well-read intellectual, clearly has a mind of his own. It is just that, having learned the lessons of Hu Yaobang and Zhao Ziyang—Deng's two ill-fated Number 2s—Hu became a past master at self-denial largely by hiding his ambitions, and very often, even his thoughts.

In an unobtrusive manner, Hu has from the late 1990s quietly prepared to take power. He used the Central Party School, which he had headed since 1993, as an experimental ground for developing new ideas of governance. According to Harvard University Asia expert Ezra Vogel, academics and researchers created a fairly vibrant and at times unorthodox atmosphere at this top institute of ideology. Vogel was among many foreign experts invited to give lectures at the CPS. He said discussions were lively and the students "spend a considerable amount of time studying the national situation and international politics and economics." Vogel has this assessment of Hu: "Those of us who have met Hu Jintao have been favorably impressed. He talks without notes, gives nuanced, well-informed answers and is personable. He is familiar with the major issues China faces domestically and internationally." As we shall see in later chapters, many of Hu's new ideas about "intra-party democracy" and other issues were first thrashed out by Hu protégés at the CPS.[23]

The other way in which Hu tried to expand his power base without incurring Jiang's jealousy was just by acting in a humble, crowd-pleasing manner. As

Confucius used to say, a virtuous official must first set a good example for his colleagues. Unlike leaders on the political stage including Jiang or even the much-admired Zhu Rongji—whose children were nonetheless often in the news as businessmen—Hu made sure that his kids kept a low profile. His daughter Hu Haiqing (aka Hu Xiaohua), who had studied in the United States, is in the biotechnology and pharmaceutical industry. And his son Hu Haifeng heads a high-tech company called Nuctech, which is associated with Tsinghua University. One of the few times when the Hu children appeared in the news was when Hu Haiqing got married to famous Internet businessman Daniel Mao in Hawaii in 2003.[24]

As veteran Hong Kong Sinologist Ting Wang indicated, Hu set an example of prudence and frugality by having only a small team travel with him when he toured the provinces. At least before he became state president in 2003, Hu gave instructions to the NCNA and official media not to mention the titles of the aides who were traveling with him. Ting added that the new supremo kept up the tradition he set in Guizhou of not giving interviews to the media; he was particularly anxious not to talk about his personal life with domestic and foreign journalists.[25]

Can Hu Outlive His Relatively Circumscribed Experience?

There is much truth to the observation that despite his moderate and even liberal persona, Hu is a quintessential Marxist and CCP cadre who is convinced that he owes it to the party to do all he can to ensure the survival and viability of its dogma, and especially, the CCP's ruling status (see Chapter 2). Perhaps most critical to the formation and molding of Hu's character and worldview were his six years at Tsinghua as a student, model CYL member, and political instructor. While his life and career were soon disrupted by the Cultural Revolution, the Ten Years of Chaos—which changed the life of perhaps the majority of China's educated class—apparently did not affect the devoted Youth Leaguer's faith in the party and Marxist ideology.

Hu's relatively smooth ride to the top has also illustrated a prominent trait of his personality: a willingness to trim his sails to suit different patrons. Party elders ranging from conservative Song Ping to ultra-liberal Hu Yaobang appreciated Hu's talents—and his obedience. Deng, who was at times liberal and at other times conservative, also considered the former CYL chief trustworthy. And ex-president Jiang, who would rather have seen his protégé Zeng Qinghong succeed him, failed during ten long years—from 1992 to 2002—to find an excuse to elbow Hu aside. Which leads to this question: will a cadre who is so adept at pleasing different factions and patrons—as well as avoiding mistakes—be imbued with a burning desire to ring in the new or to stamp his own personality on the political stage?[26]

As the leader of such a complex country as China, Hu's one obvious virtue is that he is probably acceptable to most factions and power sectors in the party and community. The disadvantage, however, is that the sixty-three-year-old leader may have been conditioned by his long years'of training to play it safe, to avoid making unpopular decisions, to cleave to the middle of the road, and to maintain "stability" at all costs. It would be most unlikely for Hu to contemplate taking big risks on either economic reform—as both Deng and Zhao Ziyang did—or political reform, as was the case with Hu Yaobang and Zhao. Instead, the new supremo would rather err on the side of caution, as the rest of this book will demonstrate.

Another important characteristic of Hu's worldview is that being an old-school party cadre, he has reservations about globalization—and Westernization. This is despite the fact that both Hu and Fourth-Generation leaders such as Wen seem to be keen supporters of the integration of the Chinese economy with the international marketplace. It is apparent, however, that in ideological, political, and diplomatic matters, Hu wants to strike a balance between leaning toward the United States and the West on the one hand, and reviving China's traditional friendship with socialist or formerly socialist countries such as Russia, and even Cuba and North Korea, on the other. It is no secret that Hu is critical of Jiang's "pro-U.S." policy—and that he wants to seek a balance between East and West by in many ways moving closer to Russia[27] (see Chapter 5).

It is no accident that Hu's "coming out" overseas tour as heir apparent to Jiang—which took place in October 2001—began in Russia. And the first country Hu visited after becoming state president in March 2003 was also Russia. An even more telling snippet that illustrated Hu's fairly orthodox views was that during his packed two-day visit to Moscow in late 2001, he took time out to visit a museum dedicated to the Ukrainian "revolutionary heroes" lionized in Nikolai Ostrovsky's *How the Steel Was Tempered,* a classic propaganda novel whose Chinese translation proved immensely popular in the China of the early 1960s.[28]

Despite Hu's relatively young age, it is evident that the Fourth-Generation honcho is much more of a "regular party man" than mavericks such as former premier Zhu Rongji, Hu Yaobang, or Zhao Ziyang. Zhu, who was labeled a "rightist" in the late 1950s for singing the praises of the radical reforms in Yugoslavia and Hungary, recognized the limitations of the CCP and the socialist order very early on in his life. And while Zhao and Hu Yaobang had been orthodox Communists in their younger days, both realized after they had reached the top that something radical needed to be done to overhaul the system.[29]

Hu's Path to Power—Skulduggery at the Sixteenth Party Congress

While the Jiang-led Shanghai Faction pretty much dominated Chinese politics from 1989 to 2002, it is significant that Hu had, in his unassuming way, assembled a formidable power network in the run-up to the Sixteenth Party Congress. Indeed, among Fourth-Generation chieftains, the ex-CYL boss had perhaps the largest following, particularly in the provinces and cities. By late 2002, a few dozen CYL alumni—plus other Hu associates, principally cadres with experience in the western provinces—had already held important positions in both the central and regional administrations.

As discussed earlier, Hu had since 1992 bent over backwards to hide his ambitions and to accommodate himself to the requirements of ex-president Jiang. As late as 2001 and early 2002, the then vice-president was at the forefront of the campaign to enshrine Jiang's "Theory of the Three Represents" in the state as well as party Constitution. An examination of how Hu could, despite daunting restraints, succeed in emerging as China's paramount leader will reveal much about the new supremo's character and statecraft.

Jiang and Hu: A Most Uneasy Relationship

A major contradiction in Chinese politics was that while Hu was to all intents and purposes the designated successor of Jiang, he was not a member of the Jiang Zemin or Shanghai Faction. After all, Hu was ordained top leader of the Fourth Generation by Deng and other party elders, such as Song Ping. Thus Hu certainly did not owe his helicopter ride to the PSC in 1992 to Jiang.

After Jiang became party general secretary in 1989, Hu went out of his way to defer to Jiang. However, the two shared mutual suspicions. Jiang had since 1992 been watching Hu closely for signs of possible insubordination, and the ex-president rarely consulted with Hu on substantial state matters. For example, the power over personnel appointments was tightly controlled by Jiang protégé Zeng Qinghong. Jiang was clearly afraid that after his retirement, his legacy might be overturned or at least revised and adulterated by Hu. And Hu realized that Jiang would actually prefer to pass his mantle to alter ego Zeng, who had helped his mentor get rid of a series of political foes that included Beijing mayor Chen Xitong, former president Yang Shangkun, and General Yang Baibing, as well as Politburo heavyweights Qiao Shi and Li Ruihuan.[30] And it was no secret that from the late 1990s, Jiang had tried to groom Zeng, known for his high-level connections as well as political savvy, as a possible counterweight to Hu.

Yet owing probably to Zeng's unpopularity—and his reputation as Jiang's ruthless hatchet man—the ex-president failed to mobilize enough support for the alternate member of the Politburo to gain full Politburo status at the fifth and sixth plenums of the Central Committee in 2000 and 2001 respectively. And there were indications throughout 2001 that the president finally decided to give Hu fuller backing in return for an implicit pledge that the Jiang legacy would be preserved intact. For example, Hu was named head of an internal steering group in charge of preparations for the Sixteenth CCP Congress, meaning the vice-president would have a big say in both ideological and personnel matters to be decided at the key conclave. Hu was also asked by Jiang to chair major party meetings to discuss such seminal teachings of the president as the "Theory of the Three Stresses" and the "Theory of the Three Represents."

However, Hu and his aides were not too happy about the fact that Jiang had largely barred the vice-president from participation in foreign and military affairs. This was despite the fact that in the Chinese context, the post of vice-president carries substantial diplomatic functions. It was not until late 2001, when Hu visited Russia, Britain, France, Germany, and Spain, that the supposed "crown prince" to the CCP throne was allowed to engage in big-time diplomacy. Some analysts also believed that Jiang had vetoed an early visit by Hu to the United States despite Washington's anxiety to schedule a trip for the up-and-coming leader. And while Hu was named first vice-chairman of the CMC in 1999, he was kept out of the loop so far as important decision making in defense matters was concerned.[31]

Moreover, Jiang and his cronies also decided to deny Hu the designation of "core" of the Fourth-Generation leadership. This was despite the great satisfaction with which the ex-president enjoyed flaunting his status as "Third-Generation core"; this would make Jiang the equal of Mao and Deng, the "core" of the First- and Second-Generation leadership respectively. In fact, Jiang had since the late 1990s asked the media not to use the term Fourth-Generation leadership or to identify Hu as its head.

Messy Infighting in the Run-up to the Sixteenth CCP Congress

Unlike the days of Mao and Deng, ideology was much weakened under Jiang Zemin. Most of the factions and power blocs within the CCP were defined not so much by distinctive ideological characteristics as by narrow self-interests. In terms of political or economic philosophies, there was not much difference between cliques such as those led by Jiang and Hu. CCP factions are thus rightly seen as interest groupings. For example, the Shanghai Faction looks after the well-being and prospects—power and status, financial resources, and business interests—of the Greater Shanghai Region (including Jiangsu and Zhejiang provinces and the lower reaches of the Yangtze River) as well as those of cadres affiliated with the rich metropolis.[32]

Owing to the fact that the Sixteenth CCP Congress would pave the way for the rise of a new generation—and a major redistribution of powers and perks—internecine bickering and back stabbing among the factions went on right until the eve of the watershed event. Thus, while Third-Generation stalwarts such as Jiang and then Parliament chief Li Peng were past retirement age, they schemed and conspired to hang onto at least one significant party or state post. And cadres who were determined to step down, such as then premier Zhu, did their best to ensure the promotion of their protégés.

Despite the rising momentum of Hu's CYL Faction as well as State Council bureaucrats headed by then premier Zhu and then vice-premier Wen, the Shanghai Faction was able to pull off a series of coups in the run-up to and at the Sixteenth Congress. First, Jiang and Zeng managed to ram through the expansion of the Politburo Standing Committee from seven to nine members. Until mid-2002, the consensus in the incumbent or Fifteenth PSC was that there would be seven PSC members, namely Hu Jintao, Chinese People's Political Consultative Conference (CPPCC) chairman Li Ruihuan, vice-premier Wu Bangguo, vice-premier Wen Jiabao, CCP Secretariat member Zeng Qinghong, law and order specialist Luo

Gan, and Guangdong party chief Li Changchun. And the major posts of party boss; chairman of the National People's Congress (NPC) or parliament; premier; CPPCC chairman; and head of the Central Commission for Disciplinary Inspection (CCDI) would go to respectively Hu, Li Ruihuan, Wen, Wu, and Luo.[33]

Just a few months before the Congress was to convene, however, Jiang maneuvered to have two cronies—Shanghai party chief Huang Ju and Beijing party boss Jia Qinglin—inducted into the PSC. This was despite the fact that except during brief periods in the Cultural Revolution, the CCP PSC usually consists of merely five to seven members so as to facilitate decision making. The inclusion of Huang and Jia—both of whom were haunted by innuendo about incompetence and corruption—however, would ensure that the nine-member PSC would have at least four dyed-in-the-wool Jiang supporters: Zeng, Wu, Huang, and Jia. Until this startling development, the expectation in political circles in Beijing was that both Huang and Jia would head off to ceremonial posts as vice-chairmen of the NPC or the CPPCC.[34]

Equally significantly, the ex-president resorted to draconian means to force former Tianjin mayor Li Ruihuan to retire from the Politburo. This was despite the fact that Li, being sixty-eight at the time, was two years shy of the generally recognized retirement age for a Politburo member. Many analysts believe that Jiang had subtly threatened to expose "black material" that would harm the reputation of the flamboyant and popular CPPCC chairman. Jiang's logic was that given Li's seniority and his perceived closeness to the CYL faction, allowing him to stay on in the PSC would tip the balance of power in favor of Hu.[35] Yet the biggest surprise that the seventy-six-year-old Jiang sprang on Hu—and other non–Shanghai Faction politicians—was his hanging on to the post of CMC chairman. This was the wily Shanghai Faction chief's way of saying that he was the equal of Deng, who also retained the post of commander-in-chief after his retirement from all party and state positions in the early 1980s. However, for reasons including his age—and the fact that he had made unofficial promises to party elders such as Qiao Shi to retire in totality—Jiang's bending of the rules proved extremely unpopular with Congress delegates as well as the majority of cadres.[36]

Yet another crucial element of Jiang-Zeng's scheme to maintain control were the frantic changes of civilian and military personnel in the year before the Sixteenth Congress. From late 2001 onward, the bulk of the party secretaries and governors of the 31 provinces and directly administered cities were reshuffled. Likewise, around 200 mid- to senior-ranked PLA posts at both headquarters units and the regional commands changed hands. Not surprisingly, the Jiang or Shanghai Faction was the major beneficiary of the personnel movement. "Zeng has been accused by cadres outside the Shanghai Faction of using regional reshuffles to boost the Shanghai Faction's share of Central Committee—and Politburo—seats," said a veteran party cadre. It is noteworthy that in 1992 and 1997, when respectively the Fourteenth and Fifteenth Party Congresses were held, large-scale regional reshuffles were not undertaken before the major conclaves. Such changes only took place in the six months or so after the congresses.[37]

It was the change of leadership of the nation's two premier cities—Shanghai and Beijing—that most raised eyebrows in 2002. Rising stars Liu Qi and Chen Liangyu replaced Jia Qinglin and Huang Ju as party bosses of Beijing and Shanghai respectively. Given that both Jia and Huang were headed for the PSC—and that the party chiefs of Beijing and Shanghai are automatically accorded Politburo status—the Jiang Faction was able to put four Shanghai Faction affiliates into the Politburo in one stroke. This was despite the fact that Chen, a fast-rising star, had only been acting Shanghai mayor for several months before his proverbial helicopter ride to the top. Other provinces and cities where Shanghai Faction affiliates made gains in the critical months before the Sixteenth Congress included Guangdong, Chongqing, Jiangxi, and Guangxi.[38]

As the party veteran indicated in late 2002, Jiang and Zeng's personnel reshuffles in the run-up to the Sixteenth Congress would deprive the new party chief of an important means of quickly firming up his grip over the party, government, and army. "In the Chinese tradition, the most effective way for a newly ensconced supremo to establish himself is through appointments and promotions," the veteran cadre said. "However, since Jiang and Zeng have already filled most of the civilian and military slots with relatively young officials, Hu may have to wait a couple of years or more before he can make another series of appointments."[39]

The Rising Fortunes of the Communist Youth League and the "Zhu Rongji–Wen Jiabao Faction"

Part of Hu's claim to being first among equals within the *disidai* leadership was that, next to senior cadres who were affiliated to the Shanghai Faction, he probably had the strongest corps of supporters and underlings. In apparent preparation for taking power, Hu had since the late 1990s been methodically elevating members from his power base, the CYL. After all, Hu first made his mark in Chinese politics as a youthful first secretary of the league in 1984. By early 2002, a sizable number of CYL stalwarts had occupied senior positions at the central and regional levels. CYL affiliates also figured prominently in the Fifth-Generation leadership—a reference to cadres now in their late thirties to late forties (see Chapter 7).

Apart from the CYL, a major component of Hu's talent pool comprises cadres who have worked in the western provinces, as well as areas with heavy ethnic minority populations. This follows from the fact that the new party general secretary spent about half of his career in the three western provinces of Gansu, Guizhou, and Tibet. Cadres close to Hu also include graduates of Tsinghua University, many of whose alumini, such as Wu Bangguo, were important members of the Shanghai Faction. And then there are members of Hu's think tanks, which were licked into shape in the mid-to-late 1990s. Most of these brain trusts are associated with the Central Party School and institutes of higher learning in Beijing such as the Chinese Academy of Social Sciences.[40]

The Hu Jintao or CYL Faction

Strengths of the CYL Faction

At the pivotal Sixteenth Party Congress, Hu managed to install several dozen CYL affiliates in the Politburo as well as in central or regional slots at the level of vice-minister, vice-governor, or above. This was no mean feat for a fifty-nine-year-old cadre who for the past ten years had been sidelined by the CCP's dominant Shanghai Faction.

On the surface, the nine-member PSC created at the Sixteenth Congress was stacked with Jiang cronies such as Zeng Qinghong, NPC chairman Wu Bangguo, CPPCC chairman Jia Qinglin, and Executive Vice-Premier Huang Ju, while the political loyalty of relatively fresh faces such as Head of the Political and Legal Affairs Commission Luo Gan (a protégé of former premier Li Peng's) and former Guangdong party secretary Li Changchun was uncertain. In the full Politburo, Jiang and Zeng could also secure the support of Vice-Premier Hui Liangyu, as well as Chen Liangyu and Liu Qi, the party secretaries of Shanghai and Beijing respectively. These were either affiliates of the Shanghai Faction or cadres who were beholden to Jiang for their promotion. The two generals represented on the Politburo—Guo Boxiong and Cao Gangchuan—were also supposed to be more favorably disposed to Jiang rather than to Hu.[41]

Within the twenty-four-member Politburo, Hu could only rely on the backing of the following: Wen Jiabao, Secretary of the CCDI Wu Guanzheng, NPC vice-chairman Wang Zhaoguo, Xinjiang party secretary Wang Lequan, Vice-Premier Wu Yi, and Head of the CCP Publicity Department Liu Yunshan. However, the momentum was definitely going the way of the Hu-Wen leadership and not the Shanghai Faction. Other things being equal, an average cadre would rather link his fate with leaders of the future than with those of the past. Thus, PSC members with no obvious factional affiliations such as Li Changchun and Luo Gan, as well as Politburo members Zhang Dejiang, Yu Zhengsheng, Zhang Lichang, and He Guoqiang, had by late 2003 begun showing signs of aligning themselves with the Hu Faction. This was despite the fact that cadres such as Li Changchun, Zhang Dejiang, and Yu Zhengsheng seemed to owe their rise more to Jiang than to Hu.[42]

Hu was also boosting the clout of the CYL clique in party and government departments—especially those in regional administrations. Take, for example, Hu's confidante and speechwriter Ling Jihua, who was in 2000 named a vice-director of the Central Committee's General Office (CCGO). It was likely that Ling, who doubled as the head of the Hu Jintao Office, would later become director of the CCGO, deemed the nerve center of the party. Zhang Xuezhong, another Hu ally, was named minister of Personnel in early 2001—and a year or so later transferred to Sichuan as party secretary. Hu first got to know Zhang when they were working in mid-ranking posts in Gansu Province. Zhang was then the personal secretary of the former party secretary of Gansu, Song Ping. Another CYL alumnus, Zhang

Fusen, was made minister of Justice in late 2000. Other Hu Faction affiliates in the central CCP and government apparatus included the following: Director of the United Front Department Liu Yandong; CYL party secretary Zhou Qiang; Minister of Civil Affairs Doje Cering; Minister of Water Resources Wang Shucheng; NCNA director Tian Congming; Vice-Chairman of the China Banking Regulatory Commission (CBRC) Yan Haiwang; and Head of the All-China Women's Federation Huang Qizao.[43]

Hu associates were also well represented in the provinces. In a strategy known as "going deep into the ocean before ascending the mountain," the then vice-president had spent much of the 1992–2002 period cultivating his regional power base. Two cadres stood out among Hu's provincially based followers: Song Defu and Li Keqiang, both former first party secretaries of the CYL. At the time of the Sixteenth Congress, they were, respectively, party secretary of Fujian Province and governor of Henan Province.

Song (born 1946), a former minister of personnel, had been deemed a strong candidate tapped for either the Politburo or the Central Committee Secretariat at the Sixteenth Congress—but he failed to make it. The Hebei native is among the few Hu associates with a solid military background. He joined the army in 1965 and rose through the ranks in the Air Force and the General Political Department before becoming a member of the CYL party committee in 1983. It was Hu who recommended that Song succeed him as CYL head in 1985. Though not famous overseas, Song was known for his political skills—and his ability to avoid controversy. At the height of the 1989 protests, many CYL cadres wanted to hit the streets in support of the students. Song tried to dissuade them from leaving the CYL headquarters—but to no avail. Just as the pro-democracy cadres left the CYL building, Song suffered a heart attack—and he stayed in the hospital until after the "counter-revolutionary turmoil" was over. Thus, the Hu protégé never had to take responsibility for those league officials who joined the student movement. Song was posted by Hu to Fujian in 2001 to take care of the mess left in the wake of the Xiamen corruption scandal. However, Song's political fortune was disrupted when he was diagnosed with cancer in 2004 (see also Chapter 7).[44]

Li Keqiang (born 1955)—one of China's youngest governors—seemed destined for a major role within the Fifth-Generation leadership. A native of Anhui Province, Li entered the Law Department of Peking University in 1977. Like Hu, Li remained in college after graduation to do ideological work. He soon joined the CYL headquarters and worked directly under Hu. Li's appointment as governor of the populous Henan in 1999 was a clear signal that he was being groomed for the top. Analysts familiar with Li's career said the Hu protégé shared personality traits with his mentor: Li kept a low profile, never lost his temper, and never spoke ill of other officials.[45]

Other Hu affiliates who had by late 2002 taken up senior regional posts include the following: Xinjiang party secretary Wang Lequan; Guizhou party secretary Qian Yunlu; governor of Yunnan Xu Rongkai; Gansu party secretary Song Zhaosu and governor of Gansu Lu Hao; governor of Tibet Legqog; governor of Jiangsu Ji Yunshi; governor of Ningxia Ma Qizhi; vice–party secretary of Jiangsu Li Yuanchao; vice–party secretary of Sichuan Liu Peng; vice–party secretary of Guangxi Liu Qibao; vice–party secretary of Qinghai Yang Chuantang; and vice–party secretary of Anhui Shen Yueyue.[46] (Most of these cadres had been promoted by late 2005.)

Analysts said Hu's evident effectiveness in elevating his protégés and putting together a national network through the 1990s would demonstrate a little-known political savvy behind his self-effacing façade. After all, the CYL and the Central Party School, which he also headed, were ideal institutions for spotting and grooming talent, as well as assembling a coterie of followers. In early 1999, Jiang tried to stop Hu's self-aggrandizement by naming Zeng director of the CCP Organization Department. And there were reports of ferocious battles between the two long-standing rivals concerning staff appointments. However, Jiang's move apparently failed to prevent Hu from building a large bloc of faithful adherents, especially at the provincial level.

Weaknesses of the Hu or CYL Faction

Traditionally, the CYL has been a training ground for party cadres—and most league affiliates who have filled senior CCP positions tend to be party affairs specialists rather than technocrats or professional managers. Not too many league alumni can be found in government departments, particularly in areas dealing with the economy, trade, and foreign affairs. This is also true for Hu's CYL protégés. The relatively few Hu associates who have worked in economic units include the Vice-Chairman of the China Banking Regulatory Commission (and former vice-governor of the People's Bank of China) Yan Haiwang and Minister of Agriculture Du Qinglin. Minister of Culture Sun Jiazhen and Minister of Minority Affairs Li Dezhu are among other State Council ministers with CYL backgrounds. At a time when economic and financial affairs have become more and more important, the Hu Faction's lack of expertise in this crucial area could be a big handicap.[47]

The president and party chief has tried to remedy the situation by forming a strategic alliance with State Council technocrats led by Premier Wen. Moreover, Hu has transferred a number of CYL members to central or provincial-level economic departments. Equally importantly, since becoming PSC member in 1992, the then vice-president inducted dozens of experts in economics, finance, foreign trade, and foreign policy into his personal think tanks. These brain trusts have been able to coach Hu and his aides about the intricacies of issues ranging from international trade to Sino-U.S. relations.

Another drawback for Hu is that the would-be core of the Fourth-Generation leadership had few close aides or supporters in the crucial police, judicial, security, and intelligence departments with the exception of then Minister of Justice Zhang Fusen and Head of the Supreme People's Procuratorate Jia Chunwang. The party chief's forte in this area is his overall control over the anti-corruption apparatus. This is thanks to his closeness to the CCDI's Wu Guanzheng as well as Minister of Supervision Li Zhilun. Hu, however, has tenuous links with the PLA and the People's Armed Police. Like Jiang Zemin before him, Hu had to move very quickly to secure the support of the army and police apparatuses once he had become CMC chairman in 2004.[48]

And what about the quality of the average CYL affiliate, particularly the ability to hack out new paths in reform? It is true that the league once boasted prominent reformers such as Hu Yaobang, Hu Qili, and Zhu Houze. Yet it must be remembered that with the majority of leaguers being specialists in Communist ideology, organization, and propaganda issues, they often consider the survival and welfare of the party as the be-all and end-all of statecraft. Indeed, there are quite a number of "leftists" among CYL affiliates such as the vice–party secretary of Jilin Lin Yanzhi, who loudly clamored against the legitimization of private enterprises. And Hu himself began his first term as party boss with a package of plans to perpetuate the CCP's ruling party status (see Chapter 2). The CCP general secretary has also been conscientiously promoting the status of party organs even in government and economic fields. In this regard, Hu represents the mainstream thinking of the CYL, whereas ardent reformers such as Hu Yaobang and Zhu Houze could only be deemed mavericks. And it is probably the younger Hu's more orthodox views on the party and on reform that endeared him to elders ranging from Deng Xiaoping to Song Ping.[49]

Alliance Between the Hu Faction and the Wen-led State Council Bureaucrats

The "Zhu Rongji Faction" of State Council Technocrats

To secure the proverbial "long reign and perennial stability," Hu and his faction had to seek an alliance with the "Zhu Rongji–Wen Jiabao Faction," a group of well-trained technocrats first brought to the fore by former premier Zhu Rongji. While Zhu was arguably one of the least factionally minded cadres in CCP history, it is an unavoidable attribute of party politics that to do his work properly, any senior cadre must cultivate his own personal clique. Although Zhu, who was born in Hunan Province, first gained international renown as Shanghai's mayor, he was not a member of the so-called Shanghai Faction. And only a portion of his trusted aides and underlings had Shanghai roots.

Most of "Boss Zhu's" men and women were concentrated in departments dealing with finance, banking, and the stock market. Well-educated and mathematically minded, these technocrats were convinced that the Chinese economy would take off much along the lines of the four Asian Dragons provided that prudent measures could be taken and unnecessary political interference avoided. Zhu's disciples believed that they should embrace market forces, on the one hand, and pursue "macroeconomic control and adjustments"—meaning fairly tight centralized control—on the other. The latter agenda, which often required old-style government fiats and diktat, was necessary to restructure the country's intractable state firms as well as to tackle negative phenomena such as corruption, manipulation in the stock market, and using bank loans to speculate on the bourses.[50]

One of ex-premier Zhu's most trusted lieutenants was then vice-premier Wen Jiabao, who hooked up with Zhu at a relatively late date. The fire-spitting prime minister was so taken by Wen's abilities that he decided by 2001 to nominate him to succeed himself. While it was well known that President Jiang had since the late 1990s tried to groom then vice-premier Wu Bangguo as well as then Guangdong party chief Li Changchun for the top government job, Zhu was known to have used his "veto power" to block the rise of both Li and Wu. As a result, Li failed to be transferred to Beijing and Wu was not given any major portfolios in the State Council.

In the run-up to the Sixteenth Party Congress, notable Zhu associates included the following: state councilor and alternate Politburo member Wu Yi (born 1936), state councillor and State Council secretary-general Wang Zhongyu (1933), People's Bank of China (PBOC) governor Dai Xianglong (1944), chairman of the China Securities Regulatory Commission (CSRC) Zhou Xiaochuan (1948), and minister at the State Economic and Trade Commission Li Rongrong (1944). Zhu also managed to groom a dozen-odd Fifth-Generation cadres who were expected to be further promoted at the Seventeenth CCP Congress in 2007. Foremost among them were then vice-foreign trade minister Long Yongtu (who subsequently left the government), then vice-governor of the PBOC Guo Shuqing, and Vice-Minister of Finance Lou Jiwei.[51]

Zhu protégés including Wu Yi and Long Yongtu were instrumental in speeding up China's application process for the World Trade Organization (WTO). Those in the financial, banking, and CSRC systems did a relatively competent job restoring fiscal discipline to and promoting transparency in the banking and stock market systems. While Wen was not a typical Zhu-style technocrat, he not only benefited from Zhu's patronage but was able to "inherit" the support of a large number of senior State Council staff whom Zhu had trained. Members of the original "Zhu Rongji faction" who are active in the first Wen cabinet (2003–2008) have included chairman of the National Development and Reform Commission Ma Kai; chairman of the State-Owned Assets Supervision and Administration Commission Li Ronggong; new PBOC governor Zhou Xiaochuan; chairman of China Construction Bank Guo Shuqing; and Finance Minister Jin Renqing as well as his deputy, Lou Jiwei.[52]

The Rise of Wen Jiabao, and the Origins of the "Hu-Wen Leadership"

There is little question that, given the constraints of Chinese politics, Vice-Premier Wen Jiabao was a most suitable candidate to succeed Zhu as premier in early 2003. More significantly, the rise of Wen would make possible perhaps the most significant collaboration between two top leaders since the Mao Zedong–Zhou Enlai show in the 1960s. Hu and Wen apparently decided to form a power pact even before the Sixteenth Congress—and they have had a near-seamless working relationship. The two Fourth-Generation leaders hit it off so well not just because they shared long years of experience in Gansu. Much more important was the fact that they had to cooperate closely to fend off challenges coming from still-powerful Shanghai Faction affiliates in the Politburo, some of whom were seen as millstones round the neck of reform. Indeed, Hu and Wen have complemented each other so well that from early 2003 onward, observers in and out of China have started referring to a Hu-Wen administration—and as though "Hu Wen" were a single person![53]

In terms of division of labor particularly after mid-2005, Hu is in charge of party affairs as well as diplomatic, military, and Taiwan matters. And according to long-standing tradition, Wen takes charge of the economy as well as the entire State Council apparatus. Given Wen's immense authority, it is instructive to examine the geologist's personality, political traits, and strong suits. First, it is not for nothing that Wen is often called a "latter-day Zhou Enlai," a reference to the late premier who is still revered for holding China together during the Cultural Revolution. Apart from the patronage of party elder Song Ping, Wen owes it entirely to his own talent and hard work that he was able to achieve the first break in his career in late 1985, when he was transferred from a vice-ministerial post at the Ministry of Geology to become vice-director of the CCP Central Committee General Office (CCGO).[54]

As China scholar Wu Jiaxiang, a former CCGO researcher, pointed out, Wen landed this vastly more influential post after going through a series of assessments and recommendations given by Organization Department officials and senior ministers. "Wen has superb administrative skills," said Wu. "Particularly given his science background, his ability to draft, handle, and refine official documents is amazing." The Tianjin native also knew how to avoid being entangled in the party's factional intrigues. His superb political sense and skills are demonstrated by the fact that Wen has since the mid-1980s served top leaders including Deng Xiaoping, the late general secretary Hu Yaobang, ousted party chief Zhao Ziyang, President Jiang Zemin, Premier Zhu, and to some extent, President Hu. His apparent closeness to Zhao—which was attested to by the photograph of Wen accompanying the ill-fated party boss to see hunger-striking students at Tiananmen Square in May 1989—almost cost him his career. But after the June 4 massacre, Wen managed to win the trust of Zhao's successor, Jiang, as well as of party elders including Deng and then president Yang Shangkun. Yang reportedly vouched for Wen's loyalty when then premier Li Peng wanted to sack the "Zhao Ziyang underling."[55]

Since moving to the State Council as vice-premier in 1998, Wen quickly proved himself indispensable to his new boss, Premier Zhu. Among the four vice-premiers, Wen held the most important portfolios, including agriculture, finance, and major projects, such as the develop-the-west program and the drafting of the Tenth

Five-Year Plan (2001–2005). Wen, along with then vice-president Hu Jintao and Director of the Organization Department Zeng Qinghong, was responsible for overall preparation for the Sixteenth CCP Congress.

A party source in Beijing commented on Wen's characterization as a "latter-day Zhou Enlai": "The Zhou Enlai nickname came about because of Wen's ability to navigate the vast government bureaucracy—and to oblige different and even rival departments to work together," said the source. "During cabinet meetings, [Premier] Zhu often asks Wen to speak toward the end, that is, to sum up the suggestions of cabinet members. Wen is much less garrulous than fellow cadres such as [Vice-Premier] Wu Banguo. But few can match Wen's ability to convert complicated issues into concise and straightforward policy recommendations." The source added that Wen spoke in a slow, measured rhythm and that he was calm and methodical, an interesting foil to the impatient and headstrong Zhu. Beijing analysts credit a number of important initiatives to Wen. In 1999, the vice-premier suggested limiting the taxes that a farmer had to pay to 5 percent of his income. In 2000, he and Zhu announced that it would be illegal for grassroots administrations to slap extra levies and charges on peasants. Wen was instrumental in expanding the stock markets—and ensuring that better-quality state-owned enterprises could go through quasi-privatization by listing on the bourses.[56]

Perhaps because of the frequency with which Wen appeared on television visiting poor peasants or handling hazardous projects such as flood control, the youthful-looking official projected a positive image among cadres and ordinary citizens. According to Beijing insiders, Wen consistently garnered the highest score in internal opinion polls conducted by the Organization Department on the popularity of high-ranking cadres. However, despite Wen's well-deserved reputation as a "can do" vice-premier and his overall acceptability to all factions, he has also come under criticism. Given that his main portfolio was agriculture, the sorry state of the countryside—the near-stagnant income of farmers and growing numbers of rural riots and demonstrations—could not but hurt his prestige. After all, Premier Zhu, his patron, also admitted at the 2002 NPC that his cabinet's main failure was in the area of ameliorating the livelihood of some 800 million farmers.

Wen's defenders, however, have pointed out that there was little the vice-premier could do given the central leadership's pro-industry and pro-coast bias since Deng Xiaoping assumed power in 1978. After the Sixteenth Congress, there were strong expectations that together with Hu, Wen might to some extent shift the focus of development away from the coast and to the central and western provinces. While most senior cadres on the political stage earned their spurs along the rich coast, both Wen and Hu spent a good chunk of their careers in the hinterland. As we shall see in Chapters 2 and 3, the Hu-Wen team has tried to enhance their national stature—and extend the CCP's heavenly mandate—by stressing their concern for the masses, particularly those living in the neglected heartland and western regions. By contrast, Shanghai's leaders have good reason to fear that the east China metropolis might not be getting as many favorable policies now that the

Jiang-Zeng faction is fading out. There were reports that Shanghai cadres tried hard to have major infrastructure projects approved while Jiang was still around.[57]

In terms of ideology, Wen was expected to steer clear of controversial issues such as political liberalization. Indeed, since his arrival at the Zhongnanhai party headquarters in 1985, Wen has concentrated on bureaucratic and economic matters, not ideology, which is deemed a minefield of risks and uncertainties. In this respect, Wen is similar to mentor ex-premier Zhu. On economic matters, the relatively young premier has also stuck to the Zhu line of market-oriented reforms coupled with strong macro-level control and adjustment. For example, while addressing an investors' forum in 2002, Wen said that China must "enthusiastically" take part in globalization. "We must grasp the trends of global international development, take firm hold of the opportunities and boldly accept challenges," the then vice-premier noted. As we shall see, however, the premier also pushed through rigorous state fiats to rein in the bubble economy in 2004.[58]

The Imminent Eclipse of the Shanghai Faction

The "Shanghai Faction" and Other Jiang Protégés

The Hu-Wen team has to vie for supremacy with a number of cliques and power blocs in the party, the most prominent of which is the Jiang Zemin or Shanghai Faction. Unlike his mentor Deng—who subscribed to the so-called five lakes and four seas theory of personnel management—Jiang had pulled out the stops to build up his own corps of loyalists, most of whom spent a good part of their career in the Greater Shanghai Region.

The most prominent *Shanghaibang* affiliate is Zeng Qinghong (born 1939). The former Shanghai vice–party secretary has become the Shanghai Faction's standard bearer after Jiang's retirement. At the Sixteenth Congress, Zeng was promoted from alternate member of the Politburo to PSC member, and given the portfolio of party affairs and head of the Central Committee Secretariat. Given that Zeng was the only PSC member who could pose a threat to Hu, the sometimes bitter wrangling between the two lasted until Jiang finally vacated his post of party CMC chairman in September 2004.[59]

Other *Shanghaibang* members who will pack a punch at least until the Seventeenth CCP Congress in 2007 include senior cadres who received promotions at the Sixteenth Congress. Foremost among them are NPC chairman Wu Bangguo (born 1941), Executive Vice-Premier Huang Ju (1938), Vice-Premier Zeng Peiyan (1938), State Council secretary-general Hua Jianmin (1940), State Councilor Chen Zhili (1942), Jiangxi party secretary Meng Jianzhu (1947), and Shanghai party secretary Chen Liangyu (1946).[60] After the Sixteenth Congress, Hu largely put an end to the practice initiated by Jiang and Zeng of "sending Shanghai cadres to fill important posts elsewhere." Yet after thirteen years of dominance in Chinese politics, the Shanghai Faction remains a force to contend with in different sectors of the polity. Moreover, there is the inescapable fact that the Greater Shanghai area has performed brilliantly since Deng's so-called Imperial Tour of Southern China in 1992. And Shanghai officials and entrepreneurs have a knack for integrating China's fast-changing socialist economy with the international marketplace.

Despite the fact that Hu has staged bitter battles with different members of the Jiang or Shanghai Clique, he—as well as sidekick Premier Wen—realizes very well that it is much better to co-opt the remnants of the ancien régime rather than to alienate them terminally. Thus, there is evidence that parliamentary chief Wu has since early 2004 been working well with the Hu-Wen group. Quite a number of Jiang Faction affiliates in the localities have also switched over to the Hu camp in the hope that they may win promotion at the Seventeenth Congress.

Showdown Between Hu and Jiang: The "Final Retirement" of Jiang in 2004

As discussed earlier, General Secretary Hu, the humble student of Song Ping, Hu Yaobang, Deng Xiaoping—and at certain junctures, even Jiang Zemin—has a Machiavellian, go-for-the-jugular streak. While remaining a colorless understudy of Jiang from 1992 to 2002, Hu began to strike out on his own from early 2003 onward. In terms of factional dynamics, one of the most stunning maneuvers by the Hu-Wen group was its successful effort to use the SARS crisis in the spring of 2003 to get rid of a number of Jiang protégés, including the much-maligned minister of health, Dr. Zhang Wenkang. Dr. Zhang was Jiang's personal physician when the latter was Shanghai major, and the incompetent physician's rise through the ranks illustrates the worst of Jiang-style cronyism.[61]

And not long after Dr. Zhang's unceremonious sacking, Hu, together with CCDI and anti-corruption chief Wu Guanzheng, lobbed a political grenade at the headquarters of the Shanghai Faction by detaining real-estate speculator Zhou Zhengyi on charges of corruption and related malfeasance. Given Zhou's sterling relations with senior Shanghai officials as well as the sons of both Jiang and Zeng, it was clear that Hu had launched all-out war against the Jiang Clique (see Chapter 4).

However, it was not until the Fourth Plenary Session of the Sixteenth Central Committee in September 2004 that the final battle was fought between Hu and Jiang—and the outcome was Jiang's retirement from his last remaining post of party CMC Chairman. Hu was able to persuade a number of senior members on the CMC, including Generals Cao Gangchuan, Liang Guanglie, and Liao Xilong, to give subtle but strong hints to Jiang that it was time for him to go. Moreover, fearing for their future—and the prospects of their sons and daughters—a number of prominent Shanghai Faction affiliates and Jiang cronies including Wu Bangguo, and later even Zeng Qinghong, persuaded the old man that it would be better for him to leave the scene at that time rather than at the Seventeenth Congress three years later.[62]

However, in keeping with what cynics call "high-level CCP etiquette," Hu is expected to keep his part of the bargain regarding the final departure of Jiang. This means essentially that the Hu leadership will assume a magnanimous attitude regarding the rumored business irregularities of Jiang's cronies and children. For example, it is most unlikely that Hu or the CCDI's Wu will go after the Shanghai officials or princelings who benefited from their commercial dealings with disgraced tycoon Zhou Zhengyi. Nor will Jiang crony CPPCC Chairman Jia have to account for his reported lapses when he was party chief of Fujian Province and later, of the Beijing municipality.[63]

Indeed, the best proof that Hu is just "one of the boys" in traditional CCP politics is that he is willing to play by the rules of the game. With Jiang finally willing to fade into the sunset, the *dangzhongyang,* or "central party authorities," could afford to take a magnanimous attitude toward both the policy mistakes and the personal foibles of Jiang and his cronies. And for the sake of factional balance, it is likely that the Shanghai Faction will still have two representatives at the post–Seventeenth Congress PSC. As things stood in 2005, NPC chairman Wu Bangguo and Shanghai party chief Chen Liangyu—who are not known for being rabid reformers—seemed set to either stay on at or be promoted to the supreme organ.

The "Gang of Princelings"

One of the less well-known political instructions that Deng Xiaoping reportedly passed on to Jiang Zemin in the early 1990s was that it was not advisable to promote too many sons and daughters of party elders, generally known as *taizidang* or "princelings," to the party's ruling Central Committee. By 2000, however, it was clear that a good number of princelings were making their way up the hierarchy.

One theory going the rounds of Beijing's political circles was that Jiang, foreseeing the imminent waning of the Shanghai Faction's influence, wanted the *taizidang* ("gang of princelings") to buttress the younger affiliates of his own clique. After all, Zeng Qinghong, whose father was senior cadre Zeng Shan, is a bona fide princeling. According to political commentator Wu Jiaxiang, the princelings could be a viable counterbalance to the CYL clique in post–Sixteenth Congress politics.[64]

Foremost among the Beijing-based princelings are Governor of the People's Bank of China and former China Securities Regulatory Commission chairman Zhou Xiaochuan (born 1948), Hebei party secretary and former minister of construction Yu Zhengsheng (1945), Beijing mayor and former Hainan party secretary Wang Qishan (1948), and Minister of Commerce and former governor of Liaoning Bo Xilai (1949). Zhou's father, Zhou Jiannan, was the patron of Jiang Zemin when both were at the Ministry of Machine Building. The younger Zhou is generally given high marks for introducing globally accepted regulations to the Chinese financial markets. Yu had good connections with Jiang Zemin, having worked in the Ministry of Electronics when Jiang was vice-minister there. However, Yu also enjoyed ties with the liberal wing of the party once headed by Zhao Ziyang. As far back as the 1980s, Yu was praised by Zhao for reforms, including liberal housing policies, that he introduced while serving in Yintai, Shandong Province. Wang Qishan is the son-in-law of former vice-premier Yao Yilin. Also a former vice-governor of Guangdong, Wang is considered a competent and reform-minded manager as well as a charismatic cadre with excellent ties to the national media. Bo is the son of famous party elder Bo Yibo, who was instrumental in helping Jiang secure power in the early 1990s. Bo made a name for himself by successfully attracting Japanese and Hong Kong investment to the northeastern Liaoning Province.[65]

There is also a strong corps of regionally based *taizidang*. Perhaps the most prominent one in this group is the party secretary of Zhejiang and former Fujian governor Xi Jinping (born 1953). Xi is sometimes rated as the most capable and popular of the princelings. And Xi, Bo, and Zhou are deemed potential candidates for the post of vice-premier after the Seventeenth Congress, which is scheduled for late 2007.[66]

By contrast, there seem to be relatively few princelings with ties to the Hu-Wen camp. One exception is Pan Yue (born 1960), the liberal and activist vice-director of the State Environmental Protection Administration who has vigorously promoted the concept of "green GDP." The big challenge for the Hu-Wen team is to co-opt those Shanghai-related princelings who can be persuaded to move out of the orbit of the *Shanghaibang*. Yet it is also obvious that the days of princelings taking helicopter rides to the top are over. Beginning in the mid-1990s, there has been a groundswell of discontent among intellectuals and cadres against the apparently unfair advantages enjoyed by the sons and daughters of top cadres. And it is instructive that *taizidang* in their thirties and forties have mostly chosen to go into the world of business rather than seeking careers in the party and government. Particularly given the Hu-Wen leadership's emphasis on a Mao-style "serving the masses" credo, being a princeling might be a liability so far as climbing up the bureaucratic ladder is concerned.

Is Hu a Chinese Gorbachev or a Chinese Putin?

Hu's Intriguing Trajectories

What kind of a leader would Hu Jintao—who is destined to rule China until at least 2012—turn out to be? Given China's affinities with Russia (and the Soviet Union) and its close ties to Asian "tigers" such as Taiwan and Singapore, it is perhaps instructive to compare Hu with a series of Soviet, Russian, Taiwan, and Singapore leaders.

First, would Hu resemble two figures influenced by Soviet communism: former party chief Mikhail Gorbachev and late Taiwan president Chiang Ching-kuo? As is well known, former Soviet party boss Gorbachev was a closet reformer who kept his liberalism close to his chest during his long rise in the Soviet Communist Party hierarchy. Then his *glasnost* and *perestroika* shook the world—and led to the fall of the Berlin Wall and the dissolution of the USSR. After becoming vice-premier in the early 1990s, Zhu Rongji was for several years labeled a "Chinese Gorbachev" by Western observers. It turned out, of course, that although Zhu played a substantial role in China's accession to the WTO, he proved much more conservative than Gorbachev in the area of political reform. Is it possible that Hu, who has fairly well formed ideas about political reform—if only in the limited areas of "elite politics" (enlarging the pool of talents from which the CCP will pick top leaders and advisers) and "intra-party democracy"—will turn out to be a Chinese Gorbachev?[67]

The career of Kuomintang (KMT, or the Nationalists) chairman and Taiwan president Chiang was in many ways as intriguing and dramatic as that of Gorbachev. While a young man in the 1930s, Chiang trained briefly with Soviet advisers at Sun Yat-sen University in Moscow, where he was a classmate of Deng Xiaoping's. Throughout almost his entire presidency in Taiwan, Chiang adopted iron-fisted methods to suppress native-Taiwanese politicians, as well as to muzzle the *dang-wai,* or underground opposition parties. Lee Teng-hui, his vice-president, would later tell the world how, even though he had been plucked from obscurity by Chiang, he had as a native Taiwanese felt stifled by the imperial carpetbaggers from the mainland. However, just two years before his death in 1988, Chiang's rule went through a sea change. The ailing supremo took steps to gradually legalize opposition groupings, which later coalesced into the Democratic Progressive Party (DPP); multiparty politics soon became possible; the ban on non-KMT newspapers and TV stations was gradually lifted; and the ailing Chiang allowed Taiwanese to travel to the mainland as tourists.[68]

Yet developments up to the end of 2005—as discussed in the rest of this book—would seem to indicate that there is more of a resemblance between Hu and Russian president Vladmir Putin. There have been moments in Putin's presidency that appeared to showcase his pro-West, pro-reform tendencies. For example, he has avidly courted Western businessmen. And partly because his cards are limited, Putin has by and large acquiesced in the relentless aggrandizement of American and European influence right at Russia's doorstep. At the same time, Putin, a former KGB functionary, has turned back the clock on domestic political reform by closing down independent newspapers and intimidating opposition politicians. Steps have been taken toward sidelining the legislature and concentrating power in the Kremlin. There are also signs that the young president has tried to boost the cohesiveness of badly divided Russians by hoisting the flag of nationalism. As we shall see particularly in Chapters 4 and 6, Hu has adopted similarly tough measures to rein in liberal, "pro-West" intellectuals and journalists in China. Hu and Putin had near-identical reactions to the series of "velvet revolutions" in Central Asian states ranging from Ukraine to Kyrgyzstan. Thus, after the original pro-Russian and pro-Chinese regime in Kyrgyzstan was overthrown in early 2005, both Hu and Putin announced harsh measures to clamp down on their nations' NGOs, particularly those with relations to the West.[69]

It is noteworthy that through 2002—the year that confirmed Hu's rise to power—quite a number of commentators in the United States did compare Hu to Putin. According to *New York Times* columnist William Safire, Hu might, like Putin, adopt iron-fisted tactics to rule China—and to pursue nationalist goals. Safire had this to say about Hu in a February 2002 article: "He is a Chinese Putin: sharp memory, agile loyalties, openly secretive." Pointing to Hu's TV statement in the wake of the NATO bombing of the Chinese Embassy in Belgrade in 1999—"hostile forces in the U.S. will never give up their attempt to subjugate China"—Safire implied that Hu might be a difficult figure for the United States and the Western world to deal with. Indeed, Hu has had many occasions to repeat similar fusillades against the George W. Bush administration (see Chapter 5). Martin Seiff, an analyst with United Press International, made similar points in a late-2001 commentary on Hu and Putin. "Both are tough and able authoritarians who had extensive experience of repressing dissent on their rise to the top," Seiff wrote. "Both of them have a far more cautious, detached and potentially hostile attitude toward the U.S."[70]

Other commentators have seen similarities between Hu—as well as other "neo-authoritarian" cadres in the CCP—and former Singapore strongman Lee Kuan Yew. Despite obvious dissimilarities between giant China and the puny city-state, the CCP and central government have since the early 1990s sent hundreds of senior civil servants to be trained in Singapore. And the Lion City's model of clean, efficient government in a climate of stern one-party rule has often been cited as a possible model for China. While Hu has never gone on record regarding his opinion of Singapore-style government, there seems little doubt that he is more eager to learn from former prime minister Lee rather than late Taiwan leader Chiang.[71]

Certainly, Hu has what it takes to be an authoritarian and supernationalist should circumstances demand. At the very least, sympathizers of the Fourth-Generation leadership would say that Hu—and other moderate, populist cadres such as Wen—might be forced to adopt a draconian agenda if the nation were to be embroiled in instability due to familiar problems such as unemployment and the disaffected classes' revolt against the corrupt, privileged elite. Even the most enlightened CCP cadre would agree that the overriding priority is still preservation of one-party rule. Should challenges to the regime increase, the Hu-Wen team might feel that it has no choice but to use strong-armed tactics to restore order—and to play the nationalism card to divert citizens' attention from socioeconomic woes as well as to foster national cohesiveness.

Given that the tenure of the Hu-Wen administration runs into early next decade, however, it is also legitimate to ask whether Hu and Wen would, given the opportunity, at least borrow from some of the liberalization policies of Chiang and Gorbachev. Should Hu decide to take the risk of thoroughgoing political liberalization, not only will one-fifth of mankind reap substantial benefits, but the CCP's heavenly mandate might be extended by quite a long stretch.

If Not Democracy, What? If Not Now, When?

For China's Fourth- and, later, Fifth-Generation leadership, "revolutionary legitimacy" is wearing thin. Honchos including Mao Zedong, Zhou Enlai, and Deng Xiaoping could say that the CPP and its leaders had the right to rule because they had apparently crushed the "triple curses" of feudalism, imperialism, and KMT dictatorship—and thanks to the adage, "he who has won heaven and earth [on the battlefield] has a right to rule heaven and earth." Jiang could claim to be a designated successor of Deng, even though that assertion had begun to ring hollow even before the patriarch's death in 1997. It is difficult to imagine what kind of legitimacy *disidai* leaders such as Hu, Wen, or Zeng could have apart from real popular support based on economic performance and service to be public. Moreover, the Hu-Wen team faces a much bigger challenge because of the impact of inchoate globalization—and the influx of new ideas due to the popularity of the Internet, at least in the cities. Not only "new classes" such as businessmen and professionals, but a growing number of workers and farmers are clamoring for a bigger say about their future (see Chapters 3 and 6). Given the fact that political reform was frozen by Jiang and his Shanghai Faction for thirteen years, it may be easiest for the Hu leadership to extend the CCP's mandate of heaven by venturing into the minefield of liberalization.

It is unrealistic to expect the likes of Hu and Wen to introduce one-person-one-vote or multiparty politics within their tenure of 2002–2012. Yet there are already signs that to broaden the CCP's power base, even conservative leaders such as Jiang had by 2001 and 2002 begun to reach out to new classes and groupings such as private entrepreneurs. Hu is expected to continue with this strategy. But he needs to do more given that decades-old problems and grievances have piled up—due to the lower classes' lack of representation at the top if not their outright disenfranchisement—and these contradictions could blow up with unprecedented ferocity.

The world will be holding its breath to see whether the Hu administration will have the determination and guts to take concrete steps toward the "last modernization," or the overhaul of the Leninist political system. This will mean not only giving workers and farmers—as well as NGOs and other fast-rising denizens of civil society—a bigger say in governance. The ban on the formation of nonofficial trade unions, farmers' groupings—as well as political parties independent of the CCP—must be lifted. Moreover, there is a crying need for relaxation of the CCP's monopoly on ideology and the flow of information, starting perhaps with the authorization of non-party-affiliated newspapers and websites.

More far-reaching political liberalization would enable the Hu leadership to reap bonanzas galore on the diplomatic—and even energy—fronts. At a time when trade makes up around 70 percent of the country's GDP—and the "world factory" is becoming dependent on fast-growing imports of oil and other resources—Beijing needs to lay to rest fears about the "China threat," which seem to be gaining ground around the world in direct proportion to the PRC's growing economic and military might. Much of the basis of the "China threat," however, has to do with the lack of democracy and transparency in the system. For example, the leadership, including the PLA, is not subject to the checks and balances that are built into a system of representative government. And this could mean that in times of crisis, China's party-state-military apparatus might react in irrational ways in both domestic and foreign policy so as to preserve the longevity of CCP rule and perhaps even the lives of its leaders.

The choice before Hu and his colleagues is as critical as it is difficult. One course of action is to move forward with the times: ride the wave of the future by making inevitable sacrifices in terms of the CCP's near-total dominance over most aspects of the country's political life. After all, the party's tight grip on society has already spawned corruption and social injustice of gargantuan proportions. The alternative is for the party to fall for illusions about never-ending prosperity and stability that its own propagandists have conjured up—and for its already much-tattered mandate of heaven to be swept away by the cruel currents of history.

There is added poignancy to the dilemma that faces Hu. Unlike Zhu Rongji, the Fourth-Generation stalwart was able to come to the fore at an early age—he was barely forty-nine when designated a "core" of the *disidai* in 1992. Yet, his apprenticeship under Jiang lasted ten long years, during which he had to practice an extreme form of self-denial so as not to be seen as upstaging senior cadres from the Shanghai Faction. The upshot is that the president and party chief can no longer afford to waste time. Given that he and allies such as Wen could take until the Seventeenth CCP Congress in 2007 to consolidate power, the Hu leadership will be left with pretty much just five years to tackle some of the most intractable problems of political reform.

Not unlike Zhu, Hu is a man in a big hurry. The window of opportunity for restructuring the party, widening the CCP's power base—and above all, modernizing and drastically pluralizing the political milieu for some 1.3 billion people—could be awfully limited. If Hu can pull this off, however, his place in history will be much more illustrious than either that of Ming Dynasty grand defense minister Hu Zongxian or modernizer Dr. Hu Shih, his two famous ancestors from Jixi, Anhui Province. And an examination of the first three years of administration under the Hu-Wen team will yield insights galore into whether the Fourth-Generation leadership is equal to this monumental undertaking.

2

The Crisis of Legitimacy

Hu Jintao's Search for a
Perennial Mandate of Heaven

New Ideas to Safeguard the CCP's "Perennial Ruling Party" Status

Despite his frequent appearances on Chinese television—and increasing numbers of forays abroad—President Hu Jintao has remained a largely mysterious personality. The same can be said of his sidekick, Premier Wen Jiabao. In the first three years after coming to power at the Sixteenth Chinese Communist Party (CCP) Congress of November 2002, Hu and Wen successfully projected the image of can-do, proactive leaders who "put people first." Yet apart from promises to take better care of the *ruoshi tuanti* (disadvantaged groupings) such as peasants and low-income workers—and to create a "harmonious society"—not much is known about the thoughts and aspirations of the two Fourth-Generation stalwarts. Of particular concern is how these relatively young and forward-looking leaders will push forward much-needed reform, particularly in the political and ideological arenas.

While it is expected that Hu and Wen will remain in power at least until the Eighteenth CCP Congress of 2012, the basic thrust of their governing philosophy and worldview had become clear by late 2005. Hu and Wen, both born in 1942, are what the Chinese call *tizhinei gaigezhe,* or relatively cautious "within-the-system reformers," not Gorbachev-like figures who are ready to overhaul the Communist system through shock therapy or other radical means.[1] Indeed, the Fourth-Generation leadership's basic philosophy is that they must balance the needs of self-preservation—meaning the perpetuation of the CCP's mandate of heaven—with the requirements of reform. And the Hu-Wen team is convinced that despite the CCP's backward ideology, plus a quintessentially Leninist political structure, it can maintain its ruling-party status and spearhead the drive to attain the age-old goal of *fuqiang* (strength and prosperity) for China.

As the following sections will show, President Hu, who spent the bulk of his career as a party affairs specialist, does not believe that there is anything intrinsically wrong with CCP ideology—especially one-party authoritarian rule and "socialism with Chinese characteristics"—or the ethos and structure of the party. He is aware, of course, of the abuses and problems such as corruption and gross inefficiency. Yet Hu, Wen, and like-minded moderates are convinced that these aberrations have taken place because of mistakes and misapplications made by individual leaders, and not due to fundamental flaws of the system. Hence their decision not to perform Gorbachev- or Yeltsin-style surgery on the CCP. The Hu-Wen team believes in the "self-perfectionism" of the party: this means that if the party's ideology, approaches, and policies can be retooled properly, the CCP's 70 million members can still lead China from strength to strength.

Hu, a former president of the Central Party School who has done thorough research on ideology and governance matters, is convinced that he and his colleagues can even raise CCP statecraft to a "scientific" level. In other words, party rule can be perpetuated—and Chinese civilization revived—through a "scientific" theory of development and a "scientific" ruling apparatus. Moreover, weaknesses and blunders like corruption and dictatorial decision making, which the outside world has ascribed to fifty-seven years of CCP rule, can basically be rectified. Hence, it is not necessary to undo or break up the system—particularly no need to introduce "Western" concepts and mechanisms such as multiparty politics or one-person-one-vote polls. As we shall see, Hu and Wen are avid proponents of limited reforms such as "intra-party democracy" as well as the streamlining of the administrative structure. But they are hardly converts to the cause of democracy.

It is significant that Hu's idea about reform, including political reform, is different from that of his supposed mentor, former general secretary Hu Yaobang, and the latter's successor, Zhao Ziyang. This is despite the fact that both Hus had headed the Communist Youth League (CYL), which was until the late 1980s famous for being a hotbed of talents and ideas. The late Hu, and especially Zhao, subscribed to a certain extent to the theory of benevolent neo-authoritarianism. As U.S. political scientist M.J. Sullivan noted, Zhao and his advisers were convinced that after a strong *zhongyang* (center) had achieved economic progress, "this political elite could implement 'top-down' political reforms to liberalize the political system without immediately threatening the CCP's central position." Zhao and his radical advisers also believed that the party could at a later stage afford to yield substantial powers to other groupings in the interest of reform. The newly deceased former party chief also thought that selective "Western-style" mechanisms such as separation of party and government as well as institutions of checks and balances should be introduced.[2] However, it is evident that President Hu's interests consist mainly of boosting CCP power so as to better consolidate its ruling mandate. And there are no provisions for genuine political liberalization or power sharing with other socioeconomic blocs and sectors.

The Lure of the New

Ex-President Jiang Zemin's Exposition of "New Thinking"

The protracted political engineering to repair the CCP's somewhat tattered mandate of heaven started in the last two or three years of the rule of ex-general secretary Jiang Zemin, whose major theoretical invention, the "Theory of the Three Represents," could be construed as a bold if belated attempt to resuscitate the party's falling political fortunes. The theory noted that to remain relevant—and to thrive—the party "must represent the foremost production forces, the most advanced culture, and the broadest interests of common people." While Jiang would like to claim personal credit for this so-called major breakthrough, advisers including Zeng Qinghong, Wang Huning, and Hu himself had chipped in with ideas and nuances.[3]

There are two main thrusts to the theory. One is that since private entrepreneurs, managers, and other professionals can be said to represent the highest-level productivity and culture, these members of the "new classes"—including the fast-rising middle class—should be admitted to the CCP and even promoted to senior positions. In a now-famous speech in July 2001, Jiang formally opened the party's door to "outstanding elements" of the "new social strata," including capitalists. The other point is that because China has entered into the era of the market economy, Marxist- and Maoist-style class struggle—which used to be integral to any communist party's raison d'être—should no longer be pursued. The corollary is that the CCP has for all intents and purposes metamorphosed into a party for all classes and all people, that is, a *quanmindang,* literally, "party for all the people."[4]

Thus, the retooled party charter endorsed at the Sixteenth CCP Congress had revised the key concept that only workers constituted the foundation of the party. The amended version said: "The CCP is the vanguard of the Chinese working class; it is at the same time the vanguard of the Chinese people and the Chinese race." This Jiang-style "new thinking" obviously contravened many orthodox Marxist edicts. Marx and Lenin insisted on the primacy of class distinction—and class struggle—meaning that proletariats should fight and vanquish the ugly, marauding capitalists. Now, as a de facto *quanmindang,* the CCP will have to justify its rule as a party that promotes the welfare of all Chinese, regardless of "class origin." Because Jiang and his colleagues were treading on treacherous ideological terrain, the then president was careful in laying out his new doctrine. While the "Three Represents" was repeated ad nauseum in the media as well as in ideological classes for cadres and workers, Jiang and company never made a clear-cut pronouncement that class struggle was now passé and that the CCP had evolved into a *quanmindang.* Nor did Jiang mention that the elevated status of proletariats such as workers and peasants was no more in the new age of the market economy.

Rather, Jiang put his emphasis on the fact that "we need new ideas for further development, new breakthroughs for reform, and new vistas for the open-door policy." Echoing the famous axiom of the late reformist party boss Hu Yaobang—that "Marxism cannot solve all the problems of today"—Jiang said in a speech at the Central Party School in mid-2002 that "it is mistaken to treat Marxism in a doctrinaire manner." Marxism required new breakthroughs, he added. In an interview with the *New York Times* in August 2001, Jiang underscored the importance of "improving" the teachings of Marx and Engels "in light of changing historical conditions."[5]

According to Chinese sources close to the Jiang Faction, the veteran leader was asked the following question during the annual leadership conference at the seaside resort of Beidaihe in the summer of 2001: "If the CCP is now a *quanmindang*—and one that pursues market economics—how different will it be from bourgeois socialist-democratic parties in Europe?" Jiang's answer was that the party must undergo a thought liberation akin to that staged by Deng Xiaoping soon after the fall of the Gang of Four.[6] In 1979, Deng launched the campaign of "seek truth from facts"—whose slogan was "practice is the sole criteria of truth"—to parry the Maoists' attack that his economic reforms had contradicted Marxism and Mao Thought. Jiang hoisted the flag of a Deng-style thought-liberation crusade in the two years before he vacated the Politburo in late 2002. "We must make progress with the times, and modernize theory accordingly," the ex-president liked to say. "If development of theory is lagging behind practice, the party's enterprise will be hurt—and it could even fail."[7]

President Hu's Emphasis on Theoretical Breakthroughs

Despite the doubts about the Hu-Wen team's commitment to reform, Fourth-Generation leaders do have new ideas—and they are determined to break out of the mold laid down by Jiang, deemed an intellectual lightweight. After all, the Fourth Generation comprises the first bunch of Chinese cadres who are arguably free from the yoke of Stalinism. Third-Generation stalwarts could not escape the past, that is, the long shadow of the Soviet model. This is even true for former premier Zhu Rongji, the supposed "Chinese Gorbachev." While unlike Jiang or Li Peng, Zhu never studied or worked in the USSR, the Soviet model of state planning had through the 1950s exerted a deep influence on the ex-premier.[8]

However, Hu and his Fourth-Generation colleagues grew up in the post–Cultural Revolution era of reform. They attended typically well known universities in Beijing, Shanghai, and other big cities in the 1960s. Hu and Wen were both thirty-six years old when Deng proclaimed the theory of reform and the open door in late 1978; at that time, Hu was a hydraulic engineer in Gansu and Wen a geologist in the same northwestern province. In the Politburo endorsed at the Sixteenth CCP Congress, only two members had Soviet roots: Luo Gan had studied in East Germany, General Cao Gangchuan in the USSR.[9] Yet almost the entire corps of Fourth-Generation cadres are beneficiaries of Deng-style reform. And on their shoulders falls the task of completing the transformation of China into a modern, nonideological, market-oriented country.

Hu's success formula is simply that cadres must break new ground in reform partly through coming up with "scientific" models for reform and development. And this became evident well before he was made party general secretary in late 2002. Take, for example, the speech given by Hu at a ceremony marking the twentieth anniversary of the celebrated 1978 campaign on "Practice is the sole criterion of truth," which set the stage for the ascendancy of Deng. "Under the guidance of scientific theories, we must boldly put into practice [our beliefs], make bold explorations . . . and liberate our thoughts in order to tackle new tasks and new contradictions," Hu intoned. While touring Shanghai in late 2000, Hu told local officials to "grasp new opportunities, face new challenges, create new conditions of superiority, and realize new developments [for the city's future]."[10]

The party chief has continued to push his doctrine of never-ending innovation after the Sixteenth CCP Congress. In a mid-2004 conference on how to make advancements in the study of philosophy and the social sciences, Hu admonished scholars and officials to delve into both Chinese and foreign works so as to "break new ground in scholarly viewpoints, in systems and institutions, and in methodology of research and development."[11] And in a Politburo session later that year, the supremo tried to strike a balance between "sticking to the socialist road with Chinese characteristics" on the one hand, and "thought liberation and keen innovation" on the other. Hu urged cadres to "ceaselessly search for new ideas, new approaches, and new methods for solving problems."[12] Hu, of course, sees no contradiction between upholding old ideals such as party supremacy and the socialist road on the one hand, and the imperative of thought liberation and "new thinking" on the other. In fact, the president and his colleagues are convinced that they can come up with innovative ways and means to attain the age-old goal of indefinitely extending the CCP's ruling-party mandate.

The Search for a Perennial Mandate of Heaven

In his capacity as head of the Central Party School and party affairs specialist, then vice-president Hu Jintao was put in charge of the task of "party construction" in 2001 and 2002. His mandate was simple: to find the formula that will enable the CCP to remain a "perennial ruling party." In internal and public speeches at the time, Hu indicated that cadres must be open-minded in their search for a new formula. "We must make progress with the times and open up new vistas," he said.[13]

A few years earlier, think tanks such as the Central Party School and the Chinese Academy of Social Sciences (CASS) had begun systematic research into stable and sturdy political parties that were long-standing ruling parties in different countries. These included the Liberal Democratic Party of Japan, the People's Action Party of Singapore, the United Malay National Organization of Malaysia, the Institutional Revolutionary Party of Mexico, the Labor Party of Canada, the National Democratic Party of Egypt, and the Constitutional Democratic Rally Party of Tunisia.[14] The conclusions of these experts were simple: democracy was not a prerequisite for a party's staying power, particularly for countries with Confucianist traditions such as Japan and Singapore. However, survivability criteria common to most of these parties included the appearance—if not also the substance—of serving the common people, an efficient administration that is relatively uncorrupt and good at quickly defusing sociopolitical crises, and an ability to nurture a relatively broad-based pro-establishment class.[15]

After taking power in late 2002, Hu and his advisers were in a better position to take a first-hand look at viable political parties all over the world. The goal was the same: to learn the relevant lessons for the CCP. As Hu put it in mid-2004, the CCP must "study and learn from the experience of other ruling parties in running the administration. We must open up new vistas so as to take a better grasp of the rules and regulations for boosting the party's governance ability." This was the background behind the CCP-sponsored Conference of Asian Political Parties held in Beijing in September 2004. Hu told representatives from eighty-three parties that the CCP would "ceaselessly improve and perfect its leadership style and governance methods."[16]

Largely with the goal of seeking the bible on "long reign and perennial stability" from other parties, Hu also asked his Politburo colleagues and other senior cadres to visit countries all over the world. In the second half of 2003 alone, three PSC members and six Politburo members called on parties in countries ranging from authoritarian Cuba and Armenia to liberal Finland and New Zealand.[17] According to Wang Jiarui, head of the CCP International Liaison Department, six points could be made about the experience of successful ruling parties in countries including the U.K., Germany, Vietnam, Singapore, and Hungary. Wang cited the following: "ability to innovate in theory [of government]; competence in organization and mobilization; decision-making power; ability to develop the economy and society; ability to handle emergencies; and ability to deal well with foreign relations."[18]

President Hu had taken into account the extensive research done by his colleagues when he thrashed out the criteria that the CCP must meet so as to consolidate its heavenly mandate. The requisite standards and goals included: "putting the masses first" through improving welfare standards for the working and farming classes; narrowing the gap between haves and have-nots, and promoting some degree of social justice as well as mobility; and expanding the power base and "recruitment pool" of the CCP. Thanks to the fact that the economy had been growing by 8 percent to 9 percent since the early 1990s, a considerable amount of wealth had been accumulated. For example, total bank deposits by Chinese reached an astounding 13 trillion yuan by 2005. Yet at least 45 percent of the nation's wealth was held by 10 percent of the richest citizens.[19] The Hu-Wen leadership's concern is to ensure a more even spread of income, thus reversing Deng's now largely discredited dictum of "letting one part of the population grow rich first."

China's Gini coefficient, a measurement of income disparity between rich and poor, has shown that the gulf between haves and have-nots in the country has increased dramatically through the heady years of reform. Thus, the index soared from 0.282 in 1990 to close to 0.5 in early 2004, a level that the *China Daily* said was "widely considered alarming." Experts estimated that when factors such as tax evasion and money laundering by the superrich are taken into account, the Gini coefficient could be even higher. Moreover, as the country gets richer, social tension has increased as the nouveau riche have more opportunities to show off glistening status-symbol objects ranging from European sedans to luxurious villas; 10 percent of the urban population owns 45 percent of properties in the cities.[20] Moreover, as the following sections will show, the administration must address regional differences in the country as well as tackle the detrimental aspects of development such as environmental depredation.

That the Hu-Wen team might be on the right track was illustrated, albeit in an oblique manner, by the shock defeat of the Bharatiya Janata Party in the Indian general elections in May 2004. While the A.B. Vajpayee administration had won kudos abroad—and within the educated, rich, and information-technology (IT)-oriented elite in India—it sorely neglected the majority of Indians who were barely literate peasants. The unexpected victory of the underdog Congress Party—allegedly because of its closer identification with the interests of the masses—would tend to confirm the validity of the "mass line" taken by the Hu-Wen leadership.[21]

Despite their dislike for Russian-style changes, the CCP elite also realizes that in the absence of Western-style political reform, the party must do more in other areas to satisfy or at least pacify the masses. This includes curbing corruption and promoting "democratic decision making," implementing some form of rule by law, and enhancing social mobility by enabling the masses to climb the sociopolitical ladder. An allied concept is the propagation of a middle class, seen as a force for stability and a potential pillar of support for the party (see Chapters 3 and 4).

"Scientific Socialism" and Scientific Development Theories

It is one of the ironies of history that Hu Jintao may have made more contribution to the world socialist movement than one of his heroes, Mao Zedong. In the 1950s and 1960s, the Great Helmsman styled himself as a leader of the global communist crusade—but got nowhere except ruining his own country as well as squandering precious resources on foreign aid to a bunch of Third World pariah states. Now Hu and his colleagues are telling the world that their distinctive China model is a smashing success owing to the Fourth-Generation leadership's having cracked the code of "scientific socialism." Deng's "socialism with Chinese characteristics," which was implemented rather faithfully by ex-president Jiang and ex-premier Zhu, proved to be effective in speeding up economic development and raising the masses' standard of living. Now, the Hu-Wen team is claiming that its unique approach known as "scientific socialism" can not only rectify the mistakes of previous socialist-Chinese administrations—such as gross corruption and social injustice—but also revive the CCP as well as Chinese civilization.

The Myth of "Scientific Socialism"

In an internal talk in 2000 on handling the problems and opportunities of the new millennium, Hu displayed a knack for cool-headed assessment of China's harsh reality. He ticked off monumental challenges, including "the severe defeat of the international socialist enterprise"; "the complex contradictions and difficulties in economic, political and cultural spheres" caused by economic restructuring; as well as the "crisis of faith" among cadres in the socialist system. Speaking two years before coming to power, Hu made no concrete recommendations on what cadres should do. However, he laid down two principles. One was that officials must follow what he called a "scientific" path. The other, related requirement was that breakthroughs must be made in different fields. And at an ideological education conference held in late 2000 to discuss ex-president Jiang's dictums, Hu said: "We must ask leading cadres to arm their brains with scientific theory." "We must come to a scientific knowledge of new situations and new tasks facing the party," the official New China News Agency (NCNA) quoted the then vice-president as saying.[22]

A key to Hu's statecraft is that even without the trappings of Western-style political institutions such as multiparty and parliamentary democracy, the CCP leadership can still get it right—scientifically right—regarding economic and social development. In a Politburo meeting in mid-2003, Hu underscored the imperative of "observing the world, China, and the CCP under the guidance of scientific theory." The president added that the scientific spirit would prod cadres into "making breakthroughs in theory, institutions, science and technology as well as culture."[23]

As we shall see in following sections, the Hu-Wen leadership has also come up with a "scientific theory of development" as well as quasi-scientific ways for running the administration, including picking the "right" civil servants and fighting corruption. Quite a few scholars, particularly those in the humanities and social sciences, are impressed by the Hu-Wen team's efforts to redress earlier administrations' pursuit of economic and technological targets at the expense of humanistic and social values. As Tsinghua University professor Xue Lan noted, "after 1949, a lot of disciplines like history, political science, and economics were subordinated to ideology." Xue was convinced that the new leadership was interested in "creating the infrastructure for public policy formation."[24]

There are, however, misgivings about Hu's penchant for "scientific socialism," murmurings that it is but a harking back to old-style Marxism. After all, this concept was first raised by early Marxists including Lenin, who wrote the classic

Utopian and Scientific Socialism. Orthodox Marxists believed that with the right formula, as well as proper social planning and engineering, a country could hit upon a fail-safe path toward democratic, egalitarian, and "scientific" development. Yet one of the points made by prominent critics of Marxism and socialism such as Friedrich von Hayek and Karl Popper was precisely that "scientific socialism" could result in a closed society if not outright serfdom.[25]

It cannot be denied that the post-1978 CCP leadership is dominated by engineers, and that despite their different philosophies, cadres such as Li Peng, Jiang Zemin, and Hu—all trained engineers—believe in the virtues of social engineering. Despite his reformist persona, Hu often lapses into the familiar rhetoric that it is best for the nation to act as one, that is, under strong party leadership. During the crisis over severe acute respiratory syndrome (SARS), for example, Hu reiterated that the entire nation should "unite their thoughts and action based on the planning of the party central authorities." "We must uphold the principles of relying on the masses, relying on science, and working hard with one heart and mind," he indicated.[26] Above all, despite experiments in "new thinking," there will be no departure from the time-tested Communist doctrine of "democratic centralism."

A Scientific View of Economic and Social Development

The Hu-Wen Fourth-Generation leadership is staking its reputation—and the future of the party—on the success of a brand-new "concept of scientific development." This is the natural culmination of President Hu's belief in the nature of "scientific socialism." As Premier Wen put it in a speech to the Central Party School in early 2004, the novel approach means "economic and social development that are comprehensive, well-coordinated, and sustainable"—as well as "development that has [the welfare of] human beings in mind."[27]

The so-called scientific theory of development is closely linked to the now-famous "five syntheses and coordination" unveiled by Hu and Wen at the Third CCP Central Committee plenary session in late 2003. This principle was a reference to well-balanced development between cities and villages, between different regions, between economic growth and social benefits, between man and nature, and between domestic growth and the open-door policy. Clearly, in the eyes of Hu and Wen, economic and other developments in the Jiang era had engendered imbalances in these five areas, for example, exacerbating regional and urban-rural disparities as well as upsetting the ecological balance. One important aspect of "scientific development" is that economic progress should not merely enrich one sector of the population or one region of the country. As Wen, deemed "the people's premier," reiterated, Beijing must see to it that the 800 million peasants—as well as disadvantaged sectors such as the urban jobless—do not feel left behind in the modernization drive. And economic growth must afford the rural central and western provinces opportunities to close the gap with the coastal cities. Latest figures showed that the gulf in the rate of economic growth between west and east China had widened from 1:1.92 in 1980 to 1:2.59 in 2003.[28]

In an address at the Central Party School in early 2004, Vice-President Zeng Qinghong criticized certain cadres' obsession with mere gross domestic product (GDP) growth. Zeng argued that "we must use a scientific spirit and a scientific methodology" to look at economic growth and national progress. In other words, while measuring China's wealth, "software elements" such as educational standards, public health, and respect for the law must be given as much weight as increase in manufacturing and exports. Or as Hu himself put it while touring Jiangsu Province in mid-2004, the right balance between man and nature, and between industrialization and ecological standards, must be sought to ensure sustainability. The party chief noted that scientific development must take into consideration "the welfare of the entire country as well as the fundamental and long-term interests of the people." "We must be concerned about the long-term development of the Chinese race as well as the welfare of our children and later generations," Hu said.[29]

An important aspect of scientific and balanced development is harmony among the three *sheng: shengchan* (production), *shengtai* (the environment), and *shenghuo* (quality of life). According to Peking University ecological expert Ye Wenhu, the mere emphasis on GDP growth has meant that China has entered into a vicious cycle of "more production, more pollution." Ye said economic growth must not be at the expense of the people's livelihood and ecological balance. He noted that production "must be attained in an environment of low waste of energy and low pollution." While China accounts for the 4 percent of the aggregate global GDP, it is using 17 percent of the world's energy supplies and raw materials. CASS environmental sciences professor Niu Wenyuan agreed. He indicated that development for the past decade had been attained at the expense of the environment as well as the livelihood of later generations. "We have spoiled the environment and sacrificed the opportunities of our offspring," he said.[30]

The Hu-Wen leadership's newfound interest in "developmental software" such as education, public health, and the environment was reinforced by the nation's near-disastrous brush with the SARS and avian flu epidemics in 2003 and 2004. The trail-blazing aspects of the Hu-Wen team's new policy could also be interpreted as a rectification of the perceived aberrations of late patriarch Deng, ex-president Jiang, and ex-premier Zhu. It was Deng who first came up with the slogan about the *yingdaoli* (unimpeachable law) of fast-paced development: that the nation must achieve a relatively high growth rate to maintain stability and prosperity. Moreover, both Jiang and Zhu, who have close ties to Shanghai, earmarked too much in the way of resources for the eastern "Gold Coast." And since there were hardly any spokesmen for rural China within the old leadership, the agricultural sector, as well as western provinces, were given short shrift. A year before his retirement, the usually arrogant Zhu indirectly admitted that his biggest mistake was neglecting peasants' welfare. "When you are talking about one single issue that causes me the worst headaches, that topic is how to increase the income of Chinese farmers," he said at the annual National People's Congress (NPC) conference in 2002.[31]

Assessing Regions and Cadres According to Criteria of Scientific Development

Many of the "unscientific" aspects of Chinese-style development are due to the fact that provincial, municipal, and county-level officials are anxious to please superiors by notching up high-GDP growth rates, even though these apparently laudable attainments were based on horrendous wastage of energy and despoliation of the environment. The Hu-Wen team has borrowed the Western concept of "green GDP," meaning that economic growth must be accompanied by not only environmental protection but also "humanistic" consideration for the overall welfare of the populace under an official's jurisdiction.[32]

Cadres at different levels were given explicit instructions in 2004 that they must never repeat the Great Leap Forward–era mentality of trying to outdo each other with superficial signs of prosperity. As Central Party School professor Liang Yanhui pointed out, some cadres had the wrong concept of development. "They have simplified the issue of development into the mere pursuit of high GDP figures," she said. The official journal *Fortnightly Chat* quoted senior cadres as saying that in assessing cadres in a particular region, the development of the economy and society as well as the welfare and spiritual well-being of local residents had to be taken into account.[33]

By mid-2004, it was clear that cadres would be assessed by standards way beyond simply boosting the local GDP or attracting foreign investment. New criteria included generating employment and lowering the rich–poor gap, maintaining environmental cleanliness, ensuring stability, and boosting democracy and rule by law. According to President Hu, economic development should not be the sole touchstone for evaluating regional officials. "We must also consider achievements in the areas of *renwen* [humanistic values], resources, and the environment," Hu said in early 2004. What the president meant was that local cadres should make sure that their charges were generally content and well educated— and that resources in areas under their jurisdiction must be efficiently exploited and used in an ecologically friendly manner.[34]

According to noted reformer Pan Yue, the assessment of cadres should be based on different sets of criteria. Pan was a senior cadre at the now-defunct State Commission for the Reform of the Economic Structure before assuming his current post as vice-director of the State Environmental Protection Administration (SEPA). "Under the scientific view of development, officials should be appraised in accordance with standards including keeping a good ecological balance, maintaining a low Gini coefficient in their localities, and providing social welfare for the destitute," he said. SEPA and the State Statistical Bureau have compiled a set of criteria for green GDP, which takes into account factors in the areas of the environment and resource distribution when governments of all levels go about planning economic development. Jiangxi party secretary Meng Jianzhu summarized his goal for building up the province: "I want mountains of gold and silver; but I also want green waters and hills."[35]

Living up to the "scientific spirit" of President Hu, various regional leaders have concocted "scientific" and quantitative criteria for assessing cadres. In late 2004, Sichuan came up with the nation's first set of standards for the annual appraisal of the performance of party and government officials. Apart from GDP growth and foreign investment, the twenty-five criteria included development in education, health, industrial safety, culture and sports, environmental protection, and social stability.[36]

An Efficient, "Scientific," and Law-Abiding Administration with Limited Democracy

As the activists of the May Fourth "enlightenment" movement of 1919 indicated, China cannot go very far down the path of economic and scientific development in the absence of democracy. On the touchy issue of reforms leading eventually to universal-suffrage elections and even multiparty politics, Hu and Wen are basically as conservative as forebears such as Deng or Jiang. And the Fourth-Generation leadership has stuck to the hackneyed view that Chinese are not prosperous or well educated enough to try out one-person-one-vote experiments. Thus, Wen said in mid-2004 that "because China is too big and populous and because its development is uneven, we can only have direct elections at the village level."[37] What is "new" about the Hu-Wen team's worldview and statecraft is their conviction that despite the slow progress in democracy, the CCP administration can still be superefficient and scientific in not just economic development but attending to the needs of the people.

An Administration of "Scientific" Decision Makers and Crisis Managers

One of the Hu-Wen team's key mottoes for efficient and "people-oriented" administration is "develop democracy, encourage the free airing of views, gather collective wisdom, and implement scientific decision making." However, it is clear that with no substantial program for democratization, the emphasis is very much on scientific decision making.[38]

The banner of "scientific and democratic decision making" was first raised in the mid-1980s by liberal leaders such as then premier Zhao Ziyang and vice-premier Wan Li. Zhao brought quite a large number of young men and women into his think tanks, notably the one on political reform. However, the tradition was lost in the wake of Zhao's ouster in 1989. While Jiang Zemin and Zhu Rongji also had their brain trusts, neither practiced wide consultation or "scientific decision making." Most of Jiang's advisers tended to come from Shanghai. And Zhu's strongman-like leadership style often meant his subordinates and advisers were afraid to contradict the "boss."[39]

One way that the Hu-Wen team is promoting scientific decision making is by picking the brains of think tanks and senior academics and professionals. For example, in the first year after Hu came to power, the Politburo and the State Council organized twelve seminars in which professors and experts from different fields expatiated on areas ranging from law and history to agriculture and technology. And suggestions from academics ranging from augmenting rural income to whittling down "administrative detention and punishment" have been adopted. According to an academic who has advised Hu, the party chief and president's desk is always piled high with papers submitted to him by officials and scholars nationwide.[40]

Nowhere is this "scientific" spirit more evident than in crisis management—forestalling disasters or putting out fires as early as possible. Hu and Wen have set up a good number of permanent or ad hoc bodies and mechanisms in Zhongnanhai—sometimes called leading groups or coordinating committees—to handle domestic and foreign crises. Subject matter and issues have ranged from the worsening shortage of energy and raw materials to the problem of declining grain yield in China's restive rural regions. And these groups are usually headed by senior ministers, including Premier Wen himself. For example, even going by official, publicized material, Wen is head of the National Defense Mobilization Committee, the Three Gorges Project Construction Committee, the State Leading Group for Science, Technology and Education, the State Leading Group for Information Technology, the State Council Leading Group for Western Region Development, the State Council Construction Committee for the South-to-North Water Diversion Project, and the State Leading Group on Energy.[41]

The underlying philosophy of *ju'an siwei* (beware of dangers while in the midst of plenitude) was spelled out by Hu in a meeting with Chinese People's Political Consultative Conference (CPPCC) members in March 2003. "The leadership collective must have a cool-headed awareness of China's conditions," Hu said. "We must boost our awareness of [possible] troubles and disasters. . . . We must positively address various risks and challenges." Hu also underscored the imperative of assessing and forestalling risks. "We must overcome difficulties and minimize risks," he said in a Politburo meeting not long after taking over the party leadership. "We must lower the adverse impact of unfavorable circumstances to ensure stable development and [national] security," the supremo added. "We'll succeed if we can forestall problems, otherwise we may fail."[42]

Plans were afoot in 2003 to put together crisis management and rapid-response "command centers" in every large and medium-sized city in the coming five years. The computer networks of these outfits would be linked with the Ministry of

Public Security as well as with each other to facilitate quick deployment of resources to resolve a crisis. The Beijing municipal party and government leadership, for example, formed a Crisis Management Command Center in the wake of the SARS epidemic in early 2003. The center is charged with handling incidents ranging from epidemics and earthquakes to terrorist attacks. Other cities that have similar facilities include Shanghai, Chengdu, Nanning, and Nanjing.[43]

Experts have also suggested establishing custom-made mechanisms or centers to handle problems and mishaps ranging from crime to road accidents. For example, Beijing-based scholar Duan Liren, a transportation specialist, proposed establishing traffic accident rapid-response centers in urban areas to deal with traffic snarls or accidents. Duan cited the fact that the death rate among those involved in road mishaps in China was 27 percent compared with 1.3 percent in the United States and only 0.9 percent in Japan. In mid-2004, the State Council rolled out a Leading Group on Rectifying the Overloading of Vehicles. Within one month, this group had deployed more than 200,000 police and other staff to "black spots" or disaster zones along the nation's highways to crack down on dangerous driving practices, particularly overloading in buses and other vehicles.[44] Other crisis-response units that have been, or are soon to be, set up include national and regional command centers to handle accidents related to the misapplication of chemicals. And coastal Fujian Province in 2004 finalized a multibillion yuan high-tech "anti-calamities system" to contend with natural disasters such as typhoons, earthquakes, fires, locusts, and other epidemics affecting crops and forests.[45]

Particularly in the wake of the recent dramatic increase of so-called "major incidents"—industrial and traffic accidents as well as other mishaps that engender deaths of over twenty people at a time—cadres are much more responsive to the need to resolve crises quickly. Even more so than past administrations, Hu and company are all-guns-blazing fighters committed to nipping the first signs of instability in the bud. On the largest scale, there are the crack PLA rapid-response units under each of the seven military regions. Even before the September 11 attacks in the United States, the People's Armed Police had set up anti-terrorist rapid-response units to deal with "urban terrorism" or other *tufa* (emergency) events such as the detonation of bombs and other explosive devices in residences, trains and buses, restaurants, and supermarkets.[46]

Symptomatic of cadres' "high degree of crisis awareness" is that from mid-2003 onward, officials of all levels have to carry mobile phones—and they are not allowed to turn them off even after midnight. There are strict stipulations from Beijing that after a major accident such as a mining disaster or big fire, responsible cadres must be on the scene in two to three hours, depending on the state of the traffic and the accessibility of the spot in question. In the four years since 2000, some 1,250 officials, including nine cadres with the rank of minister or governor, were penalized for failing to prevent or properly handle major mishaps due to lapse of safety regulations.[47]

*Ensuring Administrative Probity: Propagating Clean, Law-Abiding,
and Sage-like Cadres*

Short of being democratic, the new-look government under the Fourth-Generation leadership should at least be clean, accountable, and law-abiding. As Wu
Jinglian, a noted liberal scholar and one-time adviser to Zhu Rongji, pointed out
in early 2003, Beijing should aim for "an open, transparent, and service-oriented
government that should be answerable [to the public]." Or as cadres in the Central Party School noted, officials will have fulfilled their mission if they had paid
close attention to four points: "be close to the people; seek after concrete goals;
take the scientific approach; and abide by the law."[48]

Hu and Wen seem convinced that they can nurture thousands upon thousands
of efficient, honest, people-loving, and law-abiding cadres and civil servants even
in the absence of democratic institutions (see also Chapter 4). One key factor is
the inculcation of the ideal of "administration according to law." If officials work
within the parameters of the law—and citizens are allowed to sue officials who
have run afoul of relevant legislations—many of the negative aspects of authoritarian one-party rule can be avoided.

Certainly, no previous CCP leaders have given such emphasis to rule by law,
nor spelled out their requirements in such detail. At an early 2003 Politburo
meeting on "running the country according to law," Hu pointed out that "all
levels of cadres must assiduously boost their ability to run the administration
and to make policies according to law." And then Hu ticked off a series of goals
in this direction: "reforming the judicial and legal system, strengthening judicial supervision, upholding justice, raising the level of implementation of the
law, and ensuring the strict application of the law."[49] And in a State Council
seminar round about the same time, Premier Wen noted that rule by law would
be given the same importance as economic development. Specifically, Wen
pointed out that the government and legislature should pass timely laws on not
only economic reform but also "social management and public service." He
laid emphasis on "judicial supervision" of the government. This meant that the
masses could help rectify government policies or behavior—and seek redress
or compensation—through challenging government decisions or even suing
officials in the law courts.[50]

In terms of promoting the quality of cadres, the Hu-Wen team is continuing
with efforts begun by previous administrations to gradually introduce elements
of a Western-style civil service. From an ideological perspective, however, Hu's
requirements for a good cadre are not that different from those of Chairman Mao,
former president Liu Shaoqi, and ex-president Jiang. Mao ruled that cadres must
satisfy the twofold requirement of "redness and expertise." Liu talked about the
"virtues" that good cadres must possess in his famous 1939 tome, *How to Be a
Good Communist.* Analysts have pointed out Confucianist strains in Liu's advocacy of "self-cultivation" as a means of achieving Communist rectitude.[51] And

for Jiang, it was the "Three Emphases," meaning cadres must be strong in ideology, willing to study the Marxist canon, and mindful of "righteousness."

Hu indicated in 2004 that good cadres must be "strong in politics, be highly professional about their jobs—and that [they] must have a clean working style." Indeed, Hu and Wen have hardly departed from the traditional ideal—which predated communism—of nurturing the image of a Confucius-like sage-mandarin, the proverbial *fumuguan* or "mom-and-dad-like official." And Wen himself, with his penchant for "worrying [about the country's problems] before the rest of the world," is the near-perfect model of a caring, devoted, Lei Feng–like cadre.[52] By contrast, former party chief Zhao Ziyang and his colleagues put much less stress on the "redness," or political correctness, of cadres. For Zhao, what mattered most was *zhengji,* or performance on the job, particularly the ability to hack out new paths in reform.

Hu, together with ally Wu Guanzheng, head of the Central Commission for Disciplinary Inspection (CCDI), has taken more severe and thoroughgoing measures in fighting corruption than administrations under Deng and Jiang. But a good component of the CCDI's approach to fighting graft is no different from that of the ancien régime, that is, stressing "Marxist rectitude" and allied virtues, rather than systemic checks and balances such as vesting the power of fighting corruption in an agency that is independent of the CCP. Indeed, Hu likes to admonish officials to engage in Confucian-style "self-reflection." While talking to NPC officials from Hubei in 2003, the president said: "We must cultivate our political morality; constantly think about the damage of greed; and heed the importance of self-discipline."[53]

Seeking Regional Equality of Development

Seeking a relatively fair distribution of resources among China's disparate regions and provinces is one of the key tasks of the Hu-Wen administration. This is tied not just to economic development but also to the ideal of "scientific development," namely, a fairer distribution of resources nationwide and a more judicious balance between rich and poor provinces. However, an in-depth look at China's regional economics will reveal that political considerations are a key determinant of economic decisions, including government investment activities in different localities.

In the thirteen years of leadership under Jiang, the bulk of the attention and resources of Beijing was showered on the eastern coast, in particularly the Greater Shanghai Region of Shanghai, Pudong, Jiangsu, and Zhejiang. While both Hu and Wen were born along the eastern coast, they spent a large part of their early careers in the hinterland—and these Fourth-Generation leaders have vowed to speak up for provinces in hinterland China (the central and western provinces) as well as the "newly impoverished" northeast.

Much has been written about the "go west" program first initiated by former premier Zhu around 1998 and 1999. And the Hu-Wen team has basically taken over the Zhu initiative in resuscitating the economies of the eleven western provinces and major cities mainly through funneling more investment into the neglected heartland. For example, the majority of the China-destined funds from international financial bodies such as the World Bank and the Asian Development Bank are being used in the west. Senior central-level cadres have also played the role of salesmen and lobbyists in arranging investment tours for Western, Asian, Taiwanese, and Hong Kong businessmen. From 1999 to 2004, Beijing invested 460 billion yuan in the western provinces. This was in addition to budgetary transfer payments of more than 500 billion yuan. The GDP of western provinces went up by 8.5 percent, 8.8 percent, 10.1 percent, and 11.3 percent in the years 2000, 2001, 2002, and 2003 respectively.[54]

However, as of 2005, the east–west gap had not significantly narrowed when compared to the late 1990s. The growth rate of the coastal areas was still higher than that of the hinterland. Moreover, cities ranging from Dalian to Guangzhou are still much more successful in attracting both funds—especially foreign direct investment (FDI)—and talent. A major problem, reformist economist Chi Fulin pointed out, was that the go west policy was "government-led." "We must ensure that the future development of the west be market-oriented," Chi said in late 2004. Indeed, while the government had since the late 1990s bankrolled thirty-six multibillion yuan infrastructure projects, only one-third of these funds had been utilized by the end of 2002. This suggests that the pace of development was much slower than Beijing had anticipated. Moreover, investment by both foreign firms and private enterprises has remained weak. For example, Chongqing, the largest western city, could in 2003 only attract less than 10 percent of the FDI that was bound for Shanghai. And half of this FDI of $331 million came from Hong Kong.[55]

Resuscitating the Three Northeastern Provinces

The Hu-Wen team's determination to attain regional balance is best illustrated by their decision in early 2003 to give a facelift to the depressed economies of the northeastern provinces of Liaoning, Heilongjiang, and Jilin. While the *dongbei*, or northeast, whose industrial foundation was laid by the Japanese and then the Soviets, was the pride of Chinese industry until the 1970s, it has fallen on hard times. Weighed down by obsolete, unwieldy state-owned enterprises (SOEs), the three provinces have lagged behind the eastern coastal rim in exploiting the opportunities of the marketplace. Liaoning, once a pacesetter in industry and technology, has slipped to eleventh place in terms of provincial GDP. And the entire *dongbei* economy is no bigger than that of super-rich Guangdong.[56] Premier Wen, who spelled out instructions on revitalizing the northeast during a trip to Shenyang in August 2003, made it clear that only market forces could save the depressed region. Beijing's *dongbei* game plan could be summed up in one phrase: "policy only, no money." As government economist Gao Huiqing noted, "the central authorities will liberalize policies and introduce more market mechanisms to reactivate the *dongbei.*" Gao added that Beijing wanted to avoid the experience of its go west program, which required massive government expenditure on infrastructure.[57]

According to an economic source in Beijing, one of the Wen cabinet's recommendations was thoroughgoing privatization, meaning that more aggressive measures would be adopted to sell off SOEs to foreign companies—or to private firms from other parts of China. Customary practice dictated that fairly strict criteria must be met before an SOE could be offloaded. "A detailed assessment of the SOE's assets has to be made—and the purchase price must at least reflect a good part of the enterprise's 'worth,'" said the source. "The purchaser must also vouch to re-hire a sizable proportion of existing staff." "The new line proposed in 2003 was that as long as a 'white knight' could turn around an aging factory through an injection of modern technology and management, he could have it practically for free—nor would he be required to keep the workforce."[58]

Wen's advisers were convinced that *dongbei*'s SOEs would be of particular interest to businessmen in South Korea, Japan, and Russia. As Vice-Head of the National Development and Reform Commission Ou Xinqian put it, the infusion of private capital could foster "a highly competitive, fully energetic business environment" in the sleepy northeast. For the so-called New Dongbei Era to arrive, however, the 100 million or so residents in the northeast must, in Deng's words, "undergo a total change of mind-set."[59] As the liberal Guangdong paper *Southern Weekend* pointed out in a 2003 commentary, the northeast was home to a "special culture characterized by satisfaction with the status quo and lack of sensitivity toward the market." Or as Jilin University economist Song Donglin indicated, denizens of the northeast had an "anti-commercial mentality" owing to the residual influence of Soviet-style economic planning. And particularly for Jilin, which adjoins North Korea, potential foreign investors might be deterred by the ongoing nuclear crisis in the Stalinist country.[60]

By late 2004, it was clear that more attention—and favorable policies—from Beijing alone would still prove insufficient to lift the *dongbei* out of its doldrums. For example, Japanese and South Korean investors still preferred to go to Shanghai and Shandong respectively. Hong Kong's famously aggressive real-estate developers were nonplussed by the fact that because of the climate and other conditions, *dongbei* construction workers and sometimes even salespeople had a tradition of not working from November to April.[61] It is not surprising that the National Development and Reform Commission, headed by key Wen aide Ma Kai, had to get into the act by identifying about 100 "priority projects" for the northeast, which ranged from automobile manufacturing and shipbuilding to petrochemicals. However, owing to insufficient interest from domestic as well as foreign investors, the bulk of the $7.3 billion bill for these projects had to be footed by central coffers. Should the *dongbei* continue to have to rely on government handouts, which are reminiscent of the days of the planned economy, however, the Hu-Wen team will hardly be able to call their initiative a success.[62]

Difficulty in Striking a Balance Among the Regions

While it will take some time before the "go northeast" program can bear fruit, the Hu-Wen initiative has already upset the delicate balance among China's various regional economic blocs. While cadres and entrepreneurs in the nation's two main locomotives of growth—the Yangtze and Pearl River deltas—have pronounced themselves unperturbed by competition posed by the northeast, officials in the poor western provinces have expressed anxiety about losing their special place on Beijing's priority list.

Partly because both Hu and Wen had worked long years in the western provinces, there were expectations that the much-neglected region would finally get high-level attention, and patronage. Wen sought to reassure the western hinterland by saying that Beijing's pursuit of a "fourth nexus of growth" in the northeast was based on considerations of a more balanced regional strategy. When asked by a Shaanxi legislator in early 2004 whether Beijing would change its "go west" policy, the premier said: "You can be reassured; we have not slackened a bit in developing the west." Wen added that the *dongbei* strategy would provide added impetus to "interaction and synergy between the eastern and western regions."[63] Vice-Premier Zeng Peiyan, a former head of the now-defunct State Planning Commission, also gave a pep talk to leaders in the western provinces during a trip there in November 2004. "The party central authorities' strategy of opening up the western regions will not change, and the support given by the government to this goal will not weaken," he told cadres in the Guangxi provincial capital of Nanning.[64]

However, there were doubts in the minds of hinterland area cadres, and speculation that the Hu-Wen team was shifting the focus to the northeast because it saw no prospect of the western sector taking off any time soon, despite huge capital injections from government departments and SOEs. Diplomatic analysts said the leadership was taking a gamble because if they could not make a go of the *dongbei* quickly, Hu and Wen might come under heavy fire from both the rich coast and the impoverished west. Consider also the leaders of the six central provinces of Henan, Hunan, Hubei, Anhui, Shanxi, and Jiangxi, who felt they had been neglected due to the fact that they had received even less attention from Beijing than the western provinces. Per capita GDP in this region slipped from 88 percent of the national average in 1980 to just 75 percent in 2003. At the plenary NPC session of 2004, Li Xiansheng, the mayor of Wuhan, capital of Hubei, complained that his city had become the victim of "policy marginalization." "We don't want to see central China collapse," Li warned. Indeed, Wuhan's position as the so-called "Chicago of China" had been lost to Chongqing, the fast-rising mega-city that was tapped to be the star metropolis of the go west program. Even then Henan CCP secretary Li Keqiang, a protégé of President Hu's, groused that his province was being "forgotten." He and his colleagues lamented that Henan was being sidelined because it was "neither east nor west."[65]

It was not until early 2005 that the leaders from the six central provinces came together for a more coordinated approach to growth. Officials and deputies attending the 2005 NPC noted that since central China boasted 20 percent of the nation's science and technology personnel, there was a bright future for high-tech development. However, more needs to be done in industrial policy. For example, cities including Wuhan, Zhengzhou, Changsha, and Hefei are competing with each other in the already oversaturated area of automobile manufacturing. Moreover, central China lags behind the coast in fostering the growth of the private sector—and in ways and means to attract foreign investment.[66]

Factional Politics vs. Regional Balance

Apart from factors such as geography and availability of resources, the most important reason behind the uneven development of disparate regions has been factional politics. Given the domination of the Shanghai Clique in Chinese politics from 1989 to at least early 2003, it was hardly a secret that the Shanghai Clique affiliates—incorporating officials and entrepreneurs in the Greater Shanghai Region that include Jiangsu and Zhejiang provinces—were unhappy with the fact that Greater Shanghai was no longer the apple of the Hu-Wen leadership's eye. This feeling of loss was exacerbated by the unexpected retirement of ex-president Jiang from the Central Military Commission in September 2004.

The growing rivalry between Beijing and Shanghai came to a head during the *hongguan tiaokong* (macro-level adjustment and control) campaign of 2004, when the State Council was trying to cool down the economy. In a meeting of his cabinet in late May, Wen urged administrations of all levels to "comprehensively implement the decisions and steps of the central authorities." And as the official *Outlook* weekly magazine put it in a hard-hitting commentary: "individual regional administrations and enterprises have failed to effectively abide by the central government's instructions." "Many local units are merely stressing their 'special characteristics' while others are asking for 'special treatment' [by Beijing]," *Outlook* said.[67]

Shanghai was a good example of not-so-subtle resistance to the contraction-inducing edicts from Beijing. Lu Deming, head of the Economics School at elite Fudan University, openly disputed the wisdom of "macroeconomic control and adjustments." Lu said it would be best to let the forces of demand and supply—instead of government fiats—determine the level of economic activity. The economist pointed out that all over China, there were more than 40,000 projects involving government investment. "If the government takes action and readjusts [the levels of investment], a large number of projects will be left hanging in the air, and the tremendous losses incurred could outweigh possible gains [from state interference]," Lu asserted.[68]

For the past several years, the metropolis had been banking on earnings from sectors such as the irrationally exuberant real-estate market to finance its expansion. While the sky-high prices of apartments were sustained partly due to specu-lation-related activities by Hong Kong, Taiwan, and overseas-Chinese business-men, the Shanghai municipal government was adamant that this was not a "bubble phenomenon." Shanghai was also known to have reservations about Beijing's decision to cut down on the number of economic and technological zones in or-der to save valuable farmland. Its rationale was that business was booming in the city—and that more industrial and high-tech zones were needed to establish its claim as the "dragonhead of the world factory."[69]

For political reasons, particularly the fact that Shanghai was the bastion of the so-called Shanghai Clique led by ex-president Jiang, the Hu-Wen leadership had had difficulty imposing its will—and policies—on the East China metropolis. According to the Ministry of Construction, "prestige projects"—giant monuments and engineering marvels conceived to demonstrate the "vision" and prowess of local leaders—could be found in at least 20 percent of the nation's 660 large and medium-sized cities. Despite Beijing's repeated warnings about "monumental projects," Shanghai was set to spend 60.7 billion yuan in 2004 year on fifty-six mega-schemes of all varieties. Municipal authorities were insisting that many of their new initiatives had to do with the 2010 World Expo to be held in the city.[70]

But how about the 2.6 billion yuan stadium for Formula One car racing that was slated to be Asia's largest? Even more controversial was a 600,000–square-meter "underground city" due for completion in 2006. At thirty meters below ground, the shopping and recreation complex in downtown Shanghai would ide-ally provide a "second dimension" to the metropolis. Yet critics have noted that because of the city's relatively soft geological foundation, digging so deep would incur the kind of spending that would not make sense, particularly in a *hongguan tiaokong* climate.[71]

The Pearl River Delta vs. the Yangtze River Delta

Much of the rivalry between the Shanghai Faction on the one hand, and a number of other cliques in the party and government on the other, can be understood in light of the formation in mid-2004 of what could be China's largest economic development sphere: the Pan–Pearl River Delta Zone (PPRDZ). Dubbed "nine plus two," it comprised nine provinces (Guangdong, Guangxi, Hainan, Hunan, Fujian, Jiangxi, Yunnan, Guizhou, and Sichuan) and the two special administra-tive regions (SARs) of Hong Kong and Macau. In terms of population, the nine provinces alone encompass one-third of China's total. And if the two SARs were included, the PPRDZ would account for 40 percent of the country's GDP.[72]

The PRRDZ was initially born out of the synergy between Hong Kong and the Pearl River Delta (PRD)—the result of a process of economic integration that first started in the 1980s, when Hong Kong factories moved into Shenzhen and other cities in the Pearl River estuary. However, there was a divergence of views at the very top, meaning the Politburo Standing Committee, concerning the dramatic expansion of the PRD–Hong Kong nexus into the "nine plus two" concept. A key reason was there was no precedent for such a humongous economic zone.

Beijing sources said the PPRDZ was favored by Hu and Wen—but not by Shanghai Faction affiliates such as Vice-President Zeng or Executive Vice-Premier Huang Ju. That the zone did not have uniform Politburo backing was evident during the inaugural "nine plus two" series of meetings—the Pan-PRD Regional Cooperation and Development Forum—which took place in Hong Kong, Macau, and Guangzhou (capital of Guangdong) in early June 2004. It was intriguing that no top-level cadre from the central party and government authorities was on hand to officiate at the forum. The most senior official present was the party secretary of Guangdong, Zhang Dejiang. While Zhang had Politburo status, he took part in the forum mostly by virtue of his being the number one official of Guangdong, which first proposed the "nine plus two" idea. According to usual protocol, either Premier Wen or Executive-Premier Huang should have attended the first major function of the PPRDZ.[73]

There was also the question of geographical classification. Strictly speaking, provinces such as Jiangxi, Hunan, and in particular Sichuan had more to do with the middle and upper reaches of the Yangtze River rather than the much shorter Pearl River. Indeed, many officials in the Greater Shanghai Region would consider Sichuan a proper member of the Yangtze River Delta (YRD) economic zone.[74] It was perhaps for similar reasons that Chongqing, China's fourth directly administered city (after Beijing, Shanghai, and Tianjin) did not make it into the "nine plus two" configuration.

The Shanghai Faction was opposed to the "nine plus two" game plan for the simple reason that the PPRDZ would dwarf the Greater Shanghai Region (Shanghai plus cities in Jiangsu and Zhejiang provinces) at a time when the latter was showing signs of overtaking the PRD (basically just Guangdong in addition to Hong Kong) in importance. The PPRDZ concept would also provide the justification for central authorities to provide more investment funds to southern China rather than the YRD zone. Already, the Shanghai Clique had in private accused the Hu-Wen group of trying to use the *hongguan tiaokong* campaign to delimit Shanghai's growth.[75]

Chinese sources in Beijing have said that for the Hu-Wen leadership, the formation of the PPRDZ was, from one perspective, almost a "test of loyalty" for regional cadres. Owing to the fact that Shanghai-affiliated members of the Politburo were apparently opposed to the "nine plus two" scheme, officials of the nine provinces—in particular the Guangdong leadership—ran a considerable risk of alienating Shanghai Faction politicians by taking part in the grandiose plan. It was perhaps for this reason that then party secretary and mayor of Chongqing, Huang Zhendong and Wang Hongju respectively, had expressed reservations about joining. While not card-carrying members of the Shanghai Faction, neither Huang nor Wang yet wanted to link their political fate with the Hu-Wen leadership.[76]

The sheer size of the PPRDZ means it could take at least a few years before the fruits of synergy would become obvious. The provincial and SAR leaders talked about a "unified and well-coordinated" railway system, as well as cooperation in other aspects of transportation and logistics. Both Guangzhou and, more so, Hong Kong would play a bigger role in finance, including launching the initial public offerings of corporations based in the nine provinces.[77] What seemed probable was that the Hu-Wen team had served notice on the Shanghai Faction that the Greater Shanghai Region's domination of the Chinese economy might be frontally challenged.

Indeed, there were signs in late 2004 that Shanghai was facing increasing difficulties in maintaining its heady pace of growth. In the first three-quarters of that year, the metropolis managed to attract only US$9.2 billion in FDI, or just 3 percent more than the same period a year previous. By contrast, long-time competitor Guangdong snatched up FDI worth $13.04 billion during the first nine months of 2004, or a mammoth 36.5 percent above the same period in 2003. And in 2003, Shanghai was overtaken by nearby Suzhou in the red-hot competitive game of luring multinationals. As the Beijing-based magazine *International Herald Leader* noted, one has to ask this question: "Is Shanghai sick?" The weekly suggested that Shanghai might have succumbed to "Hong Kong disease"—fast-rising land and wage costs, which have prompted many foreign firms to set up shop in nearby Jiangsu and Zhejiang provinces.[78]

Efforts Toward Building a China-Dominated Twenty-first Century

While outwardly bogged down by the perennial problems of unemployed workers and restive peasants, the Hu-Wen team is mapping out plans to ensure China's quasi-superpower status by the end of the 2020s. The ambition of the Fourth-Generation leadership was evident in a Politburo study session in late 2003, in which several noted historians were asked to discuss "the law of the rise and fall of past empires."

Hu pointed out during the Politburo seminar that CCP cadres must study not only Marxist theories and Chinese conditions but also world history so as to "better seize the initiative in expediting our country's development." The party chief said world history had shown that a country's advancement depended on "whether it could seize the opportunity to speed up development." Hu talked about the possibility of a *kuayue,* or leap forward–style advancement, for developing countries such as China. "A backward country or people can ride the crest of the waves of the times if it can make full use of the opportunities at critical historical junctures," Hu said.[79]

Earlier in the same year, the newly installed state president repeated the same message of opportunity and urgency to a group of NPC delegates. "A key determinant of whether a party, country, or people can achieve great development is whether it can seize the opportunity and develop quickly," he said. And it was the

CCP leadership's firm belief that China was experiencing just such an opportune moment for fast-paced growth, even though the window of opportunity might not last beyond two decades.[80]

Beijing, however, is worried about "peripheral geopolitics," a reference to the current and historical relationship between major countries and their neighbors. Well-known historians and economic geographers told the Hu-Wen team that given the same availability of the usual prerequisites for power and strength such as natural and human resources coupled with sizable domestic and foreign markets, countries might be able to maintain their predominance for longer periods if they were surrounded by weak neighbors. This has certainly been true for the United States since the First World War. Neighboring countries such as Mexico and Canada have not been able to challenge U.S. supremacy. The same could not be said, for example, of France. French power, even "Gallic imperialism," could have endured if the country had not been subject to formidable threats from neighboring behemoths such as Germany and England. For a time, England was able to preserve its vast empire owing to the natural barrier provided by the English Channel. Yet the "empire on which the sun never sets" petered out during World War II when enemies on the continent such as Germany were able to develop fighter airplanes and other new weapons.

The emergence of China was only possible after twenty-five years of economic reform—and the development of the "world factory" along the eastern coast. China's vast internal market has also rendered it better able to weather global economic cycles. However, the Hu leadership is only too aware that while, on the one hand, its huge land mass would make it difficult for potential enemy forces to occupy the country for long, China is surrounded by powers such as Russia, Japan, and India, all of which have been in wars with the Middle Kingdom. And the United States, which maintains vast military bases in Japan and surrounding areas, remains a constant threat. A major foreign-policy task of the Hu-Wen team is to counter the "anti-China containment policy" supposedly spearheaded by Washington (see Chapter 5).

Renowned *People's Daily* commentator Ren Zhongping pointed out in mid-2004 that China was facing a period of unparalleled opportunity from the turn of the century until around 2020. Ren noted that the country could take off on the basis of the fruits of reform programs undertaken by Deng. He wrote: "Experts on international issues are of the opinion that when a country's per capita GDP has hit the mark of US$1,000, there may appear two prospects and two results: Some rise up and emerge [as strong states], others linger around and make no progress."[81] Of course, the twenty-year Golden Period could be cut short prematurely if one of China's neighbors were to suddenly turn into an aggressive competitor. For example, if ongoing sentiments in Japan to "remilitarize" prevail, Tokyo might have developed a sizable military force, even nuclear weapons, in less than two decades. Also, the Indian economy could take a leap forward in the coming decade in much the same way that China did in the 1990s and early 2000s. And then there is Russia, on which China relies for energy and sophisticated weapons. Russia will remain quite dependent on trade with China up through the 2010s. However, it could also become a competitor after its economy has taken off thanks to commerce with the United States and windfall from rising oil prices.[82]

For cynics, Hu's statements about fast-paced growth and seizing the moment recall the Great Leap Forward of Chairman Mao Zedong, who vowed in the mid-1950s to "overtake Britain and catch up with the U.S." in ten to twenty years through means such as smelting steel in backyard furnaces. There are also questions as to whether the leadership's repeated calls on the nation to concentrate on maintaining stability and developing the economy might not be excuses to push back already much-delayed political reform.

Above all, there is the question of whether the Fourth-Generation leadership is really committed to no-holds-barred reform. In the closed-door Politburo "study session" on history and geography, quite a few experts pointed out that the reformist spirit—or its lack—could spell the difference between prosperity and mediocrity for a country. The case of England versus Spain was cited. Both countries rose fast in the eighteenth century owing to their relatively large size and markets, and in particular, their strong navies. But, said the historians who advised the Politburo, England became a world power in the nineteenth century because it was at the forefront of innovation in technology and political systems. And Spain, being much less of a trailblazer, lagged behind. At that Politburo conclave, Hu reportedly expressed agreement. "Innovation and reform, particularly in institutions and systems, are the key to a country's progress," he said. Indeed, when he was touring Guizhou in 2000, the then vice-president already underscored the imperative of new ideas. "We shall lose the opportunity if we were to just follow old rules," he told local cadres. "We'll make no advancement if we retreat upon facing difficulties."[83] Throughout his career as an expert in "party construction," Hu had played up the importance of constantly "seeking new breakthroughs." The conclusion of this chapter will make a preliminary assessment of whether the Hu-Wen team can pass muster in this crucial arena of innovation and reform.

A Preliminiary Assessment of the Hu-Wen Team's New Ideas

Hu Jintao's efforts to craft a kind of "scientific socialism" has yet to pass the classic test embodied in the credo of "practice is the sole criterion of truth." As veteran Hong Kong–based China commentator Lu Rulue pointed out, "scientific socialism may be just a myth."[84] And while Hu may deserve praise for valiant efforts to surpass the theories of Mao, Deng, and Jiang, these attempts could turn out to be a quixotic venture if he is unwilling to make a clean break with the Leninist—and Maoist—view of the party monopoly of power.

The Limits of "Scientific Decision Making"

The Hu-Wen team's vaunted knack for "scientific" governance and crisis management has often been vitiated by undemocratic and bureaucratic decision making, which has been worsened by media censorship and cadres' tendency to hoodwink even their superiors by reporting only the good news. The Hu-Wen leadership certainly deserves credit for playing up the *yiren weiben* (putting-people-first) credo. That the lot of ordinary Chinese has not improved by much, however, is attested to by rising death figures from dangerous factories and mines, near-static wage levels for migrant workers, and the ever-increasing throngs of petitioners in Beijing. And many of these ills have to do with the problematic nature of governance and its decision-making processes.

Hu and Wen's rationale for spurning "Western-style democracy" is that even without potentially destabilizing practices such as general elections, the leadership can still hit upon the right policies based on "scientific" decision making as well as broad consultations. Yet it is well known that in the absence of real democracy and accountability, much of what senior leaders hear or read about may be an embellished version of the truth. Despite their extensive and costly intelligence-gathering network, it cannot be said that the Politburo has a good grasp of the national situation, the basis for scientific policymaking. As both Premier Wen and his predecessor Zhu have admitted, local-level cadres routinely file sexed-up reports to Beijing in order to earn promotions. In their 2004 bestseller *An Investigative Report on Chinese Peasants,* rural experts Chen Guidi and Wu Chuntao describe the many occasions on which grassroots officials pull the wool over the eyes of myriad inspectors and investigators from Beijing. For example, Wen sometimes had to shake off his entourage to make unannounced tours of the countryside in order to get at the real picture.[85]

While intellectuals and government consultants are appreciative of the attention that the Hu Politburo has accorded them, many do not think "top-down consultation" can be a substitute for democratic institutions. As Shanghai University historian Zhu Xueqin pointed out in 2004: "The issue is not how many experts you invite to Zhongnanhai each month, but when [the leadership] is going to decide to give people access to information and to allow free conversation."[86] And owing to tight censorship of the press and the websites, bold souls who dare tell Beijing the truth, such as famed Internet essayist Du Daobin, are often locked behind bars. Even relatively mild critics of the regime such as the authors of the influential *Investigative Report on Chinese Peasants* are forbidden to talk to foreign reporters.

And there is ample evidence that heavy political and ideological baggage is weighing on the "scientific" spirit that Hu is trying so hard to propagate. Out of conviction, as well as the need to pacify important factions in the CCP, Hu has paid homage to the teachings of both Mao and Jiang. This is despite the fact that the economic and political theories of Mao have been thoroughly discredited.

The president and party chief has also revived old-style *sixiang yundong,* or ideological movements, such as the early-2005 campaign to promote the "advanced nature" of party members. And the media has since 2004 revived the Maoist convention of lionizing "model cadres" and "model workers."[87]

Then there is the knowledge on the minds of intellectuals and ordinary folk that despite the Hu-Wen team's commitment to scientific and democratic decision making, powerful blocs in the country are guaranteed a lobsidedly big say in all aspects of governance. One example is the People's Liberation Army, which has a disproportionately large share of seats on powerful bodies such as the CCP Central Committee. An even more influential group is what "leftist" social scientists call the fast-emerging *guanshang,* or "clique of cadre-entrepreneurs," a reference to the collusion between businessmen and senior cadres, many of whose relatives and cronies are big bosses in the mushrooming "nonstate sector" of the economy. Scholars such as Yang Fan of CASS and Li Shuguang of the University of Politics and the Law have decried the fact that government policy is at the service of the *guanshang* class.[88] Without real democracy, there is only so far that "scientific decision making" can go in righting social wrongs.

The Problem with "Putting Out Fires"

It is a credit to the Hu-Wen team that it has proven much more responsive than the previous administration to the demands of the populace. But due to a general lack of functioning institutions able to respond to citizens' needs, it has become more frequent for Politburo members, if not Hu or Wen themselves, to personally take charge of the ways and means of alleviating "social contradictions." Wen earned immense popularity by spearheading the drive to ensure that migrant workers are properly paid by their employers. Both the president and the premier have also spent time and effort addressing the plight of urban or rural residents who have been forced to vacate their homes for urban renewal or redevelopment.

One of Wen's best-known exploits was helping *nongmingong,* or migrant worker, Zeng Xiangwan, who lived in the outskirts of Chongqing, recover owed wages of more than 2,000 yuan. This took place in October 2003, when Wen and local officials happened to be talking to Zeng's wife, Xiong Deming, during an inspection trip of the county of Yunyang. Following Wen's instructions, the county chief was able to deliver the unpaid salary to Xiong within a few hours. Wen's encounter with Xiong was nominated one of the year's top domestic news by NCNA. Xiong became a celebrity, and throughout 2004 she was visited almost daily by *nongmingong* from all over the country who had trouble collecting back pay.[89]

Liu Taiheng, a retired PLA general and the son of former military legend General Liu Bocheng, was bold enough to point out that it was less than appropriate for the prime minister of a big country to personally chase after the unpaid salaries of workers. Concerning the Xiong Deming episode, Liu said it was "a problem of the system that this type of work could not be handled by functional departments." Then there was the instance of the leaders of the city of Jixi, Heilongjiang, who provided Beijing with false figures to cover up the fact that factories in the locality had not paid workers properly. It took Wen's personal intervention—three times—before Jixi cadres finally corrected their mistakes. Wrote commentator Zhu Shugu of the *China Economic Times:* "The prime minister had to personally intervene in tackling the problem of owed wages, and the problem wasn't solved until after repeated efforts." Zhu continued, "The costs for this kind of supervision and checks and balances are undoubtedly high."[90]

China went through a scare in the spring of 2004 that was almost comparable to SARS or bird flu: the inundation of the market with nutritionless infant formula, which was responsible for the deaths of at least twenty babies and the worsening health of hundreds more infants nationwide. However, since fake liquor, foodstuffs, cosmetics, and other consumer products were already so prevalent in Chinese markets, officials in different provinces did not take this seriously until Wen issued an order to catch the culprits and stop the malpractice immediately. While the regional cadres finally swung into action, the question of "whether there be no investigation without a directive from the premier" was hotly debated on a number of website chat-rooms.[91]

Then there is the Hu-Wen team's penchant for "throwing a committee at a problem." This is a reference to the leadership's tendency to set up coordinating, crisis-management, or rapid-response commissions—or units such as "leading groups" and "working groups"—to tackle a social, economic, or political malady. The same strategy was used by previous administrations. It was interesting that the Gansu provincial party committee and government decided in early 2004 to abolish 43 out of the 70 leading groups and special coordinating committees they had set up since 2001. According to *Workers' Daily* commentator Zhou Sijun, leading groups have the harmful side effect of encouraging bureaucratism, formalism, and even dictatorial decision making. "Usually only leading cadres can sit on such committees; how can they have enough time and energy to handle so many things?" asked Zhou.[92]

Is the Hu-Wen Administration Reformist Enough?

Since becoming party chief in late 2002, Hu has aroused great expectations in and out of China through his emphasis on "putting people first" and, in particular, seeking theoretical breakthroughs and opening up vistas in reform. While discussing with historians in 2003 the factors behind the rise and fall of empires, Hu concluded that one crucial formula for nurturing powerful countries was "making breakthroughs in systems and institutions." Yet it is noteworthy that many of Hu's more conservative forebears, particularly predecessor Jiang, had also set great store by ringing in the new. For example, while pushing his "Theory of the Three Represents," ex-president Jiang urged cadres to be on the lookout for "new ways of thinking, new ways of doing things, and new mechanisms and institutions." Jiang told cadres in mid-2002 that "we must liberate our thoughts, seek truth from facts, and progress with the times."[93] Yet the former president failed in many ways to live up to his own touchstones for being an open-minded and forward-looking cadre.

While Hu and Wen have in general proven themselves more popular than Third-Generation cadres in and out of China, it is significant that both Fourth-Generation titans are best known as political survivors, not innovators. Until he became party boss, Hu was noted for being hard-working and loyal to the top leadership, but he had hardly distinguished himself as an initiator of new ideas. Take, for example, his tenure as CCP secretary of Guizhou Province from 1985 to 1988. Hu won generally high praise for having inspected all the counties in the poor province. Yet in terms of ability and reformist zeal, most local cadres would put him at least one notch below his predecessor, well-known reformer Zhu Houze. In fact, one of Hu's secrets for success was his ability to avoid making mistakes, meaning not doing or saying things deemed politically incorrect.[94]

Premier Wen has a comparable track record to that of his comrade-in-arms Hu. Wen is respected as a man of the people and, among cadres in the party and central government, as a compromiser capable of listening to different viewpoints and mediating among disparate factions. Thus, the Tianjin-born head of government is much more popular than predecessor "Boss Zhu," and many State Council old hands even call him a "latter-day Zhou Enlai" in recognition of his administrative ability. Wen's exceptional ability to ride out political storms is attested to by his having served five top cadres: Deng, Hu Yaobang, Zhao Ziyang, Jiang Zemin, and Hu Jintao. However, while Wen has proven generally proficient in solving problems and putting out fires, he has yet to demonstrate an ability to blaze new trails in reform.[95] The rest of this book will explore in greater depth and detail the areas where the Hu-Wen team has broken new ground—and more significantly, where much, much more needs to be done.

3

The Communist Party vs. Peasants and Workers

Will Hu Jintao's "New Social Contract" Work?

Reaffirming the Mass Line and Restoring Human Dignity

The new leadership under President Hu Jintao is, to some extent, reinventing the wheel. In the official media, senior cadres and official scribes are still making platitudinous salutations to the Marxist canon. Yet it is apparent to most Chinese that communism has been terminally mothballed, rendered obsolete with the last century. What is left for the Chinese Communist Party (CCP)—its only raison d'être and the basis of its legitimacy—is "serving the people." Yet with the advent of the twenty-first century—and forces such as globalization and the Internet—the CCP can no longer get away with saying that it suffices to just feed and clothe people.[1] And with the concept of protecting citizens' human rights finally written into the state Constitution in early 2004, the Fourth-Generation team has to make a commitment to raising the level of social justice and human dignity.

In a sense, Hu and ally Premier Wen Jiabao are but reviving the ideas of an earlier generation of reformist thinkers. The late philosopher Wang Ruishui, a former deputy chief editor of the *People's Daily,* raised the idea of "socialist humanism" in 1983 and 1984. Wang pointed out that since the goal of Marxism was "the liberation and full development of the individual," party and government authorities should do away with systems and institutions that inhibit people's thinking and hamper the pursuit of political freedom.[2] Wang and fellow free thinkers were attacked by hardliners during a relatively short-lived "campaign against spiritual pollution," and the respected intellectual was later kicked out of the CCP.

At the Sixteenth Congress, the CCP leadership affirmed its goal for the twenty-first century: to maintain and prolong its ruling status, or the proverbial ideal of "long reign and perennial stability." This, the Fourth-Generation chieftains hoped, would be made possible through raising the standard of living of ordinary Chinese and boosting social justice and allied "humanistic" values. This was the main thrust of the Sixteenth Congress Political Report, entitled "Building a well-off society in a well-rounded way." It is significant that "development in a well-rounded way" was soon interpreted as taking a "scientific approach to development," meaning that Beijing should aim for progress on all fronts, and not just jack up the GDP growth rate (see Chapter 2). In the two to three years prior to the Sixteenth Party Congress, ex-president Jiang Zemin had in some respects laid the groundwork for the Hu-Wen team's *yiren weiben* (putting people first) state philosophy. For example, Jiang's "Theory of the Three Represents" (that the CCP represents the highest productivity, the foremost culture, and the overall interests of the broad masses) had made clear that the CCP had morphed from a revolutionary party obsessed with class struggle to an entity for promoting the welfare of the entire people.

It was also in tune with the Zeitgeist that the Hu-Wen team should be raising the banner of populism. First- and Second-Generation titans such as Mao Zedong and Deng Xiaoping possessed some form of "revolutionary legitimacy," having taken part in the Long March and fought bloody battles to usher in the Communist administration. Third-Generation leaders such as Hu Yaobang, Zhao Ziyang, or Jiang Zemin could claim to have "legitimacy" based on having corrected the wrongs of the Cultural Revolution; they also enjoyed the "deathbed blessings" of Deng. Fourth-Generation leaders such as Hu and Wen, who lack charisma and national stature, have to base their rule on the acquiescence if not the active support of the masses.

Almost from day one, the Hu Politburo indicated its commitment to a new deal for farmers and workers, the CCP's traditional pillars of support. Hu, together with his Politburo colleagues, vowed to do something about phenomena such as the polarization between rich and poor and the erosion of the rights of workers and peasants. This flowed from a consensus among the leadership that the dire straits of marginalized sectors such as jobless peasants could wreak havoc on the CCP's fragile mandate of heaven.[3]

Hu and Wen spent almost their entire first year in office publicizing the new administration's concern for the masses and the downtrodden. The two supremos made trips to hilly backwater regions that had been neglected in the national media, for example, poor, inaccessible towns and hamlets in Hebei, Inner Mongolia, Guizhou, and Shanxi. While inspecting Inner Mongolia less than two months after taking office, General Secretary Hu told local cadres, "we must ceaselessly safeguard, promote, and develop the interests of the masses." The party chief pledged that funds Beijing had earmarked for bailing out needy families must be paid out promptly and without fail.[4] And in a series of Politburo sessions devoted to redressing the wealth gap, the Hu leadership indicated it would introduce a "sliding" or favorable policy in allocating resources so as to resuscitate agriculture and help farmers, 200 million of whom were jobless or severely unemployed. The Politburo as well as major state media reiterated in 2002 and 2003 that the party's "topmost priority is to show more concern for farmers and to support agriculture."[5]

Leading cadres and their advisers agreed that after more than two decades of fast development—and horrendous dislocations in many socioeconomic areas—Chinese society was going through a cycle of uncertainty with possibilities of cataclysmic explosions of anti-government sentiment. Studies by People's University sociologists in 2003 and 2004 concluded that China had entered a "high-risk period." Professor Li Lulu said incidents and conflicts in areas like relations between cadres and the masses, labor relations, the environment, public health, as well as law and order could tear asunder the social fabric. Peking University sociologist Liu Neng attributed the malaise to factors such as the exacerbation of social inequality, the profusion of fake products, environmental depredation, and the inadequacy of crisis-handling mechanisms.[6]

While the Hu-Wen team has done much to improve techniques and systems in detecting social crises, it is aware that the terminal solution lies in narrowing the rich-poor gap and defusing sociopolitical contradictions by boosting social equality, mobility, and justice. And whether the CCP's mandate of heaven can be extended depends on the extent to which the leadership can roll out a new deal for disgruntled peasants and workers. However, solid improvements in the lot of the underprivileged classes will require a much higher degree of powersharing—and real political reform—something that the party leadership is reluctant to do.

Hu Jintao's Reinterpreation of the "Theory of the Three Represents"

Problems with Jiang Zemin's "Theory of the Three Represents"

As we saw in Chapter 2, Jiang's now-famous "Theory of the Three Represents" meant that the CCP had become for all intents and purposes a *quanmindang*, or a party for all the people—and not just the party of the *gongnongbing* (workers, peasants, and soldiers), deemed by the likes of Karl Marx and Mao Zedong as the cream of the masses and the pioneers of the revolution.[7] This Jiang-style "new thinking" not only contradicted orthodox Marxist edicts but also threatened to alienate the CCP's traditional supporters, namely workers and farmers. The elevated social and political status of parvenu "red capitalists" has been officially confirmed. And given that members of the new classes of private businessmen and professionals can be said to be exemplars of the highest productivity and the most advanced culture, they could not only become CCP members but also be inducted into leadership ranks.[8]

According to a party source, Jiang had, in the run-up to the Sixteenth Congress, stressed that the CCP had no choice but to change from a *gongnongbing* party to one that is for all the people. Jiang and his aides cited an internal study by the party's Organization Department, which showed many private entrepreneurs were joining the eight "democratic parties" instead of the CCP. Founded in the 1940s and 1950s, these eight entities consist of non-CCP politicians, professionals, and intellectuals who have at least in theory pledged to "discuss policies and take part in politics under CCP leadership." The Organization Department document cautioned that if this trend were to go on, the party would lose hold of the most dynamic forces behind economic growth.[9] Jiang and such allies as then Organization

Department chief Zeng Qinghong indicated that the CCP must adjust itself to the new era. They noted that in the age of traditional manufacturing, when Marx wrote his revolutionary textbooks, workers were indeed at the forefront of productivity. However, in the information technology (IT) epoch, businessmen and professionals had displaced relatively less educated workers, not to mention farmers, as society's vanguard.[10]

The decision by Jiang and company to turn the CCP into a *quanmindang* that embraces the "new classes" drew fire not just from leftists, or quasi-Maoists, but also grassroots officials. Maoist ultra-conservatives, who had been sidelined since the early 1990s, took advantage of the growing class antagonism to attack free-market reforms—as well as to claw back political capital. In 2002, leftists such as former head of the Propaganda Department Deng Liqun were at the forefront of the campaign to denigrate what they called the adulteration of Marxism—and to block the red capitalists' entry into the CCP. In an internally circulated letter, Deng and a host of ultra-conservative cadres questioned the wisdom of admitting the private bosses to the CCP. "As part of the exploitative class, how can a capitalist carry on a lifelong struggle for the realization of socialism?" the document asked. And Lin Yanzhi, a senior party official in Jilin Province, also challenged Jiang openly. "Allowing private entrepreneurs to join [the party] would imply that we legitimize exploitative ideas and behavior within the party," Lin noted.[11]

Beijing was rife with stories that former party chairman Hua Guofeng, Mao's anointed successor, had threatened to quit the party if it started to let in red bosses. And nearly 1,000 party veterans reportedly held a rally in Beijing on July 1, 2002, the party's birthday, to protest against Jiang's alleged revisionism of classic Marxism and Mao Thought.[12] Jiang and his Politburo colleagues, most of whose sons and daughters were either budding red capitalists or professionals working for joint ventures, were able to defuse the challenge of the leftists. However, Jiang also realized that should factors such as polarization between rich and poor—as well as exploitation and corruption—become more serious, it was possible for leftists to form an "opposition coalition" with members of the "exploited" classes, which included a good chunk of the urban and rural jobless.

Jiang's aides tried to conciliate the opposition by coming up with media articles reassuring workers that their traditional status as "masters of the state" and "vanguard of the party" would not be affected. A mid-July 2002 commentary by the official New China News Agency (NCNA) said the CCP would "always uphold the fundamental goal of relying on the working class with all its heart and mind." The state media also quoted then Politburo member Wei Jianxing, who was in charge of labor unions, as saying that the recent reforms had not changed "the status of the working class as the masters of the state and enterprises."[13]

Unfortunately, arguments about the "peaceful coexistence" of workers and nascent capitalists ran counter to the ugly manifestations of what cynics called "the primitive stage of Chinese-style capitalism." First, there were ample reasons why "red bosses" could hardly become exemplary Marxists. The official media were replete with articles stating that nouveau riche businessmen had evaded at least 100 billion yuan in taxes a year. According to an article in the *People's Daily,* less than 20 percent of depositors owned 80 percent of the funds held in savings accounts in the nation's banks. Yet these millionaires paid less than 10 percent of all personal-income taxes. According to Liaoning University professor Yang Yuyong, the rich got away with not paying 120 billion yuan worth of taxes a year, while the government only spent 20 billion yuan in cost-of-living benefits to the urban poor.[14]

Then there was the rising spate of mining and industrial accidents, which Beijing commentators attributed to the get-rich-quick mentality of the unscrupulous private owners of mines and factories. After an accident in a gold mine in Fanzhi District, Shanxi Province, that killed at least thirty-nine workers in mid-2002, the *Legal Daily* launched an investigation into the 300–odd privately held mines in the same area. The official daily found that nearly all these mines had had at least one fatal accident in the past couple of years—and that local authorities had tolerated unsafe working conditions because they had been bribed by the owners.[15]

The *Beijing Youth Daily* said in a commentary that vicious industrial accidents were often "the result of the alliance of capital and power." The influential daily noted that particularly in remote areas such as Shanxi, Shaanxi, and Guangxi provinces, mine operators were in cahoots with local officials. Factory and mine owners ignored safety regulations because they enjoyed the protection of cronies in regional governments. The daily said the root cause of the accidents was "local cadres having been corrupted by the power of money."[16] The situation had hardly improved by the end of 2004. In the wake of a mine blast in Tongchuan, Shaanxi Province, which killed 166 miners, China Labor Watch director Li Qiang pointed an accusing finger at unscrupulous mine owners who were acting in collusion with local officials. "Mine owners, driven by profit, often violate regulations on safe practice. . . . They gang up with local officials and disregard miners' lives," he said.[17]

Little wonder that class antagonism between the have-nots and the exploited on the one hand, and "marketplace exploiters" on the other, had intensified by the early 2000s.

Hu's Modification to the "Three Represents Theory"

Apart from factional dynamics—meaning the long-standing rivalry between Jiang's Shanghai Faction and President Hu's Communist Youth League clique—it was quite obvious that Hu would, shortly upon taking over power, make major modifications to the "Three Represents Theory." Anxious to break out of Jiang's mold, Hu was also driven by his conviction that the CCP's ruling-party status would be jeopardized unless Jiang's perceived favoritism toward the "privileged classes" was reversed.

There is no evidence that the new party chief and president has reservations about raising the political status of private businessmen and the professional classes. After all, quite a few children and relatives of Hu, Wen, and other top cadres are budding capitalists. However, from the Sixteenth CCP Congress onward, Hu made the strategic decision to focus only on the third item of the "Three Represents": that is, that the CCP should promote the comprehensive interests of the broad masses. The Fourth-Generation stalwart is convinced that his close-to-the-masses dictums are more in tune with the times than the elitism implicit in Jiang's "Three Represents Theory." While Hu still cites the "Three Represents" slogan in public speeches, the Jiang mantra has for all intents and purposes been displaced by the new president's populist sayings. In fact, Hu has deftly displaced "Three Represents" with the now-famous slogan of *yiren weiben,* or "putting people first." Thus, in a September 2003 conference on studying the "Three Represents Theory," Hu noted that the essence of this theory was none other than "establishing the party for the public good and running the administration for the sake of the people."[18]

There were complaints, coming particularly from the Greater Shanghai Region, that the Hu-Wen faction was adulterating Jiang's masterpiece theoretical invention. In the eyes of some Shanghai Clique purists, there were unavoidable contradictions between protecting the interests of businessmen and those of workers and peasants. For example, Premier Wen's crusade to boost the welfare of migrant laborers (see following section) would inevitably cut into the profits, particularly of private entrepreneurs, many of whom had made their fortune out of exploiting rural work hands.[19]

It has been possible for Hu, Wen, and their colleagues to make a strategic modification of the "Three Represents Theory" because, at least on paper, it has not been identified as the personal invention of Jiang. This is despite lobbying by the ex-president and other members of his Shanghai Faction that his name should be inserted in both the CCP and the state charters when they were revised in 2002 and 2004 respectively. Opponents to putting Jiang's name next to the "Three Represents Theory" insisted that it was unusual for a living person to be cited by the party or state Constitution as having made major contributions. A compromise was struck at the last minute. The party charter merely saluted "the important Theory of the Three Represents."[20]

And this has more than academic significance. "Three Represents" would hereafter be considered a product of collective wisdom. Similar to many of the dictums of Mao or Deng, Jiang's pet theory would be adjusted according to political expediency of the day. And in spite of the fact that Jiang had at the Sixteenth CCP Congress succeeded in promoting a good number of his Shanghai Faction affiliates to the Politburo and the Politburo Standing Committee (PSC), he was unable to prevent Hu and Wen from in effect turning his theory around, if not on its head. Moreover, regional cadres who were anxious to curry favor with the new leadership, including Guangdong party secretary Zhang Dejiang, lost no time in switching over to Hu's interpretation of the "Three Represents."[21]

The Hu-Wen Team's Populism: Rehoisting the Mass Line

The Hu-Wen administration is offering a novel social contract to 1.3 billion Chinese. The new deal can be summarized as prosperity under one-party rule, more upward mobility, a relatively efficient and clean government—but no "Western-style democracy." Hu and his team have indicated that while political reform might be introduced in the latter part of the decade (see Chapter 4), the administration will put its focus on prosperity—particularly raising the well-being and the sociopolitical status of the broad masses. After all, a central message of the Sixteenth Party Congress was that China would become a "comprehensively well-off society" by the year 2020.

The party leadership is anxious to pass along the message that its mission of generating wealth for the nation will be married to the Maoist goal of being in unison with the masses. This philosophy was revealed by an unusually frank commentary in the CCP theoretical journal *Seeking Truth* in February 2002. The piece, entitled "The CCP must consolidate its status as ruling party through finding the law of [successful] administration," was believed to be close to the thinking of the Hu-Wen team. After analyzing the failure of communist parties in the former Soviet bloc and other parts of the world, the article said the CCP must focus on economic development and improving the people's standard of living. No less crucial was the party's remaining faithful to its proletarian roots. *Seeking Truth* admonished officials that "the fundamental guarantee of the CCP's ruling-party [status] is maintaining flesh-and-blood links with the people."[22]

Hu's Maoist Roots

Not much is known about Hu's debt to Maoism, except that one of his mentors was former PSC member Song Ping, a leader of the quasi-Maoist camp in the late 1990s. While the president has been projecting a generally reformist persona, he has never gone on the record as criticizing Mao's errors such as the latter's autarkist economic policy or the disastrous Cultural Revolution. It is likely that Hu harbors an opportunist attitude toward Maoism and Maoists: if Mao's teachings can be reinterpreted to consolidate CCP rule and to boost the Fourth-Generation leadership's legitimacy and popularity, there is no harm breathing new life into some of the Great Helmsman's teachings.[23]

There is thus more than symbolic significance in the fact that the first trip made by Hu after becoming party boss was a tour of Xibaipo, an old revolutionary base in Hebei Province. In March 1949, the CCP Central Committee convened a plenary session in Xibaipo barely half a year before the success of the Communist revolution was proclaimed in Beijing. And Chairman Mao's speech at the plenum contained much of the basic philosophy and statecraft with which the CCP intended to rule the new China. The Great Helmsman underscored the primacy of economic development, raising the people's standard of living, and being close to the masses. Equally importantly, Mao called upon all party members to be "modest, prudent, and self-disciplined."[24]

In a speech that was later splashed across the front pages of newspapers, Hu declared that the Sixteenth Congress's goal of "building a well-off society in a well-rounded way" was in accordance with the Maoist tradition. He indicated that while the party had achieved much in reform and modernization since 1978, "we should not be complacent and stagnant." Hu asked CCP members to bear in mind the party's sacred mission, which was serving the masses and "sharing the people's joys and sorrows." "All party members, particularly cadres, must remember their mission of wholeheartedly serving the people, and struggle for the welfare of the greatest number of people," Hu indicated. The party boss asked officials "to expand work at the grassroots level, to listen to and take care of the people and to lead them in building happy lives."[25]

In September 2003, Hu paid homage to revolutionary meccas and shrines in inland Jiangxi Province. He also visited Mao's home in Ruijin. While talking to Jiangxi cadres, Hu admonished them to "develop our party's superior revolutionary traditions, and uphold the principle of establishing the party for the public good, and running the administration for the sake of the people." He added that the formation of the "red administration" by Mao and his colleagues was for the purpose of "seeking the well-being of the people," and that party cadres must "be closely reliant upon the people."[26]

It was during Beijing's large-scale celebration of Mao's 110th birthday in late 2003 that Hu shocked his party's liberal intellectuals by his seemingly unquestioned obeisance to the Great Helmsman. After praising Mao as having "won the support of not only the Chinese but everyone in the world," the party chief went on to say that "no matter under what circumstances, we shall unswervingly uphold the great banner of Mao Zedong Thought." Given that even official party documents had faulted Mao for having made serious mistakes during the Cultural Revolution (1966–76), a number of intellectuals in Beijing thought Hu had gone too far. This was despite the high possibility that Hu might have decided to glorify Mao out of the strategy of "using Mao to upstage [ex-president] Jiang."[27]

It is significant that fire-spitting leftists, or quasi-Maoists such as Deng Liqun and his younger disciples, who had risked their pensions and perks by lambasting ex-president Jiang, have largely kept quiet after the Sixteenth CCP Congress. There were suggestions that Song Ping had used his influence to calm down the ultra-conservatives. A more plausible reason may be Hu's frequent salutation of Maoist ideals. The new supremo however, has quite inevitably angered the party's "rightist" intellectuals and cadres, who have accused Hu of turning back the clock. Criticisms that Hu had adopted the Maoist—and to some extent Deng-style—malpractice of clamping down on "pro-West" ideas mounted toward the end of 2004, when Beijing unleashed intimidation tactics to silence free-thinking intellectuals.

The "Three New Principles of the People"

It was quite a distance from the ideal of "government of the people, by the people, for the people." And it seemed unlikely that General Secretary Hu was paying direct homage to pioneer revolutionary Dr. Sun Yat-sen's "Three Principles of the People" (nationalism, people's power, people's livelihood). Yet Hu impressed observers with his fervent salute to the "people-come-first" precept while addressing an ideological study session for the CCP Central Committee in early 2003. "Power must be used for the sake of the people," Hu indicated. "[Cadres'] sentiments must be tied to those of the people; and material benefits must be sought in the interest of the people."[28] It is significant that apart from reviving Mao-style populism, Hu seemed eclectic enough to take inspiration from Dr. Sun. For while the "father of the Chinese Republic" is highly respected in the PRC and overseas Chinese communities, Dr. Sun is also widely known as the founder of the Kuomintang, or Taiwan's former ruling party.

Key to Hu's strategy for boosting his national stature—and legitimacy—was to stake out a claim as a "people's president," a spokesman for the large number of Chinese who had lost out in the course of Deng Xiaoping's nearly three decades of reform and open-door policy. These included laid-off industrial workers and the legions of jobless farmers. The theme of the first Politburo session called after the Sixteenth Congress was improving the lot of farmers. The Hu Politburo stressed that party and government policies must "tally with the realities of the village, the interests of farmers, and the requirements of rural productivity."[29] It is no coincidence that both Hu and Premier Wen had spent more than a dozen years working in grassroots-level jobs in impoverished Gansu Province in the late 1960s and early 1970s. Apart from Xinjiang party boss Wang Lequan, Hu and Wen were the only two cadres in the twenty-five-member Politburo with substantial experience in western provinces. Almost all the rest of the members of this supreme body had close ties to Shanghai and the coastal cities.[30]

Hu's "the masses come first" credo suffused a number of catchy slogans he laid down in 2003. Take, for example, the so-called threefold requirements for doing a good job, namely, that cadres must "do a good job in safeguarding, materializing, and developing the fundamental interests of the masses." Hu indicated on another occasion that all party and government units "must base their decision making and work on considerations of whether the broad masses agree with [official policies] and whether the masses will derive benefits from them." The new supremo added that "cadres must take a firm grip on questions that are of most relevance to, and that have the most direct bearing on the masses." These and other masses-oriented aphorisms were repeatedly cited by ministers and regional cadres.[31]

The goal of raising the living standards of the "underclass," or *ruoshi tuanti* (disadvantaged classes)—particularly peasants and migrant laborers in the cities—has dominated the policy pronouncements of Premier Wen. In his first press conference after becoming head of government, Wen vowed to boost the income of farmers, expand the social security net, and narrow the regional gap. Measures promised by the new cabinet included further lowering the taxes of farmers as well as curtailing the number of grassroots-level bureaucrats, who get their salaries via levies and charges on already overburdened peasants.[32] Whether Hu and Wen can make good the promises they made to the underprivileged could determine how well the CCP retains its mandate of heaven in the coming decade.

GDP Growth vs. Social Development

Much of the criticism leveled at Deng Xiaoping and Jiang Zemin was that for these Second- and Third-Generation leaders, economic growth and GDP figures were the be-all and end-all of statecraft. Not enough attention had been given by previous administrations to social development and social justice.[33] The Hu-Wen team, however, has decided to promote social well-being, "humanistic values," and environmental concerns alongside economic expansion. Hu simplified this concept as the "Theory of the Three Developments," calling it "the new thinking and path of harmonious development, comprehensive development, and sustained development." This essentially meant that development did not mean GDP augmentation alone. By "harmonious and comprehensive development," Hu was referring to the fact that the interests of different regions and *ruoshi tuanti* would be fully taken into account in the pursuit of economic growth.[34]

The gist of this new thinking on development was summarized at an academic conference in mid-2003 by one of the few heroes of the SARS outbreak, Guangdong epidemiologist Dr. Zhong Nanshan. "The degree of a country's modernization shouldn't be reflected just by GDP growth," Dr. Zhong said. "Social development is just as important." Premier Wen expressed approval in an internal policy session when he said: "One of our legs is longer than the other one." "China has always paid a lot of attention to economic development," he added. "Yet social development is lagging behind."[35] In the Chinese context, social well-being and the allied concept of social justice embrace a whole array of concerns including unemployment, rural poverty and illiteracy, public-health infrastructure, social equality, and the standard of the rule of law.

A key concept of the Third Plenary Session of the Sixteenth Central Committee held in October 2003 was "redressing imbalances," or rectifying the ancien régime's obsession with the glitzy hardware of modernization. As Wen put it, the SARS disaster had alerted Beijing to the imperative of "the harmonious and well-coordinated development of the economy and society." Wen later called the new emphasis on social well-being "government management that is based on humanitarian considerations." The plenum document contained several important initiatives. Wen wanted more attention and funds for rural China, particularly the landlocked western provinces. Central and regional governments would be asked to spend at least as much on schools and hospitals in the countryside as on new airports and office towers in urban areas.[36] In various speeches in the latter half of 2003, the premier said the leadership had to "establish a more comprehensive view on development." "We must put more emphasis on the harmonious development of the economy and society," he said, adding that there should be a balanced and coordinated approach to allocating resources among cities and villages, among the different regions, and between man and nature. The premier also indicated that more emphasis must be put on "social management and the provision of public services."[37]

Even before the pivotal Third Plenum, Beijing had begun measures to redress long-held grievances of the *ruoshi tuanti*. Take, for example, social mobility. Since early 2003, provinces and cities including Henan, Jiangsu, Guangdong, and Chongqing had been liberalizing residency permit systems, a process that would, according to Beijing officials, pave the way for 300 million peasants to move to the cities.[38] While such agrarian reforms could mean a big stimulus to domestic consumption and spending, they would also constitute a large drain on the resources of the central government. Other measures included slashing the tax burden on peasants and promoting the social status and payment of rural laborers (see following sections). There would also be a fresh impetus to improve China's long-neglected environment, whose degradation has resulted in disasters ranging from acid rain to floods and desertification.

In industrial policy, the main concerns of former administrations were nurturing high-tech sectors and attracting foreign direct investment (FDI). While Wen also wanted FDI and high technology, he was keen to foster industries and product lines—including relatively low-tech and labor-intensive ones—that would create the highest number of jobs. "I keep tabs every day on the number of new college graduates who can find jobs," Wen said in an internal meeting in late 2003. While the official urban unemployment rate that year was merely 4.1 percent, independent economists said the figure was at least twice as much.[39]

This newfound commitment to social issues could in certain areas contradict the leadership's efforts to boost market mechanisms. Take, for instance, Beijing's insistence on maintaining the existing value of the renminbi or yuan. From 2003 onward, Western governments had been putting pressure on Beijing to revalue or to float the vastly undervalued renminbi. Yet because renminbi appreciation would hurt exports—and jobs—the leadership would rather err on the side of conservatism on this issue. And the limited nature of the currency appreciation that eventually took place in July 2005—2.1 percent—was largely expected.[40]

Priority Given to Social Justice

The CCP can retain its ruling status without introducing democracy—but it has to give Chinese a decent level of social justice. This philosophy has so far informed many of the sociopolitical policies of the Hu-Wen administration. As important as pledges of more central-level attention and funds is the Fourth-Generation leadership's apparent readiness to give the so-called underclass a measure of equality and dignity through promoting *gongyi*, or social justice. As pointed out in a commentary in the liberal paper *Southern Weekend*, the objective of bringing about a well-off society must be accompanied by improvement in social justice. "Social policy must be adjusted to favor disadvantaged groupings in order to maintain social harmony," the paper said in 2003. Or as three influential social scientists, Wang Shaoguang, Hu Angang, and Ding Yuanzhu, noted at about the same time, "without social justice, there will be no way to rule a nation or have lasting peace." "To prevent income differences and class polarization, the government must become aware of inequalities and be willing to distribute wealth more fairly," they said. "The government also has to regulate social inequity and promote social justice if it wants to achieve long-term governance."[41]

Inherent in the *gongyi* ideal is the concept of fairness and dignity, which was for the first time taken seriously by the party and government leadership. In 2003, the State Council decided not to go ahead with a planned salary raise for the country's 34 million civil servants. This was largely due to the perception that it would be unfair to grant relatively well-paid civil servants a fourth pay rise in as many years when millions were hovering on the brink of poverty. After all, the three pay hikes between 2000 and 2002 cost Beijing some 307 billion yuan, about the size of the estimated budget deficit for the year. And the decision in 2004 by a couple of municipal governments to hire foreign-trained professionals at a salary of up to 500,000 yuan a year was greeted by hostile media commentaries.[42]

Of more symbolic significance were first steps taken to recognize the legal and political status of migrant laborers, who are often treated as second-class citizens. In late 2003, Zhu Lifei, a twenty-seven-year-old worker from the provinces, made history when she was elected a member of the municipal parliament in the city of Yiwu in coastal Zhejiang Province. In a commentary, the NCNA called on more regional authorities to "give migrant laborers their due recognition [in society]." While Yiwu is host to nearly 600,000 work hands from the central and western provinces, the latter had always been denied opportunities to stand for political office.[43]

Equally important are efforts to extend the social security net from the cities to the villages. Pretty much until the turn of the century, only urban residents were entitled to government handouts, including *dibao,* or the subsistence-level cost-of-living subsidy to destitute families. Zhejiang was lauded as a trendsetter for ending the decades-old practice of depriving peasants of state welfare. In late 2001, the provincial leadership promulgated a regulation on the "lowest-level livelihood guarantee" for urban as well as rural residents. The average "lowest-level income standard" for peasants was set at 104 yuan per person per month, meaning that if a farmer earned merely 50 yuan a month, he would receive a subsidy of 54 yuan from local authorities.[44]

The big question on the minds of liberal intellectuals, however, is whether real *gongyi* for disadvantaged classes is achievable in the absence of political liberalization, particularly a more equitable distribution of political power. According to Shanghai University social scientist Zhu Xueqin, political reform is necessary to right social wrongs—and to prevent the administration from slipping into a Latin American–style dictatorship. "Social injustice could engender massive social instability," Zhu said, adding that liberalization of the political structure must go hand-in-hand with market-oriented economic reforms.[45] Li Changping, a former county-level cadre who shot to fame by presenting a petition to ex-premier Zhu, noted that the roots of poverty lie in a "faultily and unreasonably designed system" of governance. Li pointed out that underprivileged classes such as peasants were discriminated against in areas including property rights, distribution of resources, the legal system, taxation, education, and welfare. "As long as peasants, who occupy the lowest strata of society, are denied access to power, they will forever remain marginalized," the reformist warned.[46]

Well-known exiled dissident Wang Juntao agrees. Wang, who was doing research at Columbia University, said that mere "favorable government policies" could not help upgrade the welfare or status of farmers. He pointed out that rural laborers must be allowed to form economic and political organizations to lobby for their welfare and benefits. The same goes for peasants' freedom to organize unions to press for their rights—including the ability to negotiate with the government on how to fix the prices of produce.[47]

Propagation of the Middle Class

When Deng first launched the era of reform in the early 1980s, his slogan was "to let one part of the population get rich first." What the Hu-Wen leadership is promising is that in two decades' time or so, almost half of Chinese will have entered the ranks of citizens with *zhongchan* or "medium-level income," the rough equivalent of the middle class in industrialized societies. There is much controversy among scholars and officials in the PRC as to the level of income that would enable a Chinese to become a middle-class person. A relatively low threshold—a household income ranging from 60,000 yuan to 500,000 yuan a year—was cited by the National Bureau of Statistics in late 2004.[48] However, foreign academics and media commentators have noted that this standard is too low, and probably set with the purpose of embellishing the quality of life of ordinary Chinese.

In any case, Hu and his Politburo colleagues seem convinced that the CCP might be able to prolong its mandate of heaven if it can successfully nurture a relatively prosperous, pro-status quo middle class. According to the Sixteenth Congress' *Political Report,* China's economy will quadruple by the year 2020—and per capita share of GDP should jump from around $800 in 2002 to $3,000. Per capita GDP in coastal cities ranging from Shanghai to Shenzhen, however, had already cleared the $1,500 hurdle by 2003.[49] Indeed, many denizens along the "Gold Coast," who in 2003 and 2004 could already afford to buy their own apartments and cars—and even send their only child abroad for education—had already entered into the ranks of the *zhongchan.* And the majority of them seemed so satisfied with their high standard of living that they had become a pillar of sociopolitical stability. It was not for nothing that the Sixteenth Congress *Political Report* indicated that China should "expand the proportion of middle-income earners [in the population], which will be beneficial to China's social stability."[50]

As well-known sociologist Lu Xueyi pointed out, members of the middle class tend to identify themselves with the ideology and policies of the ruling party. "The larger the proportion of citizens with medium-level income, the more stable a particular country will be," he said. According to Lu, who works at the respected Chinese Academy of Social Sciences (CASS), China's *zhongchan* class made up about 18 percent of the population in 2003. The sociologist added that the country should be able to add one percentage point to the *zhongchan* proportion each year, so that the latter could swell to around 40 percent by 2020.[51]

The major obstacle to the growth of a middle class is the peasantry, which still accounted for roughly 70 percent of the populace in the early 2000s. Noted CASS economist Jiang Xiaojuan indicated that China was engaged in a "gargantuan task of the mass transfer of labor forces." She figured that by 2020, about 220 million peasants will have found jobs in the industrial and services sectors, which already employ some 350 million Chinese.[52] According to London-based Sinologist Zheng Yongnian, the concept of a "well-off society" means in effect "rendering the proletarian class into the middle class." Zheng notes that "the [new CCP] goal of building a well-off society in a comprehensive way consists precisely in popularizing the *zhongchan* ideal." That this seems to go against orthodox Marxist precepts pales beside the critical CCP objective of attaining the proverbial "long reign and perennial stability."[53]

However, the improvement of living standards alone is not enough to persuade middle-class affiliates to become or to remain fans of the ruling party. Quite a number of *zhongchan* citizens are already clamoring for the kind of political clout that will enable them to protect their property, shape their own destiny, and even have a say in government policies. And to accommodate their demands, the CCP has by the turn of the century begun to broaden avenues for political participation while cleaving to time-honored one-party dictatorship. First, Jiang's "Theory of the Three Represents" has made it possible for nonstate entrepreneurs and professionals not only to join the CCP but to become relatively senior cadres. At the Sixteenth Congress, millionaire private businessman Zhang Ruimin made history when he was inducted to the party's ruling Central Committee.[54] A number of illustrious members of the *zhongchan* and new classes—including the cream of the nearly 200,000 well-trained Chinese who had returned to the country after getting advanced degrees from Western colleges—have been recruited into the civil service at relatively high levels (see also Chapters 4 and 6).

And for the past five years or so, the CCP has tried to tap new talent by selectively holding public exams to pick officials up to the level of heads of department. "The gist of the Three Represents Theory is to inject new blood into the party without having to tamper with the formula of one-party dictatorship," said a Beijing-based Western diplomat. He added that the CCP could also claim that it was serious about rectifying problems such as corruption and inefficiency because it was hiring experts and managers from disparate sectors—including returnees from abroad—to fill top-level jobs.[55]

It remains to be seen, however, whether Beijing's bid to nurture a middle class with Chinese characteristics—and to open up the government on a limited basis—could effectively prolong its mandate of heaven. Many other conditions need to obtain before the middle class can become a stabilizing, pro–status quo political force, particularly in a country without multiparty politics. Obvious prerequisites include the rule of law and a level playing field for individuals as well as for business operations. For example, Singapore, whose model of governance is much admired by CCP cadres, has relatively rigorous, British-style legal and judicial standards.

Jiang, Hu, and other leaders have made much of Beijing's commitment to legal modernization, which was played up in the Political Report to the Sixteenth Congress as an important attribute of a "comprehensively well-off society." However, what the CCP has in mind is only rule by law, which means promulgation and implementation of statutes under stern party leadership. And a growing proportion of the middle class has expressed frustration and anger at the collusion between party cadres and their children on the one hand, and business tycoons on the other.

The perception that most aspects of Chinese life are still manipulated by an arrogant, self-protecting elite that is feathering its nest through monopolizing economic resources lies behind the "revolt" of China's estimated 70 million *gumin* (individual buyers of stocks and shares) from late 2004 to early 2005.[56] During this period, the indexes of both the Shanghai and the Shenzhen bourses dropped to six-year lows, and most *gumin* were blaming inadequate government policies as well as special privileges accorded to well-connected speculators. The Chinese media estimated that about 80 percent of *gumin*—the majority of whom are members of the middle class—had lost money since the late 1990s. Many embittered stock buyers have called themselves the "new *ruoshi tuanti*," and they have blamed the Hu-Wen team for failing to take care of their welfare while claiming to "put people first." And this anger, while caused basically by economic factors, could be translated into a crusade to transform the political system into one that will do a better job guaranteeing equality of opportunity in both the stock market and other areas of life.[57]

Test Case: A New Deal for Peasants?

Not unlike Jiang Zemin, Premier Wen is given to citing ancient poetry while making speeches to domestic and foreign audiences. While the ex-president was often keen to show off his erudition, Wen is usually spot-on when using classical allusions to illustrate modern problems. During a public function at the Mid-Autumn Festival of 2003, for example, Wen recited this couplet to demonstrate his concern for the common man, in particular, the farmer: "My heart is often tormented by the suffering of farmers and growers of mulberry leaves," the premier said. "My ears are filled with the lament of the hungry and the cold."[58] Chinese policymakers have used this formulation to characterize the plight on the farm—the *sannong wenti*, or "the threefold problems of agriculture, the village and peasants." The problem of agriculture refers mostly to the quantity and quality of produce; that of the village refers to stability as well as law and order on the farm; and that of peasants refers to issues of employment, livelihood, and well-being of rural folk.[59]

According to agrarian experts, the "peasants' problem" is the most intractable among the *sannong* issues. Unless threatened by unexceptionally severe natural disasters such as floods or drought, China could in theory produce more than it needs. Since the late 1990s, however, production of grain has fallen owing to the gradual but irrevocable shrinkage of farmland owing to reasons including industrialization and real-estate development. Thus in 2003, arable land was cut by 2.54 million hectares, or 2.01 percent of total acreage, and the average plot per farmer was reduced to a miniscule 0.095 hectare. Wen repeatedly warned the nation that the nation's "grain security" was in jeopardy. This problem, though serious, could at least be theoretically remedied by imports. This is despite Beijing's marked aversion to relying on imports because of its long-standing concern for grain self-sufficiency and grain security.[60] Much more severe is the challenge of law and order—and overall stability—in the countryside, which is basically a function of whether or not peasants are happy with their lot.

Rural joblessness could remain the nation's weakest link in the first couple of decades of the century. Both government and foreign estimates say close to 200 million Chinese farmers are either unemployed or severely underemployed—meaning they can find work only during the busy harvest season. According to agronomist Wen Tiejun, the situation is even more dire. Fully 930 million Chinese are classified as peasants, nearly 500 million of whom are part of the labor force. However, even given that Chinese farms are intensely cultivated, no more than 100 million work hands are required. This means in effect that the state has to find jobs for 400 million farm hands.[61]

According to CASS sociologist Lu Xueyi, the income gap between urban and rural residents has yawned wider by the year. Thus the differential between the per capita income in the city and on the farm grew from 2.72:1 in 1995 to 3.2:1 in 2003. Lu pointed out that the basic solution for the agrarian problem was still structural reform. For example, the price of grain and other staples that peasants sell to the state—referred to as "patriotic produce" by sociologists—is fixed by the government and not by the market. Moreover, farmers also lack adequate numbers of representatives in the senior levels of the party, government, and legislature who might be able to push their cause.[62]

Farmers up in Arms

While the official media have largely desisted from detailed reports about rural disturbances, the level of discontent in the countryside has increased over issues including excessive taxation, arbitrary government policies, corruption among rural cadres, and the requisition of farmland without adequate compensation for affected peasants. Short-changed farmers have protested by means ranging from beating up tax collectors to laying siege to official buildings in villages and counties.

The plight of hard-pressed peasants is plain to all. Within five days in August 2003, two farmers in hardscrabble Xunyang County, Shaanxi Province, committed suicide—and another tried to kill himself—because of disputes with local officials over crop policies and the level of government subsidies. According to Li Liwen, the farmer who was rescued, the authorities tried to stop him from cultivating beans and sweet potato because this contravened a 1999 regulation asking peasants to quit farming in order to restore the ecological balance of the western provinces. "I was fined 560 yuan, yet our household of three people could only make less than 200 yuan a year," he told the *China Youth Daily*.[63] Other desperate cases involved suspicion that local cadres had held up relief funds that the central authorities had approved in the wake of severe flooding and other natural disasters. In September 2003, about 5,000 impoverished peasants in flood-stricken Shaanxi ransacked government premises in Hua County to protest the alleged failure by local cadres to distribute disaster relief funds and supplies.[64]

Even more serious were instances of rebellion by farmers who had not been duly compensated for "selling" land-use rights to aggressive developers—who were often backed by corrupt local officials. What happened was that while farmers who were obliged to vacate their plots were promised adequate recompense, the funds were miniscule compared to the real market value of the land, and parts of the meager payouts to farmers often ended up in the pockets of officials. Minister of Land and Natural Resources Sun Wensheng admitted in early 2004 that farmers were owed up to 10 billion yuan in unpaid or partially paid compensation fees as a result of requisition.[65]

Very often, disgruntled peasants have no alternative but to follow the centuries-old custom of trekking thousands of miles to the capital to present their petitions to the authorities. A 2003 article in *People's Daily* declared that officials must properly investigate and handle rural grievances. The party mouthpiece noted that peasants had the constitutional right to petition the government—and that cadres should not take such expressions of opinion as the proverbial "wild torrents and ferocious beasts." It added that rural petitioners felt obliged to use violent means or to take their cases to the provincial and central authorities only because grassroots cadres were "dragging their feet when handling peasants' problems."[66]

In growing numbers of rural districts, however, farmers are no longer contented with passive petitioning. Many are starting to organize themselves—or even to use violent methods to express their views. And in individual provinces such as Hunan, the influence of nonofficial peasant organizations had become so entrenched that provincial authorities had no choice but to acquiesce in their existence—and even work with them to settle rural problems.[67] Yet the Hu-Wen leadership has refused to grant farmers more political power despite Beijing's credo of "putting the people first." This obstinacy means the countryside will remain a powder keg for a long time to come. After all, Hu, Wen, and their colleagues know full well that from dynastic times to the late 1940s, numerous empires and regimes fell precisely because peasants could not bear it any more—and they took up arms to oust an administration that was deemed to have lost the mandate of heaven.[68]

Raising the Economic Standards of Farmers

At the landmark Fifth Plenary Session of the Sixteenth Central Committee in late 2005—which also endorsed the Eleventh Five Year Plan for 2006–2010—President Hu introduced the concept of "the new socialist village." This was roughly defined as a village with modern production methods, "civilized lifestyle, sufficient livelihood, and democratic management." Just as in previous major party or government meetings, CCP leaders made ritualistic pledges about improving the standard of living of peasants. Apart from the abolition of rural taxes and levies, the leadership promised to help poor children with special education subsidies. More significantly, the liberalization of the *hukou*, or household registration system, would be further speeded up to enable some 300 million peasants to migrate to urban areas—especially newly created medium-sized cities—in the coming fifteen to twenty years. And the so-called *dibao*, or minimal-level livelihood assistance payouts, would be extended from urban to rural areas to cover 100 million destitute farmers. Moreover, "social sustenance systems"—basically mechanisms for dispensing emergency social-welfare benefits—are being set up in 90 percent of the provinces and 70 percent of the counties and villages.[69] Given the sheer numbers involved, however, even the most optimistic expert would expect the improvement of the living, education, and other standards of farmers to be gradual.

Boosting Subsidies and Cutting Levies

In the early 2000s, the heaviest burden on farmers was not normal taxation by the national or regional governments but up to sixty different types of fees and levies slapped on them by local authorities. These charges, which were in theory illegal, were often arbitrarily imposed on farmers by grassroots party and government units for purposes including paying the salaries of officials, as well as underwriting education, public works, and other administrative costs. The Wen cabinet has, since its inauguration in early 2003, moved swiftly to improve the lot of the peasants. As Finance Minister Jin Renqing noted, it was time urban and industrial sectors started "paying back" the villages. "Cities must repay their [financial] debt to the countryside," Jin said in late 2003. The minister indicated that plans were afoot to remit taxes on a number of cash crops raised by farmers.[70] Moreover, state investment in rural education, culture, and public health would be increased. At the outset, however, only a handful of rich cities such as Shenzhen or Shanghai agreed to curtail rural taxes within their jurisdiction. For example, Shanghai farmers stood to make savings of 143 million yuan a year because of government largesse.[71]

It was not until the National People's Congress (NPC) of March 2004 that Wen spelled out arguably the most generous deal for farmers since 1949. The premier received enthusiastic applause from the deputies when he indicated that except for levies on special crops such as tobacco, the standard 8 percent agricultural taxes would be abolished in five years. And in 2005, Beijing upped the ante by announcing that the taxes would be cut by the end of 2006. In terms of real numbers, however, this would not amount to much. Agronomists estimated that the dispensation would enable farmers to save 100 billion yuan—or about 120 yuan per person—compared to what they had paid before 1999, when tax reforms began.[72]

Perhaps more significant were orders given by the State Council in 2003 and 2004 to individual provinces and cities to do their best to either remit taxes or boost agrarian subsidies. In good old Chinese fashion, this set off a kind of competition among regional cadres who wanted to earn Brownie points from the Hu-Wen leadership. Thus Taiyuan city in Shanxi Province vowed in mid-2004 to spend more than 1 billion yuan to promote the rural welfare. In the major agricultural province of Henan, officials pledged to cut taxes for the year by 2.19 billion yuan while boosting subsidies by 1.16 billion yuan. Heilongjiang and Jilin were among the first provinces to declare the outright abolition of all taxes on produce.[73]

Wen's cabinet also pledged to augment direct subsidies to destitute rural households so as to relieve severely destitute peasants. The rural welfare budget for 2003 was 299.9 billion yuan, which was 800 million yuan more than that of the year before—and more than double the total subsidy outlay for the five years ending in 2002. According to the China News Service, the number of farmers living in abject poverty stood at 28.2 million in 2003, while 7 million of them inhabited areas "which lack basic conditions for survival." In late 2005, CCP leaders admitted that 26 million Chinese still lived in stark poverty.[74]

While Wen has won widespread praise for his dispensation to the peasantry, quite a few scholars have raised doubts about boosting subsidies to farmers or remitting their taxes. Well-known Peking University economist Justin Lin indicated, for example, that the central government's problematic finances could not sustain perennial subsidies. "Moreover, more subventions [to the farming section] will lead to over-production of produce," said Lin. Other economists pointed out that because of China's accession to the World Trade Organization (WTO), more subsidies to farmers could lead to accusations by foreign governments that Beijing was adopting protectionist and other unfair trading policies regarding the agrarian sector.[75]

Moreover, the farmer's lot will not be improved just by cutting taxes. There are limits as to what the central government can do regarding the problem of peasants having to shoulder many of the administrative expenses of the village, town, township, and county governments, particularly the salaries of grassroots cadres. The official estimate in 2003 was that it took about twenty-five farmers to pay for the upkeep of one local rural cadre. However, there were quite a large number of villages, especially in poor areas, where eight or nine peasants had to support one local-level cadre. This was true in impoverished Huanglong County in Shaanxi. While Huanglong is a small county with only 40,000–odd people, it has more than 4,400 cadres and civil servants working in 308 departments. In the early years after "liberation" in 1949, however, the comparative ratio was only twenty-eight farmers to one official.[76]

It is because of the profusion of grassroots-level cadres and civil servants that former premier Zhu basically failed to implement his famous *feigaishui* ("tax in exchange for fees") experiment. In early 2002, the premier ordered village and township governments to stop collecting fees and charges from peasants. Instead, Beijing would make up for the shortfall by an annual rural subsidy of between 20 billion and 30 billion yuan. Yet by year's end, Zhu conceded that the *feigaishui* experiment had to be postponed owing to the "[limited] ability of state finances to cushion the shock." The reality was that many regional and grassroots administrations were complaining that without the fees, they could not even pay the teachers—and that the nine-year free-education program enshrined in the Constitution could not be sustained.[77]

After taking over the State Council in March 2003, Premier Wen admitted that the *feigaishui* problem was a tough nut to crack. He said, only half jokingly, that the person who could solve the *feigaisui* conundrum should be awarded an honorary doctorate. He cited the famous "Theory of Huang Zongxi," a reference to the Ming Dynasty thinker's reforms in rural policies. Huang had tried methods including *feigaishui* to lower taxes on peasants, but without much success. "Huang wrote that every time there was a merger of taxes and fees, the burden of the peasantry rose," Wen said. "We cannot get into this vicious cycle."[78]

It was not until the second half of 2004 that thanks to injection of more funds by both Beijing and provincial governments, the *feigaishui* experiment was extended to all provinces. However, this does not mean that peasants in the twenty-two provinces that had abolished agrarian taxes would not need to pay any levies at all. As Hong Kong Sinologist Linda Li noted, farmers living in areas where both fees and taxes were supposedly abolished still had to pay so-called one issue, one decision charges—or ad hoc levies for public services in areas including education and transport. Moreover, rural residents are burdened with taxes, fees, and charges that do not target peasants specifically, such as road-maintenance charges, license fees of all sorts, and value-added taxes for sales and purchases of different goods.[79]

Boosting the Income of Peasants

Because of the steady drop in the prices of agricultural products worldwide—and competition posed by the influx of foreign farm produce after China's WTO accession—it is unrealistic to expect that farmers' income would see substantial improvement in the foreseeable future. From 1997 to 2000, the prices of produce dropped 22 percent, and the loss to farmers amounted to between 300 million and

400 million yuan during this period. The trend was reversed in 2003 and 2004 when, owing to factors including quirky weather, produce prices jumped, in some cases by 40 percent. However, the upsurge was considered temporary, and in the longer term, Chinese farm products could be threatened by voluminous imports from Asia and North America. Soon after coming to power, the Hu-Wen team pledged that rural income would increase by 5 percent annually. In 2003, per capita rural income rose by 4.3 percent over the year before to hit 2,622 yuan; however, this percentage increase was lower than the 4.8 percent recorded for 2002. Moreover, in 2003, urban dwellers' income shot up by 9.3 percent, roughly the same rate as GDP growth for that year.[80]

According to Professor Wang San'gui of the Chinese Agricultural Sciences Institute, the future of the farm lies in "urbanization." Wang said it was illogical that while agriculture only accounted for 16 percent of GDP, it was the source of income for 40 percent of the country's laborers. "In China, the pace of urbanization is too slow," he said. "There is no way to realize a leap forward in rural income."[81] In the Chinese context, urbanization has several layers of meaning. First, farmers move to the cities and work there as "migrant laborers." Second, peasants in traditional farming areas should have more opportunities of supplementing their income by going into industry and the services.

Migration of rural workers to the cities had taken place since the mid-1980s, and by 2005, there were more than 100 million *nongmingong* (rural workers) working in the cities. However, Beijing needs to formally abolish the residence permit system, as well as provide migrant workers with *guomin daiyu* (national treatment) (see following sections). Official statistics show that in 2002, 17 percent of the income of rural households was derived from nonagricultural jobs performed by migrant laborers in urban areas. This percentage was as high as 30 in provinces such as Sichuan and Anhui, which "exported" the largest numbers of workers to the cities. Moreover, fully 41.8 percent of the increase in rural income was based on remittances from relatives working in urban districts.[82]

According to People's University Professor Wen Tiejun, the only way for government departments to boost the welfare of farmers is to end the state monopoly on a host of economic activities. They include collection and sale of produce, trading and transport, finance and insurance. "There is practically no money to be made from agricultural production," Wen said. "The profit margin is much higher from the services sector—and what's more, the profits will be plowed back to the farm." Wen suggested that the government provide loans to farmers to set up such service-oriented businesses.[83]

Another thoroughgoing solution is some form of the privatization of farmland, which has since 1949 been "collectively owned." Since real estate became a big money spinner in the mid-to-late 1990s, however, local administrations have sold land-use rights to property developers while paying a minimum of compensation to affected peasants (see following section). The Guangdong government indicated in late 2004, for example, that it owed around 2 billion yuan in unpaid land requisition fees to peasants.[84] Experts have suggested that Beijing should make it clear that farmers have a right to sell or rent the plots they occupy. This move would enable peasants—at least those living close to cities—to raise the requisite seed money for making the move to cities. Moreover, a higher degree of mechanization will be made possible since farming specialists could pull together larger plots of land through acquiring or renting plots from different households.

Raising the Education Level of Farmers

Rural poverty means that only a very small percentage of peasant children can go to technical institutes or colleges—and this lack of opportunity has resulted in farmers being mired in the vicious cycle of perennial deprivation. Twenty percent of all Chinese are considered illiterate. In his book *Telling the Premier the Truth*, rural reformer and author Li Changping writes that in his native village in Hubei, barely 20 percent of the kids were attending high school. The percentage was way lower than that thirty years ago.[85] Moreover, given blatant sex discrimination in the countryside, girls have a much lower chance of attending schools than boys. Many teenage girls are even "sold" as child brides to richer townships.

Indeed, one of the biggest failings of the Chinese Communist administration is the horrendous state of rural education. This is despite the fact that the Constitution spelled out clearly that every Chinese—rural or urban—should have nine years of free education. In a report filed in September 2003, United Nations human rights researcher on educational opportunities Katarina Tomasevski said China spent too little on education and that children of migrant workers were discriminated against in the allocation of education resources. China spends 2 percent of GDP on education, just one-third of the proportion recommended by UNESCO. Worse, most of these funds have gone to the cities. Experts estimate that in rural areas, the bulk of the funding for schools comes from local resources—very often illegal levies slapped on the shoulders of already overburdened peasants.[86]

It is a measure of Premier Wen's personal interest in the welfare of the farmer that the State Council convened a rare national conference on rural education in late 2003. Wen laid down the goal that by 2007, 85 percent of all areas in western China should enjoy free education—and that illiteracy among youths should be lowered to 5 percent. It is, however, a sad reality that the edicts of Beijing are only observed in the coastal and richer provinces. In outlying regions, horror stories of parents resorting to tragic means to support their kids' education are periodically reported in the national media. For example, parents in 1,336 households in Le Du County, Qinghai Province, had to sell their blood to earn extra income so as to pay their kids' school fees.[87]

While announcing China's Eleventh Five-Year Plan in late 2005, Beijing also noted that central and regional authorities would be spending 218 billion yuan on rural education in the coming five years. This would cover books and other expenses incurred by children in impoverished western provinces, which also owe their teachers unpaid salaries of at least 10 billion yuan. However, the urban-rural gap remains huge. For instance, it will still be a rarity for kids from poor villages or townships to go to university. College entrance exams in China are tough; high school students in the cities, many of whom can afford expensive private tutors or exam-preparation courses, generally enjoy an advantage. By contrast, poor peasant parents have to incur a huge debt in order to send their children to university. Indeed, several tragedies took place at big-name universities when rural students apparently resorted to violence to protest their being discriminated against by fellow students from the rich cities.[88]

Raising the Political Status and Powers of Peasants

The crux of the matter behind the plight of the peasantry remains power—more precisely, their pitiful lack of political power. Farmers have no voice in the leadership. As will be discussed in Chapter 4, the Hu-Wen team has refused to expand or upgrade village-level elections, which Deng introduced in 1979, to higher levels. Farmers' representation in the higher echelons of the party and government is abysmal. While some 20 percent of the party's Central Committee members are military or security officers, only a handful of cadres at that level are farmers or spokesmen for agrarian interests. Farmers' representation at the NPC is also much lower than that of city dwellers. Thus there is one NPC deputy for about 240,000 city residents, but only one parliamentarian for every 960,000 peasants.[89]

Farmers' lack of representation at the top means that central-level initiatives toward grassroots villages have often been adulterated, or not carried out at all. There have been numerous reports even in the official media that the "new deal" spelled out by Premier Wen and his colleagues has not materialized. A case in point was the No. 1 Central Document on Agriculture promulgated, in early 2004, as well as the series of dispensations that Wen unveiled at the NPC at about the same time. According to the official *Fortnightly Chat* journal, while more than 200 billion yuan of investment and welfare funds for farmers had been promised by the government that year, only "a very light drizzle" had fallen on the villages, meaning that peasants had yet to enjoy substantial benefits.[90]

By mid-2004, there were signs that the CCP leadership might be willing to give farmers at least more oversight powers. Laws and regulations were being drafted that would allow villagers to form finance management committees to oversee how the elected village administrative committees could go about spending public funds. And VAC leaders would be obliged to make public all spending on infrastructure projects as well as major issues such as the requisition of land for redevelopment. The planned regulations would also codify the procedures whereby villagers could start impeachment hearings regarding incompetent or corrupt VAC leaders through, for example, a signature campaign.[91]

Gradual Abolition of the Hukou *System and Increased Socioeconomic Mobility*

In his famous book *Looking at China with a Third Eye*, author Wang Shan laid bare an ugly facet of China's development: Mao forbade farmers to leave their land, and industry took off partly thanks to the exploitation of the lowly peasants, veritable beasts of burden whose life was brutish and short. There had been some changes by the turn of this century. For example, there was a limited but still significant relaxation of the *hukou*, or residence permit system, which was introduced in 1958. Until recently, a Chinese born in the villages could not go and live in the cities except through joining the army or job placement after graduation from college.

Partly to facilitate the migration of *nongmingong,* the *hukou* system was gradually relaxed around the year 2000. By 2004, more than half of the nation's provinces and cities had experimented with ways to break down the urban versus rural divide. Yet significant limitations remain. Almost all cities have attracted tens of thousands of migrant workers. Yet *nongmingong* are veritable second-class citizens because they can only stay for certain periods and apply for inferior menial jobs. International cities such as Beijing and Shanghai have come up with a "green card" system, which confers permanent residence status on outside residents upon payment of a hefty fee. In most regions, peasants can only settle for good in small to medium-sized cities. Although the Eleventh Five Year Plan did not give specific figures or timetables, it was assumed by Beijing experts that up to 300 million farmers will have migrated to urban areas by the year 2015 or so. According to projections by the Beijing-based Research Institute on the Development of International Cities, the urban population of China should reach 800 to 900 million by 2020.[92]

While the theories and principles behind freedom of mobility are well understood, *hukou* liberalization will only be gradually carried out for the rest of the decade. Experts such as Beijing University of Science and Technology's Professor Hu Shengdou point out that the *hukou* system is closely linked to the "vested interests of different departments and localities." For example, officials in pioneer cities such as Zhengzhou, which opened the door to peasants in the early 2000s, have found it extremely costly to expand educational, medical, and other services. Moreover, mobility of the population is only possible when enough jobs can be found for new arrivals in the cities. This explains why as of late 2005, Beijing had not announced details on, for example, which kinds of peasants were eligible to move to the large cities, and which other categories must settle in small or medium-sized cities close to their villages.[93]

So far, mobility, particularly upward mobility, has been attained with relative ease only by those peasants who have struck it rich through doing business or other kinds of nontraditional occupations. A limited number of farmers have successfully sat for civil-service entrance exams and become grassroots cadres. Thus, more than 5,000 of the 700,000 civil servants recruited from 1994 to 2003 were rural residents.[94] Moreover, Beijing has from the early 2000s onward been appointing peasant-turned-rural businessmen to at least mid-ranking party and government posts. This is a break from tradition: formerly, most senior officials at the county level were professional cadres named by the Organization Department of the relevant province. For understandable reasons, the great majority of peasants-turned-cadre were well-heeled businessmen, many of whom had already occupied positions in the local people's congress or consultative conferences. A 2003 report stated that the average peasant-cadre in Sheyang County, Jiangsu Province, had an annual income of at least 100,000 yuan.[95] However, the possibility of bona fide peasants holding high-level positions—which, paradoxically, took place during the Cultural Revolution—will remain low in the foreseeable future.

The Right to Organization

In the long run, the *sannong wenti* can only be solved through political reform. Despite more than fifty-six years of Communist rule, many agrarian areas yield the impression of being jungles where the strong—corrupt cadres, clan chiefs, and triad bosses—prey on defenseless peasants. For example, farming expert Xu Yong had this to say about officials' total neglect of the law: "It is a prevalent phenomenon in villages that cadres violate the law." "When law is useful for them, they will take rule of law as an excuse," he added. "When law is useless or even harmful for them, they will disregard law." And the lowly farmers have negligible clout to assert their rights. As Beijing-based agrarian expert Liu Yawei noted, "the current Chinese political system is such that in the halls of local and central power, taxpaying peasants have no real representatives to speak on their behalf or to monitor the government's agrarian policies."[96] The status of peasants in China is lower than that in most socialist or capitalist countries.

Deng Xiaoping took some early steps to raise the status of farmers by introducing village-level elections in the late 1970s, under which peasants can cast votes to choose members of the village administrative committee (VAC). However, the powers of the VAC are limited and there are no concrete plans by the CCP leadership to expand or elevate the elections to higher levels (see Chapter 4). The views of Wei Shengduo, the party secretary of the township of Pingba, near Chongqing, were significant. In August 2003, Wei tried to organize the first universal-suffrage election of a township chief in Chinese history. The radical reformer insisted that only when peasants could vote in their own leaders would agrarian problems be solved. "Now, all the rural cadres are appointed by superior [party] units," Wei said. "These cadres are only concerned about the views of their superior departments and their bosses. They don't have the peasants' interests at heart."[97]

A major initiative to boost the political and bargaining powers of farmers could be the formation of *nonghui*, or farmers' unions, the rural equivalent of trade unions. Many of the *nonghui* prototypes have developed out of peasants' desire for self-defense against heavy taxation or corrupt officials. CASS rural expert Yu Jianrong cited one county in Hunan, probably the province with the highest level of activism, where up to eighty volunteers had become "farmers' representatives for cutting taxation and for presenting petitions." Yu indicated that if local self-government and grassroots democracy were allowed to develop at a faster clip, these "representatives" could even become candidates for township and county chiefs.[98]

According to Beijing-based scholar Zhao Ligang, farmers' unions can make it easier for peasants to join the market economy—as well as to bargain with the government over issues including the purchasing price of produce. "Only when farmers are organized can the cost of taking part in a market economy be lowered," he said. Zhao noted that Beijing's policymaking process was more and more influenced by lobbying on the part of powerful economic blocs in society. "Without adequate organization, farmers will become the losers in government decision making," he added.[99]

CASS's Yu pointed out that a new generation of "peasant leaders" had spontaneously emerged in the course of the farmers' perennial struggle with grassroots cadres over problems such as taxation and corruption. Yu said most of these leaders were demobilized soldiers or former *nongmingong,* who had a better idea of political realities outside the villages. Yu added that *nonghui* were "organizations of political participation [by peasants] for the purpose of communication and consultation with the government." He noted that Beijing should not worry about *nonghui* because few would ever become "revolutionary, anti-government outfits." Indeed, the experience of many rural researchers is that the majority of *nonghui* leaders merely wanted to ensure that local officials abide by the central leadership's new policies toward the peasantry. Yu argued that it would be better for the government to allow peasants to organize themselves into associations instead of stifling these initiatives. The rural expert said government neglect or suppression could result in *nonghui* members taking violent means. "There is also the risk of peasant organizations becoming secret societies," he warned.[100]

Other proponents of *nonghui* have also noted that these organizations would not vitiate the power of the party and state. Beijing's Zhao added that farmers' unions could serve the purpose of propagating government policy—and that they would help maintain social stability and curtail underground criminal organizations. However, as of late 2005, Beijing had only acquiesced in the existence of quasi-*nonghui* in Hunan. At the same time, more liberal provinces such as Zhejiang have passed provincial regulations on farmers' setting up "professional cooperatives." Yet it is clear that such cooperatives are tolerated or even encouraged by local governments as long as they do not take part in politics, such as haggling with local administrations on the division of the rural-income pie.[101]

Crusading Farmers in Action

By the mid-2000s, peasants have become more aggressive and better organized in venting their grievances or holding errant cadres responsible. The most common form of resistance consisted of farmers using petitions and media exposure, as well as legal procedures, to make their cases heard. For example, thousands of farmers living in the outskirts of Changsha, the provincial capital of Hunan, signed a petition in early 2004 demanding that a golf course under construction be stopped. The petition, relayed to the provincial leadership, said the recreational facility contravened relevant provisions in the National Land Law and that farmers whose land had been taken away had not been adequately compensated.[102]

A by-product of the Hu-Wen team's effort to raise the status of the Constitution and the law is that meek, often despised peasants are able to take legal action against corrupt officials. In the spring of 2004, the Beijing leadership was shocked when about 10,000 farmers in the outskirts of Fuzhou, capital of Fujian Province, signed petitions for the censure and dismissal of a dozen-odd officials in the provincial capital of Fuzhou as well as the surrounding districts and townships of Cangshan, Minhou, Fu'an, Qingkou, Shishan, and Chengmen. While there is little the peasants can do to remove party and government officials from their posts, relevant clauses in the Constitution as well as Election Laws on the NPC and local-level people's congresses (PCs) do have provisions for impeachment of deputies. And the angry Fujian farmers were demanding that these officials, including Fuzhou party secretary He Lifeng and mayor Lian Zhiqian, be stripped of their positions as members of the NPC and local PCs.[103]

The gripes of the peasants were familiar: local officials in these five counties and townships were working in collusion with real-estate companies to secure land-use rights from farmers for redevelopment while paying the latter only a small fraction of the going price of the plots. Take the case of Shishan village, for example. On average, farmers were offered a payment of up to 30,000 yuan per *mu* (or 0.0667 hectare). But in actual fact, officials of various levels invariably took a "cut" of the compensation so it was not unusual for farmers to only pocket several thousand yuan per *mu*. The price that the officials could then fetch at public auction or through prearranged deals with property developers, however, was as high as 1 million yuan per *mu*.[104]

In the case of the Qingkou township, funds worth more than 240 million yuan that should have been distributed among nearly 10,000 peasants had since the late 1990s been ploughed into the construction of a nearby "technological zone," the East South Automobile City (ESAC). The approval of these peasants had never been sought—and each of them was only paid 800 yuan a year as "dividend" from the ESAC project. Meanwhile, the victims had been denied their ordinary means of livelihood—farming—and the most they could get from the authorities was 70 yuan a month to buy grain.[105]

The plight of peasants—and the alleged crimes of officials riding roughshod over them—was made worse by the fact that Fuzhou authorities were pulling out all the stops to suppress farmers' protest actions. According to eyewitness accounts, the petition name lists were forcibly destroyed. And Lin Zhengxu, an organizer of the petitions, was beaten up by police even though the latter failed to produce an arrest warrant. Local cadres also tried to stop petitioners from reaching Beijing.

According to Li Boguang, a Beijing scholar and lawyer who had taken up the Fuzhou cases, the authorities' tough tactics could engender a grave crisis. "The Constitution and the law are the only avenues left to farmers," Dr. Li said. If they are denied the right to use legal weapons, the lawyer said, "farmers might resort to other means to vent their anger." The Beijing-based lawyer, however, was himself detained by security personnel in December 2004.[106]

Similar cases of peasant rebellion—via the courts—have been reported in other parts of China. About 20,000 peasants near the cities of Tangshan and Qinghuangdao in Hebei took action in 2004 to strip corrupt local officials of their CP memberships. For instance, Tangshan party secretary Zhang He was alleged to have pocketed part of the 60 million yuan that was supposed to have been paid to thousands of peasants who had to be resettled to make way for a dam project. The peasant leaders had originally wanted to lodge a petition with the NPC in March 2004. Yet they were detained and sent back to Tangshan by police from that city, whom Zhang had allegedly sent to the capital. With the help of several crusading lawyers form Beijing, Tangshan peasants petitioned the NPC for the removal of Zhang's position on the local congresses.[107] As of mid-2004, the CCP Central Commission for Disciplinary Inspection had started investigations into allegations of large-scale rural corruption in Hebei, but no local officials have been penalized.

Beijing's refusal to fully recognize the political rights of farmers—and provide them with proper channels for negotiation with the government—came to a head in October 2004, when some 60,000 peasants in Hanyuan County, Sichuan, clashed with several thousand police and People's Armed Police (PAP) officers. The cause of the confrontation was inadequate compensation for the close to 100,000 peasants who would be displaced by the construction of the nearby Pubugou Dam. While the central authorities and the power company involved were said to have offered the peasants relocation fees of up to 8 billion yuan, individual households had only received a few thousand yuan. Moreover, local cadres had blocked peasants' efforts to petition higher authorities in Sichuan or Beijing. Protestors shouted "Long Live the CCP!" as they clashed with police. At one point, demonstrators surrounded the local hotel where Sichuan party secretary Zhang Xuezhong—a Hu Jintao protégé who had come for a mediation session—was staying. Local media said more than ten farmers were killed in the melee.[108]

After the thousands of PAP officers had finally dispersed the mob in early November, President Hu and Premier Wen gave orders to mollify the peasants. The leaders pledged that no "ringleaders" would be detained, and that construction of the dam would be temporarily halted pending discussion with local peasants. However, the Hu-Wen team also laid down a hard-line stipulation, namely that "stability and unity must be preserved," and that "*zhongdian* [major] hydraulic works, especially those connected with the develop-the-west strategy" must be guaranteed.[109] While compensation for peasants would reportedly be raised, no local officials have been penalized for corruption or for mishandling this major crisis. And dam construction work resumed in late 2005.

Test Case: The Plight of Workers

In theory, the lot of urban workers is much better than that of farmers. According to official statistics, the average annual income of urban workers was 16,000 yuan in 2004, nearly 5,000 yuan more than the 2001 figure. By and large, urban wages have increased at the same rate as GDP growth. Moreover, most staff of state-owned firms and factories enjoy five-day weeks, meaning that in addition to annual vacations and festivals, they are entitled to 114 rest days out of the year.[110]

The government has also extended and firmed up the social security net. Unemployment insurance for workers in state-owned enterprises (SOEs) has been increased. In the early 2000s, there was also a boost in special subsidies to workers facing difficulties. The number of recipients of *dibao,* or "minimum livelihood-assistance payouts" given by the Ministry of Civil Affairs to the jobless, reached 20,536,000 at the end of February 2003, a jump of more than 10 million over the figure just a year before. The size of the handout has also been boosted, particularly in the rich provinces. For example, Guangdong vowed in 2003 to augment *dibao* funds by 400 million yuan a year. And most cities have provided financial assistance or given tax exemption to enterprises that hire previously unemployed workers.[111]

However, most workers feel unsafe and unsure about their future. Jobs in the old manufacturing sectors are being diminished even as, thanks to globalization, employment opportunities in joint ventures along the coast are increasingly dependent on global trade cycles and investment by multinationals. Although wages have risen, most old-style welfare benefits are gone—and more and more workers have to buy their own retirement and health-insurance packages. Even worse for anxious parents, the employment rate of new high school and college graduates has gone down. The sense of insecurity and angst hitting workers was arguably the single most important factor behind the success of the Falun Gong in the late 1990s. And while the quasi-Buddhist sect was largely suppressed by ex-president Jiang, the same social malaise that contributed to its fast growth has remained—and could pose a big threat to national stability.[112]

The Politics of Fast-Shattering Rice Bowls

The Hu-Wen team was the first administration to consider lessening unemployment or generating new jobs as a "major political task." The *People's Daily* pointed out in 2003 that the employment question was at the heart of the CCP's goal of "running the administration for the sake of the people"—and the key to "the long reign and perennial stability of the country."[113] The stark reality of Chinese political economy is that, as former premier Zhu Rongji pointed out in internal speeches, China must maintain a GDP growth rate of at least 7 percent or risk grave social tension owing to unemployment. Zhu estimated that this "pressure from jobs" would remain formidable until around the year 2020, when hopefully China's population growth will have started to level off. According to the Tenth Five-Year Plan of 2001 to 2005, the economy must produce 8 million new jobs a year. This, however, will only take care of the needs of residents in the larger cities. If the demands of towns and small cities nationwide are taken into account, up to 30 million jobs have to be created each year.[114]

According to official figures released in mid-2003, the "registered unemployed" in urban areas numbered nearly 8 million people, thus resulting in a jobless rate of 4.1 percent. This was within the target set by Beijing for containing the unemployment rate within the 4.5 percent parameters. However, most independent Chinese and Western economists say the jobless rate is really around 8 percent because a good chunk of the unemployed are not registered with the authorities.[115]

And each year, the ranks of job seekers are swollen by growing numbers of high school and college graduates. This means that even assuming that the state could create 8 million jobs as mandated by the Tenth Five-Year Plan the situation becomes more and more desperate for old or new job seekers alike. The severity of the situation was reflected in the high jobless rate among graduates in 2003. As the summer ended, only half of the 2.12 million college leavers could find jobs. The plight of graduates that year was exacerbated by the fact that it was in 1999, when they entered college, that Beijing had decided to significantly boost enrollment. In 2002, there were only 1.45 million graduates—and job seekers.[116]

While Beijing has done away with many aspects of central planning and executive fiats, it still slaps job-creation quotas on different economic sectors and departments. For example, a Beijing-based agronomist said village and township enterprises (VTEs) were in the early 2000s asked to create 2.5 million new jobs a year. Yet employment for a mere 1 million people was generated by this depressed sector. VTEs, once a reliable provider of new jobs, had fallen on hard times. The agronomist said that while in the early 1990s an investment of 10,000 yuan in a typical VTE could create 12 jobs, the comparable figure for the early 2000s was down to a mere 0.67.[117]

Moreover, as China's world factory seeks to climb the technological ladder, the majority of workers are not qualified to fill the growing vacancies in high-tech sectors along the coastal cities and development zones. State statistics showed that in late 2004, barely 3.5 percent of China's 70 million urban workers could be classified as highly skilled technicians. In industrialized nations, the comparative figure is as high as 40 percent. The situation is particularly serious in the northeast and western provinces, where the government is anxious to attract foreign investment.[118]

Few Improvements in Labor Rights

Limited Role of Official Unions and Deterioration of
Working Conditions

In his address to the Fourteenth Congress of the official All-China Federation of Trade Unions (ACFTU) in late 2003, President Hu played up the fact that the legal rights of workers must be safeguarded. He warned that employers who "deduct workers' salaries, extend their working hours, neglect work safety, or infringe upon the rights of workers" would be penalized.[119] However, despite the Hu-Wen team's expressions of concern for the welfare of the working class—and Hu's campaign to promote rule by law—not much has been done to improve the legal and political status of workers.

The mammoth ACFTU was established in 1925 as the only labor organization of socialist China. It has enjoyed a fast growth since Deng's reform and open-door policy. From 1997 to 2002, ACFTU branches nationwide expanded from 1.13 million to 1.71 million, while membership mushroomed from 42.69 million to 134 million. However, although the ACFTU is usually headed by a senior cadre with Politburo status, it has been criticized by international labor watchdogs for failing to protect rights of workers such as collective bargaining.[120]

Some improvements in the "official labor movement" were made in 2003. For example, ACFTU leaders revealed plans to allow workers to directly elect grassroots-level union leaders in a few years' time. Indeed, in some rich cities such as Hangzhou, Zhejiang Province, workers had started direct election of local union leaders in 1999.[121] However, the basic nature of the official union has remained the same. It reports to the Communist Party leadership, and it does its best to encourage workers to toe the line of "maintaining stability while making self-sacrifice for the sake of the socialist enterprise." Thus, in his ACFTU address, Hu spoke of the need for "Communist Party committees of all levels to enhance and improve their leadership of trade unions."

Workers as well as farmers are denied basic civil liberties, including those of holding strikes and forming unions, for fear that the latter would cut into the CCP's monopoly on power. Patriarch Deng's fear of the "Polish disease"—the highly politicized and anti-Communist labor movement symbolized by the Solidarity Movement in Poland in the 1980s—still seems to govern the thinking of the Fourth-Generation leadership. ACFTU officials have openly said that "hostile forces both in and out of China have interfered in the labor movement" with a view to goading workers to "struggle against" the government.[122] Despite harsh criticism from Western governments as well as from international labor and human rights organizations, Beijing has refused to allow the formation of nonofficial trade unions. This is despite China having signed on to various United Nations–approved international covenants on economic and human rights. Moreover, the arrest and harassment of the leaders of non-party-affiliated or underground trade unionists has not diminished after Hu and Wen took over the reins of government.[123]

Meanwhile, conditions of laborers have deteriorated both along the rich coast and in the poor hinterland. Workers are hardly accorded basic human dignity. In August 2004, a company in Changchun, capital of Jilin Province, caused a stir when it asked trainees to practice salesmanship by kneeling down at the city's thoroughfare, Chongqing Road.[124] And factory managers who suspect certain staff members of stealing company property routinely strip-search the suspects. A 1999 survey revealed that most of the 6 million female workers in Guangdong were locked up at night and forced to work seven days a week. The situation has only marginally improved since then.[125]

There are also horror stories about workers getting prematurely old and sick due to the high levels of toxic material in their factories. Some commentators have called this phenomenon "a 30–year-old worker with the lung of a 60–year-old." For example, three workers of Fuhui Industrial Company, Guangdong Province, died in late 2002 because of long-time exposure to heavy metal as well as noxious gases. The factory did not even provide employees with facial masks. And it was unwilling to pay the medical bills of those workers who had come down with respiratory and other diseases. A mid-2004 report by the State Administration of Work Safety revealed that more than 600,000 workers nationwide were suffering from chronic vocational diseases.[126]

Workers' lack of bargaining power—and the most basic *shengcunquan* (right to life)—is best illustrated by the atrocious number of industrial accidents, particularly those in the mines. According to published statistics, 63,735 Chinese lost their lives in accidents including industrial mishaps in the first six months of 2004. (Official figures invariably lump together industrial and traffic accidents.) According to the International Labor Organization, deaths from workplace accidents in China were 11.1 per 100,000, meaning that in the early 2000s, some 81,115 laborers perished from mishaps a year.[127]

Workplace incidents increased in 2004 and 2005 as the prices of commodities and in particular coal shot through the roof. Official statistics said that around 6,000 coal miners were killed every year in explosions, shaft collapses, and other accidents in different parts of the country. However, Western watchdogs estimate that the numbers could be much higher as thousands of deaths—especially those in private pits—went unreported owing to the owners' desire to avoid trouble and punishment. Moreover, the wives of diseased miners, most of them being rural laborers, were in most cases merely given a one-off compensation of around 20,000 yuan. The authorities estimated in late 2004 that at least 51.8 billion yuan needed to be spent to improve the safety of state-owned coal mines, yet it is doubtful whether central or regional governments are willing to foot this bill.[128]

It is difficult to estimate the number of workplace-related conflicts such as rallies and protests given Beijing's anxiety to suppress news about embarrassing outbreaks of instability. The year 1999 saw the last time that Beijing publicized figures about labor disputes, which numbered 120,000, compared to 8,152 in 1992. It was not known, however, how many of such cases of altercation and flare-ups led to concrete industrial action. Human rights watchdogs estimate, however, that the number of protest actions, ranging from work stoppages to confrontation with police, is about 100,000 a year.[129]

Both state and private enterprises have come up with all sorts of draconian measures to prevent workers from venting their grievances. For instance, the state-owned Fengcheng City Electricity Co. Ltd. in Jiangxi Province tried to prevent

workers from filing petitions and other complaints with higher authorities by de-
ducting from their salaries. Thus, workers who had petitioned once would be fined
200 yuan, and two times, 400 yuan. Those who had demonstrated three times
would receive no salary for the month.[130] Many factories also employ former policemen or demobilized soldiers as security guards, one of whose purposes is to
stop workers from taking industrial action or making complaints to city officials.

Breaking the Back of Wildcat Unions

It is a measure of China's fast-improving economic and diplomatic clout that it is
getting away with all sorts of draconian action against "underground" labor unionists. Compared to dissidents, labor leaders are generally not well known overseas.
And while visiting Western dignitaries sometimes urge Chinese leaders to release
certain human rights activists, labor organizers who have been locked away are
often forgotten.

Perhaps the most telling example of Beijing's determination to crush the budding independent labor movement was what took place in the rustbelt cities of
Liaoyang, Liaoning Province, and Daqing, Heilongjiang Province, in early 2002.
In Liaoyang, a decaying industrialized city, up to 30,000 employees of about
twenty state-owned factories and mills staged demonstrations due to long-owed
salaries and pensions. The workers laid siege to the municipal government, and
law and order broke down. In the Daqing Oilfield, as many as 80,000 workers
protested over the puny size of their *maiduan gongling* (one-off retirement payout) package, which, once paid, would leave the huge state enterprise owing the
retirees nothing.[131]

The case in Daqing was solved relatively quickly because the oilfield still had a
lot of money: it partially satisfied the workers' demands by raising the retirement
payout. However, the Liaoyang protests dragged on for several weeks. The factories had absolutely no funds, while the laid-off workers, who had no prospect of
finding jobs elsewhere, had nothing to lose by confronting the authorities. Consider the bitterness behind this well-remembered lament of labor leader Yao Fuxin:
"We devoted our youth to the party, but no one supports us in old age! We gave our
youth to the party for nothing!"[132]

Beijing was particularly nervous about the Liaoyang activists for several reasons. They displayed a disturbingly high level of organization, with an association
of activists representing workers from more than twenty factories in the city. Moreover, the underground union was making political as well as economic demands
on the authorities; it was clamoring for high-level investigation into the corruption
of municipal- and even provincial-level officials.[133] The government used a mixture of brute force, persuasion, and trickery to break the movement. People's Armed
Police and anti-riot crack police teams were called in. Local cadres also tried to
break up the solidarity of the organizers by promising jobs for those who were
willing to compromise. The relatively few considered intransigent—and unmoved

by bribes—were locked up. All in all, at least four labor leaders were detained. While two were released on bail toward the end of the year, two "ringleaders" from the Liaoyang Ferro-Alloy Factory, Yao Fuxin and Xiao Yunliang, were convicted in January 2003 of "efforts to overthrow the government."[134]

Analysts said that for fear of international outcry, Yao and Xiao were not charged for running wildcat labor unions. According to a senior cadre at the ACFTU, Yao was guilty of "organizing illegal demonstrations" and "committing violent acts" including setting fire to cars during the protests. They were also accused of having links with "hostile foreign forces" and being members of the banned China Democracy Party. In May 2003, Yao was slapped with a seven-year and Xiao a four-year jail term, for which the International Labor Organization lodged protests with the Chinese authorities. Han Dongfang, director of the Hong Kong–based watchdog group, China Labor Bulletin, said: "The sentences [on Yao and Xiao] show just how little China has progressed on the path to rule of law; instead the 'law' continues to be used as a weapon against freedom of association and expression."[135]

The Hu-Wen administration has continued to play hardball against underground trade-union activists. In late 2004, police in the Jiangsu city of Yancheng arrested two female labor organizers, Ding Xiulan and Liu Meifeng, for their role in organizing protests in the Zhongheng Textile Co. in October that year. Several hundred Zhongheng workers staged demonstrations for two weeks after they were laid off—and given a meager *maiduan gongling* package of 433 yuan for every year they had worked there. The Hong Kong–based China Labor Watch organization said it was possible the two would be jailed on charges of engaging in anti-government activities.[136]

By 2004, there were signs that respected scholars and writers had taken up the plight of workers. After a spate of particularly vicious coal mine accidents—including a gas explosion in a state-owned Shaanxi Province mine that killed more than 200 miners—300 Chinese intellectuals, including well-known writers, professors, and civil rights activists such as Du Daobin, Li Jian, Zhang Zuhua, Liu Xiaobo, and Liu Junning, signed a petition in November calling on Beijing to allow workers to form independent unions. The appeal also noted that owners and managers of mines and factories with atrocious safety records should be severely punished. The Hu leadership, however, has responded to the new activism on the part of academics and writers by launching a political campaign against "public intellectuals."[137]

The Case of Migrant Workers

By 2003, close to 100 million *nongmingong* (rural or migrant laborers), about the population of Sichuan or Henan, were working in the cities. And despite growing unemployment in urban areas, about 5 million rural farmers join the ranks of the *nongmingong* each year. Because of the supposedly endless supply of migrant workers, their wage levels had until early 2004 remained substantially the same for more than a decade. In prosperous Guangdong Province, nearly half of the 26 million workers from poorer provinces earned less than 800 yuan a month.[138]

Nongmingong already form the backbone of the working class. As of late 2002, 57.6 percent of laborers in the so-called second-category production activities, or traditional manufacturing, were rural workers. They have also made inroads in the services sector, taking fully 37 percent of jobs in this field. While the *nongmingong* have made tremendous contributions to construction and other industries, rural workers are routinely disenfranchised and discriminated against. They do the so-called 3D jobs—dirty, dangerous, and demanding. And they are not protected by labor laws, few and inadequate as they are. For example, rural work hands in Guangdong usually toil for at least fifteen hours a day, seven hours more than the mandated eight-hour workday. Many are paid below the minimum monthly wage of around 500 yuan stipulated by several Guangdong cities.[139]

Premier Wen was the first top-level leader to demand a new deal for migrant workers. In the run-up to Chinese New Year in early 2003, he urged employers nationwide to pay these poor souls before they returned home to celebrate the festivities. It was estimated that rural laborers nationwide were routinely owed tens of billions of yuan on Chinese New Year's eve. After Wen's admonition, many provinces and cities scrambled to ensure that *nongmingong* within their jurisdiction would be adequately paid. It turned out that some of the worst offenders were local-government units and SOEs. For example, as of mid-2004, northeastern Heilongjiang Province still owed migrant workers salaries of 95 million yuan. Most of the culprits were government departments handling construction works as well as real-estate developers. In late 2004, the State Council passed a regulation saying employers who owed employees salaries would be penalized by having to pay their staff 50 percent to 100 percent more.[140]

It was only in 2002 and 2003 that provincial and municipal governments started promulgating regulations on the welfare of migrant laborers. Quite a few cities came up with rules saying that *nongmingong* should not be paid less than the minimum wage for ordinary laborers. Super-rich Guangzhou and Shenzhen in Guangdong Province were among the few cities in China with a minimum wage for migrant workers. In 2002, the minimum remuneration was raised by 60 yuan to 510 yuan a month.[141] And it was not until September 2003 that rural workers were formally admitted to the ACFTU. Labor law professor Yang Hanping said allowing *nongmingong* to join labor unions was "a necessary demand of social progress and a recognition of the contribution of rural workers to urban construction." Vice-Chairman of the ACFTU Su Liqing admitted that official unions should do more for the *nongmingong*. "Unions should represent migrant workers in signing labor contracts with employers or represent them in negotiations over working hours, wages, and workplace conditions," Su said.[142]

Various trade union leaders have proposed that employers of *nongmingong* must hand over to the authorities a basic level of "salary guarantee funds" before they can hire such laborers. As Gu Zhizhong, a labor union leader in the prosperous city of Kunshan, Jiangsu Province, pointed out, "we should break the back of whichever companies that do not pay migrant workers." In the summer of 2004, Kunshan started to require construction companies to deposit with the authorities "salary guarantee funds" amounting to at least 5 percent of the total cost of projects.[143]

In the final analysis, however, it was not so much the "putting people first" ethos of the Hu-Wen team as it was sheer market forces that led to the first substantial rise in the salaries of migrant workers in the past decade or so. By mid-2004, there was a shortage of *nongmingong* along the east China coast, leading to a boost in wages of 10 percent or so. And Hong Kong and Taiwan businessmen, who hire tens of millions of workers in the Pearl River Delta region, have complained about worsening labor shortages.[144] Apart from the phenomenon of the bubble economy, other factors include the rise in the prices of farm produce. The latter persuaded a proportion of rural work hands to return to their home provinces to engage in traditional agriculture.

Experts, however, are hardly persuaded that the fate of the *nongmingong* has actually improved. Individual economic sectors began showing signs of slowing down in 2005—and the demand for labor might decrease in some areas. Moreover, it was unlikely that the prices of farm produce would continue to edge up. Most importantly, the supply of migrant workers from hinterland provinces is still voluminous. This lies behind the forecasts made by cadres such as former chief trade negotiator Long Yongtu that China's cost advantages would last for a decade or more. For the *nongmingong,* however, this means that unless proper laws and regulations are in place, they will continue to remain victims of discrimination and exploitation in China's "world factory."[145]

The Plight of Other Disadvantaged Sectors

Victims of AIDS and Environmental Depredation

It was not until after the SARS crisis that the spotlight was put on the plight of HIV/AIDS carriers. The Chinese government said as of late 2003 that the number of AIDS sufferers was close to 1 million; yet experts from the World Health Organization (WHO) and other international organizations said the figure could be several times as much. Indeed, Beijing's neglect of AIDS victims bordered on criminality. The reason is simple: SARS was a highly visible disease that drove away tourists as well as foreign investors. Yet AIDS has hit mostly members of powerless *ruoshi tuanti*, or disadvantaged sectors. Apart from homosexuals, AIDS has affected mostly drug users, prostitutes, members of ethnic minorities, as well as peasants who periodically sell blood to bolster their income. Western aid agencies reckoned that as many as 1 million peasants in landlocked Henan Province might have been infected through selling blood at grossly unsanitary plasma-collection centers in the late 1980s and early 1990s.[146]

Experts said that until early 2004, hundreds of thousands of AIDS victims were practically left to die because they were denied medical care. Human Rights Watch found that drug users—a high-risk group—were merely sent to unhygienic detoxification centers, where they were in many instances forced to work in labor camp–style workshops. It was only from mid-2003 onward that Beijing began soliciting international help. The famous Chinese-American inventor of the "cocktail treatment," Dr. David Ho, was invited to give advice on anti-AIDS research. Yet for the first few months, Dr. Ho was not allowed to travel to Henan and other affected provinces.[147]

Moreover, the authorities did not allow volunteers or NGOs to get involved. Well-known AIDS activist Wan Yankai was detained by state security personnel in August 2002 for "leaking state secrets." His crime was that he had sent to foreign news agencies and human rights watchdogs an internal report on the AIDS problem in Henan. World-famous AIDS activist Dr. Gao Yaojie was subject to harassment and surveillance at least until late 2004. And consider what happened to the impoverished "AIDS village" of Xiongqiao in Henan in July 2003. Several hundred police and thugs broke into the hamlet one night, smashing property and arresting thirteen farmers. The "crime" of the villagers was that they had made a noisy protest against insufficient government economic and medical aid.[148]

The central government's attitude toward AIDS changed after Premier Wen's celebrated handshake with victims in December 2003. In February 2004, Vice-Premier Wu Yi was appointed head of a new Work Committee to Prevent and Cure AIDS. Wu announced that free medical treatment would be accorded victims who were peasants or unemployed city dwellers. As of late 2004, however, quite a few NGOs on the frontline indicated that local officials still adopted an uncooperative attitude. A well-known activist in Henan, Li Dan, who had been harassed by police, said in late 2004 that "many officials are not following the central government's policies." And foreign reporters still have difficulty getting permits to cover AIDS-related stories in far-flung provinces.[149]

Apart from "new" diseases such as SARS and AIDS, Chinese authorities must move fast to prevent the spread of both old and new sicknesses in view of environmental degradation and the breakdown of the village health-care system. A notable case is the return of snail fever, or schistosomiasis, which is a parasitic disease carried by freshwater snails that cause damage to victims' blood and liver. More than 843,000 Chinese, mostly peasants living near lakes and waterways, were infected with snail fever in 2003. Forty-three counties in seven hinterland provinces have failed to control the disease and some thirty-eight counties previously free of the illness have seen a resurgence of the scourge. Again, these and other victims of industrial pollution have only limited recourse to justice or compensation.[150]

The Phenomenon of Forced Eviction

Collusion Between Developers and Corrupt Cadres

Perhaps nothing better illustrates the growing contradiction between the haves and have-nots—and that between an insensitive bureaucracy and the suffering masses—than the thousands upon thousands of urban, and particularly rural, residents forced to leave home in the name of urban renewal or real-estate development. According to the Petitions Office of the State Council, the number of complaints and petitions related to forced eviction has risen dramatically since the late 1990s. In the first eight months of 2003, the office received 5,360 visits by citizens with grievances relating to urban clearance, up 48 percent from the same period the year before.[151]

As the case of disgraced Shanghai tycoon Zhou Zhengyi illustrated, many real-estate developers have signed under-the-table deals with local officials. It is thus relatively easy for housing companies to throw out urban or rural residents after paying minimal compensation; and those who refuse to go are sometimes chased away by police and even thugs called in by officials. In Shanghai, about 850,000 households, or at least 2 million people, moved out of their original homes to make way for urban renewal in the twenty months ending in 2002. While Shanghai officials claimed that only 300 disputes had arisen, the problem was much graver. And letters that angry residents sent to Beijing protesting against forced eviction by Zhou Zhengyi's company was one factor behind the billionaire's arrest in 2003.[152]

Things came to a head in the summer of 2003 when in the space of six months, at least three disgruntled evictees tried to commit suicide in Beijing by self-incineration. Consider the failed suicide attempt by Anhui resident Zhu Zhengliang, who tried to burn himself to death at Tiananmen Square. Forty-six-year-old Zhu, a laid-off worker in the small town of Qingyang County, was protesting what he called unfair compensation. According to his son, eviction teams sent by local authorities had destroyed his humble house, in the process smashing seven antiques left by his forebears. Zhu's wife was also beaten up, and the couple had petitioned provincial authorities five times before Zhu's fateful trip to Beijing.[153]

The liberal *Southern Metropolitan News* quoted a lawyer as saying that although in theory people affected by eviction notices possessed the same rights as developers, the former were usually outgunned by the latter. And this applied to evictees who had access to lawyers. In the case of residents forced to leave Jing'an District, Shanghai, to make way for real-estate development, their lawyer, Cheng En'chong, was even arrested by the authorities. Many of Cheng's clients were victims of real-estate projects associated with Zhou. In August, 2003, Cheng was put on trial for "leaking state secrets" and subsequently sentenced to three years in jail.[154]

As real-estate and industrial development began to take off even in central and western provinces, more farmland has been rezoned for urban development—in the process depriving peasants of their only means of livelihood. An early 2004 report in the *People's Daily* said that about 40 million farmers had been forced to give up their plots after the latter had been requisitioned for "redevelopment." Other estimates in late 2005 put the figure at close to 70 million. On the average, each member of households affected was given a one-off payment of no more than 18,000 yuan, which was barely enough for a person to live for seven years. A late-2004 CASS report entitled "Analysis and Forecast of China's Social Situation, 2004–2005" also cited "massive loss of land by farmers" as one of six major problems that bedeviled the country's development. The report warned that wanton rezoning of land for urban renewal, coupled with neglect of farmers' livelihood, could exacerbate social contradictions.[155]

Insufficient Remedial Measures

It was only by the summer of 2003 that Beijing started paying high-level attention to the plight of evictees. Senior officials began intervening to solve particularly horrendous cases. For example, Politburo member and vice-premier Zeng Peiyang gave personal instructions on how to deal with the cases of the evictees who tried to burn themselves to death at Tiananmen Square that year. Beijing also mandated leading officials in different provinces and cities to deal with the economic and political aftermath of urban redevelopment, particularly compensation for peasants forced to make way for urban renewal.[156]

In mid-2003, Hu himself made the decision to send four teams of inspectors to look at disputes relating to urban clearance in Shanghai, Nanjing, Hangzhou, and Shandong. The president reportedly instructed that tearing down the houses of the masses was "a matter of the utmost significance." "Urban development will only have the support of the masses when the public's interests are taken into account," he warned. Premier Wen also cautioned against the problem of individual cadres and developers taking advantage of loose regulations to make illegal profits.[157]

One reason for high-level concern was evidence that unlike the majority of suppressed peasants, evictee-petitioners were beginning to organize themselves. For example, Beijing resident Hua Huiqi, himself a victim of urban clearance, had become a liaison person for other groupings who made it to Beijing to present their grievances throughout 2003. Another Beijing-based organizer, Ye Guozhu, was arrested in September 2004 after he had tried to organize a 10,000–man rally in the capital against forced eviction. Ye was later that year given a four-year jail term for "disturbing law and order."[158]

Individual cities had from mid-2003 begun to lay down more clear-cut regulations to minimize the grievances of forced eviction. In Shanghai, for example, real-estate companies must make public announcements giving details of the compensation they are offering the evictees—and the criteria used for determining the values of homes. Companies must also set up offices on building sites to handle complaints. Moreover, developers must neither use force nor cut the utility supplies of affected residents as a means of intimidation. In Shanghai, a group of 152 lawyers also began providing inexpensive services to victims of urban development, including taking their cases to the local courts.[159]

Shanxi is one of the several provinces to have promulgated local regulations on issues relating to land and redevelopment. A series of public hearings was called by the provincial legislature in September 2003 to gauge the opinions of lawyers as well as citizens. These soon became platforms for the downtrodden to air their grievances against the rich and powerful. In the provincial capital of Taiyuan, many among the city's 80,000 poorest families, who were dependent on social security benefits, had been bullied by redevelopers. One evictee said he could only receive a one-off compensation of 30,000 yuan. It was merely sufficient for him to rent a small apartment for six years.[160]

Analysts said the question of forced eviction might improve because the authorities were finally becoming worried about the property bubble in big cities, especially the rampant corruption that went with it. Vice-Minister of Construction Liu Zhifeng pointed out in late 2003 that a lot of illicit money had changed hands in the areas of land development and building construction, as well as the calculation and dispensation of compensation for evictees. In 2003, the Ministry of Land and Natural Resources (MLNR) investigated some 82,400 cases of fraud involving redevelopment schemes over 747,000 hectares of land, 240,000 hectares of which had originally been farmland.[161]

The important question, however, is whether farmers' rights over their small but valued plots have been guaranteed. As of late 2004, the MLNR and other authorities claimed that they had returned to farmers 16.05 billion yuan, out of the 17.55 billion yuan that was owed them since 1999. Yet few officials handling the land portfolio have been penalized. In late 2004, the Construction Ministry introduced a regulation which said that companies wanting to tear down buildings for redevelopment must make public announcements about compensation for original residents—as well as hold public hearings to determine the proper level of payouts.[162] However, it remains to be seen whether urban residents—and defenseless rural folk—can have as big a say as developers and other powerful vested-interest groupings.

A Checkered Report Card on the "Putting People First" Crusade

As of 2005, the Hu-Wen team's *yiren weiben* credo had permeated Chinese society and brought about significant changes in people's conception of issues ranging from social justice to "green development." More attention is focused on the plight of disadvantaged classes. However, it is clear that social malaise such as the widening gap between rich and poor will not likely be healed in the rest of the decade. In fact, the population of "destitute Chinese," defined as people with a per capita income of 637 yuan a year or less—and who have difficulty feeding and clothing themselves—increased by 800,000 in 2003 to hit around 30 million. This was the first time that the number of the impoverished had increased since the start of the reform era in 1978. As of late 2003, there were 85.17 million Chinese with per capita income of 882 yuan or lower.[163]

It is true that from early 2003 onward, the Hu-Wen administration has as a whole demonstrated more sensitivity toward the personal dignity and sociopolitical rights of *ruoshi tuanti,* especially the peasants. Yet the harsh treatment that is still accorded the seemingly endless throngs of petitioners to Beijing testifies to the distance that the new leadership has to go to attain the *yiren weiben* ideal. As CASS's Yu Jianrong noted, "a major aspect of the *sannong* question did not arise from farmers themselves; one root cause is [the attitude] of administrators." Famous expert in grassroots elections Li Fan has charged that "since 1949, the central authorities have severely restricted the political rights and freedoms of the peasant."[164]

Other social critics have pointed out that while in the wake of WTO accession, foreign companies and foreign residents in China have enjoyed "national treatment," members of *ruoshi tuanti* such as peasants and migrant workers are still routinely discriminated against. And the fact that in late 2005, three years into their administration, Hu, Wen, and colleagues still found it necessary to boost control mechanisms has exposed them to accusations that their "putting people first" doctrine is mere window dressing.

The crux of the matter regarding *ruoshi tuanti* is empowerment. The lot of the politically outgunned peasants, *nonmingong,* and workers will never be improved until they have the wherewithal—especially mechanisms for organizing themselves—to bargain effectively with the "new elite" running China, that is, the "unholy alliance" between cadre-mandarins and nouveau riche entrepreneurs. By 2005, quite a few senior cadres have at least indirectly admitted that peasants are discriminated against in the distribution of national resources. For example, Health Minister Gao Qiang noted that only 20 percent of medical funds and other resources were spent in rural areas.[165] Unless farmers have the political clout to alter the power equation, dispensations from on high, such as the abolition of agrarian taxes and so forth, can only be palliatives, not thorough solutions to the social injustice that is tearing apart the body politic.

More Disturbing Signs of Discontent

Things are not looking rosy for President Hu's pledges about being "close to the masses" and "running the administration for the sake of the masses." Despite the Hu-Wen team's reassurances about doing more for society's underclasses, there are growing signs of disaffection among disadvantaged sectors. Telltale signs of social discontent have included a proliferation of *xinfang* or *shangfang* (petitioning the authorities) cases as well as suicides. In 2003, the NPC Xinfang Office received around 58,000 petitions, up 10 percent from the year before. This, however, did not take into account local-level petitions—and the fact that grassroots officials invariably spent a lot of effort trying to prevent petitioners from going to Beijing. Head of the National Xinfang Office Zhou Zhanshun admitted in 2004 that "most of the petitioners have genuine grievances." Yet officials noted that barely 0.2 percent of petitioners were lucky enough to have their cases satisfactorily settled.[166]

As for suicides, official statistics showed that some 287,000 people took their own lives in 2003, with 2 million unsuccessful attempts. This means that every two minutes, one Chinese kills himself or herself while there are eight unsuccessful suicide attempts. While the per capita suicide rate in China is not the highest in the world, it is symptomatic of an uncaring government—and shockingly unequal distribution of income and resources. According to experts at the Beijing Psychological Crisis Research Center, more than 80 percent of the country's suicides are farmers, particularly female ones.[167] As the cases of self-immolation committed by victims of "urban clearance" have shown, many have tried to end their lives as an act of protest against gross unfairness in society.

Other Chinese who feel cheated by the system, however, are not so docile. Until the late 1990s, a disgruntled, newly laid-off factory worker might choose to vent his frustration by murdering his boss. Now, aggrieved citizens might air their grievances by committing "individual acts of terrorism" such as letting off explosives in a crowded place in a big city. In the summer and autumn of 2003, numerous cases of severe urban violence were reported. Real or fake bombs and other explosives were discovered in airports, supermarkets, department stores, and fast-food chains in cities including Beijing, Shenzhen, Guanghou, Nanjing, and Wuhan. Moreover, partly as a result of market reforms, it has become much easier for would-be urban terrorists to purchase and manufacture lethal weapons. For example, a bomb costs less than 30 yuan to make. Beijing's worst nightmare is that the terminally frustrated and disaffected could band together and form guerrilla-style urban terrorist groups.[168]

Also on the rise is the use of rat poison as a vehicle of "urban terrorism." Ten yuan's worth of Dushu Qiang, a cheap but potent rat poison, could kill hundreds of people. In September 2003, more than 400 pupils and teachers in a school in Yueyang, Hunan Province—and another 75 in a Guizhou Province school—were hospitalized after eating meals laced with Dushu Qiang. A year earlier in Nanjing, 42 people, mostly college kids, were killed with the same weapon. While government officials have not released casualty figures from rat poison, the China News Service reported that in a three-month period ending January 2003, police had investigated 585 cases of criminal rat poisoning.[169]

According to a late 2003 report in the official *Chinanewsweek,* "individual terrorist crimes" have posed a big threat to Chinese society. Means used by these quasi-terrorist felons—many of whom are members of disadvantaged and marginalized sectors of society such as the chronically unemployed—have included explosives, poison, arson, hijacking, and assassination. *Chinanewsweek* quoted noted Beijing-based scholar Hu Lianhe as saying that "social contradictions have been magnified because [traditional] social adjustment mechanisms and safety valves have lost their function." Hu cited the problematic judicial and court system, poor mediation efforts by official departments, and the inefficacy of the system of government units handling petitions from the downtrodden.[170]

Beijing Boosts Control Mechanisms

Scenes like the following are taking place with alarming frequency all over China. In the early hours of July 31, 2004, about 100 policemen and riot-control operatives from Zhengzhou, Henan Province, moved into Shijiahe Village in the city's outskirts in an effort to arrest eight peasants who had organized repeated petitions to provincial and central departments. It turned out that the Shijiahe Village Administrative Committee had more than a year ago sold a sizable chunk of land to a property firm for 40 million yuan. However, VAC officials refused to distribute the money. Shijiahe folks had somehow learned about the planned action of the police, who were soon surrounded by about 3,000 angry villagers. The law officers fired rubber bullets as well as tear gas at the mob. More than thirty peasants were wounded, six seriously.[171]

Even more than frequent "disturbances" in the countryside, what worries CCP authorities are so-called acts of urban terrorism that would not only cause large numbers of deaths but also damage China's international reputation. This was a major reason behind a series of anti-terrorist exercises in cities and provinces including Beijing, Guangzhou, Jiangsu, Henan, and Shandong, held by the PAP and other security units about one year after the September 11 incident. The ostensible objective of these maneuvers was to show the world that Beijing had the ability to handle unexpected incidents during major events such as the 2008 Olympics.[172] Yet their primary aim seemed to be preventing outbreaks of urban violence perpetrated by disgruntled workers and peasants.

Of course, Beijing has always insisted that major cities are susceptible to atrocious attacks from shadowy secessionist groups in or near the Xinjiang Autonomous Region (XAR) such as the East Turkestan Islamic Movement. However, both the army and the PAP had largely tamed underground pro-independence groupings in the XAR after two years of a heavy-handed crackdown that started in 2000— and XAR authorities had by 2002 again felt emboldened to invite foreign executives to talk business in the far-off region. After watching a PAP anti-terrorist war game in the outskirts of Beijing in early 2003, President Hu said China must "resolutely prevent and combat all types of terrorist activities so as to earnestly safeguard the security of the masses and world peace."[173] What was uppermost in the minds of Hu, Wen, and other Politburo members seemed to be what some Chinese publications called "quasi-terrorist crimes committed by individuals" who harbored grievances against the authorities.

The Hu-Wen team had by late 2004 come up with multipronged strategies to keep the forces of chaos at bay. Both the carrot and the stick have been beefed up. The first was to boost the strength of anti-terrorist groups within the PAP and ordinary police. More personnel with expertise ranging from disposing of bombs to foiling hostage-taking were being hired. Tens of thousands of officers handling high-tech crimes, including cyber-cops, have been added to the public security establishment. At the same time, Beijing would provide more channels for peasants and laborers who want to present petitions to provincial and central authorities. The leadership also decided to restructure the much-maligned *xinfang* system. Instead of petitioners going to Beijing, the new line of 2005 was that the CCP leadership would ask cadres of all levels to "go down to the grassroots" to listen to grievances. New *xinfang* regulations have more clear-cut provisions on punishing officials who caused the grievances in the first place. Moreover, the Ministry of Public Security has been asked to accept petitions from the people. NCNA noted that in 2005, police offices of all levels handled more than 200,000 cases of complaints and other special requests, which resulted in "the masses receiving nearly 160 million yuan worth of compensation."[174]

After a particularly serious spate of unrest of October and November of 2004—which included massive protests in Hanyuan County, Sichuan, against the construction of a dam and related hydroelectric facilities—Beijing decided to adopt a more flexible policy toward those who dared confront the authorities. Police and PAP officers were told to avoid direct confrontation with demonstrators—and to take a conciliatory approach unless force was absolutely necessary. As Politburo member in charge of law and order Luo Gan pointed out at a late-2004 meeting, cadres should "correctly handle contradictions within the people and maintain harmony and stability in society." And police forces must try harder to "ensure fairness and justice in society." Apparently referring to the Hanyuan protests, Luo indicated that local officials should fully assess whether a forthcoming policy "would tally with the fundamental interests of the masses."[175]

However, Luo, who has the image of an uncompromising disciplinarian, left it beyond doubt that Beijing would use all necessary means to crush anti-government activities. At the meeting, he urged *zhengfa* (political and legal affairs) cadres to "boost their ability to engage in the struggle against [state] enemies and to maintain national security." After all, the Politburo was convinced that a high proportion of the protests and destabilizing incidents in society were the result of "infiltration and instigation" perpetrated by hostile foreign forces as well as anti-socialist, "bourgeois-liberal" elements within China. As we shall see in the next chapter, however, the Hu-Wen team's apparent failure to realize that much of China's worsening sociopolitical malaise has its roots in the country's archaic, Leninist party-and-state system could mean that more repression by the police-state apparatus may invite more resistance from the angry masses.

4

The Scourge of Governmental Stagnation

The Price of Holding Up Political Reform

Real Political Reform Put on Hold

China accomplished substantial results in economic reform—particularly economic integration with the international marketplace—during the administration of Premier Zhu Rongji from 1998 to 2003. The highlight of this period was the PRC's accession to the World Trade Organization (WTO) in November 2001, which signaled the country's willingness to abide by global norms in business and commerce. Given the fact that, particularly for hinterland China, complying with WTO standards is a tall order, the principal mission of the leadership of President Hu Jintao and Premier Wen Jiabao in the economic field will not be so much hacking out new paths. At least in the term of office covered by the Sixteenth Party Congress—2002 to 2007—the Hu-Wen team will have achieved a lot if they can make sure that the entire country lives up to Beijing's pledges about market liberalization, particularly in the difficult areas of finance and information.

By comparison, the one area where the Hu-Wen leadership can break new ground—and make its mark in history—is political change. It has long been a truism that economic liberalization can only go so far without commensurate restructuring of the political system. Many of the residual problems in the economy, for example corporate governance, separation of business from the party-and-government apparatus, as well as corruption, are inextricably linked with political issues. Moreover, the coexistence of twenty-first-century economic norms and a governmental structure still burdened with Leninist-era strictures has created disharmonies and contradictions that threaten to plunge the nation into crisis.

As this chapter shows, Hu and Wen projected a reform-oriented persona almost immediately after becoming top leaders at the Sixteenth Party Congress of 2002. Hu began a much-publicized campaign to bolster rule by law. There was also a lively discussion of ways to improve *dangnei minzhu,* or "intra-party democracy." Wen applied himself assiduously to the task of further streamlining the administrative structure, particularly at regional levels. The media was opened up to some extent, particularly during the period of the outbreak of the SARS (severe acute respiratory syndrome) epidemic.

Signs of a reimposition of time-honored party control, however, began to come thick and fast in the second half of 2003. Labor activists instrumental in forming nonofficial trade unions, as well as traditional "pro-West dissidents," have been locked up or put under surveillance. A group of reformist thinkers and constitutional experts has been intimidated by secret police. And again, the authorities have slapped a straightjacket on the media. Cynics refer to the taboo areas off limits to journalists and intellectuals as the "three unmentionables": constitutional reform, political liberalization, and a reversal of the official verdict on the Tiananmen Square massacre. Some cadres and intellectuals in the Hu camp have tried to shrug off responsibility by insinuating that the "cold wind of conservatism" had originated from the remnant influence of ex-president Jiang Zemin and his Shanghai Faction. More objective observers, including the victims of state harassment, however, are insistent that the Hu-Wen team not only acquiesced in the new crackdown, but took an active role in it. Indeed, tough tactics against wayward and free-thinking scholars and writers intensified after Jiang left his last post of chairman of the Central Military Commission (CMC) in September 2004.[1]

Beijing's repeated procrastination regarding political modernization is a primary reason why the country finds it hard to gain the level of international respect and leverage that is commensurate with its economic, diplomatic, and military clout. *New York Times* China specialist Nicholas D. Kristof's assessment of the country—that it is "not Communist but fascist, in the sense of a nationalistic one-party dictatorship controlling a free-enterprise economy"—is typical of the views of Western observers. Veteran Sinologist Jasper Becker made a similar observation in an article in the *New Republic*. He drew parallels between today's China and Mussolini's Italy, including a dictatorial one-party state forming alliances with big, state-controlled businesses. Becker wrote: "China today is replacing communism with something at least as bad: it is becoming a right-wing fascist state eerily similar to 1920s Italy."[2]

This chapter will examine the cautious steps that the Hu-Wen leadership has taken in areas including grassroots-level elections, legal reform, eradication of corruption, administrative restructuring, and intra-party democracy. An explanation will be offered as to why Beijing has failed to go whole hog with sorely needed reforms despite the rising costs of such foot-dragging.

The Hu-Wen Team's Limited Vision About Liberalization

To date, Fourth-Generation leaders such as Hu or Wen have refrained from talking about sensitive issues such as a time frame for political reform. This is despite the fact that in internal discussion with his aides, Hu often referred to the imperative of timely liberalization of the political structure. For example, in an early 2004 meeting, Hu reportedly told his aides that "without political reform, we may well get stuck in a cul-de-sac." This was an echo of former patriarch Deng Xiaoping's famous exhortation in 1992. During his so-called imperial tour of the south in the summer of that year, the late patriarch famously said that "without reform, there is only one road—to perdition."[3]

However, both Hu and Wen are cautious to a fault in their assessment of far-reaching measures such as general elections. In his generally well-received speech at Harvard University in late 2003, Wen claimed that his administration was eager to "perfect the election system." However, he went on to say that while elections were already being held in 680,000 villages, "we do not have the prerequisites for holding higher-level elections." He cited the familiar reason that economic development in China was uneven and that "people's cultural qualities are not sufficient." Wen asserted that his administration would not stray from the right path if it continued to allow the people to supervise the government.[4]

Moreover, there is a heavy element of noblesse oblige in Hu's approach to democracy: this means that while the ruling party is open enough to consult the divergent views of different sociopolitical groupings, it is not ready to share power with them. This top-down orientation was evident even when Hu was still vice-president. While attending a Chinese People's Political Consultative Conference (CPPCC) meeting in 2001, the Fourth-Generation leader said that the Chinese Communist Party (CCP) must "take the initiative to accept the supervision of the democratic parties, and it must be able to listen to sharp criticisms."[5] (China has eight so-called democratic parties, which were formed in the early 1950s under the behest of the Communist Party. They are still under the tight control of the CCP United Front Department.) Through 2005, the party chief and president continued to define political liberalization in terms of platitudes such as "boosting multiparty cooperation under CCP leadership" and "improving the socialist legal system."

Partial Glasnost, But Hardly Any Perestroika

There is no mistaking the fact that in the first months after the Sixteenth CCP Congress, the Hu-Wen team made tremendous efforts in the areas of administrative reform and open government, while steering clear of more thoroughgoing political-reform measures such as popular elections and power sharing.

Soon after he became party general secretary in November 2002, Hu began working on what some analysts called Chinese-style glasnost. Hu and Wen started with gestures that are taken for granted in most other countries, for example, announcing the contents of just-ended or forthcoming party and government conferences. From the days of Mao to those of Jiang Zemin, most conclaves of top-level party meetings were shrouded in secrecy—with information made available only a long time afterward. From the Sixteenth CCP Congress onward, Hu and his colleagues made it a point to announce through the New China News Agency (NCNA) meetings of the Politburo as well as the rough agenda of each session.[6] NCNA and other state media also made public the dates of major conferences such as the National People's Congress (NPC) or the plenary session of the Party Central Committee well in advance. For example, it was made known in August 2003 that the Third Plenum of the Sixteenth Central Committee would be held in October, and that the main themes would be economic reform and the revision of the state Constitution.

Hu and Wen have also bent over backward to project the image of being "cadres of the masses." Thus, on the eve of Chinese New Year in 2003, Wen joined miners in northeast Liaoning Province for a subterranean dinner of simple dumplings. On New Year's Day 2005, the premier paid an emotional visit to a child whose father had died in the horrendous coal mine disaster in Tongchuan, Shaanxi, a few months earlier. And while visiting Hong Kong in mid-2003, Wen eschewed the presidential suite—usually *de rigueur* for CCP leaders—and went about town with his aides in a minivan. Starting with his trip to Russia in May 2003, Hu abolished send-off and welcome-back ceremonies for senior officials going abroad and coming home. The president later also did away with red-carpet welcome ceremonies when he inspected the provinces.[7]

Yet the Hu-Wen leadership's most dramatic gesture in breaking with the past was the decision to abolish the annual series of top-level meetings at the summer resort of Beidaihe. Given that in the Byzantine world of Chinese politics, symbolism is sometimes as important as the real thing, Hu and Wen have won plaudits on this from liberal cadres and academics.[8] Since the early 1950s, top CCP, government, and military officials—as well as party elders—had in the summer of most years repaired to Beidaihe, a choice strip of sand in nearby Hebei Province, to discuss affairs of state. Major decisions on policy as well as personnel were made during "informal discussion sessions"—often a euphemism for behind-the-scenes skulduggery and backstabbing—in luxurious beachside bungalows. And even though party elders were supposed to have retired from their party or state positions, they still exercised undue influence in Beidaihe's cunning corridors.

The abolition of Beidaihe, which reportedly incurred the ire of ex-president Jiang, was much more than a means to save money. As former Chinese Academy of Social Sciences (CASS) sociologist Lu Jianhua indicated, what was more important was a new style of doing things, "a new effort to regularize [government] procedures and institutions." Other Beijing-based academics noted that the cancellation of the Beidaihe conferences was testimony to Hu's determination to curtail rule of personality and to run the party and country according to law and institutions.[9]

The Hu-Wen Team's Checkered Record on Liberalization

According to Bao Tong, a former aide to ousted party chief Zhao Ziyang, the Hu-Wen administration has demonstrated "a new style, but not yet a new policy." Bao, still under twenty-four-hour surveillance for his alleged role in supporting student demonstrations in May and June 1989, pointed out that the Hu team have been more efficient and effective in their administration than the ancien régime under

Jiang. "They have shown a concern for the masses," said Bao. "However, there have been no substantial changes in terms of policy and institutions."[10]

Bao's assessment is by and large correct. Partisans of the Hu-Wen team have argued, with some justification, that the Fourth-Generation leaders and their reformist colleagues have displayed a zeal unseen in the Jiang era for researching and making ready tentative initiatives in liberalizing the political structure. Some steps, albeit ginger ones, have been taken in areas including improving rule by law, promoting an accountability system in the civil service, freeing up the media, and inner-party democracy.

Yet there seems little doubt that the new leaders will not go the distance in liberalization. This is despite early signs that they might be more sympathetic toward "taboo" issues such as revising the official verdict on the suppression of the 1989 democracy movement. In late 2002, quite a few Beijing intellectuals were encouraged by the so-called Li Rui incident. In the run-up to the Sixteenth Congress, Li, a liberal intellectual and former secretary of Mao Zedong, had circulated a petition urging a reversal of Beijing's view that the democracy crusade was a "counter-revolutionary turmoil." Because of his status as a party elder, Li took part as an observer in the closing session of the Sixteenth Congress. It was a time-honored custom for the newly elected Politburo members to acknowledge the support of all participants. According to sources close to the conclave, Hu shook Li's hands warmly. The new party chief even said he had read his letter to the *dangzhongyang* (party central authorities). This was widely interpreted as a symbolic gesture that Hu, Wen, and their allies were eager to show that they had an open mind.[11]

Then there was the case of military doctor Jiang Yanyong, the now-famous whistle blower whose statements to the Western media in early April 2003 forced the government to admit to lying about SARS figures (see following section). Dr. Jiang's message was that there were hundreds of SARS cases in the military hospitals alone—not the single digits reported by Beijing officials. This led to the CCP leadership finally coming clean on the statistics—and to the sacking of two ministers for SARS-related cover-ups. However, the untold story about Dr. Jiang was that from late 2002 onward, he had written to party authorities asking for the reversal of the June 4, 1989, verdict. For at least a brief period around June 2003, Dr. Jiang was on the cover of several official magazines and newspapers. His "positive treatment" by the state media gave encouragement to fellow campaigners for overturning the June 4 verdict.[12] Equally significantly, the treatment of Bao Tong seemed to have improved during 2003. The dissident's friends said the number of intelligence officers shadowing Bao had decreased substantially so that the old intellectual could at least move about the city with less impediment. His "minders" were also less hostile after Bao had published articles in the Hong Kong press.[13]

The tide, however, had turned by early 2004. In the summer of that year, Dr. Jiang was detained for two months for circulating an open letter that gave his eyewitness account of the June 4 atrocities—and urged the CCP to come clean on its 1989 massacre. In addition to stepping up control over Dr. Jiang, state security personnel boosted surveillance over Bao. This was apparently owing to the authorities' suspicion that it was Bao who had given encouragement to his old friend Dr. Jiang. At a press conference in early June, the Foreign Ministry spokesperson used the relatively neutral term "important historical incident" to refer to the June 4, 1989, events. Yet there was no indication that the Hu-Wen team would be willing to revise the verdict even after the Seventeenth CCP Congress scheduled for 2007.[14]

Things went from bad to worse toward the end of 2004, when Hu apparently shed his pro-intelligentsia mask and cracked the whip on recalcitrant scholars and writers. The supremo gave his imprimatur to an ideological campaign against "pro-Westernization" academics, writers, and journalists who wanted a faster pace of political liberalization. In a throwback to earlier campaigns against "bourgeois liberalization," commissars in the CCP Publicity Department blasted the intellectuals for "propagating the wrong ideas of the West." A document that was circulated in November that year accused advocates of "new liberalism" of trying to undermine the socialist foundations of the party and government.[15]

Notable scholars and social crusaders under attack by Beijing's censors and commissars included Mao Yushi, Wen Tiejun, Zhang Sizhi, Gao Yaojie, Li Yinhe, Liu Junning, and Yu Jie. Mao and Liu, both respected and much-published scholars, had urged "within-the-system" democratization, while law professor Zhang was widely acclaimed for his contribution to legal reform. Wen and Gao were well known overseas for their tireless campaign for the rights of peasants and AIDS victims. State security also arrested several journalists, authors, and freelance commentators for allegedly endangering state security and leaking state secrets.

No "Western-style" Liberalization: A Moratorium on Universal-Suffrage Elections

Despite their *yiren weiben*, or "putting people first" campaign, it is noteworthy that neither Hu nor Wen has expressed sympathy for universal-suffrage elections, the most direct and reliable way through which ordinary citizens' wishes can become policy. A clear distinction can be drawn between Hu and Wen on the one hand, and predecessors such as Zhao Ziyang and Bao Tong on the other. Together with liberal colleagues such as Hu Qili and Bao, Zhao had in the mid-1980s—well before the fall of the Berlin Wall—laid down fairly concrete plans to expand and upgrade the one-person-one-vote polls being conducted in different villages all over China. Other liberalization measures on Zhao's agenda had included truncating the powers of the party, as well as promoting checks and balances at the highest levels of the party and state apparatuses.[16] With Hu and Wen, however, "Western-style" reforms have hardly emerged on the radar screen.

The Controversy over Expanding Village-level Elections

By 2004, village-level elections, where peasants select members of the ruling village administrative committees (VACs) via universal-suffrage polls, had become a viable institution all over China. Early that year, some 110 million people cast their ballots to choose the leaders of 145,000 VACs. More than 90 percent of the nation's 680,000 VACs were chosen via popular elections. The official NCNA claimed that "in the great majority of villages, the masses have picked leaders they are happy with."[17]

As of 2005, conditions of rigging and other forms of unfairness still existed in many villages. For example, the influence of clans and even secret or triad societies remained strong. Nouveau riche businessmen were also in a position to buy votes either directly or through proxies (see Chapter 6). Above all, village-level CCP committees still wielded tremendous influence in the nomination of candidates for VAC posts. At the same time, more and more unorthodox, fairly independent candidates had beaten "official" candidates favored by the party authorities. Take, for example, the poor, rural Baoyuesi Village outside the city of Zhijiang, Hubei. Veteran peasant organizer Lu Banglie outpolled the official candidate during the election for VAC head in April 2004 despite strong opposition from party and police authorities. Lu credited his unexpected victory to the fact that he had led numerous petitions to Beijing to protest against heavy taxation slapped on the village. He also tried to impeach the corrupt VAC chief in 2003, as a result of which he was badly beaten by paid thugs.[18]

Examples such as the Baoyuesi Village elections have shown that this experiment with limited democratization introduced by late patriarch Deng in 1979 reached a relatively high level of maturity. Apart from village-level polls, there are direct elections of the heads of neighborhood committees in urban areas—as well as the similar polls to pick deputies to county-level people's congresses (and deputies to district-level PCs in urban areas). Yet because neighborhood committee chiefs and county-level parliamentarians wield relatively little power, it is the possibility of expanding and upgrading village-level polls to higher levels—to enable the masses to directly pick the heads of townships (zhen), rural townships (xiang), and even counties—that has attracted domestic and international attention.[19]

According to CASS scholar Bai Guang, the upgrading of village-level elections to higher administrative levels was nothing far-fetched. Bai, usually not identified as a radical modernizer, said Deng had pointed out in the 1980s that it was possible for nationwide direct elections to take place within fifty years. "Once the affairs of a village are well run, it is feasible for [elections] to be pushed up to the level of townships, counties, cities, and even provinces," he said in mid-2003. Bai added that quite a number of NPC and CPPCC members had called on the authorities to institute direct elections up to the county level.[20]

Indeed, by the early 2000s, a large number of reformers were urging that the heads of the country's 20,226 townships and 18,064 rural townships be voted into office via universal suffrage. This would be a big step forward from the usual practice of cadres in the CCP Organization Department at the provincial level recommending candidates for township chiefs, who would then be confirmed by county-level people's congresses. Liberal officials including Wang Huning, who had advised both Jiang and Hu, had at one point or another argued for the incremental extension of universal-suffrage polls from the village to the township, county, and municipal levels. For example, a rough timetable laid out in 1998 by the Policy Research Office of the party Central Committee envisaged the direct election of the heads of townships by 2003, mayors by 2008, provincial governors by 2013, and certain national-level positions by 2018.[21]

A bold experiment was carried out by reform-minded officials in Buyun township under the city of Suining, Sichuan Province, in December 1998, when about 6,200 voters in the eleven villages that made up the township cast ballots to pick the township chief. A few days after the landmark poll, the official *Legal Daily* branded the election illegal and unconstitutional in an apparent bid to discourage other areas from following suit. However, Sichuan officials were not penalized by the CCP Organization Department, and the elected township head, Tan Xiaoqiu, was allowed to keep his post. The experiment of township-level elections spread to other areas of Sichuan—and to other provinces including Guangdong, which is adjacent to the Hong Kong special administrative region.[22]

However, the pendulum had swung toward conservatism in mid-2001, when the Organization Department came up with a circular banning the ballot box at levels higher than that of the village. The document said existing regulations about selecting township and county chiefs must be followed, meaning that CCP cadres handling personnel issues must retain their dominant say in appointments. The circular stated that one-person-one-vote elections at the township level were not in line with the Constitution. Instead, township bosses must be endorsed by local people's congresses.[23]

At the time of the document's circulation, Beijing was nervous about extending the polls to townships and rural townships out of fear of losing control and causing instability. Both central and provincial leaders underscored the imperative of maintaining stability at grassroots levels ahead of the Sixteenth Party Congress to be held a year later. Yet even after the congress had ushered in the Hu-Wen team, these Fourth-Generation leaders have hardly demonstrated any enthusiasm for pursuing this important reform. This was despite the fact that units and think tanks believed to be close to Hu, such as the CCP Central Committee Editing and Translation Bureau (CCETB), had continued to do research on higher-level elections. For example, CCETB cadre Yu Keping, also a political scientist at Peking University, indicated in late 2003 that experiments in grassroots-level democracy had gone on unabated. His colleague, Lai Hairong, added that in pace-setting provinces such as Jiangsu, Sichuan, and Hubei, the chiefs of many townships and rural townships had been indirectly elected into office by the equivalent of "electoral colleges." The latter consisted of a few thousand local personalities who were considered more in tune with public opinion than Organization Department cadres, who used to handpick candidates for these regional posts with minimal public consultation.[24]

Polls higher than those at the level of villages have continued to be held haphazardly, and in isolated areas in provinces including Sichuan, Hunan, and Yunnan— particularly those that had been exposed to similar experiments in the late 1990s. For example, Buyun residents in Sichuan held an election in December 2001 despite apparent official disapproval. After two weeks of campaigning, incumbent Tan Xiaoqiu beat rival Tan Zhibin by 527 ballots. After the balloting, Tan was confirmed as township chief by the local people's congress. Local cadres said victor Tan was reported to the higher authorities as the only candidate that was recommended by the township-level CCP committee.[25]

However, the 1999 one-person-one-vote election of the head of the town of Dapeng, close to the Shenzhen special economic zone, was not repeated. According to a report by a group of Shenzhen University academics, while the economic and education levels of Dapeng residents were higher than those in Buyun, Sichuan, "there was no commensurate enthusiasm for taking part in politics [among Dapeng residents]." The scholars noted that most of the 6,000 eligible voters in Dapeng were more interested in making money than in political reform. By contrast, the experiment in Buyun has continued because the elected leaders, including Tan, have succeeded in bringing concrete benefits to the people, who have tied their well-being to the polls.[26]

These experiments culminated in mid-2003 in the direct election of the head of Pingba Township in the outskirts of Chongqing. Given that Chongqing had been named a directly administered city, Pingba has a ranking higher than that of ordinary provincial townships. The initiative came from reformist local party secretary Wei Shengduo, who had done research on grassroots balloting. The 10,000–odd Pingba residents were about to pick front runner Ma Menglin, a dedicated teacher, to be their first freely elected leader. Yet the polls were nullified on August 29, the day of the election, by the party leadership of Chengkou County, which oversees Pingba. Wei was later fired for violating election laws. However, according to Beijing-based scholar Li Fan, examples such as the Pingba polls would encourage other places to follow suit despite Beijing's negative attitude toward such experiments. Thus seven towns and townships under Shiping County, Honghezhou District in Yunnan, held direct elections of top administrators in early 2004. Any resident could become a candidate after securing the signatures of thirty villagers; and in one township, eighteen candidates vied for the post of township chief. Party secretary of Honghezhou Luo Chongmin admitted that his colleagues had faced "great pressure" in the course of the elections.[27]

By the early 2000s, it had also become fairly normal for independent and "unofficial" candidates to run for grassroots-level legislative seats, such as deputies to county- or district-level people's congresses. The first generation of such atypical candidates consisted of private entrepreneurs who had made a name for themselves in local communities as major employers and philanthropists. Most of these "red bosses," however, had also gained the recognition and blessings of CCP organs—and they were running as party-sanctioned candidates.

Balloting for People's Congress members in Futian District, Shenzhen, in early 2003 was one of the first local-level legislative polls where an unofficial candidate beat the party-nominated one. The Guangdong media said technical college principal Wang Li'ang, one of six independent candidates, had won because of his "good background" and his service to the community. Wang, who had a master's degree in public administration from the University of California, was also believed to have the requisite international outlook. In the same year, two independent candidates in Beijing also won seats on the municipal legislature despite not having official blessings. The successful candidate representing Haidian, the famous college district, was law lecturer Xu Zhiyong. Xu had won fame for publicly opposing China's draconian system of administrative detention. While the authorities certainly did not favor the vocal academic, he had the support of the scholastic and student communities.[28] By late 2005, however, the Hu-Wen team had given no indication of any plans to upgrade the elections on a regular basis or on a large scale.

Hu's Conservative Views About "Western-style" Elections

Since Western governments and influential nongovernmental organizations (NGOs) such as the Atlanta-based Carter Center had begun scrutinizing village-level polls in China in the mid-1990s, senior cadres were careful about offering the right spin on why they had dragged their feet on electoral reform. The usual party line was that China could only move on to higher-level polls when those at the grassroots— including the election of village heads as well as county- and district-level parliamentarians—were run to the satisfaction of the authorities.

According to cadres at the Grassroots-Level Government Construction Department (GLGCD) of the Ministry of Civil Affairs, many villages even lacked proper buildings to serve as polling stations. This meant that the latter could not even set up booths to ensure secret balloting. "Secret ballots are important as they can minimize vote-buying," said Zhan Chengfu, deputy director of the GLGCD's Rural Villages Section. New regulations were issued banning candidates from privately visiting voters ahead of elections. "Candidates' interaction with voters should be done in public and at open forums," Zhan added. "We have told voters that those candidates who give you 50 yuan for a vote will likely embezzle 50,000 yuan in public funds after they are elected." The department vowed to send more discipline- and propaganda-related officials to supervise village-level polls.[29]

These wary views reflect the conservatism of the Fourth-Generation leadership. Cautious to a fault, President Hu has seldom given the public a clear-cut vision of political reform. However, Hu dropped some hints about his opposition to direct polls while meeting with a group of leading U.S. academics in early 2002. When the American Sinologists asked the then vice-president about prospects for grassroots-level elections, Hu pointed out that experience in many villages had shown that peasants usually voted along "clan" lines. This meant, Hu said, that villagers surnamed Hu would more likely than not cast their ballots for candidates with the same surname.[30] The impression the Fourth-Generation stalwart gave was that one should not put too much hope on elections as a vehicle for improving China's political system and culture.

As discussed in Chapter 2, Hu and Wen seem convinced that "scientific governance and decision making" can be attained in the absence of trappings such as Western-style elections and multiparty politics. To improve the quality of government decision making, top leaders have increased the frequency of consultation with members of elite groups such as scholars, think tank members, businessmen, and professionals. And as we shall discuss, the Hu-Wen team has limited the frame of reference of reform to administrative streamlining and rationalization as well as "intra-party democracy."

The conservative views of the Fourth-Generation leadership have been indirectly criticized by liberal intellectuals. Thus Peking University legal scholar Cai Dingzhao blamed the authorities for professing "confusing theories" to deny the people chances for higher-level polls. Professor Cai indicated that since late Qing Dynasty, even reformers such as Liang Qizhao and Dr. Sun Yat-sen had cited this so-called backwardness argument for not considering universal-suffrage ballots: "China's economy and culture are too backward; the people's quality is too low— and therefore it won't do to hold extended direct elections. Otherwise China will be plunged into chaos." Cai argued that improvements in economic and education standards under Deng's reforms had rendered the country suitable for far-reaching experiments with higher-level polls.[31]

Hu-style "Political Civilization": Rule by Law and Checks and Balances

Almost immediately after becoming party chief in November 2002, Hu laid out in a series of internal meetings the outlines of what he called *zhengzhi wenming*, or "political civilization." It could be interpreted as ways and means to modernize the political system and improve administrative efficiency without introducing Western democratic institutions. According to sources familiar with Hu's talks, the party chief wanted to sustain one-party rule through "laws and proper institutions and procedures." First, officials and citizens alike must respect the Constitution and the law. Party and government operations should be governed by well-defined rules, institutions, and procedures—and not subject to the whims of individuals. Relations among party and government departments should also be determined by sets of clear-cut regulations in order to achieve fair play, efficiency, and some degree of checks and balances.

At the same time, party cadres would be given more say in determining policies and regulations, even in choosing their leaders. This was the idea behind Hu's promotion of the ideal of *dangnei minzhu,* or "intra-party democracy." Hu and Wen also want more openness of governance and media reform—glasnost with Chinese characteristics—so that the decisions and performance of party and government units can be subject to the people's scrutiny. This section will concentrate on Hu's introduction of the concept of rule by law—and the promotion of some form of popular supervision of the government.

Rule by Law Under One-Party Dictatorship

Respect for the Constitution and the Law

Perhaps taking inspiration from the Legalists in the ancient Era of the Spring and Autumn, Hu has tried to base his new order on rule by law. This concept is to be distinguished from the familiar Western ideal of rule *of* law. What the Hu-Wen leadership has in mind is "rule by law with Chinese characteristics" because Chinese law will always reflect the decision and spirit of the party leadership. When Wen was asked by foreign reporters in early 2004 whether the party is above the Constitution and the law, the premier replied, "the party leads the people in the formulation of the Constitution," and said that party leaders and ordinary members would "set an example in complying with the Constitution."[32] In other words, unlike Western jurists and journalists, party leaders see no contradiction in Chinese-style rule by law on the one hand, and party leadership in the formulation of the Constitution and the law on the other. At the very least, however, the Hu-Wen administration must ensure that the statutes are honored by cadres and ordinary people alike.

Soon after becoming CCP general secretary, Hu initiated the equivalent of an ideological campaign to safeguard the sanctity of the Constitution and the law. This was the theme of the first "Politburo study session" that was called in December 2002, when all members of the ruling council listened to the lectures of two famous professors of law, Xu Chongde and Zhou Yezhong. "We must uphold the basic strategy of ruling the country according to law," said Hu on the occasion. "We must further raise the entire society's consciousness regarding the Constitution as well as the authority of the Constitution." Significantly, Hu linked the ideal of "administration according to law" to the oft-stated goal of "strengthening and improving party leadership."[33]

That Hu intended to wield the weapon of legalism was first evident in an address he made soon after the Sixteenth Congress to mark the twentieth anniversary of the promulgation of the 1982 Constitution. The party chief pointed out that "no organization or individual has special privileges to override the Constitution and the law." "The Constitution has promoted the construction of our country's socialist democracy," he added. "We must uphold the basic principle of running the country according to law." And in his first international press conference after the 2003 NPC, Wen cited "administration according to law" as a major initiative in political reform. "Government departments and civil servants must carry out their duties according to the Constitution and the law," the premier said. Wen elaborated his legalistic viewpoint in a State Council meeting of July 2004. "We must exercise power according to the limits and procedures imposed by the law," he said. "Our power must be subject to scrutiny; we must pay compensation if we infringe upon the [legal] rights of citizens. Those [civil servants] who run afoul of the law must be penalized according to law."[34]

Some political analysts saw a political—and factional—reason behind the Hu-Wen team's newfound interest in constitutionalism. They pointed out that one message behind Hu's legalistic offensive was that ex-president Jiang and his cronies had violated the spirit if not the letter of the law through their blatant power grab in the past few years. The former president's overweening ways were evident when he refused to step down from the chairmanship of the military commission —or when he filled a good proportion of the Politburo with Shanghai Faction affiliates—at the Sixteenth Congress.[35]

Whatever hidden agenda the Hu-Wen leadership might have in promoting rule by law, there is evidence that some results have been achieved. And this is not only demonstrated by the number of new laws being enacted by the NPC. Many of the newly enacted statutes and regional-level regulations reflected the leadership's commitment to base government behavior on legal precepts. A case in point was the Wen cabinet's speedy decision to roll out relevant legislation to fight SARS, and more importantly, to promote public health infrastructure and consciousness throughout the country. Wen said the administration must use "legal weapons" to fight SARS. In May 2003, the State Council passed a set of "Emergency Regulations on Public Health Incidents" to provide the legal framework for implementing quarantines and other health measures.[36] And in the area of "Chinese-style glasnost," different provinces and cities also enacted rules and regulations on ensuring government transparency and safeguarding citizens' "right to know."

The Case of Sun Zhigang and Changes in Regulations on
Administrative Detention

The Hu leadership's relatively brisk handling of the Sun Zhigang tragedy gave hope to intellectuals that the leadership was more committed to legal reform than previous administrations. However, the same incident also showed that China had a long way to go before an embryonic form of rule by law could be established. A native of central Hubei Province, Sun had been legally employed in Guangzhou, capital of Guangdong, as a graphic designer when he was detained by police one night in March 2003 for being a "vagrant." The only mistake of the twenty-seven-year-old—who was a gifted art student at a Hunan college—was forgetting to carry his residence permit while going to an Internet cafe. Yet officials at the Guangzhou detention center refused to let him contact his colleagues.[37]

The next day, Sun said he was ill, and he was taken to a nearby police clinic. He died soon afterward, with the postmortem showing injures caused by repeated rounds of severe beating. The Sun case merited special attention because going by past standards, similar instances of abuse of power by police were considered so routine that his maltreatment would not have made it to the local press. The nation had 833 detention centers for "vagrants and beggars." Apart from routinely roughing up members of the "under classes," center staff practiced all manners of extortion and blackmail. For example, detainees could be kept for long periods unless their relatives agreed to pay an agreed-upon "ransom" of at least several hundred yuan.[38]

Partly due to the outcry of his father and co-workers, Sun's plight caught the attention of intellectuals and journalists in Guangdong—and later dozens of prominent academics in Beijing. In a petition to the NPC, three Beijing-based law professors said Sun's detention was a violation of the Constitution and the law. Sources familiar with the Sun dossier said a couple of Politburo Standing Committee (PSC) members including President Hu and Luo Gan were alerted to the case—and Guangzhou was forced to start investigations. In early June, a Guangdong Province court slapped hefty jail terms on eighteen people accused of causing Sun's death. It was obvious that such a swift course of justice would not have been possible without intervention from the very top.

It was also clear, however, that not enough was done to bring the culprits to justice. Most of the eighteen who received jail terms of ten years or more were fellow inmates in the police clinic who were ordered by public-security and clinic officials to beat Sun up for alleged insubordination. The police officer who wrongfully detained Sun in the first place was let off lightly with a two-year jail term. And just before the trial, twenty-three Guangzhou officials, including high-level police and public-health cadres who administered the detention system, were merely given reprimands by party and government departments. There were other questionable practices by local law-enforcement agencies. Reporters were barred from the court. And Guangzhou authorities tried to silence the victim's relatives after giving them a compensation of about 500,000 yuan.[39]

Not long afterward, the Hu leadership won widespread plaudits for at least partially addressing concerns raised by the legal scholars. In late June, Beijing abolished the "Regulations on the Detention and Deportation of Vagrants and Beggars in the Cities," which was the supposed legal basis for locking up—and mistreating—vagrants and transient workers such as Sun. Introduced by government units in 1982, the regulations had never been passed by the legislature. Professor Xu Zhiyong, one of the petitioners, argued that the rules were "inconsistent with the Constitution and the laws," which at least in theory uphold citizens' civil liberties. In response to the academics' request, the leadership unveiled a new regulation called "Administrative Means to Help Vagrants and Beggars in Cities Who Have No Means of Livelihood." The Ministry of Civil Affairs converted all the 833 detention centers into Stations for Providing Succor and Help. And it was estimated that they could provide aid to 2 million people a year.[40]

Apart from the mistreatment of vagrants, there are scores of different government regulations or practices that violate globally accepted human and civil rights. Professor Xu and other legal experts wanted the Hu-Wen team to start abolishing or revising all unconstitutional laws and regulations. Examples included the *laogai* (reeducation through labor), a kind of punishment determined and administered by police authorities without court authorization. Moreover, public security authorities could hold criminal suspects for an indefinite length of time without putting them through the judicial process. It was not until late 2004 that the legal authorities decided to put restrictions on administrative detention. A proposed revision of the criminal code would stipulate that suspects for criminal offenses could not be held by police for more than thirty days. Moreover, the Supreme People's Court announced at about the same time that it had gone through nearly 900 cases of excessively long detentions, which affected about 2,500 people. It was presumed that some of the illegally detained suspects had either been released or put on trial in the courts.[41]

It is clear, however, that the restrictions on the maximum length of time that police and other law-enforcement agencies can hold suspects do not apply to "political dissidents," who continue to be incarcerated for days on end. Moreover, the notorious reeducation through labor system, which is also a form of administrative detention, has remained intact. More significantly, there are still clauses galore in the Constitution that are regularly breached. Examples include constitutional guarantees of freedom of assembly, speech, and religion. The outspoken Catholic Bishop of Hong Kong, Joseph Zen, for instance, has argued that the persecution of underground churches in the mainland has violated constitutional guarantees of freedom of faith.[42]

Constitutional Reform in 2004

In mid-2003, the CCP Politburo set up a six-member high-level committee to look into the modernization of the Constitution. The main task of this Leading Group on Revising the Constitution (LGRC) was to lay the groundwork for a thorough updating of the charter at the NPC plenary session in March 2004. The committee was dominated by stalwarts of the Jiang Zemin or Shanghai Faction who lacked a track record of reform. It was headed by NPC chairman Wu Bangguo, a former Shanghai party secretary and a long-time Jiang crony. Other members included the conservative Director of the CCP Publicity Department Liu Yunshan as well as Jiang's former speechwriter, Teng Wensheng. It was understood that one of Wu's main goals was to enshrine Jiang's "Theory of the Three Represents" in the state charter.[43]

The thirteen amendments to the 1982 Constitution were passed almost unanimously at the 2004 NPC plenary session. While this major move was much anticipated by domestic and foreign observers, the revision fell short of expectations in many ways. As anticipated, the "Theory of the Three Represents" was cited as a guiding principle of the state. The charter confirmed the legal status of private and nonstate capital as well as private-sector economic activities, adding that "the legal private properties of citizens shall not be violated." It also spelled out the importance of a social security system. And for the first time, the Constitution indicated that "the state respects and protects human rights."[44]

The constitutional revision reflected heated lobbying by various sectors, particularly the fast-growing private-business sector. However, the new charter fell short of guaranteeing the general principle of the "inviolability" of private capital and properties. For noted constitutional scholar and activist Cao Siyuan, the CCP leadership had failed to take advantage of the revision exercise to modernize many outdated concepts and practices in the body politic. Cao, who became famous for his role in introducing a law on bankruptcy, had drafted detailed proposals for constitutional reform in early 2003. For example, he wanted to abolish the opening clause of the charter, that China is a socialist country where "the people's democratic dictatorship" is being exercised by workers and farmers. "The idea of 'dictatorship' is way behind the times," Cao said. "It contradicts the spirit of the WTO and the requirements of globalization."[45]

Four revisions proposed by Cao were aimed at protecting people's rights. Cao, who had often lectured in U.S. and European universities, wanted a stipulation that "citizens' rights override everything—and that governance must be open and transparent." He argued that human rights comparable to those enshrined in international covenants must be included. "The new constitution should specify that no organization or individual can interfere with the judiciary and the due process of the law," said Cao. He also suggested that the NPC establish a constitutional court or a parliamentary commission to ensure that laws and government practices do not violate the supreme charter.[46]

By mid-2004, the Chinese parliament had established an Office for Adjudicating and Inspecting Laws and Regulations (OAILR), which had authority to check whether government departments and regional administrations had violated the Constitution. However, as University of Politics and Law professor Jiao Hongchang pointed out, this office could only make recommendations for future improvement—and was different in nature from a Western-style constitutional court that liberal academics had suggested.[47] By global standards, a constitutional court has enough authority to challenge the legality of a nation's highest executive organ, something that the OAILR could not do. It seems clear, however, that the Hu-Wen team has no desire to bring about major constitutional changes.

Imperfections in the Legal and Judicial Systems

Even if Hu is able to pull off most of his initiatives, he will only have achieved Chinese-style rule by law—not rule of law in the Western sense of the phrase. This is because the Communist Party will still be the big boss behind the NPC and the courts. As former NPC chairman Li Peng liked to say, "the legislature is formulating laws according to the will of the party." This meant that there would always be a higher authority over the Constitution and the law.[48] The clearest manifestation of the principle of "the party being above the law" was the enshrinement of the "Theory of the Three Represents" in the state charter. After all, this "important theory" is a party dogma that has relevance only for the 70 million CCP members; and it cannot be construed as a state philosophy that purports to govern the behavior of 1.3 billion Chinese. As political analyst Meng Lingwei noted in an essay posted on various Beijing-based academic Internet sites, it was "neither fish nor fowl for the Theory of the Three Represents to be considered as a guiding principle in the country's most important charter."[49]

Perhaps to ensure party leadership over the legislature, ex-president Jiang began in the early 1990s the practice of so-called cross leadership of both the party and regional party congresses. The controversial experiment had become the norm by the Sixteenth CCP Congress, after which all save seven of the thirty-one regional party secretaries doubled as the chairmen of the provincial or municipal people's congresses (PCs). In theory, cross leadership means that the status of provincial and municipal legislatures would be raised due to the seniority of the PC chief. In practice, this would result in local parliaments being subservient to the party bosses.[50]

According to an internally circulated party document on this subject, the practice of "cross leadership" had at least two merits. The first was that since local-level PCs served as a "people's chamber," the party-secretary-cum-PC-chief would have ample opportunity for feeling the pulse of public opinion. The other advantage was to ensure that China would not slip into the "Western trap" of developing a "tripartite division of power." After all, leaders including Deng and Jiang had warned that China would not opt for the clear-cut division of powers among the executive, legislative, and judicial branches of government.[51]

Equally problematic is the nature and function of one of the party's oldest and most powerful institutions, the *zhengfawei,* or Political and Legal Affairs Commission (PLAC), currently headed by Luo Gan. The PLAC has jurisdiction over law-enforcement and judicial organs such as the police, procuratorates, and in particular, the courts. That the party is riding roughshod over the judicial system is deemed unconstitutional by liberal observers because the CCP charter as revised at the Sixteenth Congress said explicitly that "the activities of the party must be within the boundaries of the Constitution and the law."[52] That the very existence of the PLAC flies in the face of the most basic demands of political reform was pointed out by a thirty-five-year-old scholar based in Hunan Province, Zhang Yinghong. In an article widely circulated on the Internet in mid-2003, Zhang said the superior status of the PLAC went against internationally recognized norms of legal governance. "Various levels of law courts are faced with the dilemma of obeying the Constitution or obeying the PLAC," he wrote. "Very often, the courts have become a hostage of the PLAC."[53]

While Zhang's views certainly raised eyebrows among orthodox party members, similar opinions had been aired before—and by none other than former party chief Zhao Ziyang. Zhao, who was deposed after the June 4, 1989, crackdown, began fine-tuning the PLAC system in 1987 and 1988 for the simple reason that some semblance of an independent judiciary was essential to even Chinese-style political reform. Zhao began dismantling several provincial and municipal-level Political and Legal Affairs Committees with a view to eventually abolishing the PLAC altogether.[54] Such reforms were mothballed after 1989. Indeed, in an interview with the official China News Service in December 2004, a spokesman of the Research Office of the Supreme People's Court stressed that "reform of Chinese courts must be based on China's national conditions"—and that there was no question of copying the Western model of the "tripartite division of power."[55]

Checks and Balances with Chinese Characteristics

Supervision by the Masses

In his first public address after becoming state president in March 2003, Hu indicated that his administration was committed to "developing democracy and doing things according to the law." He went on to add that the CCP leadership would "synthesize [the principles of] party leadership, the people being masters of their own country, and ruling the country according to law." Integral to Hu's gentler, kinder—more legalistic and mass-oriented—new order is close scrutiny of government performance by the people.[56]

Clearly, rule by law and socialist democracy would not be possible without some form of supervision by the people. While no Western-style universal-suffrage elections were anticipated, Hu's pledge that "the people will be masters of their own country" meant they would have some degree of oversight regarding the performance and integrity of senior cadres as well as civil servants. This was why Wen emphasized at the 2003 NPC that "the government will self-consciously accept the supervision of the People's Congress, the masses, and the media."[57]

Given that the leadership has already ruled out the ballot box, however, there are no established channels for the CCP's top echelon to talk to the people. One of the few institutions is regular consultation with "friends of the party" such as members of the eight so-called democratic parties and members of the Chinese People's Political Consultative Conference. Thus Premier Wen pointed out in mid-2003 that the State Council was formulating an internal "work procedure" for consultation with the nonparty elite. "Before making major decisions, the State Council will directly listen to the views and suggestions of the democratic parties, masses' organizations, experts and academics," Wen said in a meeting with leading members of the eight democratic parties. "The idea is to fully develop democracy, open up channels for expressing [divergent] views, and broadly adopt good policies."[58]

Despite the many public relations–oriented pictures that Hu and Wen have taken with workers and farmers, there are no mechanisms for regular exchange of views with proletariats. It is true that party and government departments conduct frequent public opinion surveys on what ordinary Chinese think about domestic and foreign policy. Hu and Wen also have a habit of going online to look at the views expressed in popular Internet chat rooms. And senior officials of ministries and departments—with the exception of those handling state security—have been instructed to attend online discussion sessions to explain policies to the public.[59] Yet the Fourth-Generation leadership has basically stuck to a top-down approach in their consultation exercises.

At the regional level, a number of provinces and cities have made it easier for citizens to attend regular—usually monthly—meetings of local-level people's congresses. For example, the Xian People's Congress decided in mid-2003 to allow all residents of the city to attend its sessions, and the agenda and relevant information would be publicized in the municipal press at least ten days earlier.[60] Ways that the masses exercise some form of supervision over the government include scrutiny by the media and *mingaoguan,* or ordinary folks taking legal action against the government (see following sections). It is unlikely that the Hu-Wen team will experiment with bolder forms of "popular supervision" in the foreseeable future. For example, there are no plans to encourage NGOs to contribute to policy save in less sensitive areas such as environmental or consumer protection (see Chapter 6).

Mingaoguan: *Ordinary Folk Suing the Government*

One of the more colorful instances of supervision by the masses is *mingaoguan,* or ordinary people taking the government to court over infringement upon their economic and civil rights. Such actions had become possible with the introduction in 1991 of the Law on Administrative Procedure Litigation, which allowed citizens to challenge certain types of decisions and actions by government departments. There were about 500,000 cases of individuals suing the government in the five years ending in 2002. And according to the Supreme People's Court, the number of such cases had jumped tenfold from 1991 to 2001. Moreover, the "success rate" of ordinary people winning court battles against officials is rated as high. In 2002, plaintiffs won 71.39 percent of the cases while the comparable figure was 64.07 percent a year earlier.[61]

By the mid-2000s, the variety of issues involved in *mingaoguan* cases had increased dramatically. These range from travelers suing semi-government-owned airline companies in the wake of excessively long delays to candidates in civil service exams taking a government personnel department to court for alleged discrimination. In a much-publicized case in 2003, Zhang Xianzhu of Wuhu, Anhui Province, successfully sued the local personnel department for not hiring him despite his top performance in the civil service exams. Zhang claimed that the official reason for turning him down—that he was a carrier of the hepatitis B virus—amounted to deprivation of his constitutional rights.[62]

Beijing has also allowed, if only grudgingly, citizens to take legal and other actions against people's representatives who do not make the grade. Thirty-three civil rights–minded Shenzhen residents made history in 2003 when they filed a petition to impeach an elected deputy to the People's Congress of the city's Maling District. The disgruntled citizens claimed that newly elected deputy Chen Huibin was not doing his job properly, thus "constituting a threat to the properties and safety of the masses." According to Du Gangjian, a scholar at the NPC head office, there was ample room for "innovative changes in democratic institutions" in Shenzhen. Du indicated that relevant sections of the Election Law needed to be beefed up to clarify the rights and obligations of both elected officials and deputies—and those of their constituents.[63]

Most analysts see the *mingaoguan* phenomenon as a step in the direction of democracy and rule by law. Yet as *People's Daily* writer Wang Bixue points out, many officials still regard *mingaoguan* as efforts to challenge their authority and prerogatives. Wang writes that many officials "think litigation against the government will result in the latter losing prestige and credibility—and the end result may be loss of government efficiency and even social instability." Moreover, there are growing reports on courts refusing to take up the cases, particularly of farmers who harbor grievances against local administrations. People's University legal scholar Xiao Jianguo noted in 2005 that "the number of people who succeed in filing cases against the government is miniscule."[64]

So far, the *mingaoguan* phenomenon has perhaps helped ordinary people most in two related areas. One consists of farmers taking local governments to court for misappropriation of their land. The other is related to litigation undertaken by urban residents who are unhappy over the meager compensation accorded them after they were forced to vacate their homes for urban renewal. That the law courts have failed to a considerable extent to mete out justice—and come to the rescue of the downtrodden—is evident from the large number of demonstrations and riots staged by displaced peasants and urban residents. That *mingaoguan* has hardly become an established institution is also clear from the many cases of activist lawyers being harassed by the authorities.

Checks and Balances Within the System

Compared to Zhao Ziyang and his fellow reformers, Hu and Wen have not articulated very clear concepts about checks and balances—or division of power—between party, government, military, and other units. Hu was apparently against the enshrinement of the principle of the separation of party and government in either the state or the CCP Charter. Since Hu had assumed both party and state powers, this step might lead to a dilution of his own authority and prerogatives. And personnel movements up to early 2005 confirmed that Hu had largely followed Jiang's "the party is supreme" principle by letting party apparatchiks—rather than technocrats or professional managers—run the country.[65] By contrast, both Deng and

Zhao were hardly reticent about their advocacy of the separation of party and government. Thus Zhao's now-famous Political Report to the Thirteenth Party Congress in 1987—which was endorsed by the late patriarch Deng—urged a gradual "retreat of the party" so that the CCP would concentrate on broad principles and policies and not involve itself in the nitty-gritty of governance.[66]

Some progress has however been made toward a limited degree of checks and balances for certain party and government functions. Take the labyrinthine and highly secretive *zhengfa* (political and legal) establishment, which is CCP shorthand for the departments having to do with law enforcement, state and public security, graft busting, and the judiciary. Before the current Politburo was established in late 2002, one or at most two Politburo or PSC members were given neartotal control of the *zhengfa* system. This was the case of former PSC member Wei Jianxing and his predecessor Qiao Shi. At the PSC elected into office at the Sixteenth Congress, however, Wu Guanzheng was appointed secretary of the Central Commission for Disciplinary Inspection (CCDI)—the highest anti-graft watchdog—while Luo Gan became PLAC secretary. And newly appointed police chief Zhou Yongkang was the first police chief in twenty-five years to have Politburo status. Moreover, the veteran minister of supervision He Yong, who also has responsibility for promoting clean government, was given a slot in the party Secretariat.[67] Since these four *zhengfa* heavyweights come from different factions in the party, a modicum of checks and balances will hopefully be accomplished.

At the same time, the new "elitism" espoused by the Hu administration—inducting more qualified intellectuals and professionals from disparate backgrounds into government and even party positions—could make for some form of checks and balances within the system. Traditionally, top cadres are picked from among young men and women with bona fide "red" backgrounds, namely workers, farmers, and soldiers. Even the recruitment of *haigui pai,* or returnees from abroad, for senior party and government posts would serve the purpose of making the governing system more pluralistic.[68]

The Significance of "Intra-Party Democracy"

While *dangnei minzhu* ("intra-party democracy") will in theory only affect the 70 million or so CCP affiliates, it will over the longer term have ample significance for overall political reform. At least in his "first term" of 2002 to 2007, Hu is expected to hack out new paths in this less controversial area of liberalization.[69] To some extent, intra-party democracy is the equivalent of the president and party chief's quest for constitutional and legal reform: there must be well-established institutions, rules, and procedures within the CCP—and they must be followed. Intra-party democracy is also being promoted to guarantee Hu's legitimacy, and to prevent his enemies, namely the Shanghai Faction, from using extraconstitutional and extralegal means to lay ambushes. A Hu aide indicated that the president had learned the lesson of the way in which Hu Yaobang was unceremoniously and illegally cashiered in a so-called party life meeting held in January 1987. Sources close to the Hu camp said the party chief liked to tell intimates that in theory, he could be deposed by just five senior cadres, that is, in the event that a majority of the nine PSC members expressed no confidence in the general secretary over a "grave error" in either domestic or foreign affairs.[70]

Hu also wanted to undo the perceived damage that Jiang and his chief lieutenant Zeng Qinghong had done to party institutions and regulations in their bid to fill a large number of central and regional posts with Shanghai Faction affiliates. From the mid-1990s to 2002, when Zeng assumed control over the personnel and related portfolios in the CCP, the Jiang troubleshooter had masterminded frequent reshuffles of major provincial and municipal slots with a view to strengthening the Shanghai Faction's regional network. Regional personnel "musical chairs" under Zeng were markedly more frequent than those in previous years.[71]

Much of Hu's philosophy was sounded out by Central Party School professor Gao Xinmin in the official journal *Chinanewsweek*. Writing on *dangnei minzhu,* Gao, who specializes in the theory of party construction, noted that it was necessary to boost collective leadership "so as to strengthen restrictions on [how] individual leaders exercise power." Gao argued that more power, particularly that relating to appointments, should be vested with bodies such as party congresses or entire party committees. "It will not do to let a minority of cadres select [candidates for top posts] from a minority of candidates," Gao wrote.[72] While it was not sure whether Gao was targeting Jiang and Zeng, these views were fairly typical among reform-oriented cadres.

Democratic Reforms Within the CCP

Certainly *dangnei minzhu* did not begin with the Sixteenth CCP Congress. General Secretary Hu, who has been in charge of "party construction" pretty much since 1992, has for several years asked his protégés and associates in institutions such as the Central Party School (CPS) to do research on improving democracy within the Communist Party.[73] Quite a number of liberal intellectuals have argued that the CCP should reform itself along the lines of Japan's Liberal Democratic Party (LDP). For these Chinese cadres and academics, the Japanese model means that while the decades-old party has remained Japan's predominant party, the LDP has incorporated quasi-democratic institutions that can guarantee its longevity and relevance. For example, there are time-tested check-and-balance mechanisms. Factions—usually named after major leaders—are not only allowed but regarded as a normal phenomenon of politics. Most importantly, the cliques compete openly on relatively clear-cut platforms—and not through the kind of backstabbing and bickering characteristic of CCP factionalism.[74]

Several CPS-sponsored surveys of the views of regional-level officials in 2001 and 2002 showed that most cadres were dissatisfied with the concentration of powers at the top: namely, that the party secretary of a province or city has too much power over matters ranging from policy to personnel. A number of cadres proposed that more authority be vested with the entire provincial or municipal party committee—or at least, the Standing Committee of these party organs. These reform-oriented cadres pointed out that eventually, a provincial or municipal party secretary should be elected into office by all party members of that province or city. Since the party secretary of a city or province is the highest authority in that region, this reform, if properly carried out, would have national significance.[75] In early 2002, a breakthrough was reached in Guangdong Province whereby the entire provincial party committee—around seventy senior cadres—cast their ballots to pick the heads of counties and district commissions (a district commission oversees several counties). Until this experiment, the party secretary of Guangdong as well as one or two Standing Committee members of the party committee in charge of organization had had well-nigh absolute power over appointments.[76]

Also in 2002, several avant-garde intellectuals proposed the idea of a "tripartite division of powers" among the Congress of Party Deputies (*dangdaibiao dahui*), the Central Committee as well as the Politburo, and the CCDI. In a tradition going back to Chairman Mao's days, a Congress of Party Deputies is called once every five years to elect a Central Committee; and the Central Committee in turn elects the Politburo and the CCDI, the party's highest disciplinary and anti-corruption organ. A similar arrangement takes place in the provinces, cities, and counties.

According to the CCP Charter, the Congress of Party Deputies, Central Committee/Politburo, and CCDI should be parallel units with equal authority—and there should be checks and balances among them. In fact, the Constitution says policymaking powers should rest with the party congress—and the Central Committee/Politburo should merely be an executive organ. In practice, however, all power has gone to the Politburo (and under Jiang Zemin, the Politburo Standing Committee) while the party congress is dissolved once it has fulfilled the function of electing Central Committee members once every five years. Moreover, the CCDI is often under the control of the party general secretary. Restoration of some form of checks and balances among these top organs will help prevent the overconcentration of powers in the hands of a few top cadres.[77]

Some inchoate steps along these lines have been taken in a few provinces such as Zhejiang and Sichuan. In three cities in Sichuan—Ya'an, Meishan, and Zigong—the municipal *dangdaibiao dahui,* or congress of party deputies, was in 2003 not dissolved after they had completed the basic task of picking members of the local party committee. Instead, it was decided that congress deputies should meet every year—and they could, at least in theory, be convened on an ad hoc basis—to exercise supervision over the municipal party committee. Moreover, if ten or more congress deputies raise a motion about a local problem, the party committee is duty-bound to carry out investigations and to compile a report. The *dangdaibiao dahui* can also carry out assessment of the work of the local party secretary and his senior colleagues.[78]

According to the Vice-Head of the CCP Party History Research Office Li

Zhongjie, the experiment of *dangdaibiao dahui* setting up permanent organs such as secretariats should be extended. Li pointed out that permanent party-congress secretariats had been established in eleven localities in Sichuan since the late 1990s. The academic indicated that the practice of party congresses meeting at least once a year would enable party members to exercise scrutiny and supervision over leading cadres. "This is good for the systematization and regularization of *dangnei minzhu,*" he added. By the end of 2004, permanent *dangdaibiao dahui* offices had been set up in provinces including Shandong, Shanxi, Guangdong, Guangxi, Jiangsu, and Hubei.[79]

Reaction Against the Preponderance of Party Hacks

An important party-reform issue that the Hu-Wen team has to grapple with is rectifying the tradition, begun by ex-president Jiang and former head of the Organization Department Zeng Qinghong, of career party functionaries making career gains at the expense of professional and less ideologically inclined administrators and managers. Two main reasons were behind this development. One was Jiang's insistence on party supremacy—and on the credo of "putting more emphasis on politics." The other was that the so-called Jiang Zemin or Shanghai Faction was strongest among apparatchiks and assorted party-affairs specialists. And it was in the interest of the Shanghai Faction to bolster the clout of party affairs and ideology specialists.[80] At least five out of the nine members of the PSC elected at the Sixteenth Party Congress distinguished themselves as CCP functionaries rather than ministers, governors, or mayors. Jiang Faction–affiliated party hacks who made it to this supreme ruling council included Huang Ju and Jia Qinglin. Huang and Jia's lack of a track record in economic reform had not stood in the way of their elevation.[81]

The full twenty-five-member Politburo also had a much higher percentage of apparatchiks than the previous one. A record twelve party secretaries of provinces and directly administered cities—including the former and current party bosses of Shanghai and Beijing—were inducted to the elite body at the Sixteenth Congress. By contrast, only three ministers from the State Council, or central government apparatus, made it to the Politburo. They were State Councilors Wu Yi and Luo Gan and the minister at the State Development and Planning Commission, Zeng Peiyan. It was not surprising that Premier Zhu Rongji had privately griped about the advancement of party affairs specialists at the expense of ministers. He reportedly complained that while officials such as the minister of finance or the central bank president were among the highest ranked in most countries, the new Politburo had no place for Finance Minister Xiang Huaicheng or then governor of the People's Bank of China Dai Xianglong.[82]

Party functionaries also had a field day in the spate of post–Sixteenth Congress reshuffles. A notable example was the new party boss of Guangdong, Zhang Dejiang, a former party secretary of Zhejiang Province. As the number one official of China's most market-oriented province, Zhang's brief was seen as enhancing the competitiveness of the Pearl River Delta in the face of challenges from the Greater Shanghai region. However, Zhang, a graduate of Pyongyang's Kim Il-Sung University, had handled ideological matters most of his career. And while Zhejiang had developed reasonably well under his tenure, Zhang's orthodox views about the private sector had cast doubt on his suitability for the Guangdong post. For example, in early 2001, he wrote an article in the conservative journal *Huaxia Forum* entitled "We Must Make It Clear That Private Businessmen Cannot Be Enrolled in the Party."[83]

In lower-level administrations, it has also become easier for party secretaries to land senior government jobs. For example, in the past, professional administrators such as heads of departments of municipalities had a good chance of being made vice-mayors or mayors. Under Jiang and Zeng, however, the party bosses of counties and prefectures had pride of place so far as the race up the career ladder was concerned. Political analysts see this as a ploy by Zeng and his allies to fill slots in both central and regional administrations with Shanghai Faction affiliates. "During his tenure as premier, Zhu Rongji was largely successful in vetoing the appointment of party functionaries as ministers or vice-ministers in the State Council," said a Western diplomat. "However, Wen Jiabao, who has a weaker power base in the party and government, may have to acquiesce in the party Organization Department's bid to install party affairs specialists in a number of important government posts."[84]

The rise of party hacks has caused widespread concern among reformist cadres, particularly in light of the high likelihood that Hu will repeat the same mistakes by elevating a large proportion of his cronies and former underlings from the Communist Youth League (CYL). Not unlike Jiang's protégés, most members of the so-called CYL Clique are party functionaries and specialists rather than professional administrators (see Chapter 7). The trend of favoring CCP apparatchiks in senior appointments goes against the teachings of late patriarch Deng, one of whose biggest contributions to political reform was the theory of the separation of party and government.[85]

Concrete Gestures to Democratize Party Procedures

Excitement about the possibilities of intra-party democracy were raised in the run-up to July 1, 2003, when the leadership celebrated the eighty-second birthday of the CCP. There were expectations that Hu would use the occasion to lay out a road map for *dangnei minzhu*. At least according to the first draft of Hu's address, the party chief and president would recommend that there be greater competition in the course of the selection and appointment of senior cadres. For example, mid- to senior-ranked posts would be filled through elections in which members of the party committees of particular jurisdictions would be allowed to cast their ballots—instead of having the decision made by a higher-level CCP Organization Department and endorsed by the top party secretary of the relevant level. Such experiments would amount to a drastic improvement over the principle of "democratic centralism" advocated by both Lenin and Mao.[86]

The words "intra-party democracy," however, did not even show up in the speech delivered by Hu. Instead, the party boss merely dwelled on the need to study the hackneyed "Theory of the Three Represents." As he had done since November 2002, Hu had given Jiang's pet theory his own twist by putting the emphasis on the "serve the people" credo. However, Hu's failure to offer anything concrete on *dangnei minzhu* was a disappointment for the advocates of reform, and this spelled at least a temporary setback for the Fourth-Generation stalwart.

A major obstacle to fast-paced *dangnei minzhu* had come from the camp of Jiang Zemin, who thought that excessive talk about reform smacked of "bourgeois liberalization." This way of thinking seemed to underlie a series of instructions that the director of the CCP Publicity Department, Liu Yunshan, gave to media units in June that year. Citing remarks made privately by the ex-president, Liu told media-related cadres to raise their guard against "people who are taking advantage of the outbreak of SARS to spread bourgeois liberalization." "Bourgeois liberalization," a code term for Western political ideals, had rarely been used since the late 1990s. Moreover, Jiang took advantage of the still-powerful position of the Shanghai Faction to launch yet another ideological campaign based on "a more thorough study of the Theory of the Three Represents." From mid-year, articles and seminars about the Three Represents easily crowded out calls for democracy within the party.[87]

Irrespective of whether Hu was indeed forced to make a tactical retreat, efforts related to achieving the *dangnei minzhu* goal were still being made at least in the provinces. Take, for example, Sichuan Province, which had also pioneered township-level elections. The official *Chinanewsweek* magazine reported in July 2003 that the appointment of not just grassroots-level party secretaries but also department heads in the province could only be confirmed after all standing committee members of relevant party committees had cast their ballots. Until changes introduced in the spring of that year, personnel decisions were made by the provincial Organization Department upon the endorsement of a few bigwigs on the Sichuan CCP committee.[88] And in early 2004, little-known Pingchang County, Sichuan, became the first area in China where party members freely elected the party secretary and vice–party secretaries of its nine towns and rural townships. This experiment had the blessings of top county officials, who used to have the power to appoint the party chiefs of the county's subordinate towns and townships.[89] The test for the Hu-Wen team seemed to be to ensure that such reforms would go beyond a few pioneer provinces to the rest of the country.

Hu and his colleagues made an important gesture toward *dangnei minzhu* as well as checks and balances by regularizing the institution of the Politburo giving a periodic report to the Central Committee. In a departure from history, the Third Plenum of the Sixteenth Central Committee in late 2003 began with a report delivered by the Politburo to the Central Committee. According to the official *Outlook* magazine, this gesture signified that Politburo members would submit themselves to the "oversight and supervision" of the 198 Central Committee members. Moreover, Hu indicated in the summer of 2003 that the procedure of the Politburo reporting to the Central Committee must be followed in lower-level administrations. This meant that in Guangdong, for example, the Standing Committee of the Guangdong party committee must periodically report to the entire provincial party committee. Central Party School professor Ye Duchu said this was a testimony of Hu's determination to "further develop *dangnei minzhu* and to boost the energy of the Communist Party."[90]

On the surface, Hu's decision was nothing out of the ordinary. Since the Politburo was elected into office by the Central Committee at the Sixteenth Congress in November 2002, it would seem logical for the top decision-making body to report periodically to the Committee. Yet Hu's seemingly pedestrian decision amounted to a breakthrough for *dangnei minzhu*. Jiang, who was party chief from 1989 to 2002, had pulled out the stops to render the Central Committee—and often, even the Politburo—irrelevant. Power was concentrated in the hands of the five-man Politburo Standing Committee, and sometimes in Jiang himself, along with a handful of trusted aides such as then party organization chief Zeng Qinghong.[91] Political sources in Beijing said Hu was keen to establish some degree of checks and balances among party organs such as the Politburo, the Central Committee, the CCP Congress (which elects the Central Committee every five years), and the party's anti-graft watchdog, the CCDI. For example, by ensuring that the Politburo reports to the Central Committee—and that the CCDI will have some semblance of independence—dictatorial decision making and personality cults could be avoided.

Dangnei Minzhu *at the Fourth Central Committee Plenary Session*

After establishing the principle of a "Politburo responsibility system," which means that the Politburo must at least in theory submit itself to the supervision of the Central Committee, Hu was thinking of going one step further at the end of 2004. One reform proposal that was put forward to the party chief in mid-2004 consisted of delineating the functions of the Central Committee (CC), the Politburo, and the Politburo Standing Committee. According to past practice, particularly the thirteen years under Jiang, the PSC is the supreme decision-making body; the Politburo a repository of power and authority; and the CC a council representing *minyi*, or the will of the "masses." More liberal academics and party theoreticians, however, wanted the following changes: power and authority should reside with the CC; the Politburo will be the decision-making organ; and the PSC a body for execution and implementation of the decisions made by the Politburo.[92] These liberal cadres and thinkers also wanted the *dangdaibiao*—the 2,000–odd deputies who cast their ballots to set up a new CC once every five years—to have some consultative and supervisory role to play. Under the proposed schema, the *dangdaibiao* would be the repository of party members' *minyi*. And in a 2004 article, the Chinese-run Hong Kong daily, *Wen Wei Po*, quoted party theoreticians as saying that the *dangdaibiao* should meet at least every year so as to exercise supervision over top party organs. These experts suggested that the experiment be popularized at the county level before being tried out at the municipal, provincial, and national levels.[93]

As with other *dangnei minzhu* initiatives, Hu's goal was to dilute the powers of strongman-like figures—and to boost collective decision making as well as responsibility. With the PSC turned into a body for implementing the decisions of the Politburo and the Central Committee, it will be much more difficult for the general secretary to build up an empire or to behave in a dictatorial, Mao-like manner. Just as importantly, the Central Committee, whose membership may likely be significantly increased at the Seventeenth CCP Congress in late 2007, could be playing a more proactive role in policymaking and supervision of the Politburo.[94]

Quite a few stalwarts from the Shanghai Faction were reported to have opposed Hu's proposed changes on the grounds that if sufficient power were not concentrated in the PSC or at least the Politburo, factions would emerge, particularly if there were as many as 400 CC members. Several Hu aides have countered by saying it may not be a bad thing to have factions, provided that arguments between them are rendered transparent. They added that competition among the factions might have the effect of improving, instead of disrupting, decision making.[95]

While Hu's more ambitious plans such as transforming the *dangdaibiao* congress into a regular institution—and expanding the powers of the CC—might still face opposition, there seemed little doubt that by mid-2004 a consensus had been reached for injecting more democratic elements into the appointment of senior cadres. CPS professor Liang Yanhui noted in an article in the official *Fortnightly Chat* magazine that the appointment of cadres should be rendered more transparent. Referring to the mythical equestrian trainer Bai Le, famous for his ability to pick the best horses, Liang argued that the party "must replace the system of having a Bai Le pick horses with a 'horse-racing model,'" where the best cadres would distinguish themselves through competition. Moreover, she added that the system of "a minority of senior cadres doing the picking" should be replaced by "a majority of cadres taking part in the selection" of officials for new posts.[96]

The political report that was endorsed at the Fourth CCP Plenum, entitled Resolution on Strengthening the Construction of the Party's Governance Ability (hereafter Resolution)—which fully reflected Hu's thinking and instructions—has been rightly criticized for putting excessive emphasis on upholding the age-old "the party is supreme" principle (see Chapter 7). However, the party chief did for the first time salute the overriding importance of *dangnei minzhu,* and point out specific ways to enhance democratic institutions within the party. It affirmed the generally progressive slogan of "scientific administration, democratic administration, and administration according to law." "Developing *dangnei mingzhu* is an important component of the reform of the political structure and the construction of political civilization," the Resolution said. The document added that the party must "resolutely oppose and prevent dictatorial actions by individuals." Perhaps with the impending departure of ex-president Jiang from his last post of CMC chairman, the new paramount leader had relatively more leeway to talk about ways to curtail the "rule of personality."[97]

The subsection entitled "Enhancing Reform of the Personnel System" played up the significance of "democratic recommendation and democratic appraisal" of cadres. Most importantly, Hu backed the still-controversial experiment of having members of the entire party committee of a local-level administration—for example, a province or a county—cast ballots to pick leading cadres within that jurisdiction. The Hu-drafted Resolution also indicated that the so-called margin of elimination in *cha'e* elections, where candidates outnumber the posts up for grabs, could be expanded to boost the element of competitiveness.[98]

At the same time, the Fourth-Generation leader talked openly about establishing the right kind of checks and balances among top CCP organs including the *dangdaibiao* congress, the Central Committee, the Politburo, and its standing committee. "We should enthusiastically explore ways and formats through which *dangdaibiao* can play their roles when the congress is not in session," the Resolution said. Hu endorsed experiments conducted by certain cities and counties, notably in a number of medium-sized cities in Sichuan, to establish permanent organs for *dangdaibiao*.[99] No less significant is the fact that Hu has, albeit in a roundabout fashion, made some concessions to the principle of the separation of party and government. While insisting that party committees of all levels should make decisions on "major objectives and policies" and that they should "fulfill their functions as the leadership core," the Resolution recommended that day-to-day handling, particularly of economic matters, should be left to government departments. Specifically, Hu pointed out that overlapping party and government units should be slashed or merged, and that "the number of vice–party secretaries at the regional level should be decreased."[100]

The Resolution also recommended, if only in general terms, how disciplinary-inspection units at different levels could better perform their job of cracking down on corruption and other misdemeanors. One suggestion put forward to participants of the Fourth Plenum was that the *zhengfa shuji*, or member of a regional party committee in charge of legal, disciplinary, and anti-corruption matters, should not report to the party secretary of the same committee; instead, the anti-corruption specialist should report either to the party secretary at a higher level or to the CCDI itself.[101]

There are reasons to believe that positive signals on *dangnei minzhu* released at the Fourth Central Committee Plenum have had a beneficial impact at least on individual aspects of political reform. Take, for example, Hu's concern for introducing some form of competition and election for picking regional officials. By the end of 2004, practically all party cadres at the level of mayor, municipal party secretary, and head of district commission (a district commission oversees several counties) in Sichuan and Jiangsu provinces were selected by the entire members of the provincial party committee (PPC). Moreover, the PPC members, numbering up to around eighty, cast secret ballots instead of merely coming up with a "voice vote." In the past, a few leading members of the PPC's Standing Committee, namely the party secretary and Standing Committee member in charge of organization, had a dominant say in picking lower-level cadres.[102]

Administrative Reform Under One-Party Rule: Boosting Efficiency and Elitism

Administrative reform—defined roughly as increasing efficiency of governance, bureaucratic streamlining, and expanding the basis of one-party rule by inducting more members of the elite into ruling circles—will be a major focus of the Hu-Wen team's agenda for limited political reform. Both ex-president Jiang and Hu are keen to promote so-called elitism, meaning absorbing members of the "new classes," including professionals and returnees from abroad, into the civil service. Moreover, administrative reform tallies with the post-WTO accession imperative of running China largely according to international norms.[103]

While discussing the prospects of political reform in China, Jiang said in an internal meeting in early 2002 that he did not favor the Western model of democracy. According to a politics scholar and member of Jiang's personal think tank, the former president had a high regard for the "elitist" systems in Singapore and Malaysia. He added that the major thrust of reform should consist of the popular selection—under the criteria and supervision of the CCP—of well-educated, professionally qualified elements to fill senior posts. "We have confidence in picking a whole new corps of young, professionally qualified, reformist, and [politically] trustworthy cadres," Jiang reportedly said.[104] "Jiang wants a formula that will combine one-party rule and an efficient, elitist cadre system drawn from relatively broad sectors of society including non-CCP members," the politics scholar pointed out. He added that building a new cadre system could be one of the few major political-reform initiatives in this decade.[105] The ex-president's preference for an elitist cadre system is shared by Hu and Wen.

Further impetus toward "semi-Western-style" administrative reforms was given by incidents ranging from the SARS epidemic to preparations for the 2008 Olympics. SARS forced China not just to conform to the public health criteria of the World Health Organization; many aspects of government behavior as well as the drafting and promulgation of regulations—particularly those having to do with economic and business matters—will have to be rejiggered to fit global norms (see Chapter 6). The same is true to some extent for the much-anticipated Beijing Olympics and the 2010 World Fair in Shanghai. For example, tendering and bidding for the bulk of infrastructure projects for these two events has been handled according to international standards.[106]

Open Recruitment of Officials

Key to expanding the base of the ruling elite as well as improving efficiency are experiments with open recruitment of cadres, as distinguished from their appointment by the CCP Organization Department. While no concrete timetables have been finalized, the leadership is leaning toward letting a sizable percentage of mid- to high-ranking government posts—and some party slots—be filled through public examinations. Organization Department chief He Guoqiang pointed out in mid-2004 that more senior positions should be made available to well-educated people, including non-party members and returnees from abroad. "We must enthusiastically explore the possibility of selecting and promoting non-party talent from new social strata as well as returnees from abroad for leading positions," he said in a national conference on personnel issues.[107]

The official NCNA reported in June 2002 that since 1995, more than 1,000 officials with ranks of vice-head of department or above—and more than 10,000 officials with ranks of vice-head of office—had been recruited through open exams. By 2003, about 700,000 civil servants nationwide had been hired through competitive exams. Jiangsu pioneered the practice of asking short-listed candidates for relatively senior posts to take oral exams in front of TV cameras. Thus, in September 2004, several thousand applicants took exams to contest twenty-two posts with ranks equivalent to the vice-head of provincial departments. Jiangsu party secretary and rising star Li Yuanchao said open recruitment "should be carried out on a regular basis and over a wider range."[108]

And there were signs that such recruitment exercises were attracting better-qualified applicants. In Guangdong, 13.5 people were competing for one civil service job in 2003; the ratio was 9.75 to 1 six years previously. Moreover, a lot more candidates with master's or doctorates are applying for relatively junior civil service jobs. According to one proposal for speeding up this process, one-third of all positions at the level of bureau and department head in provinces and cities should by the late 2000s be openly recruited.[109] Experiments so far conducted in several Guangdong cities have yielded interesting results. In applying for the posts, which are advertised in newspapers, CCP members are at least in theory given no preference over non-party members. In addition to a written exam on professional knowledge, candidates must sit for an oral test on political skills. Guangdong authorities have asked a number of "people's representatives," mostly deputies to local-level people's congresses and people's political consultative conferences, to be oral examiners. A Shenzhen official familiar with civil service reform said if the experiment with mid-ranking officials was successful, a proportion of cadres at the level of vice-minister and vice-governor could toward the end of this decade be selected through public examinations and other open channels.[110]

The authorities have also taken a liberal view toward the hiring of the so-called *haigui pai,* or returnees from abroad. Often, those with advanced degrees from U.S. and Western universities have been given "fast-track" positions with prospects for unusually speedy elevation. In 2001, Beijing picked veteran Hong Kong lawyer and banking regulator Laura Cha to be a vice-chairman of the China Security Regulatory Commission (CSRC), a position with vice-ministerial status. Moreover, in the wake of the Closer Economic Partnership Arrangement (CEPA) between Hong Kong and most mainland provinces and cities, more regions have sent head hunters to recruit Hong Kong professionals. So far, Shanghai and Shenzhen have stood out as the two cities that have hired the largest number of Hong Kong talents. For example, in mid-2004, fifty-one government units sent representatives to Hong Kong to hire sixty advisers and sixty-seven senior managers.[111]

Civil Service with Chinese Characteristics, and a "Cadre Responsibility" System

Adopting Elements of the Western-style Civil Service

Apart from open recruitment, Beijing is keen to incorporate other elements of a Western-style civil service under the premise of one-party rule. First, Beijing is eager to adopt the principle, observed with success in Singapore and Hong Kong, of "using high salaries to ensure clean government." For three years from 1999 to 2002, Beijing earmarked about 80 billion yuan annually for pay raises for its 45 million cadres and civil servants. Moreover, individual provincial and municipal governments are paying salaries in the hundreds of thousands of yuan a year to attract top talent. For example, the Jilin provincial administration has offered to pay top information technology (IT) personnel 200,000 yuan a year.[112] Whether the relatively high pay has effectively curtailed corruption, however, is open to question.

Second, stricter rejuvenation—and retirement—guidelines and regulations are being implemented for posts below those of Politburo members. In early 2002, two senior cadres, head of the State Economic and Trade Commission Sheng Huaren and Minister of Science and Technology Zhu Lilan, stepped down at the age of sixty-five. Under past practice, since their five-year tenure had begun in early 1998, Sheng and Zhu would have been able to serve until 2003. The Hu-Wen administration decided that as far as possible, more cadres in their mid-to-late forties would be considered for vice-ministerial-level positions, while more cadres in their early fifties would be made ministers. Analysts have pointed out that one factor prompting ex-president Jiang to retire from his last remaining post of CMC chairman in September 2004 was the groundswell of opinion among cadres and party elders alike that a seventy-eight-year-old should no longer remain in such an important position as commander-in-chief.[113]

The authorities are also working on an efficient and equitable system for assessing the performance of officials. Traditionally, incompetent officials can only be gotten rid of—or, more often than not, transferred to a less important province or portfolio—by the Organization Department. And while the department carries out frequent assessments of cadres, the appraisals often have to do with the officials' compliance with ideological, not professional, standards.

According to a party source, the new administration was considering the option of setting up a "scientific" appraisal system in every ministry, province, and city along the lines of a quasi-public tribunal. "Ideally, the tribunal should have a good proportion of nonofficials, including academics, people's congress deputies, and professionals from different fields," the source said. At the same time, various cities have started asking cadres to put down performance pledges—or lists of objectives they hope to achieve in a given year. Officials deemed to have repeatedly failed to fulfill such pledges would have to go.[114] Moreover, senior cadres at both the central and regional levels will be held to account if officials they have appointed turn out to be corrupt or to have made major errors in policymaking or implementation. This was part of the "Regulations on the Appointment of Cadres" released in early 2004. However, senior cadres can get off the hook if it can be proven that errant officials whom they had recommended only started to turn bad after their appointment, or that the mistakes they had made were due to "objective" circumstances.[115]

A Cadre Responsibility System

Former premier Zhu Rongji began in the late 1990s to introduce a cadre accountability system to, in his words, "protect the masses' property and safety and to maintain social stability." Particularly targeted were cadres responsible for *tofu* (literally "bean-curd," or shoddy) engineering projects and officials whose dereliction of duty had led to accidents with large casualties. Various provinces have come up with measures to get rid of bumbling cadres. For example, officials in Anhui who for three years in a row scored poorly in assessment tests would be subject to disciplinary action. In early 2001, CCP secretary of Jiangxi Province Shu Huiguo was demoted after an explosion in a peasant school that killed about forty students. A month later, Shaanxi governor Cheng Andong was reprimanded for a series of mishaps, including a stampede among tourists visiting the famed Huashan Mountain, in which 103 people were killed.[116]

The SARS outbreak provided a good excuse for the Hu administration to push a tougher and more thoroughgoing responsibility system. A milestone in administrative reform was reached in April 2002, when the Politburo Standing Committee decided to fire two senior cadres in connection with SARS: Health Minister Zhang Wenchang and Beijing mayor Meng Xuenong. Zhang and Meng were cashiered not just for failing to control the epidemic in the capital but for hiding information from the World Health Organization and the public.[117] In the same month, the Ministry of Personnel and the Ministry of Supervision sent out nationwide documents saying that officials who had failed to take adequate measures to prevent SARS would be fired. In all, more than 1,000 cadres nationwide lost their jobs or were severely punished because of SARS-related dereliction of duty. According to People's University professor Mao Chaohui, SARS had helped promote administrative reforms. "SARS has provided the opportunity for the civil service to develop the practice of [officials] resigning due to incompetence or poor performance," Mao said.[118]

The Hu-Wen team also went further than former premier Zhu in insisting that cadres take political as well as administrative responsibility for industrial accidents, particularly mishaps in high-risk areas such as mines and factories manufacturing firecrackers. Thus more than eighty officials, including a district-level party secretary, were penalized or cashiered in Shanxi Province on account of four industrial accidents that took place from October 2002 to March 2003. Some 180 people were killed and hundreds injured in these mishaps.[119] Yet it is obvious that the institution or culture of responsibility has not been firmly established. A commentary in the liberal-leaning *China Youth Daily* called attention to the fact that senior cadres in Shanxi had not been penalized after three mining accidents that occurred within eight days in August 2003. Nearly 100 miners and other workers were killed. The only sign of contrition displayed by senior cadres was that then governor Liu Zhenhua made a self-criticism during a State Council conference on workplace safety.[120]

By early 2004, more senior officials had resigned after taking responsibility over major mishaps. For example, the general manager of the oil conglomerate China National Petroleum Corporation resigned after a gas leak in one of the company's mines outside Chongqing had killed 243 local residents. The same was true of the head of Miyun County outside Beijing after thirty-seven people perished when a bridge in a popular park collapsed. Most importantly, a system of accountability was set up even as Beijing promulgated a "Temporary Regulation on the Resignation of Leading Party and Government Cadres." This Regulation delineated conditions under which officials who had made serious mistakes, or who had to take political responsibility for a major blunder or incident in areas under their jurisdiction, had to tender their resignations.[121]

Moreover, regulations governing specific areas of responsibility were being drafted. While giving instructions on fighting floods along the Yangtze River in mid-2004, Premier Wen pointed out that the State Council had set up a "Responsibility System for Implementation of Flood Control." Apart from combating deluges, officials must ensure the safety and health of residents along rivers, and that relief funds and material are adequately distributed among victims. Moreover, central authorities were putting together a "Responsibility System on Government Investment," which would hold cadres responsible for decisions on capital outlays that turn out to be wasteful or inefficient.[122] For Du Gang, a professor at the National College of Administration, the cadre accountability system was a concrete manifestation of the Hu-Wen team's philosophy of "putting people first." People's University expert Mao Shoulong indicated that with new regulations and practices coming into place, cadres had to take "moral, political, democratic, and legal responsibility" over their actions—and those of their underlings. By "democratic responsibility," Mao meant that "officials have to hold themselves accountable to those deputies or people who cast their votes for them."[123]

Streamlining the Bureaucratic Structure

That the Hu-Wen team is after a small government is evident from several symbolic acts of theirs in the first year of their administration. The entourage of officials and security personnel traveling with Hu or Wen either within China or abroad
is noticeably smaller than that for ex-president Jiang or ex-premier Zhu. Moreover, Hu and Wen ordered that the press corps covering the trips of PSC members
be restricted to journalists from four or five major news units. And one of the first
decisions of Wen upon becoming premier was to pledge that he would go further
than predecessor Zhu in streamlining the governmental structure, especially at the
regional level. The Beijing-based financial paper *Caijing Times* quoted economist
Xin Xiangyang as saying that administrative expenses in China were substantially
higher than those in developed countries. Xin noted that the one million tax collectors in China managed to gather 1.5 trillion yuan in taxes in 2003. While tax revenues for the U.S. government are many times higher, the United States only
employs around 100,000 taxation personnel nationwide.[124]

Premier Wen, the major force behind administrative streamlining, is determined
to go further than predecessor and mentor Zhu. "Boss Zhu" had cited lopping
away bureaucratic deadwood as one of the achievements of his five-year administration. Upon becoming premier in March 1998, Zhu slashed the number of central government ministries from forty to twenty-nine. A few hundred thousand
Beijing-based jobs in the central administration were axed. However, Zhu's fat-
trimming operations were confined to central-level units. And quite a sizable proportion of laid-off central-level bureaucrats have been reemployed in *shiye danwei,*
or quasi-government institutions, such as educational institutions and publishing
houses under State Council commissions and ministries.[125]

And the problem of superfluous or redundant civil servants is arguably more
serious in the countryside because of its direct impact on national stability. An
estimated one-third of county- and village-level governments are bankrupt: debts
incurred by these administrations totaled 400 billion yuan in 2003. The need to
pay so many civil servants means local government units have to impose extra—
and in most cases illegal—levies and fees on peasants. This, plus rural corruption,
was a major reason for riots in the countryside. In his first international press
conference, Wen cited a famous dictum from the ancient text *Daxue* (Profound
Knowledge): "Governments can only accumulate wealth when the producers of
income are numerous while the consumers are few." Wen said it was just the opposite in China. He said it was not uncommon for a county with only 120,000 or so
people to have to support up to 6,000 government employees.[126]

Wen decided very early on to abolish all layers of administration between the
counties and the villages, meaning that the *xiang* (rural township) and *zhen* (township) bureaucracies would be cut. The premier called this goal the establishment
of "a local-level administrative system with the county as basic unit." Fully 70
percent of all China's civil servants and related staff are employed by administra-

tive units at the county level or below. Apart from ordinary officials and civil servants, each county, town, and township government also has to employ staff working for units under the Communist Party, the people's congress, as well as various police, judicial, and quasi-military bodies.[127] Wen's reform has met with stiff resistance. While it might not be too difficult for laid-off central-level bureaucrats to find jobs in businesses and other sectors, grassroots civil servants have few other alternatives in terms of seeking a decent livelihood after leaving their governmental iron rice bowl. Moreover, cadres in most of the nation's 1,642 counties are opposed to abolishing townships and rural townships. Apart from the extra workload, county-level officials have to contend with the fact that there is no more buffer between the county government and the increasingly rebellious peasantry.[128]

There is evidence, however, that the premier has achieved a degree of success in his fat-trimming exercise. By late 2003, the number of towns nationwide had decreased by 375 to 20,226, while that of townships had shrunken by 575 to 18,064. Moreover, 950 towns and townships were merged. The pace of streamlining, however, has become slower from 2004 onward. In the first nine months of that year, merely 864 towns and townships were slashed or merged. It is estimated that the cancellation of a township or rural township means that from seventy to eighty local-level cadres can be taken off the payroll—and that up to 3 million yuan of administrative expenses can be saved.[129]

According to City University of Hong Kong Sinologist Linda Li, the Wen team must beware of the fact that many grassroots-level cadres are going through the motions of administrative streamlining just to please their superiors. "Take the case of the merger of two or more townships into one," she said. "It is not uncommon that the merged—and enlarged—township has merely taken over all the staff of the previous units." Professor Li noted that instead of putting the focus on merely curtailing the numbers of grassroots administrative units, a better approach would be for Beijing and provincial governments to clearly delineate the functions of individual departments under the towns and townships, so that only those departments that have no useful role to play need be cut.[130] Another Wen initative is to streamline the bureaucratic structure of cities, beginning with the curtailment of the number of the 840–odd districts directly under the big cities. Metropolises such as Beijing, Shanghai, and Guangzhou have up to ten districts, and many of the functions of the district governments overlap with those of the municipality. However, the State Council is meeting stiff resistance from powerful metropolises such as Shanghai, which do not want their bureaucracies and payrolls cut.

At the same time, the Wen team is seriously thinking of increasing the numbers of both provinces and directly administered cities (DAC). (The DACs of Beijing, Shanghai, Tianjin, and Chongqing have the same ranking as provinces and they report directly to Beijing.) Preliminary studies by the Ministry of Civil Affairs (MAC) indicate that the Hu-Wen leadership is leaning toward adding four more DACs and around ten more provinces. Leading candidates to become DACs include Wuhan, Guangzhou, Shenzhen, Qingdao, and Dalian. According to the MAC's expert on local-level administration, Dai Junliang, a DAC could become a regional hub that could expedite the growth of surrounding areas.[131]

From a political point of view, the expansion of the current numbers of provinces and DACs from thirty-two to up to fifty would mean that Beijing will be better placed to combat regionalism. Central authorities have for the past decade or so fretted over the fact that provinces and cities such as Guangdong and Shanghai have such a huge economic base that they could often refuse to toe the Beijing line. For example, if either Guangzhou or Shenzhen becomes a DAC, Guangdong will have command over many fewer economic resources, meaning it might lack the wherewithal to effectively bargain with the central government.[132]

"Not a Western-style Civil Service"

It is important, however, to bear in mind that there was no intention on the part of the CCP leadership to turn the cadre system into a Western-style civil service. This was made clear by a spokesman from the Ministry of Personnel in an interview with the official China News Service. The spokesman pointed out that in China, officials "uphold the basic principles of the CCP and are not politically neutral."[133] This meant of course, that civil servants, even those who were not party members, were supposed to be loyal to goals and principles ranging from Marxism-Leninism and to party leadership. Moreover, there is no clear-cut differentiation between political appointees and career civil servants. A draft of the Civil Service Bill to be submitted to the NPC in 2006 suggests that staff of party and government departments as well as mass organizations should be included in the ranks of the civil service. Vice-Head of the CCP Organization Department Zhang Bolin noted that this move would help strengthen the party's "unified leadership" over officials and administrative staff nationwide.[134]

It is well understood that despite rapid industrialization and modernization in the country, the CCP still calls the shots over most areas of life. And despite the Hu-Wen team's effort to streamline the party and government apparatuses, there are still overlapping CCP and government bureaucracies at both central and regional levels. In the late 1990s, the new district of Pudong in Shanghai was set up as an example where there was a minimal CCP structure and personnel establishment.[135] Yet this experiment has so far not been repeated elsewhere. As of 2005, there was more evidence that administrative reform over areas such as the assessment of personnel could not succeed in the absence of genuine political reform measures that could cut into the party—or its dominant faction's—monopoly on power. There are signs that after taking over ex-president Jiang's last remaining post of CMC chairman, Hu has sought to further bolster the political fortune of members of his Communist Youth League Faction as well as other cronies by elevating them to senior party and government posts.

Thus in a late 2004 reshuffle, a number of the Hu protégés were either promoted or given lateral transfers to more strategic posts. These included the appointments of Li Keqiang and Guo Jinlong as party secretaries of, respectively, Liaoning and Anhui, and the promotions of Yang Chuantang and Huang Xiaojing to, respectively, party secretary of Tibet and governor of Fujian. Like Hu, Li is a former first party secretary of the CYL, while both Yang and Huang are former leaders of provincial youth league committees. Li's transfer from the major agricultural province of Henan to the industrial hub of Liaoning was seen as a preparation for the fifty-year-old's promotion to the Politburo at the Seventeenth CCP Congress. However, doubts were raised as to whether these appointments were strictly based on merits—or rather whether they served mostly to bolster the authority of the CCP's dominant faction.[136]

Boosting Administrative Probity and Fighting Corruption

One primary worry of Hu's advisers soon after the Sixteenth CCP Congress was that they had difficulty licking into shape an acceptable—and laudatory—image of the relatively young president. For example, former premier Zhu was able, during his first international press conference in 1998, to present himself as a daredevil reformer who, in his own words, "fears neither minefields nor precipices." Zhu's successor Wen also succeeded in quickly establishing himself as a "people's premier" in the mold of the revered former premier Zhou Enlai. Could Hu's image consultants then portray the Fourth-Generation supremo as a "tiger-pounding, anti-graft hero"?

Despite supposedly stepped-up efforts to eradicate graft starting from the early 1990s, the situation has been deteriorating relentlessly. Mainland experts estimated in the early 2000s that economic losses due to corruption accounted for up to 14.9 percent of GDP between 1999 and 2001. One reason was the relatively cavalier attitude of ex-president Jiang and most senior members of the Shanghai Faction. This was illustrated by the heavy political interference that anti-graft personnel faced while investigating a series of major cases.[137]

The Perennial Goal of Combating Graft

Apart from jobs and living standards, ordinary Chinese are most concerned about inequity in income distribution, and corruption, which has enabled well-connected but ruthless cadres and businessmen alike to get rich quick. And the one area where they are most eager to exercise supervision over the government is rooting out "economic crime" and related malfeasance. A measurement of whether Hu has lived up to his populist and legalistic ideals would be his ability to rid the country of corruption and related felonies. Yet it is here that Hu and his allies may clash with vested interests and power blocs including the Jiang or Shanghai Clique.[138]

It is significant that Hu often talks in the same breath about rule by law, serving the masses, and promoting clean government. "Officials must come to a clear understanding that the party is there to promote the public good and that administration must be for the sake of the people," Hu indicated in a mid-2003 Central Committee speech on clean governance. The president decried "cases of corruption taking place among officials, including senior and medium-ranked officials." The party's anti-graft watchdog, the Central Commission for Disciplinary Inspection, then issued five regulations barring officials from using their power to engage in commerce. For example, cadres as well as their relatives were forbidden to buy stocks in, or to have business dealings with, enterprises directly or indirectly under their control.[139]

A party source familiar with the Hu camp believes the party chief and president, in addition to CCDI chief Wu Guanzheng, a PSC member deemed to be close to Hu, may be wielding the "anti-graft card" to beef up Hu's national stature and at the same time bludgeon political enemies. In the five years ending with 2002, more than 12,000 officials with the rank of county chief or above—including twenty-five ministerial-ranked officials—were prosecuted for taking bribes and related crimes.[140] And it seems clear that this deplorable situation would not have occurred if the ancien régime under ex-president Jiang had been serious about cracking the whip on venal cadres.

Jiang's record in graft-busting was extremely poor. Take, for example, the infamous multibillion yuan smuggling and graft scandal that erupted in the port city of Xiamen, Fujian Province, in the late 1990s. There was persistent innuendo that a number of senior cadres and "princelings," or offspring of party elders, implicated in the Xiamen case were spared prosecution owing to their affiliation with the Jiang or Shanghai Faction.[141] Indeed, the kingpin of the criminal ring, Lai Changxing, reportedly bribed scores of top-level party and military cadres, almost none of whom have been brought to justice. In early 2003, even senior cadres at the level of vice-mayor and vice–party secretary who were implicated in the Lai case were quietly let go after having been relieved of their posts and kicked out of the CCP.[142] Political analysts said while Hu seemed eager to demonstrate that he was more serious than Jiang in tackling graft, he was also a past master at using the "anti-graft card" as a potent weapon against rival CCP cliques. "Jiang has used fighting graft as a pretext to elbow aside foes ranging from [former Beijing party boss] Chen Xitong to [former Politburo member] Li Ruihuan," the party source said. "It's possible Hu is now taking a leaf from Jiang's book."[143]

That political considerations have frequently interfered with the CCP's efforts to promote clean government has highlighted the fact that the Hu administration can only go so far in pursuing rule by law without real political reform. Without checks and balances within the system, it will be difficult for the CCDI and other anti-graft organs to penalize cadres with sterling political connections. Under the "party is supreme" principle, so-called masses' bodies or supervisory organs such as the NPC and the CPPCC are toothless when it comes to investigating senior officials. And given the party's tight control over the media, the latter's function in exposing corrupt officials is often limited to mid-ranking officials.[144]

The Zhou Zhengyi Case and Its Aftermath

The first major test of the Hu administration's resolve toward cracking tough nuts was the scandal surrounding "premier Shanghai tycoon" Zhou Zhengyi. Zhou, a flamboyant, forty-two-year-old self-made boss was once named by *Forbes* magazine as the eleventh richest man in China. The convoluted case of Zhou, who made his fortune in the stock and real-estate markets, had immense political and factional significance.

Zhou was detained by Shanghai police in May 2003 and "formally arrested" three months later, allegedly for monkey business including illegally obtaining more than 1.5 billion yuan of loans from various branches of the Bank of China as well as more than ten Shanghai banks. Zhou and his socialite wife Mao Yuping, who started investing in Hong Kong properties and securities in the late 1990s, were famous for their circle of high-flying businessmen and glamorous movie stars. In Shanghai, they were also known for being on good terms with local officials, including several ranking members of the Shanghai Faction. Zhou is said to be close to PSC member Huang Ju, a former Shanghai mayor and party secretary, as well as former vice-mayor Sha Lin. More significantly, Zhou was deemed a business partner of two princelings: ex-president Jiang's son Dr. Jiang Mianheng, once known as the "IT prince of Shanghai"; and the son of PSC member Zeng Qinghong, Zeng Wei.[145]

That the Zhou case was emblematic of the power struggle between the Shanghai Faction and the Hu camp was evident from the fact that the crackdown was masterminded by Hu and CCDI chief Wu. An elite team of about 200 CCDI agents was sent to Shanghai in April to investigate Zhou. None of the investigators was from Shanghai, and local officials were not allowed to interfere with CCDI work. Hu was able to get the initial cooperation of new Shanghai party chief Chen Liangyu, a Zeng Qinghong crony. Chen sent out an internal circular urging all party and government units to cooperate with the CCDI team.[146]

Yet it was soon apparent that Wu—as well as Hu—was meeting resistance from Shanghai Faction stalwarts led by ex-president Jiang, who reportedly issued orders that investigations into Zhou's misdemeanors "should not spill over into other cases" and "should not affect the stability and prosperity of Shanghai." Jiang also insisted that Vice-Premier Huang, and not the CCDI, be put in charge of the Zhou affair. Investigations had begun to slow down by late June. The national news media was ordered to stay away from detailed reporting about Zhou's shenanigans.[147]

By late 2003, it was made clear that Zhou would be prosecuted for two relatively minor misconducts: providing false information to the securities regulatory authorities, and manipulation of stock prices. More serious matters such as how he managed to get the bank loans as well as choice pieces of real estate for development—and whether municipal officials were involved—were never delved into.[148] In mid-2004, the Shanghai court slapped a three-year jail term on Zhou, which was considered light by legal experts. None of the big-shot officials or princelings close to Zhou was implicated. The only people who got into trouble because of Zhou were a few bankers who had lent him money, including the former president of the Bank of China Hong Kong Branch Liu Jinbao.[149] From the angle of factional dynamics, the Hu-Wen team was in a position to reap important dividends from the case. Although no Shanghai Faction affiliates were publicly tainted this time around, Hu and Wu had accumulated hefty dossiers that could implicate a number of Zhou's high-placed cronies. Such material would be invaluable in a possible showdown between Hu and Shanghai Faction stalwarts including Jiang, Zeng, and Huang in the near future.[150] The Zhou case also showed that factionalist, Machiavellian calculations might have displaced respect for the law.

Fighting Graft over the Long Haul

The Zhou Zhengyi case illustrated the constraints affecting the Hu-Wu graft-busting team's attempts to go after the big fish, or in China's case, the "big tigers." However, the Hu administration made it clear in the summer of 2003, albeit in an indirect fashion, that there would be no let-up to the anti-corruption campaign. While touring Jiangsu Province in August, the CCDI's Wu gave a severe warning to "leading cadres who have a cavalier attitude toward discipline." "We must put emphasis on more scrutiny and supervision regarding clean government," the state media quoted Wu as saying. "We must deepen the work on fighting graft and building clean government," Wu added.[151]

Beijing sources close to the Communist Party said Wu and his CCDI colleagues came under heavy pressure due to their high-profile investigation of Zhou. Wu—and Hu—however, wanted to relay the message that they would continue to hit out left, right, and center. The CCDI had a field day in areas outside Shanghai. In August 2003, Jia Chunwang, the head of the Supreme People's Procuratorate, surprised observers by saying that a number of "major, earth-shattering cases" would come to light later that year.[152] A month earlier, the former party chief of Hebei Province Cheng Weigao was kicked out of the CCP for his involvement in a decades-old graft scandal. Cheng's political disgrace was remarkable in view of his high-placed patrons, who included Li Peng, the former NPC chairman, and Jiang himself. While investigations into the Cheng case had begun at least in the mid-1990s, Jiang was dragging his feet on the matter.[153]

Despite limitations due to institutional or factional reasons, it cannot be denied that Hu's track record in fighting big-time corruption has been superior to that under Jiang. It is not a coincidence that Hu himself enjoys a much better reputation as "Mr. Clean" than his predecessor.[154] From the Sixteenth Congress to mid-2004, around ten cadres with the ranking of minister and governor, or equivalent, were detained or penalized. Apart from Hubei's Cheng, they included former Hubei governor Zhang Guoguang, former president of the Liaoning High Court Tian Fengzhi, former chairman of the Heilongjiang People's Political Consultative Conference Han Guizhi, former Yunnan governor Li Jiating, former president of the

China Construction Bank Wang Xuebing, and former vice-governor of Anhui, Wang Huaizhong. The cases surrounding Cheng, Zhang, Tian, Han, and Anhui's Wang had festered for many years—and had failed to be effectively dealt with by the Jiang administration.[155]

The Empowerment of Auditing Authorities

The Hu-Wen team has beefed up the functions and powers of the National Audit Office (NAO) in an apparent attempt to make up for the shortfall of the current anti-graft regime, which revolves around the CCDI. In June 2004, the nation was stunned when the auditor-general, Li Jinhua, made public a scathing report on the lack of financial discipline, gross wastage, embezzlement, and corruption in fifty-five ministries and state commissions. For example, forty-one ministries and commissions had appropriated as much as 1.42 billion yuan of funds—which had originally been earmarked for special projects—for the construction of residential and office buildings for their own use. A particularly interesting finding was that a few years earlier, the National Electricity Corporation (NEC) had spent more than 3.04 million yuan on a three-day conference. The NEC was at the time headed by Gao Yan, a protégé of Li Peng's who was under investigation for embezzlement and corruption.[156]

While the NAO had been in existence for decades, only parts of its reports were made public and the general perception had been that the auditors treated even errant departments and officials with kid gloves. By early 2004, however, the Hu-Wen leadership made the pivotal decision that the powers of the auditor-general's office would be expanded. For example, up to late 2003, the NAO only had jurisdiction over State Council units. From mid-2004 onward, the auditors would be authorized to look at the books of all CCP and government departments, large state companies, as well as the NPC and CPPCC.[157]

Auditor-General Li Jinhua, who is reportedly close to both former premier Zhu and Premier Wen, indicated in mid-2004 that he wanted to upgrade the NAO into a unit with the same administrative ranking as the Supreme People's Court and the Supreme People's Procuratorate. Li told the Chinese media that the NAO would follow similar institutions abroad and serve as a watchdog for taxpayers. "We must tell taxpayers whether their money has been spent properly," Li said. During the first three months of what the Chinese media call the "auditing blitzkrieg," some 600 cadres lost their jobs and were subject to different kinds of punishment.[158]

The relative efficacy of the NAO, however, has illustrated yet once again that in twenty-first-century China, the success of fighting graft—as well other major party and government initiatives—still depends on the extent to which the fight has received the blessings of the two or three top PSC members. For example, in a high-profile TV appearance, Wen said in mid-2004 that all civil servants must self-consciously summit themselves to the supervision of the

NAO, and that errant officials would be "severely handled."[159] One recalls that in the late 1990s, the CCDI and other departments would not have gone as far as they did regarding Xiamen's Yuanhua case had it not been for the big push given to the anti-graft effort by former premier Zhu and former state councilor Wu Yi.

Seeking Long-term Solutions

For the long haul, Hu needed to put together more rigorous procedures and institutions in fighting corruption, deemed the number one scourge of the nation. According to an early 2005 report in the *People's Daily*, the Hu leadership had taken a new approach to eliminating graft: nurturing viable institutions and conventions. The article cited the Sixteenth Congress as a watershed in the party's long battle against the phenomenon popularly known as "the exchange of power for money." Before the conclave, the paper said, the party had relied mainly on inculcating the proper ideology and work style. Stress was now being put on "developing institutions, procedures, and systems" of clean government.[160] It was understood that the president wanted to, in the words of his aides, "institutionalize and regularize" the practice of supervision within the party, whereby ordinary cadres and even party members could blow the whistle on cadres on the take.

Moreover, more efforts have been made to check on the probity of senior cadres. For example, the CCDI, in conjunction with the CCP Organization Department, would periodically dispatch "roving inspectors" to the provinces to check on the "cleanliness" or otherwise of officials and state entrepreneurs. Thus, starting in 2003, a team of forty-five so-called imperial inspectors made the rounds of the provinces and autonomous regions. Other similar "work groups" were sent around the country a year later.[161] The Hu-Wen team expressed confidence that a viable, multipronged set of anti-graft institutions would be licked into shape with the empowerment of the auditor-general's office. As Wen noted in mid-2004, apart from the CCDI, the Ministry of Supervision, and the NAO, cadres were subject to "democratic supervision by the NPC and the CPPCC, judicial and legal supervision, as well as the scrutiny of the media and the masses."[162]

In theory, therefore, the Hu-Wen leadership has set up the proverbial *tianluo diwang* ("dragnet as extensive as heaven and earth") to ensnare corrupt and errant officials. Yet while Hu has been demonstrably more serious about combating graft than predecessor Jiang, the view of China-based foreign businessmen is that the situation has basically not improved. In its annual tally of honest versus corrupt countries, the Geneva-based Transparent International ranked China seventy-first in 2004, down from sixty-fourth a year ago. Singapore and Hong Kong were ranked fifth and sixteenth respectively.[163]

Within-the-system reforms notwithstanding, Chinese as well as foreign observers have argued that the only long-term solution to corruption is setting up a graft-fighting organ that is truly independent of the CCP. This would be similar to the highly regarded Independent Commission Against Corruption in Hong Kong or the Anti-Corruption Bureau in Singapore.[164] Yet from Beijing's viewpoint, this would amount to setting limits on the party's powers—and it is doubtful that the Hu-Wen team would seriously consider any thoroughgoing measures even in their "second term" of 2007–2012.

Assessment of the Reforms, and the Possibility of the Emergence of a Chinese-style Socialist Democratic Party

Most Sinologists have warned against excessive optimism that the Fourth-Generation leadership will launch Western-style liberalization in the near to medium term. As the party mouthpiece *Seeking Truth* pointed out in late 2003, changes in the political arena must always serve the goal of enhancing party leadership and upholding the socialist road. It stated that reform must neither lead to Westernization nor to "the truncation and negation of Communist Party leadership." And the State Council's late-2005 *White Paper on the Construction of China's Democratic Politics* further affirmed the fact that because of history and so-called national conditions, "Communist Party leadership and rule in China is an objective requirement of the country's development and progress." It added that "socialist political democracy"—meaning political reform under the stern guidance of the CCP, was "the apt choice meeting the requirement of social progress."[165] It was as though Hu, a believer in "scientific socialism," were proclaiming that it had been scientifically proven that only the CCP should go on ruling China.

The most obvious signs of a rollback in liberalization have manifested themselves in the media. In the second half of the SARS saga, foreign observers were impressed by the Hu-Wen leadership's relative commitment to a kind of "Chinese-style glasnost," including their promise that "people have the right to know." Dozens of central and local units set up a Western-style system of news spokespeople whose job was apparently to answer questions from reporters in a timely fashion. From early 2004 onward, however, the Publicity Department and other units began cracking down on liberal papers and TV stations that dared to expose the "dark side of society" or even to challenge party or socialist orthodoxy. Beijing has also pulled out the stops to police the Internet, deemed a dangerous conduit for dangerous, decadent Western ideals (see Chapter 6).

Dozens of pro-reform and pro-democracy editors, authors, and "Net-dissidents" have been arrested or placed under twenty-four-hour surveillance. The New York–based Committee to Protect Journalists indicated in late 2005 that with thirty-two journalists behind bars, China held the world record in terms of locking up news professionals. Peking University journalism professor Jiao Guobiao, who dared openly criticize the Publicity Department, was ordered to stop teaching in 2004. And relatively bold media such as *Southern Weekend* and *Beijing News* have been subjected to continual harassment by the censors.[166]

The Ideological and Institutional Limits of Reform

Putting People First or Putting the Party First?

The first three years of the Hu-Wen administration has demonstrated that it is unrealistic to expect bold steps in political reform—or even thoroughgoing changes within parameters supposedly recognized by the authorities. A good example is debate over the ostensibly noncontroversial issue of constitutional reform; it was not only one of Hu's most important initiatives since the Sixteenth CCP Congress but also one that could be accomplished without unduly upsetting the status quo.

Since the intention to have the revised charter passed by the March 2004 NPC session was made known in early 2003, intellectuals and liberal cadres thought they would have one fruitful year to discuss different proposals. Forward-looking cadres and thinkers, including constitutional scholar Cao Siyuan, prominent law professor Zhang Ping, and retired liberal cadre Zhu Houze held a nonofficial conference at Qingdao University in June 2003 to thrash out various ideals about constitutional revision. These included reforms—for example, the introduction of *cha'e* (multiple-candidate) elections for picking party and government cadres—that would not threaten the CCP's cherished one-party rule.[167]

Symptomatic of what some called "a bone-chilling frost in mid-summer," however, secret police and thought-control apparatchiks began zeroing in on free-thinking intellectuals associated with the revise-the-Constitution movement. Cao was put under twenty-four-hour surveillance and warned not to communicate with the foreign media. According to Cao, what Hu was afraid of was that "Westernized intellectuals would stir up expectations that party authorities could not deliver."[168] Cao said another reason behind the crackdown was Hu's fear that Zhu, a former head of the CCP Propaganda Department, might be spearheading a kind of "within-the-system" rebellion by the CCP's liberal faction. "While Zhu retired in 1989, he still has ample moral authority in the party," Cao said. "And as a confidante of [former party chief] Hu Yaobang, as well as Hu's predecessor as Guizhou party secretary, Zhu has a considerable following in the CCP." During the brief period of intellectual fermentation in mid-2003, Zhu had won admiration for his campaign to put an end to "rule of personality." After the Sixteenth CCP Congress, Zhu famously told a magazine that "the era of the strongmen is definitely over" and that younger leaders such as Hu and Wen should implement bolder reforms.[169]

From mid-2003 onward, "new ideas" on not only constitutional revision but other topics related to political modernization were largely barred from the official media. Part of the ferocity of the backlash against liberal opinion was that, despite their differences, President Hu and ex-president Jiang had joined forces to rein in the free thinkers. Said a Beijing source close to the legal establishment: "The former president dismissed as 'bourgeois liberalization' efforts by scholars to put into the Constitution clauses guaranteeing internationally acknowledged civil rights." And Jiang's—and Hu's—conservative underling, Director of the CCP Publicity Department Liu Yunshan, was enforcing with gusto his bosses' directive that "bour-geois liberals" be barred from airing their views on constitutional matters.[170]

Given Hu's heavy involvement in the anti-liberalization movement, there seems little substance to the claim that only the Jiang Faction was responsible for the cold winds of 2003 and 2004. Diplomatic analysts said the prestige of Hu-Wen team—and in particular Hu, who is in charge of ideological and propaganda matters—had fallen among the intelligentsia. Despite the Fourth-Generation leadership's lip service to political reform, its priority is still sustaining and strengthening the party's monopoly on power. Many of the relatively liberal measures introduced by the Hu-Wen group, ranging from promoting rule by law and curbing corruption to boosting government transparency and cadre responsibility, are meant to subserve the larger goal of raising the ruling party's "governance ability" (see also Chapter 7). Yet reform measures will be halted or scaled back as soon as they threaten the CCP's all-embracing authority.

The Deplorable Level of Human Rights

Because political reform is so inextricably linked with human rights—and because of the Hu-Wen team's *yiren weiben* motto—it is instructive to scrutinize what the leadership calls the "humanistic conditions" in the country. In March 2004, the authorities published a *White Paper on Human Rights in China*, which claimed that such rights were "at their best" in history. The document praised the leadership's focus on the dictum of "governing the country for the sake of the people." As evidence of amelioration in human rights, the paper listed a host of figures ranging from Internet availability to growth in per capita GDP, as well as improvements in peasants' livelihood.[171]

For dissidents incarcerated or under virtual house arrest, however, the civil and human rights situation is still grim. During 2004, much of the attention of Chinese intellectuals and international watchdogs was focused on the deteriorating health of former party chief Zhao Ziyang. As the 1989 democracy movement had faded from the memory of most Chinese under age thirty-five, the potential threat of the eighty-five-year-old man to the CCP leadership was becoming smaller by the day. However, Hu, Wen (once Zhao's main aide), and other PSC members were extremely wary of relaxing twenty-four-hour police surveillance over the aged leader. This prompted Zhao's former secretary, Bao Tong, to ask in April 2004: "Where are Mr. Zhao Ziyang's human rights at this point in time?" Bao, who was also under twenty-four-hour surveillance, added satirically: "Please note that now is the time when our country's human rights condition is 'at its best!'"[172]

And when Zhao passed away in January 2007, the Hu leadership decided to prevent his family members, former associates, and admirers from honoring the liberal leader. Security agents barred the bulk of well-wishers from going into Zhao's house in central Beijing, where his children had set up a temporary facility for mourning. At least several dozen Zhao sympathizers, including peasants from his hometown in Henan Province, were detained briefly. Two octogenarian writers who had published Zhao-related books in Hong Kong were put under tight surveillance. All news media and websites were forbidden to mention anything relating to Zhao's demise. And when, on the day of the minimalist funeral, the NCNA released a brief dispatch that referred to the former party chief's "grave errors" in 1989, the news item did not even mention the senior posts that he had occupied.[173]

There has hardly been any let-up in the elaborate methods that police and state-security departments employ to nip dissent in the bud. Beijing's priority targets are groups suspected of having links to "hostile foreign forces" and separatist groups in Xinjiang and Tibet, as well as wildcat labor unions and underground political parties. However, even outwardly innocuous, academically oriented "research societies" or "study groups" formed by individual college students are subject to close surveillance. After describing how the police had crushed the New Youth Study Group, which was active among a small group of Peking University students in the early 2000s, *Washington Post* Beijing correspondent Philip Pan wrote: "the CCP is engaged in the largest and perhaps most successful experiment in authoritarianism in the world."[174]

Most Western governments and watchdog NGOs have given the Hu-Wen team poor marks in the human rights area. London's Amnesty International said in a late-2003 report that "despite a few positive steps, no attempt was made to introduce the fundamental legal and institutional reforms necessary to bring an end to serious human rights violations." The U.S. State Department issued similar accusations in its 2003 and 2004 reports. For example, the Assistant Secretary for Human Rights Michael Kozak noted in late 2004 that some 310,000 people were confined in China's reeducation-through-labor camps, up from about half this figure in the early 1990s. This was despite the Hu-Wen team's alleged determination to root out administrative detention.[175]

The Fermentation of New Ideas Continues Despite Official Suppression

While intellectuals and academics recognized in 2003 and 2004 that the season for liberalization had not arrived, there were continued calls for reform. Most of these forward-looking scholars have cast doubt on the specious arguments offered by the CCP leadership that time is not yet ripe for change. Retired Peking University social scientist Shang Dewen, for example, insisted that time for meaningful change to the system was "running out." Shang said in 2003 that while political reform had been officially put on the agenda in the 1980s, what had been accomplished was merely "some tinkering with personnel reform in government departments" while "nothing has changed in the Stalinist [political] structure." Likewise, the late party chief of Guangdong and reformer Ren Zhongyi disputed the conventional wisdom that political reform would lead to instability. "Political reform won't lead to chaos," he told the official *Window of Southern Trends* magazine in mid-2004. "The great majority of people hate corruption and they want change [in the system.]"[176]

For famed economist Mao Yushi, a democratic model is the only alternative to dictatorship. Recounting how Chairman Mao had ruined the nation, Mao said a dictatorial system was fundamentally flawed "because we can never ensure that the dictator is a good person." "That's why we can't do without democratic politics, because it can [at least] prevent the worst situation from taking place."[177] Equally significantly, social commentator Wang Yi called on the authorities to show more tolerance toward *yiyi*, or "divergent and dissident views." Wang said the party leadership should expand China's "space for public politics, that is, space for [the airing of] divergent and dissident views in a nonviolent, competitive manner." The commentator said political authority must be built on the "conciliation, not suppression, of *yiyi*." It is significant that Wang's views were carried in *Chinanewsweek,* a mainstream weekly magazine. In his interview with *Window of Southern Trends,* party elder Ren went so far as to say that China should borrow the Western institution of "checks and balances among the executive, legislature, and judiciary." Ren, who passed away late 2005, said this should not be regarded as a "Western institution" because of its universal appeal.[178]

Then there are activists like Li Fan, who is instrumental in helping local officials experiment with elections. Li has for the past several years run the World and China Institute, a private think tank on grassroots democracy. The scholar was undaunted by the CCP leadership's decision not to sanction polls at higher administrative levels, because he believed that a new generation of peasants, workers, and professionals would be pushing harder for democratic rights. "Grassroots democracy may be momentarily suppressed," he said. "But once the seeds have been planted, the roots can only grow deeper and deeper before an inevitable bloom."[179]

Compared to the first generation of so-called all-out Westernizers in the mid-1980s such as astrophysicist Fang Lizhi or political scientist Yan Jiaqi, most democracy advocates of the 2000s have sought to avoid head-on confrontation with the authorities. These relatively moderate modernizers often play up the fact that political liberalization would actually bolster Beijing's authority and legitimacy, and serve the CCP's avowed purpose of maintaining stability and prosperity. It is perhaps a measure of the Hu-Wen leadership's lack of confidence that it has refused to engage in a dialogue with advocates of radical reform—let alone adopt their ideas right away.

Toward a Chinese Socialist Democratic Party?

Assuming that, as some optimists have argued, the Hu-Wen team will hasten the pace of reform after they have consolidated powers at the Seventeenth CCP Congress in 2007, is it possible that the CCP will transform itself into a Chinese Socialist Democratic Party (CSDP)? This possibility was first raised when ex-president Jiang enshrined his "Theory of the Three Represents" in the CCP Constitution in late 2002. As discussed earlier, this theory has revised key Marxist precepts by doing away with class struggle and legitimizing the concept of a *quanmindang*, or a party for all the people (see also Chapter 3). The question then arises as to whether the Fourth-Generation leadership will, by the time of say, the Eighteenth CCP Congress of 2012, push the *quanmindang* ideal to its logical conclusion.

The idea that the CCP will change its nature—if not also its name—to that of a European-style socialist democratic party is less far-fetched than it may seem. The motto of Jiang and Hu—"to progress with the times"—sounds intriguingly similar to the goal of "making progress through peaceful [evolution]" propounded by rebel cadre Xu Jiatun in 1992. A former top CCP representative in Hong Kong, Xu defected to the United States one year after the Tiananmen Square massacre. Xu, a former party boss of Jiangsu Province, argued that to stay alive and relevant, the CCP must copy the good points of capitalist systems through a process akin to "peaceful evolution."[180]

Indeed, think tanks in both the CCP and the State Council had started doing research on European social democratic parties in 2000. In the summer of 2000, then PSC member Wei Jianxing went to Germany and paid a visit to the headquarters of the German Social Democratic Party (SDP). There he discussed with SDP leaders issues such as party ideology and organization. Top SDP officials reciprocated with a trip to Beijing the same year. In late 2002, Hu, together with then Politburo member in charge of ideology and propaganda, Ding Guan'gen, made trips to several European countries, where they observed socialist democratic parties at firsthand. In mid-2002, Western diplomats in Beijing also reported that while talking with party cadres, the latter asked them numerous questions about the theory, constitution, and operation of European social democratic parties.[181]

Analysts are divided as to whether it is possible that the CCP's transformation to a CSDP can be accomplished in ten years or so. It is certain that the Hu-Wen team will be under tremendous pressure to put real political reform on the agenda. While the influence of leftists, or remnant Maoists, is expected to decline further, the voice of "rightists," or Westernized cadres, scholars, professionals, and other members of the middle class, is tipped to grow. The Hu leadership is expected to encounter ferocious lobbying from "bourgeois liberal" or pro-West intellectuals to promote political reform in order to transform party and state institutions into those that are in line with European socialist democratic parties.

Forward-looking intellectuals and officials are already saying that if the CCP has become a *quanmindang,* it should allow nonparty politicians, businessmen, and professionals to play a role in politics that is commensurate with their socio-economic clout. This significant broadening of political participation logically leads to the CCP's lifting the ban on the formation of new political parties—and ultimately to multiparty politics. Other remnants of Leninism and Maoism have also become horrendously outdated. For example, if the CCP has abandoned class warfare, the People's Liberation Army should cease to remain either a "party's army" or a tool for exercising "proletarian dictatorship."

And then there is the fact that obsolete political institutions have proven to be a millstone around the neck of economic reform and growth, which has become the sole raison d'être of the ruling party. The choice facing the CCP is as urgent as it is stark. To cope with new circumstances, it not only has to jettison age-old ideology but give up its stranglehold on power. How to manage this momentous change without undue disruption to China's already fragile sociopolitical fabric could be the Fourth Generation's biggest challenge. And it is much better for the ruling party to introduce far-reaching changes—even at the expense of some of its own power—than to have bigger and much more disruptive changes thrust upon it.

5

The Fourth-Generation Leadership's Ambitious Foreign-Policy Agenda

Diplomatic Challenges for the Twenty-first Century

Foreign and security policy is assuming ever more significance in the Chinese polity. China's fast-growing economic and military clout has better positioned the country to gradually assume a stature in the world community that befits its huge land mass and population as well as its Middle Kingdom-sized ambitions. More significantly, the Fourth-Generation leadership under President Hu Jintao and Premier Wen Jiabao is pursuing a much more assertive and multi-pronged diplomacy to ensure that the People's Republic of China (PRC) will meet its goal of economic take-off and sustained development. While lip service will still be paid to late patriarch Deng Xiaoping's early-1990s dictum about "never taking the lead," the Hu-Wen team is making sure that China's impact on international affairs will be more in line with its emerging quasi-superpower status.

That the new leadership has concluded that China is coming up against formidable diplomatic challenges in the short to medium term is evident from statements made by Hu and Wen. The president indicated not long after the Sixteenth Chinese Communist Party (CCP) Congress that cadres of all departments must pay more attention to global developments so that "China can make good preparations before the rainstorm . . . and be in a position to seize the initiative." Wen pointed out in the first meeting of the State Council, or cabinet, in March 2003, that the leadership "must keep a cool head" in domestic and foreign affairs. "We must boost our consciousness about disasters and downturns—and think about dangers in the midst of [apparent] safety," he said.[1]

President Hu, who heads the CCP's policy-setting Leading Group on Foreign Affairs (LFGA), has advocated a closer integration between foreign, security, and military policies on the one hand, and domestic concerns on the other. This is, of course to be distinguished from Chairman Mao Zedong's "pan-revolutionary" concept, which meant among other things that Chinese should tighten their belts to provide financial aid to small communist countries bullied by the United States.[2] Hu has noted that developments on the international stage would pack a big impact on areas such as energy, economic production and trade, and ultimately, people's standard of living. At a CCP Politburo study session in early 2004, the party chief and president indicated that it was imperative for officials to adopt a broad vision of the world so as to cope with new tasks and to improve the CCP's governance capability. "We need to make sound judgments of—and take a scientific approach toward tackling—volatile changes in the international situation," he said. "We must properly cope with the trends of multipolarization, economic globalization as well as scientific and technological advancements."[3]

Foremost among the Hu-Wen team's goal is to maintain a peaceful global climate—particularly good ties with China's neighbors—so as to ensure continual economic development. The LGFA is very nervous about an "anti-China containment policy" supposedly being spearheaded by Washington. Despite relatively stable relations with the United States, which are partly due to the George W. Bush administration's anxiety to secure Chinese cooperation in the global war against terrorism, Beijing is alarmed by the increasingly intimate military alliance between the United States and Japan. At the same time, Beijing must defuse fears particularly among Asian nations about economic and military threats emanating from what many perceive to be the fast-developing, fire-breathing dragon.

Also notable is the leadership's obsession with guaranteeing sufficient and reliable supplies of oil and gas as well as other minerals and producer goods. In 2003, China became the world's second largest importer of petroleum, and the leadership has gone into overdrive in waging "petroleum diplomacy" even as the price of crude reached record levels in 2004 and 2005. The Hu-Wen team has put together an elaborate strategy to ensure energy imports not just from neighboring and Asian countries such as Russia, Indonesia, and Australia, but also suppliers as far away as Africa and South America. China has also renewed efforts to exploit offshore oil and gas, in the process setting off alarm bells in Japan and member countries of the Association of Southeast Asian Nations (ASEAN). Moreover, Beijing has locked horns with India, and particularly the United States, in its ambitious effort to line up supplies and bid for prospecting rights in countries including Sudan, Canada, and Venezuela. Yet the PRC's aggressive energy diplomacy could revive the "China threat" theory even as the Hu leadership is trying to reassure neighbors about the country's win-win development formula.

This chapter will analyze Hu's "new ideas" on the diplomatic, security, and energy fronts, together with a detailed look at ties with major countries and blocs including the United States, Japan, the European Union (EU), and ASEAN. The impact of Hu's new-look foreign and security policy on domestic issues will also be examined. Clearly, possible faux pas in Beijing's efforts to reassure its neighbors of his country's peaceful intentions could exacerbate the "anti-China containment policy" and derail the PRC's ambitious development agenda.

The Hu-Wen Team's New Approach to Foreign Policy

Revisions of Ex-President Jiang Zemin's Diplomacy

Hu Jintao vs. Jiang Zemin

During his relatively long stewardship of the CCP, ex-paramount leader Jiang Zemin worked hard at trying to leave a legacy as a "foreign policy president" much in the mode of former U.S. president Richard Nixon. Jiang's thinking was that since he could not possibly rival the economic reform achievement of Deng Xiaoping— and there was nothing much the cautious and conservative president wanted to do in political reform—foreign policy (including policy toward Taiwan and Hong Kong) would be where he could claim his place in the party pantheon.[4]

While apparently observing Deng's famous foreign-policy dictum that China should "keep a low profile" in diplomacy so as to better concentrate on economic construction, Jiang began crafting a so-called *daguo waijiao* (great power diplomacy) from the mid-1990s onward. The basic idea of great power diplomacy is that while the PRC was in the 1990s not yet a global player because of its relatively limited economic, military, and geopolitical clout, it should seek to play a bigger foreign-policy role particularly in the Asia-Pacific region.[5] Jiang, who headed the CCP's LGFA until early 2003, divided the world into basically the following power blocs: the United States, the European Union, Japan, China, and Russia. Particularly after the fall of the Soviet Union, America has become the sole superpower, thus creating the situation that Chinese experts have characterized as *yichao duoqiang* ("one superpower, several powers"). While China is the only developing—and so-cialist—country among these clusters of nations or blocs, the CCP leadership was convinced that it could gradually play the role of a big power.[6]

For Jiang, the key to whether China could live up to the reality and obligations of a "great power" in world affairs depended very much on ties with the United States. And the ex-president was, in the eyes of critics among the diplomatic establishment and the Beijing intelligentsia, pursuing a "pro-U.S." policy. Put simply, this meant that Jiang and company recognized American supremacy in the world— including major parts of the Asia-Pacific region—provided that Washington would respect Chinese suzerainty over Taiwan and continue to trade with and invest in China. Despite their vastly different ideology and backgrounds, Jiang and former president Bill Clinton got along famously, to the extent that the Chinese supremo raised in 1996 to 1998 the possibility of cementing a bilateral "constructive strategic partnership."[7]

However, the partnership never took off—and frustrations on the U.S. front would perhaps mark the biggest failing of Jiang's foreign policy. This was despite the fact that at least in the eyes of non-Shanghai-Faction-affiliated cadres as well as nationalists among Chinese, the ruler of 1.3 billion people went to great lengths to ingratiate himself with the Americans. For example, in the six months or so running up to Clinton's first official visit to China in 1998, the Jiang leadership took "anti-American" books off the shelves of Beijing bookstores—and discouraged nationalistic professors from giving speeches in public. Jiang's showing off of his English facility, for example, when he recited Abraham Lincoln's Gettysburg Address in the White House in 1997—as well as his bending over backward to secure an invitation to the Bushes' Crawford, Texas, retreat a month before his resignation from the Politburo at the Sixteenth CCP Congress—was the stuff of jokes among officials.[8]

Jiang's foreign policy as well as his domestic standing, however, was dealt a body blow by the relatively frequent ways in which his good friend Clinton let China down. The American leader's decision to allow then Taiwan president Lee Teng-hui visit the United States in 1995 precipitated one of the biggest crises in the Jiang presidency. Jiang was criticized by Politburo colleagues as well as heavyweight generals for being "too soft" on both the United States and Taiwan.[9] Then came the year 1999, an *annus horribulus* for bilateral ties. Despite having made what most Chinese regarded as overly generous foreign-trade concessions, then premier Zhu Rongji failed in his U.S. trip in April to secure a trade agreement regarding China's accession to the World Trade Organization (WTO). One month later, the Chinese Embassy in Belgrade was bombed, which sparked a week of frenetic anti-U.S. demonstrations in cities ranging from Beijing to Chengdu. Foreign-trade officials such as Wu Yi and Long Yongtu, and indeed, Zhu and Jiang, were scolded by many cadres as well as large sectors of the public for being pro-American "traitors."[10]

Even before Hu came to power at the Sixteenth Congress, his aides and advisers had privately criticized Jiang for waging a "romantic" foreign policy, that is, one divorced from a more realistic, systematic, and "scientific" appraisal of the relative strengths of China and the United States. Hu and his colleagues have taken a more comprehensive, cool-headed—and in a sense Machiavellian—approach to diplomacy. For example, Hu would only characterize ties with the United States as "a constructive, cooperative partnership." While Sino-U.S. interactions will nearly always top the foreign-policy agenda of any top CCP cadre, Hu often gives observers the impression of being a "Europeanist"—or being as "pro-Europe" or "pro-Russia" as Jiang was pro-United States. And Hu has insisted in his dealings with Washington that there will have to be clear-cut trade-offs. For instance, the United States would have to acquiesce on China's harsh policies in Xinjiang and Tibet in return for Beijing's support of the global war on terrorism. Then there was the "North Korea in exchange for Taiwan" bargain, namely, that in return for reining in the nuclear ambitions of the Kim Jong-Il regime, Beijing expected Washington to put dampers on the pro-independence gambit of the ruling Democratic Progressive Party (DPP) in Taiwan.[11]

Moreover, the Hu-Wen team is aggressively using China's newfound might and status to pursue multipronged policy objectives. The years 2004 and 2005 would go down in history as a turning point in Chinese diplomacy. Suddenly, Beijing's senior cadres, diplomats, and *waishi* (foreign affairs) specialists in the army and foreign-trade departments seemed all guns blazing in different parts of the globe. Apart from isolating Taiwan—and forcing it to sue for compromise with the CCP—Beijing's foreign and security policy goals have included counteracting Washington's "anti-China containment policy," seeking a strategic partnership with EU countries in the interest of constructing a "multipolar" world order, promoting good will with China's neighbors to secure a "harmonious environment" for economic growth, building solid relationships with key countries in Africa and Latin America, and securing a long-term supply of petroleum and other precious resources.

The sea change in PRC diplomacy was first evident when Beijing took the initiative to host the six-nation talks to defuse the North Korean nuclear crisis, a bold move that boosted its leverage with Washington, Tokyo, and Seoul. Even more remarkable was the Hu leadership's daring to take on the Americans beginning mid-2004. In the initial phases of Washington's global war on terrorism, Beijing largely acquiesced in American military action in Afghanistan and Iraq. However, the CCP leadership let it be known immediately after the reelection of George W. Bush as president that Beijing would no longer go along if Washington were to "target" Iran à la Iraq. The Hu team was also more assertive in using its United Nations Security Council veto and other means to protect quasi-allies, including the much-maligned regime in Sudan.[12]

Hu and such colleagues as Wen are among the first CCP leaders to take a comprehensive approach to security and diplomatic issues. Apart from focusing on traditional concerns such as diplomacy and military affairs, Hu and company are paying a lot of attention to the foreign-policy implications of trade, economic cooperation, technology, and energy. Thus, the 2004 *White Paper on Defense* stated clearly that "questions of conventional and unconventional [national] security are closely intertwined." The paper, which bore the imprint of new Central Military Commission (CMC) chief Hu, noted that apart from foreign and military affairs, leading cadres must take into consideration areas including information technology (IT), energy, finance, and even "environmental security."[13]

The Foreign-Policy Establishment Under Hu

Before examining Hu's foreign policy, it is instructive to look at the post–Sixteenth Congress diplomatic establishment. It is safe to say that as CCP chief, state president, and commander-in-chief, Hu pays attention mainly to three areas: the general direction of the country, including the overall progress of reform—and China's emergence as a quasi-superpower; party affairs and personnel, including the "rejuvenation" of party ideology and modernization of the party structure; and foreign policy (including Taiwan and Hong Kong). By and large, economic matters are left to Premier Wen. Particularly after the resignation of ex-president Jiang from the CMC slot in September 2004—which signaled the gradual but irrevocable eclipse of the Shanghai Faction—Hu might not need to devote as much energy to factional intrigue within the party. And it is probable that with the help of senior colleagues such as Wen, who also sits on the LGFA, Hu will for the foreseeable future reserve the bulk of his energy to foreign, security, and military affairs.[14]

Soon after he became state president in March 2003, Hu was made head of both the LGFA and the Leading Group on Taiwan Affairs (LGTA), China's highest council on reunification matters. Even before the Sixteenth CCP Congress, however, Hu had played a role in foreign policy partly in his capacity as chief of the CCP's secretive Leading Group on National Security (LGNS), which coordinates policies in areas including diplomacy, defense, energy, and foreign trade. Unlike the LGFA, which meets periodically, the LGNS is convened on an ad hoc basis to attend to crisis situations. For example, the LGNS was called together after the bombing of the Chinese Embassy in Belgrade in 1999.[15] And it is in foreign affairs that Hu has displayed a hands-on approach, often tending to the nitty-gritty of strategy instead of just formulating overarching principles.

President Hu has depended quite heavily on his foreign minister, Li Zhaoxing, a former ambassador to the United States. Li is almost universally disliked by American diplomats, who complain about his doctrinaire views and stiff manners. However, he may prove to be as powerful and productive a foreign minister as Qian Qichen, even though he does not have the requisite titles of Politburo member or vice-premier. Soon after the Sixteenth CCP Congress, Li earned Hu's trust by immediately—and quite openly—switching over the from the "Shanghai Faction" to the Hu-Wen camp. While the Shandong Province native thus incurred the ire of both ex-president Jiang and his former boss, State Councilor Tang Jiaxuan, he was able to persuade Hu to give him more policymaking authority. This is despite the fact that in the Chinese context, the foreign minister is usually an executor rather than formulator of policy.[16]

After the Sixteenth Congress, the so-called Japanese Faction in the foreign policy establishment has suffered a setback. While former minister Tang was in theory promoted to State Councilor, his portfolio did not cover much beyond Taiwan and Hong Kong affairs. Another fluent Japanese speaker in the ministry, Vice-Minister Wang Yi, acquitted himself reasonably well in being China's point man on the North Korean crisis. Wang was named ambassador to Japan in late 2004, and his political fortune depended on whether he could turn around fast-deteriorating Sino-Japanese ties (see following story). In general, the LGFA is mainly relying on diplomats who are specialists in the United States and the EU, as well as experts in nontraditional areas such as energy and foreign trade.[17]

One of Hu's fortes in foreign-policy formulation is that he takes an eclectic approach to securing advice from myriad think tanks and advisers. Experts from backgrounds including the army, intelligence, finance, energy, and foreign trade get a fair hearing. For example, quite a number of specialists on the United States as well as overall security issues from the Chinese Academy of Social Sciences

(CASS) and the Central Party School have been inducted as members of Hu's personal brain trust. Think-tank members known to have offered Hu advice on Sino-U.S. policies include CASS America Institute director Wang Jisi, Peking University professor Jia Qingguo, and vice-president of the Shanghai Institute of International Affairs Yang Jiemian, who is the brother of Vice–Foreign Minister Yang Jiechi. To better position China for its take-off in the twenty-first century, Hu has consulted historians and geographers for knowledge about the rise and fall of empires through the centuries. Many of his advisers have advanced degrees from American or European universities; and quite a few are known to have offered hawkish views and recommendations—including tough tactics toward the United States and Japan—to the LGFA.[18]

Hu also began the practice of posting a sizable number of academics and experts to foreign missions so as to let trusted aides acquire firsthand experience of diplomacy. One of the academics that the Hu team picked was Su Ge, a U.S.-educated international affairs expert. Not long after the Sixteenth Party Congress, Su, then a vice-president of Beijing Foreign Affairs University, was assigned to the Chinese Embassy in Washington as minister-counselor in charge of congressional relations, lobbying, and public relations. He had under him a team of around twenty young Chinese diplomats, many of them trained in the United States and other English-speaking countries.[19]

The Theory of Balance and the Economic Card

According to Beijing-based scholars, the watchwords of the Fourth-Generation leadership's new-style diplomacy could be seeking diplomatic balance and flashing the economic card. Under the Hu-Wen leadership, the all-powerful LGFA has whipped into shape a multipronged approach to boost China's status in the international community while ensuring good relations with key powers as well as the country's neighbors.

The imperative of balance means, first, seeking cordial ties with the great powers and blocs—the EU, ASEAN, Russia, and Japan—while ensuring at least a nonconfrontational relationship with the United States. Moreover, Beijing's ability to play one country or bloc off against another would help the PRC maintain its global clout as well as a safe neighborhood. Thus, despite residual distrust between the erstwhile communist comrades, Beijing and Moscow have boosted ties in light of their common goal of checking U.S. preponderance. Indeed, while Hu is one generation younger than cadres who studied in the Soviet bloc in the 1950s, he shares to some extent a veteran party functionary's sympathy for the socialist values first propagated by the Soviet Union.[20]

And while it is obvious that Beijing accords top priority to Sino-U.S. ties, the Hu leadership is not afraid to underscore its "socialist solidarity" with quasi-Stalinist regimes such as North Korea and Cuba. Thus, in 2003, the president extended a red carpet for one of the most noted antagonists of "U.S. imperialism," Cuban dictator Fidel Castro. While hosting Castro's visit, Hu noted that China and Cuba had "shared ideals and beliefs." "Irrespective of the changes in the international situation, our faith in the future of socialism will not be shaken," Hu said. The president expressed the same enthusiasm when he celebrated the two countries' "brotherhood" on a visit to Havana in late 2004.[21]

The theory of balance is also evident in Beijing's relations with pairs of countries that are robust enemies of each other. The CCP leadership has since the 1970s maintained a "comradely partnership" with Pakistan partly with a view to checking the potential threat of India. Since the late 1990s, however, relations with India have undergone a sea change. This has led to joint naval exercises and the first tour of Tibet by an Indian military delegation.[22] The fact that Beijing can even play the role of "peacemaker" between New Delhi and Islamabad has contributed to security in China's backyard and boosted the clout of the Middle Kingdom. In the problematic Korean Peninsula, Beijing has been able to maintain relatively good ties with the two Koreas. And the Korean card is useful for Beijing in dealings with the United States and Japan.

On a larger scale, Beijing is reasonably optimistic that if it could secure a partnership arrangement with the EU—or at least "old Europe" stalwarts such as France and Germany—an inchoate "China–EU axis" could go some way toward counterbalancing U.S. influence. And this balance is essential to Beijing's conception of a "multipolar world," or a global order that is not dominated by the United States. For example, Sino-European cooperation in arenas such as the United Nations could fend off the "unilateralist" tendencies of the George W. Bush administration. Thus in its first-ever White Paper on Sino-EU relations published in late 2003, Beijing envisaged a "full strategic partnership" with the EU in areas including trade, culture, technology, defense, and space exploration.[23]

China's delicate and relatively effective diplomatic balancing act has been made possible by its mushrooming economy—and the skillful playing of the business card. As Premier Wen said while visiting the United States in late 2003, a country's foreign policy was increasingly "based on [perceptions of] national interest and economic development."[24] China had by late 2004 emerged as the third-largest trading nation in the world. American expert on the Chinese economy Nicholas Lardy estimated that from 2000 to 2003, the PRC accounted for 20 percent of the increase in global trade. Also in 2004, the PRC surpassed the United States as the largest consumer in the world. And China's huge market has proven to be an irresistible magnet even for First World countries and blocs such as the EU, and to a considerable extent, the United States and Japan.[25]

It is the economic card that has become a key catalyst for promoting Sino-EU ties. Take relations with France, perhaps China's staunchest friend in Europe. It is the desire to sell Airbuses and Mirage jets to China—as much as seeking Chinese help to ward off Bush-style unilateralism—that underlies President Jacques Chirac's "tilt" toward the PRC. And despite China's heavy dependence on the U.S. market, there are growing indications that this is no longer a one-way street. U.S. companies in areas ranging from agribusiness to aerospace are lobbying the government and Congress to pursue a more conciliatory policy toward the Beijing regime.[26]

And it is again the import card that is the backbone of China's good-neighborly policy as well as the "theory of the peaceful rise of China" (see following section). As the "world factory" grows in size, China requires a plethora of raw materials ranging from minerals to high-tech know-how. Chinese imports jumped a hefty 40 percent in 2003—and the PRC in 2004 sustained sizable trade deficits with practically all its neighbors.[27] Even countries with an overall technological edge over China, such as South Korea, have become dependent on their mounting trade surplus with the PRC. The impact of Beijing's business card is particularly felt in the relatively less well-off ASEAN. Until recently, most ASEAN countries were complaining about China taking away foreign direct investment from them. Beijing, however, has managed to partially mollify these neighbors by boosting imports—including minerals, commodities, and agricultural produce—through free-trade agreements some of which have already taken effect.[28]

Theory of Good Neighborliness and the "Peaceful Rise" Doctrine

Securing Peace in China's Backyard

China's policy of good neighborliness—or maintaining cordial ties with peripheral countries, especially those with which it has crossed swords—is closely tied to the belief by recent leaders including Deng, Jiang, and Hu that the country must take advantage of the overall peaceful international climate to focus on economic construction. While Deng played a key role in the two major events that contributed to tension with the country's neighbors, namely the 1979 Vietnam War and the 1989 Tiananmen Square massacre, he began to preach a policy of diplomatic reconciliation from the early 1990s onward. And as we saw in Chapter 2, Hu is a keen advocate of *jiyulun* (the theory of opportunity)—that China must seize the rare window of opportunity of this and the next decade to build up its comprehensive strength. This requires, of course, that Beijing make peace with its many neighbors.[29]

While Chinese rulers have through the centuries spent an inordinate amount of time pacifying the *yiman,* or barbarians, lurking at the fringes of the Middle Kingdom, Hu and his LGFA can be credited for coming up with a "scientific" approach to ensuring a productive relationship with China's neighbors. As Hu put it in an internal speech in early 2004: "China's opportunities—and challenges—lie in [its relations with] peripheral countries; the latter provide China with hope, but can also be a cause of instability."[30]

Noted international affairs scholar Wang Yizhou pointed out in 2004 that one major impediment to China's rise—as well as its attempts to secure a peaceful global environment—was that it had more than thirty neighbors, fourteen of which shared direct boundaries with the Middle Kingdom. He noted that China was involved in territorial disputes of one form or another with a dozen-odd countries. "It is almost impossible for a country with that many sovereignty disputes [with its neighbors] to emerge as a global power," he said. Wang quoted Henry Kissinger as comparing the geopolitical characteristics of China and the United States. The former U.S. secretary of state pointed out that the United States had the immense advantage of having just two immediate neighbors, Canada and Mexico, both of which were on reasonably good terms with the United States.[31]

As Beijing-based political scientist Ruan Zongze indicated, good neighborliness involved "the concept of maintaining peace with, mollifying, and enriching your neighbors." This mantra of co-prosperity was repeated by Hu and Wen on their trips to neighboring countries, when the top leaders invariably played up the huge export surpluses that almost all Asian countries were enjoying with China.[32] As of early 2005, Beijing had quite successfully boosted ties with erstwhile foes such as Vietnam, Russia, and India—in addition to members of ASEAN, which have clashed with China over the Spratly Islands and other issues. One exception is Japan. From the early 2000s onward, Sino-Japanese relations have entered a vicious cycle (see following section). Then there was Beijing's misguided attempt in early 2004 to revive the controversy over the origins of the near-mythical Koguryo Empire, which disappeared from maps 1,300 years ago. While Koreans look upon the Koguryo as the origin of modern Korea, Beijing claimed that it was but a "Chinese vassal state." Seoul saw this as a possible preemptive move by the Chinese to prevent border disputes should the two Koreas become united.[33]

Heping Jueqi—The "Peaceful Emergence of China"

Crucial to Beijing's woo-your-neighbor gambit is the concept of *heping jueqi*, or "peaceful rise," which was first raised by a group of innovative Shanghai-based academics and cadres to counter the "China Threat theory." *Heping jueqi*, which underscores the fact that China will never seek hegemony, also has a strong economic component. As former Central Party School vice-president Zheng Bijian put it, "peaceful rise" implies that "China must seek a peaceful global environment to develop its economy even as it tries to safeguard world peace through development." A former aide to the late party chief Hu Yaobang, Zheng was instrumental in putting new ideas in the ears of President Hu. Beijing's line is that far from hurting other nations, China's newfound preeminence will bring them sizable and concrete gains.[34]

As Premier Wen pointed out in his international press conference at the 2004 National People's Congress (NPC), China's emergence would come about "mainly owing to the country's own forces and in accordance with [the philosophy of] independence and self-renewal." Wen assured the global audience that China emergence, which required the work of at least several generations, "will not obstruct or intimidate other people." And at his much-noted speech at Harvard University later that year, Wen stressed that his country would observe the Confucianist ideal of *yiheweigui,* "taking peace as the highest ideal."[35] On a more practical level, Chinese theorists have drawn the distinction between the rapid expansion of China's economy in the past ten years and the take-off of Japan and that of the Four Asian Dragons (South Korea, Singapore, Taiwan, and Hong Kong) from the 1970s onward. Beijing's contention is that while the economic juggernauts of Japan and the dragons were mostly predicated upon aggressive, even predatory exports, China's growth can be attributed not just to overseas sales but also to massive domestic consumption and foreign investment.[36]

Equally importantly, China will make its door wide open to imports, particularly from less well-off countries in the region. Moreover, the "world factory" along China's coast has allowed companies from industrialized neighbors such as Japan and South Korea to take advantage of its cheap labor and land costs to manufacture high value-added items for export to the rest of the world. And Beijing has been successful in putting symbiotic economic relations with its neighbors on a permanent footing through concluding free trade agreements (FTAs) with ASEAN as well as with individual countries. For poorer countries in China's southwestern backyard such as Cambodia, Laos, Myanmar, and Vietnam, Beijing began in 2004 to implement a kind of a Chinese-style Marshall Plan, particularly in the area of infrastructure building. Thus, Beijing could claim with some justification that its *heping jueqi* plank has contributed to Asia's well-being.[37]

On the diplomatic and political front—especially regarding flashpoints such as the Spratly Islands—Hu and company have tried to sell the idea of shelving sovereignty disputes and focusing on the joint development of resources. In late 2003, Beijing signed a landmark nonaggression pact with ASEAN, meaning that sovereignty-related disagreements would be set aside so as to promote common interests. Moreover, People's Liberation Army (PLA) generals have also gotten into the act by underscoring China's peaceful intentions in the Asia-Pacific region. During a tour of Southeast Asia in early 2004, Defense minister General Cao Gangchuan noted that "China is determined to seek its emergence through peaceful means." "China will not go down the old road of some major Western countries, which embarked on an expansionist path after their rise to power," Cao said.[38]

As of 2005, however, China's *heping jueqi* gambit has only received mixed reviews from its neighbors. Certainly, there is no lack of diplomatically couched compliments coming particularly from the ASEAN states. For example, leaders in Malaysia and Thailand have characterized their giant neighbor as a "benevolent elephant"—not the predatory tiger or fire-breathing dragon with which independent academic critics in these countries would sometimes compare the newly aggressive China. Yet while the China Threat theory has been less frequently cited by Asian politicians and commentators, Beijing will have to do a lot more in winning friends and building bridges to former foes.

The image of a fast-rising China wielding formidable economic, diplomatic, and military powers in pursuit of its national interests—however legitimate the latter may be—could clash with that of an all-smiles, conciliatory neighbor. Take

China's new urgency for securing reliable supplies of oil and gas and other raw materials, seen as a prerequisite for sustained economic growth. As CASS economist Yang Fan noted, China's *heping jueqi* game plan would be restricted by internal factors such as "shortage of resources and energy as well as grain insufficiency."[39] An equally serious impediment to *heping jueqi*, however, is China's refusal to overhaul its outdated governmental structures. Thanks to the country's WTO accession in late 2001, more of China's economic operations have converged with international norms. The winds of globalization, however, have hardly touched Chinese political institutions and systems. Take the PLA, which is a major factor behind the China Threat theory. Most Asia-Pacific countries are disturbed by the PLA's lack of transparency and its "state within a state" status, particularly the fact that it reports only to the CCP's dominant faction.

And the PLA's apparent readiness to wage a "war of liberation" to reabsorb Taiwan has raised questions about the CCP leadership's policy of good neighborliness and global responsibility. As U.S. Sinologist Evan Medeiros pointed out, a vocal minority of hawkish elements in Beijing had argued that "committing to a peaceful rise doctrine could undermine China's ability to deter Taiwan" from pursuing separatism. [40] China's irresponsible handling of the SARS outbreak in early 2003 also raised the specter of a viral version of the Yellow Peril. And while the Hu-Wen team had since improved transparency over public health issues, there were accusations a year later that Beijing had been tardy in disclosing information about new SARS cases as well as the bird flu epidemic.

Cao Siyuan, a constitutional scholar, has raised queries about the viability of *heping jueqi* in the absence of real liberalization in domestic politics. "It is doubtful that foreigners will be convinced about China's peaceful ascendancy if it sticks to a nontransparent and undemocratic political system," he said. "A leadership's commitment to global fraternity and solidarity will be called into doubt if it is so reluctant to give its own people adequate human rights."[41] Owing to the many contradictions inherent in the "peaceful rise" ideal, the term was used with less frequency if not abandoned by the end of 2004. Instead, leaders such as President Hu were cleaving to the more mundane—and safer—slogan of "peace and development."[42]

Efforts to Thwart the "Anti-China Containment Policy"

Beijing's Bid to Counter Washington's "Encirclement Policy" Against China

While the September 11, 2001, tragedies convinced much of the American leadership that China was at least in the near term not Washington's number one enemy, Beijing has never abandoned its conviction that the U.S. leadership is spearheading an anti-China *weidu*, or containment policy. Not just military hawks but most cadres are convinced that Washington is trying to encircle and tame China by using allies and proxies including Japan, South Korea, the Philippines, Taiwan, Australia, and other Asia-Pacific nations.

For example, Beijing has harbored deep suspicions over the Bush administration's goal of developing a theater missile defense (TMD) system. On the surface, the Chinese leadership's opposition to TMD had weakened by 2003 and 2004—largely because it was not able to form a Beijing–Moscow united front against the "star wars" offensive. Yet Beijing has continued to raise its guard against the possibility of America's Asian allies hitching onto the TMD wagon. For example, the Junichiro Koizumi government has cited the threat of North Korean weapons of mass destruction (WMD) to argue for more funds to develop a missile-defense system.[43] And the pro-separatist Democratic Progressive Party (DPP) administration in Taiwan is eager to procure some form of TMD facility against the 600–odd PLA missiles targeting the island.

Beijing is nervous about enhanced cooperation between the United States and its Asian allies—especially Japan—to "police" the Asia-Pacific region and at the same time contain China. The LGFA was in 2004 paying special attention to reports that the Koizumi government was about to, in the words of the China News Service (CNS), "extend the Japan–U.S. alliance to the entire world." This meant that the security arrangement with the United States should not just be confined to areas immediately around Japan. Quoting the Japanese media, CNS noted that the United States wanted to turn Japan into a multiple-use base from which U.S. military units can be deployed to Asia, the Middle East, and even Africa. In a stinging critique of Tokyo, the *China Daily* all but called Japan a running dog of the United States. "Japanese Prime Minister Junichiro Koizumi is dubbed an 'Asian Blair' for 'wholeheartedly supporting' the United States launching the Iraq War," the official paper said.[44]

Moreover, the United States has beefed up military relations with individual ASEAN members with a view, in Beijing's perspective, to "containing" the Middle Kingdom. And these enhanced military ties have been accomplished under the guise of the United States aiding the counterterrorism capacities of Asian defense forces. For example, Philippine president Gloria Arroyo indicated in April 2004 that apart from training her country's military units to fight Muslim terrorists and insurgents, the United States had been coaching local soldiers to repel a possible Chinese military putsch in the Spratly Islands.[45] At the same time, U.S.-Indonesian forces hosted large-scale exercises near the strategic Batam Island, which is close to Singapore and major sea lanes. Beijing is also watching the U.S.-Vietnamese rapprochement with disquiet. For instance, Hanoi has allowed American naval vessels to use facilities at Cam Ranh Bay for reprovisioning and other logistics purposes.

The United States has also significantly bolstered its influence with China's southwestern and northwestern neighbors. Both prior to and after U.S. military action in Afghanistan, Washington has built up a semi-alliance relationship with the Kabul administration. And after the Afghan war, Washington began stationing troops in Uzbekistan, Tajikistan, and Kyrgyzstan, right in China's backyard. While Sino-Pakistan ties have remained intimate, Islamabad has become reliant as never before on U.S. economic and military aid. And such dependence will increase after Washington's decision in early 2005 to sell Pakistan F-16 fighter jets. Relations between Washington and New Delhi have also improved significantly, culminating in the White House's decision in mid-2005 to resume the sale of high-tech weapons and nuclear technology to India. This dramatic upgrading of U.S.–India ties has been attributed to Washington's desire to "contain" China.[46]

"Countercontainment," or how to protect China against the marauding "neo-imperialists," will likely be a leitmotif of the Hu-Wen team's diplomacy. Obviously, beefing up the PLA will be a major measure of defense. Military analysts have noted the emphasis that the CMC has put on submarines, jet fighters, and particularly missiles, including those that can hit U.S. aircraft carriers in the Asia-Pacific region.[47] Apart from military deterrence, Beijing is relying on diplomacy such as the vaunted good-neighborly policy to keep its borders secure—and fend off any "encirclement conspiracy."

Given America's decades-long ties with countries such as Japan, South Korea, Australia, and the Philippines, it will be difficult for Beijing to drive a wedge through Washington's alliance relationship with any one of these nations. However, Hu and his LGTA colleagues hope that Tokyo, Seoul, Canberra, and Manila can at least be persuaded that in the event of a Sino-U.S. military conflict—particularly one over Taiwan—these U.S. allies would agree not to allow American forces to use their airports or ports for military action against the PRC. Beijing also needs to ensure that in the unlikely event of the military subjugation of Taiwan, trading partners will not follow Washington's possible imposition of a trade embargo on the PRC. To some extent, this objective was achieved with Australia when Foreign Minister Alexander Downer indicated while on a trip to Beijing in 2004 that should war break out in the Taiwan Strait due to Taipei's declaration of independence, Canberra would take a "neutralist" position. The same principle was declared by Singapore shortly afterward.[48]

The main objective for the proactive role Beijing has played in sustaining the Shanghai Cooperation Organization (SCO, which groups China, Russia, Kazakhstan, Uzbekistan, Kyrzystan, and Tajikistan) is that this relatively loose outfit could somehow counterbalance the growing influence of NATO. After the September 11, 2001, events, SCO members held several joint military exercises in the interest of fighting terrorism. At least from Beijing's point of view, the six nations should form some kind of quasi-military alliance in the interest of countering U.S. predominance. Thus, during Hu's tour of Russia in June 2003—his first major trip as state president—the Chinese supremo sought not only to consolidate ties with Russia but to breathe new life into the SCO. Hu was successful in persuading other SCO states to set up a permanent secretariat in Beijing, as well as to conduct a series of joint exercises aimed at curbing terrorism and separatism.[49]

With Russian help, Beijing was able in July 2005 to enlarge the SCO to incorporate "observer countries" including Iran, India, Pakistan, and Mongolia. The aggrandizement of the SCO was celebrated in the Chinese media as a successful attempt to beat back efforts by the United States to co-opt countries in the volatile region, particularly through economic aid and the spread of democratic ideas. Both Beijing and Moscow believed that Washington was instrumental in the series of "velvet revolutions" that shook up Georgia, Ukraine, and most recently Kyrgyzstan (see following section). As Chinese scholar Xu Xiantian noted, the expanded SCO had become "the biggest and most populous security and trade-oriented organization in the Euro-Asian land mass" and would play a useful role in stabilizing the region.[50]

Beijing's Anti-Containment Policy After the Iraq War

While Beijing largely acquiesced in the beginning of the Iraq War of 2003, this dramatic display of U.S. "unilateralism" and firepower has had a profound impact on the CCP leadership's perception of the dangers of Bush-style neoconservatism. And Beijing is fine-tuning its domestic and security policies to counter American "neo-imperialism." While, given China's fast-growing economic and military muscle, it is unlikely that the PRC itself will be a target of preemptive strikes, the CCP leadership is fearful of U.S. military power projection close to its borders. Chinese strategists were shocked by the White House's National Security Strategy (NSS) of late 2002, which justified the United States taking preemptive military actions against regimes that could be developing WMDs. The NSS also noted that the United States would not allow another power to develop a level of military strength that could approximate that of the United States.[51]

As *People's Daily* commentator Huang Peizhao pointed out in March 2003, U.S. moves in the Middle East "have served the goal of seeking worldwide domination." State Council think-tank member Tong Gang saw the conflict as the first salvo in Washington's bid to "build a new world order under U.S. domination." CASS economist Zuo Dapei, who had championed against China's accession to the WTO, said the Iraq War had been an eye-opener, particularly to Chinese who still harbored illusions about American democracy. "The Iraqi people have taught Chinese the imperative of maintaining national dignity and sovereignty," Zuo said. "The war has demonstrated America's efforts at world domination—and the importance of China's ability to maintain its independence and defense capabilities."[52]

In 2003, a group of radical strategists went so far as to label Bush-style unilateralism "neo-Nazism." "Hawkish cadres in the party and army think the Bush team is pursuing more than mere unilateralism," said a Chinese source close to the diplomatic establishment. "These radicals believe that Washington is out to dominate the world through targeting countries and governments that espouse different economic and political systems." According to an internally circulated paper on "neo-Nazism," Washington was seeking world domination through not so much conquering terrain as assuming control over vital resources and technologies ranging from petroleum to IT. And while Nazi Germany had tried to exterminate so-called inferior races, Washington, according to this paper, was scheming to marginalize if not subjugate countries with alien cultures and institutions such as radical Islam or socialism.[53] While it is true that leaders such as Hu and Wen might not share this extreme view, they repeatedly expressed concern about Washington's "hegemonic expansionism" and its impact on China.

A number of Chinese strategists were convinced that if the United States could extricate itself from Iraq, Bush might in his second term shift his attention—and American power projection—to East Asia with the goal of taming North Korea and then China. For example, Washington might launch "surgical" preemptive strikes against the Democratic People's Republic of Korea (DPRK) so as to take out its nuclear-weapons facilities. Such misgivings were confirmed, at least in Chinese eyes, by Washington's announcement in mid-2004 that the United States was redeploying its forces in Asia. In a statement, the White House indicated that for the Asian region, the United States would "improve its ability to deter, dissuade, and defeat challenges through strengthened long-range strike capabilities, streamlined and consolidated headquarters, and a network of access arrangements." For example, more aircraft carriers would be stationed in beefed-up facilities in Hawaii, Japan, Okinawa, and Guam. The semi-official *International Herald Leader* reported that the Pentagon wanted to produce more F-22s, deemed as the only jet fighter that can outmaneuver the Russian Su-30s acquired by the PLA.[54]

These considerations prompted some cadres to argue that perhaps Beijing should change its long-standing geopolitical strategy: that it is best for China to follow late patriarch Deng's dictum about "seeking cooperation and avoiding confrontation" with the United States. "Now, many cadres and think-tank members are arguing that Beijing should adopt a more assertive policy to thwart potential U.S. aggression," said an academic who is a member of a Beijing-based foreign-policy think tank. "Merely avoiding confrontation would no longer do."[55] Indeed, hard-line elements in the PLA had advocated providing weapons to North Korea to help Pyongyang defend itself against a possible U.S. missile attack. Military sources in Beijing said the CMC had in mid-2004 moved more troops and heavy military equipment into the Shenyang Military Region near North Korea. Even less hawkish experts were advocating that the national security apparatus be beefed up. CASS political economist Yang Fan noted that recent global flare-ups had alerted China to the imperative of improving national security. "Equal weight should be given to economic development and national security," Yang said. "As we become more prosperous, we must concentrate our forces on defending national security and interests."[56]

Fighting Washington's "Containment Policy" in 2005

One of Beijing's worst nightmares appeared to be coming true in the first half of 2005. Having apparently steadied the course in the Middle East, the Bush administration seemed in early 2005 to be turning to Asia to tackle its long-standing "strategic competitor." While this particular term had been shelved since 9/11, there were signs at least from Beijing's perspective that Washington was spear-heading multipronged tactics to contain the fast-rising Asian giant.

In Beijing's eyes, the new doctrine of containment was spelled out during a visit by Secretary of State Condoleezza Rice to Tokyo as part of her Asian tour of March 2005. Echoing President Bush's State of the Union address, which pushed a foreign policy predicated upon "spreading democracy," Rice noted that "even China must eventually embrace some form of open, genuinely representative government." And she dropped hints that the United States would bring about a democratic China through joint actions with countries including Japan, South Korea, and India.[57] The same points were made by Bush himself during a brief visit to Beijing in November 2005. Prior to his summit with Hu, the U.S. leader worshipped at a Beijing church, after which he indicated, "my hope is that the government of China will not fear Christians who gather to worship openly." Bush later told Hu that "it is important that social, political and religious freedoms grow in China."[58]

A Beijing source close to the Chinese foreign-policy establishment said President Hu and his advisers were not surprised by Rice and Bush's less-than-subtle remarks about possibilities of containing China and "infiltrating" the country with democratic ideals. The CCP leadership had first been alerted to Bush's hardening attitude toward China by enhanced military cooperation between the United States and Japan. The source said Beijing saw the joint U.S.-Japan defense statement— released in February after a meeting in Washington between the defense and for-eign-policy chiefs of the two countries—as a turning point in China-U.S. relations. The U.S.-Japan accord referred to the looming threat of the PLA, and cited for the first time the maintenance of peace in the Taiwan Strait as a "common strategic objective" of the allies. "[The] meeting may mark the end of the extended Beijing– Washington honeymoon which came about because of 9/11," the source said. "Bush seems to have picked up the threads of his pre-9/11 agenda of containing China."[59]

Moreover, explosive events in Kyrgyzstan at about the same time were inter-preted by a number of Hu advisers as another manifestation of Bush's aggravated policy of "spreading democracy." The "Tulip Revolution" in Bishkek led to the exile to Moscow of former president Askar Akayev, deemed a good friend of Beijing's. Indeed, by early 2005, Beijing was monitoring with unease apparent efforts by the Bush administration to promote Western-style democracy in former Soviet states including Georgia and Ukraine. The CCP leadership's reaction to Washington's alleged role in the Ukrainian "Orange Revolution"—in which pro-West presidential candidate Viktor Yushchenko swept to power thanks partly to American help—was not substantially different from that of Moscow.[60]

Chinese commentators noted how Washington could kill several birds with one stone should it manage to control the Kyrgyz government. Given the 1,100– kilometer border between Kyrgyzstan and China, the fall of the Akayev regime would be no small victory for the "containment policy." Moreover, U.S. preponderance in Central Asia could pose a threat to the giant oil pipeline that is being built between Kazakhstan and the Xinjiang Autonomous Region (XAR).[61] The Beijing leadership swiftly counterattacked by providing economic and military aid to the administration of Uzbek president Islam Karimov when that country was rocked by instability two months after Kyrgyzstan. The Karimov regime has since been demanding that U.S. forces leave the strategically located country.[62] And as discussed above, Beijing and Moscow joined hands in mid-2005 to expand the SCO as a broad-based security and economic Euro-Asia bloc.

In a discussion of whether the three allies cited by Rice—Japan, South Korea, and India—would play a big role in the Washington-led anti-China game plan, a panel of *People's Daily* experts and journalists expressed optimism that "the U.S. plot to encircle China will come to no avail." The specialists reckoned that only Japan would faithfully do Washington's bidding. Korean expert Shen Lin noted that Seoul "will not damage its ties with China because of the U.S." Shen added that South Korean politicians and opinion leaders had expressed reservations about Washington's plans to use Korean-based U.S. military facilities to promote American interests in northeast Asia.[63]

New Delhi–based *People's Daily* journalist Ren Yan indicated that "India will not blindly follow the lead of the U.S." because the strategic partnership that Washington wanted to forge with the South Asian giant was "centered on American interests." One purpose of Premier Wen's trip to India in April 2005 was to cement a Chinese-Indian "strategic partnership" through means including resolving the decades-old border dispute between the two countries. Analysts said despite deep-seated suspicions between the two neighbors, the CCP leadership was confident that dramatic improvement in ties with India the past few years would at least persuade New Delhi not to become a pawn in America's anti-China machinations.[64]

By 2004, Beijing had for all intents and purposes given up Deng's adage about *taoguang yanghui*, or "taking a low profile." This was despite claims by diplomats such as Wu Jianmin that "Chinese foreign policy will uphold the *taoguang yanghui* principle over the long haul."[65] Beijing's suspicion that Bush might adopt a harsher China policy during the rest of his presidency has predisposed the Hu leadership to be more determined to boost the PLA arsenal. Hu and his colleagues are also expected to adopt multipronged measures to counter Washington's "encirclement plot." For example, Beijing might play the "North Korean card" as a means to pin down the United States and Japan. Beijing is also gunning for new "strategic relationships" with major countries in Asia—and in Africa and Latin America—for purposes including countering a U.S.-dominated world order.[66]

A People-Oriented Foreign Policy?

Will President Hu's vaunted *yiren weiben* (putting people first) credo also apply to foreign and security policies? This is one of the most crucial issues affecting how the Hu-Wen administration will handle international relations in the coming decade. Since taking over power, the Hu-Wen team has demonstrated a readiness to be more receptive to public demands as long as the Communist Party's monopoly on power is not compromised. Compared to the Jiang administration, the "masses-come-first" Hu-Wen leadership has been much faster in responding to the grievances particularly of "disadvantaged sectors" of society (see Chapters 3 and 4). But how about the people's equally vehement voices about foreign affairs, including volatile questions over the "breakaway province" of Taiwan?

Ex-president Jiang, who wants to go down in history as China's "foreign-policy president," was most scrupulous about keeping the voice of the people away from diplomacy. In determining what Chinese should—and should not—know, media censors and political commissars were at times stricter with foreign news than local developments. On a few occasions, Jiang found it useful to let "spontaneous" outbreaks of popular emotions help his diplomatic pursuit. Witness the expressions of anti-U.S. feelings in the wake of the bombing of the Chinese Embassy in Belgrade in 1999, as well as during the so-called spy plane incident of 2001. By and large, however, Jiang realized very well that while nationalism could be used to promote national cohesiveness—and to put pressure on foreign governments—it is a double-edged sword.[67]

After the Sixteenth Congress, Beijing's "putting-people-first" diplomacy has mostly consisted of promoting the transparency of diplomatic policymaking. For example, the twice-weekly meet-the-press sessions by spokesmen of the Ministry of Foreign Affairs (MOFA) were made immediately available on the Internet. Cadres in the MOFA Information Office started monitoring chat rooms to gauge popular reaction to diplomatic developments. The ministry also staged "open house" events several times a year in which senior diplomats were on hand to answer citizens' queries about foreign policy.[68]

But how about more efforts by the Hu-Wen team to ensure that popular feelings about foreign countries or diplomatic issues are properly addressed? At least as far as Japan is concerned, Beijing has, up to a point, allowed nationalists a freer hand in expressing their views about sovereignty disputes over the Diaoyu or Senkaku islands—as well as seeking war reparations. "Anti-Japanese" activists such as Tong Zeng, who were forced to lie low during the Jiang regime, have been able to openly recruit members and organize anti-Tokyo protests. Thus Tong had a field day during the three weeks of rabid anti-Japanese protests in March and April 2005. At the same time, Hu realized that letting nationalist sentiments go too far could constrict his diplomats' elbow room. This is why efforts were also taken to rein in the demonstrators as well as xenophobic websites after the nationalists' point had been made (see section on Sino-Japanese relations). However, Hu's relatively more tolerant attitude toward anti-foreign feelings has been criticized not only in Japan but in the United States and other Western countries.[69]

As international affairs expert Wang Yizhou pointed out, *yiren weiben*–style diplomacy had also manifested itself in the foreign-policy establishment's paying more attention to "people-oriented matters" such as the situation of overseas Chinese students and workers. This was despite the fact that, as noted by Luo Tianguang, director of the MOFA Consular Section, the ministry faced financial and other constraints when it tried to look after the interests of Chinese living or working overseas. Luo said embassies and consulates often had to ask for donations from local Chinese communities, foundations, and charity organizations in order to secure the funds to run programs for overseas Chinese residents.[70]

Overall, Beijing, as well as its overseas missions, has acted much more swiftly than in the past in coming to the rescue of Chinese working abroad. Notable examples included the heavy pressure that the Chinese government put on the Madrid government after Chinese shoe manufacturers based in Spain were attacked by vandals. Beijing also used diplomatic and other means to protect the safety of some 100,000 Chinese businessmen and laborers based in South Africa, many of whom were the target of burglaries and kidnappings. Sino-U.S. relations were strained when Beijing lodged strong protests after Chinese tourist Zhao Yan was beaten up after she had been picked up by American police as an "illegal immigrant." Beijing also protested vociferously in late 2005 when several female tourists to Malaysia were allegedly subject to humiliating treatment by immigration officials.[71]

Beijing has also been more willing to shoulder its global duties such as making donations to countries that have been hit by natural disasters. China's relief funds for the victims of the December 2004 tsunami were on a par with those from the United States. The Hu administration has also been making more contributions to United Nations–related projects, including peacekeeping missions in places as far away as Haiti. By the end of 2004, about 1,000 officers from the PLA and People's Armed Police were involved in UN-sponsored missions in twelve countries. Apart from demonstrating China's willingness to fulfill international obligations, this new vehicle of Chinese diplomacy will serve purposes such as putting pressure on Taiwan. For example, some observers in the United States and Taipei were worried that Beijing's new clout in Haiti would prompt the Caribbean country to consider switching diplomatic recognition from Taiwan to the PRC.[72]

"Energy Diplomacy"—The Search for Reliable Supplies of Oil and Gas

"Energy diplomacy" is expected to play an increasingly vital role in the Hu-Wen team's foreign and security policy. Compared to the Jiang Zemin administration, the Fourth-Generation leadership has put a higher priority on ensuring the reliable supply of energy, minerals, and raw materials ranging from oil and gas to water. Diplomats and cadres under the Hu-Wen group are eager to use diplomatic, economic, military, and other means to secure the friendship or at least acquiescence of foreign countries from which Beijing must acquire petroleum and other resources. As CASS expert Shen Jiru noted in mid-2004, the question of energy is "inextricably linked to state security, strategic economic interests, and foreign-policy maneuvers."[73]

Of all the resources and minerals, oil and gas stand out as the most crucial, and this section will focus primarily on "oil diplomacy." This is despite the fact that China's search for, for example, water resources has also figured prominently in diplomatic wrangling with countries including Burma, Vietnam, Thailand, and India, which occupy the lower reaches of waterways originating from western China such as the Mekong and the Nu Jiang rivers.[74]

China surpassed Japan as the second largest importer of crude oil in 2003, when China's degree of dependence on imports reached a horrendous 37 percent. In 2004, the PRC bought two million barrels of oil a day, and most estimates say that the figure could reach six million barrels by 2015.[75] Priorities for Beijing's energy diplomacy include looking for new and secure supplies of oil and gas, as well as more aggressive exploitation of such resources both within China and in peripheral waters. The oil imperative would also provide an excuse for the PLA to expand particularly its navy and air force, if only to ensure the safety of sea lanes through which China-bound tankers have to pass.[76] Given that Asian powers from Japan to India are also getting hyper-nervous about energy security, it is not surprising that the CCP leadership's newly assertive stance has engendered disputes with several countries, thereby jeopardizing the image of the "peaceful rise of China."

Securing Long-term Oil Supplies vs. Great Power Diplomacy

Given that China gets more than 60 percent of its imported crude from the Middle East, the PRC must ensure and even boost its supplies from this key oil-producing region. For reasons including the Hu leadership's reservations about direct confrontation with Bush's global anti-terrorist campaign, Beijing largely acquiesced in the U.S. invasion of Iraq in 2003. However, the CCP leadership decided to act tough regarding Iran, where China had made substantial investments in areas including oil wells and infrastructure. The Hu-led LGFA's topmost fear was that Washington would next target and subjugate Iran à la Iraq, after which the bulk of the oil resources in the Middle East could come under U.S. control.[77]

In November 2004, Beijing made it known that it objected to the issue of the Iranian nuclear program being referred to the United Nations Security Council (UNSC); in any case, Chinese diplomats dropped strong hints that Beijing would cast its veto if the UNSC were to vote on sanctions against Iran. Emblematic of Beijing's more assertive stance toward the Middle East was Li Zhaoxing's brief but high-profile trip to Tehran the same month, in which the foreign minister pledged strong support for Iran. Beijing was amply rewarded for its determination to lock horns with the United States. In October, oil giant Sinopec signed contracts with Tehran worth close to US$100 billion for items including annual imports of 10 million metric tons of liquefied natural gas for twenty-five years as well as exploitation rights to the Yadavaran Oilfield.[78] And during Li's visit, Iranian petroleum minister Bijan Zanganeh expressed the hope that China would soon displace Japan as the largest importer of Iranian crude and gas. Referring to the possibility that Bush might again start military action in the Middle East, President Hu reportedly said at a LGFA meeting in late 2004 that China "must do all it can to ensure a favorable international climate for its economic development."[79]

Beijing's efforts to secure oil and gas as well as other vital raw materials from the Asia-Pacific region—especially Australia and Indonesia—have been particularly successful, to the extent that China's huge purchases have even yielded bonus diplomatic effects. For example, Canberra has demonstrated "pro-China" sentiments on a number of issues including the Taiwan Strait (see following story).[80] Yet attempts to procure reliable supplies of oil from another major source—Russia and states bordering the Caspian Sea such as Kazakhstan—have met with unexpected difficulties. The unhappy saga of trying to get Moscow's nod for the joint construction of a 2,400-kilometer pipeline to take oil from the Siberian town of Angarsk to the northeastern Daqing Oilfield has been cited by Chinese cadres as a "negative example" in petroleum diplomacy. The pipeline was earlier billed as a landmark of the strategic partnership forged between former presidents Jiang and Boris Yeltsin. Preliminary agreements on the Angarsk-Daqing link were reached as early as 2002. A similar accord was inked one year later between Presidents Hu and Vladmir Putin. Yet Moscow seemed to be playing Beijing off against Tokyo.[81]

By late 2004, Moscow was tilting toward first satisfying the Japanese market via an Angarsk-Nakhodka line to the Pacific coast just opposite Japan. This was partly because Tokyo had offered a package exceeding $20 billion to cover both the construction of the pipeline and economic assistance to the Russian Far East. Moreover, the Putin leadership seems anxious to pursue some degree of equidistance in its relations with the PRC and Japan. A number of Russian politicians, particularly those based in the Far East, fear that the construction of an Angarsk-Daqing line would increase the already sizable presence of Chinese laborers working in that remote region.[82] After a series of meetings in late 2004 and 2005 between Putin on the one hand, and Hu and Wen on the other, Beijing was given an assurance of "ten years of supply" of Russian oil and gas. Yet neither side has revealed the exact format—for example, through a direct Angarsk-Daqing line, or via a "secondary branch link" peeling off from the main Angarsk-Nakhodka pipeline to Daqing—in which this would come about. Nor has Moscow's position softened despite the conclusion of an agreement on the delineation of the Chinese-Russian boundary that incurred the ire of Chinese nationalists for allegedly giving away huge tracts of territory to the "Russian bear."[83]

One consolation for Beijing is that work finally started on the much-delayed China-Kazakhstan oil pipeline in late 2004. The 3,000-kilometer link from Atasu to the Xinjiang Autonomous Region is set to provide western China with 20 million tonnes of Caspian Sea crude a year. Chinese authorities have claimed that owing to pressure from the United States, Beijing had been unable to raise funds on the international financial market for this project. Moreover, central and regional authorities in Kazakhstan had demanded more money from Chinese state oil companies than had been stipulated in the relevant agreements and contracts.[84]

Beijing's Diplomatic Blitz in Africa and Latin America

One relatively successful initiative launched by the Hu-Wen team is finding new sources of energy supply in Africa and South America. As CASS researcher Lu Nanquan pointed out, "China must shake off its excessive reliance on Middle East oil and work harder at diversification of its energy supply." And Tan Zhuzhou, chairman of the China Petroleum and Chemical Industry Association, indicated that China should "take its technologies and capital to Africa and South America and exploit oil there so as to diversify its sources."[85]

While Beijing started getting serious about African oil a decade ago, the historic visit by President Hu to Egypt, Algeria, and Gabon in early 2004 confirmed the country's determination to be a big player in this resource-rich continent. Other Politburo stalwarts including Wu Bangguo and Zeng Qinghong toured the continent later that year. In 2003, China bought $4.85 billion worth of African crude, up 67.5 percent from the year before. And fully 24.3 percent of total Chinese imports that year came from Africa. Beijing reckons that the African share of total oil imports could go up to 30 percent by the end of the decade. By late 2004, China had finalized relatively reliable sale-and-purchase arrangements with Angola, Sudan, Republic of the Congo, Equitorial Guinea, Cameroon, Algeria, Libya, Nigeria, and Egypt.[86]

Beijing has the edge over Western countries in Africa because it has no qualms about doing business with countries that have horrendous authoritarian traditions. A case in point is Sudan, which is shunned by the West for genocidal atrocities committed by the Khartoum leadership. Beijing has defended Sudan at the UN and other forums.[87] And the Chinese have maintained solid ties with the reportedly corrupt regime of patriarch Omar Bongo in Gabon. Moreover, established oil exporters such as those in the Middle East have well-defined rules on foreign participation in oil exploitation and exports. Chinese state oil companies have significantly more leeway in operational matters in the less regulated new African markets.

Beijing is also in a position to obtain special prices and exploitation rights in Africa through nonconventional means such as selling weapons to countries that cannot buy them on the international market. For example, China is an important arms supplier of Sudan, Angola, and Zimbabwe. Thus in mid-2004, China agreed to sell Zimbabwe fighter jets as well as military vehicles worth an estimated US$200 million. The PLA has also boosted defense ties with a number of African nations through visits by senior generals. Defense Minister Guo Boxiong was in South Africa and Egypt in July 2004. And the commander of the Lanzhou Military Region, General Li Qianyuan, toured Angola at about the same time.[88]

China's oil merchants are also harboring great expectations about Latin America.

And President Hu's trip to Latin America in November 2004, which took in Brazil, Chile, Argentina, and Cuba, showed the weight that Beijing was attaching to tapping energy and mineral resources in the backyard of the United States. Already, Beijing was close to securing supplies of oil and other minerals from Brazil, Ecuador, Colombia, and Venezuela. Apart from cash, Chinese state oil companies are, in conjunction with other government units, in a position to offer economic aid and high-quality but inexpensive technology ranging from mining to armaments.[89]

The "all-weather strategic partnership" that Hu was able to cement with Brasilia was especially noteworthy. The Brazilian state oil firm, Petrobras, expected that China would in 2004 become the third-leading destination of Brazilian crude exports, with shipments of about 50,000 barrels per day.[90] Beijing's efforts at what some analysts call the "Sinification of Latin America" were based largely on "yuan diplomacy." Hu pledged in Brazil that Chinese state firms would invest up to $100 billion in the coming decade, mainly in Latin American infrastructure and mines. Beijing has also lent support to Brazil's bid for a place on an expanded UNSC.[91]

Beijing's aggressive moves in Africa and Latin America have pitted it against a number of countries. Sino-Indian ties were strained in the second half of 2004 because Chinese state oil companies had edged out Indian ones in securing development rights to oil mines in Sudan and Angola.[92] And Beijing's high prospects for buying substantial amounts of crude from Venezuela—whose government is at loggerheads with the Bush administration—could adversely affect Sino-U.S. relations owing to the large investments American oil firms have already made in that country.

Locking Horns with Japan and ASEAN

China's energy obsession has raised problems with countries and blocs such as Japan and ASEAN. The petroleum imperative has had a particularly detrimental impact on already shaky Sino-Japanese relations. Since early 2004, Beijing and Tokyo have been at loggerheads over rights to exploit natural gas under the East China Sea, which lies between both countries. Tokyo had complained that the area, named the Chunxiao Field, where Beijing had started large-scale prospecting, was very close to the "mid-point" line of demarcation in waters between the two neighbors. And Beijing, which subscribes to the so-called continental shelf concept for ocean-boundary demarcation, has refused to entertain Tokyo's protests.[93] Moreover, disputes over the oil-rich Diaoyu Islands (known as the Senkakus in Japan) are also heating up. This is despite the commitment made by late patriarch Deng Xiaoping in the early 1970s that sovereignty-related conflicts over Diaoyu should be "left for the next generation."[94]

After a period of relative tranquility, disputes between China and ASEAN countries—mainly Malaysia, Brunei, Vietnam, and the Philippines, all claimants to sovereignty over the Spratly Islands—have flared anew. Beijing had in early 2004 criticized Vietnam's announcement that it would organize tour groups to the

Spratlys. Chinese diplomats also decried efforts by unnamed countries to invite multinational companies to prospect for oil and gas in the Spratlys. As the official *Orient Outlook Weekly* put it: "Relevant countries have mounted offensives against China over sovereignty in the South China Sea—they have strengthened their military grip over islands and sea lanes."[95]

Beijing's decision to adopt a more aggressive stance on the South China Sea seemed to be a step backward from its previous position of shelving sovereignty disputes. The CCP leadership was criticized by some of its Asian neighbors for pursuing a Machiavellian, divide-and-conquer strategy regarding the Spratlys. Sticking to its time-honored policy of seeking bilateral—but not multilateral—agreements on disputes in the South China Sea, Beijing was able to come to a one-on-one agreement with Philippine president Gloria Arroyo in October 2004 on a three-year program for joint exploration of oil in waters with undetermined sovereignty. Beijing sweetened the deal with Arroyo by adding aid packages including a $400 million loan for her country's North Rail project.[96] The Vietnamese Foreign Ministry reacted by lashing out at Beijing and Manila for bypassing other claimants in signing the bilateral agreement. Yet by early 2005, Vietnam was obliged by force of circumstances to make a compromise, which resulted in Beijing, Manila, and Hanoi setting up a joint company to exploit oil in areas with sovereignty disputes.[97]

Against this background, it is perhaps not surprising that the image of the "benevolent elephant" that Beijing hopes to project via propaganda about China's "peaceful rise" has been replaced by that of the hungry tiger or an insatiable Leviathan gobbling up everything in its way. For some, this has conjured up horror scenarios of an energy-obsessed PRC bent on grabbing hold of mines and oilfields around the world—as well as monopolizing oil and gas in territories and waters whose sovereignty is being disputed. The prices of oil and other producer goods would go up even as weak countries become subject to bullying by China's fast-growing military forces.[98]

The bogey of China as tiger on the prowl has adversely affected Chinese energy- and resources-related diplomacy. Particularly in Western countries where China's rule-of-law records are deemed deficient, several cases of Chinese attempts at acquiring major foreign companies in 2004 and 2005 have been subject to embarrassing scrutiny. Take, for example, China Minmetals Corporation's $7 billion bid to take over Noranda, a well-established Canadian mining firm. Even more spectacular was the $18.5 billion effort by China National Offshore Oil Corporation (CNOOC) to absorb the California-based oil company Unocal. The CNOOC deal met with such horrendous opposition in the U.S. Congress that the Chinese company was forced to beat a retreat. At issue was resentment among Western businessmen and politicians against Beijing's seemingly take-no-prisoners approach to safeguarding energy security.[99]

The scale of the CNOOC takeover bid, coupled with audacious attempts by PRC state firms to seize hold of resources companies in Canada, Mexico, and other U.S. neighbors, has raised fears that the anticipated showdown between the world's only superpower and its most potent would-be superpower has been brought forward.[100] It is also clear that since the United States and such major U.S. allies as Japan are also pursuing the same goal of oil sufficiency, China's assertive maneuvers in areas where America has vested interests—Asia, Central Asia, and South America—could exacerbate Sino-American contradictions.

Indeed, competition between China and other powers will be particularly strong in the Middle East and the Caspian Sea area, as well as other resource-rich Third World regions such as Africa and Latin America. Thanks to China's long-standing image as a champion of developing countries, it has an edge over the United States in quite a few developing nations. As U.S. economist David Hale pointed out, "it is too soon to speak of a new era of Chinese imperialism in the Third World, but China will certainly play a more influential role in the affairs of many developing countries," including the exploitation of natural resources.[101] Compared with more developed Asian nations such as Japan and South Korea, China has had a relatively late start in thrashing out an energy program. Yet despite its growing economic, diplomatic, and military clout, the Hu-Wen leadership realizes it must balance the aggressive search for oil and gas with a policy of mollification. Not only China's immediate neighbors but powers beyond its shores have to be reassured that the PRC is after a win-win formula of co-prosperity and joint development.[102]

China-U.S. Relations

From "Potential Enemy Number 1" to "Partner in Counterterrorism"

How 9/11 Contributed to Mending Sino-U.S. Ties

In early 2001, the Jiang Zemin team was unprepared for the hostility with which the new George W. Bush administration would be handling relations with the PRC. Going by China's own tradition, Beijing had hoped that Bush 43 would at least be as "pro-engagement" as Bush 41. Moreover, the then Chinese ambassador to Washington, Yang Jiechi, was an "old friend" of the Bush family, having served as Bush Senior's interpreter during the latter's brief posting as head of the U.S. Liaison Office in Beijing. And Beijing had studiously maintained good ties with other members of the Bush family—such as Prescott Bush and Neil Bush—who are active in China business.[103]

It soon became obvious that President Bush's so-called ABC (anything but Clinton) policy would also extend to China. The Bush team had criticized what it considered to be the excessive attention that Clinton had lavished on China—and Bush's appointments in the diplomatic and national-security fields showed that more emphasis was being put on Japan, South Korea, and Australia rather than China. There was also a dearth of China expertise among medium- to high-level officials in the State and Defense Departments and in the National Security Council.[104]

Moreover, Bush seemed more "pro-Taiwan" than either his father or Clinton. Beijing was taken aback by the new president's statement on several U.S. networks in March 2001 that Washington "would do whatever it took" to guarantee Taiwan's safety should the latter come under military threat from the mainland. Equally significant was the fact that so-called neoconservatives—who had major representatives in the administration, particularly the Defense Department—were determined that China could be tamed and de-fanged the same way that the Reagan and Bush 41 administrations emasculated the former Soviet Union. In 2001, a large number of military advisers from the Pentagon were back in Taiwan advising the local armed forces on better command-and-control operations, logistics, and other skills.[105]

Sino-American ill will came to a head earlier than expected, in the guise of the "spy plane incident" on April 1, 2001, when a U.S. Air Force reconnaissance plane was forced to land on Hainan Island after colliding with a PLA Air Force jetfighter. This alleged intrusion into Chinese territory sparked several days of anti-American demonstrations, notably outside American missions and even shops and restaurants selling brand-name U.S. goods. Other ominous developments in the first half of 2003 included plans by the U.S. armed forces to redeploy operations in Asia, which was seen by Beijing as an exacerbation of the China containment policy.[106]

September 11 was to change all that. Beijing and Washington have since cemented a "constructive, cooperative relationship" based on the global campaign against terrorism. As discussed earlier, while Beijing was alarmed by U.S. action in Afghanistan—particularly the stationing of American troops in Uzbekistan, Tajikistan, and Kyrgyzstan—it largely acquiesced in the fall of the Taliban, with whom China had just built up reasonably good ties. And while Beijing was as much opposed to a U.S. invasion of Iraq as France or Russia, it refrained from overt criticism of Washington's handling of the war-torn country. The Chinese government was instead active in lobbying for reconstruction contracts in both Afghanistan and Iraq.[107]

And what did China get in return? Chinese diplomats quickly perceived that after September 11, the Bin Laden networks as well as the Saddam Hussein regime had replaced China as America's World Enemy Number 1. Peking University international affairs professor Niu Jun pointed out even before the start of hostilities in Iraq: "Americans will be bogged down [in Iraq] and we shall have less to worry about." This was echoed by then vice-premier Qian Qichen. "After the September 11 attacks, the relationship among great powers has noticeably stabilized. Sino-U.S. relations are developing along the lines of 'cooperation, democracy, and peace,'" he said in late 2002.[108]

Both Jiang and Hu indicated appreciation for Washington's consideration of China as a close partner in the anti-terrorism campaign. Beijing also expressed thanks for Washington's agreement to designate the East Turkestan Islamic Movement (ETIM) as a terrorist organization. This move has enabled Beijing to justify its draconian measures to keep the XAR under control by claiming that many if not most of the "anti-Chinese terrorist" actions in the XAR are linked to or financed by the ETIM. This is despite the opinion of international experts on Xinjiang that most underground, anti-Beijing organizations in the region are nonreligious and nonviolent in nature.[109] During ex-president Jiang's last summit with Bush in late 2002, the U.S. president told his guest that "no nation's efforts to counter terrorism should be used to justify suppressing minorities or silencing peaceful dissent." However, while there was no indication that the Chinese were following the Americans' advice, the White House had toned down its criticism of Chinese behavior in Xinjiang and Tibet, as well as other human-rights abuses. And for the first time since the Tiananmen Square crackdown, Washington decided in 2002 not to sponsor an "anti-China" motion at the UN Commission on Human Rights at Geneva.[110]

This bilateral give-and-take seemed to be working out well. Then secretary of state Colin Powell pointed out in September 2003 that U.S.-China relations "are the best they have been since President Nixon's first visit" to China in 1972. During his tour of Asia and Australia at about the same time, Bush pronounced himself "encouraged by China's cooperation in the war on terror," particularly its role in putting pressure on Pyongyang to dismantle its nuclear program. And President Hu reciprocated the enthusiasm when he said at the same time that "developing healthy and stable Sino-U.S. relations tallies with the fundamental interests of the two peoples."[111]

Toward Some Degree of Bilateral Give-and-Take

It is a reflection of China's growing clout—and some degree of maturation in Sino-U.S. dealings—that a degree of give and take was evident in certain areas of bilateral relations. Take, for example, the issue of China's ballooning trade surplus—to the tune of an estimated $200 billion in 2005—as well as what some U.S. officials and economists considered was the "deliberate" undervaluation of the renminbi by more than 30 percent.

The Hu-Wen leadership stood up to pressure, put to bear on China by top politicians including President Bush and then U.S. Treasury secretary John Snow, that it revalue the renminbi (RMB) or yuan. At the Asia-Pacific Economic Cooperation (APEC) summit in October 2003, Bush told Hu that fair global commerce required that Beijing speed up the process of floating the RMB. Then Commerce Secretary Don Evans even noted that U.S. patience was "running thin" and that Washington "will not tolerate a stacked card." However, it was clear that the White House decided to adopt a conciliatory policy. In late 2004, the Treasury Department released a statement saying China was not manipulating its exchange rate and there was no need to take retaliatory measures.[112]

While the Chinese refused to budge on the RMB, they adopted fence-mending gestures. The practice of sending high-profile "buying delegations" to the United

States continued. For example, on the eve of Premier Wen's visit to the United States in December 2003, Beijing announced that Chinese government units and corporations would purchase $6.7 billion worth of American aircraft, jet engines, automobile parts, and other products. Officials at the People's Bank of China and Finance Ministry also indicated a willingness to speed up the procedure of rendering the yuan more reflective of market forces. The eventual appreciation of 2.1 percent in July 2005 was way below the expectations of China's trading partners. However, Chinese banking authorities did follow the advice of American experts that the yuan be pegged to a basket of currencies including the greenback, the Euro, and the yen.[113]

Another significant development was that despite the mutual distrust of the two countries' defense forces, military-to-military relations were to some extent restored in October 2002, when Defense Minister Cao Gangchuan visited the United States. Such contacts had been stopped even before the "spy plane incident" of April 2001. Bush told General Cao that he would "continue to enthusiastically show concern for and support the development of U.S.-China military ties." Beijing, however, was unable to persuade Washington to even partially lift the fifteen-year embargo on the export of military-related high technology to China. In Washington, enthusiasm for military ties with the PRC was also not high in a Defense Department dominated by neoconservatives such as Defense Secretary Donald Rumsfeld, who did not visit China until late 2005.[114]

Apart from the commercial and investment fronts, therefore, Sino-U.S. relations have remained fragile and problem-prone. There were upbeat moments when it appeared possible that the two countries could concentrate on areas of common interest rather than potential flashpoints. However, mishaps, particularly surrounding hot issues such as Taiwan, could quickly plunge relations into a crisis. This was despite the advancement in high-level communication such as hotlines between the two presidents and senior officials from both countries.

Taiwan Is Still the Key to Bilateral Ties

One major difference between the U.S. policy of Hu and that of Jiang is that at least until early 2004, the ex-president believed that China could rely on help from the White House to rein in the pro-independence gambit of Taiwan's Democratic Progressive Party (DPP). A joke within diplomatic circles in Beijing went like this: First, Beijing counted on cooperation with the Kuomintang to achieve reunification; then it pinned its hope for union on the Taiwanese people; finally, Beijing had to depend on the United States to prevent Taipei from going down the separatist road. From 2002 to early 2004, Beijing dispatched a series of high-level officials, including the director of the Taiwan Affairs Office, Chen Yunlin, to Washington to seek help in taming President Chen Shui-bian. This was despite MOFA's usual stance that Taiwan was an "internal Chinese affair that brooks no foreign intervention."[115]

President Hu has, of course, continued to call on Bush and American politicians to stop "sending the wrong message to Taipei." However, Hu is more realistic about the extent to which the White House will be cooperative on the Taiwan
issue. It is interesting that in the run-up to the November 2004 U.S. president
election, quite a few leading America experts in Beijing indicated that there was
really not that much of a difference between Bush and Democratic Party challenger Senator John Kerry on policies toward China and Taiwan. As noted
Americanologist Yan Xuetong pointed out on the eve of the U.S. polls, "both major parties in America put as their highest priority maintaining America's predominant role in world affairs," and hence their approach toward China would always
serve this goal.[116]

In internal deliberations, the LGFA had in 2004 branded Washington as "un-
trustworthy" and "duplicitous" because of the Bush administration's apparent failure to live up to its pledges about Taiwan. From Beijing's point of view, Bush and
his advisers had flip-flopped on Washington's commitment to the one-China
policy.[117] Soon after the unexpectedly fast collapse of the Saddam Hussein regime
in Iraq, Beijing was afraid that the hawks in Washington might be so carried away
by their initial success that they thought the United States could get away with
anything. And because many of these hardliners also happened to be ardent Taiwan supporters, the CCP leadership was worried that Washington would come to
the aid of the beleaguered DPP administration. The year 2003 saw more U.S. defense experts advising the Taiwan forces—and more senior Taiwan officials taking part in semi-official conferences in the United States. Such activities climaxed
with the high-level "transit visit" to New York by President Chen in September.
For the first time, the Taiwan president was allowed to give speeches in public
venues, to entertain American politicians in grand style, and to greet his supporters
in downtown New York streets. And Chen's "breakthrough" in the United States
was instrumental in boosting his reelection prospects half a year later.[118]

After many protests from Beijing, Bush appeared to give ground during the
visit of Premier Wen in December 2003. On that occasion, the U.S. president said
he was opposed to either side of the Taiwan Strait taking unilateral action to dis-
turb the status quo. Washington also pledged to prevent Chen from using the "ref-
erendum card"—a reference to the two plebiscites to be held the same day as the
presidential elections in March 2004—to pursue separatism. Wen was so satisfied
that he proclaimed this apparent concession as "a major success in Chinese diplomacy." However, Bush's supposed accommodation of Beijing's requests was followed by a series of disappointments for the CCP leadership. For example,
Washington gave full support to Chen's reelection in March 2004 despite widely
held suspicion that the DPP veteran had "staged" his own shooting one day before
the polls. Washington also put pressure on Taipei to buy a package of U.S. weapons worth a whopping NT$610 billion.[119]

Relations were briefly mended in the wake of then secretary of state Powell's
swan-song visit to Beijing just before the U.S. presidential election. The top U.S.

diplomat indicated that Taiwan was not an independent state with full sovereign powers. Powell also told the media about Washington's support for "peaceful re-unification" in the Taiwan Strait. While he later clarified that what he had meant was only the "peaceful resolution" of the Taiwan issue—not "peaceful reunifica-tion"—the Chinese were hopeful that further exertion of pressure on Washington would result in at least more rhetorical concessions.[120] Despite Washington's reas-surances, Hu has decided to go about his agenda on Taiwan while fully factoring in American military interference. The CMC chief has asked his generals to take into consideration probable U.S. intervention if the PLA were to launch a "libera-tion warfare" against Taiwan. Military sources in Beijing and Hong Kong said that as of late 2004, the generals had given the leadership reassurance that the forces could take out the bulk of Taiwan's military installations within a few days, in the process bringing the Chen regime to its knees. This short time frame would pre-sumably deny the United States the chance to intervene. PLA strategists were con-fident that they could effectively deal with up to two American aircraft-carrier battle groups that might be deployed to the Taiwan Strait in times of emergency.[121]

By the spring of 2005, Hu was sticking to the time-honored, double-fisted policy: Beijing would be projecting a more magnanimous posture to woo the "broad spec-trum of Taiwanese"—particularly Taiwanese businessmen—while intensifying "war preparation" to hit hard at the separatists. This was in accordance with the nine-character dictum he had laid down at an internal meeting on Taiwan affairs called by the LGTA in the autumn of 2004: "We should strive for dialogue; we must get ready to fight; but we don't mind waiting." On the one hand, the supremo was in effect abrogating the "2020 deadline" for the liberation of Taiwan, which had been raised by several leaders including ex-president Jiang. On the other hand, military measures would be boosted thanks to ever-bigger PLA budgets.[122] This mentality was reflected in the Anti-Secession Law (ASL) of March 2005, which spelled out the conditions—for example, Taipei taking actions that would result in "the fact of Taiwan's secession from China"—under which Beijing would use "nonpeaceful means" against the breakaway province. Beijing has emphasized that it would still opt for peace if there were even one ray of hope for peace. Yet the blood-red sword of Damocles is plain to all. The ASL, however, was deftly used by the United States, and to a lesser extent Japan, to lobby the EU not to lift its arms-export ban on China.[123]

The Tricky China–U.S.–North Korean Triangle

The furor over Pyongyang's nuclear weapons program, which first flared up in October 2002, became the first major international crisis for the Hu-Wen adminis-tration. On the one hand, Beijing wanted to preserve the DPRK as a buffer against America's perceived anti-China containment policy.[124] The Chinese leadership could also use its special relationship with the Kim Jong-Il regime as a "card" in dealings with the United States, Japan, and South Korea. On the other hand, China's influence with Kim's regime was weakening. Beijing's clout was due mainly to the DPRK's dependence on Chinese food, oil, and military technology. And Pyongyang's threat to develop WMD could encourage Japan and South Korea to go nuclear as well. The Hu leadership also feared that China might be dragged into a war it did not want: Should the Bush White House decide to take unilateral action against the DPRK, Beijing might be forced to provide its erstwhile ally with some form of military assistance under the two neighbors' still-valid mutual defense pact. Beijing was also wary of the millions upon millions of North Korean refugees who might be flooding into Jilin, Heilongjiang, and Liaoning provinces should war break out.[125]

Beijing's reaction to the Korean crisis was to depart from Deng Xiaoping's line of "never taking the lead" in diplomacy, and to play a central role in obliging Pyongyang to come to the six-party talks in the Chinese capital in mid-2003. While being opposed to actions that the UNSC might take against Pyongyang, Beijing also urged the DPRK to do its part in lowering tensions. The CCP leadership shut down its oil supplies to its long-term ally for three days in February 2003 so as to underscore its displeasure with the Kim regime's policy of nuclear blackmail. As of late 2005, nothing concrete had come out of the talks except an agreement "in principle" reached in September that Pyongyang would scrap its weapons in return for American, Japanese, and South Korean aid—and eventual U.S. diplomatic recognition. However, details as to whether the Kim regime would dismantle all WMDs—and when the economic aid would be forthcoming—were left up in the air. In spite of the uncertainties, Beijing has boosted its international standing by playing the role of "honest broker." It has particularly earned the praise of the Bush leadership for at least preventing the nuclear crisis from worsening.[126]

The Hu leadership has taken a Machiavellian approach in this China–North Korea–U.S. triangular relationship. For Beijing, there is a quid pro quo that can be summarized by the formula "North Korea in exchange for Taiwan." The Chinese leadership hopes that in return for reining in the Kim regime, Washington will play its part in putting a damper on Taipei's "creeping independence."[127] There was as of early 2004 some evidence that Washington had displayed more sensitivity on the Taiwan issue partly to pay back Beijing's "services" regarding the DPRK. Yet it was clear that for the Hu leadership, the Bush White House had to do more before Beijing would crack the whip on the Kim regime. Beijing had by mid-2004 seen more evidence of Washington's willingness to sell arms to Taiwan—and to "encircle" China by beefing up defense arrangements with Japan and Taiwan.

Beijing's posturing was evidenced by the fact that China and the DPRK seemed to have at least partially restored their "lips-and-teeth" relationship through 2004 and 2005. That the Chinese leadership had changed its assessment of the value of a revived Beijing-Pyongyang alliance first became apparent in April 2004, when Dear Leader Kim paid a three-day visit to Beijing. In an unprecedented move, all nine members of the CCP Politburo Standing Committee showed up in a welcoming ceremony. During meetings six months later with the DPRK's Head of Parliament Kim Yong-nam, Chinese officials extended North Korea another round of assistance in food and fuel. And on Hu's own trip to Pyongyang in late 2005, the Chinese supremo said both sides should "explore new ways, and open up new vistas . . . to move forward the comprehensive and profound development of Sino-Korean relations." These protestations of comradeship led many in Pyongyang to believe that the DPRK could count on Chinese support—including some form of military assistance in the event of an unprovoked U.S. attack—in the foreseeable future.[128]

According to a Chinese source familiar with Beijing's Korean policy, the LGFA had in early 2004 decided to upgrade economic and other assistance to the DPRK. "Hundreds of economic and agricultural advisers, mostly from the northeastern provinces, have been sent into North Korea," the source said. He added that Beijing hoped to enable the North Koreans to at least achieve self-sufficiency in grain and other staples. And while Kim has continued to resist Beijing's suggestion that his country follow Chinese-style economic reform, Pyongyang had agreed to allow Chinese private entrepreneurs to introduce market-oriented retailing and other commercial operations in the North Korean capital.[129]

In Bush's second term, Beijing would be looking for several U.S. concessions before it would agree to really play hardball with Kim. Apart from taking more forceful steps to rein in Taipei, Washington would be called upon to display more flexibility on Pyongyang. For example, Beijing hoped the United States would come up with a formal pledge—to be guaranteed by China, Russia, Japan, and South Korea—not to attack the DPRK on a preemptive basis. The Hu leadership had fears that neoconservatives close to the White House might push for "regime change" in North Korea through tactics including a naval blockade. According to People's University political scientist Shi Yinhong, it would be more realistic for Washington to accept proposals from both Beijing and Seoul that the six nations agree on a "partial solution," under which Pyongyang would freeze its most lethal weapons programs in return for economic aid and a guarantee of nonbelligerence. From that point onward, Shi said, pressure could be put on Pyongyang to step up economic reform, and gradually, at least partial reform of the political system after the Dear Leader's demise.[130]

The Near-Omnipotence of the "Economic Card"

An important reason why Beijing is relatively happy dealing with the George W. Bush administration is its perceived intimacy with the business community. And this goes behind the traditional coziness between Republican administrations and the corporate world. At least in Beijing's perception, the Bush family has convoluted ties particularly with firms in the defense, energy, and infrastructure fields. Many key members of the Bush team, such as Vice-President Dick Cheney and Defense Secretary Donald Rumsfeld, worked in large corporations prior to joining the administration.

While friends of individual Bush cabinet members who are defense manufacturers and contractors might favor Taiwan, the bulk of the American business community has since the late 1990s gradually but irrevocably tilted toward China. That American companies, particularly those who have invested heavily in coastal China, could be an "ally" to Chinese foreign and economic policy was evident. Most U.S. multinationals had lobbied for WTO membership for China. And their stance regarding the controversy over renminbi valuation was particularly interesting. While senior U.S. government officials had in 2003 and 2004 put pressure on China to appreciate the yuan, American companies with manufacturing plants in the PRC, as well as retail chains such as Wal-Mart that have become dependent on cheap Chinese supplies, would suffer in the event of an appreciation. Partly owing to the lobbying of these companies, Bush did not press his case too hard although trade deficits, loss of jobs, and the supposed "manipulation" of the yuan's value were hot-button issues in the 2004 U.S. presidential polls.[131]

And then there is the ever-growing attractiveness of the market with 1.3 billion people, particularly now that denizens along the coast are rich enough to buy American products ranging from wheat and fruit to computers and satellites. Vice-Premier Wu Yi blatantly flashed the business card during her 2004 visit to the United States to officiate at the inauguration of the Sino-U.S. Trade Commission. Making a pitch for the United States to open up the high-tech market to China, Wu lived up to the late Deng's famous aphorism: "When you have lots of money, your voice is much louder." "If only the U.S. abrogates unreasonable restrictions on the export [of high-tech goods and services], it is no problem at all for China to import a few 100 million dollars more—even a few billion dollars more," Wu said.[132] Being the discreet trade diplomat she had always been, Wu did not touch upon military-related technology or weapons. But Beijing was confident that once the sluice gate was opened one centimeter, the rest would follow; the most important thing was that the central government would have enough cash to back up the lobbying.

Indeed, Beijing's long-term projection for Sino-U.S. relations is that much depends on the progress of economic ties. Hu's advisers figure that there will come a point—perhaps in the year 2015 or so—when the degree of mutual dependence between the two countries will have reached parity. Foreign-trade experts in Beijing reckoned that in 2004, China still needed the United States much more than the other way round, a condition that could be reflected by a ratio of 65:35 or 60:40. When, however, the ratio becomes 50:50—denoting that the United States needs China economically as much as vice versa—diplomatic ties will be a different ball game. Beijing can use its economic leverage to put pressure on the United States on key diplomatic fronts such as Taiwan.[133] Indeed, by 2005, America was so heavily in debt that it was beholden to countries such as Japan and China for buying billions of dollars' worth of Treasury bonds. A decision by the People's Bank of China, which administers China's US$800 billion in foreign-exchange reserves, to cut down on the purchase of U.S. Treasury bonds would adversely affect the U.S. economy. As *Fortune* magazine journalist Justin Fox noted, Bush "may end up having to consult the Chinese, of all people, over his domestic taxing and spending decisions."[134]

According to a Taiwan specialist in a Beijing-based think tank, it won't be too long before the Chinese leadership can lay its cards on the table—and ask Washington to "choose between China and Taiwan." He said it was economic reasons more than anything else that underpinned the special relationship between China and a number of EU countries such as France. "As late as the 1990s, we had no guarantee that European nations which used to supply arms to Taiwan, including the Netherlands and France, would not do so again," said the expert. "Now, these countries are only interested in lifting the EU's arms embargo on China."[135]

China–EU Relations

Beijing's Great Expectations

The Fourth Generation leadership has great expectations of relations with the European Union. Among the major "great powers" and blocs—the United States, the EU, Russia, Japan, and ASEAN—Europe is perceived as the one region that poses no direct threat to China. Despite discrepancies in economic levels, and most importantly, culture and ideology, the differences between China and most European countries over diplomatic issues are much less than those, for example, between China and the United States, or China and Japan.[136]

That 2003 and 2004 will go down in history as banner years for China-EU ties is clear from the results of a landmark summit between EU and Chinese leaders in Beijing in October 2003. The two "strategic partners" agreed on a series of economic and technological joint ventures which signaled that, in the words of Premier Wen, "bilateral ties have entered a stage that is more mature, stable, and marked by strategic significance." A few months earlier, Beijing had issued its first comprehensive Policy Paper on relations with the bloc. The years 2004 and 2005 witnessed numerous visits to Europe by Hu, Wen, and other senior Politburo members and ministers. The emphasis that the LGFA is putting on Europe has prompted many observers to note that President Hu is much more "pro-Europe" than pro-America.[137]

Beijing hopes to achieve three main goals regarding Europe: building a multipolar world, securing advanced technology, and boosting trade. Good relations with the EU are essential to realizing one of China's most cherished diplomatic objectives: establishing a multipolar world, or one that is not dominated by the United States. On issues including the anti-terrorism campaign and global human rights, Beijing is hopeful that China and the EU will adopt similar or mutually compatible positions. The Chinese leadership also anticipates that better coordination with France and Russia would diminish U.S. domination over the UNSC. And closer security links between China, the EU, and Russia might lower the chances of the United States launching another unilateral attack against another "terrorist country" à la Iraq.[138]

Right before the incursion of Allied Forces into Iraq in March 2003, Beijing was happy that France and Germany—along with Russia—were able to spearhead a global anti-war movement, which resulted in some form of checks and balances vis-à-vis U.S. "hegemonism." Aggressive anti-war tactics undertaken by Paris and Moscow at the UNSC enabled Beijing to pursue its own Iraq-related agenda without having to confront Washington directly. Indeed, China seemed by early 2005 to have made progress in its goal of constructing a multipolar global order; at the very least, there was a meeting of the minds between Beijing and Paris. While touring China in late 2004, President Jacques Chirac indicated that France hoped to "boost economic and political links with China in order to balance the global influence of the U.S." He said Paris and Beijing should work together in "rebalancing the grand triangle formed by America, Europe, and Asia."[139] However, Chirac's views only represented the "radical" fringe in European thinking about the United States. There was internal opposition to Chirac's "China complex" within France itself. And Beijing faced an uphill battle convincing EU members from central and eastern Europe to share its concern about U.S. "neo-imperialism."

The Hu leadership has had more success in the relatively mundane areas of technological and trade relations with the Union. Despite the leaps-and-bounds growth in Chinese high technology and weaponry, Beijing looks to Europe as a major source of know-how, including that with military applications. At the Sino-EU summit in late 2003, it was agreed that China would take part in the EU's Galileo satellite navigation system—which will be competing with America's global positioning system (GPS)—through an initial capital injection of $236 million. The official Chinese media noted that Chinese-EU cooperation in the aeronautical sphere would "end American domination in outer space." In its *EU Policy Paper*, Beijing appealed to Brussels to lift its ban on arms sales to China so as to "remove barriers to greater bilateral cooperation in defense industry and technologies" (see following section). The CCP leadership also envisaged regular military-to-military relationships with most EU countries.[140]

Partly owing to the EU's dramatic expansion in 2004, the powerful bloc became China's largest trading partner that year. Two-way trade, which reached $177.2 billion in 2004, has been growing consistently at around 30 percent a year since the late 1990s. While Europe is only the fourth largest investor in the PRC, it is the latter's most important supplier of technology. Beijing is optimistic that progress on this front will lessen its excessive dependence on the American market. After all, China's ever-growing trade surplus with the United States has been a long-standing source of friction with Washington—as well as a root cause for China-bashing sentiments among American labor organizations.[141]

There are, of course, a number of irritants and hiccups in bilateral ties. Brussels has been putting more pressure on China to further open up its markets—particularly the infrastructure, high-tech, and financial services sectors—in view of the estimated trade deficit of $63 billion that Europe sustained in 2005. The EU has also joined forces with the United States in pressuring Beijing to revalue the yuan. However, Beijing has found that compared with the United States, European countries are more willing to give China the benefit of the doubt. For instance, then EU trade commissioner Pascal Lamy said in October 2003 that he would not push Beijing to float the renminbi because a sudden move might destabilize China's shaky financial system.[142]

There are however, a number of other issues that militate against Sino-EU friendship. One is Taiwan. Several EU members, particularly former East European countries such as the Czech Republic, think it is important to maintain an adequate level of relations with Taiwan. China's *EU Policy Paper*, however, specifically urged Europe to "prohibit any visit by any Taiwan political figures to the EU or its member countries under whatever name or pretext and not to engage in any contact or exchange of an official or governmental nature with Taiwan authorities."[143] Particularly in light of President Chen's largely successful "transit diplomacy" in the United States in late 2003, quite a few European capitals saw the Chinese position as unnecessarily stringent.

From Beijing's long-term considerations, however, hiccups and minor disagreements will not stand in the way of steady but irrevocable Sino-EU partnership. Beijing is particularly grateful that its European ties have enhanced its global position. For example, thanks to an invitation by the French, President Hu participated in mid-2003 in the South-North Leaders' Dialogue (SNLD), which was held alongside the annual Group of Eight (G8) meeting in Evian, France. It was the first time that a Chinese leader had taken part in this fringe Group of Eight function. In his SNLD address, Hu played up the imperative of "seeking peaceful coexistence [among nations] and maintaining global diversity." Analysts said it was only a matter of a few years before China would become a member of the expanded G9 nations.[144]

The "Business Card" and the Possible Lifting of the EU's Arms Embargo Against China

Beijing's skillful use of the business and import cards have played a key role in Sino-EU rapprochement and partnership. Often, this involves striking a delicate balance between buying European and buying American—and on occasion playing off one European multinational against an American one. For example, the Chinese civilian airline industry has for many years been purchasing Boeings one year and Airbuses the next.[145] Given that full resumption of technological ties with the United States is far off, Beijing is aggressively seeking high-tech products from Europe, including those with military and aerospace applications.

The best illustration of Beijing's skills in wielding the business card—and playing one country off against the other—is the issue of arms sales to China. On this crucial matter, Beijing is counting on the support of France—the one EU state that is most critical of U.S. "unilateralism"—as a model for ties with other EU members. It was no accident that France had benefited most from China's EU-related business card. In early 2003, for example, Beijing purchased thirty Airbus jets in a clear indication of its "pro-France and buy European" propensity. And the Chirac cabinet was at the forefront of the campaign to break ranks with the United States—and to lift the Tiananmen Square crackdown-related ban on the export of weapons to China.[146]

Hopes of a breakthrough on the embargo issue were raised during visits to Europe by Hu and Wen in 2004—and by return visits to China by Chirac and other European politicians later that year. One potential stumbling block was that unanimity was required among all EU members for this important decision. Quite a few European countries have raised the human rights issue, believing that the embargo should stay until China has shown marked improvements in this sensitive area. During his visit to Beijing in early 2004, then president of the EU Executive Commission Romano Prodi said "further progress on the question of human rights" might help China on the arms-embargo front."[147] EU membership was in May 2004 expanded to twenty-five with the entry of ten East European countries that are staunch allies of the United States, such as Poland. However, after the late-2004 PRC-EU summit in Brussels, officials there expressed the hope that the embargo would be lifted by mid-2005. It was the first time that EU leaders agreed to some kind of a timetable, if not a deadline, for cancellation of the ban.[148]

Moreover, Beijing was rebutting the "contain-China" voices from Washington and other places with gusto. Just prior to his European tour in May 2004, Wen reiterated that "the arms ban on China is a product of the Cold War—and was totally outdated." The Chinese leadership was mainly relying on the import card to sway Brussels. The CCP leadership had put together a huge war-chest—said to be close to $100 billion, or about one-sixth of the country's foreign-exchange holdings at the time—to buy high-tech, military, as well as "dual-use" products from France, Germany, Britain, Italy, and other EU countries. Prospects for a breakthrough in 2005, however, were dashed by Beijing's passage of the Anti-Secession Law against Taiwan in March—and widespread sentiments in Europe that it was an inappropriate time to let the PLA acquire more advanced weapons. Moreover, stunning internal political developments within the EU in 2005, particularly the failure of the French and Dutch electorates to ratify the new EU Constitution and the change of administration in Berlin, further complicated this issue. For example, foreign-policy aides of new German chancellor Angela Merkel noted on the eve of Hu's visit in late 2005 that there was no hurry to lift the arms ban.[149]

Beijing, however, was expected to continue its intensive lobbying efforts. A key motivation on the part of the CCP leadership was the perception that once the EU hurdle had been cleared, there was no way the United States could hold out for very long. "Beijing figures that after the EU has lifted the embargo, the United States may feel obliged to follow suit eventually," a Chinese diplomatic source said. "High-tech American corporations and, in particular, the defense industrial establishment, cannot afford to let their French, German, British, and Scandinavian competitors dominate the world's largest market."[150] Obviously, the United States government would prevent American firms from selling hardware such as jet fighters to China. Yet Beijing was hopeful that at least, Washington would be more liberal in granting export licenses for "dual-use" high-tech material such as computers and nuclear-power generation equipment. When Wen was touring the United States in December 2003, he complained that it was unreasonable that "China could only import soya bean and [civilian] aircraft from the U.S."[151] It is understood that a number of U.S. manufacturers of high-tech and military hardware are receptive to Beijing's blandishments—and that they are lobbying Washington for relevant trade liberalization measures.

China-EU Ties in the Rest of the Decade

The May 2004 expansion of the EU is having a major impact on Europe's relations with China. A foremost concern to the LGFA and other strategists was whether the new EU could still be counted upon to help China construct a multipolar world. However, one problem facing interactions between the PRC and the expanded EU is that while Beijing has clear-cut political and diplomatic objectives vis-à-vis Europe, many of the smaller and "new Europe" EU members are almost exclusively interested in economic and trading ties.

Indeed, the Fourth-Generation leadership is worldly-wise enough to realize that the EU itself is undergoing dramatic transformation—and there can be no question of a simplistic playing of the "European card" against the United States. For example, the Iraq War has exacerbated the dichotomy between the "old Europe"—centered on France and Germany—and the "new Europe," which includes several former Soviet bloc countries. After the change of regime in Baghdad, "old European countries" have continued to remain critical of U.S. foreign policy. And France, Germany, Belgium, and Luxembourg even contemplated in early 2004 setting up a defense-related "core group" that could exert some pressure on future decision making within the U.S.-dominated NATO.[152]

However, "new Europe" has displayed obvious pro-U.S. tendencies. For instance, Poland is developing strong economic and defense ties with the United States—and Poland and Bulgaria were among the "new European countries" to have sent at least token numbers of troops to Iraq. It is easy to understand the reason behind this. Having been freed from the grip of Moscow not that long ago, many of these former Warsaw Pact countries are anxious to consolidate their ties with the "leader of the Free World." After all, the United States is perceived to be a generous provider of aid and markets.[153]

Moreover, the development of Sino-EU ties is circumscribed by the fact that for both China and the EU, ties with the United States remain of paramount importance. While Beijing may hope that its European connections will help make way for a multipolar new world order, the Chinese leadership does not want its EU links to jeopardize the much-stabilized Sino-U.S. relations. Likewise, with the possible example of Chirac and his like-minded colleagues, most EU leaders would not want friendship with Beijing to detract from Europe's century-old solidarity with the United States. As experts in the well-known German International Security Institute pointed out: "China considers the EU as a force in counterbalancing the U.S. However, Europe may think differently as the EU still considers the U.S. as its most important diplomatic partner."[154]

Quite a few Beijing analysts are convinced that most members of the "new Europe" would follow "old Europe's" lead in asserting an economic, diplomatic, and cultural identity that was distinctly different from America's. Thus, *Guangming Daily* commentator Chen Shuren noted that an expanded EU would become a greater force toward a multipolar global order. He pointed out that a twenty-five-member EU would "exert a bigger force to counterbalance and constrain unilateralism." And CASS Europe expert Zhou Hong expressed optimism that an enlarged EU would mean that its constituents would "be less dependent on the security umbrella provided by the U.S. and NATO"—and that the Union would remain an "independent force that is distinct from the U.S."[155] Beijing scholars, however, also betrayed fears that Eastern Europe's formal entry into the "Western camp" would mean the wholesale aggrandizement of quintessentially Western political and cultural ideals. As CASS's Zhou noted, the EU's expansion represented the "spread of Western democratic and human-rights principles." He expressed worries that this new Europe might be "more aggressive" in criticizing the internal sociopolitical phenomena of countries such as China that did not share Western value systems.[156]

China–Japan Relations

Given the fast-shifting geopolitical realities of the Asia-Pacific region—particularly the rise of China—it is not surprising that China–Japan relations have plunged into a vicious cycle. Mutual ill-will culminated in horrendous anti-Japanese protests in several coastal Chinese cities in March and April 2005. Apart from familiar issues such as *lishi wenti* (the question of history) and territorial disputes over the Diaoyu Islands (also known as the Senkakus) and other areas, bilateral ties have deteriorated in large measure by Beijing's perception that Tokyo has become the number one Asian enforcer of Washington's "anti-China containment policy." And given that Beijing's bête noire, the "right-wing" Japan Prime Minister Junichiro Koizumi, will in late 2006 likely be succeeded by an equally hard-line leader, it is unlikely that relations between the two neighbors will improve in the foreseeable future. Rivalry with Japan thus stands out as a jarring exception to Beijing's generally successful "policy of good neighborliness."

The Apparently Unstoppable Vicious Cycle

There was an element of inevitability to the fact that 2005—which marked the sixtieth anniversary of the end of World War II—would be a difficult year for

China-Japan ties. For three weeks beginning late March 2005, tens of thousands of Chinese, many of them with "middle-class" backgrounds, held noisy, and at times, violent demonstrations against Japan in several coastal areas. Rocks and bottles were hurled at Japanese missions while the facades of several dozen Japanese restaurants and other business outlets in different cities suffered damage. Calls were made in cities ranging from Shenzhen to Shanghai to boycott Japanese goods, although no substantial nationwide action in this regard took place. In one vehement show of force on April 16, about 20,000 Shanghai residents milled around the downtown Japanese Consulate. As the police stood by passively, the protestors threw several thousand stones, tomatoes, soft-drink bottles, and other projectiles into the compound. This was despite the fact that one day earlier, the Ministry of Public Security had issued a warning that protestations of patriotism must be made in a "rational and legal manner." Calls for calm were subsequently made by senior ministers including Tang Jiaxuan, Li Zhaoxing, and Bo Xilai. Forty-two hooligan protestors were arrested by Shanghai police, while several radical nationalistic websites were closed down. The protests finally petered out toward the end of the month.[157]

The immediate cause of this largest show of anti-Japanese feelings since the 1940s was the stamp of approval given early in the year by the Japanese government to high school history textbooks that reportedly downplayed the Imperial Army's atrocities in China. Just prior to the protests, anti-Tokyo websites had collected some 20 million signatures from Chinese who were opposed to Japan's bid to acquire permanent membership on the United Nations Security Council (PMUNSC). Moreover, on Lunar New Year's Day in February, Tokyo announced that it had assumed control of the light-tower at the Diaoyu Islands. Disputes over the ownership of oil and gas under the East China Sea had also intensified since late 2004.[158]

The deterioration of Sino-Japanese ties has coincided with the growth of nationalistic, "anti-Japanese" NGOs, as well as the popularity of the Internet in big and medium-sized cities (see also Chapter 6). It was thus easy for anti-Tokyo sentiments to be inflated—and translated into potentially disruptive mass action. The dire straits into which bilateral ties have deteriorated were presaged by several seemingly meaningless incidents in the early 2000s. For instance, in March 2004, Zhang Yue, a popular China Central Television (CCTV) presenter, incurred the ire of large numbers of viewers when she wore a scarf that appeared to feature the Japanese "sun" national emblem. A year earlier, movie star Zhao Wei was boycotted by thousands of viewers when she showed up in a concert in Sichuan Province wearing a skirt on which was emblazoned the flag of the Japanese Imperial Army.[159]

And in September 2003, anti-Japanese comments flooded Chinese websites in the wake of an alleged "group orgy" involving about 400 Japanese employees and 500 prostitutes in the resort city of Zhuhai, Guangdong Province. The incident took place around September 18, regarded in China as a "day of shame" that marks Japan's invasion of the northeast in the late 1930s. Yet according to a Beijing-based Japanese diplomat, few Japanese under the age of forty-five are aware of the significance of the September 18 anniversary. Moreover, he indicated that there was no lack of Chinese tourists looking for prostitutes in Japan. Other ugly incidents between the two countries included the Asia Cup soccer match between the Chinese and Japanese teams in Beijing in mid-2004, in which Japanese players, fans, and diplomats were jeered at and even, in a few instances, attacked.[160]

Underlying the Sino-Japanese malaise are at least four deep-seated and intertwined contradictions between the two erstwhile foes. They include the *lishi wenti*; territorial disputes; Japan's "remilitarization" and its pivotal role in Washington's "encirclement policy" against China; and the age-old competition between China and Japan to be Asia's leader. There seems little question that the latter two factors, which are interlinked, are the major causes of the explosive situation.

The question of history is a reference to Beijing's perception that Tokyo has failed to adequately make amends for its WWII aggression against China: Tokyo has yet to make a formal, written apology to China, nor has it fully compensated for the tens of millions of Chinese victimized during the war. Tokyo's failure to look history in the eye—and make a full statement of guilt and apology—is symbolized at least in Chinese eyes by Prime Minister Koizumi's repeated homage to the Yasukuni Shrine, where a number of WWII "grade A war criminals" are honored.[161] The Chinese government—as well as several NGOs—has requested thorough compensation for victims who suffered personal damage from bombs and other toxic material left over by the Imperial Japanese Army during WWII. The issue of compensation dominated Chinese news in mid-2003 following the death of a worker in the northeast city of Qiqihar after he came into contact with a WWII-vintage mustard-gas canister in a construction site. And old bombs left by the Japanese army have been discovered in a dozen-odd cities.[162]

Anti-Japanese sentiments have also grown owing to the flare-up of territorial disputes. The years 2003 and 2004 saw ferocious attempts by Chinese nationalists to assert sovereignty over the Diaoyu or Senkaku Islands as well as the East China Sea. As discussed earlier, the new energy imperative of the Chinese leadership—finding new sources of oil and gas in peripheral areas including coastal waters—will assume more significance in China-Japan links. The petroleum angle is important because for the first time since WWII, the two countries are fighting over something tangible, and not just spiritual or symbolic matters like national honor.

It could be contended, however, that the "history" and territorial issues can be defused relatively easily. In a speech to world leaders at the Asia-African Forum in Jakarta in April 2004, Koizumi repeated the formal apology first issued by former premier Tomiichi Murayama in 1995. In any case, while visiting Tokyo in October 2000, then premier Zhu Rongji had indicated that Beijing would no longer be seeking a formal, written apology. Indeed, earlier that year, ex-president Jiang had in a high-profile manner laid down his dictum on bilateral relations: "Learn lessons from history and look to the future." During discussions on that occasion with the visiting secretaries-general of Japan's three main political parties, Jiang left it beyond doubt that Beijing would put the emphasis on the future rather than the past. It is true that visits made by Koizumi or his ministers to the Yasukuni Shrine, as well as the textbooks problem, would indicate that Japanese politicians were less than candid in their apology. However, Tokyo later agreed to the establishment of a joint Japanese-Chinese committee to look at the compilation of future history books. And while the Yasukuni issue might continue to prevent Koizumi from visiting China, it would hardly seem enough of a grievance as to provoke protests the size of those of April 2005.[163]

As for compensation, Tokyo's understanding is that both Kuomintang leader Generalissimo Chiang Kai-shek as well as Chinese cadres including Deng Xiaoping and Zhou Enlai had noted that China would not be seeking damages at the government level. Of course, Beijing has left it open for individual families as well as NGOs to press private cases against either the Japanese government or corporations. Yet the CCP leadership had until the late 1990s discouraged NGOs and individuals from doing so. And Tokyo is not entirely without justification when it insists that it is up to the courts in Japan to make rulings on such claims.[164]

And how about territorial disputes, which involve areas reportedly rich in oil and gas? It can be argued that while nettlesome, such quarrels could at least be shelved provided that the atmosphere over bilateral ties is better. Late patriarch Deng had set the example when he pointed out in the 1970s that disputes over the Diaoyu Islands should "be left for a later generation." And State Councilor Tang noted in April 2005 that it was possible for both countries to study the possibility of the joint exploitation of oil and gas under the East China Sea. Just a few months earlier, China had worked out similar compromises with Vietnam and the Philippines concerning disputed areas in the South China Sea.[165]

Tokyo as Washington's "Hit Man"—and Rivalry over Who Is Top Dog in Asia

Diplomatic observers have surmised that from Beijing's standpoint, the core reason behind Sino-Japanese mistrust and wrangling is that Japan is "colluding" with the United States, and to a lesser extent, Taiwan, to "contain" China and prevent its emergence as at least a "regional superpower." Put another way, Beijing's fears of the rise of militarism in Japan have been fanned by conspiracy theories that Tokyo is an accomplice to Washington's plot to encircle China, as well as a not-so-secret backer of Taiwan independence. As discussed above, Chinese misgivings climaxed after an early 2005 revision of the U.S.-Japan Defense Guidelines, which listed the peaceful resolution of the Taiwan Strait problem as the two allies' "common strategic objective." And Bush's visit to Japan in late 2005, which came after repeated statements about strengthening U.S.-Japan defense cooperation, further aroused

Chinese suspicions. While in Kyoto, Bush waxed eloquent about how the two allies should join hands to promote democracy in Asia. "We've got a good friend in Japan when it comes to spreading democracy and freedom," Bush noted. And Koizumi said, somewhat intriguingly, that "the stronger our ties with the U.S., the better relations we can build with China, Korea, and the rest of Asia."[166]

Fueling Tokyo's eagerness to "contain China" are apparent misgivings that Japan's position as the number one country in Asia might be overtaken by the PRC. Hence the need to enlist Uncle Sam's help to battle the common enemy. The views of Chen Xiangyang, commentator of the official *Outlook Weekly,* are representative of the thinking of the Hu leadership. "Japan fears that it will be overtaken by large, developing countries in the Asian region," Chen wrote in April 2005. "Japan has therefore bound itself to the U.S., and tried to boost its own position through the American connection."[167]

Growing disputes over the Diaoyu or Senkaku Islands have been driven by not just oil but Beijing's strategic consideration that the archipelago would be used in a U.S.-Japanese, and possibly even a U.S.-Japanese-Taiwanese, anti-China encirclement plot. The mainland and Hong Kong press has cited the possibility that the Japanese defense forces could invite American troops to stage exercises in islets close to Taiwan and Okinawa such as the Shimoji Islands or even the Senkakus.[168] Moreover, Chinese analysts believe that Japan has national-security reasons behind its alleged support of Taiwan independence. As Yu Yongsheng, commentator for the official *International Herald Leader* noted, if the mainland and Taiwan were united, "China will be in a much more advantageous position regarding territorial disputes over the Diaoyus and the East China Sea." Yu added that Beijing's control of Taiwan might threaten sea lanes which Japan-bound oil tankers had to pass through.[169]

Security reasons also underlie Beijing's opposition to Tokyo's acquisition of PMUNSC. For the Hu leadership, a PMUNSC for Japan would become a milestone in Tokyo's becoming a "normal nation," or one that possesses normal defense forces capable of being deployed around the world. After all, Tokyo would, with its PMUNSC, be justified in maintaining a much larger army so as to fulfill its global peace-keeping tasks.[170] Bilateral relations have also worsened due to the growth of nationalistic, "anti-China" sentiments not only among right-wing organizations in Japan but among also broad sectors of the Japanese general public. In December 2004, Tokyo published its National Defense Program Guideline for 2005 and after, in which China was for the first time named as Japan's main security concern. Moreover, Tokyo seems distraught with the fact that its erstwhile predominance in Asia has been eclipsed by China's fast-growing economic and diplomatic clout. The success of China in cementing free-trade arrangements with ASEAN—as well as with individual countries such as Thailand—is an indication that the momentum is going China's way.[171]

In any case, the CCP leadership is bent on pursuing a double-pronged policy toward Japan for the rest of the decade. This means that while China will recognize Japan's status as an economic quasi-superpower, Beijing will throw its weight around to ensure that Japan remains a "second-class power" in diplomatic and military arenas. Thus politically, Beijing will not regard Japan as a "top-tier power" on the order of the United States or Russia. And political and diplomatic pressure will continue to be exerted to prevent Japan from becoming a "normal country."[172] For example, Beijing has consistently opposed the augmentation of the Japan defense budget, the revision of the Japanese constitution, and other ancillary steps toward "remilitarization." The Chinese leadership also has reservations about Tokyo's playing a bigger role in international peace-keeping efforts, for example, sending noncombative forces to Iraq in 2003.

Intense Sino-Japanese mistrust and competition have overshadowed what might have been silver linings on the horizon. For instance, Beijing's peacekeeping role on the Korean Peninsula should in theory have earned the praise of Japan, which is under constant threat from Pyongyang's missiles. Yet while Japanese diplomats certainly seem appreciative of Beijing's efforts, this development has not made a dent in ordinary Japanese citizens' relatively negative sentiments about the PRC. Economically, Beijing is more than willing to work out a partnership relationship with Tokyo. According to Chinese statistics, bilateral trade in 2004 jumped 25.7 percent to $167.8 billion—and China suffered a deficit of $20.8 billion. If Hong Kong is included, China displaced the United States as Japan's largest trading partner that year.[173] A significant trend in two-way commerce since the early 2000s has been Japanese manufacturers moving relatively sophisticated production capacities to eastern China. It is true that Japanese high-tech investment still lagged behind that of South Korea by large margins. However, recent outlays by Japanese corporations in China represented quite a leap forward from the 1980s and most of the 1990s, when Japanese firms were in general leery about transferring know-how to China.

Yet there are indications that a climate of bilateral suspicion if not hostility could make economic symbiosis more difficult. Threats to boycott Japanese products during the April 2005 protests are a case in point. Equally telling is the debate within China of whether to use the Japanese Shinkansen or bullet-train technology for the important Beijing-Shanghai rail link, due to be operational by 2008. While some experts in the Chinese Ministry of Railways seemed to favor the Japanese model, the political reality would render this all but impossible. Things have come to such a point that quite a few Japanese officials and businessmen were no longer keen on seeing a Shinkansen-style rail service in China. "What if an anti-Japanese nationalist were to put a bomb on the train soon after the inauguration of the Shinkansen line?" asked a Japanese banker. "This will not only create a diplomatic incident but further poison people-to-people feelings."[174] Indeed, pessimists about bilateral relations have raised the possibility that even economic ties could falter, leading to the situation of "cold politics, cool economics." Media commentators in Beijing have claimed that the Koizumi government is encouraging Japanese corporations to invest in India instead of

China. At least up to late 2005, however, both Beijing and Tokyo seem anxious to prevent this lose-lose situation from taking place.[175]

Possibility for "New Thinking"?

At least before the outburst of anti-Japanese sentiments in 2003, quite a few well-known intellectuals created a stir in Beijing's intellectual circles by proposing so-called *xinsiwei* (new thinking) on relations with Japan. The gist of their argument was that Chinese should jettison the obsession with the "question of history"—or the goal of undermining Japan's diplomatic and political influence in Asia—by emphasizing synergy instead of competition. Speculation in Beijing's political circles was that individual leaders such as Zeng Qinghong, who was ex-president Jiang's main adviser on Japan, had at least given indirect encouragement to the *xinsiwei*.

Ma Licheng, then a renowned *People's Daily* editor, raised eyebrows by proposing in late 2002 that Chinese look at Japan from a different perspective. An unabashed advocate of Western-style political reform, the journalist-author was particularly disturbed by the "unholy alliance" between Chinese nationalists and "new leftists," or born-again Maoists. In articles and interviews in *Strategy and Management, Southern Weekend,* and other media, Ma argued that the apology issue should not stand in the way of Sino-Japanese rapprochement—and that the current revulsion against most things Japanese ran the risk of degenerating into a "Boxers-style xenophobia."[176] Ma noted that China should show the magnanimity of the victor of the Sino-Japanese War, and that officials and citizens alike should consider "the *xinsiwei* of being more tolerant and understanding" of Japan. For example, Chinese should differentiate between Japanese aspirations to become a "normal country"—including one that possesses defense forces on a par with other countries in Asia—and the so-called resurgence of militarism. The editor said Beijing should concentrate on boosting bilateral economic ties as well as the construction of a China–Japan–South Korean common market.[177]

Shi Yinhong, a U.S.-educated international affairs expert at People's University, was adroit enough to couch his *xinsiwei* about Japan in acceptable "Cold War" parlance. In an article in *Strategy and Management,* Shi pointed out that rapprochement with Japan could pave the way for a Sino-Japanese semi-alliance against U.S. "hegemonism." He noted that China should show its understanding of Japanese aspirations by shelving demands for war-time reparations, not opposing Japan's military buildup, and even supporting Japan's gaining a seat on the UNSC. The basis of Shi's argument was realpolitik: that accepting a relatively strong Japanese army is a price to pay for preventing the world's second largest economy from becoming a pawn in Washington's anti-China containment policy.[178]

Feng Zhaokui, a senior researcher at the CASS's Japan Institute, pointed out in 2004 that China and Japan should, apart from boosting already solid economic ties, try to cooperate in less contentious security issues such as guaranteeing the safety of sea routes through which both countries get their oil and other supplies from the Middle East. Feng argued that together with India, China and Japan should explore the possibility of "joining hands to deal with nontraditional security threats such as terrorism and piracy [in key sea routes]." Another famous Japan scholar, Wu Jinan, put forward the concept of an Asian Energy Development Organization (AEDO) among China, Japan, and South Korea. The three countries would reap benefits including economy of scale in the purchase and transport of crude. For example, AEDO will be in a position to acquire oil and gas at cheaper prices as Asian nations typically pay at least $1 per barrel more than American or European buyers.[179]

The spate of anti-Japanese feelings unleashed by the mustard-gas incident in Qiqihar, however, has effectively silenced the likes of Ma and Shi. By late 2003, Ma had already retired from *People's Daily,* but the paper still received calls from self-styled patriots condemning Ma's "pro-Japan" articles. And Lin Zhibo, a former colleague of Ma's in the *People Daily's* commentary department, penned an article in an early 2004 issue of *Strategy and Management* condemning both Ma and Shi for being too naïve in expecting that Japan would ever abandon its role as America's stooge in Asia. Lin alleged that their *xinsiwei* "does not represent the views of *People's Daily,* People's University, the Chinese government, or Chinese public opinion."[180]

Compounding the Sino-Japanese malaise is the fact that while there are also notable intellectuals in Japan who advocate a variant of "new thinking" toward China, they are in the minority—and are unable to affect mainstream discourse. One point of departure of China-friendly Japanese academics and researchers is to debunk the China threat theory, particularly the current version that the "world factory" along the eastern Chinese coast has taken business and jobs away from Japan. For example, veteran economist Toshiya Tsugami, who authored the book *The Rise of China* in 2003, urged Japanese to drop the China bogey. He said Tokyo should facilitate more exchanges with different sectors of Chinese citizens. For example, visa requirements for Chinese tourists and particularly private entrepreneurs should be liberalized. "There are certainly merits in a Japanese-Chinese FTA and even the integration of the two economies," he said.[181]

Likewise, Asia scholar Masuru Tamamoto pointed out that Japan and China should cooperate in the same way that France and Germany had worked together to spearhead the formation of an Asian community. "Over the long run, China and Japan need each other to deal with critical problems," he noted. For example, Tamamoto proposed that Tokyo absorb more well-educated Chinese immigrants to help cure Japan's imbroglio over its aging population. Through cooperation and not jockeying for position, the scholar pointed out, "Japan and China will become equal for the first time, and, in a sense, one and part of a larger global whole."[182]

In fact, prior to the outburst of anti-Japanese sentiments in April 2005, there were cautious optimists who saw several positive developments that could yet nudge bilateral ties toward a more benevolent cycle. In autumn 2004, Hu had signaled

Beijing's willingness to improve ties with Tokyo by sending then vice–foreign minister Wang Yi as ambassador to Japan. A fluent Japanese speaker, Wang was considered "sympathetic to Japan" by the Tokyo media.[183] And some analysts saw in the November 2004 "mini-summit" between Hu and Koizumi on the sidelines of the APEC meeting in Chile as a ray of hope. This was the two leaders' first tête-à-tête in three years. While both "agreed to disagree" on issues such as the Yasukuni Shrine, the meeting itself was deemed a sign of improvement due to the opposition to the mini-summit voiced by Chinese users of Internet chat rooms."[184]

Most significantly, Premier Wen put forward at the end of the 2005 NPC session three principles and three proposals for the amelioration of ties with Japan. The three precepts were: "To keep history in mind but look ahead into the future; to adhere to the one-China principle; and to strive for co-development." And the three proposed courses of action were: "to enthusiastically create conditions for senior-level exchanges; to initiate strategic dialogue on building long-term friendship; and to solve problems bequeathed by history."[185] This was the first time since Koizumi's 2001 visit to the Yasukuni Shrine that Beijing cited the need to work toward a resumption of high-level exchanges. Yet these relatively good vibes were shattered by the angry voices on the streets of Shanghai and Beijing a few weeks later.

Seasoned watchers of the Sino-Japanese scene reckon that at least in Beijing's assessment, the terminal solution would be for Tokyo to make some form of a pledge not to be a party to Washington's anti-China "encirclement conspiracy." This proposition—which is tantamount to asking Tokyo to choose between China and the United States—would hardly find a sympathetic reception across Japan's political spectrum. It would be quite impossible for any Japanese leader to follow in the footsteps of, say, Canberra or Singapore in declaring "neutrality" in the case of a Sino-U.S. conflict over Taiwan. While some Chinese officials may hope that whoever succeeds Koizumi in late 2006 might be more China-friendly, the odds are that his successors will continue with the "pro-U.S., anti-China" policies of the much-vilified Japanese leader.[186]

China-ASEAN Relations

Sino-ASEAN Rapprochement

As discussed earlier, China raised the concept of *heping jueqi*, or peaceful rise, to allay the fears of neighbors, particularly ASEAN countries, that its dramatic rise would not signal "neo-imperialistic" proclivities. That Beijing had achieved partial success was evidenced by its accession in 2003 to the Treaty of Amity and Cooperation (TAC) with ASEAN, which signaled that disputes over the South China Sea islands and other areas would be set aside at least for one generation. The nonaggression pact also envisaged cooperation in "politics, economy, social affairs, security, and regional affairs." And there would be enhanced cooperation in areas including the defense forces (such as that between China on the one hand and Thailand and Burma on the other) and fighting sea piracy and terrorism.[187]

President Hu in early 2004 spelled out five areas where China–ASEAN—as well as overall Chinese-Asian—ties could be promoted. They included boosting political trust and neighborliness; increasing bilateral economic cooperation with individual countries; speeding up regional economic integration; more cultural interaction; and more security dialogue, confidence-building measures, and military-to-military exchanges.[188] While several ASEAN members would have reservations about military cooperation with China, it was obvious that by 2005, economic, cultural, and diplomatic ties between China and the major regional bloc had progressed smoothly.

Commercial dealings are the most effective way for stabilizing and promoting China-ASEAN and, in general, China-Asia relations. In late 2003, leaders including President Hu and Premier Wen played dominant roles at the "ASEAN plus three" meeting in Bali and the APEC forum in Bangkok. Hu and Wen succeeded to some extent in persuading ASEAN leaders that the ever-potent "world factory" along China's eastern coast would not threaten the bloc's economic viability. By contrast, as Wen put it in Bali, a rising Chinese economy would "bring tremendous immediate and long-term benefits to Asian countries." China-ASEAN trade hit $78.2 billion in 2003, up 42.8 percent from the year before, with the PRC running a record deficit of $16.4 billion. Bilateral trade reached $105.8 billion in 2004, and the PRC is expected in a couple of years to displace the United States as ASEAN's largest trading partner. As of mid-2004, contractual investment by Chinese companies in ASEAN amounted to $1.04 billion, while actual ASEAN investment in China was $34 billion. And Beijing has told various Asian capitals that Chinese multinational companies will be investing more in the region.[189]

Details of a China-ASEAN free trade zone were firmed up and in some aspects rendered more elaborate in 2003 and 2004. At the late-2004 ASEAN conference in Laos, Premier Wen and his counterparts vowed to build "the world's largest free trade area" by 2015. This super-zone will boast a 1.8 billion population, an aggregate GDP of $2 trillion, and trade volume of $1.23 trillion. Tariffs for some 7,000 products would be lowered to under 5 percent by 2010. And thanks to an "early harvest" program, a few hundred agricultural products from individual ASEAN countries such as Thailand were able to enter China in January 2004 under much-reduced taxes. In addition, work on an infrastructure network along the Mekong River has been speeded up with a view to building a new trade zone that will take in southwest China, Thailand, Vietnam, Laos, and Cambodia. In a dispensation sometimes known as China's "Marshall Plan," Beijing is footing a disproportionately large chunk of the bill for widening rivers and building ports, airports, bridges, and related facilities.[190]

At the Bo'ao Conference in April 2004, Chinese officials laid out the vision of a pan-Asian common market with increasing cooperation in financial matters. Thus, in his keynote address, President Hu suggested better coordination in macroeconomic and financial policy, setting up regional investment entities and a bonds market, as well as other financial cooperation schemes. Former chief WTO negotiator Long Yongtu even raised the possibility of an Asian dollar zone, saying that "the Asian dollar concept is a goal worth pursuing." Countries in the Asian dollar zone would in theory enjoy zero tariffs. And the experience of the EU has proven that the introduction of the euro has dramatically improved trade among member countries.[191]

NCNA quoted Chinese experts as saying that the unitary currency could help less well-off countries in the region better cushion the impact of fluctuations in the value of the U.S. dollar and the euro. The Asian dollar would also facilitate the issuance of government bonds by individual countries. There is no doubt that in the wake of the ever-rising importance of the yuan, Beijing is contemplating a yuan-dominated Asian economic zone. By contrast, with the apparent weakening of the influence of Japan, the idea of a yen zone or a yen-dominated common Asian currency—which was fashionable in the 1980s—has become less relevant.[192]

Indeed, with most ASEAN countries chalking up considerable trade surpluses with the Middle Kingdom, Beijing has so far won the race with Tokyo in making FTAs and other special arrangements with ASEAN members. In the eyes of many ASEAN nations, China is the regional superpower on the rise. Moreover, it was only in early 2004 that Tokyo decided to speed up the process of forming FTAs with its neighbors. One stumbling block is firm objection by Japanese farmers to agricultural imports. Japan's room for maneuver regarding ASEAN has further been constricted due to its far-reaching alliance relationship with the United States. Washington sees an ASEAN-China or an ASEAN-Japan FTA as an effort to reduce American influence in the region. And Tokyo had reservations about signing a TAC with ASEAN because of its military implications, which might contradict elements of its long-standing defense pact with the United States.[193]

The China–U.S.–ASEAN Triangle: Limits of China's Political Influence in ASEAN

It is a measure of China's success in boosting economic and diplomatic ties with ASEAN that conservative commentators in the West have raised the specter of a kind of Chinese Monroe Doctrine, whereby Beijing would herd a number of its weaker neighbors into its exclusive sphere of influence. This is despite the fact that in terms of most quantifiable standards, China's influence is still dwarfed by that of the United States. For example, by the end of 2004, the PRC's cumulative investment in Southeast Asia amounted to just US$1.1 billion, compared with America's $85.4 billion. Indeed, Beijing has taken quite a leap forward in its political and economic influence in this region. For example, owing to Beijing's lobbying, ASEAN leaders shied away from using the ASEAN Forum in early 2004 to force Rangoon to improve its human rights record. And the majority of Asian officials have stopped making noises about China's plans to utilize naval facilities in Myanmar. Some analysts also see in the China-ASEAN FTA an effort to counterbalance the preponderance of the EU and the United States itself.[194]

Beijing has achieved some degree of success in banishing the "China threat" bogey from the minds of ASEAN leaders as it goes about promoting business and then political ties with this crucial bloc. There is evidence that Beijing has parlayed its newfound regional economic clout into some form of an Asian security concept that could one day challenge American "unilateralism." As Premier Wen said in the Bo'ao Conference of mostly Asian leaders in late 2003, "we should proceed from the larger interests of Asia's development, and cultivate a new security concept featuring mutual trust, mutual benefit, equality, and cooperation."[195] On private and public occasions, Chinese diplomats and defense officials have floated the idea of joint naval and other military exercises with ASEAN members. Certainly arms sales by Beijing to ASEAN members including Thailand, Burma, Laos, and even Malaysia have increased noticeably.

Diplomatic analysts say it is unrealistic for Beijing to expect that some kind of China-ASEAN security arrangement would rival that formed between the United States and long-time allies and quasi-allies such as Japan, South Korea, and the Philippines. The chances of China challenging U.S. supremacy in Asia in the foreseeable future are not high. A major reason is the predominance of U.S. naval and air power. Many ASEAN countries—including erstwhile enemies of the United States such as Vietnam—welcome American presence as a counterbalance to China's growing economic and military prowess. More importantly, ASEAN members such as the Philippines, Thailand, and Singapore have quasi-military alliance relationships with the United States, seen as the only power that can deal with the terrorism and other security threats in the region. The majority of ASEAN members harbor serious misgivings about the fast-expanding clout of the PLA. And Beijing has yet to completely win over two heavyweight ASEAN countries, Vietnam and Indonesia.

Indeed, the brief confrontation between Singapore and China in the summer of 2004 should perhaps serve as an example of how a small ASEAN country could run afoul of the rising dragon that is China. The CCP leadership huffed and puffed when then deputy prime minister Lee Hsien-loong paid a "private visit" to Taiwan in July 2004. Beijing canceled a series of bilateral visits and even postponed discussions relating to a China-Singapore FTA. The immediate cause for the confrontation was of course China's displeasure at Singapore providing support to President Chen Shui-bian. Yet a more fundamental reason could be enhanced Singapore-U.S. military ties, as demonstrated by the Lion State's support for American naval vessels patrolling the strategic Strait of Malacca.[196]

While Beijing realizes it may not be able in the near term to exert the kind of influence that the United States has over this region, it wants to prevent Asian countries from having the kind of military relationship with the United States that could hurt Chinese interests, particularly in the event of a crisis over Taiwan. For example, in the event of the United States coming to the aid of Taiwan, Beijing hopes its "strategic partners" in Asia could be dissuaded from providing air bases and other logistics support for American aircraft. And the CCP leadership is ecstatic that Australia, a staunch American ally, has indicated its "neutrality" in the event of U.S. involvement in a Taiwan Strait conflict. Canberra also broke ranks with the United States and Japan in early 2005 by not opposing the EU's lifting its arms embargo on China.[197]

By early 2005, Beijing had concluded "strategic partnership" with ASEAN countries including the Philippines, and in particular, Indonesia. This was accomplished largely through using the "business" and "benefactor" cards. For example, Beijing was generous with relief aid in the wake of the tsunami in northern Indonesia in December 2004. President Hu also pledged more imports of Indonesia minerals and produce during his visit there in April 2005. Beijing has taken full advantage of Washington's five-year-old ban on the sale of weapons to Indonesia—on account of the latter's alleged human-rights violations in the rebel province of Aceh—to successfully persuade the new administration of President Susilo Yudhoyono to buy a full package of military supplies from the PRC.[198] Despite residual mistrust between the two countries, Sino-Indonesian relations have improved largely owing to much-enhanced economic cooperation.

Beijing's ambitions about one day becoming top dog on its home continent were evident in the inauguration of the East Asian Community (EAC)—dubbed Asia's answer to the European Union—in Kuala Lumpur in December 2005. The Community consisted of the "ASEAN plus three" nations, in addition to India, Australia, and New Zealand. Although the United States, generally known as a Pacific power, was excluded, Beijing was pushing for Russia to join in 2006. While the EAC's structure and goals remain murky, it could become a platform for China to further use its "import card" to consolidate its influence among ASEAN members.[199] Indeed, Beijing strategists are already laying plans for the day—perhaps in the late 2020s—when China might be able to displace U.S. influence at least in selective areas of Asia. And if, by then, ASEAN countries will have to make a choice between China and the United States, Beijing is confident that thanks to the magnetic pull of its fast-growing economy, the PRC can secure the backing of a good number of its neighbors.

Conclusion: In Search of a New World Order with Chinese Characteristics

Three years after becoming party chief, Hu Jintao has made some headway in forging a "multipolar world order with Chinese characteristics," or a global community where China is within striking distance—say a decade or so—of playing a role that is commensurate with its huge land mass, population, geopolitical significance, as well as economic and military might. It is true that China is nowhere near catching up with the lone superpower, but the Hu-Wen leadership is realistic enough to appreciate that Beijing will have achieved a lot if it can establish close ties with major countries and blocs such as the EU, Russia, ASEAN, and increasingly, large and fast-developing countries such as India, Brazil, and South Africa.

It is instructive to look at the pivotal role that Beijing played in the Asia-Africa Forum held in Jakarta in April 2005. The conclave, attended by leaders from countries in the two relatively less developed continents, was called to mark the fiftieth anniversary of the Bandung Conference, which kick-started the nonaligned movement. Under the leadership of the charismatic Zhou Enlai, China on that occasion left a firm imprint on world diplomacy by laying claim to the role of spokesman for the Third World. As indicated earlier, the Fourth-Generation leadership would have none of the revolutionary rhetoric of Chairman Mao. However, Hu used the Jakarta conference to renew Beijing's emphasis on symbiotic, strategic partnerships with major, newly developed countries in Asia and Africa such as India, Indonesia, and South Africa, as part of Beijing's long-standing goal of nurturing a multipolar global structure. The PRC hopes to become a prime mover in this nexus of international cooperation, which is also conceived as a counterweight to U.S. preponderance.

In his Bandung speech calling for a "new strategic partnership" among Asian and African nations, Hu laid stress on cooperation based on "mutual respect, equality, trust, and dialogue" in areas including trade and economic exchange, culture, and security. Without referring to the "hegemonism" of the United States—or injustices in the current world order—Hu appealed for the creation of a "win-win international development environment" that is aimed at enhanced "South-South cooperation" and curtailing the differences between rich and poor countries.[200]

Note the distance that the Hu-lead diplomatic team has traversed from late patriarch Deng's "never take the lead" mantra. For the first time since the end of the Maoist era, there is an urgency to consolidate links with behemoths in Asia (including erstwhile enemies and potentially hostile states such as India and Indonesia), as well as those in Africa and Latin America (especially South Africa and Brazil). There are even hints that Beijing wants to put together a semi-alliance of non-Western nations such as China, Russia, India, Indonesia, Brazil, and South Africa—one that could counterbalance the so-called Western alliance, or the U.S.-led assemblage of countries incorporating the European Union, Japan, South Korea, and Australia. And it is significant that in mid-2005, China, India, and Russia decided to establish a "strategic triangular relationship" to not only boost economic, energy, and high-tech cooperation but also handle security and diplomatic challenges. For example, it is in Beijing and Moscow's interest to stop the United States from boosting its already formidable influence in Central Asian states such as Uzbekistan and Kyrgyzstan.[201]

In any event, Beijing had by late 2005 partially realized its objective of becoming a major international actor. Its bolstered ties with the EU, Russia, India, and ASEAN will enable China to have significant clout in global forums including the United Nations. For example, it is likely the PRC will gain a bigger say in ongoing reform proposals at the world body. Moreover, elements of the multipolar world order as conceived by Beijing could go some way toward countering Washington's "anti-China containment policy." The leading role that Beijing is set to play in the East Asian Community may enable the Hu-Wen team to win over more of America's traditional Asian allies. At the same time, Beijing is in a position to boost trade with fast-developing markets in countries such as Russia, India, Indonesia, Brazil, and South Africa. Reliable supplies of oil and other minerals from the far reaches of the globe can be more effectively guaranteed.

An underlying reason behind the diplomatic achievement of the Hu-Wen team is China's fast-expanding economy—and Beijing's ability to play the "business" and "import" cards. Thus, in Jakarta, Hu and his diplomats played up what the PRC could offer its neighbors and friends. In his keynote speech, Hu noted that China imported $254.1 billion worth of goods and services from Asia in 2004, up 35.7 percent from the year before. Comparable figures for Africa in 2004 were $5.7 billion and 87.1 percent. And while addressing the East Asia Summit—which is supposed to morph into the EAC—in Kuala Lumpur in late 2005, Premier Wen noted that China might be importing US$2 trillion worth of products from Asia during the rest of the decade.[202]

As discussed earlier, Wen and other leaders have pointed out that economics would be a key determinant of foreign policy. As *Outlook Weekly* commentator Yu Sui noted in a mid-2005 article, "Economic factors are most important in relations among big nations." Or as Zhu Guangyao, director of the International Department of the Ministry of Finance indicated, Beijing will wage "financial diplomacy to safeguard the country's best interests."[203] Given the leaps-and-bounds growth of the China market, it is of course advantageous for the Hu-Wen team to emphasize economics rather than politics.

And the economic and "benefactor" cards have been instrumental in helping Beijing water down old rivalries and woo new friends, especially with ASEAN countries. With foreign exchange reserves approaching $800 billion, Beijing is in a position to boost imports from developing countries—and to initiate an "Asian Marshall Plan" to help build infrastructure in the poorer Asian and African nations. Hu was able to forge "partnership relationships" with Indonesia and the Philippines during his tours of these countries in early 2005 partly through dangling economic aid as well as possibilities that Beijing would buy more from these countries.

For the PRC to really earn an exalted place in the community of nations, however, it needs to do a lot more than just distributing economic largesse or engaging in the old game of playing off Russia or the EU against a "hegemonistic" America. After all, China is still a relatively poor country. And economic reasons—for example, China's alleged dumping of cheap textile products in the EU and United States, and its taking away foreign direct investment from Asia-Pacific neighbors—are also significant factors behind the country's unpopularity with a number of nations. Moreover, there were indications by late 2005 that several developing countries including Thailand and Brazil were grousing over the relentless influx of

Chinese products ranging from fruits and garments to TV sets and computers. An even more cumbersome millstone around the neck of Beijing's diplomatic efforts consists of political factors such as Asia-Pacific countries' fear of the fast-developing PLA, especially the fact that the country's vast military and security forces are both nontransparent and not subject to popular supervision. And the rise of nationalism, coupled with the CCP leadership's apparent need to promote patriotism and sometimes xenophobic sentiments so as to maintain its mandate of heaven, has made the Middle Kingdom's foreign policy that much more unpredictable and potentially destabilizing to the region and the world.

6

The Challenge of Nationalism, and Other Ideas and Trends for the New Century

Winds of Change in the Twenty-first Century

There are increasing signs that to consolidate its mandate of heaven—and to ensure cohesiveness among 1.3 billion Chinese—the Hu Jintao leadership is using multipronged tactics to boost citizens' sense of national pride, patriotism, and nationalism. Trends toward accentuated nationalism, and sometimes even jingoism and xenophobia, first reared their head during the thirteen years under ex-president Jiang Zemin. And these tendencies could become exacerbated in the coming decade as socialist orthodoxy, as well as the Chinese Communist Party's (CCP) legitimacy, comes under increasing threat in the wake of Beijing's enhanced open-door policy. This chapter will examine the extent to which Fourth-Generation cadres led by President Hu and Premier Wen Jiabao might have to rely on the double-edged sword of nationalism to hold the nation together and to prolong the CCP's ruling-party status.

Juxtaposed against what some analysts call the "nationalistic temptation" are the equally significant trends of globalization and federalism. These two ideas, particularly thorough-going globalization, are favored by more liberal and forward-looking elements among the ruling elite, the intelligentsia, and the rising "new classes." And to the extent that educated Chinese can be persuaded to embrace a more internationalist—and tolerant—outlook in areas ranging from culture and technology to society and politics, the less desirable aspects of patriotism and nationalism could be kept at bay.

Major forces at work in Chinese society this decade also include the increasingly influential Internet and other new media. The ever-thickening traffic on the PRC information superhighway could facilitate the popularization of "Westernized," outward-looking, and pro-globalization ideas and approaches despite the CCP leadership's largely successful attempts to control the Net. At the same time, conservative groupings including nationalists have been astute in using websites and electronic signature campaigns to spread their sometimes xenophobic messages.

This chapter will also take a detailed look at the "new classes" of private entrepreneurs, "middle-class" managers and professionals, returnees from abroad, as well as non-governmental organizations (NGOs) and other elements of the civil society. These new actors on the sociopolitical stage represent in many ways the "foremost production forces" and the "most advanced culture"—elements that ex-president Jiang and, more recently, the Hu-Wen team have been eager to co-opt into the party. A sizable number of businessmen and academics have changed the political ecology by running for office in cities and counties. Professionals and intellectuals also form the backbone of the fast-expanding civil society, which includes NGOs that have packed a punch in fields ranging from legal reform to environmental protection. By and large, the Chinese intelligentsia and novel social sectors have become stakeholders in and supporters of the status quo; however, significant numbers of intellectuals and professionals remain keen advocates of political restructuring and liberalization. Whether ideas and "isms" being bandied about in academic and cultural circles, such as nationalism and federalism, can develop into substantial political forces depends to some extent on whether they have found favor with the "new classes" as well as fast-growing civil-society groupings.

Nationalism vs. Globalization and Federalism

The Double-Edged Sword of Nationalism

Nationalism as a Cohesive Force

There is much to the assertion by political theorist Wu Jiaxiang that the post–June 4, 1989, administration has deliberately drummed up nationalism to sustain one-party authoritarian rule.[1] At a time of the demise of communism and related creeds, CCP authorities are in dire need of a cohesive force to hold the huge and complex country together. And propagating patriotism, which in many areas overlaps with nationalism or even xenophobia, is perhaps an easy way for the leadership to promote a sense of unity and common purpose, which will also serve to prolong the party's mandate of heaven. Moreover, Beijing also sees patriotism and nationalism as an antidote to the harmful and destabilizing effects of globalization.

Nationalism can also be used as a diplomatic tool in the country's dealings with the United States and Japan. For example, while urging Washington officials to rein in Taiwan independence, Chinese leaders and diplomats like to point to statistics and polls showing ordinary citizens' supposed indignation at President Chen Shui-bian's pro-independence game plan—as well as their readiness to defend national unity with their lives. And despite Beijing's apparent efforts to cool down flare-ups of anti-Japanese sentiments, Chinese cadres have during meetings with Japanese counterparts cited strong popular feelings about Tokyo's perceived refusal to properly make up for its wartime atrocities.[2]

The onset of the Iraq War of early 2003 served as a good backdrop to observe Beijing authorities' skillful manipulation of Chinese nationalists' "anti-U.S." sentiments. Even before the U.S. invasion started, Beijing had slapped a ban on college students who wanted to hold demonstrations. However, in a rare move, the two main official news agencies, the New China News Agency (NCNA) and China News Service, ran stories about Iraq-related campus activities. For instance, NCNA reported in March that around forty Peking University students held a seminar entitled "Render Support to Peace: Avoid Warfare." The authorities also permitted several groups of radical intellectuals to start Internet petitions or signature campaigns condemning the rise of "U.S. unilateralism." For example, around 1,000 activists, including several well-known United States bashers, put their names on an open letter entitled "No to War on Iraq." The statement condemned Washington for its plans to perpetrate the "high-tech slaughter of defenseless Iraqi people." And in an apparent departure from Beijing's cautious attitude at the beginning of the Iraqi crisis, the authorities in late March allowed a small group of intellectuals to hold a demonstration in a downtown park to condemn U.S. "hegemonism."[3]

At least from the point of view of diplomatic observers, Beijing's adept handling the reaction of ordinary Chinese to the Iraq War could serve multiple purposes. First, it afforded people a chance to let off steam. Second, the CCP leadership, especially cadres close to ex-president Jiang, hoped to lay to rest suspicions that it was "pro-United States." Perhaps most importantly, Chinese officials were in a position to tell the United States that Beijing was doing America a big favor by pledging not to use its United Nations veto on the subject despite widespread popular sentiment against the war. And Beijing's acquiescence in America's global war on terrorism was a main reason for improved Sino-U.S. relations since the September 11 tragedies (see Chapter 5).

The Hu-Wen leadership, however, is aware that nationalism is a double-edged sword. This is true particularly when nationalism is relentlessly rising among a broad cross-section of the public. The upsurge of anti-U.S. feelings could easily translate into opposition to the country's open-door policy—especially where it involves inviting foreign, particularly American, capital to help restructure state enterprises, one result of which was the sacking of tens of thousands of laborers. It is not surprising that a sizable proportion of nationalistic intellectuals were also leftists who were opposed to late patriarch Deng Xiaoping's open-door policy.[4]

Consider, for example, the influence of a group of "left-wing nationalists" who played a major role in organizing the anti–Iraq War Internet petitions. Mostly much-published academics and journalists in their late thirties and forties, they included Wang Xiaodong, Lu Zhoulai, Fang Ning, Yang Fan, and Han Deqiang. These leftist-nationalists have warned the party and nation against leaning too close to the United States. Wang, the co-author of the famous tome *A China That Can Say No,* noted that China stood to suffer if it were to participate in the international division of labor under rules set by the United States. He pointed out in 2005 that it would be naïve for Chinese to expect that the United States would help China move up the technological chain, and that "China could end up being controlled by the United States and other developed countries."[5]

Other leftists have mixed nationalism and orthodox, near-autarkist socialism to oppose privatization of state-owned enterprises through absorbing American and Western capital. Making themselves out to be champions of workers and farmers, these radical intellectuals have claimed that the interests of the proletariat were being jeopardized through the "collusion" between cadre-capitalists and multinationals. And in private conversation or meetings, such leftist-nationalists have even scolded leaders, including ex-president Jiang, for allowing their sons and daughters to engage in lucrative cooperative ventures with American and other Western multinationals.[6]

Over the longer term, irrational growth of nationalistic and allied feelings particularly among young Chinese could have a detrimental impact on globalization. It would also detract from China's ability to function as a responsible member of the global community. A deplorable example of anti-foreign feelings run amok was the reaction to the September 11 attacks on New York and Washington. There were expressions of sympathy and support for the United States on Chinese websites immediately after the Day of Infamy. Yet there was also no lack of cynical statements saying that the U.S. had pretty much brought this about owing to its "neo-imperialist" and "unilateralist" tendencies. A group of Chinese journalists visiting the United States at the time as guests of the State Department was unceremoniously sent home because they clapped their hands upon seeing the two hijacked planes ram into the Twin Towers.[7]

Indeed, as American Sinologist Peter Gries pointed out, "the CCP is losing control over nationalist discourse." "Nationalism is a grammar that potential challengers can use to contest the CCP's right to rule," he pointed out. Looking at recent history, quite a few important patriotic and nationalistic campaigns—notably the May Fourth Movement of 1919—ended up as anti-establishment crusades because the central authorities were seen as weak, corrupt, and unable to defend China's rightful interests.[8] It would be naïve for the Hu-Wen administration to assume that outbursts of xenophobic feelings would necessarily translate into support for the CCP leadership. The phenomenal growth of anti-Japanese feelings, examined in the following sections, demonstrates the ambivalent results of nationalism run amok.

Test Case: The Unbridled Growth of Anti-Japanese Sentiment

Owing to the delicate nature of Sino-U.S. relations, it would seem obvious that the CCP leadership has qualms about allowing the anti-U.S. brand of nationalism to go too far. After all, China is still dependent on the U.S. market—and on Washington —to help rein in Taiwan's pro-independence proclivities. And large numbers of the sons and daughters of top cadres are business partners of U.S.-based multinationals. On the popular level, there is still considerable admiration for U.S. institutions and lifestyle. Take, for example, the three days or so of anti-American protests after the "accidental" bombing of the Chinese Embassy in Belgrade in May 1999. Right after the orgy of stone-throwing outside the U.S. Embassy had stopped, the long lines of applicants for American visas resumed. An early 2005 survey showed that 66.1 percent of urban Chinese said they "like Americans."[9]

Relations with Japan are different. There are theorists who have claimed that because Beijing is wary of offending the United States, the authorities think the political costs would be lower if it were to allow the populace to "let off steam" by venting xenophobic feelings against the Japanese, China's age-old enemies. Until around 2000 and 2001, Beijing had by and large tried to rein in "anti-Japanese" activities, which were focused on the following: seeking World War II–related compensation for individual families as well as for "comfort women"; protests against Japanese leaders' visit to the Yasukuni Shrine; and sovereignty disputes over the Diaoyu or Senkaku Islands as well as the East China Sea. However, by 2003 and 2004, the authorities began to allow patriotic, anti-Japanese activities to have relatively free public expression. For example, Diaoyu-related activists were permitted to set sail to waters near the disputed islands and to hold small-scale demonstrations outside the Japanese Embassy in Beijing. As leading protect-the-Diaoyus activist Tong Zeng noted in late 2004: "the new [Hu-Wen] leadership has a stronger feeling of nationalism than their predecessors, so we have more space to carry out our activities."[10]

Some Western and Asian diplomats believe that in the wake of the deterioration of Sino-Japanese relations—particularly over Japan's alliance relationship with the United States and its perceived support of the Taiwan independence movement—Beijing might want to use popular sentiments to put pressure on Japan. When Chinese officials talked to their Japanese or Western counterparts about outbursts of Japan bashing, the former usually noted that because of the profusion of the mass media, it was difficult for Beijing to do much about the situation. Individual China scholars also noted that "anti-Japanese" websites such as www.publiclaw-events.com, www.chinaeagle.org, www.1931-9-18.org, www.China918.net, and 918war.tongtu.net had "hijacked" public opinion about Japan. And more balanced views about bilateral relations propagated by liberal intellectuals such as former *People's Daily* commentator Ma Licheng and People's University professor Shi Yinhong have been suppressed[11] (see also Chapter 5).

There is evidence, however, that anti-Japanese feelings have gone too far for the good of the authorities. The ugly behavior of anti-Japanese soccer fans during the 2004 China–Japan Asia Cup final proved highly embarrassing to a leadership that was anxious to show the world it would be a good host for the 2008 Summer Olympics. And apparently irrational feelings against Japan are hurting bilateral trade and economic relations, the one bright spot on the horizon. Take, for example, the case of whether China railway authorities should use Japanese Shinkansen bullet-train technology for the Beijing-Shanghai rail link. In view of large-scale opposition to using Japanese rail expertise, the authorities reportedly decided in late 2004 to use the French model instead. As Sinologist Gries pointed out, the Beijing leadership's Japan policies "are increasingly reactive to nationalistic opinion, rather than proactive to China's national interest."[12]

There was evidence that by 2005, the Hu-Wen leadership was engaged in a tricky balancing act. On the one hand, they wanted to translate the "positive" elements of nationalism into support for the regime as well as national cohesiveness. On the other hand, the Hu-led Politburo would take measures to impose what it considered to be an adequate degree of control over the growth of xenophobia, including anti-Japanese feelings. For example, there were attempts at educating the public regarding a more rational attitude toward foreign countries. In a talk about the Olympics, Beijing mayor Wang Qishan expressed fears that Chinese among the audience might not stand up when the national anthems of certain countries were played.[13] And the official *International Herald Leader* (IHL) ran pieces attacking *fenqing* (angry young men) who advocated "using tough tactics to fight for China's interests." The official weekly publication quoted sociologist Li Mingshui as decrying how *fenqing* had indulged in "the kind of patriotism that expresses itself in bashing other countries." And the NCNA website quoted noted historian Xiao Gongqing as warning that extreme nationalism could "prompt pragmatic leaders . . . to use hard-line methods to solve complex international questions." In yet another commentary, IHL pointed out that "if nationalistic sentiments are being exploited by people with ulterior motives, the results would be disastrous."[14]

Beijing's Problematic Handling of the April 2005 Anti-Japan Protests

The Hu-Wen leadership's clumsy handling of the ferocious anti-Japan demonstrations from late March to mid-April 2005 illustrate fully the socialist regime's difficulty in wielding the double-edged sword of nationalism. It is assumed that state-security units kept a close tab on the activities of nationalistic NGOs and anti-Japan websites. However, except for the case of smaller outbreaks in places such as Guangzhou and Hangzhou, the leadership made no effort to control either the number of demonstrators or their actions.[15] One consideration might be that as in the past, Beijing wanted to put pressure on the Japanese government by flexing the "people opinion" card. And the Hu leadership was right in thinking that the massive show of anti-Japan feelings—coupled with similar activities in South Korea as well as among overseas Chinese communities abroad—could torpedo Tokyo's gaining a permanent seat on the UN Security Council.

Yet the perception in not only Japan and the United States but other countries was that Beijing had provided at least indirect encouragement and support to this remarkable outburst of xenophobia. TV footage of Beijing, and especially Shanghai, police looking on passively as the protestors hurled stones at the Japanese missions did a lot toward smearing China's international reputation. Some commentators even suspected that the CCP's maladroit handling of the demonstrations, together with its tolerance of some form of xenophobia, could have a detrimental impact similar to that of the passage of the Anti-Secession Law a month earlier.[16]

Even more significantly, the anti-Japan protests managed to alienate a broad cross-section of the Japanese public. This was against Beijing's long-standing "united front" policy of targeting only "right-wing militarists" but wooing the majority of Japanese. As veteran diplomat Wu Jianmin noted, "we must differentiate between a minority of right-wing elements [in Japan] and the broad masses of Japanese." "Being anti-Japanese does not mean you are patriotic," he added.[17] However, it was not until the second half of April that Beijing began taking action by arresting some rock-throwers and closing down several excessively inflammatory websites. Both the official media and senior officials began to dwell on the fact that while patriotism should be affirmed and encouraged, Chinese should remain rational—and they should follow the law in their expressions of nationalism. For example, NCNA ran a series of articles entitled "Patriotism, While Aroused by Feelings of Justice, Should Be Restricted by Reason." NCNA and *People's Daily* also carried pieces calling on the public to "bear the entire situation [of the country] in mind and help safeguard stability." And Commerce Minister Bo Xilai explained to the hotheads among protestors that boycotting Japanese products could hurt China as much as Japan.[18]

Efforts to rein in the radicals climaxed with an editorial in the Shanghai-based *Liberation Daily* on April 27, about ten days after the worst phase of the demonstrations was over. The article slammed the rallies and protests as an "evil plot" with "ulterior motives." "The facts have shown that the marches that occurred in some localities were an attempt to achieve hidden goals," the paper said. "Communist Party members must clearly see through to the essence of this struggle and understand its gravity."[19] In the Chinese context, the *Daily* was railing at the fact that unspecified "plotters" were trying to change the nature of the protests—and that they were targeting the CCP instead of the Japanese.

Yet why had the Beijing leadership not sounded the alarms and warnings earlier? There is speculation among foreign observers that members of the ruling Politburo Standing Committee were divided over the issue of Sino-Japanese relations. However, a more straightforward answer could be that the Hu-Wen team was afraid that a too-early intervention—without having given the crowds a chance to let off steam—would be equally dangerous. In May 1999, when anti-American protestors went on a rampage after the bombing of the Chinese Embassy in Belgrade, the leadership was able to call off their action with relative ease. Six years later, however, Beijing's ability to exercise control over nationalistic crowds has become much less effective.[20]

Beijing's Dilemmas over the "Nationalistic Temptation"

The CCP leadership faces tough challenges in instilling in its citizens a fair and balanced view of foreign countries. This is despite the fact that party hacks have prided themselves on the effectiveness of official propaganda. As explained in Chapter 4, CCP politicians and historians have refused to come clean on a large number of less-than-glorious incidents in the party's convoluted history. For example, to nurture the "right" attitude toward Japan, Beijing must explain to the public why First- and Second-Generation leaders such as Mao Zedong, Zhou Enlai, and Deng Xiaoping took a largely tolerant and magnanimous stance toward Tokyo, including giving up the right to demand compensation for war-time damages. Deng also decided in the early 1970s to temporarily shelve efforts to assert Chinese sovereignty over the Diaoyu or Senkaku Islands.[21]

Similarly, much remains hidden regarding China's complicated relationship with the Soviet Union and Russia, including the widely held perception that CCP leaders from Mao to Jiang had for a variety of reasons let Moscow get away with holding on to substantial pieces of Chinese territory along the two countries' long borders. And the Hu Jintao leadership refused to disclose the details of the settlement reached with Moscow in late 2004 concerning the demarcation of the two countries' boundaries.[22] A full disclosure of factors behind a number of key events in recent Sino-Japanese and Sino-Russian relations, however, might result in several revered CCP figures being denigrated by rabid nationalists—as well as an overall fall in the party's prestige. And this is hardly something that the ever-cautious Hu-Wen team would consider doing.

The same also holds true for relations with the United States. Circumstances concerning the nation's most traumatic "interaction" with America—the Korean War of the 1950s—are still shrouded in secrecy. The preliminary but substantive World Trade Organization (WTO) accord that former premier Zhu Rongji negotiated with Washington during his trip there in April 1999 was never publicized in the official media. The apparent reason was the leadership's fear that concessions made by China might provoke ferocious opposition from the public as well as regional officials. And the official media have never reported the business dealings, particularly those with American and European companies, of former officials or the children of senior cadres.[23]

President Hu's somewhat ham-fisted effort to drum up patriotism—and to play up the lips-and-teeth relationship between the Chinese and Russian peoples—on the occasion of the sixtieth anniversary of the end of World War II is a good example of how Beijing's propaganda fusillades are often hampered by its dubious views on history. While attending a gathering of world leaders in Moscow in May 2005, Hu met a group of Soviet soldiers who had fought alongside Chinese against the Japanese Imperial Army in the northeastern provinces. The president celebrated the "life and death" friendship of Chinese and their Soviet friends. While in Moscow, Hu also lay emphasis on the fact that "history is a mirror that illuminates reality." Yet the Fourth-Generation stalwart's words somehow rang false because he and his predecessors had hidden crucial information about Sino-Soviet relations just several years after 1945, especially how Stalin half-bullied, half-cheated Mao into making the disastrous decision to get into the Korean War. That lapse in judgment of the Mao leadership was responsible for the deaths of tens of thousands of ill-equipped Chinese soldiers in ice-cold Korea.[24]

According to liberal scholar Ren Bingqiang, a key difference between Chinese and Western nationalism is that "Western nationalism grew up during liberal revolutions in the creation of national states while Chinese nationalism arose as a reaction to foreign invasion." Ren's point jells with those of other observers who have commented on the heavy dosage of "victimization complex" behind Chinese nationalism. Ren pinpoints the xenophobic streak among Chinese nationalists, adding that they did not have "constructive policy suggestions" apart from boosting state power and asserting China's strength internationally.[25] Yet this situation could be hard to remedy because there are moments when the CCP leadership needs to exploit the victimization complex. Moreover, as long as much of the country's relations with foreign countries are locked up in airtight archives, it is difficult for the party leadership to inculcate in citizens unbiased views about Chinese statehood and foreign policy in general.

The Forces of Globalization

New—and Mostly "Western"—Ways of Doing Things

China's accession to the WTO has given a big impetus to globalization, which is evident not only in economic and business but also in cultural and sociopolitical dimensions. While nationalism—in many ways the obverse of globalization—is also on the rise, American and Japanese fads and products ranging from couture and cuisine to entertainment software are fast gaining fans along the coast as well as in central cities such as Wuhan and Chongqing. Not just Hollywood but South Korean TV dramas and movies are tugging at the heartstrings of a new generation of high school and college students. Moreover, with the lifting of pretty much all restrictions on Chinese tour groups visiting countries in Asia, Europe, and even Latin America, Chinese are in a position to take in foreign ideas and institutions firsthand.[26] And in the wake of the State Council's determination to promote Western-style corporate governance, not only government departments and state firms but also private businesses are trying hard to adopt internationally recognized accounting and auditing procedures. At the government and policy levels, the Hu-Wen leadership has by and large cleaved to the standard line espoused since Deng of "learning from the best fruits of world civilization."

In tandem with fast-growing economic and cultural ties with the United States, Beijing has shown signs of using elements of the U.S. model in economic, foreign-trade, and certain administrative areas. After all, dozens if not hundreds of rising stars among central and regional officials are being sent annually for half- or one-year courses at Harvard and other institutions in America. Several of the hottest programs in top Chinese universities, such as MBA and master's in public policy courses, are based substantially on American syllabuses. In the case of business programs, the teachers are often professors of American universities, many of which have set up joint MBA programs with Chinese colleges. That the U.S. system has in some instances displaced the "Singapore way" as a model for emulation was evidenced by the fact that in 2003, the central government created a new—and American-style—Ministry of Commerce as well as a Center for Disease Control, which is based on the famous CDC in Atlanta.[27]

In the run-up to the passage of the Civil Service Law in 2005, individual National People's Congress (NPC) members and scholars had advocated that provisions be made for hiring foreigners. While their suggestion was ignored, these liberal intellectuals have argued that in the Tang Dynasty (618–907), a few hundred Europeans, including missionaries, were hired by the emperor as teachers or scientists. This practice continued until the end of the Qing Dynasty in 1911. And in the past decade, a number of ethnic Chinese with foreign passports have become government advisers and even senior officials (see following section).[28]

Perhaps ironically, the SARS battle throughout much of 2003 could turn out to be a milestone for globalization in China. For fear of disasters including a drastic drop in foreign investments and tourists, the CCP leadership was forced to accede to the demands of the World Health Organization (WHO) in reforming its medical system. For several months, WHO inspectors were given VIP treatment as well as relatively thorough access wherever they went in China. At one point during the outbreak, then acting Beijing mayor Wang Qishan even said he would make available an office—next to his own—to WHO experts. This was to ensure that whatever the Beijing municipality did on the medical and epidemiological fronts would fit global requirements.[29] Given that the public health arena is intimately tied to decades-old communist-style rule, the leadership was making a concession that could have wide-ranging repercussions.

In the area of environmental protection, there were also suggestions that perhaps only international organizations and personnel would have the requisite methodology—and immunity from political influence—to do the job properly. In an article on efforts made by the China branch of Greenpeace to prevent a multinational company from excessive logging in Yunnan Province, the official *International Herald Leader* asked the intriguing question, "Do we need 'foreign inspectors' to protect China's environment?"[30] The reasoning behind this query is the fact that Chinese officials and environmental specialists may lack the skills needed to successfully navigate the corridors of vested interests and political patronage.

Yet the CCP leadership is still trying its level best to ensure that globalization will not vitiate the core of the political system—that is, one-party rule. This means in effect that while different aspects of culture and society may become Americanized, Europeanized, or even "Japanized," Chinese citizens' faith in "stability" backed by stern one-party rule must never be shaken. Thus, in his speech at the pivotal Fourth Plenary Session of the Sixteenth Central Committee in late 2004, Hu sounded alarms about the intelligentsia succumbing to the mindless wave of "bourgeois liberalization." At the same time, Li Changchun, the Politburo Standing Committee member in charge of ideology and propaganda, issued warnings about "infiltration by Western enemy forces" even as he called for a campaign to counter the forces of Westernization and boost national cohesiveness.[31]

The Political Impact of WTO Accession and Globalization

Despite their fears about excessive Westernization, CCP leaders might sooner or later have to come to terms with the fact that, to borrow Mao Zedong's imagery, globalization is not a dinner party. Much has been written about the impact of China's hard-earned WTO status on the country's economy policy and ways of doing business. However, it is probable that WTO accession and globalization in general will gradually but inexorably chip away not only at Beijing's "economic sovereignty" but also at the power base and prerogatives of the party and cadre elite. As well-known Peking University political scientist Yu Keping put it, "globalization has increased the economic and political risks of the country." He warned that if the country failed to take "the right response toward global forces," state sovereignty would be damaged.[32]

About a year before China's entry to the WTO, the CCP and State Council set up a special team to study the accession's impact on domestic politics. While the group's findings have not been publicized, it was evident that from the CCP leadership's viewpoint that economic and trade globalization would pose a severe challenge to the authority of the party and state apparatus. In a prescient paper written soon after the dissolution of the Soviet Union in the early 1990s, a group of sons of party elders argued that to avoid the fate of the USSR, the CCP must never lose control over the economy and business.[33] There seems little doubt, however, that both the party and the central government have to sever links with enterprises in the post–WTO accession order. Not only has the number of state-owned enterprises (SOEs) been reduced, but different economics-related ministries have curtailed the number of fiats and regulations that had been used for decades to exert control over the economy.

WTO accession will hasten the separation of party and business—something that the Hu-Wen leadership is still reluctant to do. After all, the *dangzhongyang* (party central authorities) still have leading groups and other units handling different aspects of finance, commerce, and foreign trade. And the CCP leadership frequently passes along edicts via party cells in most state as well as nonstate enterprises. In various WTO-related protocols that China had signed with foreign countries, however, it was stated clearly that Beijing should ensure the party's withdrawal from the business field as early as possible. Yet there are signs that despite the CCP's unwillingness to beat a retreat, the party's reach is gradually being truncated. For example, the CCP's ability to start and operate party cells in joint ventures and wholly owned foreign concerns could be challenged by overseas businessmen. This is despite the fact that CCP departments have insisted that party cells should be set up in private or foreign-owned firms, according to relevant laws and regulations. The CCP-led All-China Federation of Trade Unions (ACFTU), China's only permitted trade union, has also been rebuffed in its efforts to set up branches in multinationals including Wal-Mart, Dell, Samsung, and McDonald's.[34]

The very concept of a party-dominated legal system will also be imperiled. It is an open secret that since 1949, the courts and procuratorates—as well mechanisms for legal and juridical interpretation—are under the thumb of a secretive CCP organ called the Political and Legal Affairs Commission (PLAC). In an attempt to pacify foreigners, Beijing has set up special courts in big cities to handle commercial disputes and other cases involving foreign residents.[35] Yet it is only a matter of time before the increasingly resourceful expatriate community, which includes ethnic Chinese "returnees" from abroad, will challenge the age-old system of the CCP domination of the law and the courts. Another pillar of CCP domination—control over information—could also be jeopardized. This is despite the fact that WTO protocols so far signed with the United States and the European Union (EU) have made no provisions for joint-venture newspapers or TV stations. Yet these WTO agreements do allow for joint-venture Internet companies, although foreign partners cannot hold more than 49 percent of total shares. Analysts say Beijing will find it difficult a few years post–WTO accession to resist pressure to open up the news business, even though initially foreign partners may only be allowed to handle advertising, marketing, and distribution.

Also under threat is Beijing's vaunted ability to guard "state secrets" from foreign eyes. For example, the CCP leadership has refused to allow Western companies to conduct information-related businesses such as polling and market research, for the obvious reason that such activities can yield a bonanza of politically sensitive data. After joining the WTO, Beijing may no longer be able to maintain the bamboo curtain. By 2004, quite a number of Hong Kong–based firms, many of which have injections of foreign capital, were already conducting operations akin to polling and opinion surveys in Guangdong and other provinces.[36]

Indeed, police and state security departments are keenly aware that many Western-style commercial operations can have heavy political overtones. A case in point is *chuanxiao,* direct or door-to-door marketing through close-knit, quasi-pyramid networks of salespeople. In the mid-1990s, Beijing asked several foreign firms in the areas of cosmetics and household products to stop direct-sales activities. An internal paper cited the political implications of such tightly organized marketing teams, which often boasted several tens of thousands of salespeople. The document said law and order, a euphemism for CCP control over everyday life, might be threatened if "hostile foreign forces" including quasi-religious bodies, were able to use such sales networks to pursue anti-Beijing goals. Injunctions against direct selling were repeated by police and other departments in the early 2000s. However, by early 2005, not only foreign *chuanxiao* firms but also local companies based on similar models were thriving at least in the large cities.[37]

In the age of globalized business, the CCP leadership also has to yield its monopoly over education to foreign learning institutions, including commercial operators. By 2002 or so, more and more nouveau riche parents in cities ranging from Shenzhen to Shanghai started sending their kids to international schools, where Marxism-Leninism is hardly taught. Beijing has also in theory agreed to limit restrictions on the establishment of private universities. And it is quite clear that to attract students, these new institutions will be using Western, probably American, syllabuses. Moreover, a dozen or more big-name American and European universities have secured official permission to open branch campuses along the eastern coast.[38] Above all, the party's worst nightmare is that globalization could engender changes in people's thinking. As a Beijing-based social sciences professor put it, if everything is now being done according to international—in many instances, Western and American norms—more people will cast doubt on CCP ideology. "It will soon become clear that values and systems such as socialism and 'dictatorship of the proletariat' run counter to global trends," the professor said.[39]

Of course, WTO accession will, in theory, not affect the party's hold over control mechanisms such as the army, the People's Armed Police, and the police. Yet a pluralistic market milieu will afford ordinary folks ample opportunity to thumb their noses at the CCP—and with devastating effect. For example, well-trained personnel including scientists, engineers, and mangers can vote with their feet by working for foreign or joint-venture firms instead of government departments or SOEs. As various leaders have indicated, globalization means first of all a fight for talent between government units and SOEs on the one hand, and multinationals on the other. People can also vote with their pocketbooks. If Chinese have lost faith in the authorities, they may put their money in foreign banks, patronize foreign insurance companies, purchase foreign stocks instead of local ones—and, well before the end of this decade, buy the *Global Daily* instead of *People's Daily*.[40]

As of 2005, the Hu-Wen team was still brimming with confidence that a relatively high growth rate—plus achievements such as putting three astronauts in orbit and winning thirty-two Olympic gold medals—would convince most Chinese to stay with the CCP. The police and thought-control squads are sparing no effort to crack down on dissident opinions. The CCP leadership was confident that, in the words of Peking University's Yu, "China should participate actively and intuitively in globalization processes while never becoming Westernized."[41] Over the long haul, however, there seems little doubt that the forces of economics and social change will be effectively eroding outdated dogmas—especially those that serve only a privileged minority.

The Ideal of Federalism

A New Look at Federalism

The partial revival of Maoism under the Hu-Wen administration has served many purposes, including the leadership's desire to play up the Great Helmsman's achievements in unifying the diverse and chaotic country under the *dangzhongyang*. Beijing's emphasis on a system of efficient, centralized control became more apparent in the wake of the resistance that the State Council met in cooling down the economy throughout 2004. On the cultural level, there is famed movie director Zhang Yimou's 2003 hit, *Hero*, which did much to glorify the exploits of the First Emperor Qin Shihuang in ending the Era of the Warring States and building up a unified, apparently tightly knit empire.[42]

The centripetal imperative became even more palpable as a result of what Beijing perceived as disturbing events in Taiwan and Hong Kong: the pro-independence gambit of President Chen Shui-bian as well as the call for one-person-one-vote elections in the Hong Kong Special Administrative Region (SAR). The Hu-Wen leadership has tried to squash separatism in Taiwan through a mixture of diplomacy —mainly asking Washington to rein in Taipei—and intimidation backed by military threat (see Chapter 5). In Hong Kong, the Hu leadership has stressed the value of patriotism even as mainland authorities have helped buttress the SAR economy through a series of favorable policies.[43]

However, while Third- and Fourth-Generation leaders have put the utmost emphasis on "national cohesiveness," discussion about the virtues of a quasi-federalist political structure has been going on unabated. Because of the sensitivity of the subject, the words "federalism" and "confederation" seldom come up in public discourse or the official media except in a pejorative light. However, largely owing to the need to solve the Taiwan conundrum, a think tank in Shanghai that enjoyed the patronage of two of its former majors—Wang Daohan and Jiang Zemin—carried out studies about the federal system and its suitability for China in the 1990s. In this period, federalism was also a subject for research and discussion in the relatively liberal Central Party School, which was headed by then vice-president Hu.[44]

Starting from the late 1990s, numerous articles on the subject of federalism and confederalism have been written by overseas-based scholars, including dissidents active in the 1989 democracy movement. These writings are easily accessible to Internet users in China. One part of the debate concerns how the benevolent application of the principle of federalism and power sharing could help Beijing achieve a "win-win" situation in its relations with Taiwan, Tibet, and Hong Kong. Equally significant is the viewpoint that many of China's internal problems can probably be better tackled if the country the size of Europe were in some ways split administratively into subsystems that are given autonomous authority on a par with those in states or provinces in the United States or Canada.

The point of departure for the federalist argument is that revolutionaries of the early twentieth century including Dr. Sun Yat-sen and Mao Zedong were, at least in the early stages of their careers, sympathetic to the idea of federalism if only as a means to pacify the ethnic minorities. American historian Leslie Chen contended that the federalism favored by relatively benevolent warlords of the 1920s and 1930s jived with the reality of China much better than the Soviet-inspired nationalism of Sun or Kuomintang leader Chiang Kai-shek.[45] Wu Jiaxiang, a former researcher in the CCP Central Committee General Office, has done detailed studies on early Communist leaders' thinking on federalism. He noted that CCP founder

Chen Duxiu advocated the formation of a "Chinese Federalist Republic," so as to better unify mainland China, Mongolia, Tibet, and Xinjiang. Moreover, Chen had buttressed his theory with Lenin's own precepts about federalism as a vehicle to solve the problem of minorities in the Soviet Union. However, Mao nixed these ideas, wrote Wu, owing to "his extreme leftist views about the state system as well as relations among the nationalities."[46]

Moreover, Wu argued that Deng Xiaoping practically revived the ideals of federalism in his epoch-making "one country, two systems" model, which was concocted in the 1980s to solve the Taiwan and Hong Kong issues. It is important to note that the "autonomous powers" granted to Taiwan under this model, which includes the right to maintain an army and to implement certain quasi-diplomatic functions, are more considerable than those enjoyed by provinces or states in federalist countries such as Canada and the United States.[47] Analysts have suggested that at least for Deng, something akin to "one country, many systems" could be reconciled with the concept of "socialism with Chinese characteristics"—and that this idea enjoys the support of a considerable number of liberal cadres. Indeed, the successful development of the EU, particularly its expansion in 2004 to incorporate twenty-five countries, has prompted forward-looking thinkers in Beijing to consider whether some form of EU model could be used to solve the Taiwan problem. For example, at the initial stage of a "trial union," the mainland and Taiwan could go after EU-style economic integration by adopting common economic policies and even a common currency. And matters of political affiliation or integration could be left for a later stage.[48]

Other vocal advocates of federalism such as exiled scholar Yan Jiaqi have indicated that Beijing's commitment to a federal, "one country, many systems" model will not only help to mollify disparate nationalities but also help political reform through improving administrative efficiency and devolving power from the center to the regions and social groupings. Yan, a former head of the Chinese Academy of Social Sciences' (CASS) Political Science Institute, noted that decentralization was "a logical step in the entire course of liberalization," which was unfortunately reversed during the Jiang Zemin era. Yan indicated, however, that economic diversity in the wake of globalization would promote added momentum to a kind of de facto federalism. Moreover, as Gabriela Montinola and other U.S. Sinologists have argued, given the difficulty of developing democracy in China, federalism "may be one of the few ways in which a large, non-democratic state can provide credible limits on its behavior."[49]

Principles of Diversity in the Constitution—and the Future of Limited Federalism

Despite the recentralizing tendencies of recent and current leaders including Jiang Zemin, Zhu Rongji, and the Hu-Wen team, it is important to note that early-generation CCP leaders' tolerance for regional diversity is fully reflected in the

Chinese Constitution. Following President Hu's stress on strict constitutional rule, scholars have challenged the conventional wisdom that the supreme charter has spelled out explicitly that the country is a unitary, highly centralized state where sovereignty and administrative powers reside solely with the central authorities— and where localities owe their powers entirely to these authorities' largesse.

An examination of the Chinese Constitution, as well as the dynamics of inter-actions between the *zhongyang* (central authorities) and the regions, would invalidate the unitary state argument. China is of course not a federalist nation like the United States, where state governments enjoy a high degree of autonomy apart from sovereignty-related matters such as defense and foreign affairs. However, the Chinese charter makes it clear that while sovereignty resides in the *zhongyang* alone, there is a sizable division of political and administrative powers between Beijing and the regions.

Nowhere in the document is it stated that China is a "unitary state" or that all or most local administrative powers are derived from Beijing. It highlights instead the need to balance "the unified leadership of the central authorities" on the one hand, and "giving full play to the initiative and enthusiasm of the local authorities" on the other. The section on regional administrations sets out unequivocally that "local people's congresses [PCs] at different levels are local organs of state power," and that "local people's governments at different levels are the executive bodies of local organs of state power as well as the local organs of state administration."[50]

Moreover, the Constitution prescribes that deputies to provincial and municipal PCs are either directly or indirectly elected into office by local residents. And governors as well as mayors are picked and endorsed by PCs of relevant levels. In practice, of course, the CCP leadership has tried to arrogate all powers to itself. And the party Politburo, China's highest-ruling council, has a dominant say in the nomination of not only regional party secretaries but also governors and mayors. However, since the early 1990s, there have been increasing numbers of CCP-nominated candidates for mayor and even governor—for example, those of Guizhou and Zhejiang provinces—who have failed to make good because they failed to command the support of delegates to local PCs. Even more significantly, a number of townships in provinces ranging from Sichuan to Guangdong have held one-person-one-vote elections to select their top administrators or party chiefs without the *zhongyang's* approval. This is despite the fact that since the late 1970s, universal suffrage polls for local leaders are only allowed at the village level (see also Chapter 4).[51]

The tug-of-war between a Leninist-style CCP leadership-cum-*zhongyang* and regions given to centrifugal tendencies has become more acute in recent years. As a result of decentralization induced by market and other reforms, China has developed what some Western scholars call "de facto federalism with Chinese characteristics." As U.S.-based economist Qian Yingyi noted, fiscal federalism had made it possible for individual provinces along the coast to get rich first. "If there had been no large-scale regional power-sharing, local-level enterprises would not have developed so prosperously," Qian noted.[52] And despite the relative success with which the Hu-Wen leadership has imposed its stamp on the country since late 2002, the *zhongyang*'s grip over localities is substantially less tight than in the days of charismatic, helmsman-like figures such as Mao and Deng.

Pro-federalism scholars like Wu Jiaxiang have pointed out that de facto financial and economic federalism would be a good start in persuading CCP leaders to consider the benefits of power sharing with the provinces. However, an important caveat is that as the Hu leadership becomes more nervous about losing its mandate of heaven, strong centripetal tendencies will always remain. Then there is the ever-growing energy imperative, the need for the *zhongyang* to dominate the exploitation and use of petroleum and other precious minerals. For instance, it would be unimaginable for Beijing to allow Xinjiang to have a bigger say in the disposal of its petroleum reserves. Hu's decision to elevate ally Wang Lequan, party secretary of Xinjiang, to the Politburo, seems to attest to the leadership's desire to maintain ironclad control over the resource-rich and trouble-prone autonomous region.[53]

Indeed, on the political front, Beijing's tendency to tighten its grip over Xinjiang and Tibet has become more obvious, at least in the eyes of pro-independence elements in these two regions. Crackdown on so-called terrorist organizations in Xinjiang has intensified under the banner of "participation in the global alliance against terrorism." And negotiations over Tibet with the proxies of the Dalai Lama have made no progress. International watchdog organizations have charged that the central authorities are boosting time-honored programs to move Han-Chinese to the western provinces. And the soon-to-open rail link into Tibet is expected to smooth the process of the "Han-Chinese transformation" of the Tibet Autonomous Region.[54]

The Challenge of the New Media

The Rise of the Internet and Other New Media

The Internet has been hailed as a potent weapon that could empower dissidents, intellectuals, and ordinary citizens in their fight for free expression if not political democratization. According to liberal sociologist Deng Weizhi, the Net could provide three channels to bolster democratic governance: elections of certain government posts could one day be held via the Net; "Net forums" could ensure freedom of expression; and citizens could use the Internet to supervise government cadres.[55] More significantly, the Net, which has an estimated 100 million aficionados nationwide, has enabled relatively small and weak groupings to stage "asymmetrical warfare" against the authorities. Thus it was the information superhighway that enabled the numerically out-gunned Falun Gong members to wage the equivalent of a guerrilla battle against the CCP administration. And the Net has made it possible for underground dissident cells to communicate with human rights organizations overseas and to galvanize global support for those detained by the government.[56]

One of the most famous of these "dissident" Internet writers was twenty-three-year-old Liu Di, a female Beijing Normal University student who went by the pen name "Stainless Steel Mouse." Although she mostly wrote about relatively innocuous subjects such as corruption and government bureaucrats' insensitivity to public demands, Liu was picked up by police in late 2002 for allegedly "endangering state security." Liu's case became a cause célèbre in Chinese intellectual circles because of her youth—and the fact that she did not have any intention of overthrowing the government. Many of her supporters continued to risk their safety by writing supportive essays on the Net until her release more than one year later.[57] Also consider the case of Li Zhi, a thirty-two-year-old government employee in faraway Sichuan Province who was arrested in September 2003 for posting his views on political reform on Internet bulletin boards and chat rooms. Li was accused by police of maintaining links with overseas anti-Chinese dissident organizations. He was later charged with "conspiracy to subvert state power," which could bring with it a jail term of up to fifteen years. According to the president of Human Rights in Asia, Liu Qing, "Monitoring email and Internet chat-rooms is an unacceptable invasion of privacy, and a reprehensible method of gathering evidence for prosecution of a political crime."[58]

Apart from being a forum for the expression of opinion, the Internet has proven to be a potent means for mobilization that cuts across geographical and socioeconomic boundaries. For example, the Net is a powerful vehicle for blowing the whistle on corruption and seeking *shehui gongyi* (social justice). Take the sensationalist case of the "bullet-proof vest party secretary" Huang Jingao, a party boss of Lianjiang County outside Fuzhou, Fujian Province, who claimed in mid-2004 that he had been wearing special protection gear for the past six years to ward off possible assassins. In an e-letter to the media, Huang said he had tried to stop an urban development project that was the product of collusion between greedy real-estate developers and corrupt officials. Lacking support from higher authorities, however, Huang said he lived in fear of reprisals and that his only course of action was seeking the help of the media. Within a couple of weeks, more than 100,000 Netizens had written to different websites expressing support for the courageous Huang.[59]

Then there was the even more remarkable case of Shandong-based Li Xinde, who set up his own anti-graft website in late 2003. Li, a retired soldier, became a Net activist, or Netivist, after having endured several trips to Beijing to present petitions on behalf of his friends and relatives. His website, www.yuluncn.com, received a constant stream of letters from farmers and workers who wanted to expose the corruption of local officials. Li scored a victory in August 2004 when the vice-mayor of the city of Jining, Shandong, Li Xin, was detained for corruption after the activist had presented the official's dossier to the Central Commission for Disciplinary Inspection. However, graft buster Li had received many death threats and his website was often sabotaged from official Net police.[60]

At the same time, China's 350 million mobile-phone users have turned text messaging into an artful—and often subversive—means to air their frustrations and grievances. Throughout 2004, Chinese sent close to 220 billion text messages, an average of some 7,000 per second, or more than the rest of the world combined. Perhaps the single most potent expression of "short message service [SMS] power" was the "election" in mid-2005 of Li Yuchun as top "Super-girl" in a national TV singing contest in which viewers cast their ballots via short messages. Li, a cool, somewhat androgynous crooner, garnered 3.5 million votes—and even appeared on the cover of the Asian edition of *Time* magazine as one of the "heroes of Asia."[61] From the political viewpoint, SMS messages allow citizens to let off steam. Many of the politically oriented messages have to do with gossip, which ranges from corruption allegations surrounding unpopular officials to the sex lives of senior cadres. Ex-president Jiang is a favorite target of SMS users due to his flamboyant, buffoon-like personality—and because of disgust at his refusal to give up the limelight. Jiang's alleged special relationship with a PLA singer was often an inspiration for playful cell phone owners to compose short but mischevious messages.

The role played by SMS messages in exposing the real picture of the SARS disaster in early 2003 fully demonstrated the political significance of this very simple and innocuous communication tool. After all, text messaging had played an even bigger role in political events in the Philippines and Indonesia. And it is hardly surprising that the authorities began a thorough crackdown in 2004. In a week-long sweep in June that year, the police closed down twenty SMS providers and fined ten of them for failing to filter out politically incorrect items. Earlier that month, during the sensitive anniversary period of the Tiananmen Square massacre, many SMS users discovered that texts containing the numbers "6" or "4," or words such as "Tiananmen" and "Zhao Ziyang" failed to get through. Officially, all the authorities said was that they were increasing control over text messaging due to a proliferation of pornography as well as commercial-fraud cases.[62]

Of course, the Internet and SMS messaging could also be a force for dubious social and political causes. The full force of the Internet revolution was evident in 2003 and 2004, when nationalistic groupings were successful in mobilizing nationwide support to seek war-time damages from Japan or even to boycott certain types of Japanese products and technology. Moreover, the party and police authorities are also adept at policing the Net and preventing websites from spreading heretical or "subversive" messages about subjects ranging from Western-style democracy to federalism.

The State vs. The Net: The Battle Intensifies

Beginning in the early 2000s, several party and government units including the Ministry of Public Security (MPS) and the Ministry of State Security (MSS) initiated a multipronged counterattack against the "harmful side-effects" of the new medium. Cyber divisions were set up in police departments in every city—and the strength of cyber-policemen nationwide was estimated at more than 50,000. The

MPS and MSS also began offering high salaries to recruit IT graduates from famous universities in the United States and Europe. In a particularly interesting case, a teenage "genius hacker" who had been caught after repeated offenses was in 2003 recruited by the Shanghai police with the understanding that after graduating from college on a government scholarship, he would become a star Net-policeman. And after the dissolution of the illegal "Hackers' Union"—reportedly China's largest such organization—in late 2004, National Defense University professor Zhang Zhaozhong said some of the IT talents in the union could be absorbed into the government "to boost the country's IT security."[63]

Beijing's control over the Net is made relatively easy by the fact that at least officially, all Chinese Internet users have to register with the government and use officially approved or government-run Internet service providers. A study by the Harvard Law School in 2002 found that China had the most extensive Net censorship in the world. Of the 200,000 popular websites tested by the researchers over a period of six months, China blocked 19,000 all the time and 50,000 some of the time. By the early 2000s, the government was also able to benefit from the help of multinational companies in developing Net-policing software such as firewalls for use against politically incorrect or subversive material. Cyber-cops now have the means to quickly hunt down proxy servers that allow users to circumvent firewalls. Moreover, the government has developed keyword-searching software to block out websites that contain subversive material on topics ranging from political reform to Taiwan and Tibet. And censors can employ filtering techniques to excise offensive e-mails.[64]

Net-nannies are also swooping down on Internet cafes, once deemed an oasis of freedom of information. First, taking advantage of the public outcry against a series of horrendous fires and other accidents that had broken out in many such hangouts for teenagers and college students, the government started closing down thousands of them in 2001 and 2002. Internet cafes nationwide were in late 2002 reduced to 110,000, half the number of just a few years earlier. Second, cultural departments began in 2003 to run so-called healthy Net cafes that feature innocuous and squeaky-clean cultural products. It has also become routine for Internet entertainment units to be policed by plainclothes Net cops. Many cyber-cafes boast surveillance cameras, which swing into action during sensitive political seasons such as the period around June 4. And outlets in several cities have asked patrons to activate computers with personalized swipe cards that bear ID card numbers.[65]

The most effective way of policing the cyber-superhighway is rigid control of websites and draconian measures against Netivists. Beijing has from the late 1990s been arresting IT-related private entrepreneurs and technicians who are bold enough to start politically or news-oriented websites. As a result of strict official surveillance, popular news sites such as sina.com or sohu.com stopped breaking news stories that could be deemed embarrassing to the CCP. And beginning in 2002, dozens of Net-based intellectuals, ranging from college students and professors to civil servants, have been warned, harassed, and arrested for posting supposedly subversive articles on the Net. Apart from using high-tech means to build firewalls, the authorities have from mid-2004 encouraged Internet users to blow the whistle on pornographic and politically incorrect websites. A center to handle complaints about "illegal and unwholesome" sites was set up for the purpose. As American expert on the Chinese Internet John Palfrey noted in early 2005, "China has been more successful than any other country in the world to manage to filter the Internet despite the fast changes in technology."[66]

The jury, however, is still out on whether CCP authorities can effectively control the Net. The relative success with which activist groups in and out of China were able to fight for the release of—or at least a reduction in the penalty for—several big-name Internet dissidents has shown that there is a lot of sympathy for Netivists and other professionals committed to using the new medium to break the party's monopoly on information. And when Hu and his commissars closed down popular BBS (bulletin board system) sites at Peking and Tsinghua universities, a surprisingly large number of students dared to issue protests at the truncation of intellectual freedom. Moreover, the Net has been spawning new modes of expression such as blogs—and the thought police have found it difficult to keep track of the country's 10 million bloggers.[67]

Political Impact of the "New Classes"

The Rise of "Red Businessmen"

An influential 2002 study by the CASS divided China into ten social strata, with due recognition given to the "new classes" of businessmen and professionals as the cream—and future—of the country. By contrast, proletariats, the erstwhile "pace-setters of the revolution," risked being marginalized as more workers and farmers joined the ranks of the unemployed.[68] And it is clear that the way of thinking and political affiliation of members of these new classes will determine which way the country will be going in the first decades of this century.

The CCP leadership has been ambivalent concerning the rise of the new classes—particularly what political role they should play in the twenty-first century. It is noteworthy that when ex-president Jiang declared in July 2001 that the CCP would open its door to private businessmen, about 20 percent of the nation's 1.8 million private businessmen had already become party members. These included former state employees such as SOE managers who had retained their party affiliation after they had taken the proverbial dive into the sea of business. Given their economic clout and experience, private businessmen are hardly a negligible force in the CCP.[69]

And even before the party and state constitutions were revised in November 2002 and March 2003 respectively to further legitimize the status of "red" businessmen, Jiang and his aides had raised the status of businessman–party members. In the second half of 2002, entrepreneurs, professionals, and joint-venture staff in

Guangdong, Beijing, and a number of other cities and provinces were for the first time elected to regional party congresses. And a dozen-odd of the more prominent chiefs of private enterprises or firms with mixed ownership were made delegates to the Sixteenth CCP Congress. As of late 2004, however, private entrepreneurs' representation in major political bodies was miniscule: 55 out of 2,985 NPC deputies, 65 out of 2,238 Chinese People's Political Consultative Conference (CPPCC) members, and 10 out of 2,154 delegates to the Sixteenth CCP Congress.[70]

At the same time, the Jiang, and later the Hu-Wen, leadership was unwilling to let the business class rise too high too soon. One reason is fear that granting political rights to the "new classes" of businessmen and professionals would exacerbate feelings of jealousy and betrayal among the *gongnongbing,* a reference to workers, farmers, and soldiers, who have been the party's traditional pillar of support. And still-powerful leftists or quasi-Maoists in the party have never ceased decrying the "evil class nature" of private entrepreneurs. Moreover, relatively traditionalist and forthright cadres such as former premier Zhu Rongji were unhappy about the special privileges—and misdemeanors—that the new millionaires were getting away with. In an internal speech in 2002, Zhu decried the fact that most of the 100 Chinese multi-millionaires listed by U.S.-based *Forbes* magazine did not need to pay taxes. "I earn just around 800 yuan a month," Zhu thundered. "How come I'm paying taxes and they [the nouveau riche] don't? Why is it that the super-rich pay the least taxes?"[71]

More importantly, the party leadership is disturbed by signs that the "red bosses" are using aggressive—and politically destabilizing—means to grab power. Bearing in mind that in the run-up to the June 4, 1989, massacre, the nation's inchoate private sector had supported the student radicals, CCP authorities have always been wary of an "unholy alliance" between businessmen and liberal, reform-minded academics. Beijing rightly fears that should intellectual hotheads manage to get financing from businessmen, the ruling elite's authority could be challenged.

A little-known episode in the southern city of Guangzhou in early 2003 showed that China's flourishing private businessmen had yet to enjoy the trust of the party leadership. The Guangzhou Association for Research on the Development of the Nonstate Economy had invited a number of noted scholars and retired cadres from Beijing to take part in a forum on the future of private enterprises. These liberal economists and thinkers included Li Rui, Zhu Houze, Yu Guangyuan, and Du Runsheng. While having retired from party and academic posts, they were well-known advocates of radical economic as well as political reform. For example, Li, a former secretary of Chairman Mao Zedong, was an outspoken critic of what he called "dictatorial decision making." And Zhu, a former head of the party's Publicity Department, was partly responsible for the short-lived Beijing Spring of the mid-1990s.[72]

The party leadership having gotten wind of the guest list, cadres from the provincial Publicity Office and other units put pressure on the organizers to withhold the invitations. The upshot was that while most of the liberal scholars did show up in Guangzhou, they went as "tourists" and could not attend the opening ceremony of the conference. "Apparently to satisfy the authorities, the organizers suggested that we go to the local zoo to make us look like tourists," said a Beijing economist who attended the session. "It is quite laughable that with China having gotten into the World Trade Organization, Beijing should want to stop the free flow of ideas between different cities in the country."[73]

The real reason for the leadership's nervousness was that "red capitalists," having been fed liberal ideas by the intellectuals, might feel emboldened to lobby for political power that was commensurate with their fast-growing economic clout. For example, at another forum on the nonstate economy held in Shenzhen in late 2002, more than 100 owners of nonstate firms asked for an amendment of the Constitution guaranteeing the inviolability of private property. They complained that while foreign companies were granted national treatment post–WTO accession, private businesses still suffered multiple forms of discrimination when compared with SOEs. For example, nongovernment firms faced more difficulty in securing loans from banks or in being listed on the country's two stock markets.[74]

In a manifesto endorsed at the Shenzhen meeting, the "red capitalists" demanded more representation in the political system, at least within the NPC, China's parliament. According to social scientist Cao Siyuan, who was an adviser to private businessmen and a forum speaker, it was high time that Beijing recognized the political rights of practitioners in the nonstate economy, which accounted for about 60 percent of the nation's GDP. "Both the party and state constitutions should be revised to take note of the rising status of nonstate businessmen," Cao said. "Moreover, given Beijing's commitment to market forces, the pace of privatization should be speeded up. There should, for example, be private banks, which might be in a position to treat private businessmen better."[75]

Political Aspirations of the "Red Bosses"

As of early 2005, the red bosses lacked institutional means to influence major state policies, including economic decision making. As American Sinologist Richard Bush pointed out regarding the political channels of private entrepreneurs, "aside from the limited routes that have opened up since the beginning of reform— associations and collusive personalistic ties—there is precious little [in the way of channels] at their disposal."[76] One example of the personal influence of high-profile businessmen was the relationship between IT executive Jiang Mianheng and his father ex-president Jiang. Until his retirement from politics in 2004, Jiang had sought the advice of his son—and the latter's business friends—on formulating the country's Internet and telecommunications strategies.

The CCP leadership is not particularly anxious to come up with mechanisms for recruiting bright and trustworthy business executives into the higher circles of the party or government. In a tradition going back to the 1950s, entrepreneurs have been inducted into the CPPCC and other advisory bodies. And those who have distinguished themselves in the eight *minzhu dangpai,* or the so-called democratic parties, particularly the All-China Federation of Industry and Commerce (ACFIC), may be given senior positions in the NPC or CPPCC. For example, agribusiness tycoon Liu Yonghao, one of China's richest men, with assets of over 8.3 billion yuan, is active in political circles as a leader of the ACFIC as well as the CPPCC.[77] Yet the average businessman seems to lack a burning ambition to get into the political process. According to an early-2003 investigation by the popular *Caijing* financial magazine, only a minority of non-state-sector bosses or managers exhibited a desire to take part in politics. "Although quite a few [private bosses] have accumulated considerable economic prowess, they have not demonstrated strong political aspirations," the biweekly noted.[78]

However, this picture might be changing in a few years' time. While few entrepreneurs or managers have illusions of becoming top-level government or party cadres, an increasing number of red bosses are eager to acquire administrative or even figurehead government positions to help protect their hard-earned gains—and to lobby for the interests of the business class in general. Despite the changing attitude of the leadership on the status and contributions of the private sector, many "red capitalists" feel insecure. In 2002 and 2003, dozens of renowned private bosses ranging from Shanghai tycoon Zhou Zhengyi to film star Liu Xiaoqing were detained for alleged corruption and illegal speculation. Some of these suspects blamed lax and sketchy laws on tax and business activities in general for the ease with which they could be entrapped.[79] According to tabulations by international journals such as *Forbes,* most of the nouveau riche magnates are in the age group of thirty to fifty. And while few of them would want to endanger their ties with the authorities by advocating political reform, these energetic bosses do want to expand their influence beyond the economic world. And many are disdainful of so-called flower vase or decorative slots such as government adviser or CPPCC member.[80]

Dozens of cases of red bosses buying up political positions have since the early 2000s been reported in provinces ranging from well-heeled Guangdong to poor Shaanxi. Posts acquired ranged from deputy to a seat in local-level people's congresses to the vice-mayor or even mayor of a medium-sized city. Moreover, even prosperous cities such as Shenzhen are becoming increasingly dependent on taxation from fast-expanding private firms. "In rich as well as poor regions, the owners of a big private company are in a position to hold the local administration hostage by threatening to move to a rival city," said a Guangdong province economic planner. He added that while Beijing was happy that total taxation had been increasing rapidly since the late 1990s, the leadership was keenly aware that much of the revenue was coming from the private sector.[81]

Maiguan (buying posts) scandals have been widely reported in the official media. According to an investigation by the business newspaper *Fazhan Daobao* (Development Herald) into the *maiguan* phenomenon in the city of Yuncheng, Shanxi, nouveau riche bosses were snapping up positions for three reasons: to enhance their political standing, to facilitate business, and to seek a "protection umbrella" for dubious deals. In many cases, big-spending bosses have replaced traditional, Lei Feng–like model farmers as local-level administrators. The mass-circulation *China Youth Daily* said in an August 2004 article that "more and more rich people with experience will become rural officials." The daily cited the case of the head of the village administrative committee in Changhe Village outside Chongqing, Shi Changrong, who had been reelected to her position several times since the late 1970s. While Shi had devoted herself wholeheartedly to her job—to the extent that her husband divorced her a few years ago—she lost to construction company boss Yan Dalin in late 2003 by a large margin.[82]

By early-to-mid-2003, the phenomenon of savvy folks wearing two hats—being both cadres and businessmen—had become common in a number of east China provinces and cities. Take Anhui Province, which led the nation in rural reform in the early 1980s. The official *Zhongguo Jingying Bao* (China Business Times) cited Anhui cadres as saying that it had become usual practice for talented and success-ful businessmen to be recruited by party authorities as county administrative heads or even municipal party chiefs. For example, Jian Xialai, the party secretary of the industrial city of Wuhu, was the chairman of a good-sized automobile factory. *Zhongguo Jingying Bao* quoted local officials as saying entrepreneurs who had surrendered a certain amount of taxes to local coffers were automatically consid-ered for a senior posting in many cities.[83]

The special status of red bosses was even more pronounced in a number of rural provinces. In relatively backward Qinghe County, Hebei Province, any entrepreneur who has paid more than 1 million yuan of taxes for three years in a row qualifies for the post of a department head in the local administration. Qinghe folks like to cite the case of millionaire entrepreneur Zhang Lidong, who had merely had primary school education. Owing to the huge taxes he paid every year, Zhang was made vice-president of the County High Court. No attention was paid to possible conflicts of interest. Thus, of the ten-odd businessmen who were rewarded with senior slots in the county, several were in charge of its economic, business, or labor bureaus.[84]

As of early 2005, there was no sign that the Hu-Wen administration was taking measures to check the *maiguan* phenomenon. One reason was that the posts avail-able to the red bosses were still mid-ranking provincial slots. Anti-graft agencies such as the Central Commission for Disciplinary Inspection (CCDI), however, have been more pro-active in investigating cases of private businessmen greasing the palms of senior officials to further their economic or political interests. And in early 2004, the CCDI as well as the CCP Organization Department promulgated rules to check the phenomenon of cadres becoming so-called red-hat businessmen.[85]

The Power of "Returnees"

Immediately after China's accession to the WTO in November 2001, then Premier Zhu Rongji said his main task would be the search for talent. As of 2005, up to half a million vacancies existed in areas including senior management, the law, foreign trade, accounting, and auditing. Obviously, holders of foreign degrees, many of them in their thirties, are a major talent pool for leaders anxious to speed up China's integration with the international marketplace. And collectively speaking, this *haiguipai* (corps of returnees) has emerged as a new subclass that is packing political and economic punch.[86]

In the early 2000s, about 25,000 students a year went abroad for college, at both the undergraduate and graduate levels, making China the country with the biggest contingent of students studying overseas. In fact, more than 700,000 have since the mid-1980s gone abroad for higher education in North America, Europe (mainly the U.K.), and the Asia-Pacific region (mostly Japan and Australia). About 180,000 of these *haiguipai* have since returned, with more than 20,000 resettling in the PRC in 2003 alone.[87]

A key reason for the move-back trend is, of course, the luster and opportunities in megacities such as Shanghai and Guangzhou. Moreover, ministries and departments including the police, the Ministry of Personnel, the Education Ministry, and the Ministry of Science and Technology have since 2001 come up with policies to lure back holders of foreign degrees. These incentives include pay according to international norms, and special help with housing and other perks. Those wanting to set up businesses may be given tax privileges and dispensations including funds for developing high technology, and guarantees of intellectual property rights. And returnees who want to retain their overseas citizenship are eligible for multiple-entry and work visas. By late 2004, a number of liberal intellectuals and cadres had even proposed that Beijing consider allowing Chinese to hold dual citizenship. The prospect for this happening, however, is not high in the coming decade or so.[88]

The majority of graduates from American and other Western universities have found gainful employment in Chinese universities as professors and researchers. Others have flourished in business, particularly cutting-edge areas such as IT startups. However, it is a measure of the head-hunting eagerness of both ex-president Jiang and the Hu-Wen team that they have made special efforts to smooth the career path of *haiguipai* cadres. At the regional level, quite a few provincial and municipal administrations have given preferential treatment to applicants with advanced degrees or professional qualifications from foreign universities.[89]

Fourth-Generation or Fifth-Generation cadres with Western qualifications such as doctorates, MBAs, or law degrees have already attained vice-ministerial-level positions or above. They include Minister of Education Zhou Ji (born 1946), a graduate of the City University of New York; Vice-Chairman of the National Council for the Social Security Fund Gao Xiqing (born 1953), who holds a J.D. from Duke University; Vice-Governor of Jiangsu Zhang Taolin (born 1961), who has a doctorate from Bonn University; and the Vice-Director of the National Foreign Languages Bureau Zhou Mingwei (born 1955), a Harvard graduate. Most of these Western-trained cadres are employed in departments having to do with finance, law, the stock market, or foreign trade.[90]

Liu Hong and Fang Xinghai, in their early forties, are billed as among the youngest returnees who have enjoyed a meteoric rise up the bureaucracy. Liu, who has degrees from Oxford and Harvard, headed the China Securities Regulatory Commission's (CSRC) Department of Legal Affairs before he went into private business in 2000. Fang, a Stanford Ph.D., went in the opposite direction. He first worked for a private securities firm before joining the Shanghai Stock Exchange as assistant to the general manager in 2000. He was promoted to deputy general manager in 2002. Indeed, heads of ministries and commissions have allowed a growing number of bright and reliable returnees from the United States to take the proverbial "helicopter ride" to the top.[91]

At the same time, more sons and daughters of a number of Fourth-Generation leaders are making their influence felt in economic and political circles. For example, the daughter of President Hu and the son of Premier Wen were trained in the United States. Like the offspring of Jiang Zemin or Zhu Rongji, these Western-educated children of Fourth-Generation cadres are expected to play a big role, particularly in joint ventures with multinationals.[92] This is despite the fact that owing to intensive anti-corruption measures launched by Hu in 2003 and 2004, most "princelings" have chosen to maintain a low public profile.

A subset of the *haiguipai* consists of ethnic or overseas Chinese from Hong Kong, Taiwan, and even Western countries such as the United States who have returned for gainful employment in the mainland. While most of the *huaqiao* (overseas Chinese) returnees are running businesses, they exert an indirect influence on governance through being advisers to central or regional cadres. And quite a few have even been absorbed into government departments. The most high-profile of these *haiguipai* mandarins was lawyer Laura Cha, who was CSRC vice-chairman from 2001 to 2004. And Beijing has made the absorption of *huaqiao* talent easier by not insisting that they give up their foreign citizenship, except for posts with the rank of vice-minister or above.[93]

Major cities such as Guangzhou, Shenzhen, Shanghai, and Beijing have also used multinational head-hunting firms to find talent in places ranging from Hong Kong to New York. For example, the target for Beijing in the early 2000s was to sign up at least 5,000 overseas-trained personnel, and for Shanghai, up to 30,000. Shanghai, Shenzhen, and Chongqing have also worked out arrangements with Hong Kong to launch recruitment exercises in the special administrative region. The bulk of *huaqiao* professionals hired will be working in commercial enterprises. Shanghai and Chongqing, however, have indicated a desire to appoint a Hong Kong or overseas Chinese to government posts as senior as assistant mayor. And in early 2005, the State-owned Assets Supervision and Administration Commission advertised in China and overseas for candidates to fill twenty-five senior posts in SOEs and research academies under the central government.[94] Salary packages in China are still much lower than those in Hong Kong or New York. Yet many *huaqiao* and *haiguipai* personnel are convinced that promotion prospects are higher in the mainland.

The most significant question concerning the *haiguipai* trend is whether these well-educated and "Westernized" officials and professionals are well-placed to spearhead reformist changes in party and government policy. As far as new ideas are concerned, those working in finance and commercial departments—particularly regulatory organs such as the CSRC—have distinguished themselves by introducing much-needed global and corporate-governance practices. For example, *huaqiao* and *haiguipai* talents such as Cha and Anthony Neoh, a Hong Kong–based adviser to the CSRC, have made substantial contributions to improvements in laws and regulations dealing with foreign trade, joint ventures, insurance, and the stock market.[95]

In more sensitive departments dealing with politics and foreign policy, however, returnees from the West have a tendency to take a cautious or at least noncontroversial line for the obvious reason of self-preservation. There are examples of *haiguipai* officials who have been sidelined for advocating policies deemed too "soft" or politically incorrect. For example, the Harvard-educated Zhou was removed in 2003 from his more high-profile post of vice-director of the Taiwan Affairs Office reportedly because he had taken an excessively conciliatory line toward Taiwan and the United States. One of Zhou's portfolios was to liaise with U.S. government officials on Taiwan matters.[96]

The Political Role of the Middle Class, the Intelligentsia, and the Civil Society

In the former Soviet Union as well as Eastern European countries such as Hungary, Yugoslavia, and Poland, dissident intellectuals, academics, and professionals played a decisive role in destabilizing the Marxist regimes and spreading the gospel of political reform and Western-style liberalization. After using an iron fist to crack down on liberal opinion in the two to three years after the Tiananmen Square massacre of 1989, the CCP leadership has largely been able to co-opt the educated classes—or at least steer them away from politics and into economics, meaning the pursuit of material gains.

Thus by the early 2000s, the Chinese middle and professional classes, ranging from cadres and professors to lawyers and doctors, can hardly be described as agents for radical change in the sociopolitical arena. And it is for this reason that, as discussed in Chapter 3, the CCP leadership has laid out a detailed plan to expand the middle class's share of the population by around 1 percent every year. Yet a number of China analysts are convinced that members of the middle and professional classes will still be in a position to ring in the new, even regarding the sensitive area of political reform. Moreover, the undernourished Chinese civil society is showing signs of life as more NGOs and other groupings—which consist mostly of college-educated activists with a middle-class background—are influencing policies and events, albeit in an indirect and oblique fashion.

The Dubious Political Orientation of the Middle Class

For a long time, observers in the West have cherished the hope that the ever-widening open door in China, coupled with the growth of the middle class, would speed up the pace of democratization. This has yet to take place in a dramatic fashion more than four years after China's accession to the WTO. And analysts are divided about the extent to which members of the Chinese-style middle class can act as catalysts in engendering basic changes to the system. The most crucial factor is that compared with counterparts in other Asian countries, members of the Chinese middle class are much more dependent on the ruling party for their livelihood and sociopolitical status. As discussed earlier, even the billionaire bosses of huge private firms—who can be perhaps be considered members of the "upper classes"—are anxious to seek CCP patronage. Moreover, as Singapore journalist Huang Jiahua noted, in capitalistic societies, "members of the middle class have a relatively strong sense of responsibility to society." He cast doubt on whether affiliates of the Chinese middle class—many of whom had accumulated their wealth through dubious means—would have a serious social consciousness.[97]

As in the case of private entrepreneurs and "red bosses," members of the nascent middle class such as professionals and academics want to bolster their political status and expand their ability to influence policy so as to preserve their vested interests. However, middle-class folks by and large have no desire to challenge the authority of the *dangzhongyang* or the principle of one-party dictatorship. Their foremost concern is improving market-force mechanisms—which would ensure that they and their children will be in a better position to compete on a level playing field with other social sectors.

Beijing-based social scientist Li Zhengtong thinks that middle-class social sectors will provide an added impetus for economic reform because they are the product—and beneficiaries—of the age of the reform and open-door policy. "Members of the middle class will be the supporters and implementers of reform and modernization," he wrote in mid-2004. However, Li agreed with the prevailing opinion that while the middle class supports reform—mostly economic liberalization—it would not want to rock the boat or try to "make revolution." Instead, the sociologist indicated, the middle and professional classes would be "an important force for maintaining social stability."[98] Likewise, U.S. Sinologist Orville Schell noted in 2004 that open markets did not necessarily lead to open societies. "There are examples where Leninist capitalism works quite well and where the middle class that you might expect to be lobbying for greater freedom and democracy is happy enough as long as the economics cohere to just let things be the way they are," he pointed out. Schell cited Italy and Germany during World War II as countries where members of the middle class acquiesced in the ultra-rightist policies of the ruling parties.[99]

Beijing-based social scientist and historian Wang Sirui, however, gravitates toward the view that the middle class can considerably expedite political change.

Wang argued in late 2004 that in addition to seeking economic development and market reforms, the middle class "wants to gradually expand the space for public [debate] and enlarge the possibilities of political participation." Wang dismissed what he called the "fatalistic" view that the middle class was necessarily pro-establishment. He pointed out that a key factor was "whether the ruling echelon adopts a conciliatory attitude toward the middle class expanding its participation [in politics]—or whether the former wants to suppress such participation."[100] As of now, however, it seems obvious that CCP leadership is reluctant to allow middle-class affiliates to clamor for thoroughgoing political liberalization.

Political Aspirations of the Intelligentsia

Two of the best-selling books of 2003 and 2004 were, respectively, *The Final Years of Zhou Enlai,* by U.S.-based retired party historian Gao Wenqian, and *The Demise of Empire: Cataclysm in the Late Qing Dynasty,* by Guangzhou historian Yuan Weishi. A powerful point made by Gao in *Zhou Enlai* was how shamelessly cadres and intellectuals submitted themselves to the tyranny of Chairman Mao and the Gang of Four during the Cultural Revolution. And one of the controversial conclusions of *Empire* was that Chinese civilization could only be resuscitated by an intelligentsia that refuses to become a tool of the party. As author Yuan said, intellectuals must "uphold civil liberties and the ideals of democracy and rule of law."[101]

While scholars and writers played a sizable role in the brief Beijing Spring in the mid-1980s, their ability to be catalysts for change has declined drastically. According to a Beijing-based social sciences professor, the authorities have very successfully co-opted intellectuals and academics, who make up a large portion of the middle class. "Most college teachers and graduate students are not interested in politics," he said. "Their focus is finding more lucrative second jobs, projects, and consultancies, or, for the more senior ones, memberships on the boards of newly set up companies."[102] Indeed, it is not uncommon for faculty members of the twenty or so big-name universities in Beijing, Shanghai, Chongqing, or Guangzhou, particularly those in the finance, legal, and high-tech fields, to earn well over 1 million yuan a year. And these elite academics are aware of the fact that they are the "darlings" of—and holders of vested interests in—the age of market reforms.

The CCP-inspired depoliticization of the middle and professional classes is most evident when the situation today is compared to that of 1988 and 1989, when professors and college students were eager to throw themselves headlong into the reform process. These social-activist intellectuals differed in their worldviews and methodologies: some wanted a relatively radical overhaul of the system, while others, including "black hand" dissidents Wang Juntao and Chen Ziming, merely advocated evolutionary-style changes within the CCP hierarchy.[103] Yet there was a consensus that change was in the air, and that if necessary, these intellectuals were willing to make personal sacrifices to expedite the liberalization process.

According to avant-garde writer Yu Jie, the bulk of well-educated Chinese, including scholars and professionals, have become what he calls an "appendage of the powers that be." "Most intellectuals curry favor with party leaders and they will even tell lies and expose the 'political errors' of their colleagues and friends," he said. A graduate of Peking University, Yu has been a freelance writer since the early 2000s because he refuses to accommodate himself to the stifling political culture of government or academic institutions. His best-selling book *I Refuse to Tell Lies* reveals the many instances in which academics and journalists unthinkingly toe the party line on issues ranging from politics to morality.[104]

The influential *Southern People's Weekly* (*SPW*) pointed out in a special feature in 2004 that despite the relatively tight political climate, a few dozen-odd "public intellectuals" were in a position to exert influence in society. *SPW* noted that academics, thinkers, and experts such as economist Mao Yushi and political scientist Liu Junning were "idealists who have a critical spirit and moral responsibility." The liberal magazine, however, deplored the fact that while in the 1980s, socially conscious intellectuals were "shining stars," "the kaleidoscopic market economy has relegated them to the margins of society [in the past few years]."[105]

The Political Influence of a Nascent Civil Society

Beijing Frowns on Politically Active NGOs

In its official report for 2003, the Ministry of Civil Affairs (MCA) asserted that *minjian* (nonofficial or mass-based) organizations in the country were "developing healthily." As of late 2003, there were 142,000 social, unofficial, and non-party-affiliated organizations in the country, up 6.8 percent from the previous year. However, there were only 1,736 *minjian* units that could be classified as nationwide or cross-provincial in nature—or merely 49 more than in 2002. Moreover, it is well understood that the bulk of the *minjian* units have subtle affiliations with party or government departments. As such, these outfits are markedly different from what is usually known as an NGO in the West or other parts of Asia. As Peking University political scientist Yu Keping noted, Chinese civil-society organizations (CSOs) are typically "government-led," and most of them are "too dependent on the party and government organs of political power."[106]

It is clear that the authorities do not want too many politically oriented mass organizations—particularly those that have direct or indirect ties to dissident intellectuals or foreign governments. Thus the MCA pointed out that it was focusing on nurturing *gongyixing* (charitable and public interest–oriented) organizations, as well as business units such as chambers of commerce and professional associations. The leadership's newfound interest in *gongyixing* organizations was directly related to the Hu-Wen administration's concern for improving public health, education, and other "developmental software." It was after the SARS crisis in 2004 that Beijing grudgingly acknowledged the role that civic organizations and volunteers had played in alleviating the suffering of AIDS patients in Henan Province and other places.[107]

The most popular NGOs and citizen advocacy groups are those that are nonpolitically motivated—or at least unlikely to challenge CCP supremacy. These include consumer rights and health-promotion organizations, including those that monitor the profusion of fake food products. From mid-2003 onward, consumer groups have published regular print and electronic bulletins on the quality and safety of goods, and they have occasionally taken shady or irresponsible manufacturers to court.[108]

Perhaps the most vigorous among the fast-growing NGOs are groups devoted to the environmental cause. The country now boasts some 2,000 green NGOs, up from just a few in the mid-1980s. For obvious reasons, most of them take a nonconfrontational stance toward the government. Yet several such groupings can be construed as politically oriented and their lobbying efforts have had an impact on official policy. Thus, the Snowland Great Rivers and Environmental Protection Association is lobbying for public support for preserving rivers in the Tibet region, which is also the origin of the country's biggest waterways. Action by several green groups such as Green Earth Volunteers was a factor behind Beijing's decision in mid-2004 to postpone the construction of thirteen dams and hydro-stations on the Nu or Salween River in Yunnan Province, which flows into Myanmar and Thailand. And the NGOs vowed to fight the State Council's decision a few months later to go ahead with the construction of at least four out of the thirteen dams. The central government has also agreed to change the routes of the "south-north water diversion" project in order to avoid environmental damage.[109]

Meanwhile, the green groupings were fighting a pitched battle to protect another pristine waterway in Yunnan, the sixteen-kilometer Jinshajiang River. Provincial authorities and the state electricity giant Huaneng Corporation—which is headed by Li Xiaopeng, the son of former premier Li Peng—had decided to build a 276 meter dam at the picturesque Hutiaoxia Gorge without consultation with the local populace, several million of whom would have to be resettled. This time, not only green activists but famous scholars and writers in Beijing including Tsinghua University professor Wang Hui signed a petition to party authorities to stop the project. They were joined by eight vocal professors at Yunnan University, who alleged that provincial officials as well as Huaneng had "robbed the public of their right to know" about this horrendous scheme.[110]

The CCP—as well as the Hu-Wen team—has so far maintained a murky attitude toward the *gongmin shehui,* or civil society. For example, no senior official has gone on record saying that civil-society groups can contribute to building a *xiaokang shehui,* or a comprehensively well-off society. According to the *Wen Wei Po,* a Beijing-run Hong Kong paper, senior party think tanks had in 2004 been studying how the party should make adjustments to cope with changes in the civil society. *Wen Wei Po* quoted "party construction experts" as saying that as the *gongmin shehui* developed, the CCP must "raise the level of its ability to coordinate and control social [groups]." The unnamed experts said that the Beijing leadership must boost efforts in "guiding and leading" NGOs and other civil-society groups. For example, the CCP leadership hoped that party cells could be established in most of the influential NGOs and mass-based groups.[111]

Over the longer term, quite a few influential intellectuals believe that CSOs and NGOs will exert a bigger influence on society irrespective of the leadership's inclinations. Among them is Peking University's Professor Yu, who is said to be a member of Hu's think tank. "As the market economy is gradually established and the political and legal environment undergoes changes, all kinds of civil organizations are bound to emerge," he noted. "Their emergence will play a positive role in improving democratic governance in urban and rural areas."[112]

An Inchoate Network of "Pressure Groups"

If one were looking for evidence of NGOs and other civil-society groupings exerting pressure on the party and government, the best example might be groups of scholars and lawyers lobbying the government on behalf of *ruoshi tuanti*, or disadvantaged sectors. Take, for example, the issue of the forced eviction of urban or rural residents by developers who are often acting in collusion with corrupt local officials. Cases involving poor urbanites or peasants driven from their homes—and without adequate compensation—accounted for a good portion of petitioners who flocked to Beijing from 2002 to 2004.

The most famous of the anti-eviction lobbyists is Zheng Enchong, a forthright lawyer whose campaign on behalf of the residents of Jing'an District, Shanghai, was a factor behind the detention of "premier Shanghai tycoon" Zhou Zhengyi (see Chapters 3 and 4). Zheng was in late 2003 slapped with a three-year jail term for allegedly sharing an internal NCNA report with foreign human rights organizations. Human rights activists estimate that more than 400 lawyers were detained between 1997 and 2004 for defending clients. This, however, has not deterred other legal professionals from taking up the cases of penniless and powerless evictees. A group of Shanghai lawyers started a free legal service in 2003 for evictees who wanted to seek a higher level of compensation from developers. And in late 2005, after People's Armed Police officers killed an estimated twenty villagers in Dongzhou, Guangdong while they were protesting against illegal requisition of their land, lawyers Teng Biao, Wang Yi, and other intellectuals in Beijing petitioned the authorities on the need to protect farmers' rights.[113]

Lawyers have been at the forefront of efforts to abolish or moderate outdated and draconian laws and regulations such as the administrative detention of "vagrants and beggars." It was the lobbying efforts of ten or more law professors and other academics in Beijing and Guangzhou that led to the punishment of police and other personnel who beat graphic designer Sun Zhigang to death in early 2003. The scholars' appeal prompted the Hu-Wen team to revise the law books (see Chapter 4).

No less significant was the success with which a dozen or so lawyers and academics were able to attract national sympathy for philanthropic rural businessman Sun Dawu, who was detained in 2003 for "illegally" raising funds from well-to-do peasants. Sun, dubbed "Robin Hood" by his admirers, had used profits from his agribusiness to finance welfare schemes for the poor in Hebei Province. Yet he antagonized Beijing because of his repeated criticism that the party had neglected farmers—and that the official banking system was so corrupt he had to use unconventional methods to raise capital from his own workers. Defenders of Sun included famous law professors Jiang Ping and Xu Zhiyong, as well as lesser-known academics. Sun was eventually given a "suspended" three-year jail term, a surprisingly light sentence that reflected the effective work of his academic friends.[114]

Indeed, acting as individuals or groups, socially committed lawyers have even dared to challenge the authorities on taboo areas such as Beijing's suppression of the Falun Gong spiritual group. For instance, Beijing lawyer Gao Zhisheng, who had taken up a number of human rights cases in the past, penned a petition to NPC chief Wu Bangguo in late 2004. Gao noted that punishments meted out to Falun Gong affiliates, including "reeducation through labor," had violated relevant clauses in the Constitution. Moreover, Beijing-based lawyers including Fan Yafeng and Zhang Xingshui defended the rights of organizers of house churches on the grounds that freedom of worship was written into the Constitution.[115]

Indeed, different groups of intellectuals were by 2004 pressing Beijing for the release of political dissidents and assorted individuals who had run afoul of the authorities. Much of this protest action took place on the Internet, which allowed for a certain degree of anonymity. After famous Netivist Du Daobin was arrested in late 2003 for posting articles on the Internet that were deemed to have endangered state security, some 1,000 intellectuals put their names down on an Internet petition for his release. Du was in mid-2004 given a suspended jail term of three years, which was lighter than expected. Chengdu University law professor Wang Yu, one of Du's attorneys, said he had no doubt that "public pressure was the key to the release of several Netivists."[116]

Also weighing in are a bunch of private think tanks, which started having an impact on political and economic issues in the early 2000s. Owing to pressure from the authorities, there is but a handful of nonofficial think tanks in Beijing and Shanghai. And there is evidence that the Hu-Wen team has started cracking down on the more avant-garde among these research units. For example, Cao Siyuan and Mao Yushi, central figures of the Siyuan Social Sciences Research Center and the Unirule Economic Research Institute, respectively, were subjected to harassment by different party and government units. Mao was unable to circulate a book advocating Western-style freedoms, while Cao was put under twenty-four-hour surveillance for his role in lobbying for radical constitutional changes.[117]

Owing to political and economic constraints, most of these private brain trusts have remained miniscule. Two of them, Li Fan's China and the World Research Institute (CWRI), and economist Zhong Dajun's Beijing Dajun Economic Observation and Research Center, had barely a couple of full-time employees. While the influence of these outfits is restricted to the intelligentsia, some of their proposals have either been partially adopted by the authorities or at least become a factor that Beijing has to take into consideration when making policies. For example, it is true that Li's effort to popularize grassroots elections has not found favor with the Hu-Wen team. However, on a practical level, the indefatigable campaigner has provided much-needed intellectual and spiritual support to peasants and cadres in Sichuan and other provinces in their pursuit of local-level democracy. And because of CWRI's influence overseas, the authorities have to think twice before penalizing local officials who have gone the distance in conducting township-level polls.[118]

7

Conclusion

Where Is the New Thinking?

China at a Crossroads

China, a bafflingly complex country, can be neatly summed up by Charles Dickens's famous line: "It was the best of times; it was the worst of times." The key behind the bundle of contradictions that is twenty-first-century China is that there are in fact two Chinas. There is the country that, according to domestic as well as foreign academics, is an economic juggernaut that will overtake Japan by 2010 and the United States before 2030. Peking University professor Justin Lin predicted that by 2030, 20 percent of the Fortune 500 companies would be hailing from the PRC.[1] And optimists are confident that owing to the "putting people first" strategy of the Hu Jintao–Wen Jiabao administration, this wealth will enable the leadership to defuse dangerous contradictions in Chinese society. The apparent concern that the Fourth-Generation leadership has shown for *ruoshi tuanti* (disadvantaged sectors) ranging from peasants and migrant workers to HIV carriers seems to demonstrate that a debilitating class war and an implosion of the "market-authoritarian regime" might be avoided.

Yet there are also disturbing signs that time is running out, even as the Hu-Wen leadership has failed to demonstrate an iron-clad resolve to go the distance in reform. As well-known sociologist Lu Xueyi noted in early 2005, "China is at a crossroads." "It can either smoothly evolve into a medium-level developed country or it can spiral into stagnation and chaos," the Chinese Academy of Social Sciences (CASS) scholar said. Another "within-the-system" reformer, Beijing professor Yang Peng, quoted President Hu as saying in late 2005 that "we face many problems that we cannot avoid—and we must tackle them instead of delaying further."[2] And it is clear that only in-depth and far-reaching reforms, including political liberalization, instead of palliatives dispensed by Confucian-style sage-emperors, could minimize the possibility of an ugly confrontation between the privileged elite and the *ruoshi tuanti*. Signs of social upheaval—what some analysts have called the Latin-Americanization of China—are increasing despite the Hu-Wen team's apparent decision to use conciliatory measures to bring about a "harmonious society."

Indeed, the more desperate among the nearly 200,000 petitioners flocking to the capital in a typical month have adopted drastic measures to dramatize their plight. These range from blowing up bombs to threatening to jump from tall buildings. The official *Orient Outlook Weekly* admitted that cases of farmers who had not been adequately compensated for land requisitioned by corrupt local officials and greedy developers had mushroomed along the coast, leading to "worsening social instability." Take, for example, the mid-2004 case of peasant Zhang Mingchun, who murdered multi-millionaire developer Ge Junming in a rural county in Sichuan Province. Convinced that Ge had used dirty tactics to cheat him of his piece of land, Zhang detonated a self-made bomb in Ge's office, which killed both instantly. Zhang wrote in a note that he had no other recourse save "mutual and simultaneous destruction."[3]

The last few months of 2004—which witnessed large-scale confrontation between the masses and paramilitary police in provinces and cities including Sichuan, Chongqing, Yunnan, Henan, and Guangdong—provided ample evidence that the overstretched social fabric was close to the breaking point. These included a standoff between several tens of thousands of peasants and People's Armed Police (PAP) officers in southwestern Sichuan over the seizure of farmland for the construction of a dam, and a vicious fistfight between Han Chinese and Muslims in Henan Province. Even minor mishaps could ignite a full-scale explosion. Consider how 50,000 residents of Wanzhou District, Chongqing, clashed with riot-control police in October 2004. Windows of the Wanzhou government office were smashed and police cars burnt. Yet the melee started simply because a lowly porter was savagely beaten up by a local official whose wife was bruised by the laborer's "coolie pole." The cadre told onlookers he could have the porter killed by "paying a small fee of 200,000 yuan." The crowd went berserk when police sided with the highly connected couple. Thousands of Wanzhou residents—mostly laid-off workers—gathered outside the district office premises. They were only dispersed when elite PAP forces were called in.[4]

Yet perhaps the worst nightmare for the Hu leadership is that chinks in the armor of China's much-ballyhooed world factory are showing. Doubts have been cast about the so-called China model of growth. While there is a near consensus that the strength of the nation and the standard of living of large sectors of Chinese have increased in the past twenty-five years, China's approach to economic development and modernization in general have bred ill effects galore. These include unprecedented environmental degradation and the rise of the incidence of different types of cancer and epidemics. Moreover, economic expansion has not been accompanied by a commensurate augmentation in "soft power," originality of thinking, and cultural vibrancy. Instead, a wave of crass commercialism and materialism—as well as fake products and bogus college degrees—is sweeping the land. Should Chinese-style growth prove unsustainable—thus exacerbating already volatile social conflicts—the party's mandate of heaven could be torn asunder even as the nation is plunged into chaos.

The single most important question facing the nation is whether the Hu-Wen team's reform can somehow rectify defects of the China model. The Hu administration's many efforts to restructure the economic and political systems have been hampered by its obsession with maintaining the CCP's monopoly on power. At a CCP Central Committee plenum in September 2004, Hu called for a no-holds-barred effort to raise the CCP's "governance ability" so as to sustain the party's legitimacy and heavenly mandate. This chapter looks at the price that the Hu-Wen team has to pay for putting the party ahead of reform—and the people. Moreover, the Hu leadership's apparent determination to root out "heretical" or "bourgeois-liberal" thinking has inhibited the flowering of new ideas that might one day resolve China's many contradictions.

It is, of course, still possible for the Hu-Wen team to hack out new paths in the rest of this decade. Yet its rather disappointing performance so far has prompted Chinese as well as foreign observers to pine for the next, or Fifth Generation of leaders, who could take the baton around the year 2012. The concluding chapter of this book will examine whether a fast-rising corps of relatively young and forward-looking cadres—as well as members of the nonparty elite—might be able to cut the Gordian knot of reform while simultaneously maintaining the requisite level of stability and economic well-being.

Hu's Obsession with Holding Power vs. the Seeds of Real Reform

Improving "Governance Ability" and Consolidating One-Party Rule

The late-2004 Central Committee's Resolution on Strengthening the Construction of the Party's Governance Ability (hereafter Resolution) made it clear that for President Hu, the administration's foremost task and raison d'être consists of maintaining the CCP's ruling status. Other goals such as economic development and political reform would only subserve this leitmotif. The document, delivered at the Sixteenth CCP Central Committee's fourth plenary session in September 2004, amounted to the fullest—and perhaps frankest—statement of the worldview and governing philosophy of Hu, Premier Wen, and their Fourth-Generation colleagues. Its main ideas reflect Hu's concerns, going back to the mid-1990s, for finding a magic formula to resuscitate the party's staying power.[5]

As discussed in Chapter 1, one notable drawback to the career and background of Hu is that he has been a party apparatchik most of his adult life. This means that his specialty is the traditional mix of ideology, organization, and propaganda. Since becoming a Politburo Standing Committee (PSC) member in 1992, Hu has paid more attention to economics, foreign trade, and foreign affairs. Yet he sees his primary role as consolidating party ideology, worldviews, "ruling methods," and especially the CCP's ability to maintain its "long reign and perennial stability."

The Resolution reflected Hu's fervently held belief that through what the document called "a scientific leadership system and leadership method," the party can "put forward and implement correct theories, lines, goals, policies, and strategies" to run China well and forever maintain the CCP's mandate of heaven. Unlike the Long March generation of leaders, Hu and Wen did not take for granted the CCP's status as ruling party. As discussed in previous chapters, the Hu-Wen team introduced populist concepts and policies such as "building up the party for the public good and putting people first." Hu and his colleagues also vowed to "run the administration in a scientific manner, and to administer democratically and according to the law."[6]

At the party Central Committee plenum, Hu urged cadres of all levels to acquire and improve five types of "governing ability," namely, the ability to *jiayu* or "take control over" the socialist market economy; to develop "socialist democratic politics"; to build "socialist advanced culture"; to build a "socialist harmonious society"; and to deal with the global situation. Yet the party chief has yet to explain to party members or the world the ways in which his "socialist democratic politics" and "socialist advanced culture" would differ from the tight control that the CCP has exercised over ideas, culture, and the media since 1989.

In fact, the word "democracy" was cited many times in the Resolution, such as in the context of "democratic elections, democratic decision making, democratic management, and democratic supervision." However, the Hu-Wen team did not deign to mention political reform in the sense of an equitable power sharing between the party and other political groupings or socioeconomic blocs, now or in the future. And there was no reference to concrete measures such as boosting election mechanisms in the party and country, by, for example, holding polls to pick heads of townships and counties.

The much-discussed document merely revived the shibboleth of perfecting "the multiparty cooperation and political consultation system under CCP leadership." It is common knowledge that the eight so-called democratic parties—which on the surface are supposed to provide some form of competition to the CCP—are largely run by party cadres as well as dependent on state financial support. Indeed, in a Chinese People's Political Consultative Conference (CPPCC) meeting called after the Fourth Plenum, conference chairman Jia Qinglin noted that members of the top advisory body—which included many members of the eight "democratic parties" as well as non-CCP intellectuals—should "resolutely rally behind the leadership of the CCP."[7]

Particularly disturbing for Chinese intellectuals was the fact that in both the Resolution and other policy statements in 2004 and 2005, Hu laid the utmost store by party supremacy. The Resolution indicated, for example, that "the party should strengthen leadership over legislative work." It pointed out that relevant party committees should "fulfill the function of the leadership core in organizations such as people's congresses, [different levels of] administrations, and people's political consultative conferences." Obviously, party domination of legislative and judicial work runs against the much-praised ideal of "rule by law" and "respect for the Constitution" raised by Hu and his colleagues in the first six months of their administration. It is noteworthy that in a speech after the Fourth Plenum, the nation's chief judge Xiao Yang indicated the courts' obeisance to party leadership. While noting that the courts must "uphold judicial authority," Xiao pledged that cadres and staff in the judicial system would "uphold the authority of rule by law, as well as the authority of the CCP."[8]

The Central Committee document also underscored the imperative of party control over information and the media. It said that the CCP must "uphold the principle of the party managing the media," which should focus on "making propaganda for positive [sociopolitical developments]." Just as predecessor Jiang, Hu has obviously forgotten the gist of the *Political Report* to the Thirteenth CCP Congress of 1987, which reflected Deng's dictum about the importance of the separation of party and government as well as party and economic activities. The Resolution does not mention the Four Cardinal Principles, a reference to Deng's insistence on rigid obeisance to stern party leadership, Marxist-Leninist precepts, the socialist road, and the "dictatorship of the proletariat." However, Hu asked fellow cadres and party members to raise their guard against "the strategies of hostile foreign forces to try to Westernize and divide up China." In the field of culture and the arts, the document urged responsible cadres to "combat the infiltration of corrupt capitalist ideas and culture."[9]

Then in January 2005, Hu launched a year-and-a-half campaign to *baoxian,* or to safeguard and bolster the "advanced nature" of party members and cadres. In a Politburo study session at the time, the party chief noted that CCP authorities would "severely educate, severely manage, and severely supervise" the moral and political standards of members and officials. Hu added: "we must implement in various kinds of work the ideal of establishing the party for the common good and administering [the country] for the sake of the people." As with other crusades of orthodoxy such as ex-president Jiang's campaign of the "Three Emphases" ("putting stress on studying the Marxist canon, on righteousness, and on political rectitude"), the *baoxian* exercise was aimed at weeding out "bourgeois liberal" ideas from the West. As the *People's Daily* noted in an editorial about the *baoxian* campaign, "hostile powers have not changed their conspiracy to Westernize our country and divide us up."[10]

The Campaign to Build a Harmonious Society, 2004–2005

A major initiative unveiled by the CCP leadership at the Fourth Central Committee Plenum was "building a socialist harmonious society." Going one step further than the ideal of "putting people first," the Hu-Wen leadership vowed to "adequately mediate among the interest relationships of various sectors, and to correctly handle inner contradictions within the people." More resources would be spent on "resolving contradictions and lessening the difficulties" of disaffected sectors of society. While the CCP leadership stopped short of pledging not to use force against groups with grievances, it vowed to use legal and economic methods as well as vehicles such as "consultation and reconciliation" to handle and otherwise mollify the masses' complaints and grievances.[11]

At a special session at the Central Party School (CPS) in early 2005, Hu noted that the construction of a harmonious, socialist society should be "organically integrated" with the other objectives of economic growth and developing political and spiritual civilization. The party chief told CPS students that "a harmonious society will feature socialist democracy, rule by law, equity, justice, sincerity, amity, and vitality." "We must correctly handle contradictions within the people and other social contradictions, and adequately mediate among different interest relationships," Hu added.[12]

According to People's University professor Zheng Gongcheng, the concept of a harmonious society signaled that China had entered the "late reform-and-open-door era." This meant that as much emphasis was being put on social development and social justice as on GDP growth. Or as sociologist Li Qiang put it, if the first twenty years of China's reform era were concerned with economic problems, the priority for the second twenty years would be social issues.[13] Other commentators have pointed out that the newfound stress on harmony has grown out of a "neo-Confucianist" strain of thinking within the Hu-Wen leadership (see following section on Confucianism). Senior cadres ranging from Hu to former PSC member Li Ruihuan are convinced that under the guidance of "wise rulers," sociopolitical harmony can be attained through caring for disadvantaged sectors and reconciling differences among power blocs and interest groupings.

While it is certain that compared with the leadership in the Jiang era, the Hu-Wen team has lavished more attention and funds on *ruoshi tuanti,* the political clout and wiggle room that the CCP leadership is willing to give peasant and labor groupings is not much bigger. For example, the Resolution and other statements by CCP leaders still cite improving the *xinfang* or *shangfang* (petition system) as a way to alleviate the suffering of the masses. This is despite the official admission that the authorities lack the resources to investigate the petitioners' grievances, let alone redress whatever wrongs they have suffered. Through late 2005, the CCP leadership breathed no word about the possibility of legalizing independent labor unions or farmers' organizations.[14]

There have also been efforts to tackle the immediate causes of the *ruoshi tuanti*'s grievances. Take, for example, a more cautious attitude by the State Council in approving new hydroelectric projects, which have often led to massive protests by peasants forced to leave their land on short notice and without adequate compensation. Thus, the State Environment Protection Administration (SEPA) announced in early 2005 that thirty projects, mostly having to do with power and hydroelectric plants, had to be stopped pending improvement in relevant standards. Projects affected included the Xiluodu hydroelectric station in the Three Gorges area and the proposed "cascade of dams" along the Nu River. However, powerful energy companies, working in connection with local leaders, still seem to enjoy the upper hand. For example, local officials have estimated that the Nu River projects would be resumed in 2006.[15]

The campaign to build a harmonious society also dominated the Fifth Plenary Session of the Central Committee in October 2005, as well as the Eleventh Five-Year Plan (2006–2010) endorsed in the same session. Following upon the Hu-Wen team's earlier pronouncements about "scientific development" and balance between economic growth and social welfare, Wen noted at the plenum that more efforts would be made in nurturing a harmonious society. The premier indicated that "employment, social security, poverty reduction, education, medical care, environmental protection, and safety will be given priority" in the coming five years. Referring to oft-repeated statistics that the richest 10 percent of the population owned 40 percent of society's total assets, senior officials and government advisers pointed out that "common prosperity"—the original goal of Chinese socialism—was achievable along the road map delineated by the Hu leadership. As President Hu indicated, after per capita GDP had reached around $3,000, "the economy would develop further, democracy would become more comprehensive, science and education more advanced, culture more prosperous, society more harmonious, and the life of the people more fruitful and substantial."[16] However, apart from recommendations similar to the "five balances"—striking a better balance between rich and poor, coast and hinterland, prosperity and environmental protection, and so forth—which had been raised in 2003 and 2004, Hu and Wen did not spell out many new ideas.

Growing Doubts About the "China Model"

The Economic, Environmental, and Human Costs of Progress

By early 2005, China looked set to accomplish the goal put forth at the Sixteenth CCP Congress of November 2002: that is, to achieve by the year 2020 a "relatively well-off society in a comprehensive manner." Per capita share of GDP had reached US$1,000 by late 2003—and this figure was on course to triple by the year 2020. Moreover, discounting the up to 900 million rural-based Chinese, denizens along the coast are not too far from hitting the magic $5,000 per capita mark. Most domestic and foreign economists reckon that the high growth rate of around 8 percent first attained in the early 1990s could go on at least through the year 2010. The country's financial goals would seem even more attainable if the purchasing-parity yardstick is used—and if the huge "underground" or "black" economy is taken into account.

By 2004 and 2005, however, doubts about the efficacy of the "Chinese growth model" had become voluminous. Put simply, the PRC's no-holds-barred growth has mainly been achieved not through breakthroughs in productivity or the efficient use of resources, but through capital input. China's investment is approaching 45 percent of GDP, as against comparable figures of 20 percent to 30 percent for most developing countries. Capital outlays include those from the government and state banks—Chinese have the highest savings rate in the world and banks are swelling with some 13 trillion yuan worth of savings deposits—as well as record-breaking levels of foreign direct investment.[17] Moreover, the long-term economic efficiency of many mammoth projects in infrastructure and other arenas are in doubt. After all, the "high growth rate strategy" has been mandated by the party and state in large measure to serve the political purpose of maintaining a relatively high level of employment and, in some instances, keeping powerful provinces and cities happy.

One corollary of such a *cuguang* (rough and quantity-based) approach to development is vast wastage of energy and other resources, as well as environmental depredation. The rate of efficiency with which China is using petroleum, coal, water, and many other mineral resources is about one-third that of the United States and one-sixth that of Japan. Chairman of the National Development and Reform Commission Ma Kai, a top aide to Wen, admitted in early 2004 that the PRC's growth had been achieved at the expense of a profligate use of resources. Thus, while the country accounted for 4 percent of global GDP growth in 2003, it consumed 40 percent of the world's cement, 27 percent of its steel, and 31 percent of its coal. "Our high-input, high-consumption, high-emission, crude method of growth remains unchanged," Ma said at a press conference.[18] This wastefulness was partly responsible for the global shortage of oil and other minerals from 2003 onward.

Moreover, inefficient use of minerals and energy has led to pollution and other hazardous conditions for Chinese in urban and rural areas. Overexcavation of coal has resulted in the subsidence of land in provinces ranging from Shanxi and Heilongjiang. For example, 300,000–odd residents in northeast Heilongjiang had to be relocated to safer areas in 2003 and 2004. And the relentless lowering of the water table nationwide has engendered dangers for large numbers of cities. This is due to water shortage caused by rapid industrialization and ecological imbalance. Shanghai, China's most glamorous city, is believed to be slowly sinking, in part because of this new scourge.[19]

By 2004, a few mainstream media were bold enough to occasionally run scary—and politically incorrect—headlines about imminent disaster scenarios. Most of these warnings concerned the human costs of development: the horrid living conditions of the disadvantaged classes coupled with the widening gap between the filthy rich and the neglected poor have engendered well-nigh explosive conditions. The Ministry of Public Security admitted that in 2004, there were 74,000 cases of "mass incidents," a euphemism for demonstrations and riots, compared with just 10,000 in 1994.[20]

A research group at Peking University noted in early 2005 that the country might enter a "multiple-crisis phase" around the year 2010. This was the opinion of 66 percent of the ninety-eight professors and experts that the group consulted. The unit's leader, Professor Ding Yuanzhu, cited the usual flashpoints such as growing poverty, environmental imbalance, and the bad debts sustained by banks. Yet Ding's most startling point was that despite two decades of apparently satisfactory economic development, the masses had lost faith in the leadership. "People have lost confidence and trust in the government as well as the efficiency and transparency of its decision making," Ding said. The study group decried phenomena such as "corruption and a depraved party style" as the main causes for loss of trust in the CCP authorities. Another noted social scientist, People's University professor Li Lulu, claimed that "China has become a 'risk-prone society,' perhaps even a 'high-risk-prone society.'" Tsinghua University scholar Li Mei expressed the fear that the root of the malaise was that reform had reached a dead end. "The easier parts of reform have all been handled," he noted. "What's left in the reform process consists of difficult-to-tackle elements." It is possible that these outspoken experts were hinting at the fact that the Fourth-Generation leadership might lack the determination to tackle a thoroughgoing makeover of the system.[21]

Gnawing Fears About the "Latin-Americanization" of China

Foreign observers have since the late 1990s sounded warnings about the possible "Latin-Americanization" of the PRC. In a much-noted article in 2004, U.S. scholars George J. Gilboy and Eric Heginbotham express fears that China might be morphing into a country with distinct and antagonistic classes of haves and have-nots—one that is held together by draconian, dictatorial, even quasi-fascist means. Gilboy and Heginbotham describe the yawning gap between rich and poor, as well as the failure to liberalize the political system. They cite benchmarks for South American–style malaise: "political leaders could settle into a collusive relationship with business and social elites; a semi-permanent have-not class might engage in a constant and economically costly low-level war with the entitled minority." While the authors take note of efforts by the Hu-Wen team to alleviate the poverty of peasants, they conclude that "Beijing is in a race against time."[22]

The same alarm bells have been rung by Chinese analysts. Take dissident Bao Tong, the former aide to ousted party chief Zhao. In an essay published in the Hong Kong media in 2002, Bao noted the dangers inherent in "the collusion between power and money," which was based on the fact that the CCP was merely "providing cover for the newly rich minority." The fiery critic pointed out that the nation's legions of peasants—"second-class citizens without property rights, political rights, and personal rights"—could rise up in revolt. Earlier sections of this book have already described how cadres and developers have colluded to cheat peasants of their land. Other examples of the "unholy alliance" between cadre-mandarins and the newly rich include the fact that as of late 2005, 4,878 officials nationwide had illegally invested 737 million yuan to become directors or joint owners of coal mines, including those with inadequate safety equipment.[23]

For Beijing-based social scientist Lan Pingyi, China is facing a watershed in its development. If the gap between haves and have-nots, the powerful and the dispossessed, continue to widen, he warned in mid-2004, the country will be heading toward Latin-Americanization. Lan said similar conditions already obtained in China and quite a few South American countries. These include "the situation of a fortress of unequal distribution where capital is monopolized by a small minority." "While the upper classes have integrated themselves with the global economy, at least 50 percent of the people are mired in the abyss of perennial poverty," he added.[24] Similarly, a commentary in the official *Beijing Review* noted the dangers inherent in the juxtaposition of a class of haves versus one of have-nots. The article said that "a look at China today can show similarities between China's unemployment rate—and the number and income levels of its impoverished population—and those of Latin American countries." It also noted that quite a few European countries were able to avoid the crisis of polarization because "Europe's socialist movements helped countries . . . to use law to protect laborers' rights and interest and increased social security and welfare."[25]

Focusing on purely economic and social factors such as the Gini coefficient, however, explains only half of the picture. A key contributor to the Chinese malaise is stagnation on the front of political reform, which alone holds the promise of empowering *ruoshi tuanti*—especially allowing workers and peasants to form labor unions and other political organizations—to the extent that they will have the requisite bargaining power when battling political and business elites. Lack of liberalization and powersharing is also the main cause behind phenomena such as corruption, which, as Peking University's Professor Ding pointed out, led to the bankruptcy of the authorities' *chengxin*, or trustworthiness.[26]

While Latin-Americanization may have hit other Asian countries with severe degrees of corruption and wealth gaps, this scourge can better be understood in the Chinese context when we also consider the allied phenomenon of Singaporeanization. This refers to efforts to copy at least those aspects of the city-state that have found favor with CCP leaders from Deng Xiaoping onward: a seemingly never-ending mandate of heaven enjoyed by a sole political party; some degree of dynastic politics; and rigid control of the political activities of citizens coupled with the flowering of market-oriented commerce and foreign trade.[27] There are, however, aspects of the "Singapore model"—particularly a largely corruption-free and efficient administration—that seem beyond the reach of even the most zealous CCP reformer. The Hu-Wen team has, for example, refused to let go of the party's control over major aspects of the economy, as well as the army and the legal system.

Horrific Damage to the Environment and to the Quality of Life

Glaciers in the Tibetan plateau are shrinking at a rate of 7 percent a year. Certain segments of the Yellow River, cradle of the Chinese civilization, have dwindled to the size of a stream. Each year on August 18, according to the lunar calendar, tens of thousands of tourists rush to the majestic Qiantang River in Zhejiang Province to witness a huge wave crest. In 2004, however, there was no wave crest in part because of weak rainfall earlier that year. Meanwhile in Gansu Province, the world-famous Moon Tooth Springs near the Dunhuang Caves is drying up. Its water level has fallen by 11 meters in forty years. And look at the world-renowned pine trees in Huangshan Mountain in Anhui Province, which are the darlings of tourists and the stuff of legends. In recent years, so many of the "godly wooden creatures" have died that officials have to put up fake ones to satisfy tourists.[28]

Indeed, yet another tragedy of post-reform China is that ecological damage in this once-beautiful country may have become irrevocable despite belated efforts by the Hu-Wen team to establish the concept of a "green GDP" as well as standards for sustainable development. And while in the old days, for example, during the Cultural Revolution, the results of pollution and related damages might take a generation or so to manifest themselves, it has taken a much shorter time for acts of environmental degradation to be translated into grievous and often lethal damage for people, livestock, and the economy. The World Bank estimates that the economic toll of pollution could eat up between 8 percent and 12 percent of China's GDP. This includes the impact on crops of acid rain and soil degeneration, lower yields of aquatic products, medical bills, lost productivity due to illnesses, relief funds for flood victims, and so forth.[29]

Consider the worsening climatic pattern—as well as the sorry state of the great rivers, which have nourished the Chinese race since time immemorial. Each summer almost without exception, massive flooding takes place along the Yangtze River, inflicting a heavy toll on at least several tens of millions of people. Take, for example, the year 2004, when flooding was relatively mild. Even then, 50 million people were at least temporarily dislocated and economic losses of more than 15 billion yuan were incurred. In all, 70 percent of China's fixed assets and 40 percent of the population are threatened by flooding from various rivers every year. At the same time, drought has persevered in about ten northern provinces, including districts around Beijing. Latest statistics showed that 2.62 million square kilometers of land nationwide has turned to desert, and desertification is costing the country 54 billion yuan a year.[30]

Experts seem to have given up hope of resuscitating the Yellow River. Yet two other major waterways, the Yangtze and the Huai, are likewise imperiled. The official NCNA warned in a late-2004 story that owing to multipronged ecological damage, "the Yangtze could become another Yellow River in ten years' time." The official agency quoted experts such as Professor Ai Feng of the China Development Research Institute as saying the Yangtze was being buffeted on different fronts. Trees along the waterway are being depleted. Pollutants from nearby factories are so serious that large segments of the Yangtze are not only unsuitable for drinking but could damage hydroelectric facilities. "The Yangtze is so dirty that the natural cleaning ability of its water is being lost," Ai said. Moreover, several species of fishes and aquatic life unique to the Yangtze are about to go extinct.[31]

The Huai, which affects the livelihood of some 170 million people, is also on the brink of disaster. This is despite the fact that the State Council and local governments have spent some 60 billion yuan since 1994 to "cure" the river. While the volume of the Huai is only 3.4 percent that of the nation's total waterways, it has to irrigate some one-sixth of China's arable land. The result is that the "utility ratio" of Huai water for irrigation and other purposes is an astounding 71.6 percent, compared to the 30 percent recommended by global bodies. A major scourge is the expansion of village and township enterprises, most of which lack sophisticated pollution-treatment facilities. Moreover, the population along the Huai has grown by 20 million in the past decade. According to an investigation by the Beijing-based *Economics Daily*, fifty-seven water treatment plans have been built since 1994, but for one reason or another, plans for eighty-five more have been delayed. There is also massive corruption. "Only when the officials are clean can the Huai water become clean," has become a popular saying in this area.[32]

A Hobbesean Life for the Underprivileged?

For the nouveau riche minority of Chinese, life seems to be seventh heaven. They patronize well-appointed private clubs, send their kids to international schools, go skiing in Japan or Switzerland, and can look forward to retirement in exclusive houses in choice districts of Shanghai and Beijing, or even overseas. Yet for the majority of Chinese, there is a disturbingly Hobbesean ring to life, which is often brutish and short.

On the surface, that many Chinese are living dangerously could be due merely to the teething pains of development. For example, in 2003, more than 104,000 Chinese died on the road in some 660,000 accidents. A study released by NCNA in late 2004 said about 75 percent of residents in large cities ranging from Guangzhou to Beijing suffered from ill health. "The worrying trend of early death in China has left authorities searching for ways to deal with the problem," the official agency said. However, there seems to be little Beijing can do since typically socialist benefits such as free or hugely subsidized medical care was abolished in the 1990s. An early 2005 survey by a semi-governmental unit said 25 percent of Chinese did not have enough money to seek adequate medical treatment. The number of Chinese without medical insurance jumped from 900 million to 1 billion in 2003. Medical authorities have also noted that mental illness—which affects about 16 million Chinese—has become a "major public health problem." Other official sources even said that mental cases accounted for 20 percent of all diseases in China.[33]

Yet much of the suffering endured by the *ruoshi tuanti* can be directly related to the "Chinese model" of growth. Owing to insufficient—and poorly enforced—labor regulations, working conditions, particularly for rural and migrant workers, are hazardous to the extreme. As discussed earlier in this book, quite a number of workplace disasters in coal mines, fireworks factories, and the like could have been avoided if both the national and regional administrations had come up with ways to rein in what cynics have called the primitive stage of capitalism with Chinese characteristics.[34]

The Hu-Wen team's newfound concern for social justice notwithstanding, not enough is being done to preserve basic human dignity. The shabby treatment accorded the thousand upon thousand of petitioners to both Beijing and the provincial capitals is shocking even by Third World standards. The same goes for victims of diseases such as AIDS. Despite the decision by the Wen government in late 2003 to fully recognize the problem—and the pledge to offer massive state assistance particularly to HIV carriers in the villages—international agencies and experts decry a high degree of coverup and callousness, particularly relating to sufferers who are members of ethnic minorities. Environmental degradation is another factor behind the brutality of life. A 2004 study by the popular magazine *Orient Outlook Weekly* showed that respiratory diseases in the country, including lung cancer, accounted for 25 percent of the world total. One reason could be that one-third of all cigarettes produced in the world are consumed by China. However, air pollution seems to be the main culprit. Studies have found that in practically all industrialized cities, the incidence of lung cancer and related diseases is abnormally high.[35]

Starting in the early 2000s, more and more districts nationwide have experienced higher incidences of cancer as well as an assortment of hard-to-define but lethal diseases. For example, Ci County and She County in predominantly rural Hebei Province, as well as Linzhou County in Henan Province, have cancer rates several dozen times the national average. The same is true for a number of townships and villages along Huai River tributaries such as Huangmengying, a village of 2,400 people in Henan. Local officials say the rate of both stomach and rectal cancer has increased dramatically since the 1990s. Consider the plight of peasant woman Kong Heqin, who said she began falling ill soon after marrying into a Huangmengying family ten years ago. Kong was soon saddled with a debt of 70,000 yuan in a bid to cure a rectal tumor. Medical experts quoted by the mainstream press said the problem with almost all "cancer villages" and "death zones" was pollution caused by factories in the vicinity.[36] However, it is difficult for victims to seek compensation or to initiate legal action.

Then there is the return of "old" diseases that were supposedly gotten under control before the 1980s. For example, the number of tuberculosis patients is going up by 1.45 million a year, making China the second worst-hit nation in the world. And in Dongting Lake and along the Yangtze River, deadly schistosomiasis, or snail fever—an epidemic spread by a parasite carried by snails—has made a comeback after it was pretty much wiped out in the 1950s. Officials estimate that more than 1 million peasants and fishermen, mostly in Hunan and Hubei provinces, might be affected.[37]

A Half-Baked Strategy for Reform and Liberalization

Reform Is Not a Buffet

Reform is not a dinner party—particularly not a buffet where would-be reformers can pick only the fancy or easy-to-digest fare. The problem of Chinese modernization from the late Qing Dynasty onward, however, is precisely that while its rulers are aware of the desperate need to do something, they refuse to go the distance by making a clean break with the past. The tradition of half-hearted reforms was evident in the late–Qing Dynasty elite's attitude toward Westernization, or learning from European, and later American, values, institutions, and technology. Famed minister Zhang Zhidong (1837–1909) coined the classic slogan about this ambivalent approach to modernization: "Chinese learning for fundamental principles and Western learning for practical applications."[38] This meant essentially that the path for modernization would consist in retaining the Chinese—basically a quasi-Confucianist, autocratic, anti-democratic, and to some extent autarkist—system while adopting "Western" scientific, engineering, and technological know-how. For example, in the 1890s, Qing ministers immersed themselves in developing a Western-style navy (even though much of the funding was siphoned off by the hated Empress Dowager Cixi to build the Summer Palace in the outskirts of Beijing). By comparison, the "Meiji Restoration" in Japan, which began in 1868, represented a relatively more thorough attempt by the Tokyo imperial court and elite to study not just Western science and weaponry but law, culture, and philosophy.[39]

China's half-baked, nonholistic approach to the modernization or Westernization drive was briefly interrupted during the May Fourth intellectual movement of 1919, when college students and professors boldly demanded that Mr. De (democracy) and Mr. Sai (science) be welcomed into the country simultaneously. However, the dualistic, near-schizophrenic strain in China's attitude to Western culture and science reasserted itself under the Communists. Mao Zedong and his cohorts would characterize their approach to statecraft—and to epistemology in general—as *yifen wei'er* (divide a phenomenon into two aspects), a kind of dialectical materialism with Chinese characteristics.[40]

On the surface, of course, Mao and his colleagues seemed to be fervent followers of Marx and Engels, prominent social scientists and thinkers who had been nurtured by Western philosophy and economics even as they went about transforming a good segment of these disciplines. In actual fact, the Great Helmsman had rejiggered Marxism and adapted it into a version of Oriental despotism. The Maoists never paid much attention to the liberal and democratic elements in the teachings of Marx and Engels, such as those dealing with the free development of the individual and the relationship between the individual and the state.[41] In fact, it can be argued that Mao drew more inspiration about governance from Chinese classics such as the *Shi Ji* (Historical Memoirs, by Sima Qian, 145?–190? B.C.E.), or *Zizhi Tongjian* (Compendium on Governance, by Sima Guang, 1019–1086), which he had reread dozens of times. And while, like Zhang Zhidong before him, the Red Emperor craved European or Russian weapons and technology, he would have nothing of the progressive ideas of equality and egalitarianism contained in Western Marxist or socialist literature.[42]

This mind-frame of marrying one-party dictatorship on the one hand and Western technology and business practices on the other is found in practically all CCP chieftains after the Cultural Revolution, namely Deng Xiaoping, Hu Yaobang, Zhao Ziyang, Jiang Zemin, Hu Jintao, and Wen Jiabao. Former party chief Zhao, who died in 2005 after fifteen-odd years of house arrest, however, deserves credit for trying to break new ground in political reform partly through borrowing Western institutions and beliefs. For instance, Zhao and his associates discussed in internal brainstorming sessions in 1987 and 1988 the extent to which such Western concepts as the tripartite division of power could be applied to China.[43]

Then there were the initiatives undertaken by Deng, whose contribution to Chinese thought and statecraft remained substantial despite obvious aberrations such as the suppression of the 1989 student movement. During his so-called liberal phase—a reference to the period from the late 1970s to early 1980s—the late patriarch was able to transcend the kind of dualistic approach to and artificial compartmentalization of knowledge that was evident in scholars and cadres from Zhang Zhidong to Mao Zedong. Take, for example, his "white cat/black cat" theory, or the dictum about "crossing the river while feeling for the boulders." Or his insistence that "a policy is okay if it works—and irrespective of whether it is sur-named socialist or capitalist." In the 1980s, he also admonished his colleagues to *buzhenglun*—to stop splitting hairs over the ideological or philosophical nature of a policy or an approach. It was this enlightened approach that enabled Deng to hammer out original ideas such as the "one country, two systems" or "one country, many systems" model for the reunification of Hong Kong and Taiwan.[44]

Taking Deng's holistic teachings one step further, Chinese reformers might come to the conclusion that there is no problem with borrowing even political and philosophical principles from the West as long as these ideas work in China or can promote the welfare and well-being of Chinese. Unfortunately, Deng's thinking changed markedly after the student demonstrations in December 1986, and particularly, the 1989 "counter-revolutionary turmoil." The "New Helmsman" would subsequently underscore the juxtaposition between reform and the open-door policy on the one hand, and the "four cardinal principles" of orthodox Marxism on the other.[45]

And what about Hu and Wen? As of late 2005, these Fourth-Generation leaders had yet to display the clarity and breadth of vision of either Deng (or at least his "liberal persona") or Zhao Ziyang. As we saw in Chapters 3 and 4, Hu and Wen have basically cleaved to the time-honored approach to reform: that is, certain "Western" principles and systems are not applicable to China. Thus, in his address in the ceremony marking of the fiftieth anniversary of the founding of the NPC, Hu said that copying Western political ideals such as multiparty politics and the tripartite division of power would "get China into a blind alley."[46] Given their relatively limited exposure to Western social science heritage, it is not surprising that both Hu and Wen have often turned to the Chinese tradition for inspiration. Hu has gone overboard with his revival of many aspects of Maoism. And Wen has a habit of lacing his speeches with liberal citations of ancient philosophers and scholars ranging from Confucius to Sima Qian of the Western Han Dynasty (206 B.C.E.

to 25 C.E.).[47] At least as far as political ideology is concerned, Hu and Wen seem to be much more comfortable with the tradition of the "sage mandarin" than modern ideas of democracy.

Economic Policy: Battling Residual Obstacles to Full Liberalization

China's Search for Full Market Economy Status

The debate that flared up in 2004 over China's qualifications for full market economy status (FMES) has illustrated residual doubts among Western economists and officials about Beijing's commitment to market reforms three years after China's accession to the World Trade Organization (WTO). The FMES recognition by the United States, the European Union (EU), and other major Western countries would, among other things, make it easier for China to defend itself against mushrooming accusations of dumping. After all, it is much easier for a country with strong residual central-planning mechanisms to influence elements such as pricing. Yet for Beijing, FMES is more than a mere weapon in world-trade maneuvers: FMES confers upon the country the status of having cleared the final hurdle to global recognition of more than twenty-five years of arduous economic reforms. As of the end of 2005, Beijing had persuaded more than thirty countries, including Russia, New Zealand, Brazil, South Korea, and members of the ASEAN regional bloc, to recognize its FMES qualifications. Yet the United States and the EU have so far refused to do so.[48]

While China took some fifteen years in its convoluted process to win accession to the WTO, many observers say it could also take aggressive lobbying—plus more thoroughgoing reforms—for China to be considered a full-fledged market economy. This is despite contentions by the likes of former chief trade negotiator Long Yongtu that China's qualifications for FMES were "self-evident." Officials such as Long have claimed that about 90 percent of the prices in China's markets are determined solely by the forces of supply and demand.[49] Moreover, thousands of national and local-level state fiats and regulations on the economy have been abolished since China's WTO accession. Soon after taking over power, the Hu-Wen administration signaled its commitment to market-oriented liberalization by pushing through an ambitious blueprint for structural changes at the third plenary session of the CCP Central Committee in October 2003. The document, entitled "Decision on Improvement of the Socialist Market Economic System" (hereafter cited as the Central Committee "Decision") listed more than forty areas of the economy where further integration with the international marketplace would take place. Another landmark was the revision of the State Constitution in March 2004. For the first time, the charter recognized the rights of the nonstate sector to compete on an equal footing with the "wholly people-owned sector."[50]

To a considerable extent, China further opened up the market to multinationals, particularly those in the service sector, from 2003 to 2005. Upon seeing the usual brand names associated with a globalized economy—Starbucks, Nike, Louis Vuitton, Wal-Mart, Home Depot, and so forth—a casual visitor to Shanghai and Guangzhou would consider eastern Chinese cities as no different from Hong Kong, Singapore, or even Tokyo. And the Hu-Wen team has opened the door wider even in hitherto disputed areas such as banking, insurance, and stock brokerages. For example, big-name multinationals such as HSBC and Goldman Sachs were allowed to buy into Chinese banks or set up joint-venture financial institutions.[51]

Beneath the surface, however, it is still true that the party and government apparatus maintains considerably tight control over the economy. While the old-style State Planning Commission as well as production targets have been long abolished, Beijing still imposes "guidelines" to achieve an array of political and economic objectives. These include the imperative of job generation and maintaining a sufficiently high degree of grain and energy self-sufficiency. And given that trade accounts for up to 70 percent of GDP, Beijing has also pulled out the stops to maintain annual export growth rates of 30 percent or so. The result is that in many ways, China's economy still remains a *cuguang* one, where growth is often achieved at the expense of efficiency and gross wastage of raw materials.[52]

That the state's highly visible hand is still running a good part of the show was most evident in the controversial *hongguan tiaokong* (macroeconomic control and adjustment) measures taken by the Wen cabinet to cool down the economy through much of 2004. Despite his pro-market proclivities, Wen and his team mainly relied on executive fiats to restrict bank loans to "undesirable sectors" such as cement, iron, and steel, as well as to curtail land-use rights for industrial development. Around 5,000 economic or technological development zones, in addition to hundreds of huge infrastructure projects were axed by the State Council. And it was not until October of that year that Beijing agreed to use standard fiscal levers: the overall interest rate for bank loans was raised by 0.27 percent.[53]

It is also significant that during his first trip to Shanghai since 2000—a brief visit in mid-2004—President Hu tried to pacify disgruntled Shanghai cadres by saying that Beijing followed the policy of *youbao youya* (guarantee some, suppress some) when carrying out its contraction-oriented economic policy.[54] The point, however, was that it was essentially the party-state machinery in Beijing that decided which sectors or areas to safeguard and which to discourage or whittle down.

More Impetus for Market Reforms: New Deal for the Private Sector

Overall, Western government officials and economists have given the Hu-Wen leadership high marks for its encouragement of the no-holds-barred development of the nonstate sector. The CCP Central Committee "Decision" indicated that private firms should be given the same rights as state-owned enterprises (SOEs) in areas including investment, finance, taxation, land use, and foreign trade. "Nonpublic capital should be allowed to enter infrastructure, public utilities, and other sectors not prohibited by laws and regulations," it said. Official economists anticipate that in about ten years' time, the so-called wholly publicly owned sector's share of GDP would decline from the current 33 percent to no more than 20 percent.[55]

Under Beijing's new dispensation, private firms have had relatively better access to resources, in particular bank loans. However, it cannot be said that there is a level playing field in the Chinese economy. Liu Yonghao, one of China's richest entrepreneurs, has been lobbying for the promulgation of a Law on Investment. His point is that certain types of companies, for example, multinationals or joint ventures, still enjoy special privileges such as tax exemption. Liu said in 2004 that under WTO regulations and global norms, all enterprises should be treated the same way.[56] Private enterprises were a major victim of efforts in 2004 to cool down the quasi-bubble economy. Particularly for the three sectors deemed excessively overheated—iron and steel, cement, and aluminum—orders were issued by central authorities to discourage if not shut down medium-sized or small factories, most of which turned out to be nonstate owned. In early 2004, Beijing promulgated new criteria for the registration of iron and steel enterprises. For instance, new plants must have at the least a 1,000–cubic-meter main furnace —and no more than seven tons of coal could be used for turning out one ton of steel. The official *China Business News* quoted a number of owners of medium-sized plants as saying that the new strictures were discriminatory against smaller, nonstate enterprises.[57]

One major imperfection in the area of privatization concerns land, particularly land-use rights in rural areas. Since 1949, all agricultural land has been deemed the "property of the collective." In theory, land-use rights for a specified duration can only be bought and sold under strict government regulation. In practice, local officials—often corrupt ones acting in conjunction with savvy real-estate businessmen—have made available sites close to the cities for property development. This practice has become a prime cause of instability in the countryside (see Chapter 3). Liberal-minded academics have lobbied since the early 2000s for the privatization and sale of rural land whereby the rights of farmers would be safeguarded. Proceeds from the commercialization of this land bank, worth an estimated 25 trillion yuan, could be used to underwrite social security for peasants and rural laborers. According to Beijing-based economist Professor Hu Xingdou, the wealth generated could also become a kind of "seed fund" to enable peasants to make the necessary adjustments while moving permanently to the cities.[58]

Restructuring SOEs, Banks, and Other Institutions

Another major thrust of economic reform under the Hu-Wen team is the restructuring of state-sector firms and factories. At the end of 2005, the number of fully state-owned and partially state-held businesses was around 138,000, down from close to 240,000 in 1998. Sixty percent of the 4,223 large-scale SOEs had already undergone restructuring into shareholding companies of different forms. And the post–Sixteenth Congress CCP leadership has made it clear that the great majority of the state-invested firms will eventually be turned into "mixed-ownership shareholding companies" with investment from diverse sectors including private firms and individuals. Indeed, one of the key theoretical advancements under the Hu-Wen administration is the official recognition that "socialist state ownership should most efficiently manifest itself in shareholding companies." The Central Committee "Decision" said official management of the economy should consist mostly in "providing services for the market and creating a good environment for development"—not direct interference.[59]

Yet it is also clear that at least for the foreseeable future—say the coming twenty years—the state would directly control around 170 mega-SOEs deemed to be strategically important. This was the rationale behind the formation in early 2003 of the State-owned Assets Supervision and Administration Commission (SASAC), which was headed by a top adviser to former premier Zhu, Li Rongrong. Li indicated in 2003 that SASAC would "supervise and manage" 196 firms—which included the oil and steel monopolies as well as transport and telecommunications behemoths—with total assets of 6.9 trillion yuan. And he indicated that the state would not give up control over these conglomerates, which he called "the basis of CCP rule." In 2005, SASAC's giants, whose number had shrunk to 169, contributed half of the total taxes surrendered by all SOEs.[60]

On the surface, of course, this industrial strategy known in the Zhu Rongji era as "getting a firm grip on large [SOEs] and letting go the small ones," seemed to be working. Thus in 2005, SASAC's 169 mega-firms made profits in excess of 600 billion yuan—which accounted for most of the revenues of China's state-sector firms. However, concern has been raised by Western economists as to whether SASAC's "flagship SOEs" have been making giant profits owing to their monopolistic positions—and that the state's refusal to yield control over this big chunk of the economy would impede the development of relatively more competitive private firms or shareholding companies with mixed ownerships. Questions have also been asked about the advisability of the "big is beautiful" doctrine underpinning Beijing's penchant for putting together "aircraft carrier–type" conglomerates.[61]

The Hu administration is also primed to grasp the nettle on the unwieldy banking system, deemed the soft underbelly of the economy. The Central Committee blueprint said the process of off-loading nonperforming loans (NPLs) should be speeded up to enable a number of state banks to be listed on the stock market. Domestic media reported in early 2004 that the Big Four banks had requested a "final" injection of 800 billion yuan to tackle the problem of NPLs, officially estimated at 2 trillion yuan and unofficially at 3.5 trillion yuan or more. Officials of the Ministry of Finance and the central bank—People's Bank of China (PBOC)—noted that the requisite sums might be raised through means including issuing bonds and digging into the country's foreign exchange reserves. Critics, however, have pointed to the less-than-satisfactory results of a similar state rescue operation in 1997 and 1998, when the state injected 270 billion yuan into the so-called Big Four (Bank of China, China Construction Bank, China Industrial and Commercial Bank, and Agriculture Bank), and the latter "sold" 1.4 trillion yuan worth of NPLs to four government-assisted asset management companies.[62]

The State Council was also proceeding with the listing of three of the Big Four banks. As of early 2005, at least eleven banks nationwide had attracted investments from multinational financial institutions including HSBC, IFC, and Citigroup. For example, HSBC held a 19.9 percent stake, worth $1.75 billion, in the Bank of Communications, China's fifth largest. However, industry analysts said foreign banks were wary of plowing huge sums, particularly into the Big Four. In October 2005, the China Construction Bank (CCB) raised $8 billion in its IPO in the Hong Kong Stock Exchange, even though regulatory agencies in the United States were for the time being holding up its application for listing on the New York bourse. But the IPO of Bank of China (BOC), originally scheduled for late 2004, was postponed to 2006. Banking officials claimed that by 2005, the NPL ratios of both the CCB and BOC had been reduced to around 5 percent. Yet foreign economists remained suspicious about the accuracy of these figures, particularly given the fact that "bubbles" in the real estate and other overheated sectors might have created new bad loans in recent years.[63]

To convince the world community of its reform fervor, Wen's State Council has to not only adopt global norms in supervising banking operations but also promote transparency regarding how authorities such as the China Banking Regulatory Commission (CBRC) go about investigating financial scandals. The authorities admitted that in 2003, the PBOC carried out investigations into 4.7 trillion yuan worth of dubious transactions. And during inspections of the Big Four in 2005, CBRC investigators uncovered questionable loans worth 588.5 billion yuan. Yet despite the Hu-Wen administration's commitment to transparency, few details were divulged.[64] A case in point was the series of corruption and mismanagement problems that plagued the BOC and CCB from the late 1990s to 2004. These graft-related irregularities led to the incarceration of ten or so high-level executives in various BOC branches. For example, the flamboyant CEO of the BOC's Hong Kong branch, Liu Jinbao, was nabbed in early 2004 for alleged fraud and corruption. And in March 2005, former CCB chairman Zhang Enzhao was detained for alleged business irregularities. Yet few details of their "crimes" have been released. And there is speculation that the arrests were made so that State Council officials— and their big-name overseas sponsors and PR companies—could prepare for the two banks' IPOs with a clean slate.[65]

Areas of Remnant—and Strong—State Control

While addressing the EU Secretariat during his European tour of mid-2004, Premier Wen pointed out that one major factor behind the lack of market-compatible phenomena in the Chinese economy was outdated "systems and institutions."[66]

Indeed, a major institutional drawback for reform is the still-considerable party-and-state interference in the operations of the market, a problem that is part and parcel of China's political reality. And despite the Hu-Wen team's vaunted ability to douse fires and preempt crises, it has been slow in tackling age-old problems for fear that bolder and more thoroughgoing measures will affect sociopolitical stability. Examples include the artificially low pricing of oil and electricity; the snail's pace in reforming utilities such as the railway system; and lack of courage in off-loading state-held shares in listed companies.

In terms of industrial strategy, the Wen cabinet is to some extent still pursuing former premier Zhu Rongji's long-standing policy of nurturing large, *chaebol*-like conglomerates. This is despite the fact that the negative aspects of *chaebol*-style management have already been amply demonstrated in Japan and South Korea.[67] Close to 200 selected state firms, as well as listed companies where the state is the major shareholder, still have priority access to capital as well as favorable government policies. For example, it is much easier for firms favored by state agencies to get listed on the stock markets both in China and abroad. And the state is committed to giving aid to a select number of "aircraft carrier-like enterprises"—which may be either SOEs or companies with mixed ownership—to become multinationals.[68]

As of 2005, major heads of SOEs and other quasi-official corporations in China, ranging from the banks to the oil companies, were still appointed by party and government units. Although the heads of such firms have assumed Western-style titles such as CEO and CFO, they retain traditional party and administrative rankings. Some are members or alternate members of the CCP Central Committee. And just as in the past, the CCP Organization Department—which recommends candidates for all central and regional-level party and government posts—still has significant say in naming the couple or so top executives of large SOEs.[69]

There are, of course, significant differences between old-style SOE chiefs and executives in the mid-2000s. For example, the salary levels and promotion prospects of the latter are more dependent on market forces—especially the performance of their companies—rather than traditional factors such as ideological purity or relationship with the top leaders. Yet the bulk of government-appointed or government-affiliated business executives—including those of SASAC's films—still cannot freely conduct their business as in Western economies. As U.S.-based economist Qian Yingyi has indicated, many top executives of the biggest banks were party and government officials rather than professional bankers. "The environment in which these senior cadres work means they must put their focus on political matters," he said. "Political factors play a big part in the management of the big banks."[70]

Part of the reason for Beijing's support for the large-scale conversion of SOEs into mixed-ownership shareholding concerns is that the new management—which consists of a Western-style board of directors and professional managers—will have more leeway in operating their businesses according to market and global norms. Moreover, the heads of the transformed companies must be accountable to the shareholders, including minor ones. Yet as Chinese University of Hong Kong business professor Tang Fangfang has pointed out, a good proportion of the members of the boards of directors of Chinese shareholding companies are appointed or recommended by government departments. And there is no mechanism for ordinary shareholders to exercise supervision over the board or the senior management. "In theory, shareholders control the board; but in reality, it's still government control," notes Tang.[71]

Beijing's obsession with control of a substantial number of "aircraft carrier–type" enterprises is also illustrated by its reluctance to share state holdings in companies listed on the two stock markets. As of early 2005, the government still held more than 60 percent of the shares of listed SOEs, which together accounted for 96 percent of the capitalization of the two bourses. A mid-2005 decision by the State Council to incrementally sell off the state-held shares has been criticized as too little, too late. As SASAC's Li indicated, Beijing must be extra-cautious about off-loading state assets because of the need to "protect the interests of both the state and public investors." However, reformist cadres such as NPC vice-chairman Cheng Siwei believe that the stock market must "get out of the 'strange cycle' of a government policy–dominated market." He notes that "serious defects still remain in the market" if it is under undue influence from the policy of the day.[72]

Similar political considerations have affected Beijing's decision to postpone the reform of the foreign-exchange system—particularly the convertibility of the yuan. This was despite the fact that major trading partners including the United States and the EU had been putting pressure on Beijing to either appreciate or float the currency. PBOC governor Zhou Xiaochuan admitted in late 2004 that "there is no timetable for [the completion of] foreign-exchange reform." And Premier Wen added later that decisions on the yuan were a matter of China's "financial sovereignty," a matter that brooked no foreign intervention. Wen had apparently forgotten that the Chinese economy is inextricably tied to the globalized world! While a small appreciation of the yuan did take place in July 2005, it is understood that the ultimate step—letting the exchange rate be fixed by market forces alone—still depends on the leadership's perception of economic and political stability.[73] A key consideration is that if the yuan is revalued at too high a level, exports—and employment—will be dealt a body blow. This is despite the fact that in the early days of reform, more radical economists had suggested that the yuan be rendered fully convertible by 1995, or 2000 at the latest.

While reviewing the economy at the Fifth Central Committee Plenary Session in 2005, Hu and Wen underscored the imperative of innovation, that is, coming up with technology and brands that are uniquely Chinese. As the Eleventh Five-Year Plan document noted, China must "base itself on scientific development and pay the utmost attention to *zizhu chuangxin* [uniquely Chinese innovation]." "We must create a bevy of superior enterprises that have strong global competitiveness, and that have their own intellectual property rights and well-known brands," it said.

Hu later noted that "only with a strong capacity for innovation can a country win the initiative in global competition," adding that "real core technologies" can only be developed by Chinese experts, not bought from abroad. Latest figures showed 39 percent of China's economic growth was due to technological improvements; the comparative figure in advanced countries was 70 percent. And Beijing announced in late 2005 that research-and-development-related (R&D) investments would be boosted from the current 1.23 percent share of GDP to 2.5 percent of GDP by the year 2020.[74]

Yet as the ensuing discussion on Chinese achievements in the arts and sciences will make clear, the crux of the matter is not money or hardware. The ideology, institutions, and control mechanisms of the party-and-state apparatus, which suppresses freedom of expression and awards conformism, do not foster the kind of Silicon Valley–style values that encourage innovation and risk taking in either R&D, marketing, or capital-market maneuvers. This is the main reason why the "world factory" has lagged behind in R&D as well as in confecting world-famous brands. For example, the World Economic Forum said in its *World Competitiveness Report* for 2005 that China's competitiveness had declined by three rungs—to 49th place out of 117 economies surveyed—largely owing to institutional drawbacks including corruption and bureaucratic interference. And while China produces more than 250,000 science and engineering graduates a year, their ability to innovate has been affected by the authorities' anxiety to, in Hu's words, "improve the political thinking of university students." The problem of brain drain is serious, and it is mostly researchers who have gone abroad who have made a name for themselves or their industrial setups.[75]

Finally, there is the residual problem of the military control of still-significant parts of the economy. This is despite the 1998 order given by the Central Military Commission to all army units to sever links with business operations. It is true that in the late 1990s, most companies ranging from trading firms to hotels and karaoke bars run especially by regional and provincial PLA units were surrendered to their civilian counterparts. However, headquarters-level PLA units still own sizable business operations. Much of the industry in the northeast provinces is inextricably linked with PLA concerns such as munitions factories, aircraft manufacturers, and shipbuilding yards. Shenzhen University economist Guo Shiping has argued that a key reason behind the leadership's decision to resuscitate the northeastern region—particularly the heavy industries—is to ensure a "solid base" for development of military plants.[76]

Lacking a Strategy for Democratic Development

Foot-Dragging in Political Reform

In industry, science, technology, and military matters, the CCP leadership has made much of a *kuayue*-style (leap forward) progress. In the 1950s, Mao waxed eloquent about "overtaking Britain and the U.S. in twenty years." After the First Gulf War of 1991, and particularly the Iraq war that began in 2003, PLA strategists under Jiang Zemin and Hu Jintao decided to take the leap into high-tech warfare, particularly the digitization and informatization of weapon systems and command structures.[77]

In political matters, particularly areas dealing with democratization, however, the go-slow, play-safe mentality has prevailed. Many experts have doubts about the argument professed by Chinese cadres the past twenty years for not granting universal-suffrage rights to their charges: that the economic and education levels of Chinese are too low for them to meaningfully participate in elections, which might only lead to chaos. In 2004, large-scale polls were held in Asian countries with comparable socioeconomic conditions to China, including Indonesia and Mongolia. Moreover, also in the same year, the "serve-the-people" leadership under Hu and Wen denied Hong Kong residents—who have one of the highest per capita GDPs in the world—the chance to pick their chief executive by one person, one vote.[78]

In the two years since arriving at the pinnacle of power, Hu and Wen seem to have neglected the advice of more liberal cadres about making up for lost time. According to a social science academic close to top-level think tanks in Beijing, Hu was told not too long after the Sixteenth CCP Congress that he could not afford to imitate ex-president Jiang by putting political liberalization on the back burner. "For thirteen years Jiang kept postponing political reform and he largely got away with it," the scholar said. "But Hu was reminded by his advisers that he could not afford to put off the inevitable for that much longer."[79]

Indeed, liberal party veterans have pointed out that even before 1949, the underground Communist media had loudly proclaimed the CCP's readiness to promote democratic ideas—which were not that different from Western ones. For example, the CCP mouthpiece *Xinhua Daily* editorialized in July 1945 that "the Great Wall and the oceans could not block global trends." "Today is the century of the people, the era of democracy," the paper added. "No one country can isolate itself from the great torrents of democracy. That is why China must—and will definitely—implement democracy."[80] In the early 1950s, none other than Mao Zedong made promises to the non-Communist elite in China that some form of "multiparty politics" would be practiced. For example, a number of non-Communist politicians and intellectuals, as well as those who belonged to the "eight democratic parties," were made ministers of the State Council.

In a perceptive article in the party journal *Outlook Weekly* in mid-2003, deputy party secretary of Hunan Province Sun Zaifu cited two main challenges facing the party: globalization and democratization. "Domestic and foreign experience has told us that if a socialist country led by a Communist party lacks energy, it is because the [party leadership] has failed to pass muster in the tests of the market and democracy," Sun wrote. The cadre pointed out that the party and country would face a devastating defeat if they could not handle the challenges of market competition and political democratization. "It will be futile to avoid these two tests," he added. "It is much better to take the initiative to storm the fortress rather than reacting [to the challenges] passively." Peking University's Yu Keping agrees. Yu noted in 2004 that he was opposed to the "shock therapy" carried out in Eastern Europe in the 1990s, adding that a gradualist, incremental approach was better. However, the professor issued the caveat that gradualism did not mean that "political and economic reform should always be implemented slowly." "We should resolutely go after a breakthrough when breakthroughs are called for," he indicated. "We should not hesitate even if there were to be localized and short-term shocks."[81]

As discussed in earlier segments of this book, the Hu-Wen team has come up with meager initiatives in pushing democracy. As University of Victoria Sinologist Wu Guoguang pointed out, Hu did not seem to empathize with the forward-looking ideas that were developed during brainstorming sessions on reform that were sponsored in the mid-1980s by then party leaders Zhao Ziyang and Hu Qili. In effect, even during the more progressive phases of the thirteen-year Jiang administration, the ex-president's liberal advisers had at least studied possible ways to speed up the democratization timetable. For example, during the short-lived Beijing spring of 1998—which coincided with Bill Clinton's visit to China—relatively open-minded Shanghai Faction affiliates such as Liu Ji and Wang Huning had put forward proposals for liberalization. Thus Wang, a former Shanghai political science professor, suggested extending and upgrading the level of universal-suffrage elections from the village to that of townships, counties, and even provinces in twenty years or so.[82]

At his press conference at the end of the 2004 NPC, Premier Wen waxed eloquent about the leadership's eagerness to launch political reform. He noted that a holistic approach was needed for reform because "experience of the past and present" had cast doubt on the validity of "reform that depends on the success of only one aspect." "Taking the medium to long term, the reform of the economic system and that of the political system—which includes people's mind-set—cannot be separated from each other," Wen avowed.[83] Unfortunately, Wen and his colleagues have not lived up to their commitments.

At least from one perspective, however, the Resolution on Strengthening the Construction of the Party's Governance Ability of late 2004 represented Hu's game plan for extending the CCP's mandate of heaven in the absence of liberalization. The document made it clear that the Hu leadership was aiming at the "self-perfection of socialism"—as well as beefing up the role of the party in organs and departments including the legislature, mass organizations, and economic entities. On the one hand, Hu and Wen have stressed the need to "put the people first," even "democratic administration and democratic supervision." Yet this is at most a kind of noblesse oblige. As Vice-President Zeng Qinghong put it, boosting the party's ruling ability meant "running the administration well and holding power well for the sake of the people."[84] Yet there was no provision for the possibility that the people might be able to throw out the leaders of the party, let alone discard the CCP and form another ruling entity.

The Hu-Wen Team Hones Control Mechanisms

In its explanation of the significance of the Resolution, the official NCNA lumped, on the one hand, "running the administration for the people" and "ensuring that the people are masters of the country," together with, on the other hand, "perfecting the people's democratic dictatorship" and "upholding the principle of democratic centralism." [85] It must be remembered that in a CCP tradition that goes back to the days of the Yanan caves, enforcing "people's democratic dictatorship" has meant, in actual practice, using force to crush dissent. And "democratic centralism" is a euphemism for concentrating power in the *dangzhongyang* (party central authorities.)

Indeed, it was at an internal talk at the end of the Fourth Plenum—when the idea of a "harmonious society" was introduced—that Hu indicated for the first time that the "Gorbachev road" was no good for either China or the socialist enterprise. The party chief told Central Committee members and other senior cadres that "Gorbachev is a traitor to the socialist cause, and the main culprit for the fall of the Soviet bloc." He added that the CCP must guard against the mindless Westernization and bourgeois-liberal tendencies evident in Gorbachev's Soviet Union. While Hu has never given any public assessment of Vladimir Putin's policies, it seems evident that he has been following the ex-KGB officer's tough tactics to muzzle dissent. Particularly after the "color revolutions" in Central Asian countries such as Kyrgyzstan and Ukraine in the first half of 2005, Hu repeatedly warned of the danger of dissident groupings and NGOs—which might be in cahoots with "anti-China forces abroad"—undermining the CCP's predominance.[86]

The security apparatus's crackdown on dissent has intensified since Hu took over the CMC chief's post in September 2004. As BBC commentator Haoyu Zhang put it, "achieving 'harmony' seems to have meant that any dissenting voices are dealt with [by the authorities] swifter and harsher than ever before." A couple of party documents issued in late 2004 further restricted the maneuvers of not only avant-garde intellectuals but also octogenarian elders who used to work with late party chiefs Hu Yaobang and Zhao Ziyang. A Publicity Department document released in November carried President Hu's injunction that "we must learn from Cuba and North Korea in managing ideological and media circles." In December, three writers and activists well known in Hong Kong and the west, Yu Jie, Liu Xiaobo, and Zhang Zuhua, were detained for a day apparently as a warning to the entire intellectual community. And at least twenty-odd writers and retired liberal cadres were harassed and detained in the run-up to and after the death of late party chief Zhao in January 2005.[87]

The authorities were also targeting NGOs as well as activist intellectuals such as lawyers who were at the forefront of seeking social justice for *ruoshi tuanti*. In early 2005, for example, Guo Guoding, a Shanghai lawyer who had defended many dissidents, had his office ransacked by police. Another socially conscious attorney, Gao Zhisheng, said he had been served repeated warnings by police. "Many lawyers are thrown into jail each year in China, because the more attention they attract [while defending the suppressed], the more likely they'll expose the inherent evils in the current legal system," Gao noted. Other activists blacklisted by the authorities, such as Tsinghua University professor Qin Hui, were active in marathon campaigns to halt the construction of several dams in western China that were seen as damaging the environment.[88]

By late 2005, there were disturbing signs that cadres and police in various localities were resorting to force to put down demonstrations, and that they were connived at if not encouraged by Beijing. Two such cases took place in prosperous Guangdong Province just next door to Hong Kong. In early October, police—together with members of the local mafia—arrested and beat up dozens of residents of Taishi Village after they had demonstrated against the reinstatement of a director of the local Village Administrative Committee who had been impeached for corruption. Several lawyers who had helped the farmers were also detained. Things got worse in December after thousands of peasants and fishermen in coastal Dongzhou protested against the construction of a coal fire station in the village. PAP officers called to the scene sprayed tear gas—and then live bullets—at the protestors, killing twenty villagers, according to eyewitnesses. While the local deputy police chief was detained, the official NCNA report claimed the demonstration was a "serious crime" engineered by "a small group of instigators." Western commentators pointed out that the Dongzhou bloodbath was the first time after 1989 that paramilitary police opened fire on unarmed protestors.[89]

The Dearth of "Soft Power," New Thinking, and New Ideas

Given Beijing's anxiety to dispel the "China threat" bogey—and to popularize the "peaceful rise" theory (see Chapter 5)—much attention has been paid to projecting the country's soft power. Chinese analysts have largely followed Harvard professor Joseph Nye's definition of hard and soft power: the former refers to economic, technological, and military prowess, and the latter to culture and ideas. Not surprisingly, pro-government as well as relatively independent theorists and academics are convinced that cultivating *ruan quanli* (soft power) is an ideal way for China to emerge as a quasi-superpower in a nonthreatening manner. Moreover, extending the influence of contemporary Chinese thinking and culture would blunt the criticism that fifty-five years of CCP rule has detracted from rather than added to the glories of Chinese civilization. As *Outlook Weekly* commentator Zhao Changmao noted in a mid-2004 article, the country must "boost the attractiveness of its culture and ideas as well as the ideals of harmony and reconciliation."[90]

Since the early 2000s, the Beijing leadership has, in terms of what is known in party jargon as "overseas propaganda work," been concentrating on "soft" elements such as Chinese culture and performing arts. For example, the Chinese cultural festival in Paris in early 2004—which coincided with President Hu's visit—was given front-page treatment by the global media if only because the French decided to flood the Eiffel Tower in a red tinge. Two other, more colorful, events in 2004 highlighted the potentials of Chinese *ruan quanli* even more. One was the Beijing team's triumphal performance at the Summer Olympics in Athens in August 2004, in which they were three gold medals short of displacing the United States as the world sports superpower. The other event, the celebration of the 600th anniversary of the start of the voyages of famed Ming Dynasty mariner Admiral Zheng He, inspired animated discussion about different ways of achieving—and popularizing —Chinese greatness. Eunuch seafarer Zheng (1371–1435) made history in the fifteenth century when he undertook seven voyages over twenty-eight years to lands as far away as Africa. As Lawrence Ho, a Phoenix TV commentator, said, Ming Dynasty China could at that time have become an imperialistic power by occupying dozens of different countries. Yet, Ho added, China was content with spreading its culture, arts, and sciences.[91]

Both Third- and Fourth-Generation leaders have laid stress on reviving Chinese culture and boosting its global appeal. Thus, in 2001, ex-president Jiang admonished artists and writers to "make Chinese culture more attractive and inspiring to people everywhere." And while visiting the United States in late 2003, Premier Wen waxed eloquent about "the rich and never-ending reach of Chinese culture." Wen pointed out that the core of Chinese culture and values was harmony, and in particular, *he'erbutong,* or "seeking harmony in spite of differences."[92]

Certainly, China's cultural and other kinds of "soft" influences have been spreading quickly in tandem with its fast-developing economic might. The number of Asians, including South Koreans and Japanese, studying Chinese language and culture both in their own countries and in China has shot up exponentially in the past five years. This trend is also spreading to the United States and Europe. An estimated 30 million foreigners were studying Chinese in 2004, and the figure was expected to grow to 100 million by 2007. Beijing's official Chinese-language proficiency test—the equivalent of the TOEFL (Test of English as a Foreign Language)—is now being administered in more than thirty-six countries. Most importantly, despite China's controversial record in areas such as trade and human rights, China's image in the global village is generally positive. A poll conducted in twenty-two countries by the BBC World Service in early 2005 showed that 48 percent of respondents welcomed the expansion of China's role in the world. The corresponding figure for the United States was only 38 percent.[93]

It remains to be seen, however, whether China can charm its neighbors—and the world—with its soft power without the country going through the necessary modernization and democratization processes. For example, the "China threat" theory will continue to hold water for many governments in the region as long as transparency about the PLA remains low, and the country's nationalism as well as global power projection continue to expand relentlessly.

Insufficient New Thinking on Political Philosophy and Foreign Policy

Whether the Fourth-Generation leadership is equal to the task of revitalizing Chinese civilization and spreading Chinese soft power, however, hinges on their ability to encourage creativity and new ways of thinking. The large-scale celebration of the birthdays of Mao and Deng in 2003 and 2004 respectively has betrayed the lack of originality on the part of the Hu-Wen leadership. On both occasions, President Hu heaped exaggeratedly generous praise on his predecessors. Totally glossing over the blunders of these CCP forebears, Hu has vowed to continue in their footsteps (see Chapter 1 and 2). Given their anxiety to uphold orthodoxy, Hu and like-minded twenty-first-century cadres might have difficulty convincing their countrymen and foreigners of their ability to forge new paths in governance and political philosophy.

But perhaps Hu and Wen are not to blame. Deng, perhaps the most original thinker in Communist China, never worked out a viable system or cosmology to "modernize" Marxism-Leninism. His response to the collapse of the Soviet bloc in the early 1990s was effective but hardly trail-blazing: concentrate on building the economy while arrogating more power to the party. By contrast, Communist leaders in Russia and Eastern Europe came up with out-of-the-box notions to re-tool their unwieldy political and economic mechanisms. It is arguable, of course, whether methods such as the "shock therapy" tried out in Russia and other former Soviet-bloc nations in the 1990s were successful—or applicable to China. Certainly, official Chinese academics and commentators are scornful of the experiments conducted by most members of the former Eastern bloc. Yet the likes of Boris Yeltsin, Lech Walesa, and Vaclev Havel tried at least to ring in the new, whereas cadres in China have to some extent contented themselves with wallowing in the ruts of dynastic politics.[94]

In diplomacy and reunification matters, Deng came out with the highly original idea of "one country, two systems," which has been touted as a formula for solving not only the Taiwan and Hong Kong "problems" but also differences between the two Koreas. At least before the Tiananmen Square massacre, Deng was liberal in his interpretation of the "two systems" mantra. Thus, he once proposed that Beijing did not need to station troops in the special administrative region (SAR). And the patriarch invited two of Hong Kong's fervid democrats, Martin Lee and Szeto Wah, to sit on the Drafting Committee for the Basic Law, Hong Kong's mini-constitution. Things, however, have changed dramatically after 1997—and especially after the watershed July 1, 2003, demonstration by more than half a million SAR citizens, which eventually led to the resignation of the unpopular chief executive Tung Chee-hwa in early 2005. Beijing has been criticized for overplaying its hand in efforts to restrict the speed of democratization in the SAR.[95] A similar pattern of gradual tightening up can be detected regarding Beijing's treatment of Taiwan.

As discussed in Chapter 5, the Hu-Wen team's foreign policy has contained forward-looking elements. It can even be argued that, backed by the country's fast-growing economic and military clout, Fourth-Generation leaders have been much more daring and imaginative in diplomacy than in domestic affairs. For example, there are laudatory elements in the concept of *heping jueqi,* the "peaceful rise of China." The Hu leadership has displayed initiatives aplenty in mending fences with erstwhile enemies such as India and Vietnam. Beijing has made strides in cementing ties with faraway countries in Africa and Latin America. And its decision to consolidate a "strategic triangular relationship" with Russia and India seems a stroke of diplomatic acumen. The country has also made a switch toward multilateralism—and played a more active role in international diplomacy, including the solution of regional problems such as the Korean nuclear crisis (see Chapter 5).[96]

Yet the Hu-Wen team has broken no new ground with the United States and Japan. It can be argued that the Hu and Wen are less flexible than, say, the late Zhou Enlai and Hu Yaobang, in handling relations with Tokyo. For example, both Zhou and former party general secretary Hu were able to build bridges to disparate elements in Japanese politics. While Beijing is probably on the mark in sounding alarms about the rise of right-wing sentiments in Japan, its perceived Japan bashing seems to have alienated a broad cross-section of Japan society. An opinion survey released in Japan at the end of 2004 noted that the proportion of the Japanese public that felt "close to China" had slipped to 37.6 percent from 47.9 percent the year before. And anti-China feelings have risen since the three weeks of anti-Japan demonstrations in March and April of 2005.[97]

Regarding relations with the United States, veteran diplomatic scholar Liu Jianfei has proposed, among other things, the original idea of "enthusiastically pushing forward political structural reform" as a means to relax tension between the two powers. While stressing that China would not copy Western models, Liu noted that "the progress of China's democratization is nonetheless a major factor in influential Sino-U.S. ties." He added that while China was not obliged to accommodate American demands, the country "can absolutely push forward solid political-structural reform within permissible conditions."[98] The problem with the Fourth-Generation team, however, is that it has proven lily-livered even in circumscribed areas of liberalization.

Dubious Achievements in Culture, the Arts, and Science

China is a country with the longest continuous civilization in the world; it is also one where parents are willing to sacrifice a lot to ensure that their children will have the best education. It is true, of course, that much of the originality and inventiveness of the intelligentsia has been destroyed or at least inhibited by decades of Marxist regimentation, especially during the Cultural Revolution. Yet even after more than twenty-five years of the reform and open-door policy, this nation of 1.3 billion people has not been able to produce a sizable body of world-class talents in culture, the arts, and science.

Chinese have so far failed to win a single Nobel Prize. The self-righteous official press has sometimes put it down to a Western "bias" against socialist achievement. Yet Beijing's negative reaction to a Chinese-French writer, Gao Xingjian, snatching the literature award in the year 2000 exposed much of the underlying reason for the dearth of creativity in the country: lack of tolerance for diversity, and the tendency to take a "pan-political," censorious attitude toward unorthodox academic and cultural pursuits. The official media largely ignored Gao's prize, and the novelist and dramatist was discouraged from attending gala functions hosted by Paris on the occasion of President Hu's visit in early 2004. To this day, Gao's trail-blazing work has hardly been mentioned in nonpolitical venues such as literature and cultural magazines. This is particularly jarring because Gao has studiously tried to avoid politics since leaving his native land for France in the mid-1980s.[99]

It is also not a coincidence that perhaps the best-known cultural icons hailing from China in the past decade or so are figures who are either supporters of the regime, such as film director Zhang Yimou, or stars whose professions do not touch on politics, such as basketball legend Yao Ming. Perhaps this also explains that the one cultural arena where China has excelled most is sports. In terms of training and endurance, Chinese athletes have blazed trails in areas ranging from gymnastics to volleyball. However, Chinese achievement in sports, which was given due recognition at the Athens Olympics, hardly qualifies as an element of "soft power." The global media has focused on "state regimentation"—for example, sending ten- or even eight-year-olds from their peasant homes to the county or provincial sports school for several years of vigorous, bone-crushing training—rather than the beauty and grace of the world-class athletes.[100]

In literature, which is intimately linked to politics, China's performance has been singularly lackluster. The several literary lions who distinguished themselves before 1949, notably novelists Qian Zhongshu and Shen Chongwen, basically stopped writing serious creative works in the mid-1950s. Many of the most promising writers among the younger generation have chosen to settle in the West, and in some cases, taken up English as their language of choice.[101]

While discussing China's soft power, *Outlook Weekly*'s Zhao claimed that "China's attempt to build up soft power and to boost its international influence has been subject to interference by American cultural hegemonism." And while trying to explain why quite a few notable Chinese men of letters had failed to win the Nobel literature award, revered martial-arts novelist Jin Yong claimed that the Nobel committee was primarily looking at Western literary works.[102] Yet what some Chinese commentators have failed to recognize is that Asian countries ranging from rich Japan to relatively poor India have since the 1940s had an influence on the global cultural scene that is arguably more substantial than China's. One can cite, for example, the widely admired Japanese cinema, which established a world-class reputation as early as the 1960s, when the Japanese economy had hardly taken off.

Take a look also at China's checkered, and generally disappointing, report card in scientific achievement. Fourth-generation leaders such as Hu still like to play up the "innate superiorities of socialism," for example, in the area of mobilizing people to build infrastructure projects or to *gongguan* (seek breakthroughs) in scientific pursuits. There are quite a few examples of scientific and technological discoveries under state sponsorship and regimentation. Examples in the past few years have included the invention of various types and makes of silicon chips under the so-called China chip engineering project, one of whose leaders was Dr. Jiang Mianheng, the son of ex-president Jiang. Beijing has also become a world leader in genetics and biotechnology. State-funded scientists have been able to decode the genome of materials including rice and silkworms in a matter of months. The government is spending more on R&D: close to 2 percent of GDP, as compared to 3 percent in the United States. Coastal cities have also benefited from laboratories set up by multinationals such as Microsoft and Intel.[103]

There are also obvious advantages to scientific development in socialist or non-democratic countries. For example, there are fewer inhibitions about research in ethically controversial areas such as cloning and stem cells. And even in the post–WTO accession environment, government departments can up to a point help to popularize products based on new discoveries, thus enabling at least well-connected high-tech firms and labs to break even much earlier than is usually the case in the West. Yet these advantages are no substitute for the spirit of freedom of expression, which is the soul of first-class research.[104] For the past decade or so, the phenomenon of politics hampering academic research has vastly diminished in the hard sciences—and to a lesser extent, in areas in the humanities and social sciences that do not have a direct bearing on ideology. Yet a new impediment to academic excellence has emerged: it is common for professors in Chinese universities to spend a good chunk of their time on boosting relationships with officials as well as making money in "extracurricular activities." As Harvard mathematics professor Shing-tung Yau has pointed out, corruption, influence-peddling, and even plagiarism have made huge inroads in Chinese academe. Yau, who has helped train Chinese academics, warns that unless such undesirable trends are stopped, "the quality of Chinese research could retrogress significantly." In 2005, a number of famous professors left big-name universities such as Tsinghua for reasons including college administrators' insistence on students passing exams in political ideology.[105]

The Dearth of New Ideals and the Rise of Materialism

Failure to Construct an Alternative Philosophy

The phenomenon known to Chinese thinkers as the dearth of philosophy has worsened in the Hu-Wen administration. After the death of communism in the wake of the Tiananmen Square bloodbath as well as the collapse of the Berlin Wall, all that Deng could do was to offer Chinese a kind of crass consumerism: the late patriarch was convinced that people would be happy with Chinese-style socialism if poverty could be eliminated and their standard of living kept rising.

While Premier Wen is in many ways different from Deng, he gave more or less the same message when he told an audience in Brussels during his mid-2004 EU tour that his government's ability to feed 1.3 billion people was "China's big contribution to human civilization."[106]

It is a truism in social sciences, however, that material goods alone are insufficient to keep the people happy. Chinese, particularly those who have become disillusioned by the Cultural Revolution and other ugly political campaigns, yearn for something meaningful to fill their spiritual vacuum. The emergence of the Falun Gong, which had a special appeal for disadvantaged sectors such as the unemployed and hapless retirees, should serve as a warning to the leadership. The rise of Christianity is another major sign of the times. Conservative estimates state that by the early 2000s, there were 12 million Catholics and 30 million other Christians in the country—not counting the tens of millions of adherents to underground religious orders and organizations. This is despite the CCP leadership's constant harassment of underground house churches.[107]

For quite a sizable portion of Chinese who have not converted to any religion, money-worship seems to be the in thing. One of the most eloquent critics of a Mammonism-driven society is reformer Mao Yushi, a senior member of a private think tank in Beijing. "Rich people in our society are not necessarily happy, but grievances are piling up in the hearts of the poor," Mao said. "However, the main goal of the authorities is to increase material wealth—and this means money has become the yardstick for measuring success and status in society," he added. "The total quantity of happiness in society has actually decreased as a result of crass consumerism."[108]

Peking University scholar Wang Yuequan thinks that Chinese society is entering "a period of no beliefs." "The middle and white-collar classes are merely pursuing materialistic satisfaction," Wang said. "They have fallen into the abyss of faithlessness." The social sciences professor added that many youths were merely chasing after the "three American items"—potato chips, silicon chips, and movies. Moreover, Wang argued, the millions of peasants who have entered the cities as migrant workers have been cut off from their rural roots. Tension in society has increased because while the rural laborers have picked up urban-style consumerism, they do not have the means to satisfy their longings.[109]

Examples of the most tacky commercialism that is being splashed across the front pages of growing numbers of Chinese tabloids could make Mao or even Deng turn over in their graves. There were, for example, cases of female college students becoming prostitutes or agreeing to be impregnated by childless millionaires for fees of up to 500,000 yuan. Then there was the craze of women of all ages undergoing plastic surgery, even in clinics that had dubious doctors and equipment. And the first-ever beauty pageant tailored for "artificially made belles" in late 2004 became the talk of the town in many cities. Among the contestants was sixty-two-year-old Liu Yulan, who had embellished six parts of her body. As Chinese University of Hong Kong scholar Lang Hanping noted, the "man-eat-man

phenomenon" in China has worsened to a degree "not seen in 5,000 years" because all types of faiths, beliefs, and traditions have been wiped out by a relentless
wave of commercialism and materialism.[110]

The Halfhearted Revival of Confucianism

The year 2004 marked a sizable revival of Confucianist culture with a series of
seminars and exhibitions marking the 2,555th birthday of the Great Sage. Officiat-
ing at an international symposium on Confucianism, CPPCC chairman Jia Qinglin
noted that the CCP and the government had always underscored the importance of
preserving and developing "superior traditional culture" including Confucianist
ideals. "We must use a scientific attitude and use scientific methods to diligently
delve into and study Confucianist culture in order to absorb its essence and shed
its imperfections," Jia said.[111]

Jia, an official saddled with rumors of corruption—and hardly known for his
erudition—would hardly seem to be an appropriate official spokesman for Confucianism. However, it is true that quite a number of relatively liberal cadres have
urged a reexamination of Confucianism. These cadres included former CPPCC
chairman Li Ruihuan; Gu Mu, the "father" of the special economic zones; and
former Guangdong governor Ye Xuanping. Li, a Politburo Standing Committee
member who retired at the Sixteenth CCP Congress, is a long-time advocate of the
tradition of the Golden Mean, especially the concepts of harmony and peaceful
co-existence. Li, who was once close to Hu, is thought to have had a big influence
on the Hu-Wen team's philosophy of "putting people first" and "harmonious social development." For example, in his speech as CPPCC leader in early 2002, Li
urged members to "display a dynamic role in maintaining social harmony, stability, and well-coordinated development."[112]

The Confucianist creed was also applied by Li to foreign affairs. In a meeting
with Singapore president S.R. Nathan in 2001, Li indicated that the Confucianist
belief of "harmony is supreme" was the antithesis of "hegemonism." "Do not do to
others what you would not have them do to you," Li quoted the Great Sage as
saying. More recently, this ethos was reflected in a statement by Premier Wen
while marking the fiftieth anniversary of the establishment of the "Five Principles
for Peaceful Coexistence" in mid-2004. Wen cited a Confucian saying: "10,000
different things are nurtured [by the Creator] and they do not harm each other
while going about their own ways."[113]

Harvard professor of Chinese philosophy Wei-ming Tu has argued that a kind
of neo-Confucianism informs much of the thinking of the Hu-Wen administration,
including the principle of *yiren weiben* (putting people first) and *goujian hexieshehui*
(building a harmonious society). Tu, known as "the father of neo-Confucianism,"
noted that "putting people first" was taken directly out of the *Book of Mencius*—
Mencius being one of Confucius' closest disciples. He noted that Premier Wen
was familiar also with the ideas of Confucianists down the ages, such as the famed

scholar Zhang Zai (1020–1077). Thus, in his lecture at Harvard University in December 2003, Wen cited Zhang's famous dictum, "Establish a [humane] purpose for heaven and earth; build up a good life for the people; and open up the vista of peace for millennia." Tu noted that various quasi-Confucianist ideals proposed by Hu and Wen for improving the ruling ability of the party and running China in general represented "an intellectual consensus [among the Chinese political elite] with [a] broad cultural basis."[114]

The big question, however, was whether the CCP leadership could successfully propagate the ideals of neo-Confucianism as interpreted by masters such as Professor Tu, for example, by putting emphasis on humanitarian values and tolerance for divergence. And how about the pro-democratic ideals of Confucius and Mencius? These sages lived, of course, before mechanisms of democracy such as elections were popularized. Confucius, for example, noted that the people had a right to throw out rulers who had lost their mandate of heaven. And Mencius emphasized that virtuous emperors and leaders must base their administration on the wishes of the people.[115]

Moreover, quite a few Beijing intellectuals fear that the Hu-Wen team is only after an adulterated type of "authoritarian Confucianism." It is widely noted, for example, that in the early 1980s, the Lee Kuan Yew administration in Singapore spent a lot of resources on reviving Confucianism to encourage compliance with the city-state's patriarchal style of governance. And insofar as Hu and Wen's partial revival of Confucianism is motivated by somewhat Machiavellian and opportunistic purposes, it might be difficult for Beijing to ensure that "neo-Confucianism" will win the support of the populace let alone exert a substantial influence on neighboring countries.[116]

The Great Chengxin Crisis

While many analysts have focused on unemployment, the shaky financial sector, or the ever-worsening environment as the biggest obstacles to China's stability and prosperity, not as much attention has been paid to something more serious: the across-the-board bankruptcy of trust and good faith in Chinese society. The profusion of dubious and fake practices in governance and business—as well as in everyday life—has impeded China's economic globalization as well as political reform.

What Beijing journalists call the crisis of *chengxin* (honesty and trust) has hit areas of life ranging from sports and education to politics. The severity of the *chengxin* problem is most obvious in the commercial world. The official media have reported that the dishonesty factor has been responsible for damages of up to 600 billion yuan a year.[117] This figure includes losses incurred by victims of shoddy products and business deals—as well as wasted commercial opportunities because of failure to construct a credit regime. If a high percentage of companies and customers alike have a tendency to cheat, credit cards and similar systems that are pillars of a modern and increasingly web-based economy cannot be erected. As former NPC vice-chairman Jiang Chunyun put it, *chengxin* and creditworthiness are the basis of the market mechanism that China is trying so hard to build. "It is necessary to encourage healthy trends, fight bad tendencies, and punish those who are dishonest and who violate business rules and sabotage the economic order," NCNA quoted Jiang as saying.[118]

Up to the mid-1990s, most *chengxin*-related transgressions manifested themselves in fake household goods, liquor, or medicine. In recent years, thousands of investors have been bilked of billions of yuan by the questionable practices of companies ranging from private, fly-by-night operations to big-name, listed corporations. Well-educated but unscrupulous stockbrokers have turned the bourses into casinos. Various valiant attempts have been made by businessmen and professionals to meet the *chengxin* challenge. For example, quite a few accounting firms have publicized "pledges of honesty" to customers. They have promised not to cook the books and to go by advanced international norms. And provinces and cities including Zhejiang, Guangdong, Shanghai, and Wenzhou have set up web-based credit networks. Lists of honest and law-abiding companies, as well as those given to double-dealing, are posted on websites for the benefit of consumers as well as institutions such as banks and credit-rating agencies.[119]

The *chengxin* curse is more difficult to exorcize outside the business world. Take the culture of chicanery that seems prevalent in the lucrative sector of soccer, China's most popular sport. The early 2000s witnessed dozens of scandals involving so-called black whistles—or referees who accepted bribes to rule in favor of a certain team. Fakery and deception have eaten into more established pillars of society such as schools and institutes of higher learning. Departments including the Ministry of Education, the Communist Party's Organization Department, and the police have joined forces in cracking down on the growing phenomenon of bogus diplomas—many of which are purchased at big expense by senior cadres. Indeed, a 2004 investigation by relevant departments found that 15,000 cadres nationwide were holding bogus or faked diplomas.[120]

Even the Central Party School, the highest custodian of Marxist canon, has been slammed for liberally giving away master's and doctoral degrees to officials who hire ghost writers for their dissertations. Each year, the Education Ministry has to dispatch thousands of inspectors nationwide to check whether students, sometimes with the aid of teachers as well as newfangled, IT-enabled equipment, are cheating at college entrance examinations. In mid-2004, the hundreds of thousands of high school graduates had to sign a "*chengxin* exam pledge" before taking part in perhaps their lives' most important test.[121]

There are doubts as to whether the *chengxin* nut can be cracked until CCP authorities have demonstrated a willingness to be honest and above board. Evidence that the central government is not above a dirty trick or two goes beyond its well-documented penchant for embellishing production and GDP statistics. Beijing has routinely used information—or disinformation—campaigns to influence the stock market for economic as well as political purposes. Top officials have in the past few years used editorials in *People's Daily* and other mouth-pieces to send bullish, buy-at-all-costs messages to the country's 70 million or so *gumin,* or stock buyers.[122]

And what about *chengxin* at the highest level of politics? Former president Jiang ran afoul of party regulations and traditions when he refused to step down from the CMC chairmanship at the Sixteenth CCP Congress. Attempts by Jiang and his cronies to promote even unqualified Shanghai Faction affiliates to senior posts also constituted a violation of the people's trust. And how about Jiang's much-ballyhooed "Theory of the Three Represents," which made possible the empowerment of "new classes" including private entrepreneurs? For many of the country's disadvantaged groups, including peasants and laborers—who are still deemed the "vanguard of the revolution"—Jiang's decision to welcome members of the "new classes" into the party smacked of the most iniquitous betrayal of trust and good faith.

Indeed, the CCP's gravest crisis could be that the people have lost faith in its ability to reform itself. In a survey of 109 leading experts conducted by the CASS in early 2004, 73 percent said that of all social sectors, party and government cadres were the biggest beneficiaries of reform measures. This meant essentially that when drafting and implementing policies, officials sought to take care of them-selves before bringing benefits to the masses. Another survey of residents in Shang-hai later that year showed that nearly 60 percent of respondents thought ongoing anti-corruption measures—including pledges made by leaders to implement clean government—were either "of no use" or "do not have obvious results."[123]

Waiting for the Fifth Generation

Challenges Awaiting the Next Generation of Leaders

The concept of *zhizheng nengli* (governance ability) was actually first raised well before the September 2004 Central Committee Plenum. In late 2001, the Beijing-based *Guangming Daily* carried an interesting commentary on how the CCP should "improve its ruling methods so as to raise administrative standards." The official paper noted that administration must be based on rule by law, extermination of graft, and the ideal of "small government, big service." It said the CCP must "ab-sorb into its ranks the most distinguished members of the Chinese race." The piece added that the authorities should be "more enthusiastic in learning from the supe-rior fruits of the political culture of capitalist democracy."[124] Can the *disidai,* or Fourth-Generation leadership, acquit itself of these tasks? Equally significant is whether the *disidai* elite could go one step further in pluralizing the ruling system and society—if not actually legalizing non-CCP parties—and in privatizing the economy. But do they have enough determination, time, and the requisite socio-economic milieu?

The one question that most haunts members of the Fourth-Generation leadership may be: will theirs be a mere transitional epoch? In other words, owing to constraints of ideology and force of circumstances, the likes of Hu and Wen might not have the opportunity to demonstrate their worth and come up with thoroughgoing reformist agendas during the decade allotted them from 2002 to 2012. (At the time of the Eighteenth CCP Congress in 2012, Hu and Wen will both be seventy, meaning that they will have to step down from the Politburo if existing criteria on rejuvenation are followed.) Constraining factors include not only socioeconomic instability but also the unwillingness of the ruling elite—what some call the "collusive" bloc of CCP cadres and business leaders—to introduce changes that may vitiate their monopoly on power.

The argument can be made that because of their background and training, in addition to shifting international realities, *diwudai,* or Fifth-Generation cadres, might be better placed—and better timed—to finish the new long march of reform. While no definition of the *diwudai* has been given by official sources, the Fifth Generation can generally be characterized as cadres now in their late thirties to early fifties. Most *diwudai* cadres attended college in the mid-1970s and 1980s, and joined the CCP from the late 1970s onward. In terms of education and professional experience, *diwudai* cadres are better qualified than their forebears. Many have master's or doctorates, and in the social sciences, not just engineering. While most of them were trained in Chinese universities, many have attended at least short-term courses or worked in Western or other Asian countries. Most have had ample experience interacting with Western businessmen or academics, and quite a few can speak English with ease. The single most important influence in their life and career is Deng Xiaoping's reform policies rather than earlier events such as the Cultural Revolution.[125]

Compared with their predecessors, Fifth-Generation cadres have had much more exposure to the West. Among the estimated 380,000 Chinese who have gone abroad for education since the early 1980s, around 180,000 have returned to work in China. A good number of these so-called returnees, or holders of American and foreign degrees, might be inducted to leadership circles toward the end of the present decade. It is possible that given their knowledge of the Western economy and society, reform in a wide variety of areas could be speeded up. Moreover, it is likely that owing to factors including the spread of the Internet and enhanced contact with foreign culture since WTO accession, Chinese as a whole may be more attuned to the requirements of globalization. Compared with their *disidai* predecessors, *diwudai* stalwarts might have a better understanding of the fact that it would be quite impossible—if not also self-destructive—for the CCP to maintain the kind of monopoly on power, resources, and information that was still possible in the early 2000s.

However, progress on both the economic and political fronts during the tenure of the *disidai*—and the *diwudai*—depends on how well the masters of Zhongnanhai are handling social unrest, particularly in the countryside. Even optimistic observers reckon that the fruits of the Hu-Wen team's *yiren weiben* and "scientific" development theories will take several more years to have an impact on the worsening social polarization—if not class warfare—that is symptomatic of the "two Chinas" scourge. Given that the knee-jerk reaction of the average CCP cadre, including one who has attended college in the West, is to beef up control and suppression mechanisms, whether Fifth-Generation leaders are in a position to introduce genuine political reform remains a big question.

The younger generation of leadership also has to deal with the responsibilities that come with China's emergent "regional superpower" status in the Asia-Pacific region. Competition between China on the one hand, and the United States and Japan on the other, will heat up further by the early 2010s. For reasons including securing the requisite requirements for economic development such as energy supplies—plus the imperative of reining in Taiwan's pro-independence movement—Beijing is poised to play a more assertive role in diplomacy (see Chapter 5). A big test of the *diwudai*'s ability to advance the course of reform will be whether they would succumb to the growing demands of nationalism.

Traits of the Fifth-Generation Leadership

The Fifth-Generation leadership is tipped to begin running China from the early 2010s. In the wake of China's WTO accession in late 2001—and the need for the party, government, and enterprises to recruit thousands upon thousands of English-speaking, globally minded professionals—the proportion of senior posts being given to officials in their early forties or even late thirties is expected to increase dramatically. By the end of 2005, there were already several cadres aged forty-five or below—including Secretary of the Communist Youth League (CYL) Central Committee Zhou Qiang (born 1960) and Vice-Governor of Jiangsu Province Zhang Taolin (1961)—who had been appointed to senior posts. The youngest provincial party secretary, that of Qinghai, Zhao Leji, was only forty-eight.[126]

Given that most *diwudai* cadres have developed their careers in the epoch of market reforms, it seems reasonable to assume that it is in their vested interests to continue with economic liberalization. This is particularly true for cadres with experience in departments such as foreign trade or financial regulatory agencies, which either did not exist or were not considered important in the pre-reform era. Yet by 2005, few among the bright young men and women had yet displayed a knack for bold thinking or novel problem solving.

A key factor behind the quality and outlook of Fifth-Generation cadres is their background and political affiliations. By 2005, it was obvious that quite a few traditional nurturing grounds for leaders might be losing their effectiveness. Take, for example, the talent pool usually known as the "gang of princelings," or the sons and daughters of senior cadres. By the early 2000s, a large number of these "high-born" cadres had gone into business rather than the much more risky world of politics and government. Examples include Li Xiaolin, whose father, former premier Li Peng, is known among Chinese and foreigners alike as the "Tiananmen Square butcher." Daughter Li has emerged as a successful businesswoman in the electricity sector.[127]

Prominent princelings in their mid-forties to mid-fifties who have already occupied vice-ministerial positions or above include Zhejiang party secretary Xi Jinping (born 1953), Chinese Academy of Science vice-president Jiang Mianheng (1957), Vice-Head of the State Environmental Protection Agency Pan Yue (1960), and newly promoted political commissar of the Academy of Military Sciences Liu Yuan (1951). They are, respectively, the son of party elder Xi Zhongxun, son of Jiang Zemin, son-in-law of General Liu Huaqing, and son of the late president Liu Shaoqi. However, as Chinese society has become more pluralistic, the public's antipathy toward "dynastic politics" has increased. And most sons and daughters of the current Politburo have kept a low profile at least in the political field.[128]

Another source of talent, the "Shanghai Faction," is tipped to decline in importance following the full retirement of ex-president Jiang in September 2004 and the expected retirement from the Politburo Standing Committee and Politburo of a number of Shanghai Faction stalwarts at the Seventeenth CCP Congress in 2007. For obvious reasons, unpopular Shanghai Faction affiliates with excessively close ties to ex-president Jiang are expected to fade away. Foremost among them is Jiang's eldest son Jiang Mianheng, who is widely thought to have leapfrogged up the business—and political—ladder owing to his father's special position.[129]

Indeed, the Shanghai Faction's decline seems probable despite the fact that *Shanghaibang* stalwarts such as Zeng Qinghong and Wu Bangguo have been grooming potential *diwudai* leaders from the early 2000s. As of 2005, younger-generation Shanghai Faction affiliates with potentials for promotion include Shanghai mayor Han Zheng; Party Secretary of Jiangxi Meng Jianzhu, Director of the CCP General Office Policy Research Unit Wang Huning, and Executive Vice-Mayor of Chongqing Huang Qifan. Most members of this group, such as Meng (born 1947), are already in their mid-fifties, and only Han (1954) and Wang (1956) enjoy a relative age advantage. Given the fact that Shanghai-related politicians and intellectuals have played such a big role in Chinese politics since the 1960s, it would be a pity if the Hu-Wen leadership were to penalize the clique simply for factionalist considerations. After all, quite a few former underlings of ex-president Jiang have displayed reformist tendencies. For example, Wang, a former professor, fed ex-president Jiang a number of forward-looking proposals for political reform. These ranged from expanding village-level elections to modernizing the structure of the PLA.[130]

Faring better than the Shanghai Faction will be a solid body of financially oriented technocrats who first gained prominence as the bright young men and women working under former premier Zhu Rongji and former vice-premier Wen Jiabao. Most of them have had long experience in departments such as the Ministry of Finance, the banks, foreign-trade units, and regulatory bodies such as the China Securities Regulatory Commission (CSRC). A number of Zhu—and Wen—affiliates who straddle the Fourth and Fifth Generations have risen to senior posts. Prominent among them are Head of the National Development and Reform Commission Ma Kai (born 1946), Executive Vice-Minister of Finance Lou Jiwei (1951), Chairman of the China Construction Bank Guo Shuqing (1956), and Vice-Chairman of the National Council for the Social Security Fund Gao Xiqing (1953). Up-and-coming Fifth-Generation Zhu Faction affiliates also include PBOC vice-governor Wu Xiaoling and Vice-Minister of Commerce Yi Xiaozhun.[131] However, these technocrats will probably function more as executors of policy rather than originators of new ideas on reform, particularly sociopolitical reform.

It is not surprising that among various CCP factions, the CYL Clique has been most successful in propagating *diwudai* successors. After all, the very function of the league is to identify potential leaders from the younger generation. The political fortune of the faction has gone up following the rise of President Hu. A number of Beijing-based cadres who are in their late thirties to mid-fifties are CYL alumni and considered to be Hu protégés. Foremost among them are Vice-Director of the CCP General Office Ling Jihua (1956); Justice Minister Wu Aiying (1951); the executive vice-director and vice-director of the CCP Organization Department, respectively Shen Yueyue (1957) and Huang Yaojin (1953); and President of the Chinese State General Administration of Sports Liu Peng (1951).[132]

Having himself served for long years in the provinces, Hu has been particularly conscientious in grooming CYL alumni for important regional slots. By 2005, there were more than twenty league affiliates holding jobs such as party secretary, governor, or mayor—or the relevant deputy positions. The regional strength of the CYL Faction was boosted following a spate of reshuffles after Hu became CMC chief in September 2004. Young turks with potential included Party Secretary of Liaoning Li Kejiang (1955), Party Secretary of Jiangsu Li Yuanchao (1950), Party Secretary of Chongqing Wang Yang (1955), Party Secretary of Tibet Yang Chuantang (1954), Governor of Inner Mongolia Yang Jing (1953), Governor of Fujian Huang Xiaojing (1946), Governor of Qinghai Song Xiuyan (1955), Vice-Party Secretary of Guangxi Liu Qibao (1953), Vice-Party Secretary of Shaanxi Yuan Chunqing (1952), Vice-Party Secretary of Beijing Qiang Wei (1953), Vice-Party Secretary of Shandong Jiang Daming (1953), and Mayor of Lhasa Luosang Jiangcun (1957).[133]

Among CYL rising stars, Li Keqiang and Li Yuanchao have attracted the most attention. Sources close to the Hu-Wen team think it is possible that one of the two Lis could be appointed to the Politburo, even the PSC, at the Seventeenth CCP Congress. Li Keqiang is a distinguished Peking University graduate who built his career in the CYL, rising to party secretary in the mid-1990s. President Hu posted Li to Henan, China's most populous province, in 1998 to test his mettle. And Li's transfer to Liaoning in late 2004, so that he can gain experience running a large industrial province, is a considerable leap forward for his career. Li Yuanchao, another former CYL luminary, has a similar background to Henan's Li. As boss of the rich coastal province of Jiangsu, Li Yuanchao has earned praise for rooting out high-level corruption and promoting a more transparent way of selecting cadres.

However, given the critical importance of age, the younger of the two Lis—who is said to have a temperament almost identical to that of his boss—has a higher chance of emerging as Hu's successor. This is despite criticism that Li Keqiang had neglected the serious problem of Henan peasants contracting AIDS while selling blood to eke out a living. In late 2005, there was widespread speculation that Hu was contemplating transferring Li from Liaoning to a senior slot in CCP headquarters—and that there was resistance to Hu's maneuver.[134]

As discussed in Chapter 1, what some critics call the intrinsic deficiencies of the leaguers still remain. This is a reference to the fact that owing to their background and experience, most CYL alumni are career party functionaries and party affairs specialists well versed in areas including ideology and propaganda. While some of them may have been exposed to market forces—and are supporters of economic liberalization—league affiliates almost invariably take as an article of faith not only the imperative of the CCP's ruling-party status but also the fact that party organs should play dominant roles in almost all aspects of the polity.

Moreover, there is evidence that after cataclysmic events including the suppression of the 1989 pro-democracy movement and the fall of the Soviet bloc, a wave of conservatism has swept the CYL and its affiliates. Bona fide liberals such as Hu Yaobang and former head of propaganda Zhu Houze—who was put under surveillance in 2003 on orders from President Hu—seem to have become quite a rarity. As of 2005, there was little to support the optimistic projection that younger-generation CYL stalwarts such as the two Lis of Liaoning and Jiangsu possess the breadth of vision and willingness to embrace the new that characterized Hu Yaobang and Zhu Houze.[135]

Equally significantly, cadres and intellectuals not affiliated with the CYL have begun to criticize the blatant factionalism practiced by Hu, especially his promotion of dubiously qualified leaguers to top-level jobs. A case in point is the new justice minister, Wu Aiying, a career apparatchik who spent the bulk of her career as a CYL and CCP functionary in Shandong Province. With no law degree or formal training in judicial matters, Wu's suitability for her post is questionable, particularly in light of the Hu-Wen team's emphasis on rule by law.[136]

Reflecting what some cynics call the "unholy alliance" between cadres and China's new breed of savvy entrepreneurs, a dozen-odd cadre-entrepreneurs as well as "red capitalists" are being groomed for the party and government leadership. By late 2005, the Hu-Wen leadership was grooming—and in some cases had already elevated to senior slots—several entrepreneurs who straddled the Fourth and Fifth Generations. They included the general manager of the China Aerospace Science and Technology Corporation, Zhang Qingwei (born 1961), newly appointed party secretary of the central city of Wuhan, Miao Yu (1955); President of China Industrial and Commercial Bank Jiang Jianqing (1953); and the president of China's famous First Auto Works, Zhu Yanfeng (1961). Zhang, who has ties to the CYL, is already a Central Committee member, while Wuhan's Miao is former general manager of the high-profile Dongfeng Automobile Company.[137] Given China's fast-developing economy, it is probably necessary for the Hu-Wen team to follow the global trend of naming successful businessmen to senior posts. Yet the CCP leadership's failure to give a bigger say, or even senior positions, to the leaders of peasants and workers—as well as activist academics or heads of NGOs—has demonstrated the limits of Beijing's championship of the *ruoshi tuanti*.

The Paradox of President Hu's Siege Mentality

The relative lack of reformist talent in the Hu-Wen camp—particularly within the CYL Clique—has highlighted a major paradox in President Hu's statecraft. The harder he tries to preserve the "advanced" ideological nature of party members and cadres—while at the same time suppressing dissident or bourgeois-liberal views among the intelligentsia—the more difficult it is for the leadership to sustain the vitality and innovativeness of the party. In his early 2005 message on boosting the "advanced" characteristics of the party, Hu urged his colleagues and underlings to "materialize the spirit of the times . . . and to be rich in creativity" so that the party "can always be in sync with the development of the times." Hu and his colleagues reiterated that what the party needed most was "creativity, cohesiveness, and combat ability."[138]

However, a late-2004 article in the liberal *Orient Outlook Weekly* revealed the shocking results of a survey done earlier that year among 100,000 party members and cadres in Sichuan Province. Thirty-four percent of the respondents noted that leaders within their units spent the bulk of their time and effort currying favor with superiors through "anticipating their wishes." The study, commissioned by the Sichuan party committee, revealed that some party cadres "no longer have firm beliefs and ideals, and they only have a faint consciousness of the objectives" of the party and government. The poll tallied with the results of another study done in 2000 by the CCP Organization Department to discern the worldview and inclinations of 300,000 party members.[139] These surveys have demonstrated the near-futility of repeated efforts by Jiang and Hu to use quasi-Maoist campaigns to elevate CCP members' morality and worldviews.

An overwhelming question has arisen: If the Hu-Wen team were to succumb to their siege mentality and ask party members to focus on orthodox Marxist values—while fending off potentially dangerous ideas from the West—how could officials, particularly the younger ones, develop the kind of originality and creativity required for keeping up with the times?

By early 2006, however, Hu, Wen, and their advisers seemed convinced that the somewhat contradictory path they had chosen—safeguarding one-party dictatorship and Chinese-style socialism while simultaneously seeking innovation in industry, trade, and technology—would help usher in a prosperous, harmonious, and *chuangxinxing* (innovative) China by the year 2020. The Fourth-Generation leadership's high level of confidence can be gauged from a series of articles that the orthodox party journal *Guo Feng* (The National Spirit) published on the "secrets" behind the staying power of ruling parties worldwide.[140]

The conclusion of the CCP researchers was essentially the same as what Hu and his colleagues in the Central Party School had discovered around the turn of the century. Thus, theoretician Zhu Xijun noted that successful ruling parties must have "governing mechanisms and policies that are in accordance with the law," good relations with the masses, "reasonable use of the media," as well as the "modernization of party construction." Again, democracy and political reform were not mentioned. Xiao Feng, another expert writing in *Guo Feng,* even saluted the leaders of the Cuban Communist Party for "upholding resolute beliefs and unbendable spirits." It is instructive that in the interest of modernizing party doctrine and organization, Hu ordered in late 2005 that more funds and resources be devoted to the study of Marxism and socialism, as well as "party construction." "New situations and new tasks have demanded that we boost the construction of the party's advanced nature . . . and further implement the great engineering project of party construction," the president said in a conference on party theory.[141]

In September 2004, the Guangzhou-based liberal magazine *Southern People Weekly (SPW)* caused a stir by selecting fifty distinguished "public-arena intellectuals" in the Chinese-speaking world. The bulk of them were mainland-Chinese academics, writers, and NGO organizers who had dared to propagate bold, and at times, anti-establishment ideas. Examples included thinkers and proponents of radical reform such as economist Mao Yushi, political scientist Liu Junning, activist legal scholar Zhang Sizhi, agrarian lobbyist Wen Tiejun, and media reform advocates Lao Yaogang and Hu Shuli. Social activists honored by the magazine included AIDS campaigner Dr. Gao Yaojie, green-movement guru Liang Congjie, and Wang Xuan, who leads the movement to seek war reparations from Japan. Given the CCP's decades-long search for talent, one might wonder if the Hu leadership shouldn't consider inducting some of them into official think tanks and even governing councils—instead of squashing their basic rights of expression.[142] It is, of course, doubtful whether liberal intellectuals would turn out to be successful leaders of political parties or governments, especially in the case of China. However, it is significant that avant-garde academics and social activists have made a triumphal transmutation to politicians in former Soviet-bloc countries such as Poland, the Czech Republic, and to some extent, Russia.

The fact that several among the "*SPW* 50"—for example, Liu Junning and Mao Yushi—cannot even publish their works without official harassment has demonstrated a real danger in CCP-style politics, especially the critical issues of political participation and succession. This is despite the fact that almost all of these controversial activists are "within-the-system reformers" who do not advocate direct confrontation with the authorities. The lack of tolerance displayed by President Hu and his colleagues shows that they might prefer to groom as Fifth-Generation successors obedient cadres who toe the party line unthinkingly—or even worse, opportunists whose only interest is gaining promotion and power. And this hardly bodes well for the country's tortuous reform enterprise, upon whose success so much of the future of Asia and the world depends.

Notes

Preface

1. Cited in "Premier: GDP to exceed $1.85 trillion in 2005," *China Daily* (an official Chinese newspaper), October 20, 2005.
2. Cited in "EU: No trade war with China over textiles," *China Daily,* May 5, 2005.
3. "The main goals of the 11th FYP raised by the Fifth Plenary Session of the 16th CCP Central Committee," New China News Agency (NCNA) (an official news agency), October 11, 2005.
4. Liu Hongbo, "Polarization of rich and poor is tearing asunder the consensus of society," *Beijing News* (an official Beijing paper), September 27, 2005; Jiang Wenran, "Social costs of China's prosperity," *The Standard* (a Hong Kong newspaper), January 26, 2006; Ye Jianping and Nie Sun, "Public accidents and related incidents cause death and injury to more than 1 million people each year," NCNA, November 27, 2005.
5. "Li Yizhong: 4,000 coal mines to be closed within the year," China News Service (CNA) (an official news agency), December 11, 2004.
6. "Wen Jiabao: Comprehensively raise the country and society's ability to counter risks," China News Service (CNS) (an official news agency), July 24, 2005.
7. Cited in "Structural reform and innovation should be given higher priority in the 11th Five Year Plan," *Outlook Weekly* (an official newsweekly), September 29, 2005.
8. Qiao Xinsheng, "Why has South Korea surpassed China in science and technology?" *People's Daily* (an official Beijing paper), September 2, 2005.
9. David Lague, "With less of a safety net, Chinese practice thrift," *International Herald Tribune,* June 14, 2005.
10. For a discussion of Beijing's early efforts to offload state-held shares, see "Sectors report: Stock by stock," www.chinaeconomicreview.com (a pro-Chinese, Hong Kong–based website), October 1, 2005, www.chinaeconomicreview.com/subscriber/articledetail.php?id=810.
11. Cited in Yu Jingbo, "The Eleventh Five-Year Plan should be closer to the livelihood of ordinary people," CNS, October 1, 2005.
12. "Wen Jiabao accepts interview by *Le Figaro*," CNS, December 3, 2005.
13. A good example of the coalition of cadres, businessmen, and thugs bullying and dispossessing peasants was the case of Dongzhou Village, Guangdong. Eyewitnesses said about twenty villagers were killed during a protest in December 2005. See, for example, Edward Cody, "Police open fire on rioting farmers, fishermen in China," *Washington Post,* December 8, 2005.
14. "The Five Principles of Peaceful Coexistence remembered," *People's Daily,* June 28, 2004.

Chapter 1

1. For a discussion of ex-president Jiang's reluctance to hand over the CMC position—and his subsequent decision to retire in 2004, see, for example, Qiu Ping,

The Chinese Communist Party's Fifth Generation (Hong Kong: Xia Fei Er Press, 2005), pp. 353–355.

2. For a discussion of Hu's education and earlier career, see Ting Wang, *The Leader of Beijing in the 21st Century* (Hong Kong: Celebrities Press, 2001), pp. 55–104.

3. While most official biographies list Jixi, Anhui, as Hu's birthplace, this is only the town where his ancestors came from. The president was in fact born in Taizhou, Jiangsu. See, for example, Xia Xiangren, "Hu Jintao and his bitter banquet of injustice," *Asia Times Online* (a Hong Kong–based news service), August 27, 2004, www.atimes.com/atimes/China/FH27Ad02.html.

4. For a discussion of Hu's life and career at Tsinghua University, see, for example, Yang Zhongmei, *Hu Jintao: The Chinese Communist Party's Cross-Century Successor* (Taipei: China Times Press, 1999), pp. 38–64.

5. For a description of Hu's career in Gansu Province, see Su Li, *Hu Jintao: Crown Prince of the Communist Party* (Hong Kong: Xia Fei Er Press, 2002), pp. 74–102.

6. For a study of Hu's patrons, including Song Ping and Hu Yaobang, see, for example, Ian Seckington, "Who's Hu?" *China Review* (a London journal) (Spring 2002).

7. Ting Wang, *The Leader of Beijing*, pp. 105–160.

8. For a discussion of Hu's successful effort in building a network of faithful followers while he was CYL chief, see, for example, Qiu Ping, *The Chinese Communist Party's Fifth Generation*, pp. 23–30.

9. For a discussion of Hu's early career in Guizhou and the Youth League, see, for example, Yao Jin, "Hu Jintao: The bird that keeps its head down," *China Brief,* Jamestown Foundation, Washington, D.C., November 21, 2001.

10. For a background description of Hu's appointment to Tibet and his activities there, see, Yang Zhongmei, *Hu Jintao*, pp. 131–156.

11. "The legacy of Hu Jintao in Tibet," Tibet Information Network, London, November 19, 2002, www.tibetinfo.net/news-updates/2002/1911.htm.

12. Hu's basically tough attitude toward Tibetans can be seen by his conclusion in 1989 that the anti-Beijing disturbances were a result of conspiracies "by separatists both within and outside the country, who have been aided by hostile forces abroad." The then party secretary of Tibet said the authorities had to be "prepared for a long-term struggle" to restore stability in the autonomous region. See "Hu Jintao on the situation in Tibet," New China News Agency (NCNA) (an official news agency), December 23, 1989.

13. Author's interview with Chinese sources in Beijing, November 2003. For a discussion of Hu's participation in quelling the riots in Lhasa, see, for example, Cai Jia, "The role of Hu Jintao in suppressing the rebellion in Lhasa," *Open Magazine* (a China-watching Hong Kong monthly), December 2002.

14. The official death toll for the March riots was 16, but Tibetan sources said at least 60 locals perished. See "Tibet, the outsiders," *The Economist*, August 12, 1989.

15. For an assessment of Hu's years in Tibet, see John Tkacik, "A biographical look at Vice-President Hu Jintao," *Heritage Research,* Heritage Foundation, Washington, D.C., April 19, 2002, http://new.heritage.org/Research/AsiaandthePacific/HL739.cfm.

16. For the background of Deng Xiaoping's elevation of Hu, see Yang Zhongmei, *Hu Jintao*, pp. 158–169.

17. For a discussion of Deng's dissatisfaction with Jiang, see, for example, Willy Wo-Lap Lam, *China After Deng Xiaoping* (Singapore and New York: John Wiley & Sons, 1995), pp. 236–238.

18. For a discussion of the special relationship between Deng Xiaoping and Hu Jintao, see, for example, Su Li, *Hu Jintao: Crown Prince*, pp. 211–220.

19. Cited in Zong Hairen, "The low-profile Hu Jintao," *Hong Kong Economic Journal* (a Hong Kong paper), April 29, 2002.

20. Author's interview with West European diplomat, Beijing, September 2003.

21. Author's interview with former CYL official, Beijing, April 2003.

22. For a discussion of the career of Wang Huning, see, for example, Li Cheng, "The 'Shanghai Gang': Force for stability or cause for conflict?" *China Leadership Monitor,* Hoover Institution, Stanford University, no. 1 (Winter 2002).

23. For a discussion of the Central Party School as a think tank and talent-hunting ground for Hu, see, for example, Charles Hutzler, "New guard: China's next leaders keep a low profile as they push reform," *Wall Street Journal,* January 3, 2002.

24. Kathy Chen, "China elite wedding a class act," *Wall Street Journal,* November 8, 2003.

25. Author's interview with Ting Wang in Hong Kong, November 2003.

26. That Hu's "true identity" remains mysterious even after he has been in the spotlight for years is most probably due to his refusal to take a strong stance on weighty issues. For a discussion of Hu remaining a "mystery man" three years after taking office, see Geoffrey York, "Chinese leader still a mystery man," *The Globe and Mail,* September 8, 2005.

27. For a discussion of Hu's possibly hostile views of the United States, see, for example, John Tkacik, "A sour record: Hu's hostility to the U.S.," Heritage Foundation Press Commentary, Heritage Foundation, April 29, 2002, www.heritage.org/Press/Commentary/ED042902.cfm.

28. For a note on the influence of Ostrovsky's great novel, see, for example, Carlos Rule, "Essential Reading," *The Guardian* (London), September 22, 2004.

29. For a discussion of the "leftist" mistakes made by Zhao in the earlier parts of his career, see Jin Zhong, "The revolution has devoured its sons," *Open* magazine, February, 2005.

30. For a discussion of Zeng's career as adviser to and hatchet man of Jiang Zemin, see, for example, Wen Yu, "Zeng Qinghong: A potential challenger to China's heir apparent," *China Brief,* Jamestown Foundation, November 21, 2001.

31. Jiang was so anxious to hang on to his military powers that he waited until the very last moment before handing over the post of CMC chairman to Hu. For a discussion, see, for example, Brian Rhoads and Benjamin Lim, "China military chief drags feet on retirement," Reuters, September 10, 2004.

32. For a discussion of the factions and power blocs in the party by the time of the Sixteenth Congress, see Zhiyue Bo, "The 16th Central Committee of the Chinese Communist Party: Formal institutions and factional groups," *Journal of Contemporary China* (a U.S. journal) (May 2004), pp. 223–256.

33. For a discussion of the composition of the "original version" of the seven-member Politburo Standing Committee, see Andrew Nathan and Bruce Gilley, *China's New Rulers* (New York: New York Review Press, 2002), pp. 65–90.

34. Willy Wo-Lap Lam, "Storm of controversy over CCP jockeying," www.cnn.com, October 29, 2002.

35. Jeremy Page, "China congress gives first clues to new leadership," Reuters, Beijing, November 12, 2002; H. Lyman Miller, "Where have all the elders gone?" *China Leadership Monitor,* no. 10 (Spring 2004).

36. For a discussion of Jiang's remaining CMC chief at the Sixteenth CCP Congress, see, for example, James Mulvenon, "The PLA and the 16th Party Congress: Jiang controls the gun?" *China Leadership Monitor,* no. 5 (Winter 2003).

37. Author's interview with party sources in Beijing, April 2003.

38. For a discussion of the power struggle between Jiang and Hu in the run-up to the Sixteenth CCP Congress, see, for example, Zong Hairen, *China's New Leaders: The Fourth Generation* (New York: Mirror Books, 2002), pp. 3–33; Willy Wo-Lap Lam, "Jiang determined to hang on to power," www.cnn.com, August 21, 2001.

39. Author's interview with party sources in Beijing, April 2003.

40. See Ren Zhichu, "The power base, decision determinants, and image of Hu Jintao," *China Strategy*, CSIS International Security Program, Center for Strategic International Studies, Washington, April 30, 2004, www.csis.org/isp/csn/040430.pdf.

41. For a discussion of the identities and orientation of the nine-member Politburo Standing Committee, see Norihiro Sasaki, "Transfer of power from Jiang to Hu," in *China's New Leadership*, ed. Yasuo Onishi (Tokyo: Institute of Developing Economics, Japan External Trade Organization [JETRO], 2003), pp. 15–24.

42. For a discussion of Hu's allies in the Politburo, see Qiu Ping, *Power Struggle Within the Fourth Generation Leadership* (Hong Kong: Xia Fei Er Press, 2003), pp. 61–91.

43. For a discussion of CYL stalwarts under Hu, see Qiu Ping, *Power Struggle*, pp. 214–246.

44. For a discussion of Song Defu's career, see Li Cheng, "Hu's followers: Provincial leaders with backgrounds in the Communist Youth League," *China Leadership Monitor*, no. 3 (Summer 2002).

45. For a discussion of the career and performance of Li Keqiang, see, for example, Zong Hairen, *China's New Leaders*, pp. 421–465.

46. For a discussion of provincial leaders who are CYL rising stars see Cheng, "Hu's followers: Provincial leaders with backgrounds in the Youth League."

47. For a discussion of the characteristics of CYL-affiliated officials, see Willy Wo-Lap Lam, "Enter the Fifth Generation," www.cnn.com, December 3, 2001.

48. Since Hu has never been a professional soldier, most of the PLA officers he is familiar with are those he got to know while serving in the provinces of Guizhou and Tibet. General Liao Xilong, the Head of the General Logistics Department of the PLA—who spent several years in western China in the 1980s—is one of just a handful of PLA officers with whom Hu has established a relatively long-term personal relationship.

49. In fact, there is evidence that Hu has tried to distance himself from prominent CYL liberal cadres including Hu Yaobang and Zhu Houze. At the very least, the new supremo has done nothing for the family members of his mentor Hu. For example, Hu Yaobang's wife has been unable to publish a collection of the articles and speeches of her famous husband. And Hu's aides have issued a severe warning to Zhu for trying to take part in a mass-based movement to demand a liberal revision of the 1982 Chinese Constitution. For a discussion of Lin Yanzhi's leftism, see Wang Dan, "China trying to redefine the party," *Taipei Times* (a Taiwan paper), July 5, 2001.

50. For an analysis of the traits and policy orientation of Zhu's technocrats, see Willy Wo-Lap Lam, *The Era of Jiang Zemin* (Singapore: Prentice Hall, 1999), pp. 372–373.

51. Tim Healy and David Hsieh, "Zhu's technocrats," *Asiaweek* (a Hong Kong–based newsweekly), March 13, 1998.

52. For a discussion of Wen's aides and think-tank members, see Long Hua, *The Inside Story of the Wen Jiabao Administration* (Hong Kong: Hong Kong Xinhua Colour Press, 2004), pp. 277–323.

53. For a discussion of the common points between Wen Jiabao and Hu Jintao, see, for example, Ma Ling and Li Ming, *Wen Jiabao: His Emergence and Administration* (Hong Kong: Ming Pao Publishers, 2003), pp. 102–132.

54. For a discussion of Wen's rise from humble civil servant to central-level cadre, see ibid., pp. 40–71.

55. Cited in Willy Wo-Lap Lam, "Wen Jiabao: A reformer at heart?" *China Brief*, Jamestown Foundation, March 28, 2002.

56. For a discussion of Wen's statecraft, see Long Hua, *The Inside Story*, pp. 219–276.

57. For a discussion of Shanghai's less privileged position in the Hu-Wen era, see, for example, Li Cheng, "Cooling Shanghai fever: Macroeconomic control and its geopolitical implications," *China Leadership Monitor*, no. 12 (Fall 2004).

58. Cited in Willy Lam, "Wen Jiabao: A reformer at heart?"

59. For a discussion of the rise of Zeng, see, for example, Ting Wang, *Zeng Qinghong and the Strongmen of the Sunset Race* (Hong Kong: Celebrities Press, 2001), pp. 171–196.

60. Chen Liangyu, who may be further promoted at the Seventeenth CCP Congress, has generally reformist credentials. He is credited with pioneering the IT industry in Shanghai. For his views on governmental reform, see, for example, "Shanghai to restructure its government," *China Daily,* August 5, 2003.

61. For a discussion of the relationship between Jiang Zemin and Jiang Wenkang, see Yang Long, "Jiang Zemin must bear responsibility for the SARS disaster," www.washingtonchinareview.org, Washington, April 25, 2003.

62. For a discussion of the role played by the generals in Jiang's retirement from the CMC, see Liu Tong, "Generals force Jiang to yield military power," *Open* magazine, October, 2004. For a discussion of the overall background of Jiang's retirement, see Zhu Zhan, "The Chinese puzzle: Jiang's retirement," *Asia Times* Online, September 18, 2004, www.atimes.com/atimes/China/FI18Ad07.html; Leslie Fong, "Behind the red curtain—power struggle in China," *Straits Times* (a Singapore paper), September 16, 2004.

63. Ex-president Jiang also made a promise to Deng Xiaoping in the early 1990s that he would not pursue the corruption-related allegations leveled at the late patriarch's children, particularly his son Deng Zhifeng.

64. Author's interview with Wu Jiaxiang, Beijing, March 2003.

65. For a discussion of the prospects of various princelings after the Sixteenth Congress, see Zhiyue Bo, "The 16th Central Committee of the Chinese Communist Party."

66. For a discussion of the career and performance of Xi Jinping, see, Zhong Hairen, *China's New Leaders,* pp. 389–420.

67. Bruce Einhorn, "Hu Jintao: China's Gorbachev," *Businessweek,* October 27, 2003.

68. For a discussion about the "Taiwan model of democracy" first introduced by late president Chiang Ching-kuo, see, for example, Xiao Gongqian, "Six political choices found in China's 100 years of modernization," transcript of discussion held at Beijing Unirule Research Institute, Beijing, April 2, 2004, http://bbs.sjtu.edu.cn/bbsgcon?board=SIPA&file=G.1099119069.A.

69. America's complaints about Putin's failure to promote liberal reforms were evident during U.S. secretary of state Condolezza Rice's visit to Europe in early 2005. Rice ticked off a list of areas where Moscow had failed to promote liberalization, including a dictatorial decision-making system and a censored press. See, for example, "Rice: Russia Must Improve Democracy for Better Ties," Reuters, February 5, 2005. For a discussion of Putin's views on NGOs, see Nick Wash, "Russia says 'spies' work in foreign NGOs," *The Guardian,* May 13, 2005.

70. Martin Seiff, "Hu was here; but who is Hu?" *National Review* (a Washington monthly), May 3, 2002.

71. For a discussion of the "Singapore model" in the context of China's possible paths of democratization, see, for example, Wang Sirui and He Jiadong, "The 'world trends' of democracy and their 'Sinicization,'" www.zisi.net, May 24, 2005, www.zisi.net/htm/wwzh/2005-05-24-23032.shtml.

Chapter 2

1. For a discussion of Hu's supposed affinities with Soviet and Russian leaders, see, for example, Pan Hu, "A Chinese Andropov?—Communist totalitarianism has staying power," *National Review* Online (a U.S. e-publication), October 4, 2004, www.nationalreview.com/voices/pan_hu200410040853.asp.

2. For a discussion of the impact of "neo-authoritarianism" on recent Chinese politics, see, for example, M.J. Sullivan, "The impact of Western political thought in Chinese political discourse," *World Affairs* (a U.S. monthly), vol. 157 (Fall 1994).

3. Most Chinese media have identified the "Theory of the Three Represents" with Jiang; see, for example, "CCP members called on to freshen mindset for breakthrough in theory and practice," *People's Daily* (an official Beijing paper), June 27, 2002. However, the fact that Jiang was not identified as the author of the "Three Represents" in the new party charter of 2002 demonstrated that there was resistance in the party's upper echelons against Jiang claiming to be the sole originator of the "important theory."

4. For a discussion of the significance of the concept of a "party for all the people," see, for example, Willy Lam, "China progresses with the times," www.cnn.com, September 5, 2001.

5. "In Jiang's words: 'I hope the Western world can understand China better,'" *New York Times*, August 9, 2001.

6. Author's interview with Chinese sources in Beijing, November 2003.

7. Cited in Willy Lam, "China's leaders battle for their place in history," www.cnn.com, September 17, 2002.

8. For a discussion of Zhu Rongji's background and economic viewpoints, see, for example, Yang Zhongmei, *A Biography of Zhu Rongji* (Taipei: China Times Press, 1988), pp. 210–248.

9. For a study of the careers of Luo Gan and Cao Gangchuan, see H. Lyman Miller, "Hu Jintao and the Party Politburo," *China Leadership Monitor,* Hoover Institution, Stanford University, no. 9 (Winter 2004).

10. "Hu Jintao makes an appeal to boldly explore new tasks," New China News Agency (NCNA) (an official news agency), May 10, 1998.

11. "Hu Jintao on the development of philosophy and the social sciences," NCNA, May 29, 2004.

12. "Hu Jintao: The Chinese-style socialist road tallies with China's national conditions," NCNA, December 2, 2004.

13. For example, in remarks marking the sixtieth anniversary of the end of World War II, Hu urged Chinese to continue the "innovative and pioneering spirit of blazing new trails." "We should do our best to carry forward in a way that fits the new situation of the times," he said. Cited in "Chinese President's speech on war victory commemoration," *People's Daily,* September 3, 2005.

14. For a study of the CCP's research on the "secrets" behind the world's ruling parties, see, for example, Willy Lam, "Hu moves to consolidate power," *Asian Wall Street Journal,* June 3, 2004.

15. Ibid.

16. "Hu Jintao: "We must study and learn from the beneficial experience of other ruling parties in the world," China News Service (CNS) (an official news agency), June 30, 2004; "Hu Jintao: Various political parties unite to revive Asia," NCNA, September 3, 2004.

17. Liu Yameng, "CCP-originated diplomacy has become more and more busy," *Wen Wei Po* (a Chinese-run daily in Hong Kong), September 3, 2004.

18. Wang Jiarui, "It is worthwhile to learn from the experience of foreign ruling parties," CNS, November 15, 2004.

19. "China's income gap widens," *China Daily* (an official Beijing daily), June 19, 2005.

20. "GDP catches up at a price," *China Daily,* November 24, 2004; "Five major problems in China's income distribution" *People's Daily,* June 19, 2003.

21. For a discussion of the reasons behind the failure of the Bharatiya Janata Party in the Indian election, see, for example, Alex Perry, "The Sonia shock," *Time* Asia edition, May 17, 2004.

22. "Hu Jintao summarizes six experiences from education relating to the 'Three Stresses,'" CNS, December 17, 200.

23. Cited in "Why do central authorities raise the viewpoint of scientific development?" NCNA, February 26, 2004.

24. Cited in Howard French, "China opens the window on the really big ideas," *New York Times,* June 2, 2004.

25. For a discussion, see Piers N. Turner, "Remembering Karl Popper," *Hoover Digest,* Hoover Institution, no. 1 (2000).

26. "Hu Jintao says the nation should unite its thought and action based on the planning of the party central authorities," CNS, April 29, 2003.

27. Cited in Willy Wo-Lap Lam, "President Hu pushes theory of scientific development," www.cnn.com, February 24, 2004.

28. Xu Yu, "Rich-poor polarization in China has reached brink of danger," *Wen Wei Po,* August 25, 2005.

29. "Hu Jintao: We must implement the view of scientific development in solving China's developmental problems," NCNA, May 6, 2004.

30. Ye Wenhu, "Scientific development must balance production and ecology," *Ming Pao* (an independent Hong Kong daily), March 12, 2004; Zhao Xiaohui and Wei Wu, "The mainland has given up the one-sided pursuit of a high growth rate," *Hong Kong Economic Journal* (an independent Hong Kong daily), March 8, 2004.

31. Cited in "Chinese premier fails farmers," BBC news service, March 15, 2002.

32. "Chinese president urges [cadres] to build energy-efficient and environment-friendly society," *People's Daily,* March 13, 2005.

33. Cited in "The key is to establish the correct view of administrative achievement," NCNA, February 25, 2004.

34. Zhong Xuebing, "Green GDP concept included in assessment of local officials," *Wen Wei Po,* July 8, 2004.

35. Peng Kailei, "Pan Yue: Selecting officials according to results in achievements in environment-related work," *Wen Wei Po,* May 8, 2004; "China counts biological costs in pursuit of green GDP," www.getgd.net, March 9, 2004, www.getgd.net/gd_trend/english/2004/3/greengdp.htm.

36. Li Wei, "Sichuan has come up with a set of 25 criteria to quantify the assessment of party and government leaders," *Sichuan Daily* (an official daily), November 3, 2004.

37. Cited in "Conditions are not ripe for high-level elections," *Central News Agency* (Taipei), April 30, 2004.

38. Cited in "Proposals of college students put on the premier's desk," NCNA, November 23, 2003.

39. For a discussion of former premier Zhu's advisers, see, for example, Xiao Zhengqin, *The Think-tank of Premier Zhu Rongji* (Hong Kong: Pacific Century Press, 1999), pp. 299–378.

40. Author's interview with a senior social scientist in Beijing who often advised Hu, Beijing, November 2003.

41. *China Directory* (Tokyo: Radiopress Inc., 2004), pp. 179–186.

42. "Hu Jintao stresses the importance of seizing opportunities in order to push forward development," *People's Daily,* January 29, 2003.

43. Zhong Xuebing, "Beijing studies crisis management mechanisms," *Wen Wei Po,* March 28, 2004; Sun Fangcan, "Beijing prepares for establishment of crisis management command center," CNS, June 23, 2003; "Rapid-response systems to be set up in the cities in five years," *Ming Pao,* May 24, 2004.

44. "200,000 staff deployed to crack down on traffic accidents," *Ming Pao,* June 21, 2004; "Expert proposes setting up a crisis management mechanism to handle traffic accidents," NCNA, May 15, 2004.

45. Staff reporter, "Fujian establishes multi-billion yuan anti-calamity system," *Wen Wei Po,* September 8, 2004; staff reporter, "Mainland to set up a safety system to handle chemicals-related incidents," *Wen Wei Po,* September 5, 2004.

46. Hong Dao, "China boosts strength of rapid-response troops in its western border

regions," *The Mirror* (a pro-Chinese Hong Kong monthly), May 2004. For a discussion of China's various anti-terrorist squads, see, for example, Martin Andrew, "Terrorism, riots and the Olympics: New missions and challenges for China's special forces," *China Brief,* Jamestown Foundation, September 13, 2005.

47. "The State Council has penalized nine governor-level officials for responsibility over safety-related mishaps," NCNA, August 25, 2005.

48. Wu Jinglian, "Build up an open, transparent and responsible government," *Caijing* (an influential Beijing-based financial magazine), June 20, 2003; "Chinese officials draw their conclusion on changes in 2003: Be close to the masses, seek concrete goals, take the scientific approach, and abide by the law," CNS, December 16, 2003.

49. "Hu Jintao puts emphasis on administration according to law," CNS, April 27, 2004.

50. "Premier Wen chairs State Council seminar on rule by law," NCNA, March 31, 2004.

51. In his 1939 text, Liu made references to the teachings of the Chinese sages while emphasizing the imperative of studying Marx and Lenin. See excerpts of *How to Be a Good Communist* at www.marxists.org/reference/archive/liu-shaoqi/1939/how-to-be/ch01.htm.

52. "Hu Jintao on the development of philosophy and the social sciences," NCNA, May 29, 2004.

53. "Hu asks cadres to improve their morality and self-discipline," *Wen Wei Po,* March 15, 2003.

54. "Economies of western provinces have gone up," NCNA, February 4, 2004.

55. Fang Guang, "Chi Fulin advocates legislation on the development of western regions," *Wen Wei Po,* November 20, 2004; Peng Kailei, "Policy on development of the west will undergo slight adjustment," *Wen Wei Po,* January 30, 2004; Richard Tomlinson, "The new wild west," *Fortune,* October 4, 2004.

56. "Liaoning to achieve a GDP of 1 trillion yuan in five years," NCNA, September 8, 2003.

57. Cited in "Developing the northeast depends on market forces," *Southern Weekend,* (a Guangzhou-based weekly publication), September 18, 2003.

58. Cited in Willy Wo-Lap Lam, "Reinvigorating China's sleepy northeast," www.cnn.com, October 7, 2003.

59. Cited in "Private capital is a new vehicle for reforming state-owned enterprises," *Wen Wei Po,* September 30, 2003.

60. "Developing the northeast depends on market forces," *Southern Weekend.*

61. Guan Po, "Why the northeast has said no to Hong Kong," *Wen Wei Po,* June 22, 2004.

62. Dexter Roberts, "Grinding the rust off the northeast," *Businessweek,* July 19, 2004; Xu Jingyao, "The National Development and Reform Commission on full-scale support for revitalizing the northeast," NCNA, September 25, 2004.

63. "Premier Wen: There will be no de-emphasis on development of western areas," CNS, March 9, 2004.

64. Xu Jingyao, "Zeng Peiyang: We must open up new vistas for the western regions," NCNA, November 18, 2004.

65. Xu Jinpo, "Central provinces need to catch up," CNS, March 14, 2005; "Henan seeks breakthrough through developing central-China cities," *Wen Wei Po,* April 9, 2004; "Li Xiansheng: Beware the collapse of the central [provinces]," *Wen Wei Po,* March 14, 2004.

66. Zou Zhengui, "Six provinces vying to become the king of central China," *Wen Wei Po,* March 9, 2005.

67. Cited in "Premier Wen issues warnings to 'warlords,'" *Wen Wei Po,* June 25, 2004.

68. Author's telephone interview with Professor Lu, Shanghai, March 2004.

69. For a study of efforts by Beijing to cool down the Shanghai economy, see, for ex-

ample, Cheng Li, "Cooling Shanghai Fever," *China Leadership Monitor,* no. 12 (Winter 2004).

70. Bill Savadore, "Shanghai plans HK$217 billion spending spree," *South China Morning Post,* May 23, 2003.

71. Jim Yardley, "Shanghai Journal: Splendid skyline, do you feel something sinking?" *New York Times,* October 14, 2003.

72. For a discussion of the potentials of this delta region, see, for example, "If China's Pearl River Delta Region wants to retain its dynamism, it has to expand hugely," *The Economist,* November 20, 2004; "Regional cooperation," *Beijing Review,* no. 29 (2004); "Pan Pearl River Delta: A new common market emerges in booming southern China," www.china.ahk.de website, August 2004, www.china.ahk.de/articleslibrary/0408_special.pdf.

73. No senior officials from the State Council were on hand at the official launch of the Pan–Pearl River Delta Region in mid-2004; see "Pan–Pearl River Delta Region forum opens," NCNA, June 1, 2004. NCNA called this superzone "the largest-scale regional cooperation in China since the founding of the People's Republic of China in 1949."

74. The influential Shanghai–Hong Kong Council for the Promotion and Development of the Yangtze, for example, counts Sichuan Province as a member of the Greater Yangtze River Delta Region; see, for example, their website, www.yangtzecouncil.org/region_introduction.asp.

75. For a discussion of the competition between the Pearl River and Yangtze River deltas, see, for example, Zhu Wenhui and Zhang Yubin, "On four regional policy readjustments since reform and an assessment," China Development Institute, Shenzhen, Occasional Papers no. 1, 2004, www.cdi.com.cn/publication/pdf/cdireview_200401_zhangyb.pdf.

76. Former Chongqing party boss Huang Zhendong, sixty-four, is deemed closer to the Shanghai Faction; for a look at his biography, see the www.Chinavitae.com site, www.chinavitae.com/biography_display.php?id=83.

77. For a discussion of the future of the Pan–Pearl River Delta Zone, see Guo Yecheng, "The 'nine plus two' concept has re-jiggered regional cooperation in China," *Wen Wei Pao,* July 28, 2005.

78. "Is Shanghai sick?" *International Herald Leader* (a Beijing newsmagazine), November 30, 2004.

79. "Hu Jintao makes major speech at the Politburo's Ninth Study Session," NCNA, November 25, 2003.

80. "Hu Jintao: Seize the strategic opportunity and speed up development," *People's Daily,* March 5, 2003.

81. Ren Zhongping, "Work hard for another 20 years," *People's Daily,* July 3, 2004.

82. For a discussion of the comparative advantages of China and India—and whether India could overtake China in economic development—see, for example, Meghnad Desai, "India and China: An essay in comparative political economy," paper presented at the IMF Conference on India and China, New Delhi, April 2004; "India might overtake China economically in long run: NIC," *India Daily* (a New Delhi paper), February 5, 2005.

83. "Hu Jintao: We'll lose opportunities if we just follow old rules," CNS, March 7, 2000.

84. Lu Rulue, "Hu Jintao's search for the myth of scientific socialism," *Hong Kong Economic Journal,* December 18, 2000.

85. Cited in Pepe Escobar, "The peasant Tiananmen time bomb," *Asia Times* Online, January 22, 2005, www.atimes.com/atimes/China/GA22Ad01.html.

86. Cited in Sushil Seth, "The emperor's new clothes are old," *Taipei Times,* September 22, 2004.

87. The propaganda machine has been recycling stories about Mao-era "models" such as Lei Feng and Zhang Side, the 1940s soldier paragon who was behind Mao's famous

"serve the people" dictum. See "The model for serving the people," NCNA, March 17, 2004.

88. See, for example Li Shuguang's point that the "privatization" of many giant state enterprises will only encourage corruption; "Expert has decried the pillage of state assets by managers," *Legal Evening Post* (an official Beijing paper), September 29, 2004.

89. Geng Yinping, "The efficiency of the premier vs. the efficiency of the county chief," *Guangming Daily* (an official Beijing paper), October 26, 2003.

90. "Son of Li Bocheng: The PM should not be involved in chasing after owed salaries of workers," *Ming Pao,* March 10, 2004; Zhu Shugu, "Why the leaders of Jixi did not implement the instructions of the prime minister," *China Economic Times* (an official Beijing paper), July 22, 2004.

91. Cited in "What if there were no directives from the premier?" NCNA, April 23, 2004.

92. Zhou Sijun, "Time to end bureaucratism in our government," cited in CNS, January 22, 2004.

93. Cited in Willy Wo-Lap Lam, "Jiang pushes new thought liberation," www.cnn.com, May 29, 2002.

94. For a discussion of Hu's tenure in Guizhou, see, for example, Ma Ling and Li Ming, *Hu Jintao: Where Is He Heading?* (Hong Kong: Ming Pao Press, 2002), pp. 133–162.

95. For a discussion of the rise of Wen, see Ma Ling and Li Ming, *Wen Jiabao's Rise and His Administration* (Hong Kong: Ming Pao Press, 2003), pp. 40–71.

Chapter 3

1. For a discussion of the orthodox CCP views on human rights, see "China issues White Paper on human rights progress," *People's Daily* (an official Beijing paper), March 30, 2004.

2. For a discussion of Wang Ruoshui and other liberal intellectuals' ideals, see, for example, Wenfang Tang, "Party Intellectuals' Demands for Reform in Contemporary China," Hoover Essays in Public Policy, Hoover Institution, Stanford University, 1997, www.hoover .stanford.edu/publications/epp/97/97b.html.

3. For a discussion of legitimacy-related issues in the PRC, see, for example, Vivienne Shue, "Legitimacy crisis in China?," in *State and Society in 21st-century China: Crisis, Contention and Legitimation,* ed. Peter Hays Gries and Stanley Rosen (London: RoutledgeCurzon, 2004), pp. 24–29.

4. Erik Eckholm, "China's new leader works to set himself apart," *New York Times,* January 12, 2003; "Hu Jintao stresses importance of re-employing laid-off workers," New China News Agency (NCNA) (an official news agency), January 5, 2003.

5. "President Hu stresses need to raise farmers' income," *People's Daily,* December 18, 2003; "Politburo meets to boost work on rural construction," NCNA, December 26, 2002.

6. Yuan Tiecheng, "Experts say China has entered into a 'high-risk society,'" China News Service (CNS) (an official news agency), July 19, 2004.

7. For a discussion of the concept of "a party for all the people," see, for example, Willy Wo-Lap Lam, "CCP 'evolving' to embrace all Chinese," www.cnn.com, November 12, 2002.

8. For a discussion of the new phenomenon of private bosses joining the party, see, for example, Elena Meyer-Clement, "Institutional change under the impact of an evolving private sector in the PRC—the case of opening the party to private enterprises," *Asien* (a German journal), July 2004, www.asienkunde.de/articles/MeyerClement92.pdf.

9. Author's interview with Chinese source in Beijing, August 2003.

10. Cited in Willy Lam, "Class warfare in the offing," *China Brief,* Jamestown Foundation, Washington, D.C., July 18, 2002.

11. Lin Yanzhi, "Private entrepreneurs should not be allowed to join the party," *Zhenlide Zhuiqiu* (In Pursuit of Truth) (a conservative Beijing journal) (May 2001).

12. For a discussion of leftists' opposition to Jiang's quasi-capitalist theories, see Xu Yufang, "Jiang's last hurrah?" *Asia Times* Online, August 9, 2001, www.freerepublic.com/forum/a3b715a15669b.htm.

13. Cited in Willy Lam, "Beijing reassures workers ahead of new era," www.cnn.com, July 16, 2002.

14. Yang Yuyong, "The poor can be saved through recuperating 120 billion yuan worth of evaded taxes," *Ming Pao* (an independent Hong Kong paper), June 4, 2003.

15. Cited in "China miners told to pack bags," BBC news website, July 5, 2002, http://news.bbc.co.uk/1/hi/world/asia-pacific/2097783.stm.

16. Cited in Willy Lam, "Class warfare in the offing?" *China Brief,* Jamestown Foundation, July 18, 2002.

17. "Latest mine blast traps 166 coal miners," *Asian Labour News* website, November 29, 2004, www.asianlabour.org/archives/003083.php.

18. "Hu Jintao: Our decision-making must [help] realize the wishes of the people," CNS, September 4, 2003.

19. Author's interviews with officials in charge of ideology and propaganda in Shanghai, November 2003. The Shanghai media, which is controlled by local party chief Chen Liangyu, a staunch supporter of Jiang Zemin, has been remarkably reticent in reporting on the "putting-people-first" activities of Hu and Wen.

20. Part of the reason why Jiang could not claim to be the sole author of the "Three Represents" theory was that it was licked together with input from a handful of cadres including Zeng Qinghong, Wang Huning, and Hu Jintao himself. By contrast, many of the aphorisms linked to Deng, such as his "Two Cats Theory," bore the distinct mark of the late patriarch.

21. It is significant that many major regional cadres also began toeing the Hu-Wen line when talking about the "Three Represents." Thus, Politburo member Zhang Dejiang, also Guangdong party chief, pointed out in mid-2003 that whether an official had grasped well the "Three Represents Theory" could be gauged by how well they went about fulfilling the goal of "establishing the party for the public good, running the administration for the people, and serving the masses with all their hearts and minds." Cited in "Leading cadres must set an example in 'establishing the party for the public good and running the administration for the people,'" *Nanfang Daily* (an official Guangzhou paper), July 19, 2003.

22. Cited in Willy Wo-Lap Lam "China toys with de-Jiangification," www.cnn.com, September 4, 2004.

23. For a discussion of Hu Jintao's debt to Maoism, see, for example, Dong Xun, "Will Hu Jintao declare a national holiday to honor Mao Zedong?" China Study Group website (Seattle), December 10, 2003, www.chinastudygroup.org/article/67/; see also Willy Wo-Lap Lam, "China's leaders turn to Mao," www.cnn.com, November 18, 2003.

24. Cited in "Hu Jintao visits revolutionary base," *People's Daily,* December 9, 2002.

25. Ibid.

26. "Hu Jintao on administration for the sake of the people," CNS, September 2, 2003.

27. Ching Cheong, "Hu rekindles Maoism," *Straits Times* (an English-language newspaper in Singapore), February 7, 2004.

28. Cited in "Hu Jintao makes pledges for the staff of the new government departments," CNS, March 18, 2003; see also Ren Huiwen, "CCP theoreticians explain Hu Jintao's new three principles for the people," *Hong Kong Economic Journal,* August 22, 2003.

29. "Politburo meets to boost work on rural construction," NCNA, December 26, 2002.

30. "The Politburo Standing Committee studies ways to solve the livelihood problems of masses with difficulties," NCNA, December 13, 2002.

31. "Hu Jintao on safeguarding, materializing and developing the fundamental interests of the masses," NCNA, January 5, 2003.

32. Cited in "Materializing [the principle of] 'putting people first,'" *People's Daily,* March 5, 2004.

33. For a discussion of the differences between Hu's and earlier leaders' approaches to development, see, for example, Wang Yongzhi, "Between the [pursuit of] GDP growth and [the goal of] putting people first," CNS, June 29, 2003.

34. "President Hu speaks on comprehensive and sustained development," CNS, September 2, 2003.

35. Cited in Willy Wo-Lap Lam, "China focuses on social well-being," www.cnn.com, July 29, 2003.

36. For a discussion of the significance of the Third Plenary Session of the Sixteenth CCP Central Committee, see, for example, Joseph Fewsmith, "The Third Plenary Session of the 16th Central Committee," *China Leadership Monitor,* Hoover Institution, Stanford University, no. 9 (Winter 2004).

37. "Premier Wen: We must establish a comprehensive view on development," CNS, July 28, 2003; "Premier Wen on the scientific approach to development," NCNA, September 15, 2003.

38. For a study of the issue of social mobility among peasants, see, for example, Chi Hung Kwan, "How to solve the three agriculture-related problems—Labor mobility holds the key," Occasional Papers, Research Institute of the Economy, Industry, and Trade, Tokyo, August 25, 2004; Willy Wo-Lap Lam, "China focuses on social well-being."

39. Staff reporters, "Putting people first instead of singlemindedly pursuing GDP growth," *Wen Wei Po* (a Chinese-controlled Hong Kong paper), February 17, 2004.

40. For a discussion of the impact of a renminbi revaluation on employment and other socioeconomic conditions in China, see, for example, Linda Lim, "Why China should not revalue the yuan," *Straits Times,* September 15, 2003.

41. "Focus on social justice in China," *Southern Weekend* (a relatively liberal paper in Guangdong Province), September 20, 2003; Wang Shaoguang, Hu Angang, and Ding Yuanzhu, "Behind China's wealth gap," *South China Morning Post (SCMP)* (a Hong Kong English-language paper), October 31, 2002.

42. Hua Ming, "Do we need civil servants with an annual salary of 500,000 yuan?" NCNA, December 27, 2004.

43. Cited in Zhang Yuxuan and Li Ling, "Peasant workers: The rise of a new class," *Chinanewsweek* (an official Beijing newsweekly), August 9, 2004.

44. Xie Chunlei, "Peasants have been granted the right to 'minimal livelihood expenses subsidy,'" *Southern Weekend,* December 31, 2002.

45. Zhu Xueqin, "Political reform is the correct path to attaining social justice," *Southern Weekend,* December 31, 2002.

46. Li Changping, "Poverty originates from an unreasonable system [of governance]," www.Boxun.com website, July 30, 2004.

47. Author's interview with Wang Juntao in New York, August 2002.

48. Staff reporter, "5,000 yuan a month puts families in middle class," *SCMP,* January 20, 2005.

49. Per capita GDP in China reached $1,000 by the end of 2003. Taking into consideration the fact that the yuan is undervalued by as much as 30 percent, the $3,000 goal should be reached well before the year 2020.

50. Actually, the idea of the augmentation of a Chinese-style middle class was raised before the Sixteenth Congress, See, for example, "The authorities advocate the expansion of citizens with middle-level income," *People's Daily,* January 31, 2002.

51. Cited in "Middle class, urban poor numbers increasing," *China Daily,* August 2, 2004; "China's middle-income class in the making," NCNA, March 26, 2004.

52. Tian Junrong, "Jiang Xiaojuan on the farming population decreasing by 220 million in 20 years," *People's Daily,* November 26, 2002.

53. Zheng Yongnian, "The CCP's views on the middle class," *Hong Kong Economic Journal*, November 19, 2002.

54. For a discussion of the business and political career of Zhang Ruimin, see, for example, David Lynch, "CEO pushes China's Haier as global brand," *USA Today*, April 2, 2004.

55. Author's interview with Western diplomats in Beijing and Hong Kong, September 2004.

56. For a discussion of the dicey nature of the Chinese bourses, see, for example, Yongyan Li, "China's equity markets: Buyer beware," *Asia Times* Online, May 9, 2003, www.atimes.com/atimes/China/EE09Ad01.html; "Foundation of China's stock market is in danger of collapse," www.Chinanews.cn (an official website), January 19, 2005, www.chinanews.cn/news/2004/2005-01-19/1125.shtml.

57. Staff reporter, "Frustrated *gumin* have become members of the disadvantaged classes," *Sichuan Finance and Investment Paper* (a Chengdu paper), January 22, 2005; Li Xuebin, "The government has to take responsibility for the drastic fall of the stock market," *China Commercial Daily* (a Beijing paper), January 22, 2005.

58. "Premier Wen on the people's livelihood," CNS, September 11, 2003.

59. For a discussion of the *sannong* problem, see, for example, Lu Xiaobo, "Taxation, protest and (in)stability in rural China," Asia Project Special Report, Woodrow Wilson International Center for Scholars, March 2003.

60. "National arable land decreased by 2 percent last year," *Ming Pao*, April 4, 2004; "Grain need should mainly be solved domestically," NCNA, August 11, 2004.

61. Wen Tiejun, "The 'threefold problems of rural areas' are not entirely a question of the system," www.shehuixue.cn website, August 15, 2005. For a study of the political implications of rural unemployment, see also Michael Szonyi, "Potential for domestic instability in the PRC in the medium-term (2001–2006)," Commentary no. 79, Canadian Security Intelligence Service, Canadian Government, November 2000, www.csis-scrs.gc.ca/eng/comment/com79_e.html.

62. Lu Xueyi, "Take a coordinated approach to the development of city and countryside," NCNA, February 25, 2004.

63. "Farmers try to commit suicide in Beijing," *China Youth Daily* (an official Beijing paper), August 12, 2003.

64. "5,000 peasants attack government offices in central China," Agence France-Presse, September 14, 2003.

65. Zhao Shengyu, "Farmers owed nearly 10 billion yuan in compensation and resettlement fees after their land has been requisitioned," CNS, April 21, 2004.

66. Ma Zhizhong, "Petitions by peasants must be properly considered," *People's Daily*, September 14, 2003.

67. For a study of the potentials of agricultural organizations in Hunan and other provinces, see, for example, Yu Jianrong, "Political crisis in rural China: Manifestation, origin and policy prescription," speech at Peking University Yanyuan Seminar, April 1, 2003, www.chinastudygroup.org/article/28/.

68. For a discussion of the role of the peasant rebellion in China's "dynastic cycles," see, for example, Qin Hui, "The 'tenant myth' and the 'clan myth': The history and reality of Chinese peasant issues," polyglot.lss.wisc.edu website, February 27, 2004, http://polyglot.lss.wisc.edu/east/Events/2004Fall/MythTalkEng.pdf.

69. Li Li, "What is the new socialist village?" *Economics Daily* (an official Beijing paper), December 7, 2005; "How to go about building the new socialist village," NCNA, December 11, 2005; "Farmers' lowest livelihood guarantee system to be established," NCNA, November 22, 2005; "90 percent of provinces to set up basic framework for social sustenance systems," NCNA, November 18, 2005.

70. "Finance minister on lightening the burden of farmers," CNS, September 3, 2003.

71. Regular agricultural taxes for most provinces, save for poor ones such as Tibet and Xinjiang, had been cut by mid-2005. For a background of the government's efforts to relieve rural taxes, see, for example, Joseph Kahn, "China to cut taxes on farmers and raise their subsidies," *New York Times*, February 3, 2005.

72. "China to scrap agricultural tax in five years," *China Daily*, March 5, 2004; "Agriculture tax in China to be gradually abolished," Associated Press, March 10, 2004; "Remission of rural taxation means farmers can each save 120 yuan," *China Youth Daily*, December 31, 2005.

73. Zhang Yulan, "Taiyuan to use 1 billion yuan to solve rural problems," *Wen Wei Po*, May 14, 2003; Yang Xiaohui, "Burden on peasants in Henan decreases by 65.4 percent," *Wen Wei Po*, May 12, 2004; Jiang Kaini, "Heilongjiang and Jilin to lead the nation in abolishing farm taxation," *Hong Kong Economic Journal*, October 29, 2004; "Twenty-two regional administrations have abolished rural taxes," NCNA, January 17, 2005.

74. President Hu said in late 2005 that there were still 26 million poor people in the countryside; see "Hu Jintao's speech at the banquet given by London mayor," NCNA, November 10, 2005; "China to earmark 29.9 billion yuan for helping the poor," CNS, June 20, 2003; "90 million Chinese under poverty line," NCNA, May 28, 2005.

75. "Beijing to boost subsidies to rural sector," *Southern Weekend*, July 17, 2003.

76. "Administrative reform in Huanglong County, Shaanxi," NCNA, August 30, 2001.

77. Cited in Willy Wo-Lap Lam, "Beijing reassures farmers of support," www.cnn.com, April 3, 2002. For a discussion of lack of fees for rural education, see, for example, Guo Zi, "Free compulsory education for all," *China Daily*, January 17, 2005.

78. "Premier Wen Jiabao meets the press," NCNA, March 8, 2003.

79. Author's interview with Professor Linda Li, Hong Kong, December 2004. For a discussion of the problems of the tax-for-fee program, see also Jean C. Oi, "State responses to rural discontent in China: Tax-for-fee reform and increased party control," Asia Project Special Paper, Woodrow Center International Center for Scholars, March 2003.

80. "Rural income rises, but growth slows," *China Daily*, January 26, 2004.

81. Cited in Zou Jianfeng, "It is possible to stop the fall in the income of farmers," *China Economic Times* (Beijing), July 11, 2003.

82. "Nearly 100 million farmers will work as laborers in cities," CNS, July 31, 2003.

83. Wen Tiejun, "Boosting rural income by cutting government monopoly," *Ming Pao*, June 5, 2003.

84. Staff reporters, "Guangdong to return 1 billion rmb in owed fees to farmers," *Wen Wei Po*, September 19, 2004.

85. Paul Mooney, "Falling farther behind," *Newsweek* Asia edition, December 2, 2002; Dong Degang, "Culture gap widens income gulf," *China Daily*, December 27, 2005.

86. "UN official says China spending too little on schools," Associated Press, September 18, 2003.

87. "Wen Jiabao emphasizes strengthening rural education work," *Liberation Army Daily*, September 20, 2003; Wang Shengzhi and Wang Fan, "More than 1,000 households have to resort to blood-selling to support the schooling of their kids," *Fortnightly Chat*, November 4, 2004.

88. Matthew Forney, "China's school killings," *Time* Asia edition, December 6, 2004; "China tries to fix growth problems," Reuters, December 28, 2005.

89. Zheng Yongnian, "Structural and democratic reforms in the Chinese village," *Hong Kong Economic Journal*, February 3, 2004.

90. "Rural problems rank first among the ten risks facing the nation before 2010," *Fortnightly Chat* (an official biweekly magazine), September 2, 2004.

91. Josephine Ma, "Reforms to give power to the people," *SCMP*, May 29, 2004.

92. Cheng Hongjin, "300 million farmers to move to the cities," NCNA, July 25, 2003; Jiang Xiaoqing, "China to build 200 cities in 15 years," *Wen Wei Po*, December 15, 2004.

93. Tang Yaoguo, "Obstacles to *hukou* reform mainly due to questions of vested interests," *Outlook* weekly, November 21, 2005.

94. "More than 60 percent of the public wants to move into upper echelons of society," CNS, August 9, 2004; "China embarks on civil service reforms," *China Daily,* September 23, 2003.

95. "Entrepreneur-cadres in Sheyang County have annual income exceeding 100,000 yuan," *Jiefang Daily* (an official Shanghai paper), September 9, 2003.

96. Xu Yong, *Village Autonomy in Chinese Villages* (Wuhan, China: Huazhong Normal University Press, 1997), p. 156; Liu Yawei, "Crisis in the hinterland, rural discontent in China—The Chinese countryside in the era of self-government," Special Report, Woodrow Wilson International Center for Scholars, March 2003.

97. Cited in Wang Jiaoli, "An aborted direct township election," China Center for Rural Studies website, www.ccrs.org.cn, September 6, 2003.

98. Yu Jianrong, "Organized resistance by peasants and its political risks," *Strategy and Management,* vol. 3 (June 2003).

99. Josephine Ma, "Peasant leaders emerge to fight graft," *SCMP*, June 16, 2003.

100. Yu Jianrong, "Organized resistance by peasants."

101. Bian Jun, "The birth of the first regulation on peasant cooperative organization," *Wen Wei Po,* November 18, 2004.

102. "Changsha peasants protest construction of golf course," *China Labour Bulletin* (a Hong Kong–based publication on the workers' movement in China), February 24, 2004.

103. Wang Jianmin, "10,000 Fujian farmers sign petition to impeach officials," *Yazhou Zhoukan* (a Hong Kong newsmagazine), May 16, 2004.

104. Ibid; staff reporter, "More than 10,000 peasants petition to remove corrupt officials," *Ming Pao,* April 22, 2004.

105. Wang Jianmin, "10,000 Fujian farmers sign petition."

106. "Fujian men who organized petitions are kidnapped," *Ming Pao,* April 21, 2004.

107. "Large-scale petitions lodged by Hebei and Fujian peasants," Radio Free Asia broadcast, May 4, 2004.

108. Jiang Xun, "60,000 peasants battle police as they chant 'Long live the CCP,'" *Yazhou Zhoukan,* November 21, 2004; Kathy Chen, "Chinese protests grow more frequent, violent," *Wall Street Journal,* November 6, 2004.

109. For a discussion of the resolution of the Hanyuan riots, see Clifford Coonan, "Beijing alarm as riots against poverty spread," *Times of London,* December 9, 2004; Hu Ping, "On Hu-Wen's instructions to solve the Hanyuan affair," www.secretchina.com website, December 12, 2004.

110. "Workers' wages have gone up more than five times in 13 years," CNS, November 11, 2002; Fu Jing, "Measures urged to close income gap," *China Daily,* December 12, 2005.

111. Li Qiang, "China's labor unrest," China Labor Watch website, June 14, 2003, www.chinalaborwatch.org/voices/030614.htm; Wu Jianfang, "Guangdong increases minimum welfare payouts by 400 million yuan a year," *Wen Wei Po,* September 25, 2003.

112. For a discussion of the social roots of the Falun Gong phenomenon, see, for example, John Pomfret, "'Hateful' cult plotters held," *Washington Post,* July 23, 1999; Terry McCarthy, "Chasing shadows," *Time* Asia edition, August 9, 1999.

113. "Employment-related work is a major political task," *People's Daily,* August 16, 2003.

114. Cited in Willy Lam, "Hu's new deal," www.cnn.com, December 3, 2002.

115. "Eight million workers jobless in the cities," CNS, July 17, 2003.

116. "One million graduates face unemployment in July," *People's Daily,* June 12, 2003; Sarah Schafer, "Degrees but no jobs," *Newsweek* Asia edition, September 22, 2003.

117. Cited in Willy Wo-Lap Lam, "Beijing fears Argentinian-style unrest," www.cnn.com, January 3, 2002.

118. Hai Yan, "Jobless rate fixed at 4.6 percent for 2005," *Wen Wei Po,* December 15, 2004.

119. "Hu Jintao: Boosting and improving the work of labor unions," CNS, September 28, 2003.

120. For a discussion of the government's role in the labor movement, see, for example, Philip P. Pan, "Government stifles labor movement," *Washington Post,* December 28, 2002.

121. "China trade union to allow direct election of shop leaders," Associated Press, September 27, 2003.

122. Cited in "An independent union," *China Labor Bulletin,* February 6, 2002.

123. For a discussion of Beijing's suppression of wildcat unions, see, for example, Philip. P. Pan, "In China, labor unions offer little protection," *Washington Post,* October 16, 2002.

124. The manager of the company, Li Jinghua, said this was to help them "get rid of their shyness." However, Jilin University sociologist Liu Shaojie said the company had "infringed upon the human dignity of their staff," who could take legal action against their employers. See Chen Xi, "Staff asked to practice kneeling down during training course," *Wen Wei Po,* August 12, 2004.

125. Josephine Ma, "Millions of women 'locked up in Guangdong factories,'" *SCMP,* December 22, 1999.

126. Josephine Ma, "600,000 fall victim to workplace illnesses," *SCMP,* July 21, 2004; Chen Ji, "The incident of the death of three workers in Huizhou has attracted attention," NCNA, December 25, 2002; Ma Longsheng, "How come some factories can be so dictatorial?" *People's Daily,* December 31, 2002.

127. "China: Industrial accident and death statistics," *Asian Labour News* website, www.asianlabour.org, January 10, 2004; Xing Zhigang, "China's mining sector sounds the alarm," *China Daily,* December 3, 2004; Antoaneta Bezlova, "China's deadly mining industry," *Asia Times,* July 26, 2003.

128. Willy Lam, "Dying to make China successful," *Asian Wall Street Journal,* December 15, 2004; "51.8 billion yuan need to be spent on coal mine safety in coming three years," CNS, December 27, 2004.

129. Cited in *China Labour Bulletin,* June 10, 2003.

130. "Jiangxi SOE punishes petitioning workers by withholding salaries," *Ming Pao,* September 17, 2003.

131. Jasper Becker, "Workers in a state of disunion," *SCMP,* March 23, 2002; for a study of the rash of labor unrest in northeastern China, see, for example, "Paying the price: Worker unrest in northeast China," Human Rights Watch Report (New York), vol. 14, no. 6 (August 2002); Thomas Bernstein, "Unrest in rural China, a 2003 assessment," Center for the Study of Democracy, University of California, Irvine, Paper 04–13, 2004, http://repositories.cdlib .org/cgi/viewcontent.cgi?article=1043&context=csd.

132. Philip P. Pan, "Government stifles labor movement," *Washington Post,* December 28, 2002.

133. "Prototype of an independent union," *Ming Pao,* February 28, 2002; Willy Lam, "Stability at the expense of reform," *China Brief,* Jamestown Foundation, April 11, 2002.

134. "China sentences two labor leaders to jail," Associated Press, January 1, 2003.

135. "Appeal for the release of Liaoyang Two," *China Labor Bulletin* website, May 9, 2003, www.china-labour.org.hk/public/contents/campaign?revision%5fid=17458&item%5fid=7217.

136. "Two women arrested in eastern China for organizing labor protests," Associated Press, October 26, 2004.

137. Despite the suppression of "public intellectuals," more socially conscious groups of lawyers, professors, and other professionals have stood up to fight for the human rights of society's downtrodden; see, for example, Willy Lam, "Why Beijing is afraid of the civil society," *Apple Daily* (an independent Hong Kong daily), September 1, 2005.

138. Staff reporter, "Nearly half of migrant workers in Guangdong earn less than 800 yuan," *Ming Pao*, July 7, 2004; "South China faces shortage of migrant labor," Associated Press, September 9, 2004.

139. "Unions' new approach puts workers' rights first," NCNA, September 11, 2003; Yan Wuyou, "Low pay and owed salaries in Guangdong," *Wen Wei Po*, August 1, 2004.

140. "Heilongjiang has paid back 400 million yuan of owed salaries to workers," NCNA, August 8, 2004; "Employers who owe their staff salaries to be penalized," NCNA, November 14, 2004.

141. Ray Cheung, "Minimum wage rise will benefit migrant workers," *SCMP*, January 2, 2002.

142. "The question of induction of *nongmingong* into trade unions for the first time written into ACFTU Report," CNS, September 24, 2003.

143. Zhang Xiaosong and Li Jianhong, "Trade union representatives are concerned about three hot-button issues," NCNA, September 21, 2003; Willy Wo-Lap Lam, "New deal for migrant workers," www.cnn.com, September 22, 2003.

144. "South China feels acute labor shortage," NCNA, March 3, 2005; "40 percent of Guangdong's employers consider paying more," NCNA, February 26, 2005.

145. Yan Wuyou, "Low pay and owed salaries in Guangdong."

146. "China: Discrimination fuels HIV/AIDS crisis," Special Report by Human Rights Watch (New York), September 3, 2003; "WHO: 10 million Chinese to be infected with AIDS in seven years," *Ming Pao*, August 19, 2003; J. Kaufman and Jun Jing, "China and AIDS: The time to act is now," *Science*, June 28, 2002.

147. Brad Adams, "Waiting for death in China," *Asian Wall Street Journal*, September 3, 2003; Leslie Chang, "China may apply lessons of SARS to fight AIDS," *Asian Wall Street Journal*, August 4, 2003; Rupert Wingfield-Hayes, "China's forgotten AIDS victims," BBC news website, November 12, 2003, http://news.bbc.co.uk/2/hi/asia-pacific/3269269.stm.

148. Leigh Jenkins, "AIDS activist 'detained for leaking secrets,'" *SCMP*, September 7, 2002; "AIDS campaigner refuses to be silenced," AFP, March 8, 2004.

149. "Wu Yi heads Work Committee to Prevent and Cure AIDS," CNS, February 26, 2004; "Hundreds of police storm AIDS village," AFP, July 4, 2003; Philip P. Pan, "China meets AIDS crisis with force," *Washington Post*, August 18, 2003; Josephine Ma, "AIDS workers appalled by hostility of local officials," *SCMP*, November 27, 2004.

150. "China to break snail fever by 2008," *People's Daily*, November 8, 2004; "Rural health expert writes to Vice-Premier Wu Yi on the return of schistosomiasis," *Wen Wei Po*, December 24, 2004.

151. For a study of rural petitions as a result of forced eviction and other causes, see, for example, Thomas Bernstein, "Unrest in rural China: A 2003 assessment," Center for the Study of Democracy, University of California, Irvine, Occasional Paper 04–13; "China to better protect petitioners' rights," NCNA, January 18, 2005.

152. Bill Savadore, "Shanghai moves to ease rows over urban clearance," *SCMP*, July 26, 2003.

153. "Reason behind the self-incarceration of Anhui Peasant at Tiananmen Square," *Southern Metropolitan News*, September 17, 2003.

154. "Public proceedings initiated against jailed lawyer," *Hong Kong Voice of Democracy* website, August 19, 2004, www.democracy.org.hk/EN/2003/aug/news_03.html.

155. "40 million farmers have lost their land," *People's Daily*, February 2, 2004; Joshua Muldavin, "In rural China, a time bomb is ticking," *International Herald Tribune*, January 1, 2006; Wang Yu, "Six problems bedevil China's development," *Wen Wei Po*, December 14, 2004.

156. Li Kunhui, "Zeng Peiyan gives instructions on how to handle the self-incineration case," *Wen Wei Po*, September 17, 2003.

157. Cited in "Eviction team destroys house and beats up people," *Ming Pao,* September 19, 2003; "Four teams of inspectors to look at disputes surrounding urban renewal," *Ming Pao,* September 28, 2003.

158. Melinda Liu and Anthony Kuhn, "Petitioning the Emperor," *Newsweek,* September 29, 2003.

159. Bill Savadore, "Shanghai moves to ease rows over urban clearance."

160. Liu Yunling, "A public hearing on urban clearance in Shanxi," NCNA, September 5, 2003.

161. "Ministry of construction says massive corruption involved in urban renewal," *Hong Kong Economic Journal,* September 19, 2003; Jiang Xun, "Filthy background behind the red-hot real estate market," *Yazhou Zhoukan,* October 12, 2003.

162. "Public hearing needs to be called involving urban re-development and eviction," NCNA, February 11, 2005.

163. "Number of destitute Chinese has increased by 800,000," *People's Daily,* July 18, 2004.

164. Li Fan, "The political choices of peasants," World and China Research Institute Special Report, 2004, www.bjsjs.net/news/news.php?intNewsId=791.

165. Cited in "Gao Qiang: Farmers take up 20 percent of the resources," CNS, December 26, 2005.

166. "Political reform from the angle of the high numbers of petitions," *Hong Kong Economic Journal,* July 8, 2004.

167. Lan Yan, "More than 80 percent of China's suicides are peasants," *China Youth Daily,* November 21, 2003.

168. For a discussion of the leadership's fear of acts of "urban terrorism," see, for example, Willy Lam, "Beijing faces winter of discontent," www.cnn.com, September 30, 2003.

169. "China has confiscated 110,000 kilos of rat poison," CNS, March 23, 2003; "Rat poison takes 5 lives in Sichuan," *Ming Pao,* February 14, 2003; Deng Yifan and Wang Ying, "Rat poison breakfast: 69 people hospitalized," *Wen Wei Po,* September 27, 2003.

170. Wang Yi, "The 'civil rights movement' is just one centimeter away from us," *Chinesenewsweek* (an official newsmagazine), November 24, 2003.

171. "Henan riot police fire on protesting farmers," Radio Free Asia broadcasts, August 3, 2004.

172. "More than 30 wounded in clash between Henan police and peasants," *Wen Wei Po,* August 3, 2004; "Zhengzhou police opened fire on protesting farmers," *Ming Pao,* August 2, 2004.

173. Cited in Willy Lam, "Beijing faces winter of discontent"; for a discussion of China's augmentation of PAP and police forces against terrorism, see, "China deploys nationwide forces to fight terrorism," *Chinesenewsweek,* November 4, 2004.

174. "New *Xinfang* regulations spell out criminal liability of officials," *Ming Pao,* January 18, 2005; Ren Huiwen, "CCP about to reform *xinfang* system," *Hong Kong Economic Journal,* November 12, 2004; "Police begin accepting petitions from the masses in 2005," NCNA, December 29, 2005.

175. "Luo Gan on creating a just and efficient law-and-order system," NCNA, December 8, 2004.

Chapter 4

1. For a discussion of Hu's crackdown on intellectuals in late 2004, see, for example, Jiang Xun, "China's intellectuals face bleak winter," *Yazhou Zhoukan* (a Hong Kong–based newsweekly), December 19, 2004; Liu Tong, "Hu Jintao has strengthened dictatorship [over intellectuals]," *Open Magazine* (a Hong Kong China-watching monthly), November 2004.

2. Nicholas D. Kristof, *New York Times (NYT)*, June 3, 2003; Jasper Becker, "Mussolini Redux," *The New Republic* Online, June 23, 2004, www.tnr.com/doc.mhtml?i=20030623&s=becker062303.

3. For a discussion of the impact of Deng's exhortation of reform in 1992, see, for example, Orville Schell, "With an official O.K., capitalism takes off," *Time* Asia Edition, September 27, 1999.

4. "Premier Wen gives speech at Harvard University," China News Service (CNS) (an official news agency), December 11, 2003; "Premier Wen: Let the people supervise the government," *Wen Wei Po* (a Chinese-run Hong Kong daily), December 12, 2003.

5. "Hu Jintao: The CCP has to listen to criticisms," CNS, March 4, 2001.

6. The official New China News Agency (NCNA) also carries fairly detailed accounts of each Politburo meeting, including the so-called Politburo study sessions that are conducted more or less on a monthly basis; see http://news.xinhuanet.com/zhengfu/2003–08/13/content_1024721.htm.

7. "Wen visited relatives of Shaaxi coal mine," *Beijing News* (an official Beijing paper), January 4, 2005; "President Hu did away with the red carpet while visiting the Pearl River Delta," NCNA, December 24, 2004.

8. "The media heaps praise on the leadership's decision not to go to Beidaihe this summer," CNS, August 30, 2003.

9. Author's interview with sociologist Lu Jianhua, Beijing, November, 2003.

10. Bao Tong, "The ins and outs of the Hu-Wen New Policy," *Open Magazine*, September 2003; Bao Tong, "Faking Reforms at the Communist Party Congress," *NYT*, November 23, 2002.

11. Cited in Willy Wo-Lap Lam, "Lessons from China's SARS debacle," www.cnn.com, April 24, 2003.

12. For a discussion of the treatment of Dr. Jiang Yanyong, see, for example, Geoffrey York, "China cool toward MD who told SARS truth: Whistle blower treated both as hero and political threat," *Globe and Mail* (a Toronto paper), May 23, 2003.

13. Author's interviews with friends close to Bao Tong, Hong Kong and Beijing, August 2003.

14. Joe McDonald, "China urged to rethink Tiananmen Square," Associated Press, March 15, 2004; "Foreign Ministry spokesman holds press conference," CNS, June 1, 2004. After the death of Zhao Ziyang in January 2005, the Foreign Ministry spokesperson again noted that there would be no reassessment of the June 4 verdict.

15. For a discussion of Hu tightening control over the intelligentsia, see, for example, Philip Pan, "Hu tightens party's grip on power," *Washington Post*, April 24, 2004.

16. For a discussion of political liberalization under Zhao Ziyang, see, for example, Wu Guoguang, *Political Reform Under Zhao Ziyang* (Hong Kong: Pacific Century Institute, 1997), pp. 98–187.

17. "110 million people take part in elections," NCNA, May 5, 2004.

18. Staff reporter, "Rebel peasant elected village chief," *Ming Pao* (an independent Hong Kong newspaper), May 14, 2004.

19. For a discussion of the significance of township elections, see, for example, Jiquan Xiang, "Self-government in Chinese villages: An evaluation," *Perspectives*, Overseas Young Chinese Forum (U.S.), vol. 1, no. 4 (February 29, 2000); Jamie P. Horsley, "Village elections: Training ground for democratization," *The China Business Review*, U.S.-China Business Council, Washington, D.C., March–April 2001.

20. Cited in Yang Fan, "The level of direct elections may be elevated," *Wen Wei Po*, May 20, 2003.

21. For a discussion of the "timetable" for promoting elections in China, see, for example, Willy Wo-Lap Lam, *The Era of Jiang Zemin* (Singapore and New York: Prentice-Hall, 1999), pp. 392–393.

22. Josephine Ma, "Township poll defies ban on direct elections," *South China Morning Post* (*SCMP*) (an English-language Hong Kong paper), January 31, 2002.

23. For a discussion of the evolution of grassroots elections, see, for example, Tony Saich and Xuedong Yang, "Selecting within the rules: Institutional innovations in China's governance," paper presented at Conference on Local Government Comparisons in India and China, Beijing, January 2003.

24. Author's interview with Yu Keping, London, November, 2003; author's interview with Lai Hairong, London, November 2005.

25. Sha Lin, "Three years after the direct election of village chief in Buyun," www.chinaelections.org website, April 20, 2002; Josephine Ma, "Township poll defies ban on direct elections," *SCMP*, January 31, 2002.

26. Zou Shubin, Huang Weiping, and Liu Jianguang, "Comparison between electoral reforms in Dapeng Town and Buyun Township," *Contemporary China Research* (a Beijing-based monthly journal) (January 2003).

27. John Pomfret, "Chinese reformer risks livelihood for elections," *Washington Post,* September 27, 2003; Wang Qiaoli, "An aborted township direct election," China Center for Rural Studies website, www.ccrs.org.cn, September 6, 2003; Charles Hutzler, "Town's election plans form ripples in Beijing," *Asian Wall Street Journal,* September 16, 2003; staff reporter, "Direct elections held to pick the chiefs of seven towns and township in Yunnan," *Ming Pao,* November 10, 2004.

28. Verna Yu, "Congress delegate elected without party's backing," AFP, May 22, 2003; Tao Xiao, "Returnee from abroad elected Shenzhen PC member with high number of votes," *Wen Wei Po,* May 21, 2003; "Two independent candidates become deputies to Beijing legislature," *Ming Pao,* December 17, 2003.

29. For a discussion of difficulties encountered in the early phase of village-level elections, see, for example, Susan V. Lawrence, "Village elections," *Far Eastern Economic Review,* January 27, 2000; "Chinese farmers elect village heads," *China Daily,* January 10, 2000; James Robinson, "An election with Chinese characteristics," *Asia Times* Online, (a Hong Kong news service), February 17, 2000, www.atimes.com/china/BB17Ad01.html.

30. Cited in Melinda Liu and Paul Mooney, "Turning the Page," *Newsweek* Asia edition, February 11, 2002. For a discussion of Hu's inclinations on political reform, see also Bruce Einhorn, "Hu Jintao: China's Gorbachev?" *Businessweek* Asia edition, October 27, 2003.

31. Cited in staff reporter, "Peking University professor urges political reform," *Wen Wei Po,* October 24, 2003.

32. "Wen Jiabao's press conference at the end of the 2nd session of the 10th NPC," NCNA, March 15, 2004; for a discussion of Chinese-style "rule of law" see, for example, Fong Tak-ho "China's rule of law in theory, not practice," *Asia Times* Online, January 22, 2004, www.atimes.com/atimes/China/GA22Ad03.html.

33. Cited in H. Lyman Miller, "Hu Jintao and the Party Politburo," *China Leadership Monitor,* Hoover Institution, Stanford University, no. 9 (Winter 2004).

34. "Premier Wen: Administration according to law means strict adherence to the Constitution," CNS, March 31, 2004; "Wen Jiabao advocates administration according to law," CNS, July 22, 2004.

35. For a discussion of the power struggle between the Jiang and Hu factions in the run-up to and after the Sixteenth Congress, see, for example, Qiu Ping, *Power Struggle Within the Fourth-Generation Leadership* (Hong Kong: Xia Fei Er Press, 2003), pp. 19–72.

36. "State Council passes regulations on public health," CNS, May 15, 2003.

37. "Examining China's unconstitutional investigation system through the Sun Zhigang case," *Outlook Weekly* (an official Beijing weekly), June 5, 2003.

38. Staff reporter, "Death of one [innocent] victim has led to the end of a nasty regulation on custody," *Ming Pao,* June 25, 2004.

39. Fong Tak-ho, "Payout for family of fatal beating victim," *SCMP,* June 9, 2003;

"Sentences given out on the Sun Zhigang cases," NCNA, June 10, 2003.

40. Wang Junshou, "Minister of Civil Affairs says stations for providing succor and help nationwide can help 2 million people a year," *China Youth Daily,* July 28, 2003; Wang Pan, "Guangdong abolishes regulation on custody and sending back [vagrants]," CNS, July 25, 2003.

41. Li Zishun, "China has cleared up 868 cases of administrative detention," CNS, December 17, 2004.

42. "Interview with Bishop Zen," Cable News (a Hong Kong TV station) newscast, May 31, 2003.

43. For a discussion of the constitutional revision process, see Ren Huiwen, "Wu Gangguo starts fourth constitutional revision process," *Hong Kong Economic Journal* (an independent Hong Kong paper), July 18, 2003; Murie Dickie, "China's communists call for protection of property," *Financial Times,* December 22, 2003.

44. Cited in "NPC tables revisions to the State Constitution," CNS, March 8, 2004; staff reporters, "Principle of protection of private property written into Constitution," *Wen Wei Po,* March 9, 2004.

45. Cited in Cao Siyuan, "Ten proposals for a better Constitution," www.cipe.org website, November 30, 2003.

46. A couple of Cao's suggestions dealt with political processes, including holding "elections" to pick party and government officials. For example, without saying that he was after one person, one vote, Cao indicated that the principle of *cha'e xuanju*—that the number of candidates should outnumber the positions available by a reasonably large margin—should be enshrined in the charter. "So-called elections where there is only one candidate for one job—or where the candidates only outnumber the posts available by a few percentage points— are bogus ones," he said in an interview with the author, Beijing 2003.

47. "NPC sets up office to check on anti-constitutional behavior of regional administrations," *Wen Wei Po,* June 22, 2004.

48. For a discussion of the controversy over party supremacy over the Constitution, see, for example, Nailene Chou Wiest, "Party's supremacy versus the Constitution," *SCMP,* February 25, 2004; Willy Wo-Lap Lam, "Hu girds for political reform," www.cnn.com, January 14, 2004.

49. Staff reporter, "Scholar criticizes 'Theory of the Three Represents' getting into the Constitution," *Ming Pao,* March 10, 2004.

50. Cited in Willy Wo-Lap Lam, "Hu Jintao earns his place as role model," www.cnn.com, January 28, 2003.

51. Cited in Ren Huiwen, "The CCP on party secretaries doubling as people's congress chairmen," *Hong Kong Economic Journal,* May 23, 2003.

52. For a discussion of the powers of the Political and Legal Affairs Commission, see, for example, Bryan Edelman and James T. Richardson, "Falun Gong and the law: Development of legal social control in China," *Nova Religio* (U.S. journal), no. 6, vol. 2, 2003, pp. 312–331.

53. Staff reporter, "Hunan scholar suggests improvements in judicial system," *Ming Pao,* July 30, 2003.

54. For a discussion of Zhao's efforts to whittle down party control of the courts, see, for example, Willy Wo-Lap Lam, *China After Deng Xiaoping* (Singapore and New York: John Wiley & Sons, 1995), pp. 269–270.

55. Zhu Daqiang, "Reform of Chinese courts to be based on national conditions," CNS, December 7, 2004.

56. Cited in Willy Lam, "Turning a crisis into an opportunity," www.cnn.com, April 29, 2003.

57. "Wen Jiabao holds first State Council meeting," NCNA, March 21, 2003.

58. "Wen Jiabao on listening to the views of democratic parties," CNS, April 12, 2003.

59. "Hu and Wen go online to monitor people's views and wishes," NCNA, November 12, 2004.

60. "Xian residents to attend meetings of the People's Congress," *People's Daily,* January 6, 2003.

61. "More citizens use litigation method to seek their rights," *China Daily,* March 22, 2003.

62. He Cong, "Plaintiff wins in 'Hepatitis B discrimination case' in Wuhu," *People's Daily,* April 5, 2004.

63. "Shenzhen residents use legal means to remove post of People's Congress deputy," *Wen Wei Po,* June 5, 2003.

64. Wang Bixue, "A step forward for *mingaoguan,*" *People's Daily,* March 28, 2001; Joseph Kahn, "China courts turn deaf ear to peasants' cases," *NYT,* December 28, 2005.

65. For a discussion of the career paths of affiliates of the Youth League Faction, see, for example, Willy Lam, "Is Hu Jintao a reformer?" *Apple Daily* (an independent Hong Kong daily), December 27, 2004.

66. For a discussion of reform elements in Zhao's Report to the Thirteenth CCP Congress, see, for example, Willy Lam, "Waiting for 'real reform' to blossom," www.cnn.com, October 8, 2002; Also see Andrew Nathan, "Authoritarian resilience," *Journal of Democracy* (a U.S. monthly journal), January 2003.

67. For a discussion of Luo Gan and other major figures in the "security and legal establishment," see, for example, Zhong Hairen, *China's New Leaders: The Fourth Generation Leadership* (New York: Mirror Books, 2002), pp. 211–261.

68. For a discussion of the "returnees" on personnel changes in the upper echelons of party and government, see, for example, Li Cheng, "Bringing China's best and brightest back home: Regional disparities and political tensions," *China Leadership Monitor,* no. 11 (Summer 2004).

69. For a discussion of Hu's push for intra-party reform, see, for example, "What price reform: Hu Jintao's consolidation of power does not mean that democracy is in the cards," *The Economist,* September 23, 2004.

70. Author's interviews with a couple of Beijing cadres who were close to the Hu camp, April 2004.

71. For a discussion of the career and strategies of Zeng Qinghong, see, for example, Ding Wang, *Zeng Qinghong and the Strongmen of the 'Sunset Race'* (Hong Kong: Celebrities Press, 2001), pp. 171–196.

72. "Leadership echelons should go one step faster in *dangnei minzhu,*" CNS, July 10, 2003.

73. For a discussion of Hu's aspirations for intra-party democracy, see, for example, Willy Wo-Lap Lam, "Chinese leaders set out wish list," www.cnn.com, October 15, 2003.

74. For an official Chinese view of the political structure of the LDP, see, for example, Jin Dexi, "Political restructuring in Japan after the Cold War," *Japan Studies,* no. 3, Chinese Academy of Social Sciences, Beijing, 1996.

75. "Central Party School professor: Party and government officials should be elected via competitive elections," CNS, June 1, 2004.

76. Liu Yueshan, "Several provinces have used 'the system of casting ballots' to choose regional-level cadres," *Wen Wei Po,* August 11, 2004.

77. For a discussion of the division of power among various top CCP organs, see Wang Guixiu, "The tripartite division of power within the party is an important element of intra-party democracy," *Chinanewsweek* (an official newsmagazine), January 19, 2004.

78. *China Youth Daily,* May 31, 2003; Wen Han, "Experiments conducted in rendering party congresses into permanent institutions," *Wen Wei Po,* December 9, 2003.

79. Peng Kailei, "CCP Party Congresses to have permanent organs," *Wen Wei Po,* August 27, 2003; Zhang Jin, "Experiments on permanent *dangdaibiao dahui* offices have been expanded," *Wen Wei Po,* December 29, 2004.

80. For a discussion of the career advantages of party hacks, see Willy Lam, "China's qualified give way to party hacks," www.cnn.com, December 26, 2002.

81. For a discussion of the rise of Jia Qinglin and Huang Ju, see, for example, Ed Lanfranco, United Press International, November 15, 2002; Qiu Ping, *Power Struggle Within the Fourth-Generation Leadership,* pp. 61–64.

82. Cited in Willy Lam, "China's qualified give way to party hacks."

83. Zhang Dejiang, "Private entrepreneurs must not be allowed to enter the party," *Zhenlide zhuiqiu* (Seeking Truth) (a Beijing-based monthly), May 2001. For a discussion of the ideas of Zhang and other leftists, see Joseph Fewsmith, "Is political reform ahead?" *China Leadership Monitor,* no. 1 (Winter 2002).

84. Author's interview with Western diplomats in Beijing, November 2003.

85. Under reform policies introduced by Deng Xiaoping and Zhao Ziyang in the mid-1980s, professional managers and administrators were given more authority vis-à-vis party secretaries and functionaries in units including government departments, factories, and universities. For a discussion of Deng and Zhao's political reforms, see, for example, Steven Mufson, "Debate blossoms in Beijing Spring," *Washington Post,* April 19, 1998; "Zhao's legacy," *The Economist,* January 20, 2005.

86. Several articles in major Western media discussed *dangnei minzhu* reforms that Hu would supposedly introduce in July or August 2003. See, for example, Oliver August, "Hu puts 'democracy in the party' on agenda," *Times of London,* June 9, 2003; John Pomfret, "China to open field in local elections," *Washington Post,* June 13, 2003.

87. For a discussion of a comeback of Jiang's "Three Represents Theory" and other conservative ideas, see, for example, Willy Wo-Lap Lam, "Setback for China's constitutional reform," www.cnn.com, September 2, 2003,

88. Su Qi, "On China's practical process of democratization," *Chinanewsweek,* July 21, 2003.

89. Li Tao, "Direct elections of party secretaries of towns and townships in Pingchang County, Sichuan," *Wen Wei Po,* January 11, 2004.

90. "Party school scholar on developing intra-party democracy," *Ming Pao,* September 18, 2003.

91. For a discussion of ways in which Jiang circumvented the Central Committee and concentrated power in his inner circle, see Willy Wo-Lap Lam, *The Era of Jiang Zemin,* pp. 86–88.

92. Wen Shan, "Party congresses may become permanent institutions," *Wen Wei Po,* July 13, 2004.

93. Wen Han, "The system of party congresses having permanent offices should be extended," *Wen Wei Po,* December 12, 2003.

94. The Central Committee (CC) created at the Sixteenth CCP Congress had 198 full and 158 alternate (nonvoting) members. Party insiders said in late 2004 that Hu and his aides were gravitating toward expanding both the full and alternate CC members at the Seventeenth CCP Congress. They said full CC members could be augmented to about 400 by then; for example, all provincial governors and most ministers and heads of central-level commissions would be eligible for full membership.

95. Author's interviews with cadres and scholars in Shanghai, November 2003.

96. Cited in "Party affairs expert: Competitive elections should be held for party cadres," CNS, June 1, 2004.

97. Cited in "Resolution of the Fourth Plenary Session of the 16th Central Committee," NCNA, September 27, 2004. Despite the long-standing rivalry between Jiang and Hu—as well as that between their respective factions—the latter was extremely careful about making even oblique criticisms of the Third-Generation patriarch. Hu's reference at the Fourth Plenum to "dictatorial actions by individuals" was his first pointed critique of the Jiang era.

98. "Resolution of the Fourth Plenary Session of the 16th Central Committee."

99. Ibid.

100. Ibid. Party sources indicated, however, that senior party cadres at the provincial and municipal level were reluctant to carry out instructions that the number of vice-party secretaries of a province and city—which could be as many as six or seven—be cut.

101. For a discussion of improvement of supervision of senior cadres, see, for example, Ren Huiwen, "CCP to implement supervision regulations regarding party bosses," *Hong Kong Economic Journal,* January 16, 2004.

102. Zhang Xin, "Party committees in more than half of the provinces cast ballots to select officials," *Wen Wei Po,* December 12, 2004; "Senior party, government posts open to competition," www.chinaview.cn website, September 9, 2004.

103. For Western and Chinese views on administrative and civil-service reforms, see, for example, "China needs far-reaching reforms in public and corporate governance," Organization for Economic Cooperation and Development (OECD) (Paris) news release, September 7, 2005, www.oecd.org/document/53/0,2340,en_2649_201185_35316789_1_1_1_1,00 .html; "China embarks on civil service reforms," *China Daily,* September 23, 2003.

104. Author's interview with a CASS political science scholar, Beijing, April 2003.

105. Ibid.

106. For a discussion of the open bidding system for projects related to the 2008 Summer Olympics, see, for example, Paul McKenzie and Jacqueline Teoh, "Bidding on Beijing 2008," *China Business Review* (a Washington-based bimonthly), vol. 30, no. 1 (January–February 2003).

107. Zhang Shuping, "China explores possibility of promoting members of the new classes as well as returnees from abroad," CNS, August 25, 2004.

108. "China embarks on civil service reforms," *China Daily,* September 23, 2004; Bao Xinyan, "Cadres get their post via election," *China Daily,* September 29, 2004.

109. "Open exams to pick officials in Guangdong Province," *Wen Wei Po,* June 12, 2003; "Candidates with higher qualifications contest for civil-service posts," CNS, August 12, 2003.

110. Author's interview with planning officials in Shenzhen, Guangdong, August 2004.

111. Luo Aiwen, "Shenzhen units come to Hong Kong to hire high-level staff," *Wen Wei Po,* July 4, 2004.

112. "Jilin pays high salaries to attract professionals," *Wen Wei Po,* June 12, 2003; "Higher pay to create cleaner civil service?" *China Daily,* December 20, 2000.

113. For a discussion of reasons behind Jiang's retirement, see, for example, Wang Jianmin, "An inside look at Jiang's sudden retirement," *Yazhou Zhoukan,* October 3, 2003; Zhu Zhan, "The Chinese puzzle: Jiang's retirement," *Asia Times* Online, September 18, 2004, www.atimes.com/atimes/China/FI18Ad07.html.

114. Author's interview with party cadre in Guangzhou, Guangdong, August, 2004; also see "19,374 civil servants fired to clean up government," NCNA, July 5, 2004.

115. Zhang Jin, "Cadres who have made mistakes in personnel appointments may be held to account," *Wen Wei Po,* December 18, 2004.

116. "Three Gorges Dam–related bridges branded 'tofu,'" Reuters, Beijing, June 7, 1999. For a discussion of the careers of Shu Huiguo and Cheng Andong, see Willy Wo-Lap Lam, "China's 'disaster zones' under pressure to bring justice," www.cnn.com, August 9, 2001.

117. Willy Wo-Lap Lam, "Lessons from China's SARS debacle," www.cnn.com, April 24, 2003; however, Meng was in 2004 reinstated to a vice-ministerial-level position in the office supervising the diversion of water from southern to northern China.

118. "SARS has helped promote administrative probity," *Wen Wei Po,* July 24, 2003

119. Cited in "Chinese officials increasingly punished," *People's Daily* (English edition), June 10, 2003.

120. "Shanxi cadres should take responsibility over serious accidents," *China Youth Daily,* August 31, 2003; "China mine toll rises," Associated Press, Beijing, August 20, 2003.

121. "Risks for cadres have become higher under regulation on the resignation of officials," CNS, July 12, 2004; "CNPC general manager resigns to take responsibility over Chongqing mine accident," CNS, April 15, 2004.

122. "Cadre responsibility system on government investment in the pipeline," *Caijing Times,* September 2, 2004; "Premier Wen on a responsibility system on flood control," NCNA, July 21, 2004.

123. Cited in staff reporter, "Cadre responsibility should be systematized," *Ming Pao,* April 21, 2004.

124. Cited in Willy Wo-Lap Lam, "Hu pulls the purse strings," www.cnn.com, June 9, 2003

125. For a discussion of Zhu Rongji's administrative reforms, see Zhiyong Lan, "The 1998 administrative reform in China: Issues, challenges and prospects," *Asian Journal of Public Administration* (a U.S. journal), vol. 21, no. 1 (June 1999).

126. Cited in staff reporters, "Local governments owe debts totaling 400 billion yuan," *Ming Pao,* March 12, 2005; "Premier Wen Jiabao's press conference at the NPC," NCNA, March 18, 2003.

127. "Premier Wen stresses importance of administrative streamlining," NCNA, May 30, 2003.

128. For a discussion of local-level opposition to Wen's bid to curtail towns and townships, see Xu Yong, "The orientation of town- and township-level administrative structural reform," *Strategy and Management* (a Beijing monthly journal) (April 2003).

129. "Ministry of Civil Affairs: The merger of towns and townships speeded up in 2003," NCNA, May 8, 2004; "800 million yuan saved through cutting and merging 864 towns and rural townships," CNS, November 15, 2004.

130. Author's interview with Professor Linda Li, Hong Kong, December 2004.

131. Zhong Xuebing, "How many directly administered cities should China have?"*Wen Wei Po,* April 1, 2004

132. For a discussion of possible additions of provinces and directly administered cities, see Long Hua, "China may finish reform of administrative divisions in 2005," *Hong Kong Economic Journal,* May 10, 2004.

133. "Interview with Ministry of Personnel spokesman," CNS, August 17, 2003.

134. Qi Bing, "China to include as civil servants staff of party and government departments as well as mass organizations," CNS, December 25, 2004.

135. For a discussion of experiments in governmental streamlining in Pudong and other cities, see, for example, Dali Yang, "Rationalizing the Chinese state," future-china.org website, April 8, 2004, www.future-china.org/csipf/activity/19990408/mt9904_4–2.htm.

136. For a discussion of the consequences of the late 2004 personnel reshuffle masterminded by Hu, see, Willy Lam, "Is Hu Jintao a reformer?"; Li Cheng, "Hu's policy shift and the *tuanpai's* coming of age," *China Leadership Monitor,* no. 15 (Summer 2005).

137. For a discussion of Jiang's cavalier attitude toward fighting graft, see, for example, Willy Lam, "New 'honesty' rules for top China leaders," www.cnn.com, January 14, 2004.

138. For a discussion between the power play between the Hu Jintao and Jiang Zemin group see, for example, Zong Hairen, "The relative influence and power of Hu Jintao and Jiang Zemin," *China Strategy,* a newsletter published by the Center for Strategic and International Studies (CSIS) International Security Program, Washington, D.C., April 30, 2004.

139. "Anti-corruption legal system to be set up in China," *People's Daily* (English edition), November 8, 2003.

140. "Hu calls on officials to clean up act," *China Daily,* February 20, 2003.

141. For a discussion of the involvement of "princelings" in the Xiamen graft scandal, see, for example, Nisid Hajari, "Fall of an empire," *Time* Asia edition, February 7, 2000.

142. Author's interview with Qiu Ping, a Hong Kong–based journalist and author who

has written two books on the Xiamen smuggling and corruption case, Hong Kong, December 2004.

143. Author's interview with Chinese sources in Beijing, April 2004.

144. For a trenchant analysis of the nature of Chinese corruption, see, for example, "Ten characteristics of Chinese corruption," a report by the Chinese Academy of Social Sciences and Tsinghua University, www.China.org.cn website, June 11, 2003, http://unpan1.un.org/intradoc/groups/public/documents/APCITY/UNPAN016642.pdf.

145. Joseph Kahn, "China and Hong Kong investigate a well-connected real estate tycoon," *NYT*, June 2, 2003; Liu Xiaobo, "The Zhou Zhengyi case and financial corruption," *Hong Kong Economic Journal,* June 16, 2003.

146. Li Bin, "Chen Liangyu: We should act according to the law and get rid of interference [in graft-related investigations]," *Shanghai Security News* (a Shanghai paper), June 7, 2003.

147. For a discussion of Jiang Zemin's alleged interference in the Zhou Zhengyi case, see Willy Lam, "Chinese corruption crusade causes new factional infighting," *China Brief,* Jamestown Foundation, January 20, 2004.

148. Staff reporter, "Zhou Zhengyi sentenced to three years in jail for market manipulation," *Ming Pao,* June 2, 2004.

149. For a discussion of Zhou's alleged links with Wang Jinbao and other Shanghai officials, see Cheng Li, "Cooling Shanghai fever," *China Leadership Monitor,* Hoover Institution, no. 12 (Fall 2004); "Former bank chief tried on corruption charges," *China Daily,* July 14, 2005.

150. Willy Lam, "Chinese corruption crusade causes new factional infighting."

151. "Wu Guanzheng pushes anti-corruption work among Party members," NCNA, August 20, 2004; Willy Wo-Lap Lam, "Setback for China's constitutional reform," www.cnn.com, September 2, 2003.

152. Cited in "China handled in the first nine months of the year the cases of 2,189 criminal suspects who were medium-ranked or senior officials," NCNA, October 30, 2003.

153. "Disgraced officials highlight chinks in the system," *China Daily,* August 15, 2003.

154. While Hu's two children run medium-scale businesses, they adopt a low profile and have not attracted the kind of derogatory remarks and innuendo associated with the children of both ex-president Jiang and late patriarch Deng Xiaoping. For a discussion of the activities of Hu's daughter, Hu Haiqing, see, for example, Cathy Chen, "China's elite wedding a class act," *Wall Street Journal,* November 8, 2003.

155. "One cadre at the level of provincial chief penalized every month," *Oriental Outlook Weekly* (Shanghai), December 29, 2003; "Ironclad measures lead to senior officials being given jail terms," *Wen Wei Po,* March 11, 2004.

156. Yu Zhenjia, "Misuse of funds uncovered in four ministries," *Wen Wei Po,* November 11, 2004; "Curbing corruption," *Shanghai Star* (an official, Shanghai-based English-language paper), July 8, 2004.

157. Staff reporter, "'Auditing storm' to hit large state firms," *Hong Kong Economic Journal,* July 8, 2004; Ren Huiwen, "The auditing storm is new breakthrough for transparency of government," *Hong Kong Economic Journal,* July 4, 2004; "Interview with the Auditor-General Li Jinhua," *Chinanewsweek,* July 18, 2003.

158. Yan Shiyu, "600 officials have lost their posts in three months of NAO investigation," *People's Daily,* June 14, 2004.

159. "Premier welcomes audit report on government departments," *People's Daily,* July 5, 2004.

160. "China enters new phase of institutional anti-corruption," *People's Daily,* January 12, 2005.

161. "Party central authorities start investigation of senior cadres in the provinces," *China Youth Daily,* July 13, 2004.

162. Sun Haifeng, "Wen Jiabao: Problems discovered in the course of auditing should be seriously rectified," *People's Daily,* June 29, 2004.

163. At least according to Transparent International tabulations, Hong Kong's ranking has declined since its reversion to Chinese rule in 1997, see "Hong Kong slips to no. 16 in global ranking of clean governments," *Ming Pao,* October 21, 2004.

164. For a discussion of the relative effectiveness of anti-corruption agencies in Hong Kong and Singapore, see "Independent anti-corruption agencies," *Transparency International Source Book, 2000,* Transparency International, Brussels, www.transparency.org/sourcebook/11.html.

165. Cited in Willy Lam, "China toys with de-Jiangification," www.cnn.com, September 24, 2003; "The Information Department of the State Department publishes the *White Paper on the Construction of Chinese Democratic Politics,*" NCNA, October 19, 2005.

166. See Jiao Guobiao, "Blasting the Publicity Department," *Yazhou Zhoukan,* April 18, 2004. For a discussion of Beijing's control over the media and the Internet, see, for example, "Control tightens as Internet activism grows," *Country Report,* Amnesty International, London, January 28, 2004; "Cyber-dissident held for past two months on libel charge," Reporters sans Frontières (RSF) news, Paris, July 28, 2005; Robin Kwong, "Deadly attacks on journalists continue with impunity," *SCMP,* January 11, 2006.

167. For a discussion of Hu's decision to stop intellectuals from discussing constitutional reforms, see John Pomfret, "China orders halt on debate on reforms," *Washington Post,* August 27, 2003.

168. Author's telephone interview with Cao Siyuan, Beijing, January 2004.

169. Cited in Zhong Guoren, "Expectations about Hu Jintao must be realistic," *Ming Pao,* October 15, 2004.

170. John Pomfret, "China orders halt on debate"; Willy Wo-Lap Lam, "Setback for China's constitutional reform," www.cnn.com, September 3, 2003.

171. "The State Council Information Office publishes *White Paper on Human Rights,*" NCNA, March 30, 2004.

172. Bao Tong, "The 'best' period for human rights?" cited in www.Chinesenewsnet.com website, April 6, 2004.

173. "Mourners attend Zhao funeral under heavy state security," Reuters, Beijing, January 29, 2005; "China dissident who tried to see Zhao family held—activist," Reuters, February 12, 2005.

174. Philip P. Pan, "A study group is crushed in China's grip," *Washington Post,* April 23, 2004.

175. "Serious human rights abuses continue in China, Kozak says," U.S. State Department website, December 16, 2004, http://usinfo.state.gov/eap/Archive/2004/Dec/15-236300.html; Amnesty International Country Reports, 2004, December, 2003, http://web.amnesty.org/report2004/chn-summary-eng.

176. Nailene Chou Wiest, "Time for democracy is 'running out,'" *SCMP,* July 24, 2003; Guan Shan, "Ren Zhongyi: Courage is needed for political reform," *Window of Southern Trends* (an official magazine), Haikou China, July 16, 2004.

177. Mao Yushi, "On Bai Le picking horses and God exercising dictatorship," *Ming Pao,* March 14, 2004.

178. Wang Yi, "Dissident views provide statesmen with opportunity to win support," cited in CNS, July 27, 2004; Guan Shan, "Ren Zhongyi."

179. Matt Forney, "Taking a stand," *Time* Asia edition, March 1, 2004; Li Fan, "Grassroots democracy in China," www.project-syndicate.org/commentaries, December 2001; author's telephone interview with Li Fan, April 2004.

180. Cited in Willy Wo-Lap Lam, "China progresses with the times," www.cnn.com, September 3, 2001.

181. For a study of official-level research into Western socialist democratic parties and

other new institutions, see, for example, Elizabeth Rosenthal, "China's Communists decide what they stand for," *NYT*, May 1, 2002; Willy Wo-Lap Lam, "China progresses with the times"; Dinkar Ayilavarapu, "Communist Party of China Inc," *Asia Times* Online, August 16, 2002, www.atimes.com/atimes/China/DH16Ad03.html.

Chapter 5

1. "Premier Wen chairs first meeting of the State Council," New China News Agency (NCNA) (an official news agency), March 22, 2003.

2. For a discussion of the diplomacy and worldview of Mao and early revolutionaries, see, for example, Lu Benlong, "Evolution of the new China's international identification," occasional paper, Shanghai Institute of International Studies, February 2004, www.siis.org.cn/english/journal/2004/2/Lu%20Benlong.htm.

3. "Hu Jintao discusses world affairs at tenth group study session of the CCP Politburo," NCNA, February 23, 2004.

4. For a discussion of Jiang as a "foreign policy president," see, for example, Willy Lam, "Jiang Zemin: Challenged on both domestic and foreign fronts," *China Brief,* Jamestown Foundation, Washington, D.C., December 10, 2001.

5. As late as 2005, many diplomats and diplomatic scholars still argued that China should stick to a foreign policy of modesty and nonaggressiveness as first preached by Deng in the early 1990s. See, for example, an article by the president of the Chinese Foreign Policy Institute, former ambassador Wu Jianmin, "Chinese diplomacy will uphold the goal of 'taking a low profile to concentrate on domestic development,'" China News Service (CNS) (an official news agency), July 24, 2005.

6. Cited in Willy Wo-Lap Lam, "Jiang rolls last diplomatic dice," www.cnn.com, September 24, 2002.

7. For a discussion of the "constructive strategic partnership" forged between Jiang and Clinton, see, for example, Harry Harding, "The Clinton-Jiang Summits: An American Perspective," speech given at the Asia Society Hong Kong Center, May 28, 1998, www.asiasociety.org/speeches/harding.html.

8. It is instructive that during President Hu's first trip to the United States as head of state in September 2005, the top leader did not ask for the "Texas ranch" treatment. Hu was eager to avoid giving the impression, associated with ex-president Jiang, that he was "pro-U.S."

9. For a discussion of Jiang Zemin's allegedly "pro-U.S." proclivities, see, for example, Willy Lam, "Hu Jintao: Emerging from the semi-shadows," *China Brief,* Jamestown Foundation, February 28, 2002.

10. For a discussion of the consequences of the 1999 bombing of the Chinese Embassy in Belgrade, see, for example, Ralph A. Cossa, "Can Sino-U.S. relations be salvaged?" *PacNet Newsletter* #20, Pacific Forum, Center for Strategic and International Studies, Honolulu, May 21, 1999; Zhang Xiaobo, "The anger runs very deep," *Time* Asia edition, June 7, 1999.

11. For a discussion of Hu's more assertive foreign policy, see, for example, Evan S. Medeiros and M. Taylor Fravel, "China's new diplomacy," *Foreign Affairs,* Washington, November/December 2003; James Przystup, "China's great power diplomacy: Implications for the U.S.," *PacNet Newsletter* #42, Pacific Forum, October 6, 2002.

12. For a Chinese viewpoint on Beijing's efforts to provide diplomatic help to the Khartoum regime, see "UN Security Council in Africa to push Sudan peace," *China Daily* (an official English-language paper), November 18, 2004.

13. Cited in "Beijing releases White Paper on National Defense," NCNA, December 27, 2004. For a discussion of Beijing's concept of defense for the new century, see, for ex-

ample, David M. Finkelstein, "China's 'new concept of security'—retrospective and prospects," paper presented at the National Defense University Conference, "The Evolving Role of the People's Liberation Army in Chinese Politics," Washington, D.C., October 30–31, 2001.

14. For a discussion of the division of labor in the Politburo, see H. Lyman Miller, "Party Politburo processes under Hu Jintao," *China Leadership Monitor,* Hoover Institution, Stanford University, no. 11 (Summer 2004).

15. Ching Cheong, "Hu takes charge of national security body," *Straits Times* (a Singapore newspaper), December 19, 2002.

16. For an official profile of Foreign Minister Li, see "Profile: Li Zhaoxing," www.en.Chinabroadcast.cn website, March 18, 2003, http://en.chinabroadcast.cn/144/2003–3-18/28@5214.htm; unofficial profiles said Li was a leader of a radical Red Guard Clique within the Foreign Ministry during the Cultural Revolution; see, for example, Paul Lin, "China's backdoor politics will fail," *Taipei Times*, March 10, 2001.

17. The so-called Japanese Faction within the Foreign Ministry has declined in importance partly because of the sorry state of Sino-Japan relations. Front runners to succeed Li Zhaoxing as foreign minister in 2008 include a couple of U.S. specialists, such as former and current ambassadors to the United States Yang Jiechi and Zhou Wenzhong, respectively.

18. For an analysis of these think-tank members, see, for example, "Who's who in China's economic policy: TIE's biennial survey of the backroom power structure," looksmart.com website, Summer 2004, www.findarticles.com/p/articles/mi_m2633/is_3_18/ai_n6276701/print.

19. For a discussion of the congressional lobbying unit under the Chinese Embassy in Washington, see Bill Gertz and Rowan Scarborough, "China influence unit," *Washington Times,* January 2, 2004.

20. For a study of Hu's Marxist and Soviet roots, see, for example, Julie Chao, "Leader seeks China's Marxist roots," Cox News Service (U.S.), January 28, 2005.

21. "China, Cuba seek closer ties," BBC news, November 23, 2004.

22. For a discussion of the potentials of India–China relations, see, for example, "Indian PM: India, China can build partnership," *People's Daily,* June 22, 2003.

23. Cited in "China issues EU Policy Paper," NCNA, October 13, 2004.

24. Cited in Cheng Dawei, "China is ushering in the era of commercial diplomacy," *Outlook Weekly* (an official Beijing magazine), January 10, 2005.

25. Cited in David Lynch, "China risks 'hard landing,'" *USA Today,* November 26, 2004; Kevin Morrison, "China outstrips U.S. appetite for consumption," *Financial Times,* February 17, 2005.

26. For a discussion of the background of U.S. businesses lobbying for China, see, for example, Jim Mann, "Big business comes to aid of China," *Los Angeles Times,* November 10, 1999.

27. China sustained a record overall trade deficit of more than $8.4 billion in the first quarter of 2004, although it still enjoyed a comfortable surplus of close to $32 billion for the entire year. "China posts $8.43 billion trade deficit in first quarter," *People's Daily,* April 12, 2004. From 2005 onward, however, the country is expected to pile up substantial surpluses again.

28. For a discussion of China's growing economic and diplomatic influence in Asia, see, for example, Fareed Zakaria, "Mishandling the China challenge," *Newsweek,* August 15, 2005; Chalmers Johnson, "Coming to terms with China," Japan Policy Research Institute, Working Paper 105, March 2005, www.jpri.org/publications/workingpapers/wp105.html.

29. For a discussion of the background of Hu's policy of good neighborliness in diplomacy, see Willy Lam, "Beijing's new 'balanced' foreign policy: An assessment," *China Brief,* Jamestown Foundation, February 20, 2004.

30. Cited in Xiao Shi, "*Heping jueqi* strategy has become state policy," *The Mirror* (a pro-Beijing Hong Kong monthly journal) (May 2004).

31. Wang Yizhou, "On prospects for Asian regionalism," paper presented at the Conference on Nationalism and Regionalism in Asia, Waseda University, Tokyo, December 2004, www.waseda-coe-cas.jp/symposium/pdf0412/wang0412.pdf.

32. Ruan Zongze, "Chinese foreign policy after the 16th CCP National Congress," *People's Daily,* December 18, 2002; the formula of "befriending, reassuring and enriching your neighbors" was cited by Premier Wen while visiting Kuala Lumpur in late 2005. See "Wen Jiabao addresses the East Asian Summit in Kuala Lumpur," NCNA, December 12, 2005.

33. James Brooke, "Reviving a Korean kingdom," *New York Times* (*NYT*), August 24, 2004.

34. "Peaceful rise: Strategic choice for China," NCNA, April 24, 2004; Zheng Bijian, "China's peaceful rise and opportunities for the Asia-Pacific region," presentation at Bo'ao Asia Forum, Hainan Island, April 2004, www.csis.org/isp/us_china_sd/0404_zheng.pdf.

35. "Full text of Premier Wen's speech at Harvard," *China Daily,* December 11, 2003.

36. Li Wen, "The theory and practice of China's peaceful rise," *China Youth Daily* (an official Beijing paper), May 16, 2004.

37. "Beijing to boost economic cooperation with ASEAN countries," *Wen Wei Po* (a Beijing-controlled paper in Hong Kong), November 28, 2004; for a discussion of a possible "China-led development model" for ASEAN, see, for example, Eric Teo, "Strategic relevance of Asian economic integration," paper presented at the conference "Building a New Asia: Towards an Asian Economic community," Research and Information System for Non-Aligned and Other Developing Countries, Tokyo, Japan, November 18–19, 2004.

38. Luo Yinwen, "Chinese defense minister talks about the 'peaceful rise' road in a speech in Thailand," CNS, March 31, 2004.

39. Duo Wei, "Expert suggests that the *heping jueqi* goal requires adjustments in economic strategy," *Ta Kung Pao* (a China-run Hong Kong daily), March 31, 2004.

40. Evan S. Medeiros, "China debates its 'peaceful rise' strategy," www.YaleGlobal.org, June 22, 2004.

41. Author's interview with Cao Siyuan, Hong Kong, June 2004.

42. There was also speculation that a few months before stepping down as CMC chairman in September 2004, ex-president Jiang advised Hu to abandon the concept of the "peaceful rise" because it did not jell with reality. Cited in Matthew Forney, "First or equals," *Time* Asia edition, September 20, 2004.

43. For a Chinese viewpoint on Japan's rationale for boosting its military prowess in order to combat "emergencies" arising from Asian flashpoints, see, for example, Li Daguang and Niu Baocheng, "Japan to use several hundred billion yen to tackle [crises] in neighboring areas," *Global Herald* (a Beijing-based official magazine), August 10, 2005.

44. "U.S., Japan establish military alliance." *China Daily,* April 13, 2004; "Japan, U.S. may increase base sharing," *Yomiuri Shimbun* (a Japan paper), August 22, 2004; Kosuke Takahashi, "Japan to become 'Britain of the Far East,'" *Asia Times* Online, February 24, 2005, www.atimes.com/atimes/Japan/GB24Dh03.html.

45. "Joint U.S.-Philippine exercises in the Spratly Islands," Associated Press, April 3, 2004.

46. For a Russian view of the U.S. involvement in the Ukraine elections, see, for example, Alexandra Volkova, "How the Americans 'created' the Orange Revolution," *Pravda* (Moscow), February 14, 2005; Fred Weir, "Will Kyrgyzstan's protests follow Ukraine's lead?" *Christian Science Monitor,* March 22, 2005; Jeremy Page, "Poll protest in Kyrgyzstan echoes Orange Revolution," *The Times of London,* March 16, 2005. For a discussion of reasons behind Washington's resumption of the sale of nuclear technology to India, see, for example, "Indo-U.S. nuclear deal is a major U.S. policy shift," Press Trust of India (an Indian news agency), November 11, 2005.

47. Cited in Andrew Perrin, "What Taiwan wants," *Time* Asia edition, March 15, 2004.

48. For a discussion of Australia's possible involvement in a Taiwan Strait war, see, for example, Robert Ayson, "Will we go to war over Taiwan?" *The Age* (an Australia paper), August 21, 2004.

49. "SCO opens permanent secretariat in Beijing," *People's Daily,* January 15, 2004.

50. Cited in Willy Lam, "Hu's central gamble to counter the U.S. 'containment strategy,'" *China Brief,* Jamestown Foundation, July 5, 2005. For a discussion of the future of the expanded SCO, see Pan Guang, "The Chinese perspective on the recent Astana Summit," *China Brief,* August 16, 2005; Tang Shiping, "Anti-terror body not a dead duck just yet: Future of Shanghai Cooperation Organization," *Straits Times,* October 12, 2002.

51. "National Security Strategy Report, September 2002," www.globalsecurity.org, September 20, 2002.

52. Huang Peizhao, "Motives behind U.S. moves in Iraq," *People's Daily,* March 22, 2003. Author's interview with Zuo Dapei in Beijing, November 2003.

53. Cited in Willy Wo-Lap Lam, "China toughens Iraq stand," www.cnn.com, March 4, 2003.

54. Ching Cheong, "U.S. redeployment seen as targeting China," *Straits Times,* August 27, 2004; Zheng Yongnian, "U.S. strategy realignment and pressure on China," *Hong Kong Economic Journal* (an independent Hong Kong paper), August 24, 2004; "U.S. intends to use top-of-the-line stealth jets to counter China's Su-30 jet fighters," *International Herald Leader* (an official Beijing magazine), April 22, 2004.

55. Author's interview with member of a diplomatic think tank in Beijing, March 2004.

56. Author's interview with Yang Fan, November 2003.

57. "Rice makes call for democratic China," Agence France-Presse, March 19, 2005. It was Condoleezza Rice who first coined the term "strategic competitors" to characterize U.S.–China relations; see Condoleezza Rice, "Campaign 2000: Promoting the national interest," *Foreign Affairs,* January/February, 2000.

58. "Bush pushes China on rights, trade surplus," Associated Press, November 20, 2005; "Bush presses Hu on trade, religious freedom," Reuters, November 20, 2005.

59. Author's interview with a senior Chinese security source in Beijing, March 2005.

60. For a discussion of Beijing's views on political changes in Kyrgyzstan, see, for example, Nury Turkel, "People power sends a message to oppressive regimes," *Wall Street Journal,* April 21, 2005.

61. For a discussion of the Tulip revolution and the future of the SCO, see John Daly, "Sino-Kyrgyz relations after the Tulip revolution," *China Brief,* Jamestown Foundation, April 26, 2005; Willy Lam, "Beijing's alarm over new 'U.S. encirclement conspiracy,'" *China Brief,* Jamestown Foundation, April 12, 2005.

62. For a discussion of the Karimov regime's disenchantment with the U.S., see, for example, Erich Marquardt and Yevgeny Bendersky, "Uzbekistan's new foreign policy strategy," *Power and Interest News Report* (U.S.), November 25, 2005, www.pinr.com/report.php?ac=view_report&report_id=404&language_id=1.

63. Zhang Lixia, Shen Lin and Ren Yan, "America's plan to contain China will be to no avail," *People's Daily,* March 23, 2005.

64. For a discussion of the new Sino-Indian friendship, see Martin Sieff, "India looks to China, not just U.S.," United Press International, May 27, 2005; John Lancaster, "India, China hoping to 'reshape the world order' together," *Washington Post,* April 12, 2005; "China and India decide to construct a relationship of strategic partnership," NCNA, April 12, 2005.

65. Cited in "Wu Jianmin: Chinese foreign policy will uphold the *taoguang yanghui* principle for the long haul," CNS, July 24, 2005.

66. For a discussion of Hu's propensity to spend more on military modernization, see, for example, Willy Lam, "Hu Jintao: Driving influence on Chinese military modernization," *China*

Brief, Jamestown Foundation, August 2, 2005; for an overall assessment of Beijing's "anti-containment" policy, see "Beijing blocks U.S. strategy abroad," *China Economic Review* (a semi-governmental website), October 2005, www.chinaeconomicreview.com/subscriber/articledetail.php?id=803.

67. A good example of Jiang trying to discourage expressions of popular nationalism was official suppression of the campaign to assert Chinese sovereignty over the Diaoyu or Senkaku islands in 1996. For an analysis, see, Peter Hays Gries, "Popular nationalism and state legitimization," in *State and Society in 21st-century China,* ed. Peter Hays Gries and Stanley Rosen (London: RoutledgeCurzon, 2004), pp. 183–185.

68. "Foreign Ministry opens house to public," *China Daily,* April 16, 2005.

69. For an analysis of reasons behind Beijing's support for anti-Japan demonstrations, see, for example, Murray Scot Tanner, "Beijing's dangerous game," United Press International, May 12, 2005; "Chinese nationalists use net in anti-Japan campaign," Associated Press, April 5, 2005.

70. Staff reporter, "Scholar says Chinese foreign policy will follow the put-the-people-first principle," CNS, May 2, 2003.

71. Yuan Hua, "Lives of 100,000 Chinese living in South Africa under threat," *International Herald Leader,* October 26, 2004; Liao Yameng, "Ministry of Foreign Affairs to boost protection for Chinese living overseas," *Wen Wei Po,* July 4, 2004; "Malaysia probes abuse of Chinese women," Reuters, November 27, 2005.

72. "Annan applauds China's role in UN," *China Daily,* October 12, 2004; Bill Gertz, "China to send troops to Haiti," *Washington Times,* September 6, 2004.

73. Lin Tianhong, "Expert: China must have a strategic concept of 'petroleum diplomacy,'" CNS, July 27, 2004.

74. Cited in Willy Lam, "China's energy obsession," *Asian Wall Street Journal (AWSJ),* July 30, 2004.

75. For an analysis of China's long-term energy needs, see, for example, Matthew Forney and Susan Jakes, "China's quest for oil," *Time* Asia edition, October 25, 2004; "Daqing to lower crude oil production," www.chinaview.cn, March 23, 2004; "China: Surging oil demand changes energy scene," *Oxford Analytica,* February 26, 2004; Brian Bremner and Dexter Roberts, "China and the great hunt for oil," *Businessweek,* November 15, 2004; "China petroleum strategy picks up speed," *Wen Wei Po,* March 13, 2004.

76. For a discussion of the assertion of Chinese naval power in the South China Seas and other regions, see, for example, David Hale, "Will China need a blue water navy to protect commodity imports?" www.chinaonline.com website, April 5, 2004, www.chinaonline.com/commentary/; A. James Gregor, "China, the United States, and Security Policy in East Asia," *Parameters* (a U.S. journal), (Summer 1996), pp. 92–101.

77. Tang Zhichao, "China and Iran pursue normal cooperation as the U.S. gets nervous," *International Herald Leader* (an official Beijing newsmagazine), November 12, 2004.

78. For a discussion of the energy and diplomatic impact of Sino-Iranian cooperation, see, for example, Robin Wright, "Iran's growing alliance with China could cost the U.S. leverage," *AWSJ,* November 18, 2004; Paul Rogers, "Iran's nuclear politics," *Energy Bulletin* (a U.K. journal) (December 3, 2004).

79. Author's interviews with Chinese diplomatic sources in Beijing and Hong Kong, November 2004.

80. For a Chinese viewpoint on thriving Sino-Australian cooperation in the energy and resources sector, see, for example, "China, Australia enhance energy cooperation," NCNA, April 7, 2004; "Hu Jintao: We can all move forward through respect, cooperation and trade," address to Australian Parliament, October 24, 2003, www.onlineopinion.com.au/view.asp?article=835.

81. For a discussion of Beijing's troubles in securing Russian oil, see, for example, John

Helmer, "Dances with bears: Oil to China is a race against time," *Asia Times* Online, October 25, 2002, www.atimes.com/atimes/Central_Asia/DJ12Ag01.html.

82. Charles Hutzler, "Halt of Yukos oil comes at bad time for Beijing," *Wall Street Journal,* September 21, 2004; Martin Sieff, "Russia calls oil shots with China," United Press International, October 20, 2004; for a discussion of Russians' fears of Chinese encroachment in the Far East, see John Daniszewski, "Far East void eats at Russia," *Los Angeles Times,* July 19, 2001.

83. "Successful demarcation makes strong Russia ties," *People's Daily,* October 15, 2004. For a discussion of accusation that Beijing had let Moscow get away with huge chunks of Chinese territory, see, for example, Ching Cheong, "One thing about which Jiang Zemin should render an explanation to the Chinese people," *Ming Pao* (an independent Hong Kong paper), September 30, 2004.

84. For a discussion of China–Kazakhstan cooperation in oil exploration, see, for example, staff reporter, "A turn-around in China's overseas petroleum strategy?" *International Herald Leader,* February 2, 2004; "China, Kazakhstan to start building eastern section of oil pipeline within year," *People's Daily,* May 18, 2004; Sergei Blagov, "Oil-rich US ally Kazakhstan looks to China," *Asia Times* Online, February 27, 2004, www.atimes.com/atimes/Central_Asia/FB27Ag01.html.

85. Cited in "Experts: China has an eye on African, South American oil," *People's Daily,* February 28, 2004.

86. For a discussion of the energy-related reasons behind the Beijing leadership's attention to Africa, see, for example, Xu Shengru, "Hu Jintao visits three African nations: Petroleum diplomacy has thrown into sharp relief China's energy gameplan," *21st Century Economic Herald* (a Guangzhou paper), February 2, 2004; "Sino-African petroleum cooperation," netease.com website, July 14, 2004; Howard French, "A resource-hungry China speeds trade with Africa," *NYT,* August 9, 2004.

87. Stephanie Ho, "China's oil imports from Sudan draw controversy," Voice of America news, July 21, 2004.

88. "Military cooperation between Angola and China under discussion," Angola Press Agency (Luanda), August 9, 2004.

89. Geraldo Samor and Alex Keto, "China cuts Latin American deals," *AWSJ,* November 22, 2004.

90. "Petrobras expects to boost crude oil experts to China," Dow Jones news wires, May 26, 2004; Andrew Hay, "Brazil recognizes China as a 'market economy,'" Reuters, November 12, 2004.

91. "President Hu pledges stronger strategic partnership with Brazil," NCNA, November 17, 2004.

92. "China and India go toe to toe over West Africa's oil," AFP, October 16, 2004.

93. For a discussion of China–Japan disputes over the Chunxiao fields and related areas, see, for example, Mao Feng, "More disputes between China and Japan over energy issues," *Yazhou Zhoukan* (a Hong Kong newsweekly), July 18, 2004; Liu Yameng, "China suggests 'joint exploration' to solve disputes over East China Sea oil fields," *Wen Wei Po,* July 11, 2004.

94. For a discussion of the Sino-Japanese conflict over the Diaoyu or Senkaku islands, see, for example, Reiji Yoshida, "Is the Senkaku row about nationalism—or oil?" *Japan Times* (Tokyo), March 27, 2004. For a discussion of Deng Xiaoping's "pledge" about the Diaoyu islands, see Xu Yu, "Diaoyu islands can be solved by the next generation," *Wen Wei Po,* November 6, 2004.

95. Cited in Willy Lam, "China's energy obsession."

96. Alan Boyd, "Oil worries lubricate South China Sea pact," *Asia Times* Online, September 4, 2004, www.atimes.com/atimes/China/FI04Ad04.html; "Arroyo's China trip a tribute to Beijing clout," news.1chinastar.com website (Manila), August 30, 2004.

97. "Philippines to allay Vietnam's fears over Spratlys oil plans," AFP, September 10, 2004; for a discussion of the tripartite cooperation among China, Vietnam, and the Philippines in oil exploration, see, for example, Huang Qing, "All-win rational choice," *People's Daily*, March 18, 2005; "Beijing, Manila and Hanoi strike deal over Spratlys' oil," asiannews.it website, March 15, 2005, www.asianews.it/view_p.php?1=en&art=2771.

98. For a discussion of how China's fast-growing resource demands could drive up the prices of oil and other resources, see, for example, "The Oiloholics," *The Economist*, August 25, 2005. Beijing, however, has consistently denied the link between Chinese demands and the rising prices of energy.

99. "Editorial: China's disquieting bid for Noranda," *Toronto Star*, October 5, 2004; Geoffrey York, "China set to buy Canada's resources," *The Globe and Mail*, October 21, 2004; "Unocal won't be the last, so set the rules now," editorial, *Businessweek*, July 11, 2005; Paul Krugman, "The China challenge," *NYT*, June 27, 2005.

100. For a discussion of potential Sino-U.S. conflict over the supply of oil from Canada and other areas, see, for example, Irwin Stelzer, "America stymied as governments bid to control oil," *Sunday Times* (London), January 30, 2005; Kevin Carmichael, "Canada, wary of China, might tighten foreign investment rules," Bloomberg news agency, January 26, 2005; "Sinopec, CNPC to invest in Canadian oil firms," *Shenzhen Daily* (an official paper), December 31, 2004.

101. Author's telephone interview with Hale, April 2004.

102. As of 2004, leading officials such as National Development and Research Commission chief Ma Kai have tried to reassure the world that China's overall energy self-sufficiency rate remained at 94 percent—and that the nation would be working on energy conservancy. See "China will not overtax global energy sources," www.chinanews.cn, April 25, 2005.

103. For a discussion of the friendship between Yang Jiechi and the Bush family, see, for example, Wang Li, "Chinese diplomat accompanies Bush on his 1977 China tour," www.china.org.cn (an official website), November 26, 2003.

104. Asia experts in the first and second terms of President George W. Bush are mostly Japan and Korea specialists rather than veteran China hands. For example, the assistant secretary of state for Asia-Pacific affairs in the second Bush administration, Christopher Hill, is a former ambassador to South Korea.

105. Barry Hillenbrand, "Bush backs arms sales with tough talk," *Time* Asia edition, April 27, 2001.

106. For a discussion of Sino-U.S. relations since the late 1990s, see, for example, Thomas J. Christensen, "Potential roadblocks to long-term PRC cooperation with the U.S.," in *Asian Aftershocks*, ed. Richard J. Ellings and Aason L. Friedberg, (Washington, D.C.: National Bureau of Asian Research, 2002), pp. 61–67; Robert L. Suettinger, *Beyond Tiananmen: The Politics of U.S.–China Relations, 1989–2000* (Washington, D.C.: Brookings Institution Press, 2003), pp. 358–442.

107. For a discussion of Beijing's Iraq strategy, see, for example, Yufeng Mao, "Beijing's two-pronged Iraq policy," *China Brief*, Jamestown Foundation, May 24, 2005.

108. Cited in staff reporter, "Qian Qichen speaking at Peking University: September 11 has stabilized ties among great powers." *Ming Pao*, September 11, 2002.

109. "China appreciates U.S. decision to put ETIM on terror list," *China Daily*, August 28, 2002.

110. For a discussion of U.S.–China relations in the wake of the war on terrorism see, for example, David M. Lampton and Richard Daniel Ewing, "The U.S.–China relationship facing international security crises," Nixon Center Monograph, 2003, www.nixoncenter.org/publications/monographs/USChinaRelations2003.pdf.

111. "Bush says Sino-U.S. relations full of vitality," NCNA, September 23, 2003; Willy Lam, "China seeks payback for North Korean efforts," www.cnn.com, September 16, 2003.

112. Edmund Andrews, "White House defends China on currency," *NYT*, December 4, 2004.

113. For an American viewpoint of the appreciation of the yuan, see, for example, Stephen Roach, "Give China credit: Beijing's shift in currency policy is great news for the global economy," *Time,* Asia edition, August 1, 2005.

114. Rumsfeld made his much-postponed visit to China in late 2005, when he was allowed to see the headquarters of the PLA missiles unit. However, no concrete breakthrough was achieved in areas including the resumption of the sale of more "dual-use technology" to China. For a discussion of the background of U.S.–China military ties, see, for example, "Officials seek 'constructive spirit,'" *China Daily,* February 3, 2005; Andrew Tully, "Why Rumsfeld wants to engage China," *Asia Times* Online, February 12, 2005, www.atimes.com/atimes/China/GB12Ad01.html. For a discussion of the recent evolution of Sino-U.S. military relations, see Jing-Dong Yuan, "Sino-U.S. military regions since Tiananmen," *Parameters* (a U.S. journal) (Spring 2003), pp. 51–67.

115. For a discussion of Sino-U.S. interactions—including Chen Yunlin's visit to Washington in 2003—regarding Beijing's bid to rein in Chen Shui-bian, see, for example, David Brown, "Pernicious presidential politics," *Comparative Connections,* third quarter 2003, Pacific Forum, Center for Strategic and International Studies (Washington), www.csis.org/pacfor/cc/0303Qchina_taiwan.html.

116. Sun Yuting, "The election will not change America's basic policy toward China," CNS, November 6, 2004.

117. Cited in Willy Lam, "The end of the Sino-U.S. honeymoon?" *China Brief,* Jamestown Foundation, June 24, 2004.

118. Lauri Li, "A good trip and a diplomatic success," www.sinorama.com.tw (a Taiwan government website), December 9, 2003.

119. For a discussion of Wen's visit to Washington in December 2003, see, for example, Kathrin Hille and James Kynge, "Bush changes tack in Strait of Taiwan," *Financial Times,* December 11, 2003.

120. Huang Tai-lin, "Powell reversal seen as 'positive' by [Taiwan] government," Central News Agency, Taipei, October 29, 2004.

121. Author's interviews with sources close to the army in Hong Kong and Beijing, November, 2004.

122. Cited in Ye Pengfei, "China's new strategy: To be predominant in Northeast Asia without fighting a war," *Lianhe Zaobao* (a Singapore paper), November 7, 2004.

123. "Anti-Secession Law adopted by NPC," *China Daily,* March 14, 2005.

124. For a study of second Bush administration's much tougher policy toward China, see, for example, "Taiwan independence may trigger conflict among China, the U.S. and Japan," editorial, *Yazhou Zhoukan,* March 27, 2005.

125. For a discussion of the delicate Sino-DPRK relations, see, for example, Anthony Spaeth, "Going nuclear: It's a crisis," *Time* Asia edition, February 24, 2003.

126. For a discussion of China's role as "honest broker" in the six-party talks on North Korea, see, for example, Paul Kerr, "U.S., North Korea jockey for China's support as working group nuclear talks approach," *Arms Control Today* (a U.S. monthly), Arms Control Association (Washington), May 2004; for a discussion of controversies over the agreement reached at the fourth session of the talks, see, for example, Todd Walters, "The Fourth Round of the Six-Party Talks," *Power and Interest News Report* (U.S.), September 5, 2005, www.pinr.com/report.php?ac=view_printable&report_id=360&language_id=1.

127. Willy Wo-Lap Lam, "China seeks payback for North Korean efforts," www.cnn.com, September 16, 2003.

128. "President Hu applauds deep China–DPRK relations," *China Daily,* October 20, 2004; "President Hu holds talks with Kim Jong-Il," NCNA, October 28, 2005.

129. For a discussion of investments by Wenzhou merchants in North Korea, see, for

example, "Chinese companies invest more in the DPRK," korea-is-one.org website, August 17, 2004, www.korea-is-one.org/article.php3?id_article=817.

130. Author's interview with Professor Shi Yinhong, Vancouver, Canada, September 2004.

131. For a discussion of how economic relations between China and the United States impact on bilateral diplomatic ties, see, for example, Pete Engardio, "The China price," *Businessweek*, December 2, 2004.

132. For a discussion of the significance of Wu's U.S. trip, see Kevin Nealer, "Assessing the Wu Yi visit," *Asia Report*, #64, Japanese Institute for Global Communications, Tokyo, April 20, 2004; "Wu makes high stakes U.S. trade mission," *China Daily*, April 19, 2004.

133. For a discussion of the mutual dependence of China and the United States in economic and other fields, see, Banning Garrett, "Strategic straitjackets: The United States and China in the 21st century," Atlantic Council Occasional Papers, Washington, D.C., October 2003, www.acus.org/Publications/occasionalpapers/Asia/GarrettStrategicStraitjacketOct03.pdf.

134. Justin Fox, "Congrats sir! Now please fix the $50 trillion mess we're in," *Fortune*, November 29, 2004; see also "The passing of the buck?" *The Economist*, December 4, 2004.

135. Author's interview with a senior member of an official think tank, Beijing, April 2004.

136. For a discussion about the dramatic improving in Sino-EU ties, see, for example, David Shambaugh, "China and Europe: The emerging axis," *Current History*, September 2004, www.brook.edu/dybdocroot/views/articles/shambaugh/20040901.pdf; Stefan Theil, "Dangerous liaisons," *Newsweek* international edition, December 13, 2004.

137. Cited in Tracey Boles, "Lifting Chinese arms ban is economic threat to Europe," *The Business* (a London-based financial paper), December 12, 2004.

138. Wang Yan, "The Chinese economy will be hurt if the U.S. were to invade Iran," *The Globe* (an official Beijing magazine), November 5, 2004; as a sign of U.S. unhappiness over Chinese involvement in Iran, Washington imposed fines on eight PRC companies in early 2005 for allegedly helping to improve the capacity of Iranian ballistic missiles; see, for example, "U.S. targets Chinese firms over Iran," Associated Press, January 19, 2005.

139. Peter Qiu, "Questions concerning China–EU strategic cooperation," *Hong Kong Economic Journal*, October 27, 2004.

140. Ambrose Evans-Pritchard, "EU viewed by China as world power to rival US," *Daily Telegraph* (London), October 14, 2003; "China maps out objectives for its EU policy," *People's Daily*, October 13, 2004.

141. Peter Gumbel, "Pack your bags for the Orient Express," *Time* Asia edition, October 18, 2004; Zhao Shengyu, "Sino-European trade is complex and sweet," CNS, December 7, 2004; Huang Jing, "China–EU relations: More vigorous, more mature," *People's Daily*, December 16, 2005.

142. "China should consider linking yuan to a basket of currencies: EU's Lamy," AFP, October 31, 2003.

143. "China maps out objectives for its EU policy," *People's Daily*.

144. "Chinese President makes proposals for world development, cooperation," *People's Daily*, June 2, 2003.

145. Chinese purchase of Airbuses is expected to surpass that of Boeings for the first time in 2005; see Stephan Theil, "Dangerous liaisons"; "China ousts Boeing," *Pravda* (Moscow), April 18, 2002.

146. For a discussion on the views of France and other EU members on the arms embargo issue, see Wu Liming, "Divergence of views within the EU on lifting arms embargo against China," *Outlook Weekly*, October 20, 2004.

147. "The EU presses China on human rights," Reuters, April 13, 2004.

148. Shi Hongtao, "Will Poland become the key to the lifting of the arms embargo against

China?" *China Youth Daily,* July 26, 2004; Goh Sui Noi, "EU not lifting China arms embargo," *Straits Times,* December 9, 2004.

149. See Mark Beunderman, "Berlin signals end to support for lifting China arms ban," *EU Observer,* www.euobserver.com, November 8, 2005. With new and less "anti-American" leaders emerging in both Paris and Berlin, Beijing would not be getting the kind of special treatment accorded China by French president Jacques Chirac and former German chancellor Gerhard Schroeder. For example, new German chancellor Angela Merkel, who grew up in Communist East Germany, is considered more "pro-U.S." than Schroeder.

150. Author's interview with Chinese diplomatic sources, Beijing, March 2004.

151. "China has signed contract for buying $1.6 billion worth of U.S. products," CNS, December 18, 2003. The purchased products were made up almost entirely of soybeans and mechanical parts.

152. For a discussion of the possible creation of a European defense force, see, "Europe: European defense policy. What is at stake in the debate about a European defense force?" Council of Foreign Affairs (New York) *Backgrounder* 7729, www.cfr.org/pub7729/esther_pan/europe_european_defense_policy.php.

153. For a discussion on the "pro-U.S." stance of the Warsaw government, see, for example, "Poland politics: Between Iraq and a hard place," *Economist Intelligence Unit* (London), October 14, 2004.

154. Cited in "China wants to link up with Europe to fight U.S. influence," *Wen Wei Po,* May 3, 2004.

155. Chen Shuren, "Will an expanded EU be another U.S. or an antagonist of the U.S.?" *Guangming Daily* (an official Beijing paper), April 30, 2004; "Impact of the eastern expansion of Europe," NCNA, April 30, 2004.

156. Ibid. For a discussion of how certain EU member countries may differ with China over issues including human rights, Taiwan, and so forth, see Liu Wenxiu, "Several factors that affect China's foreign-policy strategies toward Europe," *China's Foreign Affairs* (an official Beijing monthly), February 2005.

157. Bill Savadore, "Anti-Japan rampage in Shanghai," *SCMP,* April 17, 2005; "Waiting for May," *The Economist,* April 30, 2005; "Li Zhaoxing makes report on Sino-Japanese relations," NCNA, April 19.

158. "Troubling events in China," editorial, *Japan times,* April 13, 2005; "More than 10 million oppose Japan's UN campaign," NCNA, March 29, 2005.

159. "Chinese pop singer under fire for Japan war flag dress," *China Daily,* December 13, 2001.

160. Jim Yardley, "In soccer loss, a glimpse of China's rising ire at Japan," *NYT,* August 9, 2004.

161. For a discussion of Koizumi's "dilemma" over visits to the Yasukuni Shrine, see, for example, Jiang Xun, "Will Koizumi stop visiting the Yasukuni Shrine?" *Yazhou Zhoukan,* January 9, 2005.

162. "Gas victims demand Japan compensation," *China Daily,* August 11, 2003.

163. For a discussion of the impact of former premier Zhu's visit to Japan in 2000, see, for example, James J. Pryzstup, "The Zhu visit and after . . . Efforts to steady the course," *Comparative Connections,* Pacific Forum, fourth quarter 2000, Center for Strategic and International Studies, Washington, www.csis.org/pacfor/cc/004Qjapan_china.html; "Japan's Koizumi apologizes for World War II," Associated Press, April 22, 2005.

164. For a discussion of the issue of war reparations, see, for example, Frank Ching, "Removing the thorn from Japan–China ties," *Japan Times,* September 19, 2004.

165. "Tang Jiaxuan: China–Japan relations are at a crossroads," CNS, April 16, 2005; staff reporter, "Japan may tap gas fields with China," *Yomiuri Shimbun,* April 22, 2005.

166. "Bush, Koizumi reaffirm alliance," Kyoto News Agency, Tokyo, November 16, 2005; Toshiyuki Ito, "Japan, U.S. to upgrade strategic dialogues," *Yomiuri Shimbun,* May 5, 2005.

167. Chen Xiangyang, "Four opportunities and four challenges facing the peaceful development of Asian and African countries," *Outlook Weekly,* April 25, 2005.

168. Yu Yongsheng, "Beware of Japan interfering in Taiwan," *International Herald Leader,* January 10, 2005; Patrick Goodenough, "US reportedly eyes island near Taiwan as military base," www.cnsnews.com (U.S.), October 14, 2004; Edward Cody, "China protests U.S. – Japan accord," *Washington Post,* February 21, 2005.

169. Yu Yongsheng, "What the U.S. is interested in is dominance, and the Japanese, geopolitical advantage," *International Herald Leader,* April 11, 2005.

170. For a discussion of Beijing's worries about "defense collusion" between Japan and the United States, see, for example, Denny Roy, "Stirring samurai, disapproving dragon: Japan's growing security activity and Sino-Japan relations," Occasional Paper, Asia-Pacific Center for Security Studies, Honolulu, September 2003; "The background behind the U.S. urging Japan to revise its peace charter," CNS, August 18, 2004; Toshisyuki Ito, "Japan, U.S. to upgrade strategic dialogues," *Yomiuri Shimbun,* May 5, 2005.

171. "Japan envisages three scenarios under which it may be attacked by China," *Ming Pao,* November 9, 2004; Robyn Lim, "Can Japan counter China's growing influence in Southeast Asia?" *China Brief,* Jamestown Foundation, January 6, 2004. For a discussion of Sino-Japanese rivalry for being top dog of Asia, see, for example, Chalmers Johnson, "No longer the 'lone' superpower: Coming to terms with China," Working Paper No. 105, Japan Policy Research Institute, Tokyo, March 2005.

172. Willy Lam, "Anti-Japanese protests pose long-term challenges for Beijing," *China Brief,* Jamestown Foundation, April 26, 2005.

173. "Sino-Japanese trade flourished in 2004," NCNA, February 15, 2005; "China replaces US as Japan's top trade partner," *Asahi Shimbun,* January 27, 2005.

174. For a discussion of the background behind Chinese nationalists' opposition to the Japanese bullet train, see, for example, Hannah Beach, "Patriot games," *Time* Asia edition, November 22, 2004.

175. The semi-official Japan External Trade Organization (JETRO) noted in early June 2005 that China-based Japanese firms were less bullish about the PRC market as a result of the growth of anti-Japan sentiments among Chinese; cited in "The Koizumi government has poured cold water on Japan–China economic and trade relations," *International Herald Leader,* June 10, 2005.

176. For a discussion of the "new thinking" on Sino-Japanese relations, see, for example, Xiao Zhou, "New thoughts, old grudges," *Beijing Review* (an official magazine), April 15, 2004; Yang Ruichun, "An interview with Ma Licheng," in *Southern Weekend* (an official paper), February 27, 2003.

177. Author's interview with Ma Licheng, Hong Kong, September 2004.

178. Cited in Chi Hung Kwan, "China's confidence in its 'new thinking' on Sino-Japanese relations," website of Research Institute of Economy, Trade and Industry, Tokyo, May 30, 2003, www.rieti.go.jp/en/china/03053001.html.

179. Feng Zhaokui, "China–Japan–India axis strategy: An all-round economic and political cooperation," *People's Daily,* April 29, 2004; Leslie Fong, "Will oil woes lead to Asian EU?" *Straits Times,* October 20, 2004.

180. Lin Zhibo, "Views on certain questions in current Sino-Japanese relations," *Strategy and Management* (an official journal), vol. 2 (2004).

181. Author's interview with Professor Tsugami in Tokyo, February 2004.

182. Cited in Masuru Tamamoto, "After the tsunami, how Japan can lead," *Far Eastern Economic Review,* February 2005.

183. For an explanation of the significance of Wang's appointment, see Fang Zhou, "One step to thaw chilly relationship with Japan," *China Daily,* October 18, 2004.

184. "Koizumi warned over war shrine," BBC News, November 24, 2004.

185. Cited in "Premier Wen meets the press after the closure of the NPC," NCNA, March 14, 2005.

186. For a Chinese viewpoint on the predominance of "right-wing" politicians in the post-Koizumi era, see, for example, "It is hard to rectify the rightward turn in Japanese politics," *International Herald Leader,* August 12, 2005. For a discussion of a couple of possible "right-wing" politicians who may succeed Koizumi, see, for example, "News analysis: Koizumi's new cabinet features reformers, hawks," NCNA, November 1, 2005.

187. "China to join ASEAN Friendship Treaty," *People's Daily,* April 29, 2003. For a discussion of China–Southeast Asia relations, see, for example, Brantly Womack, "China and Southeast Asia: Asymmetry, leadership and normalcy," *Pacific Affairs,* vol. 76, no. 3 (Winter 2003–2004).

188. Jason Liew, "Hu's peace pledge: China is a partner, not a threat, to Asia," *Straits Times,* April 25, 2004.

189. Yang Shenghua, "China and ASEAN to sign trade agreement," *Wen Wei Po,* November 3, 2004; "China to speed up FTA process with ASEAN," NCNA, November 3, 2004.

190. "China and ASEAN to form the world's largest free trade area," CNS, November 29, 2004.

191. "When will an 'Asian dollar' come true?" NCNA, June 26, 2004.

192. For a discussion of the relative merits of the yuan and yen as a regional currency, see, for example, Carsten Hefeker and Andreas Nabor, "Yen or yuan? China's role in the future of Asian monetary integration," Hamburgisches Welt-Wirtschafts-Archiv Discussion Paper 206, Hamburg Institute of International Economics, 2002.

193. "Japan speeds up process of forming FTAs with neighbors to counter China," Associated Press, April 3, 2004.

194. Amy Kazmin and Victor Mallet, "ASEAN will take no action against Burma," *Financial Times,* November 29, 2004; "China–ASEAN bloc bids to become world's no. 1," editorial, *European Times* (a pro-Beijing Chinese-language paper in Europe), December 1, 2004; Liu Zhenting, "The rise of ASEAN as counterweight to the U.S. and the EU," *Yazhou Zhoukan,* December 12, 2004; Sheng Lijun, "Great game plays on in Asia," *Straits Times,* November 28, 2005.

195. Michael Vatikiotis, "A diplomatic offensive," *Far Eastern Economic Review,* August 5, 2004.

196. For a discussion of the implications of Singapore's support of a U.S. role in policing the Malacca Strait, see Eric Teo, "The China–Singapore row and Sino-U.S. rivalry," *PacNet* Newsletter No. 44, Pacific Forum, October 7, 2004.

197. Greg Sheridan, "PM defies Bush over China arms," *The Australian,* February 12, 2005.

198. For a discussion of Beijing's new clout in Indonesia, the Philippines, and other ASEAN member nations, see, for example, Hannah Beech, "Deals and diplomacy," *Time* Asia edition, May 30, 2005; Dana R. Dillon and John Tkacik, Jr., "China and ASEAN: Endangered American primacy in Southeast Asia," *Backgrounder,* Heritage Foundation, Washington, D.C., October 19, 2005. It is significant that Washington resumed arms sales to Jakarta in late 2005, perhaps as a reaction to the inroads made by Beijing in Indonesia.

199. For a discussion of the significance of China's role in the inchoate East Asian Community, see Willy Lam, "Beijing's strategy to counter U.S. influence in Asia," *China Brief,* Jamestown Foundation, December 6, 2005; Edward Cody, "East Asian Summit marked by discord," *Washington Post,* December 14, 2005. Tokyo and Canberra have already made known their desire to prevent Beijing from dominating the EAC.

200. Li Jing, "Hu Jintao suggests building a new form of strategic partnership relationship among Asian-African countries," CNS, April 22, 2005; Grant Ferrett, "Leaders praise Asia–Africa deal," BBC news, April 23, 2005.

201. For a discussion of the significance of the "triangular relationship" between Beijing,

Moscow, and New Delhi, see, for example, "China, India, Russia to join forces to boost regional security," AFP, June 2, 2005; "India, Russia and China issue a joint communiqué," Press Trust of India, June 2, 2005. The bulk of the diplomatic activities of the Politburo Standing Committee members in 2004 and 2005—for example, trips taken by Hu Jintao, Wen Jiabao, Wu Bangguo, Zeng Qinghong, and Jia Qinglin—were focused on countries and areas including ASEAN, Russia, Africa, and Latin America.

202. "Hu Jintao's full speech to the Asia–Africa Forum," NCNA, April 22, 2005; "Wen Jiabao addresses the East Asian Summit at Kuala Lumpur," NCNA, December 12, 2005; "China a boon to Asia," Associated Press, December 13, 2005.

203. Yu Sui, "New trends in the world situation," NCNA, May 8, 2005; "China to promote financial diplomacy this year to protect the country's best interests," CNS, June 7, 2005.

Chapter 6

1. Cited in Nicholas Kristof, "The China threat?" *New York Times* (hereafter *NYT*), December 20, 2003.

2. In early 2005, Beijing successfully used the "public opinion" card to postpone if not derail Japan's bid to become a permanent member of the UN Security Council; see, for example, Patrick Goodenough, "History, rivalry cloud Japan's hopes for UN Security Council seat," www.cnsnews.com, April 5, 2005.

3. Cited in Willy Wo-Lap Lam, "Beijing bans anti-war protests," www.cnn.com, March 11, 2003.

4. For a discussion on the relationship between China's leftists and nationalists, see, for example, Feiwen Rong, "Chinese allowed to speak their minds on Iraq," *Taipei Times* (English-language paper in Taiwan), May 10, 2003; Willy Wo-Lap Lam, "China's leaders turn to Mao," www.cnn.com, November 18, 2003.

5. "Chinese nationalism under the background of globalization," speech delivered by Wang Xiaodong at the London School of Economics, London, February 7, 2005.

6. Author's interviews with noted leftist-nationalists Yan Fan and Wang Xiaodong, Beijing, November 2003.

7. Cited in John Tkacik, "Time for Washington to take a realistic look at China policy," *Backgrounder* #1717, Heritage Foundation, Washington, D.C., December 22, 2003.

8. Peter Hays Gries, "Popular nationalism and state legitimization," in *State and Society in 21st-Century China*, eds. Peter Hays Gries and Stanley Rosen (London: RoutledgeCurzon, 2004), pp. 180–181.

9. "Global Times survey: How Chinese regard Sino-U.S. relations," *People's Daily* (an official Chinese paper), March 2, 2005.

10. Justin McCurry and Jonathan Wats, "China's angry young focus their hatred on an old enemy," *The Guardian* (London), December 30, 2004.

11. Ma Licheng, Shi Hanhong, and Chinese Academy of Social Sciences Japan expert Feng Zhaokui were denigrated as the "three big traitors" by anti-Japan and nationalistic groupings in China.

12. Staff reporter, "One million netizens put down their names to seek war-time compensation from Japan," *Ming Pao,* (a neutral Hong Kong newspaper), September 15, 2003; Peter Gries, "China's 'New Thinking' on Japan," *China Quarterly* (London) (Spring 2005).

13. "Mayor fears Olympics expectations too high," *China Daily,* November 12, 2004.

14. Long Tao, "Will nationalistic feelings get involved in commercial operations?" *International Herald Leader* (an official Beijing-based weekly magazine), February 7, 2005; "Who are the nationalistic angry youths?" *International Herald Leader,* November 9, 2004;

"Explaining the 'angry youth' phenomenon: Loving your country or derailing it?" New China News Agency (NCNA) (an official news agency), November 18, 2004.

15. Joseph Kahn, "China pushing and scripting Japan protests," *NYT*, April 15, 2005; "China's reckless nationalism," editorial, *International Herald Tribune*, April 13, 2005.

16. "Japanese blame Chinese nationalism," Associated Press, April 26, 2005. For a discussion of the international fallout of the anti-Japan protests, see, for example, Willy Lam, "Anti-Japanese protests pose challenge for China," *China Brief*, Jamestown Foundation, Washington, D.C., April 29, 2005.

17. "Wu Jianmin: Only when the fundamental interests of the nation are safeguarded can real patriotism be achieved," China News Service (CNS) (an official news agency), April 22, 2005.

18. Liu Feng, "Patriotism, while aroused by feelings of justice, should be restricted by reason," NCNA, April 18, 2005; Vivian Wu, "Don't boycott Japanese goods, says minister," *South China Morning Post* (*SCMP*) (an English-language Hong Kong newspaper), April 23, 2005.

19. Joseph Kahn, "State-run Chinese paper lashes anti-Japan protests as 'evil plot,'" *NYT*, April 27, 2005.

20. See Willy Lam, "Anti-Japanese protests pose challenge for China," *China Brief*, April 29, 2005. For a discussion of a divergence of views among the top leadership on ways to handle the protests, see, for example Wang Dan, "Rivalry between Hu and Jiang still going on," *Apple Daily* (a neutral Hong Kong daily), May 12, 2005.

21. For a discussion of Deng's views on the Diaoyu/Senkaku Islands, see, for example, Charles K. Smith, "Senkaku/Diaoyu Island dispute threats amiability of Sino-Japanese relations," www.pinr.com, May 3, 2004.

22. For an official account of the signing of the border agreement, see "China, Russia agree on borders, WTO entry," *China Daily* (an official English-language daily in Beijing), October 15, 2004. However, the details of the border pact have never been released.

23. For a discussion of the secrecy concerning the Korean War, see, for example, Howard W. French, "Was the war pointless? China shows how to bury it," *NYT*, March 1, 2005.

24. Cited in "Hu Jintao meets old Soviet soldiers," NCNA, May 9, 2005. For a discussion of Hu's refusal to face up to the truth about Sino-Soviet relations, see, for example, Willy Lam, "Hu wants alliance with Russia to fight the U.S. and Japan," *Apple Daily*, May 12, 2005.

25. Ren Bingqiang, "The waves of nationalism since the 1990s: Criticizing the nationalist views of Wang Xiaodong," in *Undercurrents: Criticisms and Reflections on Narrow-minded Nationalism*, ed. Le Shan (Shanghai: Huadong Normal University Press, 2004).

26. "Chinese tour groups given green light to visit Europe," AFP, August 31, 2004.

27. The United States is still the favorite country for Chinese students going abroad for advanced education, and despite the fallout of the September 11, 2001, attacks, the influx into America of Chinese students and experts taking courses of all kinds, including government and administration, has continued unabated. See "U.S. visas to Chinese students set to top record," *China Daily*, June 17, 2005; Louis Lavelle, "China's B-school boom," *Businessweek*, January 9, 2006.

28. Liu Ningzhe, "Experts advocate hiring foreigners as civil servants," *Wen Wei Po* (a Beijing-controlled Hong Kong daily), February 3, 2005.

29. Zhong Xuebing, "WHO experts work in an office close to that of the mayor," *Wen Wei Po*, May 1, 2003.

30. Staff reporter, "Does China need foreign inspectors to protect its environment?" *International Herald Leader*, November 30, 2004.

31. Wang Jianmin, "Li Changchun on combating Westernization and efforts to divide up China," *Yazhou Zhoukan* (a Hong Kong newsweekly), October 31, 2004.

32. Yu Keping, "On the 'Beijing consensus' and China's development model," *The Contemporary World and Socialism* (a Beijing journal) (May 2004).

33. Cited in Willy Wo-Lap Lam, "WTO winds blow away the old China," www.cnn.com, July 3, 2001.

34. Zhou Xiaozheng, "ACTFU officials say efforts to set up unions in foreign enterprises have often been obstructed," NCNA, October 24, 2004.

35. The first specialist court handling non-Chinese firms was set up within the Shenzhen Intermediate Court in 1988. In the first few years, this "Overseas Economic Court" mainly dealt with cases involving Hong Kong and Taiwan companies. See "Shenzhen Intermediate Court protects the rights of Taiwan firms," *Shenzhen Daily* (an official paper in the Shenzhen municipality), July 11, 2002.

36. Author's interview with Hung Ching-tin, director of Hong Kong Polling Associates, a Hong Kong–based opinion polling company that has done surveys in southern Chinese provinces.

37. "Legislation on direct selling expected this year," NCNA, February 10, 2004.

38. Nottingham University in the U.K., for example, is setting up a 4,000-student campus in Ningbo; see Jane MaCartney, "University establishes an English outpost in China," *Times of London,* September 16, 2005; author's interview with Gary Rawnsley, Nottingham University professor in charge of the project, Hong Kong, August, 2004.

39. Author's interview with a Beijing-based social sciences professor, March 2004.

40. For a discussion of how foreign banks in China will be able to attract more customers and talents, see, for example, staff reporter, "WTO forces domestic banks to mature," *People's Daily,* November 20, 2000.

41. Yu Keping, "From the discourse of 'Sino-West' to 'globalization': Chinese perspectives on globalization," Working Paper, Institute on Globalization and the Human Condition, McMaster University, Canada, March 2004.

42. For a discussion of the political and nationalistic overtones of Zhang Yimou's *Hero,* see, for example, Tzu-hsiu Chiu, "Public secrets: Geopolitical aesthetics in Zhang Yimou's *Hero,"* E-ASPAC newsletter, Pacific University in Forest Grove, Oregon, 2005, http://mcel.pacificu.edu/easpac/2005/tzuchiu.php3.

43. For a study of the possible impact of democratization in Hong Kong on the rest of China, see, for example, Minxin Pei, "Democratic contagion?" *Newsweek* Asia edition, March 22, 2004.

44. Wang Daohan, an adviser of former president Jiang Zemin and chairman of the Association for Relations Across the Taiwan Strait, is a well-known dove on reunification issues. Before bilateral ties went into a tailspin with the advent of the "Green" administration in Taipei, Wang had told Taiwan emissaries that even the future name and anthem of a reunited China can be discussed by the mainland and Taiwan as two equal partners.

45. Leslie H. Chan, "Nationalism, federalism and China's search for modernization—An historical perspective," paper presented the 39th Annual Meeting of the Southeast Regional Conference of the Association for Asian Studies, Duke University, January 14–16, 2000.

46. Author's interview with Wu Jiaxiang, Beijing, April 2003; Wu Jiaxiang, "The three waves of federalism in China," paper presented at the Conference on Constitutionalism in Modern and Contemporary China, Sydney, Australia, January, 2003, cited in www.ncn.org website, February 9, 2003.

47. Wu Jiaxiang, "A cat with federalist stripes: Deng Xiaopoing's creation of a multi-layered political system for China," www.ncn.org website, November 15, 2001.

48. Wang Xiangwei, "An EU road map for Taiwan Strait?" *SCMP*, November 2, 2004.

49. Gabriella Montinola, Yingyi Qian, and Barry Weingast, "Federalism, Chinese style: The political basis for economic success in China," *World Politics* (a U.S. journal) (October 1995); author's telephone interview with Yan Jiaqi, December 2002.

50. For example, Article 96 of the Chinese Constitution points out that "Local people's congresses at different levels are local organs of state power."

51. For a discussion of the dynamics of central-regional power sharing as deduced from the Constitution, see, for example, Willy Lam, "China's tussle with the provinces," *Asian Wall Street Journal*, April 22, 2004.

52. Li Limin, "Interview with Qian Yingyi," *Economics* (an official Beijing journal) (January 2004).

53. For a discussion of the Xinjiang policy of Hu Jintao and Wang Lequan, see, for example, Stephen Schwartz, "The coming Chinese jihad," *Weekly Standard* (London), June 17, 2004.

54. For a discussion of Beijing's policies on Tibet and Xinjiang in 2003 and 2004, see, for example, Alex Perry, "A conversation with the Dalai Lama," *Time* Asia edition, October 25, 2004; Nicolas Becquelin, "Criminalizing ethnicity: Political repression in Xinjiang," *China Rights Forum*, Human Rights in China, no. 1, 2004, www.hrichina.org/fs/view/downloadables/pdf/downloadable-resources/b1_Criminalizing1.2004.pdf.

55. "Deng Weizhi pushing Net-based democracy," *Wen Wei Po*, March 4, 2004.

56. According to Frank Lu, head of the Information Center for Human Rights and Development in Hong Kong, the Internet remains a useful tool for dissidents in China to keep in touch with the outside world. Author's interview with Frank Lu, Hong Kong, August, 2004.

57. Josephine Ma, "Author held after work goes online," *SCMP*, December 20, 2002.

58. "Sichuan Internet dissident arrested," Reuters, September 24, 2003; "China formally arrests Internet dissident on subversion charges," AFP, September 24, 2003.

59. "'Bulletproof vest party secretary' spills more beans," *Legal Evening Post* (a Beijing paper), August 12, 2004.

60. Staff reporter, "Shandong man vows to risk his life to fight corruption," *Ming Pao*, August 8, 2004.

61. For a discussion of the "Super Girl" phenomenon, see Susan Jakes, "Li Yuchun loved for being herself," *Time* Asia edition, October 3, 2005; "China rockin' to 'Super Girl,'" *China Daily*, August 30, 2005; Jiang Xun, "China leads the world with SMS economic miracle," *Yazhou Zhoukan*, February 27, 2005.

62. Joseph Kahn, "China is filtering phone text messages to regulate criticism," *NYT*, July 3, 2004; "The whole nation to crack down on SMS networks," CNS, June 1, 2004.

63. Zheng Hailong, "China's largest hackers' association is dissolved," *Wen Wei Po*, February 8, 2004.

64. Joseph Kahn, "Net censorship is the world's tightest," *NYT*, December 4, 2002; Paul Mooney, "China's cyber crackdown," *Newsweek* Asia edition, December 16, 2002.

65. Staff reporter, "Internet cafes cut by half nationwide," *Wen Wei Po*, February 21, 2003.

66. "Chinese control Internet by sophisticated means," Associated Press, April 15, 2005; "Living dangerously on the Net," Reporters Without Borders report, www.rsf.org, May 12, 2003.

67. For a study of the background of official censure of influential BBS, see, for example, Xiao Qiang, "Students protest restrictions on most influential BBS," *China Digital Times*, Graduate School of Journalism, University of California, Berkeley, May 13, 2005; for an assessment of China's blogging phenomenon, see Nicholas Kristof, "Blogs are strangling Chinese communism," *NYT*, May 25, 2005; Jiang Xun, "Blogging has changed China's way of life," *Yazhou Zhoukan*, January 15, 2006.

68. For a discussion of the "ten-tier" class structure first publicized by the CASS in 2002, see, for example, Li Minqi, "China's class structure in the world system perspective," www.chinastudygroup.org, April 1, 2003.

69. Cited in John Pomfret, "China balances power and freedom," *Washington Post*, October 3, 2002.

70. Citied in Richard Bush, "China's business leaders: Assuming a political role?" in

Brookings Northeast Asia Survey 2003–2004 (Washington, D.C.: Brookings Institution, 2004), p. 115.

71. Cited in Willy Wo-Lap Lam, "Premier Zhu fights for his legacy," *China Brief,* Jamestown Foundation, October 10, 2002.

72. See the 2005 article by Li Rui, "The voice of a 'sensitive writer,'" for a sampling of the liberal ideas of the famous party elder, www.observechina.net/info/artshow.asp?ID=35175&ad=5/19/2005.

73. Cited in Willy Wo-Lap Lam, "Dictatorial decision-making," www.cnn.com, January 9, 2002.

74. Ibid.

75. Author's interview with Professor Cao, Beijing, November 2003.

76. Richard Bush, "China's business leaders," p. 10.

77. For a study of the significance of the Liu Yonghao phenomenon, see, for example, "China: Communist Party touts billionaire capitalist role model," Stratfor.com website, January 25, 2002.

78. Staff reporters, "An investigation into China's private enterprises," *Caijing* (a Beijing financial biweekly), February 20, 2003.

79. Wu Zhong, "Rich pickings: Greed and official corruption are taking their toll on the mainland's wealthy," *Hong Kong Standard,* December 2, 2003.

80. For a discussion of China's young millionaires, see, for example, Tim Luard, "China's jet set takes to the skies," BBC news, November 17, 2003.

81. Author's interview with Guangdong official, Guangzhou, December 2003.

82. Tian Wensheng, "Villagers in Chongqing cast their ballets for rich people," *China Youth Daily,* August 19, 2004.

83. Cited in "Red bosses make no differentiation between politics and business," *Ming Pao,* June 22, 2003.

84. "Businessmen who pay lots of taxes can become officials in Hebei and Jilin," *Ming Pao,* February 13, 2004.

85. "NPC and CPPCC members concerned about the phenomenon of 'red-hat business-men,'" *China Commercial Times,* March 1, 2004.

86. For a discussion of the role of the *haiguipai,* see, for example, Ariane Berthoin Antal and Jing Wang, "Organizational learning in China: The role of returners," discussion paper SP III 2000–103, Wissenschaftszentrum Berlin fur Sozialforschung, http://skylla.wz-berlin.de/pdf/2003/iii03–103.pdf.

87. Staff reporter, "Looking for 'returnees' from all over the world," *China Youth Daily,* October 16, 2004.

88. For a discussion of the dual nationality controversy, see "Demand for dual national-ity has risen," *International Herald Leader,* December 7, 2004.

89. For a discussion of the long tradition of *haiguipai* intellectuals appointed to senior positions in the government, see, Li Liang and Dong Shuhua, "Illustrious 'tenth-genera-tion' *haiguipai* officials," *Southern Weekend,* April 14, 2005.

90. For a study of the careers of prominent returnees, see Li Cheng, "The status and characteristics of foreign-educated returnees in the Chinese leadership," *China Leadership Monitor* no. 16 (Fall 2005). For a discussion of the rise of Zhou Mingwei, see, for example, "China names new official for Taiwan relations," Reuters, July 6, 2000.

91. For a study of why Fang Xinghai and some of his contemporaries returned to work in China, see, for example, Robin Ajello and Rose Tang, "Homeward bound," *Asiaweek,* July 17, 1999.

92. For example, Zhu's son, Levin Zhu, forty-six, who was trained in the United States, is a senior executive in the China International Capital Corporation (CICC), a high-profile joint venture investment bank affiliated with Morgan Stanley. CICC has been active in the listing of China's major SOEs. See, for example, Cathy Chan, "China International lands top IPO," *Hong Kong Standard,* March 11, 2005.

93. For a discussion of Cha's career, see "Iron supervisor bows out," *Beijing Review,* September 23, 2004.

94. "412 overseas candidates have applied for senior management positions in enterprises under central government control," CNS, June 29, 2005.

95. Author's interview with Anthony Neoh, Hong Kong, April 2002.

96. Many *haiguipai* cadres were taken aback when senior colonel Xu Junping defected to the United States in 2000. Xu had undergone a six-month training at Harvard University, where he reportedly developed a liking for Western culture and values.

97. Huang Jiahua, "Who are members of China's middle class?" *Lianhe Zaobao* (a Singapore paper), December 31, 2004.

98. Li Zhengtong, "The rise and practice of China's middle class," Beijing Social and Economic Sciences Research Institute website, August 1, 2004, www.sociology.cass.net.cn/shxw/shjgyfc/P020040628482601872939.pdf.

99. Cited in "The next great leap, 2004–2005," *Uncommon Knowledge* program, American Public Television, July 15, 2004, www.uncommonknowledge.org/900/908.html.

100. Wang Sirui, "The formation of the middle class," Beijing Social and Economic Sciences Research Institute website, September 1, 2004, cited in www.yannan.cn/data/detail.php?id=6563.

101. Cited in Shi Yanzi, "Chase away the mist of history and smash the prison of thought," *Yazhou Zhoukan,* September 12, 2004.

102. Author's interview with a U.S.-graduated *haiguipai* social scientist teaching in a Beijing university, Beijing, November 2003; for a discussion of the role of Chinese intellectuals, see, for example, Ding Dajun, "The role of Chinese intellectuals in the Hu-Wen era," *China Strategy,* a newsletter of the CSIS International Security Program, Washington, D.C., vol. 1, January 30, 2004.

103. Author's interview with Wang Juntao, New York, August 2003.

104. Author's interview with Yu Jie in Hong Kong, July 2003.

105. "Who are public intellectuals," *Southern People's Weekly* (a Guangzhou magazine), September 7, 2004.

106. Yu Keping, "The emergence of Chinese civil society and its significance to governance," cccpe.com website, Winter 2002, cited in www.ids.ac.uk/ids/civsoc/final/china/chn8.doc.

107. For a study of social welfare-oriented NGOs in China, see Yiyi Lu, "The limitations of NGOs: A preliminary study of non-governmental social welfare organizations in China," Centre for Civil Society, London School of Economics, International Working Papers #13, 2003, www.lse.ac.uk/collections/CCS/pdf/IWP%2013%20%20Lu%20Yiyi.pdf.

108. More than 100 provinces and cities in China have set up consumerism-oriented NGOs, which are affiliated with the umbrella China Consumers Association.

109. Peter Wonacott, "Green groups move to clean up China," *Asian Wall Street Journal,* June 14, 2004; Ray Cheung, "Project is trimmed from 13 to four sites," *SCMP,* November 2, 2004.

110. Liu Songshi, "Intellectuals and peasants are fighting against the son of Li Peng," *Yazhou Zhoukan,* November 21, 2004.

111. Zhang Jin, "CCP makes provisions for new developments in the civil society," *Wen Wei Po,* September 6, 2004.

112. Yu Keping, "The emergence of Chinese civil society and its significance to governance."

113. Dorinda Elliott, "The last frontier," *Time* Asia Edition, June 19, 2005; "Defender of the rights of housing—Zheng Enchong," Amnesty International news release, June 16, 2005. For a discussion of the contribution of activist lawyers, see Ji Shuoming and Wang Jianmin, "Chinese lawyers protect the rights of citizens and pioneer rule of law," *Yazhou Zhoukan,* December 25, 2005.

114. Joseph Kahn, "A Chinese Robin Hood runs afoul of Beijing," *NYT,* August 24,

2003; "Academics and lawyers urge authorities to clarify laws surrounding the Sun Dawu case," *Ming Pao,* August 5, 2003.

115. Benjamin Youngquest, "China attorney appeals for Falun Gong," *Epoch Times* (a U.S.-based Chinese-language paper), January 5, 2005; Wang Jianmin, "A legal battle to protect freedom of worship," *Yazhou Zhoukan,* December 25, 2005.

116. Nailene Chou Wiest, "Suspended jail term for Internet dissident," *SCMP,* June 12, 2004.

117. Liu Kegang, "Mao Yushi and Cao Siyuan focus on political reform," *Ming Pao,* October 12, 2004.

118. Liu Kegang, "Beijing's mass-based think tanks exert more influence in China," *Ming Pao,* October 11, 2004; author's interview with Cao Siyuan and Li Fan, December 2003, Beijing and Hong Kong.

Chapter 7

1. Many Chinese and Western analysts believe that if "purchasing power parity" standards are used, and taking into consideration the undervaluation of the yuan, the Chinese GDP has already overtaken those of Germany and Japan. For example, the CIA World Fact Book said that in 2003, China's economy was the second largest in the world. See www.cia.gov/cia/publications/factbook/geos/ch.html.

2. Xing Zhigang, "Experts discuss a harmonious society," *China Daily* (an official English-language paper), March 4, 2005; Yang Peng, "What are the main contradictions in Chinese society now?" *China Youth Daily* (an official Beijing paper), November 16, 2005.

3. Staff reporter, "Land related protest activities increase in the villages," *Ming Pao* (an independent Hong Kong daily), September 7, 2004; Liu Kegang, "Six petitioners threaten to jump out of building near the Zhongnanhai party headquarters," *Ming Pao,* August 20, 2004; "Multi-millionaire bombed to death by Sichuan man," China News Service (CNS) (an official news agency), June 23, 2004.

4. Wang Jianmin, "The inside story of 50,000 [people] surrounding government premises in Chongqing," *Yazhou Zhoukan,* (a Hong Kong–based weekly newsmagazine) November 7, 2004; staff reporters, "More than 10,000 people stage riot in Chongqing," *Ming Pao,* October 20, 2004.

5. Zhang Shutong and Sun Chengbin, "On the drafting of the 'Resolution on the Construction of the Party's Governance Ability,'" New China News Agency (NCNA) (an official news agency), September 27, 2004.

6. "Party Chief Hu: Building a democratic, law-based and harmonious society," CNS, February 19, 2005.

7. "Expert: Boosting the construction of governance ability has touched the heart of the reform of the political structure," CNS, September 28, 2004; "Jia Qinglin: Resolutely rally behind CCP leadership," CNS, September 25, 2004.

8. Xu Yu, "Xiao Yang appeals for the upholding of judicial authority," *Wen Wei Po* (a Chinese-run Hong Kong daily), October 9, 2004.

9. The "separation of party and government" platform was put forward by Zhao Ziyang with the full support of Deng Xiaoping. Even after the 1989 Tiananmen Square crackdown, Deng said "not one word of the 13th Congress document should be adulterated."

10. "Hu Jintao: The party's *baoxian* construction will bring benefits to the people," NCNA, January 25, 2005. "Boost the party's construction relating to governance ability," *People's Daily* (an official Beijing paper), January 6, 2005.

11. For a discussion of more "humane" ways to resolve conflicts and to construct a harmonious society, see, for example, "A road map for building a harmonious society," *21st Century Economic Herald* (an official Guangzhou paper), March 4, 2005.

12. "Party General Secretary Hu: Building a democratic, law-based and harmonious society," CNS, February 19, 2005.

13. Cited in Sun Yuting, "China has entered the 'post-GDP era,'" CNS, March 6, 2005.

14. Huang Zhong, "Should the *xinfang* system be abolished?" *Chinanewsweek,* December 13, 2004; Cathy Chen, "Chinese protests grow more frequent, violent," *Wall Street Journal,* November 11, 2004.

15. "Editorial: Environment watchdog shows it's ready to bite," *South China Morning Post* (a Hong Kong English-language paper), January 21, 2005; He Xianghong, "Hydroelectric projects may be 'defrozen' next year," *Wen Wei Po,* December 11, 2004; "Work on Xiluodu hydroelectric station to stop," CNS, February 7, 2005.

16. "Hu Jintao: Per capita share of GDP to reach US$3,000 in 15 years," NCNA, October 15, 2005; "Premier: GDP to exceed US$1.85 trillion in 2005," *China Daily,* October 20, 2005; "China approves proposals on 11th Five-Year Plan," NCNA, October 11, 2005.

17. Zhou Tianyong, "Finding a better growth model," *China Daily,* October 27, 2004.

18. Cited in Anthony Kuhn, "The death of 'growth at any cost,'" *Far Eastern Economic Review* (a Hong Kong–based journal) (April 1, 2004); Wang Yongqian, "Time to change the way economic growth is attained," *Bimonthly Chat* (an official Beijing magazine), October 9, 2005.

19. Shi Lucheng, "Large-scale land subsidence in four areas of Heilongjiang," *Wen Wei Po,* June 15, 2004.

20. Cited in "Chinese villages, police clash," Reuters, August 5, 2005.

21. Cited in Wang Lei, "China to enter into a phase of multiple crises by 2010," *China Youth Daily* (a relatively liberal Beijing paper), September 3, 2004.

22. George J. Gilboy and Eric Heginbotham, "The Latin Americanization of China?" *Current History* (a U.S. journal) (September 2004).

23. Cited in Willy Lam, "China's dangerous class divide set to stay," www.cnn.com, September 2, 2002; Di Wei, "Senior officials in Guangdong and Shaanxi disciplined over coal mine disasters," *Wen Wei Po,* December 24, 2005.

24. Lan Pingyi, "Watershed for Chinese development," *Oriental Outlook Weekly* (an official Chinese magazine), August 6, 2004.

25. "Critical Point," *Beijing Review* (an official English-language magazine), September 9, 2004.

26. Wang Lei, "China to enter into a phase of multiple crises by 2010."

27. Singapore has run large numbers of short- and medium-term management courses for Chinese cadres. Former Singapore prime minister Lee Kuan Yew thinks Beijing is keen to learn aspects of the city-state's administration, see "Lee Kuan Yew reflects," *Time* Asia edition, December 5, 2005.

28. Jonathan Fenby, "China's industrial revolution a great leap into polluted water," *The Observer,* August 18, 2004; "Glaciers in Tibet receding," NCNA, May 10, 2004; "Famous spring in Dunhuang drying up," NCNA, July 9, 2004.

29. "A great wall of waste," *The Economist,* August 21, 2004.

30. "70 percent of China's fixed assets and 40 percent of its population subject to threats from floods," CNS, August 20, 2004; Wang Yu, "One-sixth of China's cities seriously lacking in water," *Wen Wei Po,* November 16, 2004; "2.6 million square kilometers of land have become deserts," *Ming Pao,* February 28, 2005.

31. "Ecological damage to the Yangtze becoming more serious," NCNA, October 12, 2004.

32. Cited in "170 million people affected by pollution in the Huai River," NCNA, September 22, 2004.

33. "Mental illness becoming a major problem in China," Reuters, October 12, 2004; "25 percent of Chinese lack funds to seek medical treatment," *Ming Pao,* February 28, 2005; "China approves proposals on 11th Five-Year Plan," NCNA, October 11, 2005.

34. After a spate of horrendous coal mine accidents in two Guangdong counties in August 2005, the Guangzhou government decided on the draconian—but effective—solution of closing down all such mines within the province; see, for example, "Guangdong shuts down coal mines for checks," *China Daily,* August 11, 2005. However, it must be noted that, Guangdong being a super-rich province—and mines not being a "pillar industry" in that province—it was relatively easy for Guangzhou to make that decision.

35. "China has become high-incidence area for lung disease," *Wen Wei Po,* April 7, 2004.

36. "Dirty river linked to cancer," *China Economic Net,* October 5, 2004; Zhang Kang, "Cancer village," *Caijing* magazine (a Beijing-based financial weekly), October 4, 2004.

37. Jim Yardley, "A deadly fever, once defeated, lurks in a Chinese lake," *New York Times* (hereafter *NYT*), February 22, 2005; Zhong Xuebing, "Snail fever threatens 60 million people," *Wen Wei Po,* December 22, 2004; "Tuberculosis sufferers increase by 1.45 million a year," CNS, March 23, 2005.

38. For a study of the ideas of Zhang Zhidong and the overall differences between the Chinese and Japanese approaches to reform, see Xiao Lang and Tian Zhengping, "A comparative study on the 1898 reform of China and the Meiji Restoration," *Journal of Zhejiang University* vol. 1, no. 1 (2000), pp. 105–110.

39. It was due to the relative success of the Meiji Restoration, which started in 1868, that the first generation of Chinese revolutionaries and modern thinkers, including Lu Xun, Guo Morou, and Liu Chengzhi, spent time in Japan studying that country's approach to modernization. For a study of Chinese attitudes toward Japanese modernization in the late nineteenth and early twentieth centuries, see, for example, Samuel C. Chu and Kwang-Ching Liu, eds., *Li Hung-chang and China's Early Modernization* (New York: East Gate Books, 1994); Samuel C. Chu, "China's attitudes toward Japan at the time of the Sino-Japanese War," in *The Chinese and the Japanese: Essays in Political and Cultural Interactions,* ed. Akira Iriye (Princeton, NJ: Princeton University Press, 1980).

40. For a discussion of Mao's *yifen wei'er* dialectics, see, for example, Ping Toupo, "On Mao Zedong's idea of 'dividing one into two,'" xslx.com website, September 21, 2002, www.xslx.com/htm/sxgc/mlyj/2002-9-21-10015.htm.

41. For a discussion of Mao's distortion of Marxism and other "leftist" errors, see, for example, Wang Ruoshui, *The Newly Discovered Mao Zedong* (Hong Kong: Ming Pao Press, 2002), pp. 599–631.

42. For a modern Chinese version of Mao's efforts to manufacture nuclear weapons, see, for example, Yao Lan, "Hard-earned success," *Shanghai Star* (an official English-language paper), October 16, 2003.

43. For a discussion of Zhao's political-reform proposals, see Wu Guoguang, *Political Reform Under Zhao Ziyang* (Hong Kong: Pacific Century Institute, 1997), pp. 122–317.

44. Some of Deng's most liberal statements on economic reform, such as "stay away from controversy," were uttered during his tour of southern China in 1992. See "Records of Comrade Deng Xiaoping's Shenzhen tour," *People's Daily,* January 18, 2002.

45. One of Deng Xiaoping's central precepts is that the party and country must adopt a "double-fisted" policy of laying equal emphasis on the reform and open-door policy on the one hand, and the Four Cardinal Principles of Marxism-Leninism and stern party leadership on the other.

46. "Western systems a 'dead end' for China," NCNA, September 15, 2004.

47. For example, in his report to the NPC in March 2005, Wen cited short excerpts from Tang Dynasty poetry as well as Han Dynasty historian Sima Qian's *Historical Memoirs;* see, "Ancient texts cited by Premier Wen," NCNA, March 14, 2005.

48. For a discussion of the country's search for FMES, see, for example, Stephen Green, "China's quest for full market status," *China Brief,* Jamestown Foundation, Washington, D.C., August 5, 2004; Pete Engario, "Wielding a heavy weapon against China," *Businessweek,*

June 21, 2004; Lou Yi, "The debate on full market status," *Caijing,* June 20, 2004.

49. "Long Yongtu: China's status as a market-economy country does not need other countries' recognition," *China Youth Daily,* June 16, 2004.

50. For a discussion of the significance of the constitutional change, see, for example, "Amendments protect private property," *China Daily,* January 4, 2004.

51. Andrew Browne, "China lets brokerage firms hire foreigners in top posts," *Asian Wall Street Journal,* October 28, 2004.

52. Shen Jiru, "China must reduce its dependency on foreign trade," *Fortnightly Chat* (an official Beijing magazine), September 21, 2004.

53. Wen Han, "Chinese banks raise interest rate by 0.25 percent," *Wen Wei Po,* October 29, 2004; Wen Han, "Macro-economic controls have moved from executive fiats to market means," *Wen Wei Po,* October 30, 2004.

54. "Hu urges Shanghai to 'go on taking the lead,'" NCNA, July 29, 2004.

55. "China's burgeoning private sector," *China Business Times* (an official Beijing paper), February 9, 2005; "Private sector boosted," *China Daily,* December 3, 2003.

56. "China's richest man: Private property must be protected," *Wen Wei Po,* March 4, 2004.

57. Cited in staff reporter, "Beijing raises the threshold for the steel industry," *Ming Pao,* May 9, 2004.

58. Author's interview with Professor He Kaiyin, director of the Center for Rural Issues, Anhui University, in Hong Kong, October 2004; Hu Xingdou, "Pay attention to the deprivation of farmers' rights," www.houxingdou.com.cn, August 6, 2004.

59. "China's SOE reform on right track and to make headway," *People's Daily,* September 30, 2004.

60. Li Rongrong, "SASAC's responsibilities and targets," *People's Daily,* May 22, 2003; "Centrally controlled enterprises expected to earn 500 billion yuan this year," NCNA, December 22, 2005.

61. For a discussion of SASAC's mega-firms, see, "Li Rongrong: Centrally administered enterprises to make more than 500 billion yuan of profits this year," *People's Daily,* September 25, 2005; "Spurring performance in China's state-owned enterprises," *The Mckinsey Quarterly,* (U.S. journal), April 11, 2004.

62. For a discussion of Chinese banks' bad loans problems, see, for example, Frederick Balfour, "Reform picks up speed," *Businessweek,* March 8, 2004.

63. Staff reporters, "Investors wary of China's banks," *Asian Wall Street Journal,* October 29, 2004; staff reporter, "Enterprises pile up new debts as bad assets amount to 1.5 trillion yuan," *Hong Kong Economic Journal,* July 15, 2004; David Barboza, "IPO of Chinese bank marks a watershed," *NYT,* October 27, 2005.

64. Staff reporter, "The PBOC investigates suspicious transactions worth 4.7 trillion yuan," *Ming Pao,* July 24, 2004.

65. "China banks told to act on fraud," BBC news, March 28, 2005; "New BOC chairman Li Lihui says speed and quality equally important," *Wen Wei Po,* August 27, 2004; "588.5 billion yuan's worth of questionable loans in the Big Four banks," *Ming Pao,* December 28, 2005.

66. Cited in "Wen Jiabao interviewed by Reuters," NCNA, April 29, 2004.

67. For a discussion of Beijing's concept of forming *chaebol,* see, for example, Willy Wo-Lap Lam, *The Era of Jiang Zemin* (Singapore: Prentice-Hall, 1999), pp. 378–380.

68. For a study of the problem of corporate governance and market listing in Chinese enterprises, see, for example, Chen Chien-hsun and Shih Hui-tze, "Initial public offerings and corporate governance in China's transitional economy," Working Paper 9574, National Bureau of Economic Research, Washington, D.C., March 2003.

69. For a study of the role of the party and government in the appointment of senior SOE executives, see, for example, Jian Chen and Roger Strange, "The evolution of corporate

governance in China," The Management Centre Research Papers, King's College, University of London, Research Paper #25, April 2004; Laurence Lau, "Twin problems facing SOE reform," *Caijing*, October 31, 2005.

70. Cited in Li Liman, "Which of China's reform measures need to be radical, which moderate?" *Economics* (a Beijing monthly magazine), January 2004.

71. See Tang Fangfang, "Problems of corporate governance in Chinese firms undergoing structural transition," *Hong Kong Economic Journal*, May 10, 2004.

72. Li Rongrong, "State share sales will be delayed," *Shanghai Daily*, November 12, 2003; Cheng Siwei, "Come out of the strange cycle of a policy-dominated market," *Caijing*, October 18, 2004. For a study of the Chinese stock market and its recent downturn, see, for example, Matthew Forney, "China's market maladies," *Time* Asia edition, February 7, 2005; "Capitalization of the Shanghai and Shenzhen stock markets shrunk by 150 billion yuan in 2004," *China Industrial and Commercial Times* (an official Beijing paper), January 6, 2005.

73. For a discussion of Chinese views on the yuan's value, see, for example, "Zhou Xiaochuan takes part in G7 finance ministers meeting," NCNA, October 1, 2004; "Pressure on renminbi will not help: Wen," *China Daily*, May 16, 2005. For a discussion of ways to make the renminbi more responsive to market conditions, see, for example, David DeRosa, "Basket, float or peg for the yuan?" *International Herald Tribune*, December 29, 2003; "China: Yuan won't rise sharply," Reuters, March 5, 2005.

74. Cited in "The main goals of the 11th FYP raised at the Fifth Plenary Session of the 16th CCP Central Committee," NCNA, October 11, 2005; Chua Chin Hon, "China's great innovation push," *Straits Times*, January 10, 2006; "China's goal for the coming 15 years: To build an innovative country," NCNA, January 9, 2006.

75. See Matthew Forney, "Requiem for reform?" *Time* Asia edition, January 31, 2005; Tang Jing, "China's competitiveness has declined owing to corruption and other factors," *People's Daily*, September 26, 2005; "China losing best college graduates abroad," www.chinanews.cn, November 15, 2005. Among the 500 most successful "world brands" cited by international business magazines, only four are Chinese. See "Dearth of brands: Fast-rising exports can't hide structural problems," NCNA, December 12, 2005.

76. Guo Shiping, "Superpower dream behind China's heavy industry push," *Straits Times*, November 19, 2003.

77. For an analysis of the PLA's ambitious plans to digitalize operations, see, for example, the Pentagon's annual report, *The Military Power of the People's Republic of China, 2005* U.S. Defense Department, Washington, D.C., pp. 15–19.

78. Examples of Beijing's efforts to stifle democracy in Hong Kong included a statement by the NPC Standing Committee in April 2004 that there would not be general elections to pick the chief executive in 2007. NPC Chairman Wu Bangguo said the NPC Standing Committee's decision had contributed to the "healthy development of democracy" in the SAR; see "Wu Bangguo delivers report on NPC work," *People's Daily*, March 10, 2005.

79. Author's interview with a political scientist in Beijing, April 2004.

80. "Fighting for democracy is the entire people's business," *Xinhua Daily* (the underground paper of the Communist Party before it came to power), July 3, 1945.

81. Cited in "Sun Zaifu: Two challenges facing the party," CNS, August 6, 2003; Yu Keping, "On the 'Beijing Consensus' and the model for China's development," *The Contemporary World and Socialism* (a Beijing journal) (May 2004).

82. For a discussion of the democratic ideals of Liu Ji, see, for example, Todd Crowell and David Hsieh, "China loosens up," *Asiaweek* (a Hong Kong newsmagazine), June 26, 1998.

83. "Premier Wen: Reform must be comprehensive, including economic and political aspects," CNS, March 24, 2004.

84. "Zeng Qinghong: 'Strengthen the CCP's governance ability, run well the administration and hold power well for the sake of the people,'" NCNA, September 24, 2004.

85. Zhang Shutang and Sun Chengbin, "The birth of the 'Resolution on Strengthening the Construction of the Party's Governance Ability,'" NCNA, September 27, 2004.

86. Cited in Yu Wenxue, "Hu gave hard-line speech at inaugural session," *Open* magazine, December 2004; Willy Lam, "Hu's recent crackdown on political dissent," *China Brief*, Jamestown Foundation, June 7, 2005.

87. For a discussion of Hu's new regime of intolerance, see, for example, Haoyu Zhang, "China's intolerance of dissidents," BBC news, March 7, 2005; Yu Wenxue, "Putting the lid on the party's liberal elements," *Open* magazine (a China-watching publication in Hong Kong), March 2005; Luis Ramirez, "China cracks down on intellectuals," Voice of America news, December 14, 2004; Willy Lam, "Hu's reforms and the Zhao Ziyang fiasco," *China Brief*, Jamestown Foundation, February 4, 2005; Robyn Meredith, "Alarms over China," *Forbes* magazine, June 8, 2005.

88. Haoyu Zhang, "China's intolerance of dissidents,"; for a discussion of Qin Hui's role as an activist environmentalist, see, for example, Mark Magnier, "A watershed role for farmers," *Los Angeles Times*, January 16, 2005.

89. For a discussion of the two riots in Guangdong, see, for example, Tim Luard, "China village democracy skin deep," BBC news, October 10, 2005; Howard French, "Beijing casts net of silence over protest," *NYT*, December 14, 2005; Willy Lam, "China's spiraling unrest," *Asian Wall Street Journal*, December 14, 2005; Hannah Beech, "Village killings highlight Beijing's dilemma," *Time* Asia edition, December 14, 2005.

90. Zhao Changmao, "China's peaceful rise must be anchored upon the enhancement of soft power," *Outlook Weekly* (an official Beijing magazine), June 10, 2004.

91. For a description of China's massive "culture week" held in Paris in early 2004, see, "Culture week to kick off in Paris," *China Daily*, January 8, 2004; author's interview with Lawrence Ho, Hong Kong, September 2004.

92. "President Jiang on the development of the arts, culture in China," *China Daily*, December 19, 2001.

93. For a discussion of the widening influence of Chinese culture, see Jane Perlez, "China's reach," *NYT*, November 18, 2004; "China's influence seen as positive," BBC news, March 5. 2005; "China's rise and the popularity of Chinese-language learning," CNS, May 23, 2005.

94. The Chinese translations of Lech Walesa and Vaclav Havel were available, via "underground" channels, to Chinese intellectuals from the 1980s onward. And in the early to mid 1980s, Deng Xiaoping repeatedly warned against the "Polish disease," a reference to the Solidarity movement, spreading to China. For a discussion of Deng's views on Lech Walesa and the "Polish disease," see Robin Munro, "Who died in Beijing, and why?" *The Nation* (a U.S. journal), vol. 250 (June 11, 1990).

95. For a discussion of Beijing–Hong Kong relations, see, for example, "The last tycoon," *Newsweek* Asia edition, March 14, 2004; Willy Lam, "Setbacks for 'one country, two systems,'" *Apple Daily* (an independent Hong Kong paper), March 11, 2005.

96. For an official view of China's new approaches to multilateralism, see "China urges multilateralism in maintaining world peace," NCNA English service, August 19, 2004.

97. Cited in Jiang Xun, "Koizumi not to visit the Yasakuni Shrine?" *Yazhou Zhoukan*, January 9, 2005.

98. Liu Jianfei, "The trends of Sino-U.S. relations and China's strategies," *Theoretical Trends* (an internal journal of the Central Party School, Beijing) (December 10, 2004).

99. For a discussion of Gao's relationship with the Chinese government, see, for example, Yu Sen-lun, "Gao Xingjian gets warm Taipei welcome," *Taipei Times*, February 2, 2001.

100. Hannah Beech, "The price of gold," *Time* Asia edition, August 16, 2004.

101. Apart from Gao Xinjian, famous Chinese writers who have settled in the West include the prize-winning novelist Ha Jin, and London-based author Jung Chang, originally

from Shanghai. Chang, of *Wild Swan* fame, co-wrote a remarkable biography of Mao Zedong that came out in 2005.

102. Cited in "Jin Yong on China's Nobel prospects," *Wen Wei Po,* October 8, 2004.

103. Feng Xiaofeng, "Mass breakthroughs in the 'China chip engineering project,'" NCNA, October 6, 2004; Ye Guobiao, "China has manufactured own chips," CNS, September 6, 2004.

104. For a discussion of the future of Chinese science, see, for example, David Stipp, "Can China overtake the U.S. in science?" *Fortune,* October 18, 2004.

105. Cited in Huang Jinjia, "Top Chinese-American professors debate the quality of Chinese scholarship," *Wen Wei Po,* December 17, 2005; staff reporter, "Professor resigns to protest systems and institutions at Tsinghua," *Ming Pao,* March 25, 2005.

106. Cited in "Premier Wen's opportune visit to Europe," *People's Daily,* May 10, 2004.

107. For a discussion of the state of Christianity in China, see, for example, Sarah Schafter, "Onward, Christian soldiers," *Newsweek* Asian edition, May 10, 2004; Jason Kindopp, "Fragmented yet defiant: Protestant resilience under Chinese Communist Party rule," in *God and Caesar in China* ed. Jason Kindopp and Carol Lee Hamrin (Washington: Brookings Institution Press, 2004), pp. 122–145.

108. Mao Yushi, "Reform should not put money first," *Ming Pao,* October 16, 2003.

109. Cited in Yu Yunxi, "Changes in the class struggle are worrisome," *Wen Wei Po,* August 11, 2004.

110. "Beijing holds first-ever beauty contest for artificially embellished women," CNS, December 14, 2004; Lang Hanping, "Harmony is needed to cure the man-eat-man phenomenon in Chinese society," *Yazhou Zhoukan,* November 11, 2005.

111. "Jia Qinglin's address at the international seminar marking the 2555th birthday of Confucius," NCNA, October 9, 2004.

112. Cited in "CPPCC annual session closes in Beijing," *China Daily,* March 14, 2002.

113. "Premier Wen delivers speech at 50th anniversary of enunciation of the 'Five Principles for Peaceful Co-existence,'" CNS, June 28, 2004.

114. Author's interview with Professor Tu, Barcelona, June 2004.

115. For a study of the democratic roots of Confucianism, see, for example, Xu Keqian, "On the compatibility between Confucian principles and democracy," paper presented at the conference "Democratic Issues Within the Framework of Political Philosophy," Beijing, April 27, 2004.

116. For a discussion of the Confucian movement in Singapore, see, for example, John Wong, "Promoting Confucianism for socio-economic development: The Singapore experience," in *Confucian Traditions in East Asian Modernity: Moral Education and Economic Culture in Japan and the Four Mini-Dragons,* ed. Tu Wei-ming (Cambridge, MA: Harvard University Press, 1996), pp. 277–293.

117. "Economic cost of lack of *chengxin* up to 600 billion yuan a year," CNS, June 16, 2002.

118. "NPC vice-chairman calls for sound credit system," *People's Daily,* June 17, 2002.

119. Cited in Willy Lam, "A question of faith," www.cnn.com, July 10, 2002.

120. Wang Li, "Organization Department and other units find that 15,000 cadres hold false diplomas," NCNA, July 4, 2004.

121. Staff writer, "Students taking college entrance tests sign pledge of *chengxin,*" *Wen Wei Po,* June 8, 2004.

122. "China Securities Regulatory Commission to strike out against false information," NCNA, August 13, 2001.

123. Staff reporter, "40 percent of Shanghai residents think officials' clean-government pledges have failed to produce effect," *Wen Wei Po,* October 16, 2004; He Yan, "Survey: Officials are the greatest beneficiaries of reform," *Wen Wei Po,* February 22, 2004.

124. "The party must improve its ruling methods," *Guangming Daily* (an official Beijing paper), October 12, 2001.

125. For a discussion of the characteristics and political traits of the Fifth-Generation

leadership, see, for example, Qiu Ping, *Fifth-Generation Leaders of the Chinese Communist Party* (Hong Kong: Xia Fei Er Press, 2005), pp. 225–324; Willy Lam, "The generation after next in Chinese politics," in *Chinese Leadership in the 21st Century,* ed. David Finkelstein and Maryanne Kivlehan (Armonk, NY: M.E. Sharpe, 2003), pp. 251–270.

126. For a discussion of Hu Jintao's young protégés, see, for example, Willy Wo-Lap Lam, "China's new star in the making," www.cnn.com, April 25, 2001.

127. For a portrait of Li Xiaolin, chief of China Power International, see, for example, Nellie Huang, "Li Xiaolin, star power," *Time* Asia edition, December 13, 2004; Li's brother Li Xiaopeng is also making waves as head of the mammoth Huaneng energy company.

128. For a discussion of the potentials of Xi Jinping, see, for example, Zong Hairen, *China's New Leaders: The Fourth Generation* (New York: Mirror Books, 2002), pp. 389–420.

129. For a discussion of the Shanghai Faction princelings, including the sons of Jiang Zemin, see Willy Lam, "Factional politics in the CCP," *China Brief,* Jamestown Foundation, March 8, 2004.

130. For a discussion of the career prospects of Han Zheng, Wang Huning, and other Shanghai-related officials, see, for example, Qiu Ping, *Fifth-Generation Leaders,* pp. 132–138, 175–184.

131. For a discussion of the potentials of younger members of the "Zhu Rongji clique," see, for example, Willy Wo-Lap Lam, *The Era of Jiang Zemin,* pp. 366–368.

132. For a discussion of Beijing-based CYL elite, see, for example, Ting Wang, *Hu Jintao and the Successors of Communist Youth League in China* (Hong Kong: Celebrities Press, 2005), pp. 303–334.

133. For a discussion of Hu's provincial followers, see, for example, Li Cheng, "Hu's followers: Provincial leaders with background in the Communist Youth League," *China Leadership Monitor,* Hoover Institution, Stanford University, no. 8 (Fall 2003); Li Zi, "Major shake-up of officials," *Beijing Review,* March 2, 2005; Ching Cheung, "Hu moves his allies to key positions," *Straits Times,* January 7, 2002.

134. For a study of the career of Li Keqiang, see, for example, Qiu Ping, *Fifth-Generation Leaders,* pp. 92–105; Willy Lam, "China's new star in the making," www.cnn.com, April 25, 2001; "Chinese official moved as Hu consolidates power," Reuters, December 13, 2004.

135. For a study of the liberal ideas of Hu Yaobang and Zhu Houze, see, for example, Stanley Rosen, "China in 1987: The year of the Thirteenth Party Congress," *Asian Survey* (an American journal), vol. 28, no. 1 (January 1988), pp. 35–51.

136. For a discussion of the career and traits of Minister Wu, see, for example, Ma Yu, "Three dark-horse candidates being groomed by Hu," *Frontline* (a China-watching monthly in Hong Kong), August 2005.

137. For a discussion of the careers of businessmen who may be promoted to party and government posts, see Li Cheng, "The rise of China's yuppie corps: Top CEOs to watch," *China Leadership Monitor,* no. 14 (Spring 2005).

138. "Hu Jintao: The party's *baoxian* construction will bring benefits to the people," NCNA, January 25, 2005.

139. "Why a survey of the thoughts of 300,000 party members has disturbed party authorities," NCNA, November 23, 2004.

140. Cited in "China's goal in the coming 15 years: To build an innovative country"; Zhu Xijun, "On the successes and pitfalls of ruling parties in the world," *Guo Feng* (a Beijing party journal) (September 2005).

141. Xiao Feng, "Why has Cuba been able to withstand pressure?" *Guo Feng,* September 2005; "Hu Jintao lays emphasis on boosting theoretical research on party construction," NCNA, December 30, 2005.

142. "List of 50 public-arena intellectuals who have influenced China," *Southern People Weekly,* September 22, 2004.

Index

With more than thirty years of experience in writing about China, **Willy Wo-Lap Lam** is a recognized authority whose books have been translated into Chinese and Japanese. Educated at the University of Hong Kong, the University of Minnesota, and Wuhan University, the veteran Sinologist has published five books on China, including *The Era of Jiang Zemin* (1999) and *China after Deng Xiaoping* (1995).

Dr. Lam has worked in senior editorial positions in international media including *Asiaweek* newsmagazine, *South China Morning Post*, and the Asia-Pacific Headquarters of CNN. He was an accredited Beijing-based foreign correspondent from 1986 to 1989. In early 2004 he was appointed Professor of China Studies and Global Studies at Akita International University, a new English-language liberal-arts university in Japan. He has held several visiting fellowships and is a frequent lecturer and commentator on contemporary Chinese affairs.